Adjustment and Personality

McGRAW-HILL SERIES IN PSYCHOLOGY

HARRY F. HARLOW, *Consulting Editor*

BARKER, KOUNIN, AND WRIGHT · Child Behavior and Development
BEACH, HEBB, MORGAN, AND NISSEN · The Neuropsychology of Lashley
VON BÉKÉSY · Experiments in Hearing
BERLYNE · Conflict, Arousal, and Curiosity
BLUM · Psychoanalytic Theories of Personality
BROWN · The Motivation of Behavior
BROWN · The Psychodynamics of Abnormal Behavior
BROWN AND GHISELLI · Scientific Method in Psychology
CATTELL · Personality
CRAFTS, SCHNEIRLA, ROBINSON, AND GILBERT · Recent Experiments in Psychology
DEESE · The Psychology of Learning
DOLLARD AND MILLER · Personality and Psychotherapy
DORCUS AND JONES · Handbook of Employee Selection
FERGUSON · Personality Measurement
FERGUSON · Statistical Analysis in Psychology and Education
GHISELLI AND BROWN · Personnel and Industrial Psychology
GILMER · Industrial Psychology
GRAY · Psychology Applied to Human Affairs
GRAY · Psychology in Industry
GUILFORD · Fundamental Statistics in Psychology and Education
GUILFORD · Psychometric Methods
GUILFORD · Personality
HAIRE · Psychology in Management
HIRSH · The Measurement of Hearing
HURLOCK · Adolescent Development
HURLOCK · Child Development
HURLOCK · Developmental Psychology
KARN AND GILMER · Readings in Industrial and Business Psychology
KRECH AND CRUTCHFIELD · Theory and Problems of Social Psychology
LAZARUS · Adjustment and Personality
LEWIN · A Dynamic Theory of Personality
LEWIN · Principles of Topological Psychology
LEWIS · Quantitative Methods in Psychology
MAIER AND SCHNEIRLA · Principles of Animal Psychology
MILLER · Language and Communication
MISIAK AND STAUDT · Catholics in Psychology: A Historical Survey
MOORE · Psychology for Business and Industry
MORGAN AND STELLAR · Physiological Psychology
PAGE · Abnormal Psychology
REYMERT · Feelings and Emotions
SEASHORE · Psychology of Music
SHAFFER AND LAZARUS · Fundamental Concepts in Clinical Psychology
SIEGEL · Nonparametric Statistics: For the Behavioral Sciences
STAGNER · Psychology of Personality
TOWNSEND · Introduction to Experimental Method
VINACKE · The Psychology of Thinking
WALLEN · Clinical Psychology: The Study of Persons
WATERS, RETHLINGSHAFER, AND CALDWELL · Principles of Comparative Psychology
ZUBEK AND SOLBERG · Human Development

John F. Dashiell was Consulting Editor of this series from its inception in 1931 until January 1, 1950. Clifford T. Morgan was Consulting Editor of this series from January 1, 1950 until January 1, 1959.

ADJUSTMENT
and
PERSONALITY

Richard S. Lazarus

PROFESSOR OF PSYCHOLOGY

UNIVERSITY OF CALIFORNIA, BERKELEY

McGRAW-HILL BOOK COMPANY, INC.

New York   Toronto   London

1961

ADJUSTMENT AND PERSONALITY

36796

III

To My Wonderful Wife
BERNICE

Preface

An author usually writes a textbook because he feels dissatisfied with the existing ones and because he believes he has unique things to offer. Either he conceives his field differently from other textbook writers, or he thinks that other books are pitched at too high or too low a level to employ successfully. In formulating lectures to supply what is needed, he finds himself with the makings of a new text. This has been true in my case.

Next to an introductory course in psychology, one of the courses most frequently offered in colleges and universities is on the psychology of adjustment. The course, variously described as "adjustment," "mental hygiene," and "personality development," is not necessarily directed toward students who intend to major in psychology but toward the large number of students drawn toward the subject matter out of curiosity or personal need. This popularity is not surprising in view of the increasing public awareness of psychology and the universality of problems of adjustment.

Great interest in the psychology of adjustment is indicated not only by the high frequency of college courses on the subject but also by the considerable number of lay books, from the early best seller by Dale Carnegie, *How to Win Friends and Influence People,* through a succession including Overstreet's *The Mature Mind,* Bishop Sheen's *Peace of Soul,* Rabbi Leibman's *Peace of Mind,* and Norman Vincent Peale's widely read book, *The Power of Positive Thinking.* Most newspapers throughout the country include columns offering advice on interpersonal relations, analyzing personal problems, and suggesting child-rearing practices guaranteed to make youngsters healthy and interpersonally competent. Along with cancer and heart-disease research, mental-health programs are beginning to be the order of the day.

As I have been at pains to show in Chapter 15, these books and articles that strive to advise the reader on matters of adjustment, although hungrily read by the public, have very little significant effect

on the adjustment processes of their audiences. They also rarely offer
genuine understanding of the complex processes of personality and adjustment as these are presently understood by psychologists. They are
easy to read and inspirational rather than educational.

Unfortunately there has been a great tendency for this type of inspirational book, suggesting some formula for effective living, to become the
standard source book in a college course in adjustment, although it is
apt to be tailored to the college setting and provided with the affecta-
tions of a text. Rather than stimulating the student to knowledge and
thought about the fundamentals of the subject matter, these "texts" are
accepted because they are popular and easy and seem relevant. When
writing for this market, one is often advised to leave out difficult theoretical and methodological matters and to present what is appealing
rather than educational, although these values need not be antithetical.

Instructors in adjustment courses offered in the best colleges and universities often express impatience with most of the textbook material
they are offered. Because the courses are usually at the beginning level,
the higher-level books on personality, and its theories and methodology,
are understandably too difficult. The books that seek the lowest common
denominator are also not satisfactory. Books that seek a middle ground
in sophistication and yet are suitable for a second- or third-level course
in psychology are very hard, if not impossible, to find.

In consequence of this, *Adjustment and Personality* was written with
certain objectives in mind. First, it was not intended to embrace any
particular point of view. Rather, it concerns ways of looking at personality and adjustment. In the case of controversial issues, I have tried
to take the position generally held among the specialists most concerned
with the problem.

Second, the book was written with the conviction that too much
time is apt to be spent on the detailed data of psychology and not enough
on the psychological problems and the ways they are approached. This
is not to say that in a science data are not the ultimate basis for ideas,
but I believe that the beginning student can too easily lose the forest
for the trees. As a consequence, some teachers will find references to
experimental research somewhat more sparse than they are accustomed
to. For nonmajors and nonprofessionals especially, most of the facts will
soon be forgotten, but the larger issues at which the fact getting is aimed
will, hopefully, be retained longer. In the main, this is a book about the
current ideas of psychologists concerning adjustment and personality.

Third, I think most writers, at least implicitly, recognize the indivisi-
bility of the fields of adjustment and personality, even though one typically finds some books ostensibly on adjustment alone and others dealing

only with personality. I have tried to integrate the two fields by regarding adjustment as an interpretation of behavior that stresses how persons resolve their problems and the internal pressures to which they are subjected as biological and social organisms. One might say, in fact, that personality itself is made up largely of the more or less stable and organized processes of adjustment. One cannot adequately develop one topic without the other

With this conception of the unity of the fields of adjustment and personality, and having eschewed (or at least tried to eschew) any particular theoretical point of view, it was unthinkable not to include a major section on personality theories. Beginning students are likely to find the five chapters (3 through 7) explicitly dealing with theoretical approaches to personality the most difficult in the book. And yet it seems to me that a real understanding of the field requires a thorough knowledge of at least a single conceptual scheme and how it integrates the main observations, and a grasp of the variety of viewpoints as well. In this book I have surveyed this variety. If the student goes further, he can invest more heavily in one or more of the theories. To do this effectively, he will have to go directly to the primary sources. I believe that it would be advantageous to use the writings of some major personality theorist along with this textbook, especially for students who are majoring or minoring in psychology. Then depth as well as breadth would be ensured.

I am indebted to the many artists, writers, and publishers who have permitted the reprinting of their material and to the professional and editorial consultants who have given their assistance and encouragement. I am especially grateful to my wife, Bernice, for providing a life situation that facilitated writing the book and for being a sounding board for testing ideas. I also thank my children, David and Nancy, who are still too young to appreciate how much their respect of my work place and schedule meant to the completion of the manuscript.

Richard S. Lazarus

Contents

xi

Psychotherapy and Psychological Theory. Psychotherapy: A Doubtful Panacea.

Implications of Control over Human Behavior. Personal Applications. Some Other Fields of Application.

I

THE CONCEPTS OF
ADJUSTMENT AND PERSONALITY

PSYCHOLOGISTS APPROACH their subject from two somewhat different although related perspectives. The traditional, general experimental psychologist is concerned mainly with an analysis of the various separate
psychological functions that characterize human beings. Thus he studies
the properties of motives, emotional states, and cognitive processes such
as perception, learning, thinking, and communication. He seeks to understand man by discovering the laws that apply to each of these functions
individually, assuming usually that the laws appropriate to one function
differ from those appropriate to another. In a sense, psychological man
is the combination of these discrete processes.

The psychologist of personality, in contrast, is concerned with the
study of persons not merely as collections of separately analyzable
psychological functions but as organized wholes, the parts of which are
merely convenient abstractions arbitrarily separated out of an integrated,
purposeful system. It is the integrated, purposeful system that he wishes
to describe and understand, even though he must often approach it
analytically in terms of identifiable classes of process, such as motivation,
emotion, and cognition.

The systematic study of the whole man is undertaken in two inseparable fields, identified as the psychology of adjustment and the psychology
of personality. Adjustment and personality are unifying concepts because they include the various subordinate processes of motivation,
emotion, and cognition. For example, adjustment is accomplished through
the exercise of cognitive activities such as perception and thought,

1

processes by which the person has transactions with the world about him. But these processes are not the person. To the psychologist of personality, the *organization* of the subordinate processes is the essence of personality. In Part I, we take up separately the concepts of adjustment and personality. In Chapters 1 and 2, these two central and related ideas are introduced and analyzed.

1

Basic Problems

One of the unique attributes of man is his self-awareness and capacity to understand himself. In past centuries his preoccupations were determined mainly by the need to survive physically in a world of constant danger. Western man has now succeeded to a remarkable degree in controlling his physical environment, so, instead of nature, he is beginning to consider other men, and even himself, as his greatest enemy. Although social existence has produced physical dangers such as war, there are important psychological problems uniquely associated with living in society, which result, in the extreme, in mental illness. There are also questions of the attainment of basic satisfactions from competence in interpersonal relations and through some degree of inner harmony. Man has, accordingly, become increasingly interested in psychological adjustment and the nature of personality.

During his history, man has devised many ways of viewing himself in relation to the world in which he lives. To consider his behavior from the point of view of adjustment is in the tradition of the modern, *naturalistic* view of man, which regards behavior as governed by natural laws of cause and effect. In earlier times, human action was seen as governed by *demons* or spirits, both good and evil. Man's religious views in both ancient and modern times have been often cast in terms of the determination of thought and action by gods, God, or the devil. Both the naturalistic and demonological conceptions are attempts to explain the nature of man and the world. Modern science has strongly empirical (observable) bases, and one can test ideas about the world by observing whether they accord with the empirical facts.

In the seventeenth century, Francis Bacon proposed an inductive system called *natural science* for obtaining knowledge about the world in place of recourse to authority, whether based on magical or theological views. There followed in the seventeenth and eighteenth centuries increasing emphasis on developing natural laws that could be tested by means of empirical evidence. The method shifted from Bacon's entirely inductive procedures to setting up hypotheses from which specific consequences could be deduced and then verified by observation and experimentation. With respect to behavior, the naturalistic approach evolved into consideration of the organic and functional bases of behavior, stressing physical structure on the one hand and environmental stimulation on the other. Modern psychology recognizes the importance of the interaction of organic and functional factors as determinants of behavior.

While some of the "idols" that Bacon attacked centuries earlier are still among us in the form of modern superstitions and cults, our formal systems of psychological theory are guided by the naturalistic principle and by the requirement that our interpretations of behavior accord with observable facts. Concepts about man that cannot be empirically verified are rejected, although at any early stage in formulating principles it is difficult to distinguish between sound and unsound notions. We are always moving from inadequate conceptions to better supported and more useful ones, and the exciting challenge of the science of psychology, as in other sciences, is to advance the frontiers of knowledge about man and the world. We still are, and always will be, seeking explanations in order to understand ourselves.

THE CONCEPT OF ADJUSTMENT

The concept of adjustment was originally a biological one and was a cornerstone in Darwin's theory of evolution (1859). In biology the term usually employed was *adaptation*. Darwin maintained that only those organisms most fitted to adapt to the hazards of the physical world survive. Biologists have continued to be concerned with the problem of physical adaptation, and many human illnesses are thought to be based on the processes of adaptation to the stress of life (cf. Selye, 1956). Such illnesses include diseases of the circulatory system that produce coronary attacks and cerebral hemorrhages as well as disturbances of the digestive tract such as ulcers and intestinal colitis.

Man's behavior can be described as reactions to a variety of demands or pressures that are brought to bear upon him. The clothing he wears varies with the climate in which he lives and represents, at least partly, an adaptation to weather. Architectural forms also depend upon climatological and topographical factors, and man has shown great ingenuity in adapting the raw materials of his environment to his need for shelter and warmth. This is dramatically illustrated by the remarkable feat of the Eskimos, who build houses out of ice and snow (in adapting to the rigors of life in the Arctic). We can understand a great deal of human behavior by conceiving human actions as adaptations to various kinds of physical demands.

Just as a person adapts to physical demands, he also adjusts to social pressures, that is, demands that arise from living interdependently with other persons. When he is an infant, his parents make demands upon him to acquire the proper values and behavior patterns. When he is adult, they continue to have expectations of his marriage, his career, or where and how he lives. Wives have certain expectations about their husbands, husbands about their wives, employers about their employees, and children about their parents. These expectations function as powerful pressures upon the individual.

The biological concept of adaptation has been borrowed by the psychologist and renamed *adjustment*. The psychologist is more concerned with what might be called "psychological survival" than physical survival. As in the case of the biological concept of adaptation, human behavior is interpreted as adjustments to demands or pressures. These demands are primarily social or interpersonal, and they influence the psychological structure and functioning of the person.

It was said that adjustment involves a reaction of the person to demands imposed upon him. The psychological demands made upon the person can be classified into external and internal.

ADJUSTMENT TO EXTERNAL AND INTERNAL DEMANDS

There are a large number of *external demands* that arise from the physical conditions of existence. From the psychological viewpoint, however, those pressures arising out of our existence as social beings are of greater importance. From early childhood we are confronted with the demands of other persons to do some things and not others. At first, these demands deal with relatively primitive actions. For example, we are required to feed ourselves, not to hit other children, and not to damage property. Between two and three years of age we must learn to control the sphincter muscles of the bladder and bowel according to social custom. As we mature, the demands of others become more subtle and include conceptions, values, and more complex patterns of social behavior. Our failure to comply with these demands results in disapproval and negative consequences, and our conformity to them leads to approval and positive consequences. When we incur the disfavor of our parents and other persons who are significant to our welfare, strong anxieties are aroused. We learn that certain forms of behavior lead to approval, and hence the reduction or elimination of anxiety, and that other forms of behavior have the opposite effects.

This process of *socialization* in response to anxiety and social pressures has been very effectively discussed by Allison Davis, who has been concerned with the influence of social-class factors in the development of personality. He writes (1944, pp. 203–204):

The intensive study of normal personalities leads inevitably to the recognition of the tremendously vital role of this type of socialized anxiety in the integration and direction of the personality, notably in the development of individuals of middle status. One of the certain gains for social science, in the recent studies of normal individuals living in their social contexts, has been the discovery that many concepts of personality economy developed by psychopathology do not hold for individuals in our own culture who are not mentally ill. The tendency of the psychopathologist to extend the concept of the neurotic, maladaptive, irrational type of anxiety, for example, to all anxiety has been a dangerous generalization. In the same way many other concepts of maladaptive functions, based upon clinical study of the delinquent, the criminal, or the mentally ill have been applied wholesale to the analysis of the personality dynamics of normal people by mental hygienists, psychiatric case-workers, and by other students of personality development. These supposedly symptomatic traits include, among others, such motivations as hostility, guilt feelings, intimidation, inferiority feelings, chronic frustrations, as well as anxiety.

The fact is, however, that all of these motivations not only appear in the normal range of human personalities in American society, but these instigations may be all culturally useful and may be integrated in some form into the adaptive behavior of the well-adjusted and socialized child or adolescent. For example, most young children of middle-status families are trained in the basic cultural forms with regard to property, exploration of the adult world, and aggression largely through those feelings of shame, of age inferiority, of guilt, and of anxiety which are instilled by the parents and other adults in accord with the necessary modes of child training *in a society like that of American middle class*. Even aggression and hostility must be taught to the child through culturally approved forms. With regard to overt aggression, the middle-class boy must learn, for example, (1) to fight when attacked by another boy, (2) not to attack a boy unless he has been struck, (3) not to attack girls or supervisory adults under any circumstances, but also (4) not to withdraw when in a normal, approved competitive situation. A child without the culturally approved, adaptive type of aggression in a competitive and status-structured society like ours is himself abnormal.

We are born, as human beings, with a great many *internal needs*, the frustration of which leads to discomfort and sometimes death. Many of these are physiological. If we don't eat, we become hungry and uncomfortable. If we don't drink, we experience the unpleasant reaction of thirst. Other such physiological, internal needs are sleep, defecation, and temperature regulation. In childhood we soon discover that there are certain ways of gratifying these needs, and we behave accordingly whenever an unpleasant state of tension associated with some need exists. In the course of development, additional internal needs emerge, which are primarily social rather than physiological. We need human company, social approval, a sense of self- and social esteem, and love. These needs, like the basic ones of hunger and thirst, are experienced as internal pressures or demands, which direct individual behavior in certain ways. The frustration of these socially oriented needs also results in discomfort.

Experiments dealing with internal needs have most often dealt with physiological ones, because these are more easily manipulated than social needs like approval, love, and esteem. These studies show that needs such as hunger and sleep, when thwarted, produce significant effects on behavior.

For example, during World War II, Brozek and collaborators (1951) exposed thirty-six conscientious objectors, who had volunteered as subjects, to a study of prolonged semistarvation, severely limiting their food intake for a period of months while requiring from them normal physical labor. Observations of the men indicated marked personality changes and continual preoccupation with food. Many of the men had fantasies that after the experiment they would become cooks or restaurateurs, and they used magazine pictures of various tasty dishes as pin-ups. Studies such as these have shown how greatly individual activities, perceptions, and associations can be governed by the activation of strong internal needs.

The individual behaves in such a way that as many internal needs as possible, and especially the strongest ones, will be gratified. In the same way, he responds to external pressures by eliminating them or altering them or accommodating to them in some way. Part of his development as a human being involves the acquisition of particular methods of managing the large variety of these demands. Special problems are produced by conflict.

CONFLICT BETWEEN DEMANDS

The process of adjustment is complicated because the way an individual responds to one demand can conflict with the requirements of another. Conflict can arise because two internal needs are in opposition, because two external demands are incompatible, or because an internal need opposes an external demand.

Suppose, for example, a person desires social prestige but at the same time needs love and approval. He may conceive that prestige is most likely to be achieved by economic success in direct competition with others. In a sense, then, this person must win hundreds of competitive battles with other persons who are seen as striving equally hard to be successful. But victory for oneself could mean defeat for one's competitor, evoking hostility on the part of the latter. Therefore, in the gratification of his need for prestige, the individual may fear the loss of love and approval. Conflict has occurred because the gratification of two internal needs seems to this person difficult to achieve simultaneously; the outcome can be the frustration of one or another of the two, or even both, depending upon the type of resolution attempted.

In a similar way, two external pressures may be in conflict. A boy may be encouraged by his father to be masculine and aggressive and a successful athlete, and the mother may strongly urge him in more artistic directions, frightening him away from fighting and sports because she fears he will be injured. If he responds positively to one of these pressures, the other must be countermanded. Consider Aesop's fable in which a hapless man who is traveling with his family and an ass is berated by onlookers no matter what he does. If he rides and his wife and child walk, he is criticized for his inconsideration to his family. When his wife rides, he is criticized for not taking the proper role as master of his household. When the whole family rides, he is attacked for his cruelty to the ass. His efforts to please everyone eventually lead to disaster.

Figure 1. This photograph was snapped at a boxing match at St. Nicholas Arena in New York City. Notice the young man who, carried away, stands up and punches the air as he vicariously experiences the fight from his place as a spectator. In this way he is able to discharge aggressive impulses in a socially accepted manner. Although the other member of the audience in the center background is amused, he does not disapprove. Moreover, most of the spectators take no notice of his phantom fight. (*Wide World Photos.*)

Finally, there exist conflicts between internal needs and external demands. It is this type of conflict that occurs most often in the social development of the child. Many of our impulses cannot be gratified readily because they are disapproved or dangerous. For example, our sexual needs often conflict with social taboos (especially in adolescence) because the gratification of these needs is acceptable only through certain highly institutionalized forms such as marriage. Similarly, certain forms of aggression, such as direct assault, are rarely accepted in our culture. Sports like boxing and wrestling are socially approved and institutionalized forms to permit the discharge of aggressive impulses. Very commonly, the individual has impulses the gratification of which cannot be accomplished without considerable modification in response to external social pressures.

As we shall see more clearly in later chapters, conflict presents special problems of adjustment, because the gratification of one of the needs or pressures which oppose each other implies frustration of the others. In this way, a conflict can be resolved only by ignoring or frustrating one of its sources. However, failure to gratify a strong need or to respond to an important external demand results in painful tensions. These, in turn, can disturb psychological comfort, produce physical symptoms, or result in pathological behavior. Because conflict is widespread if not universal, the way it is handled is a chief distinction between the adequately and inadequately adjusted person.

ADJUSTMENT AS ACHIEVEMENT OR PROCESS

There are two important aspects to adjustment. The first has to do with its quality or efficiency. Adjustment is regarded as an *achievement*, which is accomplished either badly or well. It is a very practical way of looking at adjustment, one that makes it possible to compare individuals in terms of their adjustive adequacy. The second aspect is the *process* or processes by which the person adjusts. We ask: "How does he adjust? What are the modes of adjustment by which he responds to various demands?"

In essence, the two aspects of adjustment reflect different purposes. The first is emphasized when we are evaluating, the second when we want to understand rather than evaluate. Let us examine more closely these two ways of looking at adjustment.

ADJUSTMENT AS ACHIEVEMENT

The most widely emphasized aspect of adjustment is *achievement*. This makes sense to the businessman who must hire personnel who will be most effective at the job, often under adverse circumstances; to military leaders who must select men who can adjust to the stressful conditions of military combat and to the psychological deprivations that are sometimes associated with military service; to educators because educational opportunities can be wasted by a person who is failing to make a satisfactory school adjustment; to society in general, which must pay the cost of widespread maladjustment. In the form of neuroses, psychoses, and character disorders, defects of adjustment waste the manpower resources of the community and require huge custodial and therapeutic expenditures. The widespread psychological misery that stems from inadequate adjustment is reason enough to study the problem in the hope that adjustive failures can be understood and prevented or successfully treated when they do occur.

If we talk about adjustment in terms of achievement, that is, how good or bad it is, then we must consider criteria to determine the quality of adjustment. Such criteria have been provided by our culture in terms of its own particular value system. We must recognize that in other cultures or in other generations other criteria are often utilized, and some of the present indices of good adjustment might conceivably become signs of psychological illness in future generations. In some ancient societies, being psychotic and having hallucinations identified a person as like a god and someone to be revered. In others, it meant that he was possessed of devils and should be destroyed or imprisoned. Developing serviceable criteria of adequate adjustment requires value judgments, which are not scientifically derived but which depend on our beliefs as members of a particular society.

Criteria of the Adequacy of Adjustment

We can identify four main classes of criteria for evaluating the adequacy of adjustment. We can consider how comfortable psychologically a person feels, the effectiveness of his functioning in terms of skilled or intellectual performance, the presence or absence of physiological symptoms of tension, and the degree to which his behavior is socially desirable or undesirable. Let us examine each of these criteria individually and consider how they are used in assessing the adequacy of adjustment of any person.

Psychological comfort: One of the most compelling signs of adjustive failure is that a person is psychologically uncomfortable in some way. Examples of such discomfort include states of depression, chronic or acute anxiety, obsessive thoughts of guilt, or fears of illness or dying. If these states of mind occur so much of the time and to such a degree that the person is in great distress, they may stimulate him to seek help. Seeking professional assistance is likely to depend upon how much discomfort a person is willing to tolerate. Experiencing this discomfort often implies some inadequacy of psychological adjustment, although, as we shall see later, the difficulty may be considered well within normal limits in a statistical sense.

Work efficiency: Another sign of adjustive difficulties is impaired ability to make full use of occupational or social capacities or skills. A person may be failing in school, or chronically poor performance may result regularly in the loss of jobs. Such a person may be able to work consistently but only at a level far below his capabilities. He is sometimes unaware that he is functioning below par and may have difficulty understanding why he is failing occupationally or socially.

In actuality, reduced work efficiency is often attributable to states of stress, which can impair the ability of the individual to function up to his capacity. Figure 2 shows an instance of the experimental production of decrements in skilled performance under stress. The experimenters, Carlson and Lazarus (1953), harassed subjects in the experimental (or stressed) group, resulting in a performance curve considerably below that of a control (unstressed) group. The problem of psychological stress and adjustment will be taken up in greater detail in Chapter 11.

Physical symptoms: Sometimes the only evidence of inadequate adjustment appears in the form of damage to body tissues. The field of psychosomatic medicine has developed because of increasing recognition that physiological damage can be brought about by psychological malfunctioning. Disturbances of digestion, for example, are one of the most common ways in which difficulties of adjustment and their consequent

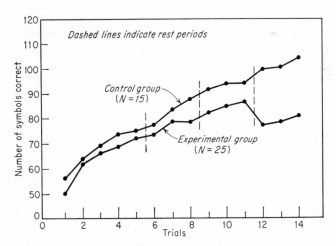

Figure 2. Digit-symbol test performance for the control and experimental groups. (*From Carlson & Lazarus, 1953.*)

tension states manifest themselves. The formation of ulcers, impairment of appetite, and persistent diarrhea are some of the symptoms that frequently reflect disturbances in psychological economy. That some of these symptoms can have a psychological origin is often vehemently denied by the patient, who may not recognize the existence of adjustive problems. That such physical symptoms have psychological origins is often ascertained by the fact that no physical basis for them can be found, and the disturbance may respond to psychotherapy.

Social acceptance: Some kinds of adjustments are socially acceptable and quite useful, that is, they are what other persons want. Supporting oneself by working at a legitimate job is socially desirable, whereas responding to financial necessity by stealing or other antisocial behaviors is not. Similarly, the discharge of sexual tension by assaulting women or children or being a Peeping Tom will lead to imprisonment, whereas obtaining sexual satisfaction through marriage is quite acceptable to society. The person whose mode of adjustment leads him to behave in ways that are dangerous to himself or to others will ultimately be hospitalized or imprisoned by modern society. The person whose processes

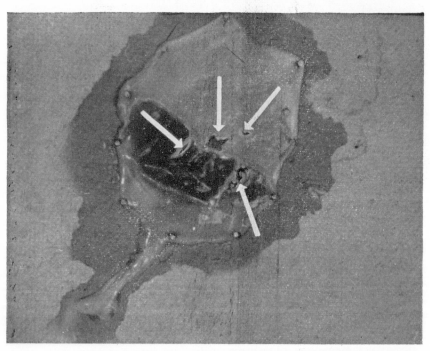

Figure 3. Rat's stomach with numerous ulcers produced by stress. Dark spots on inside of stomach wall are the ulcers. (*Plate contributed by W. L. Sawrey, based on research reported in Sawrey et al., 1959.*)

of adjustment lead to behavior that is a public nuisance may be criticized or shunned at the very least. In other words, some adjustments are poor simply because society regards them as poor.

It is interesting that acceptable behavior in one community may not be acceptable in another. For example, in the Samoan culture (cf. M. Mead, 1928), it is considered quite normal and acceptable for adolescent boys and girls to engage in homosexual activity prior to marriage. In our own society, however, we look upon homosexual behavior as reprehensible and even pathological. There is a certain amount of arbitrariness in the designation of particular behavior patterns as good adjustment or poor adjustment on the basis of their social desirability. This arbitrariness limits the scientific applicability of this criterion in the assessment of adjustive adequacy.

Application of the Criteria

There are a number of dilemmas in applying these four criteria to the adjustment of any individual. The cultural variation in standards mentioned above is one. Another difficulty is that a person can be considered well adjusted by one criterion and poorly adjusted by another. For example, in the case of a particular neurosis known as *conversion hysteria*, the patient may appear quite comfortable psychologically, but he must be considered seriously maladjusted from the standpoint of physical symptoms.

To illustrate, a student was referred to the medical clinic on a college campus with the complaint of being unable to swallow food. He was rapidly losing weight but upon examination showed no evidence of any physical pathology that might account for his symptoms. On this basis, he was referred to the psychological clinic. When asked about the nature of his school adjustment, he indicated that his relationships with other students and his professors were most pleasant and that he had absolutely no problems. An exploration of his relationships with his family brought the same kind of denial of conflict. "I don't have any psychological problems," he maintained. "Everything is fine. It's just that I can't swallow."

The nature of this student's illness was such that his symptom appeared in a physical way, although he seemed to remain psychologically comfortable. Clinical workers have called this unawareness of conflict in hysterical patients *la belle indifférence*. The presence of the symptom (inability to swallow) showed the existence of adjustment failure just as surely as if he had complained of depression or anxiety. It is therefore difficult to evaluate the adequacy of adjustment by a single criterion. The particular signs of maladjustment that characterize a person can relate to one or several of these criteria.

Can we regard a person who is psychologically comfortable but has physical symptoms as more poorly adjusted than a person who is in a state of psychological distress without such symptoms? This question cannot be answered without placing some kind of differential value upon the types of maladjustment symptoms. The types of symptoms that are considered especially serious tend to be a matter of opinion rather than a matter of scientific assessment. We are better able to describe individual adjustment by certain criteria than to determine in any objective way the desirability of such adjustment.

Another problem faces us when we try to assess adequacy of adjustment. It was noted before that depression or anxiety was a sign of difficulty in adjustment. How uncomfortable need a person be and for how long must he suffer before we say that he is maladjusted? Similarly, how socially undesirable must his behavior be in order to be considered pathological? What degree of psychosomatic symptom shall we consider as evidence of adjustive disturbance? How efficient must a person be socially or occupationally to pass as well adjusted?

The essential problem is to establish a *standard* against which to evaluate a person with respect to each of the four criteria of adjustment. This standard can be achieved in two ways. In one case, we can make interindividual comparisons. That is, we can compare a person with others and consider how adequately he is adjusted with respect to them.

These others can be an average or norm for the population at large. Thus, if one student obtains mostly A's as college grades, we would say that a B student is performing less effectively, although he still may be operating at a level above the average for the entire college-student population. In the same way, because most persons have a certain amount of anxiety, the presence of small amounts in a person would not seem pathological.

There is a difficulty in utilizing interindividual comparisons to assess the adequacy of adjustment. The difficulty is clearly seen in the case of the comparison of the college students' grades. How can we properly compare the two students in terms of effectiveness if the A student has far greater intellectual capacity than the B student? It may actually turn out that the B student is making more use of his intellectual potentialities than is the A student. In other words, the standards that we apply to different persons should not always be the same. In a similar way, an individual living in extremely adverse circumstances may appear more anxious or maladjusted than an individual who lives in very favorable environmental circumstances. The difference in their adjustment may be not a matter of differential ability to adjust but rather the result of differences in the demands made upon them.

The difficulty in applying interindividual standards to the assessment of adjustment can be partially resolved by utilizing an *intraindividual standard* as well. Thus, instead of comparing a person with others, we examine the same individual from time to time or under different conditions. In other words, we compare him with himself. If we know that a person has once carried the responsibility of a family and an important position in a high-level occupation and we now observe that the only type of job he can hold is one calling for minimum skill and responsibility, then we have rather significant evidence that his present adjustment is a poor one for him. This can be the case even though he is still functioning at a level above that of the average person in society. Similarly, the student in college may be getting B grades in his course work, which is certainly above average for the college population in general. However, this may represent a serious decline in his level of functioning from his previous record of A. The intraindividual evaluation of adjustment is an important source of information about a person's functioning, which, in combination with the interindividual approach, may greatly improve our ability to apply the criteria of adjustment adequacy.

There has been increasing dissatisfaction with the achievement approach to adjustment because of the many problems it raises. Chief among these problems is that to speak of good or bad adjustment requires some value judgment concerning how we should feel or act. Thus, if a person deviates from the immediate behavior norm, he is apt to be labeled as peculiar or even sick. This tendency has gone so far that even the crusaders who have fought social injustice, such as Florence Nightingale or Susan B. Anthony, the suffragette, are often identified in retrospect as maladjusted persons merely because they would not accept the *status quo* of a society that contained many evils. The term "well adjusted" has become almost synonymous with "conformist" (cf. Lindner, 1952). If a person goes along with the crowd, he is likely to be well regarded. If he attempts to produce social change, the modern, scientific epithet for him is the word "pathological." Struggle for all change or reform comes to be regarded as pathological, and in this way science unconsciously may ally itself with conservative or reactionary movements.

There is no way out of this dilemma of cultural relativism. The closest we can come to a solution is to focus on the ways in which persons adjust rather than on how successfully they do so. If we are to regard individuals as differentially effective in adjustment, we must try to consider success from the point of view of the nature of the modes of adjustment manifested rather than from the perspective of social norms or values. We must make an effort to be independent of our cultural traditions and take a cross-cultural frame of reference. So far as possible, we must consider adjustment as process.

ADJUSTMENT AS PROCESS

In the analysis of behavior as a *process* of adjustment, it is possible to take a longitudinal view of the problem and consider the genesis of the characteristic ways in which a person copes with demands made upon him. We can examine the gradual emergence and maturation, from infancy on, of psychological functions such as perception, abstraction, and self-control, which give a person progressively more mastery over his impulses and his external environment. The nature of his adjustment at any point in time will depend upon the form this development has taken and will be based upon biological factors in growth as well as upon his social experiences.

Some Psychological Functions Involved

The child at birth has a very limited *perception* of the world in which he lives. The primitive state of his perceptual apparatus makes him perceive objects and events around him in a diffuse and global fashion. In such a state he can do little to adjust effectively to changing circumstances, and he remains almost totally dependent upon benevolent adults. In the course of the growth and maturation of his nervous system, and through learning processes, he becomes able to articulate the details of his environment and develop a conception of himself as distinct from others. Eventually this articulation of the world becomes integrated into more complex perceptions and conceptions.

An experiment by Hemmendinger (1951) nicely illustrates this pattern of perceptual development. He employed amorphous ink-blots as stimuli and systematically observed the kinds of percepts that were given by 160 children between the ages of three and eleven. The task was to look at the blots and decide what they looked like or might be. The youngest children gave responses that were predominantly amorphous, diffuse, and confabulated. With increasing age (and presumably level of development), more precisely formed percepts were given, which clearly articulated separate parts. In the higher-age brackets, larger portions of the blots (and the whole blot frequently) were analyzed and differentiated into parts and then integrated into an organized totality. This research supported the concepts of Werner (1940) and others that the development of perception proceeds from the global and diffuse to the articulation and integration of parts, although psychologists are not altogether in agreement that the evidence is sufficient to support this assertion.

Along with this development of the perceptual function, other capabilities emerge. For example, initially the individual is bound to the concrete stimulus and can respond only to the immediate circumstances. He learns the structure and functions of particular objects and ultimately becomes capable of *abstractions,* so that the particular object becomes a member of a class of objects. In this way, the person is freed from concrete dependence on the immediate situation. He acquires the capacity to think and therefore to control his own actions and the events in which he participates.

The development of the capacity to *control* himself and his environment is one of the most remarkable aspects of man's behavior. When the small child experiences an impulse to pick up a fragile glass on the coffee table, he has little or no capacity to inhibit or delay this action. If the mother wishes to preserve her fine glassware, she must physically restrain the child. In his enormously popular book on baby and child care, Spock recognizes this lack of capacity for self-control in the very young child in the following way:[1]

How do you keep a year-old baby from hurting himself or the household furnishings, anyway? First of all, you can arrange the rooms where he'll be so that he's allowed to play with three quarters of the things he can reach. Then only a quarter have to be forbidden. Whereas, if you try to forbid him to touch three quarters of the things, you will drive him and yourself mad. If there are plenty of things he can do, he's not going to bother so much about the things he can't do. Practically speaking, this means taking breakable ashtrays and vases and ornaments off low tables and shelves and putting them out of reach. It means taking the valuable books off the lower shelves of the bookcases and putting the old magazines there instead. Jam the good books in tight so that he can't pull them out. In the kitchen put the pots and pans on the shelves near the floor and put the china and packages of food out of reach.

In the course of development, the child becomes capable of inhibiting the action of grasping the glass. Eventually he no longer acts on impulse but is able to interpose thought between the impulse and the action. In this way he becomes capable of controlling himself and managing events that are external to him. Psychological functions have developed that enable the child to make adjustments to a variety of circumstances. The form this development of psychological functions takes and the degree of such development determines the nature of the adjustive processes.

Two Broad Types of Adjustive Processes

When a conflict occurs between an individual's internal need states and external demands, two broad classes of adjustment patterns seem to be possible. The individual can modify or *inhibit the internal impulse*, or he can attempt to *alter the environmental demand* in some way so as to eliminate the conflict. Where the conflict is entirely internal or external the problem is somewhat different, but there remains a similar

[1] *Baby and Child Care,* by Dr. Benjamin Spock. Copyright 1945, 1946 (c) 1957 by Benjamin Spock, M.D. Published by Pocket Books, Inc., New York City.

problem of choice of which pressures to bow to and which to attempt to alter or modify.

With respect to biological adaptation, the organism can modify his own state in some way or attempt to alter the environment. As an example of the former, the bear hibernates during the bitter winter. He is so developed that an amazing complex of physiological changes takes place including a marked reduction in physiological activity such as heart rate and metabolism and a lowering of body temperature. These changes permit the animal to survive the winter in a sleeplike state without need for food or water. Unable to modify the environment to suit their needs, hibernating animals modify their needs so that they can survive. In contrast with the animals that hibernate, the human being has a greater capacity to alter the environment to ensure his survival and comfort. He builds a house, fashions clothing, and produces artificial heat.

Psychologically, we can find instances in which individuals change themselves rather than their environmental circumstances in the face of conflict between the two. For example, when a person finds that he believes differently from others concerning a social issue, he may alter his own views, sometimes without being aware of this, so they no longer conflict with others.

Asch (1952) has performed a fascinating experiment on the effects of social pressure on perceptual judgments. The subject in his experiment was required to match a visually presented series of lines with comparison lines of different lengths. In the same room with him were other persons who the subject thought were also being tested but who, in reality, were allied with the experimenter and said what they had been rehearsed to say when they were asked publicly to make their judgments. A large proportion of the time they gave incorrect answers so that the actual subject often found himself a minority of one. Even though the correct answers were quite obvious, tremendous social pressure was exerted on the subject to modify his judgment in favor of the group.

As Asch (1952, pp. 4–5) wrote, "There was a marked movement toward the majority. One third of all the estimates in the critical groups were errors identical with or in the direction of the distorted estimates of the majority. The significance of this finding becomes clear in the light of the virtual absence of errors in the control group, the members of which recorded their estimates in writing." The relevant data about the critical (influenced) group and the control group (uninfluenced) are presented in Table 1.

In response to this situation, the subjects conformed to the pressure of the group about 30 per cent of the time. In fact, some subjects, when questioned later, seemed to be entirely unaware that they had responded to this pressure, believing that they actually perceived the lines in the same way as the majority. The degree of conformity evidenced by the subjects depended upon the extent to which they were a minority, being less when an ally or two was inserted into

Table 1

DISTRIBUTION OF ERRORS IN EXPERIMENTAL AND CONTROL GROUPS
OF ASCH STUDY ON GROUP PRESSURE

Number of critical errors	Experimental group* ($N = 50$)	Control group ($N = 37$)
0	13	35
1	4	1
2	5	1
3	6	
4	3	
5	4	
6	1	
7	2	
8	5	
9	3	
10	3	
11	1	
12	0	
Mean	3.84	0.08

* All errors in the critical group were in the direction of majority estimates.
SOURCE: Asch, 1952, p. 5.

the situation. However, whereas some subjects modified their own perceptual judgments in accordance with the pressure, others did not, presumably choosing to permit the conflict to remain or perhaps reducing the tension by being critical of the judgments of the majority. Under other circumstances, these latter subjects might have attempted to modify the views of the others in order to eliminate the conflict.

Many writers on psychology have recognized the two general adjustive modes to which we have been referring. For example, Piaget (1952), who has been greatly concerned with the development of adaptive intelligence, has utilized the terms *accommodation* and *assimilation* to represent the alteration of oneself or the environment, respectively, as means of adjusting. In a colorful analogy, Lerner (1937) referred to the two groups as chameleons and beavers. The *chameleons* adapt immediately to the situation, changing themselves to suit the circumstances. *Beavers,* in contrast, continue gnawing through the trees regardless of what happens. Riesman (1950) described the *inner-directed person* as one who carries his values and standards of conduct around with him, maintaining these in spite of major changes in the social climate. In contrast with this is the *other-directed person,* who must take his standards from the social context, changing his beliefs in accordance with the altered values of the persons and institutions around him. The former person is the beaver, the assimilator, and the latter is the chameleon, the accommodator.

These two polarities of adjustment by no means exhaust the richness and variety of adjustment processes, but they provide us with useful abstractions in describing life styles. In later chapters specific adjustive mechanisms (such as repression and intellectualization) will be examined in greater detail. We might like to evaluate the two basic modes of adjustment, accommodation and assimilation, as to their adequacy, but, like applying the four main criteria of adjustment, what is good or bad is difficult to assess scientifically.

Both accommodation and assimilation produce resolution of conflict. It is interesting that, as we move up the phylogenetic scale from lower animal forms to man, we find an increase in the availability of means of assimilating. Lower animals can do little to alter their environments, and man is supremely effective in this regard. Lower animals are tied to the here-and-now stimulus, and man has the capacity to manipulate events mentally through symbols and thus see the consequences of his behavior before it occurs. The helpless human infant must accommodate and only later develops the means of altering external demands. The entire process of *socialization,* by means of which the child acquires the values and conduct patterns of the culture, is a process of accommodation, in which the child learns to inhibit and modify his impulses in favor of environmental pressures, and develops new ones that are culturally determined. It is doubtful whether creativity can occur in the context of complete accommodation, because accommodation involves accepting whatever exists externally and altering oneself accordingly rather than making new combinations of ideas. The artist who follows existing dogmas concerning art can be commercially successful, and the one who blazes new trails risks ridicule and conflict. But he sometimes emerges as a creative person.

In view of these considerations, it is tempting to consider accommodation as a more primitive form of adjustment than assimilation. Although the question is an interesting one, it cannot be settled here and it is subject to the criticism that the relative merits of either requires the making of value judgments pro or con. The human being, in order to adjust successfully must do some accommodating and some assimilating, and it is probable that an extreme of either goes along with maladjustment. The useful question for the psychological scientist is how does the individual adjust rather than how well?

INTERPERSONAL COMPETENCE

Some writers on adjustment, impatient with the traditional achievement concept of adjustment but convinced that different degrees of adjustive skill or capacity exist, have stressed the notion of social adequacy or interpersonal competence. They do not mean by this that particular traits or habits of response to specific situations differentiate the more adequate from the less adequate person. Rather, certain qualities that operate under many circumstances characterize an individual and make him effective in controlling the pattern of interpersonal relationships. Such persons are more capable of producing intended effects and achieving self-realization, gratifying their highest needs under a wide variety of circumstances.

For example, Phillips (1953) attempted to evaluate psychiatric patients in terms of their *social adequacy* prior to becoming ill. He used such criteria as the amount of economic, occupational, or family responsibility the individual accepted, his sexual maturity, and the degree of psychological independence he had shown toward his family. He found that those psychotic patients in mental hospitals who had histories of generalized social inadequacy are less likely to recover from the psychotic episode than those who had displayed evidence of greater effectiveness but who became ill because they could not cope with some immediate crisis.

Foote and Cottrell (1955) proposed the term *interpersonal competence* to stand for those little-understood social skills that give the individual control over his interpersonal affairs and increase the likelihood of optimal personal development along self-chosen lines. They pointed out that, at the level of common sense, persons differ markedly in their aptitude for dealing with others. They suggested, further, that such competence depends upon the uniquely human processes of suspended action, memory, reverie, foresight, reflection, and imagination, by means of which a person from birth onward escapes progressively from the control of his immediate environment and, in turn, begins to control it. Freedom from irresistible instincts and external stimuli that claim the responses of lower animals enables man to modify his surroundings, plan, create, and have a history and a future. This detachment from the present situation makes it possible for him to declare his own identity as an adult. The competent person is better able to accomplish this detachment and to develop values of his own.

Variants of this point of view will be found in the writings of Adler (1924), Horney (1937), Sullivan (1953), Fromm (1941), Erikson (1950), and Maslow (1954), from which Foote and Cottrell have borrowed ideas.

Piaget (1952) maintained that a guiding principle of development is the progressively increasing freedom of the person from the concrete event and the increase of such distance by means of man's capacity for symbolization or representation of it. In their emphasis on power or control, Foote and Cottrell seem also to be saying that assimilative modes of adjustment are more adequate or higher level than accommodative. The achievement of self-identity cannot be brought about by accommodation alone; it must involve the manipulation of the world in relation to one's own needs.

It is interesting to note how much in recent years the emphasis has shifted from accommodative to assimilative values in considering the adjustive process. Writers on this subject have tended more and more to eschew the philosophy of the ideal, well-adjusted man as one who passively accepts the social world about him and "adjusts" himself to it. An extreme version of this passive view of adjustment had filtered down from psychology to the lay public. It led people to feel ashamed of their anxieties and dissatisfactions with their life circumstances. One now hears increasingly often, however, criticism of the "cult of conformity" and attacks on comfort seeking as opposed to dedicated striving and self-sacrifice. This shift occurs at a time when, professionally, there is more and more tendency to view mental health as positive striving. Terms like competence are increasingly often introduced into treatises on adjustment.

In recent years, Jahoda's (1958) approach to mental health, which stresses positive striving, has received considerable interest and attention. She presents a series of criteria of positive mental health that includes acceptance of the self, growth and self actualization, a unifying outlook on life, autonomy, the perception of reality that is free from need distortion, and mastery of the environment. Notice the deemphasis here on conformity to social demands or socialization and psychological comfort. The focus is clearly on assimilative adjustive efforts.

An even more recent statement of the importance of the concept of competence has been made by White (1959) in a penetrating review and critique of current approaches to human motivation. White proposes the thesis that a variety of behaviors, including visual exploration, grasping, crawling, walking, attention and perception, language and thought, curiosity and manipulation of the environment, is part of the process by means of which the person (and lower organisms as well) learns to interact effectively with the environment and develops "competence" to change or control the environment for his own ends. Thus, in White's timely discussion we again see the important role in human development and adjustment that is played by the concept of competence. The socially oriented psychologist of personality conceives of competence primarily in terms of interpersonal relationships, that is, as concerned with trans-actions with the social aspects of the environment. But the essential point remains the same. Effective adjustment requires competence to affect, manipulate, or control the environment.

The difficulty with the notion of social adequacy or interpersonal competence is that such concepts tend to be vague and unspecified with respect to the particular processes that make up competence or adequacy. What are the operations or measurable qualities that result in or contain competence? Such qualities surely cannot be taught in the simple sense, because they do not involve specific acts like driving a car but rather a variety of acts, which may vary from circumstance to circumstance. Rigid adherence to some formula of interpersonal interaction (e.g., Carnegie, 1937) results only in awkwardness or frustration. Yet if the notion of interpersonal competence is to be useful and meaningful to us, we must be able to specify operations that characterize competence and incompetence regardless of the culture or circumstance.

Foote and Cottrell suggested six components to interpersonal com-petence: health, intelligence, empathy, autonomy, judgment, and creativ-ity. Their analysis is interesting, but it is still a long way from thorough clarification of the processes associated with the notion of competence. More thought and research are necessary to evaluate the concept. On the face of it, the idea appears to have considerable merit; there are great individual differences among persons in their adequacy to cope with interpersonal relations, differences that are not reflected in the analysis of mental health in terms of comfort, social acceptability, efficiency, or absence of physical symptoms. Should the point be reached where we can more clearly specify what the specific qualities of interpersonal competence are and how they are determined, we would be in a far better position to influence constructively the mental health of the population.

In our society, change is the order of the day. Society is no longer rela-tively immobile and stable. Flux characterizes our laws, family organiza-tion, customs, residence, and values. Such flux places a tremendous burden on families and individuals to adjust and move constructively toward higher personal and social development. Knowledge about what character-istics make for such effective adjustments would be of enormous value in helping us to meet the crises that such continuing change brings about in the modern world.

The Nature of Personality

After being oriented toward the concept of adjustment in the first chapter, you may wonder at what seems to be a digression into the area of personality. You may ask: "What has personality to do with adjustment? Aren't they two different ways of interpreting behavior? You have whetted my appetite concerning adjustment, and the topic is suddenly dropped."

In a certain sense, it is correct to say that personality and adjustment are two different interpretive frames of reference about behavior. However, they are intimately related, and it is difficult to consider one without the other. This is especially true when adjustment is viewed as process, that is, as methods of dealing with internal and external demands. These methods depend upon the structure and organization of personality, the stable attributes that a person carries around with him, so to speak, which determine his approach to the problems of living. The notion of adjustment as process leads us directly into the field of personality, because it is the process aspect of the structure of personality.

For this reason, we must now embark on a more detailed consideration of the nature of personality. Moreover, as we shall see, there are many ways of conceptualizing personality and its development, and we must understand the most important of these in order to feel at home with the issues of adjustment that we shall deal with again later. After a systematic orientation into the field of personality and its development, we shall return to such matters as failures of adjustment and their treatment.

THE CONCEPT OF PERSONALITY

The human being lives in continuously changing circumstances to which he must respond and direct his actions. His behavior is extremely varied because of the variety of situations to which he responds. If he is verbally insulted, he is likely to react differently than if he is complimented. Similarly, in one social situation he is expected to speak out, and in another, silence is more appropriate. Man's actions are continually attuned to the internal as well as external conditions to which he is exposed.

On the basis of the common-sense relation between the stimulus and behavior, it would be natural to seek understanding of man's actions in the transitory milieu in which he is always embedded. Changes in personal behavior would be attributed to changes in stimuli. Because the external stimuli are easier to identify, they are apt to become overemphasized as the mainsprings of behavior.

The fact is that we cannot understand behavior simply by reference to the external circumstances in which it occurs. It is true that variations in action and feelings do tend to follow external events to some extent, but there is also a remarkable degree of consistency or identity to an individual. Persons seem to carry around with them dispositions to think or act in certain ways that are independent of the situation. For example, we find one individual who practically never evidences anger, even under extremely provoking circumstances. Another person carries a chip on his shoulder, so to speak, becoming angry or hostile for the slightest reason.

In the first illustration, we cannot attribute the absence of hostile behavior to the external circumstances, because they provoke hostility in most other persons. In the second instance, we cannot blame the anger on the situation alone, because it occurs independently of the circumstances. The hostile behavior or its absence in both these cases shows consistency from situation to situation. We must attribute it to characteristics within the person, dispositions to act in certain ways, which a person carries with him. The pattern or organization of these dispositions is what we call *personality*.

We should make an important qualification at this point. It is correct to say that without understanding the nature of an individual's personality we cannot fully understand his behavior. It is equally true, however, that a knowledge of personality without reference to the circumstances in which a person behaves also provides limited understanding. This is why making statements about future behavior on the basis of an analysis of personality structure alone is so hazardous. We rarely know what the future external conditions of this behavior will be. Therefore, statements about future behavior do not represent scientific predictions on the basis of a knowledge of all the relevant conditions. The personality of an individual makes certain behaviors highly probable and others improbable, and our predictions are essentially statements about these probabilities. The actual future behavior of a person is determined by the interaction of both his personality structure and the social and physical circumstances in which he acts.

GENERAL LAWS OF BEHAVIOR AND THE INDIVIDUAL CASE

Science advances by formulating general principles about the events in the world. All sciences systematize the multiplicity of facts by including many events under a relatively small number of concepts. Without such systematization, the world would remain a chaotic and unmanageable collection of facts. The problem for the personality theorist is to provide such a manageably small number of rules that apply to persons in general and enable us to comprehend their varying behaviors.

There are millions of persons in the United States and several billions of persons in the world. Each is unique and different from every other person, although they are also similar to each other in certain respects. To have separate principles for each person would require too many to be convenient. Scientists try to determine general principles that can apply to the universe of cases. Such abstract or general principles will necessarily tend to overlook or obscure minor variations between persons, and an apparent gap between general principles and the individual specimen will always exist.

Let us illustrate this gap by considering the growth of trees. There are countless numbers of trees on earth. Each tree is different from all others, just as human beings differ. But there are general principles that apply to all trees regardless of the species or particular specimen. We know, for example, that all trees absorb moisture and mineral substances from the ground through their roots and convert these substances into tissues (foliage and wood) by means of photosynthesis. The nature of this absorption process and of photosynthesis is essentially the same for all trees. They constitute general botanical principles. They are so general that they apply to other botanical classes as well as trees.

The question arises whether these general principles can be applied to an individual specimen of tree. To a certain extent, they certainly can, but they cannot be accurately applied to predict the rate or characteristics of growth of the tree unless very detailed information about the particular tree and its conditions of life is provided. The general laws obscure differences in individual trees or species of trees. For example, rates of moisture absorption differ, and the soil conditions that are most suitable for one specimen are not so suitable for another. The kinds of life experiences, in terms of weather, injury, etc., vary from tree to tree. Thus, the specific characteristics of the absorption and growth processes will depend upon the unique combination of events in one particular case. Such events are always lawful and describable in general terms, but application to an individual case presents a complicated problem. It requires a large number of specific bits of information from which to predict the particular event.

The scientist of personality is interested, fundamentally, in general laws about behavior and its underlying structure. The botanical scientist is concerned with general laws about plants. There are times, however, when understanding and predicting the behavior of an individual case is of paramount practical importance. For example, in our back yard there may be a sick or retarded tree in which we have an economic as well as aesthetic investment; or one of the members of our family may be mentally ill. A knowledge of the general principles of pathology will not reassure us, if they cannot be applied to the individual tree or person about which we are concerned.

This gap between general laws (sometimes referred to as a *nomothetic orientation*) and the practical application of knowledge to an individual specimen (*idiographic orientation*) represents the gap between the pure scientist and the applied scientist or practitioner. It is true wherever we have a practical stake in the operation of the world about us. The distinction is manifest between the primary interests of the biologist and the physician, the physicist and the engineer, the theoretical psychologist and the clinical practitioner faced with the task of helping a person in trouble. The problem of the individual case is keenest in the human specimen where individual variation is great and where the welfare of the individual person is so important.

Another problem in applying general laws to a particular case has to do with the availability of the necessary information. We may be able to make precise predictions in some applied scientific fields on the basis of our knowledge of the important factors, but the measurements that would make such prediction possible are not readily available. Take the example of the meteorologist who is trying to forecast the movements of a dangerous hurricane. If all the relevant conditions for its movement were known, such as the path of the jet stream far above the earth's surface and the pressures and air currents along the course of the storm, the forecaster might be far more accurate. Often however, he does not have such information. In recent years, greater effort has been expended to get it by using radar, high-altitude balloons, and airplanes that enter the storm and plot atmospheric conditions.

Though the meteorologist may have a well-documented theory about weather, we are acutely aware of his failures in forecasting because weather is so important to us personally. The same problem exists in psychology, where psychological illness or the activities of political leaders or of various interest groups are so vital to our national and personal welfare. Precise application of scientific laws is often less important in other fields, and we make fewer demands on their theories. For example, no one would ask the physicist to predict the exact course of a falling snowflake. The problem of the individual case exists in physics, but it does not bother us as much. The following was recently written about the magnetic properties of metals by de Klerk (1953, p. 4): "Some substances, for example, iron and nickel, show a rather complicated magnetic behavior at room temperature. When placed in a magnetic field, they show a magnetic moment which not only is a function of field and temperature, but which also depends on the history of the specimen; that is, it depends on the fields and temperatures in which the substance has been before."

In other words, to predict the magnetic behavior of an individual specimen of metal, it is necessary to have precise information about the nature of the specimen, including its history. Although the general laws of magnetics are known, each specimen is unique in terms of the conditions to which it has been exposed and it has to be studied as such. This is exactly what we say about personality. Although we may have a great deal of knowledge about the general principles of behavior, each person has a unique history and is different from every other person. To consider the personality of an individual, we must examine his unique history and properties in the light of the general principles about personality organization and development.

PERSONALITY: AN INFERENCE FROM BEHAVIOR

If we asked the question: What are people like?, we might receive many answers. They might include physical appearance, emphasizing the similarities and the variations in physical structure. We would need some descriptive terms, and these terms would depend on the nature of the physical attributes that we consider important or worthy of description. Such dimensions as height, weight, bodily proportions, and skin color might be included. Instead of anatomy, the physical functions that persons can perform might be emphasized. Thus, instead of describing the muscle and bone structure, we could talk about the postures and movements of which this muscle and bone structure is capable (process). Structure always represents the more or less permanent arrangement of things, whereas process refers to what they do and how they interact, develop, or change.

Suppose the same question were asked in the psychological sense. We could then describe the characteristic behavior of the person, that is, how he acts in most situations. For example, he is dominant, aggressive, shy, uncertain, or optimistic. We would have some difficulty, however, in talking about the structure underlying this behavior. Physical functions such as walking, digesting, and speaking must have an anatomy or structure, and it is easy to observe this anatomy because often definite organs can be referred to, although the control and organization of these processes (e.g., through activity of the nervous system) is a more difficult matter. It is extremely difficult to recognize the structures underlying psychological functions, although such structures must exist. Sometimes we have to imagine what the underlying structure is like, because it is not directly observable. When we try to go beyond the description of behavior to the underlying structures, we find considerable difficulty and enter the area of theory construction.

It is important to recognize that personality is not simply how the person acts. If we say that a person is aggressive, we refer to an observation that he behaves aggressively. By saying that he is aggressive we are merely describing or interpreting his superficial acts without reference to the personality determinants that produce them. These determinants are what we are trying to describe and comprehend. Because personality involves the stable characteristics that determine action, our problem is to describe them adequately and state how they work.

The problem of identifying the psychological structures underlying behavior is difficult because these structures are not directly observable. The psychological structures must be inferred from the behavior itself. The problem is the same for the physicist concerned with the nature of matter. The wood in the chair you are sitting on appears stationary and solid enough, and it seems fanciful to propose that this solid object is made up of atoms and subatomic structures that are in constant motion. These atomic structures cannot be observed, yet they are conceived to be the basic building blocks for all matter and are thought to function in certain ways. Theorizing about these structures has proved fruitful and has resulted in the construction of atomic and hydrogen bombs and in the creation of industrial power plants. These are practical consequences of hypothetical structures that have never been seen.

In a similar way, human behavior can be understood by postulating the existence of certain hypothetical structures which can never be seen directly but which power and direct action. Just as the concept of the atom has been useful to the physicist in explaining matter and energy and in controlling the physical world, psychological theories of personality structure aid us in understanding human behavior.

SOURCES OF INFORMATION
ABOUT PERSONALITY STRUCTURE

There are two main and overlapping sources of information about personality structure: the individual's verbal report (to reflect inner states), on the one hand, and other forms of observed behavior, on the other. These, of course, are not strictly separate, for both are behaviors that someone observes. However, we can treat the verbal report as a direct reflection of a private psychological experience. In a sense, it is thus an introspection. If we are concerned with organisms lower than man, the verbal report of inner experience is, of course, not available. Many times the inference that we draw from one is not the same as the inference we might draw from the other. For example, let us consider a young man who has been out on a date and who returns to his room unusually early the same evening. His roommate, noting his friend's crestfallen appearance and the early hour of his arrival, questions him about the evening. The young man offers the information that he has been jilted by the girl he has been dating.

"Oh," says the roommate, "that's too bad. You must feel awful."

"Not at all," says the young man. "I didn't care about her one bit. It doesn't bother me at all." And for the next two hours, to his roommate's dismay, the jilted young man protests how indifferent he is to the girl who rejected him.

What can we learn about the underlying feelings and motivation of this young man from his reported introspections and his other behavior? If we take his report at face value, we must believe that he doesn't care about the loss of the girl. But such an interpretation fails to ring true in the face of his crestfallen appearance and lengthy denial of distress. He protests too much. As we appraise the situation, we are led to believe that, in spite of the fact that he maintains the contrary, he is quite shattered by the rejection. Thus, the combination of manifestations of strong emotion and overprotestation and reported introspections including denial of concern leads to a different interpretation about his feelings than would be obtained by simply asking him how he felt and taking his report at face value. Moreover, distress is the reaction we might reasonably expect under these circumstances. Shakespeare, in *Hamlet,* has given us a line to illustrate the mechanism inferred here. At one point, Hamlet's mother says, "The lady doth protest too much, methinks." In describing this same kind of psychological event, Freud used the term *reaction formation* to refer to the process of concealing unacceptable motivations by the steadfast insistence on the opposite.

In the same way that we can be wrong in literally taking a person's verbal report to stand for the actual psychological process, we can also misinterpret the actions of the person. We notice, for example, that someone maintains an air of great confidence and self-assurance. He readily criticizes others and takes credit for being highly superior. Such behavior can lead us to infer that this person has a great sense of security and perhaps even considers himself superior to others. It comes as a great surprise when he reports that he is easily frightened in social contexts and is only able to put up a confident front by dint of great effort. Through his reported introspections, which he may communicate to a close friend or therapist, we get the picture of someone who feels inadequate and insecure and who is surprised, though pleased, that his bravado is successful and that others look upon him as self-assured.

Because interpretations of personality are inferences from verbal introspections and other forms of behavior, great care and ingenuity are

Figure 4. Look at this picture and try to infer what the two boys are thinking and feeling on the basis of the situation portrayed and the expressions on their faces. The actual story is printed upside down, below. See whether you have sized up the situation correctly. (*Wide World Photos.*)

"Please, Spade, don't sit down now." The boy at the left bursts into tears as his huge collie decides to stage a sitdown strike just as Spade, his entry, was being judged in a school pet show. The boy on the right observes sympathetically.

called for on the part of the psychological scientist or practitioner who uses them. Because the underlying personality structures and processes are scientific conceptions, there are alternative ways of theorizing about behavior. Thus, one finds a variety of theoretical systems, all of which attempt to describe and explain behavior. They attempt to conceive the stable structures and processes underlying human behavior and to develop models of how they operate to produce the observable aspects of our psychological life.

THE CONSTRUCTION OF THEORY

The scientific step of creating hypothetical constructs about personality structure (anatomy) and process (function) is referred to as *theory construction*. For a good understanding of adjustment and personality (or any scientific enterprise, for that matter), one must grasp the nature of theoretical constructs. Let us look more closely at this matter of scientific theory construction, especially as it applies to personality.

Three kinds of statements are made about the biological, physical, social, and psychological world. One kind might be called "nonscientific," because such statements are not dealt with by scientists and no attempt is made to check them empirically. They depend upon faith. An example might be religious dogma, such as "God is omnipotent."

A second kind of statement might be called "empirical." Such statements include the observable facts of a science or the hypotheses about observable relationships that are found in the world in which we live. These empirical statements are directly testable. In psychology, they refer to behaviors of human beings and animals and the observable conditions under which these behaviors occur. Thus, it takes a simple experiment to determine whether a score on a test (however this score is interpreted theoretically) is related to academic grades in college.

The third kind of statement might be called "theoretical," because it represents the concepts of any science, which are devised to make the empirical events of the world understandable. They bring order to chaotic facts and enable us to account for as many of them as possible. Whereas an empirical statement can be directly tested because it always deals with observables, theoretical statements have to do with imaginary constructs (like electricity or the atom in physics, neural mechanisms in physiology, the chemical activation of cell differentiation by genes in biology, and roles in social psychology) and they must be tested indirectly by a process of deduction. These deductions are "if . . . then" statements; that is, if the system of constructs applies, then we should find certain directly observable and measurable consequences of them.

We then arrange experiments to see whether the empirical consequences we deduced from the theoretical statement actually are found. If the empirical facts do not accord with the deduction from our theory, then (assuming we have performed an adequate experiment, using satisfactory measurements of the variables), we must discard the theory or revise it to conform better to the facts.

Let us consider an example of this kind of scientific procedure in the study of personality. You will recall the concept of "reaction formation," which was illustrated (the overprotestation in *Hamlet* and by the student who had just been jilted). This is an example of a hypothetical construct (i.e., a theoretical statement). We do not observe the reaction-formation process, but we observe some behavior that is consonant with and defines the process. The observable behavior breaks down into two aspects: the denial of concern or feelings of loss about the breakup, and the exaggerated amount of effort and emotion expended in the denial. One asks: "Why, if he doesn't care, does he keep talking about the matter?"

Theoretically, it has already been suggested that persons attempt to protect their self-esteem and reduce anxiety by sometimes disguising their true feelings from themselves and others. From this point of view, denial of a feeling does not always correctly represent the actual process underlying the behavior; under certain conditions it reflects the defense mechanism of affirming the opposite state of affairs. Thus, we can understand the excessive emotion that goes along with the denial by referring to the construct of "reaction formation." We have interpreted the observed event in terms of a hypothetical process embedded in a particular theory or set of constructs about personality.

But this does not illustrate how such a construct might be tested experimentally or by systematic observations. Some recent work (Lazarus, 1959) illustrates how this problem comes up in experimental research.

Experimental subjects were shown two motion-picture films, one benign, the other highly stressful. During the presentation of the films, measures were taken of the subjects' heart rates and skin resistance to electric current. These autonomic nervous system indices are extremely responsive to emotional states such as fear and anger. After the film, the subjects were asked to indicate their reactions to the films. Many of them noted extreme distress in response to the stressful film. Others gave no evidence of any involvement, sometimes even stating that it didn't bother them in the slightest (see Table 2).

The critical question here is whether the denial of disturbance represented an accurate statement about the subject's emotional state or whether it had the character of a defensive maneuver designed to conceal and reduce the distress. An examination of the heart rates and skin resistances of these subjects, in many instances, showed the latter. The

Table 2

DIFFERENT REACTIONS OF ELEVEN EXPERIMENTAL SUBJECTS EXPOSED TO THE SAME STRESSFUL FILM[*]

Subject	Interview statement of reaction
1	"I accept it as life but I didn't think that this sort of practice still existed on earth today."
2	"God, I'm shocked! and nauseated. It made me sick."
3	"I was completely disgusted to the point of almost being ill."
4	"Shocked—disgusted—I felt like vomiting and wanted to leave."
5	"Wished I had never seen it for now I feel extremely tense and nervous."
6	"Interested in customs; disliked poor sanitary conditions of surgery; confused as to basis of custom and its function; curiosity about function of fires; amusement at the dancing; appreciation of stoic control of subjects."
7	"There were many puzzling parts and I found myself wishing there was sound accompanying it."
8	"At first I was curious, then I became very interested in what was going on."
9	"I was bored with the film and felt that watching it was a complete waste of time."
10	"I thought that it was a rather interesting movie. As a premedical student I was especially curious about the techniques."
11	"The film was unusual, but it didn't bother me a bit."

[*] The diversity of feeling expressed here is interesting when it is considered that all these subjects saw exactly the same film about subincision rites in an Australian tribe, initiating its adolescents into manhood. The ritual shows an operation on the penis and scrotum of the young men by means of a stone knife, along with some tribal ceremony.

No consistent differences were found between these subjects in evidence of emotional reaction as indicated by autonomic nervous system measures of heart rate and skin resistance. Most of the subjects, even those denying verbally that they were upset or expressing relaxed attitudes, showed marked physiological reactions indicating they were strongly aroused.

SOURCE: Lazarus & Speisman, 1960.

same subjects who denied distress often displayed arousal of the autonomic nervous system (innervating the heart and sweat glands of the skin) of great magnitude. This suggested that, in spite of the denial, there was considerable stress. Indicators of emotional reaction supported the notion that a defensive mechanism of denial was operating and that the subjects were attempting to deceive at least the experimenter, if not themselves. The use of such autonomic nervous system indicators as heart rate and skin resistance is the basis of modern lie detection in criminology.

Shaffer and Lazarus (1952, pp. 43–44) describe the process of personality-theory construction and verification as follows:

Psychologists for a long time have observed cases of physical symptoms in people who have had no signs of organic injury or disease. In order to account for this observation the existence of a process called "conversion hysteria" was postulated in which some individuals were thought to respond to emotional problems by developing a physical symptom. This symptom served the purpose of disguising for the patient the true nature of the problem. The patient was said to have repressed the traumatic events and to have "converted" the dammed-off energy into a physical symptom.

It should be clear to the reader that all that can be observed directly in patients with conversion hysteria is the physical symptom for which the patient has come for medical assistance. Any explanation of this symptom in terms of some psychological processes can scarcely be tested directly. One cannot see the defense process or measure it. The concept of defense mechanism is an imaginary (hypothetical) construct which is introduced to make the behavior which we have observed meaningful. For such an explanation to be proved reasonable it is first necessary to demonstrate that the hysterical patient's symptoms are in some way different or distinguishable from the symptoms of the patient with real organic pathology and to set up empirical models which are appropriate to the theoretical statement of defense mechanism which must be tested. The real question in any of this activity of model-making is whether the empirical model is appropriate or is a good analogy to the construct from which it is derived.

The work of Hilgard and Wendt (1933) and Cohen, Hilgard, and Wendt (1933) illustrates the manner in which a hypothetical construct may be handled by the use of an empirical model. It was found possible to show that a hysterical patient (who reported that he was blind in part of his visual field) could actually perceive light sensations in the reportedly blind areas. The authors (Cohen, Hilgard, and Wendt, 1933) demonstrated with this patient that a light which preceded a sudden sound altered the patient's normal eye-wink reflex to sound whether the light was presented to the blind or unimpaired visual area. This phenomenon could not be produced in the blind part of the visual field of a patient who was known to have had hemianopsia (genuine organic blindness in part of the visual field) with a history of organic injury (Hilgard and Wendt, 1933). Moreover, it was also shown that the hysterically blind part of the visual field could be conditioned to give responses to a light stimulus. It was possible to conclude from these experiments that, in the hysterical patient, blindness was not the result of an organic defect and should be accounted for by some psychological mechanism (hypothetical) which could not be directly observed. These experiments represent empirical models which serve as support for the notion that certain psychological defense mechanisms are operating in hysterical conditions.

SURFACE, DEPTH, AND UNCONSCIOUSNESS IN PERSONALITY THEORY

By now it should be clear that the concept of personality is not equivalent to observable patterns of action of the person, but it has to do with unobservable (hypothetical) constructs that are inferred from that behavior. Of course, it is still possible to offer a description of a person that is strictly behavioral and nontheoretical, that is, what an individual does or says in a variety of contexts. This has been referred to as a *surface* definition of personality. In contrast, we have been offering the more common *depth* interpretation. Allport (1937), over twenty years ago, wrote an excellent treatment of the surface-depth distinction in the field of personality.

When we refer to the underlying structure of personality—the aspects of it that are deep, inner, or central—we are in one sense saying that they are not accessible to direct observations. But in doing this we have not entirely exhausted the meaning of "depth," at least as it is commonly used by personality theorists and in the typical clinical description of personality. We can speak not only of inaccessibility to direct observation but also of inaccessibility to the person himself. It is implied that the forces that energize and direct behavior have the quality of being *unconscious*. They exist and proceed to organize behavior without the awareness of the person. In fact, they are often thought to remain unconscious because of mechanisms that prevent them from becoming conscious.

Sanford (1956) recently suggested that this quality of unconsciousness is the essential one underlying the surface-depth distinction. He implied that we cannot ask the person about the underlying structure of his personality because it is inaccessible even to him. Certainly this is what Freud and the later psychoanalytic theorists meant by the underlying structure of the personality. We must recognize, then, that the constructs of personality have this dual meaning, sometimes referring primarily to their properties as theoretical models and at other times having this added property of depth or unconsciousness.

It is methodologically very difficult to test the notion of unconscious determination of behavior (especially when our view of unconsciousness implies that material is being actively prevented from attaining consciousness). One of the critical difficulties is to differentiate between the simple reluctance or refusal of a person to communicate his real feelings to someone else and actual instances of self-deception. For example, in the experiment of Asch (1952) that was briefly reported in Chapter 1, subjects had the task of judging lengths of lines while subjected to tremendous group pressure. The planted allies of the experimenter kept publicly giving the wrong answers, and the subject, who had to make his judgment after the others had made theirs, frequently went along with the group, often when his private judgment was contrary. However, when Asch interviewed the subjects afterward, he found some persons in this situation who appeared to be totally unaware that they had been influenced by the group. Were they really unaware of the situation, or did they simply not wish to share verbally with the experimenter their willingness to conform to the group pressure? In other words, were they unconscious of their response to the pressure or simply unwilling to admit it?

The only way the problem can be solved experimentally is to find situations in which there appears to be no reason for the subject consciously to withhold information; even here there can be no absolute proof, because our judgment about what is conscious always depends upon the subject's report, usually verbal. What we can say is that there are many instances, especially in the clinical situation where one is dealing with neurotic patterns of behavior, where an individual *appears* to be totally unaware of influences directing his behavior. It is theoretically reasonable, then, to infer the existence of processes of which an individual is unconscious. It is postulated that awareness of these processes is highly disturbing and is avoided by the person.

The therapeutic situation is one instance that provides evidence of unconscious processes. States of amnesia and hypnosis and many neurotic manifestations are consistent with the interpretation of unconscious processes, although there are always alternative interpretations possible. The notion of unconscious processes is a theoretical one, and personality theorists, especially those working in the clinical setting, have continued to find it most useful in accounting for many of the phenomena they observe. For this reason, the notion, which was originally elaborated by Freud, has survived for many decades.

CONSISTENCY

The science of personality depends upon the consistency of the individual. A person must carry some attributes with him from situation to situation that influence his behavior. However, in referring to consistency, we must ask: "What is it that is consistent?" Do we mean that the person performs the same or similar acts under different conditions? Or can his actions be quite dissimilar and still reflect some constant underlying structure? The problem of consistency is so important to personality theory that it deserves some further elaboration.

Consistency of Acts

The question of personality consistency in terms of acts (a behavioristic or surface approach to personality) has interested psychologists for a long time. Because in this form the problem is rather easily handled by exposing the person to different conditions and observing whether certain acts are repeated, the problem of consistency was first studied experimentally in this way. For example, in 1928, Hartshorne and May reported an extensive study of consistency of moral behavior. Among the questions that Hartshorne and May sought to answer were whether persons behave honestly or dishonestly in response to specific situations, and whether moral character resides within a person independently of the circumstances.

A large number of preadolescent children were studied under a variety of circumstances. Tests were constructed that permitted the children to act honestly or dishonestly in a variety of situations. For example, in one such test cheating was measured by giving the children a school examination, returning it to them, and asking them to grade their own papers. The teacher read aloud the correct answer to each question, and each child indicated on his own paper whether his answer was right or wrong. As a child saw no obvious external danger of being caught, he had an excellent opportunity to change his answers and improve his grade. Unknown to the child, however, a wax impression had been made of his original set of answers, and any changes could be identified by comparing a child's corrected paper with the original. In some instances a child could take his examination home to grade. Similar situations were constructed in competitive sports. By comparing behavior in different circumstances, it was possible to tell whether a child who acted honestly in one situation was also likely to act honestly in another.

Hartshorne and May found only slight consistency (an average correlation of about 0.30) in children's moral behavior from one situation to another. Arguing from these results, the authors propounded the "doctrine of specificity," which stipulated that honesty was not a character trait of the individual but rather that there were only honest acts in response to particular situations.

The Hartshorne and May studies were models of experimental ingenuity, but they can be severely criticized as missing many of the crucial points in the problem of consistency. For one thing, the use of preadolescent children offers some limitations because such a population has not yet developed a stable personality organization to the same degree as adults. Character is still forming in early adolescence and behavioral consistency is less likely to be found than at a later age. It can also be pointed out that the "doctrine of specificity" ignores the fact that there were some tendencies, although small, to act consistently from one situation to another. In fact, there was a small proportion of children who acted honestly in all the experimental situations and of others who behaved dishonestly in any experimental situation that permitted it. Furthermore, such factors as religious training, intelligence, and socioeconomic status played a role in determining whether a child would behave honestly or not, suggesting that some underlying factors arising out of a child's experience were important in determining his behavioral honesty.

Of greatest importance, however, is the fact that Hartshorne and May defined consistency in a behavioral sense only. That is, they asked whether honest or dishonest behavior would be repeated from situation to situation. They did not, however, consider the underlying reasons that determined the behavior. For example, it was found that brighter children cheated less than duller children. One might say that the brighter children had less reason to cheat because they knew their work and were confident of doing well. The tests probably resulted in differential motivations on the part of the children to succeed, and no doubt they provoked a great deal of fear of doing poorly. Thus, although a child may have behaved inconsistently from situation to situation, the underlying reasons for the behavior were probably characteristic of the child's personality. A child who was highly motivated to succeed and knew the material well in one test situation might not cheat, but given a test that threatened him with failure, he might behave dishonestly. Thus, the superficial behavior might be different from situation to situation, but the underlying structure, the child's pattern of motivation, might be very stable in spite of changes in the external conditions. This underlying personality structure leads to different behavior as a function of the nature of the external conditions. The Hartshorne and May studies demonstrated a degree of inconsistency in behavior, but they failed to address the problem of the possible constancy of personality structure.

Consistency of Expression

Psychologists have observed another form of behavioral consistency that can be called *consistency of expression or style.* In contrast to purposeful or intentional acts, style or expression represents the form that any intentional act can take. We can easily recognize a popular vocalist by the style that characterizes him apart from the song or the circumstances in which he sings. These styles are sometimes so characteristic and unique that they can be widely imitated by others. In the same way, the act of lighting a cigarette can be performed in qualitatively different ways by different persons and we can recognize one way as characteristic of a particular person. The act itself does not differentiate the two individuals, or one person under different conditions, but the style or form of expression may. The term "style" can include the tempo of our acts, as in the case of handwriting, where our letters can be large and expansive or small and cramped. Another example is the degree of emphasis in our motor behavior, such as the extent to which we bear down on the pen or pencil or give gestures that are definite or uncertain and delicate.

There can be no question that forms of expression exist and appear consistently in the same person from circumstance to circumstance. Allport and Vernon (1933) have performed perhaps the best-known set of experiments dealing with the question of the consistency and organization of these forms of expressions, which they have called *expressive movements*. They have been able to show that certain of these forms of expression tend to go together and to be consistent for an individual under different conditions. But like our actions themselves, these expressions are relatively superficial manifestations and cannot be understood without reference to underlying structures, which must be hypothesized and investigated.

Consistency of Internal Structure

The problem of the consistency of underlying structures in the person is a difficult one to explore because, as has been said, these structures are not directly observable but are inferred from behavior. We assume that these structures exist and that they have a certain degree of stability. They represent the dispositions of a person to act in certain ways. It is the enduring dispositions rather than the transient ones that form the essence of what we mean by personality.

An experiment by Lazarus and Longo (1953) illustrates one of the ways in which the consistency or stability of these underlying processes has been studied. A group of students were given the task of unscrambling a number of sentences, the words of which were all mixed up. Half of these scrambled sentences could not be solved at all; the words could not be put together to form a meaningful sentence. The other half could be readily solved. The students were told that this was a test to measure their intellectual competence and should indicate their potentiality for academic and vocational success. The subjects were unaware that some of the sentences could not be unscrambled. A time limit was set for each sentence. Some students who were allied with the experimenter were mixed in with the group of regular subjects. When a scrambled sentence impossible to solve was presented, these false subjects each put their pencils down to convey the impression that they had completed the sentence, while the experimental subjects continued trying unsuccessfully to find the answer.

At the end of this part of the experiment, the subjects were asked to recall as many of the solvable and unsolvable sentences as they could. Some of them remembered predominantly the sentences on which they had been successful, and other subjects recalled predominantly those sentences on which they presumably had failed. It was argued that this selective forgetting was the way in which the subjects had protected their self-esteem. For some subjects their self-esteem was best protected by forgetting all about the unpleasant experiences of failure. For others, the defense of self-esteem was attempted through rumination about the failures—the symbolic repetition of the threatening experiences over and over again so that they could be neutralized. This resulted in better recall of the failures than of the successes.

The question was whether this differential recall of successes and failures represented a consistent defense mechanism (hypothetical construct) that the subject would employ under other conditions of psychological threat. Those

Table 3

MEAN PERFORMANCE OF Ss AS RELATED TO THE TENDENCY TO SHOW
SUPERIOR RECALL FOR SUCCESSFUL OR UNSUCCESSFUL SENTENCES

Group	Recall in terms of per cent of total *		Relearning by number of trials	
	S†	N	S	N
Superior recall of successes	56.1	74.0	3.12	2.55
Superior recall of failures	72.1	60.0	2.60	3.34

* This comparison results in a difference between groups by a chi-square two-by-two analysis that is significant beyond the 0.01 level of confidence.
† Refers to shock syllables and N to nonshock syllables.
SOURCE: Lazarus & Longo, 1953, p. 497.

subjects who had shown an extreme tendency to recall their successes, and other subjects who showed an extreme tendency to recall their failures, were selected for a further experiment. They were presented a list of nonsense words to learn. Each word was paired with another word so that when the first word was presented the other word had to be remembered. Half these nonsense words were followed by the presentation of a painful electric shock regardless of whether the subject gave the right response or not. Only these latter word pairs ever led to the shock. The subjects were never shocked on the other word pairs. Again, at the end of this experiment, the subjects were asked to recall as many of the shocked word pairs and nonshocked word pairs as they could.

It was found that the subjects who had previously protected their self-esteem by recalling their successes rather than failures tended to recall predominantly the words without shock. On the other hand, those who had recalled mostly failures remembered the shocked words best during the second experiment. These subjects presumably carried with them the tendency to remember selectively either unpleasant or pleasant experiences, and this characteristic was independent of the nature of the experimental circumstances. Some process underlying behavior was operating (was consistent) in the two situations that was characteristic of the subject himself and that could be considered as a way of dealing with threat in the two different situations. The essential findings cited above can be seen in Table 3.

MOTILITY

Up to this point we have been emphasizing the identity of the person from situation to situation. If there really were a high degree of consistency in a person's actions, we would have to consider his behavior as rigid and mechanical. He would be at the mercy of certain underlying structures, and it would be difficult to conceive of him rising above these to adapt to his environment. Total consistency of acts would entail a view of human behavior similar to the tropistic concepts employed in biology. In such a view, human behavior would be similar to that of the moth, which is irresistibly attracted to the light and can destroy himself as a consequence of his mechanical, phototropic response. If we expected very great consistency from a person, we would of necessity have to expect considerable restriction in his capacity to control his life. Such control or direction calls for motility or variation as well as consistency.

Although we must assume a certain degree of stability in personality structure, we must leave room as well in our theory of personality for progression or change. Psychotherapy assumes that personality structure can somehow be altered; otherwise, we would have to be quite fatalistic about the possibility of treating maladjustment. If we assumed that the personality structure was so rigid as to be impervious to change, then we could have little hope of doing much for a person whose personality has developed in pathological or deviant directions.

We generally assume that the development of personality structure involves a progressive increase in stability and organization with age. The child is most susceptible to influence. With advancing age, the structure becomes relatively rigid, and an older person is a poor risk for psychotherapy because of this inability to change. The older person is less able than the young person to survive personal and social change or upheaval.

Some personality theorists emphasize the early age at which personality structure has been formed and stabilized, and others stress the continuing development and change that can take place throughout most of life. Reality exists somewhere between these two extremes. In adult life the personality structure is quite stable and somewhat resistant to change. However, this stability need not be rigid or unchangeable, particularly in the most mature person or under conditions of great stress. Persons can be very adaptable to the changing demands of life. Their most cherished systems of values or patterns of motivation and the forms of control exerted over behavior are subject to some modification. If this were not so, then social change, which is always a characteristic of our society, would leave most of us in a totally maladaptive state.

SOME BASIC CONSTRUCTS OF PERSONALITY

We have discussed the idea that certain hypothetical structures underlie observable behavior, and we have considered some of the problems associated with this idea. Let us direct our attention briefly toward some of the particular structures that are commonly conceived and consider how they function to determine behavior. Different theories of personality tend to emphasize different kinds of underlying processes in describing personality, but there are two classes of constructs that are found in some form or other in a great many theories. These two constructs are *motivation* and regulation or *control*. Let us examine them more closely.

Motivation

From a common-sense point of view, a concept like motivation is easy to accept. We find ourselves wishing that certain things would happen. We sense an intentionalness about our behavior; that is, we desire or intend to do something. We want to bring about some result or state of being, and we engage in behavior aimed at such a result. For example, we want to see a certain movie, and so we arrange our affairs accordingly and gratify our wish. The action of going to the movies seems logically to be the result of the desire to see the movie.

There is *direction* to our acts: direction toward eating, toward drinking, toward winning in a competitive game, toward seeing a particular movie, and so on. This direction has a dimension of *intensity*. For example, we speak of wanting something very badly or only slightly. We observe a person striving toward some goal with great doggedness in the face of obstacles. We speak consequently of strong motives and weak motives. When motivations are strong, they crowd out anything else in our behavior. Efforts to gratify them persist in spite of discomfort.

The hypothetical concept that stands for the underlying force that impels behavior and gives it direction is *motivation*. All theories of personality postulate some such underlying force, although its nature is not identically conceived by different theories. The terminology of motivation varies, but whether one speaks of motive, drive, need, impulse, id, wish, want, or valence (some of the terms used), there is a common implication—the existence of a force of some degree of intensity activating or arousing behavior. The object or goal of this force defines its direction and determines how we label it.

This problem of critically examining the arousal and directional aspects of behavior that define the presence of a motive state is not a simple one. The rules of operation of motives must be based upon the observable conditions that define them. Let us examine a little more closely what this means. What are some of the conditions that identify the existence of hunger motivation? We know from our observation and experimentation that, when a person is deprived of food, certain changes are observable in his behavior. We find that he becomes more preoccupied with thoughts of food as the degree of deprivation increases. The experiments of Brozek et al. (1951) on human semistarvation, mentioned in Chapter 1, showed that subjects living for many weeks on inadequate, low-calorie diets began to think more and more about food and eating. They would search magazines for illustrations of food and plan future careers as cooks and in other occupations associated with food handling. In addition to these introspective changes, we find increased energy directed at food-seeking activity. Thus, the arousal of a state of hunger motivation could be inferred from the antecedent condition of deprivation of food and from the behavioral consequences of such deprivation—activity intensively directed toward finding and eating food. Observing such antecedent and consequent conditions, we can state that the person has a strong state of hunger motivation.

When motivational states are physiological in nature and are essential for physical survival (hunger, thirst, sleep, etc.), it is not so difficult a matter to identify the antecedent conditions and the behavioral consequences from which this state can be inferred. It is much more difficult to do this in the case of social motivations. It is quite a problem to identify conditions of arousal of the need for love, achievement, prestige, and support. What is more, the goal-seeking behavior is far more obscure and embedded in many other patterns of goal-oriented behavior. However difficult the problems, the task is essentially the same as with physiological motivations. To identify a motivational state in a person, it is essential to know what conditions produced this state and what the effects of this state are on behavior.

In one of many experiments designed to show the influence of social motivation in behavior, Atkinson (1953) divided subjects into those who had strong achievement motivation and those whose achievement motivation was weak on the basis of an analysis of stories told about a series of pictures (Thematic Apperception Test). The subjects were required to perform a series of routine tasks under three conditions: *task orientation,* in which no effort was made to create any specific experimental atmosphere and in which the tasks were simply presented to the subjects to be performed; *relaxed orientation,* in which the importance of the tasks was minimized and a jovial and casual atmosphere was created; and *achievement orientation,* in which the tasks were presented as measures of important high-level abilities and in the context of evaluating the subjects. The subjects were made to fail to complete half of the tasks but were permitted to complete the other half. After the performance, they were asked to recall as many tasks as they could. When the instructions clearly indicated that completion of the task meant success and incompletion meant failure (the achievement-orientation condition), those who were high in achievement motivation recalled relatively more uncompleted (unsuccessful) tasks than subjects who were low. Under the relaxed condition in which little or no references were made to success and failure, the opposite trend was observed, with the results

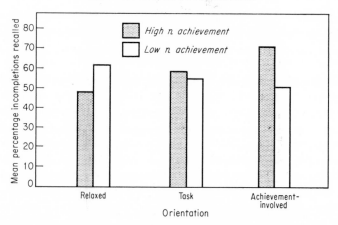

Figure 5. Mean percentage recall of incompleted tasks by subjects above and below the mean achievement score under three types of instructional orientation. (*From McClelland et al.,* 1953.)

of the more ambiguous task-orientation condition falling in between. Thus, motivational characteristics of the subjects partly determined their relative recall of completed and uncompleted tasks.

Other problems arise from our efforts to explain behavior in motivational terms. What are the motives that direct human behavior? How many are they? Are these motives shared by all persons or merely by some? Are they all equally important, or are some more critical than others? Do the patterns of motives vary in different persons? What is the origin of motive states? What happens when a motive is not gratified? What aspects of behavior do motives control or influence? These are some of the questions with which the psychologist interested in motivation must deal. They are also some of the issues that any theory of personality must address. Later we shall see how some of the main theoretical approaches to personality answer these questions. At this moment, however, the important thing to remember is that, in most theoretical systems dealing with personality, some conception of motivation remains a key hypothetical construct.

Control

The notion of motivation in personality involves primarily excitation or the impelling of action toward a goal. It must also be recognized that any goal can be reached by a variety of routes. Social prestige can be obtained by economic success or by preeminence in science or in politics. These routes or means to ends distinguish individuals as much as the goals toward which they are striving.

Moreover, at any time some motives can be gratified and others have to be inhibited. Because many motives exist in an individual simultaneously, his behavior would be chaotic if he attempted to discharge all the motivated impulses simultaneously. As you read this book, you may also be experiencing hunger or you may wish to go to a movie or out on a date. Somehow you are successfully inhibiting a variety of motives as you currently study the text material. The activity of reading is impelled by the momentarily stronger motive of becoming educated or passing an examination on the subject matter of the text. Regardless of the term used to describe these inhibiting processes and choice of routes through which gratification of motives is sought and accomplished, regulating or controlling structures are important aspects of personality theory. Regulation, control, inhibition, ego control, ego defense, and style of life are some of the terms that have been used to refer to these structures. The goal aspects of personality are motivational; the control aspects refer to the manner in which the goal is attained and the selective inhibition of impulses.

The importance of control can be readily seen when we consider what would happen if behavior was determined solely by impulse. It was pointed out earlier that as the child develops he gains the capacity to regulate his behavior. In early childhood the presence of an impulse is tantamount to the act. Later the child is able to inhibit action when it is dangerous or undesirable or conflicts with a stronger motive. In this way, control, which was originally external, becomes an aspect of the inner organization of the personality. Living together harmoniously depends upon our ability to regulate impulses in relation to the needs and expectations of others.

Some writers have treated these processes of control as a motivational system in itself. Instead of postulating the existence of motivational states on the one hand and forces that regulate the expression of these motivational states on the other, they have suggested that control represents a kind of impulse or motivational state in itself. One motive may not be expressed because another motive is in conflict with it or is more powerful. Thus, the impulse to attack someone may be less strong than the wish to be liked or accepted by him, and it is consequently not discharged. This type of formulation is merely another way of conceptually describing the activating and regulating forces that govern behavior. It occurs partly because of a degree of conceptual imprecision in defining motivation in terms of direction as well as arousal. The concept of control seems also to include directional elements. Personality theorists have not always been precise on the overlap between motivational and controlling forces.

One of the many experiments illustrating the role of regulating factors in the personality on behavior has been performed by Block and Block (1952). On the basis of personality-assessment procedures (questionnaires about behavior), three kinds of subjects were identified: overcontrollers, appropriate controllers, and undercontrollers. The first group was considered to exercise excessive control or inhibition with respect to the expression of their needs, and the third group exercised insufficient control.

The experimental procedure was essentially simple. Subjects were given a dull, repetitive task of filling a tray with spools. When the tray was filled, it was immediately emptied by the experimenter and the subject again began to pack the spool box. The subjects were told that when they didn't want to do it any more they could stop. But when a subject indicated that he wished to discontinue the task, the experimenter responded, "Don't you want to do some more?" If the subject answered "No," the experimenter said, "You really want to stop now?" If the subject insisted that he still wished to stop, the experiment was terminated. If he went on with the task, the same sequence was followed each time he indicated his desire to stop. Those subjects who continued the spool packing were considered to have submitted to the experimenter's authority and those subjects who did not, to have stood up to it.

The experimenters predicted that overcontrollers would most frequently continue spool packing and that undercontrollers would most readily discontinue the task. Their reasoning was that undercontrollers exercised little inhibition over their impulses, and when faced with the desire to quit, they would do so without restraint. In contrast, overcontrollers, in spite of their wish to discontinue, would inhibit this in response to the social pressure of the experimenter. The results confirmed this prediction and are consistent with the hypothesis of the determination of impulse discharge by the process of ego control.

However the problem is stated, at least two types of forces in personality must be postulated: those that impel the person to a particular action, and those that inhibit this action or impel behavior in directions incompatible with the first. I shall refer to motivation and control (excitation and inhibition) as the essential processes governing behavior. Whether personality theorists call the regulating or inhibiting processes

Table 4

THE RELATIONSHIP BETWEEN REACTIONS TO AUTHORITY AND EGO CONTROL

	Subjects continuing spool packing	Subjects not continuing spool packing	Total
Overcontrollers	10	10	20
Appropriate controllers	7	11	18
Undercontrollers	1	15	16
Total	18	36	54

SOURCE: Block & Block, 1952, p. 95.

motives of a special type or employ other terminology, the existence of such conflicting forces in personality is assumed by all theoretical systems.

Organization

There is one more general concept to be discussed in considering the nature of personality. Two basic hypothetical constructs have been outlined: motivation and control. In discussing motivation, the existence of a variety of motives that activate behavior was implied. In discussing control, it was implied that motives are regulated (inhibited) as to when and how they are gratified. The question arises whether personality is best understood as a collection of discrete structures or whether there is some organization that functions as a total integrated system. There is often a tendency to conceptualize personality as many motives and controlling forces functioning in isolation. Each of these forces has its unique effects on behavior and can be isolated for purposes of analysis from other aspects of personality. This segmentation of psychological structures is less easily seen in considering control processes than in dealing with motives, because the former already imply a governing or organizing process.

It is convenient for purposes of exposition and experimentation to discuss personality as a number of discrete processes, but this introduces a great deal of artificiality into our conception of personality by considering these functions as separate and independent. The behavior of a person seems quite coordinated, and most of the time he does not act as though the various components of the personality operated independently. Thus, for example, there was some kind of overriding organization implied when Freud, dealing with the regulation of impulses, used the analogy of the censor who stood guard at the gate of consciousness, permitting some impulses to gain admission and others not. As will be noted in later chapters, other writers have postulated such a governing or organizing principle in the form of the self concept.

The notion of organization in personality has been severely criticized because it can easily appear mystical and because it is rather difficult to examine scientifically the observable conditions that define its operation. If there is a kind of little man within us who tells us what to do, as is often the image perceived in the case of Freud's censor, who tells the little man what to do? The postulation of such a self of selves leads to an infinite regress and to the questionable practice of explaining behavior as the vagaries of some magical little entity within us.

On the other hand, it is equally unsatisfactory to consider personality as a collection of discrete and unorganized structures. It is sensible to postulate the existence of some organization by which the various parts (structures of personality) somehow work in unison. No one would seriously propose, however, that some magical agent or demon produced this organization. Like any other scientific principle, the laws of this organization must be potentially discoverable and should ultimately be stated in terms of their empirical antecedents and consequences. But it is difficult to consider as complicated a matter as organization without having firsthand knowledge of the individual structures and their functions, which make up the totality.

THE DEFINITION OF PERSONALITY

It was previously stated that personality is the organization of stable structures within a person that disposes him to act in certain ways. These structures are in reality hypothetical constructs that are inferred from behavior. Some of the fundamental constructs have been illustrated in the discussion of motivation and control. Essentially, we have been talking about the formal nature of personality, but the reader has, as yet, no clear picture of a systematic set of constructs with which to think about personality substantively. The form has been presented, but not the content. You can still legitimately ask: "Well, what *is* the nature of personality? I understand that it is an inference and that it involves various constructs, organized in a certain way. But what are these constructs specifically, and how are they organized?"

There is not one answer but many to these questions. The content of the hypothetical system of constructs making up the personality depends upon which theory is espoused. Freud set up one particular set of constructs in attempting to build a theoretical model. He developed a special terminology for these constructs and postulated a particular set of principles about their organization. Jung, Adler, Rank, Horney, Fromm, and Sullivan have offered well-known alternatives to Freud's system. There are many other theorists who have ventured into the realm of personality-theory construction, more or less elaborately. Which set of constructs should we espouse? It seems more appropriate in such a text as this to avoid accepting any special system but rather to attempt to give the reader a sense of the nature of personality as it is conceived by the most important theorists. In a sense, therefore, these theoreticians can speak for themselves and provide their own ideas concerning the specific nature of personality. The subsequent chapters offer a panorama of personality theory.

II

PERSONALITY THEORY

WITH MAN SO COMPLICATED an organism it is not surprising that many schemes would exist for conceptualizing his personality. However, this multitude of schemes also attests to the early stage of our present knowledge, for science normally progresses by dropping poor theories that do not conform to the empirical world and developing more advanced ones that do a better job of encompassing all that is known. Most of the theoretical systems that we are about to explore are products of the early twentieth century, although they all have roots that go far back in the history of ideas. As our knowledge broadens, the present theories will be replaced or modified to keep pace with it. These refinements will be better stated and lead us more successfully to specify the biological and social conditions of life on which personality depends. The theories that we shall explore should be regarded as halting, beginning steps toward understanding personality, taken only recently in a modern science less than one hundred years old.

A few special words of guidance for the next five chapters should be provided. Chapters 3, 4, and 5 present what might be called "frames of reference" from which to view personality: specifically, trait and type, association learning, and phenomenology. Strictly speaking, a frame of reference is not a theory but only a start toward one, in which the kinds of units of description and the general perspective have been determined. Within any of the frames of reference many specific theories, varying in content, are possible. Thus, in the trait-and-type frame of reference one can find more specific theories; for example, those of Cattell and Eysenck. Both writers offer somewhat diverse theoretical systems, with somewhat different assumptions, but yet they share the main perspectives. Similarly, for the association-learning point of view, there are many ways of detailing the learning process, and only the most influential view is presented here, that of Dollard and Miller. With respect to the phenomenological frame of reference, eight divergent views, which share a phenomenological outlook, have been described.

The reader should also recognize that theories vary in degree of elaborateness or completeness. They may be in early stages of development with only the most basic postulates available. This may be because a theorist did not know how to proceed further or did not have the opportunity (for example, Prescott Lecky died before getting very far with his views) or for any number of other reasons. Of all the theoretical systems to date, Freud's psychoanalysis is by far the most extensive and elaborate. Other psychoanalytically oriented writers, such as Horney, have been content to eliminate parts of psychoanalysis as unacceptable or to add concepts without altering many of the basic elements of the total system. It will become apparent that some writers have said a great deal and others have said little, adding only a few but significant ideas to the total picture.

Finally, it should be said that no point of view can be as completely presented here as in the original source or even as in the best secondary source books that survey in greater detail the field of personality theory. The reader is urged to explore later some of these fuller and more advanced accounts. I wish to commend especially one recent source, on which I have leaned heavily for my summaries because of the generally accurate and well-organized treatment of the great majority of theoretical points of view. This is *Theories of Personality* (Hall & Lindzey, 1957). I have made particularly heavy use of this source in Chapters 5, 6, and 7. Another book well worth recommending in this regard is *Schools of Psychoanalytic Thought* (Munroe, 1955), which I have liberally consulted, especially for the material on Otto Rank, in Chapter 7.

Theories always consist of speculations, but they are, along with known facts about the world, fundamental parts of science. The real essence of adjustment and personality is contained in the ideas presented in the next five chapters, and knowledge in this field must be considered very limited without an awareness of the broad scope of material encompassed by personality theory.

CHAPTER
3

Personality in Terms of
Trait and Type

In our day-to-day attempts to denote stable human qualities we have available an extensive trait vocabulary. For example, we describe a person as lazy, ambitious, melancholy, happy, aggressive, or dependent. In a study of trait names in the English language, Allport and Odbert (1936) found nearly 18,000 terms used to describe human characteristics. The systematic use of such descriptive terms is one of the commonest ways of talking about personality and identifies the trait approach.

Persons can also be classified into types by their pattern of traits. For example, a person who has the traits of being impressed by the objective facts of the world, behaving according to expediency, accommodating readily to new situations, and being relatively indifferent to his physical welfare can be called an *extrovert*. In contrast a person who is oriented subjectively rather than objectively, whose conduct is governed by absolute standards and principles instead of expediency, who is relatively inflexible and lacks adaptability, and who is overattentive with respect to his physical well-being can be classified as an *introvert*. This dichotomous division of persons into extroverts and introverts is based on Jung's theory of types and is one of many such classification schemes found in the psychology of personality.

The trait and type approaches to personality are logically related. The first part of this chapter is concerned with the concept of trait; personality typology will be developed later.

THE TRAIT APPROACH

As pointed out in Chapter 2, the essence of a science of personality is the consistency or stability of the person. To say that a person has a particular trait implies such consistency. If the trait applies in one particular situation but not in any other, it has no generality and is not a useful way to describe the person. If we say that Jack is belligerent, we

53

mean not that Jack is belligerent at one particular moment or situation but rather that Jack behaves belligerently under a wide variety of circumstances. Thus, a trait involves consistent patterns of reaction that are typical of the person.

In Chapter 2 it was noted also that consistency could be considered at several levels of analysis: consistency of acts, consistency of expression or style, and consistency of the underlying structure of personality identified by inferences from behavior. In the same way, traits can refer to consistent patterns of action, expression, or underlying, depth characteristics of the personality. For example, we say that a man has the trait of honesty, meaning that he is consistently honest from situation to situation. Similarly, from the point of view of expressive qualities, we can describe a person's tempo of action as rapid or slow. This too can be regarded as a trait. Lastly, when we say that a man is ambitious for power, we are making an inference about an underlying motivational construct, a trait that directs his actions from circumstance to circumstance, even though the acts themselves appear inconsistent. Thus, in one situation he might behave obsequiously to someone in authority, and in another he might mercilessly and publicly attack authority figures. These superficially diverse reactions can reflect an underlying ambition to be powerful, which the individual tries to accomplish in different ways depending upon the circumstances. Although the behavior itself seems inconsistent, the enduring motive trait of ambition for power is stable and postulating it helps us relate these diverse action patterns. A variety of situations and a variety of responses on the part of the individual have been made equivalent by the inference that some underlying trait has determined them.

There is a very practical reason for speaking of personality in terms of traits apart from the reason of understanding behavior. It has to do with the problem of anticipating or predicting what an individual may do in the future on the basis of what we know about him in the past. Such predictions are a rather important part of our everyday social behavior, although this is not always apparent to us. For example, we depend upon the stability of the social world in which we live—so when we return home after a day's work we will find our family acting in a predictable manner toward us. We expect our mother and father to behave in certain accustomed ways. We expect our teachers to continue their lectures in the direction in which they started and on the appropriate topic. Imagine what a world it would be if we could not in some rough degree anticipate the behavior of the persons closest to us and that of our associates with whom we work or play. The fact that they have stable personality traits makes this predictability possible.

How Traits Are Discovered

The discovery of traits is a relatively simple matter when we are considering the superficial level of acts or expression and much more difficult when we are dealing with the underlying structures (theoretical) that are the sources of action. Let us consider, for example, the surface trait of shyness. The behavior of the shy person is characterized by reticence with strangers, and the term "shyness" simply identifies this kind of behavior. If we are observing the person's behavior in one particular social situation, we may note that he acts shyly. At this point, however, it would be dangerous to generalize that shyness in social situations characterizes his behavior. Perhaps some particular factor in this social situation (such as the presence of a parent or some specifically embarrassing relationship with one of the persons involved) is constraining the person to behave reticently. It is therefore necessary to observe the same person in other social situations. If it turns out that under numerous stimulus conditions he displays shy behavior, we have good reason to attribute to him the trait of shyness. We have, in a sense, eliminated or reduced in importance the external-stimulus variable as the determinant of his behavior because we see the same reactions occur under a variety of circumstances.

The identification of the underlying sources of behavior can be accomplished in a similar fashion with one added step, the logical process of inference about what factors might be responsible for the observable patterns of behavior under different circumstances. Suppose that we find that several surface characteristics seem to go together (be positively correlated) in persons under a variety of circumstances. These characteristics might be a large vocabulary, ability in arithmetic, and tactfulness in social situations, to illustrate from Cattell (1950), a prominent trait theorist. This is a broad surface trait including three patterns of behavior that go together under varying conditions. The question now arises: What are the underlying sources that determine the presence of this surface trait? One possibility is that general intellectual capacity is involved in all three of these action patterns. That is, vocabulary size, arithmetical ability, and tactfulness all depend upon intelligence. All three characteristics spring from a single root. Thus, by inference, we say that the underlying source of these surface characteristics (which together form a broad trait) might be general intelligence. This theoretical reasoning can be checked by seeing whether independent tests of intelligence predict the three characteristics. The inference cannot be tested directly, because it is based upon theoretical speculation about an unseen construct: intellectual capacity. The step of going from surface-level traits (behavioral) to underlying or depth traits (hypothetical constructs) is a theoretical one.

Trait Dimensions

There are a number of dimensions along which traits can be classified. These dimensions have to do with different kinds of traits that writers have postulated for the adequate description of personality. They include such distinctions as common versus unique traits, surface versus underlying traits, broad versus narrow traits, and whether the content of the trait involves abilities, motivational and control processes, or expressive or temperamental qualities. These distinctions will be discussed more fully.

Common versus unique traits: Some traits are found widely distributed through the population or among certain groups. Therefore, we can speak of traits that an individual shares with others. Trait terms like honesty and aggressiveness are used by society to evaluate the behavior of persons in general and are sometimes called *common traits*. A particular person may be the most aggressive or most honest individual in his group, and this relative position may be consistent in a wide variety of situations. The trait terms aggressiveness or honesty can be applied along a scale of degrees to all individuals or groups.

In contrast, we can talk about individual or *unique traits,* referring to patterns of behavior or characteristics of personality that have no interpersonal reference but apply only to a single person. Frequently, the common trait terms are not useful for describing certain consistent attributes of a particular individual that are not shared in any degree by others. The consistencies from which the unique trait is inferred are intraindividual rather than interindividual. That is, the person behaves in a particular manner or has some characteristic that is unique to him and characterizes him much of the time. Allport (1937), in his important book on personality, has argued for a sharp distinction between common and unique traits, focusing on the uniqueness of the individual.

An interesting problem arises with unique traits because we cannot think of terms that are recognizable to others to describe such traits. If they are unique to a single person, they represent a way in which he is different from all others. Thus, such a term would not be applicable to anyone else. In other words, terms like honesty, aggressiveness, submissiveness, dependency, and pessimism all have interpersonal reference and are common traits. If we speak of an individual as aggressive, this aggressiveness is compared with the degree of aggressiveness of other persons as well. It is easy to describe persons in terms that have interindividual implications, even though such terms tend to force everyone into a common mold. Although we can recognize abstractly that each individual has combinations of characteristics unique to him and unlike any other, it is difficult to apply this distinction in practice because a different set of terms would be required for each individual and we could not relate the terms used for one person to the terms used for another. For this reason trait descriptions in practice generally depend upon some common social reference; that is, the traits apply more or less to everyone.

Surface versus depth traits: Most writers about traits have recognized a further distinction with respect to trait dimensions, one that should be readily understandable in the context of the previous discussion of theory construction and consistency of underlying personality structure. Traits considered at the behavioral or action level are called *surface traits* as opposed to underlying or *depth traits* (constructs). In the illustration used previously in this chapter, size of vocabulary, arithmetical ability, and tactfulness in social situations might be considered as surface traits because they describe behaviors that are directly observable. Tactfulness is a disposition to perform certain acts in social situations that are interpreted as tactful; similarly, size of vocabulary and score on an arithmetic test are directly derived from behavioral responses. On the other hand, the underlying sources or structures that determine these behavior characteristics must be inferred rather than directly measured. General intellectual capacity in the earlier illustration is a substance trait accounting for the observed surface manifestations.

Writers have used a variety of terms to make the same distinction between surface and depth traits. Cattell (1950), for example, referred to "surface" and "source" traits. Allport borrowed the terms "genotypical" and "phenotypical" from Lewin, who took them from the field of genetics and applied them by analogy to the surface-depth dimension. Allport presented the distinction with great clarity, as follows (1937, pp. 324–325):

It is obvious that what seems to be the *same* trait may, in different people, have quite diverse origins. Shyness in one person, for example, may be due to hereditary influences that no amount of contrary pressure from the environment has been able to offset; in another person, shyness may stem from an inferiority feeling built by an abnormally exacting environment. In spite of dissimilar histories, in appearance and in effect, the shyness of these two persons may be very much alike. Conversely, two youths suffering some shocking experience of grief or bitter disappointment, objectively alike, may be affected very differently. One of them becomes morose and ineffectual, lost in his trouble; the other stiffens his back and becomes more realistic and aggressive. The same fire that melts the butter, hardens the egg.

Lewin has shown this general problem of appearance versus underlying cause to be of considerable importance in the investigation of personality.

Description in terms of here-and-now attributes are phenotypical; explanatory accounts, seeking underlying motives and stresses are genotypical.

Broad versus narrow traits: Another dimension along which traits can be considered has to do with the number of types of behavior that can be considered under a particular trait term. For example, in Cattell's system of classifying traits the smallest behavior fragments or narrow traits are called *trait elements.* Cattell wrote: "The dictionary gives the trait of 'manual dexterity'; but this could be split into 'dexterity in shuffling cards,' 'dexterity with a screwdriver,' and so on." In other words, many trait elements make up broad or general traits like manual dexterity, which can include a wide variety of specific acts (namely, dexterity in shuffling cards, etc.). Each of these specific acts could be considered a minor trait. However, these individual behaviors tend to cluster together to form a relatively large constellation of acts, which is classified as a *broad trait.*

It would be an endless and impractical task to try to describe personality in terms of the thousands of narrow traits that can be identified. It is more economical to look for groups or clusters of traits that ordinarily go together. There is clinical and statistical evidence to show that persons who are dominant in their relationships with others tend also to be assertive, egotistic, tough, vindictive, and hardhearted. Thus, trait elements or narrow traits are grouped together in such a way that specific behavior patterns can be organized under a single, more general heading of a broad trait.

Dynamic, stylistic, and ability traits: This consideration of trait dimensions emphasized formal characteristics of traits, that is, their scope or breadth, their surface or substance characteristics, and the extent to which a trait is common or unique. Traits can also be classified by content, that is, the kind of behavioral characteristic to which they apply. For example, Cattell (1950) identified three rough modes for source traits. He spoke of *ability traits* such as general intelligence, which concern "how well the person makes his way to the accepted goals." *Dynamic traits* primarily concern enduring or stable motivational patterns and regulative or controlling characteristics of the personality. *Temperament traits* have to do with the style or manner in which an individual functions within the context of his capacities and motivations. Temperament traits in Cattell's system are largely constitutional in nature and include speed or tempo, energy, and emotional reactivity.

Many writers have objected to this inclusion of dynamic as well as stylistic characteristics under the concept of trait. For example, McClelland (1951) reserved the term "trait" to apply to characteristics that are essentially stylistic, and he used the separate term "motive" to apply to the forces that power behavior. Thus, whereas Allport and Cattell are willing to speak of motive traits, McClelland speaks of traits and motives separately. For present purposes, this is a terminological distinction rather than one of any important functional significance.

Organization of Traits

As pointed out earlier, it is economical to group trait characteristics on the basis of those qualities that tend to go together in the same individual. It is possible by such grouping to reduce them to a practicable number, which can be managed readily and used for the description of personality. The nearly 18,000 trait names found in the English language include many duplications and many characteristics that, although related to separate behavior patterns, tend to be found together. Thus, being an outgoing person in social situations tends to be associated with being good-natured and adaptable; these three separately described traits can be organized into a single trait, which can then be given a name that refers to the characteristics included.

One of the recently developed statistical methods used to identify patterns of traits that go together is *factor analysis*. Factor analysis has a mathematical basis that need not concern us here. However, it is a statistical variant of a logical method for studying the organization of traits and can be readily understood as such.

Factor analysis depends upon the concept of *correlation*. Two traits can vary together so that a person who has a high degree of one is likely to have a high degree of the other as well. This going-togetherness of two characteristics represents a positive relationship or correlation. In a previous illustration arithmetical ability and size of vocabulary were positively correlated, meaning that, if a person has a large vocabulary, he is also likely to be good in arithmetic. The extent to which these two traits are related or correlated can be expressed quantitatively by the mathematical term "coefficient of correlation."

If the relationships between a number of traits were studied, it might be found that five traits are all positively correlated with each other, and four other traits are not correlated with any of the first five but are, in turn, correlated with each other. The five correlated traits have something in common, as do the four traits. Some more basic factor underlies the five correlated traits, but this factor is not found in the four correlated traits, which are themselves unified by some different underlying factor. Through studying such patterns of correlation, by factor analysis one can determine how many factors are needed to explain the pattern of relationships found between a large number of traits. Thus, in any factor analysis a large and unwieldy number of traits can be reduced to a relatively small and manageable number of basic factors, which are

Table 5

CATTELL'S FORMULATION OF PRIMARY TRAITS OF PERSONALITY*

I. Cyclothymia	vs.	Schizothymia
Outgoing		Withdrawn
Good-natured		Embittered
Adaptable		Inflexible
II. Intelligence	vs.	Mental defect
Intelligent		Stupid
Painstaking		Slipshod
Deliberate		Impulsive
III. Emotionally mature	vs.	Demoralized
Realistic		Evasive
Stable		Changeable
Calm		Excitable
IV. Dominance	vs.	Submissiveness
Assertive		Modest
Headstrong		Gentle
Tough		Introspective
V. Surgency	vs.	Melancholy
Cheerful		Unhappy
Placid		Worrying
Sociable		Aloof
VI. Sensitive	vs.	Tough poise
Idealistic		Cynical
Imaginative		Habit-bound
Grateful		Thankless
VII. Trained, socialized	vs.	Boorish
Thoughtful		Unreflective
Sophisticated		Simple
Conscientious		Indolent
VIII. Positive integration	vs.	Immature, dependent
Mature		Irresponsible
Persevering		Quitting
Loyal		Fickle
IX. Charitable, adventurous	vs.	Obstructive, withdrawn
Cooperative		Obstructive
Genial		Cold-hearted
Frank		Secretive
X. Neurasthenia	vs.	Vigorous character
Incoherent		Strong-willed
Meek		Assertive
Unrealistic		Practical
XI. Hypersensitive	vs.	Frustration tolerance
Demanding		Adjusting
Restless		Calm

Table 5 (*Continued*)

Self-pitying		Self-effacing
XII. Surgent cyclothymia	vs.	Paranoia
Enthusiastic		Frustrated
Friendly		Hostile
Trustful		Suspicious

* Each trait is defined by a pair of opposed qualities, with descriptive words to clarify the meaning.
SOURCE: Cattell, 1946, pp. 313–316.

independent of each other and which underlie the relationships found among the large number of traits.

The factor-analysis method in the study of personality traits can be illustrated with a study by Cattell (1946), who is one of the scientists responsible for the development of factor analysis of personality. Originally, Cattell began with a list of 4,000 trait names. He was able to reduce this list to 171 by eliminating qualities that overlapped (duplicated terms) or were extremely rare. By means of preliminary correlation, he further reduced the list to 35 clusters of traits, which accounted for most of the variation found in the 171 and which represented pairs of opposed qualities such as sociable-seclusive. A sample of 208 adult men were rated on each of the traits included. Correlations were obtained among the traits and the underlying factors were isolated. Included in the study also were data from personality questionnaires, from objective tests, and from clinical case studies. Twelve basic factors were identified by Cattell, which are presented in Table 5. These factors represent primary traits, which can be described along a dimension that includes the extremes of a scale of measurement from one end of the factor to the other. For example, factor 2 is intelligence–mental defect. A person can be rated on a scale of high intelligence to low intelligence or mental defect, as in the case of any other of the twelve dimensions or primary traits of personality. Under each end of the continuum of each factor are a number of adjectives that illustrate the meaning of the factor suggested by Cattell.

There are a number of limitations to the factor-analysis approach to the study of personality. For one thing, the nature of the factors derived from such studies depends upon the types of tests or behavioral data that are sampled in the population being studied. Questionnaires, for example, or the observations derived from short samples of the behavior offer rather restricted views of the personality being studied. There are likely to be many characteristics of great importance in personality organization that do not appear in such samples. Therefore, important traits can be overlooked.

Another defect is that a factor analysis, which produces a number of independent factors or primary traits of personality, does not answer the important question of how these traits are organized within the personality. For example, a person who is hypersensitive and intelligent will be a very different kind of person from one who is hypersensitive and intellectually dull. There is a tendency, in this type of approach to personality, to treat personality as a collection of independent traits that have no relationship to each other, thus fragmenting the human being into a number of isolated attributes and ignoring the integrity and organization of the whole.

However, the use of factor analysis does represent an objective systematic approach to the assessment of traits and their relationship and has great usefulness in reducing the tremendous overlapping among the many trait names we use commonly in the description of personality.

Trait Generality

The psychologist who attempts to describe personality in terms of traits confronts an especially interesting problem—the generality of traits. If behavior were determined entirely by internal dispositions or structures (the extreme of generality), then a knowledge of them would enable us to predict behavior regardless of what type of situation a person was in. If behavior was highly specific to the situation, then a trait approach would have little value in predicting behavior. Let us consider more fully and concretely what this really means.

For many years psychologists have been interested in how persons protect themselves against threatening experiences. One of the fundamental constructs that has been developed is the defense mechanism. An individual acquires certain methods (defenses) of dealing with threats to his self-esteem or integrity. They deceive him (and perhaps others) about the true nature of motives that, if expressed or gratified, would produce disturbing emotional states. One defense mechanism, first postulated by Freud, is called *repression*. Repression is the process of keeping out of consciousness the dangerous or unacceptable impulses. An individual with hostile impulses can repress them. He is then unaware of their existence and is to some degree protected from the anticipated threatening consequences of having them.

Now the question arises: To what extent is the tendency to repress threatening impulses a consistent trait characteristic of particular persons? Can we say, for example, that some persons tend usually or habitually to use the mechanism of repression whenever threatening impulses arise? Or does the use of the mechanism depend heavily upon particular circumstances, such as the nature and degree of the threat?

If we took the extreme trait-generality position, we might argue that any threatening impulses will be repressed by an individual. In contrast, we could maintain that the mechanism of repression will only be evoked when certain particular impulses are aroused or when the conditions involved are favorable to the defense mechanism of repression.

If the former position were sound, the identification of the trait or disposition to repress would be tremendously useful, because one could expect that, with any kind of threat, an individual would repress. We would be in a very favorable position to predict behavior that is a consequence of repression. If the latter position were adopted, we could only predict relevant behavior if we could specify precisely a number of specific stimulus conditions. For example, repression might be evoked only when the stimulus conditions aroused sexual impulses but not when the external conditions stimulated hostile feelings. The greater the generality of any trait, the more readily can we infer it from a limited sample of behavior and the more readily can we use it to predict behavior in a wide variety of circumstances.

Let us consider one additional example of this problem of degree of generality of a trait. Some persons have very strong motivation to achieve, and others have relatively weak tendencies to strive for achievement. The former are characterized by the ever-present desire to excel in their performance against some standard of excellence. In college, for example, they study more than persons with low achievement motivation, and their aspirations with respect to college grades and future careers are consistently high. Now the question might be asked at this point: How general is such achievement motivation? Does the desire to excel against some standard apply to any type of task that we give such persons to perform, or is it limited to only certain types of performances and certain types of situations? Does the person whose efforts are greatly mobilized by comparison with others in the area of mathematics or chemistry become equally involved when we compare him with others in, say, musical or artistic appreciation, or is the achievement motive restricted to achievement in certain fields?

The answers to these questions require more systematic research than is available. However, a number of observations from research literature as well as from common sense suggest that, for most persons, an in-between position is most reasonable. There may be some rare persons who are challenged by any comparison or competition with others. There may also be those who will not strive for achievement in any situation. Most of us, however, have achievement motives that are applicable over certain broad classes of situations—situations that have something in common—and we do not blindly strive to achieve in every context.

Neither extreme position, arguing for generality or specificity of traits, is totally sound. It is necessary to study what classes of situations are appropriate to the particular trait characteristics. A trait approach to the description of personality that emphasizes only enduring characteristics within the person and ignores the limiting external conditions can only go part of the way in permitting us to predict behavior. Its success must then depend upon the generality of the traits abstracted, and, except for the rare individual, it must be in error a large part of the time.

Sometimes, in individual cases, we can identify a trait so broad, so central in importance, and so general in scope that we speak of a consistent *style of life* that characterizes the person. For example, we may find a person whose interpersonal relations are characterized by a passive-dependent attitude. In most social contexts he tends to place himself in such a position that the initiative for action comes from others. He usually takes the role of the dependent person who requires support from others. Having inferred the existence of such a trait by observing some of his interpersonal relations (say, with respect to his employer or immediate supervisor), we will have expectations about other relationships into which he enters, for example, marriage. We expect him to choose a wife who is dominant and aggressive and to establish a relationship with her that might be characterized as passive-dependent.

Although such characterizations of life style are often useful, they are gross oversimplifications in most cases. They overlook the variations in pattern of behavior that are dependent upon particular external stimulus conditions. For example, no matter how passive-dependent an individual might be, he will meet other persons who cannot be forced into a role compatible with his passive-dependent characteristics. The trait approaches have their advantage in a certain amount of simplicity. However, this is their great disadvantage, because behavior is rarely determined by trait characteristics alone.

THE TYPE APPROACH

Traits or combinations of traits can be so broad in scope that they are often referred to as *types*. Because persons have certain very broad traits in common with many others, they are identified as belonging to the same type. For example, we can say that a particular person is seclusive, socially uncomfortable, and shy, thus describing him in terms of a number of traits. We can observe, however, that persons who are seclusive are usually quiet, socially uncomfortable, and shy. These characteristics seem to go together. Persons who have all these characteristics might be called "introverts." They are members of the same class of persons, because they share the same pattern of traits. They belong to the introvert type.

When we shift from a trait-oriented description of personality to a type-oriented one, there is a subtle qualitative change in our form of

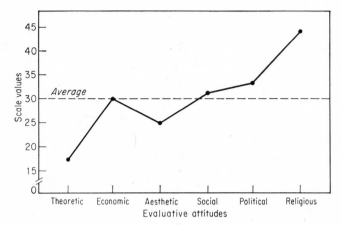

Figure 6. Profile of the evaluative attitudes of Jonathan Swift. (*From Ferguson,* 1952.)

thinking. In the case of trait descriptions, the mode of thought is analogous to a psychogram. A psychogram involves positioning an individual in relation to others on the basis of a series of trait dimensions. That is, he has a great amount of some traits and very little of others. This patterning of traits for an individual is a representation of his personality.

An example of such a psychogram is found in Ferguson (1952) and shows a hypothetical profile of values for the satirist Jonathan Swift. Using the values found in Vernon and Allport's *A Study of Values* (1931), the trait pattern of the famous writer, based upon his writings and available biographical data, was estimated. This pattern or psychogram provides a picture of Swift's values (traits) and is presented in Figure 6.

When we are dealing with typologies, on the other hand, the psychogram model is abandoned in favor of a broad classification or pigeonholing scheme in which, on the basis of the patterning of traits, a person is placed in one of several categories. He is considered to share the pattern of traits with a large class of others. The description is simplified by the use of a few categories, e.g., extrovert or introvert. Persons who have a pattern of traits in common are described as belonging to a particular type classification. The logic of trait descriptions and type classifications is closely related, but the form of representation of the information is somewhat different.

Examples of Psychological Typologies

Because typologies are simple means of classifying persons, they have a long history and a tradition that flourishes even at the present time. It will be useful at this point to illustrate psychological typing with some of the classical and current typologies.

Typologies of some sort have existed since ancient times and are found in the writings of the Greeks. Theophrastus, who lived at the same time as Aristotle, did a remarkably effective job of describing thirty personality types. But the best known of the ancient personality typologies was set forth by Hippocrates in the fifth century B.C. and dealt primarily with the emotional aspects of personality. In that era the body was thought to contain four fluids or humors: yellow bile, black bile, phlegm, and blood. Hippocrates theorized that these humors determined the fundamental personality characteristics of the person, depending upon which of them predominated. If yellow bile (or *choler*) predominated, an individual would show a *choleric* temperament, characterized by irascibility. If black bile predominated (*melas* and *choler*), an individual would be *melancholy*. Such a person was characterized by a depressed, slow, and pessimistic outlook on life. If phlegm (referring to mucus) predominated, an individual was called *phlegmatic* and was temperamentally sluggish and apathetic. Finally, the predominance of blood (*sanguis*) would make an individual *sanguine*, or cheerful, hopeful, active, and quick. Hippocrates believed that the normal personality resulted from a balance of all these humors.

Hippocrates's concept of personality types has had a considerable influence over many centuries, although the specific typology he espoused is no longer maintained. Typologies, even if implicit, are readily noted in literature. Perhaps one of the most frequently cited is from Shakespeare's *Julius Caesar*. Caesar expresses suspiciousness of Cassius by pointing out that Cassius has a lean and hungry look and stating that such men think too much and are dangerous. In his remarks, Caesar indicates his preference for men in his command who are fat. They are presumably more affable and open. Also in Shakespeare's *Henry IV*, the character Falstaff is presented as fat and jovial, reflecting the popular notion, which still exists, that stout persons are generally good-natured and thin persons are introverted, serious, and of poor disposition.

A huge variety of psychological types have been proposed by writers throughout the ages and even by current psychologists. We cannot possibly elaborate all these typologies here. Most of those mentioned subsequently can be found in Table 6 presented later. To mention some, William James (1890), the great philosopher-psychologist, spoke of the rationalist and empiricist types: the *rationalist* is tender-minded, guided by general principles and abstract ideas and tending to be idealistic and religious; the *empiricist* is tough-minded, a practical person who is influenced primarily by realistic considerations and expediency. Kraepelin (1907) distinguished between the manic-depressive and dementia-praecox (or schizophrenic) types and developed a classification system or typology for mental illness. Rosanoff (1938) described three types of personalities: the *antisocial,* characterized by criminal tendencies and pathological lying; the *cyclothymic,* showing fluctuations of mood and emotional instability (similar to the manic-depressive described by Kraepelin); and the *schizoid* (like Kraepelin's dementia-praecox), manifesting a separation of intellect from emotional activity, withdrawal from social contacts, and a chaotic and disturbed sexual adjustment. The German philosopher Spranger (1928) propounded a typology in which persons were divided into six fundamental attitudes or dominant value orientations: theoretical, economic, aesthetic, social, political, and religious. In more recent years, Allport, Vernon, and Lindzey (1951) have adapted Spranger's six value types in developing a useful test of personality called the "Study of Values."

Some psychological typologies have had greater influence on current thought than others. Among these are the typological systems of Jung and Freud, which are presented in some detail below.

Jung's Typology

In the early part of his career, Jung was a close follower of Freud, with whom he later disagreed, developing his own conceptual system for viewing personality. The theory of psychological types proposed by Jung (1922) is one of the best known and most influential psychological typologies among both lay persons and professional workers.

Jung identified two broad organizations of psychological traits: the *extrovert,* whose primary orientation is toward the external world, and the *introvert,* whose orientation centers on himself and his subjective world. Jung further argued that these external and internal orientations could also be divided into rational processes, which emphasize the examination or verification of experiences by logical analysis, and irrational processes, which are determined largely by chance, accidental perceptions, or illogical associations. The rational processes are further divided into two subfunctions, thinking and feeling. The irrational processes can be divided into the functions of sensation and intuition. The rational processes, thinking and feeling, are characterized by reasoning and judgment, whereas the irrational processes, sensation and intuition, are characterized by intensity of perceptions. Thus, each of the two broad types, extrovert and introvert, is organized around the four subfeatures of thinking, feeling, sensation, and intuition.

From Jung's point of view, one of the four subprocesses can be particularly differentiated or well developed in a person and play a dominant role in his adjustment or orientation to life. Eight special classes of personality can be derived from this analysis: the extroverted thinker, the extroverted feeling type, the extroverted sensation type, and the extroverted intuition type, and the same subcategories applied to the introvert class. Thus, although Jung is most remembered for what might be called a "dichotomous typology," that is, a twofold classification of extrovert-introvert, his system of classification is really an eightfold one and somewhat more complicated than is typically realized.

The *extroverted thinker* is largely oriented to facts and logical classification, with the emphasis upon the actual construction of reality and the tendency to check logical analysis against the external objective facts. He is somewhat like James's empiricist. The *introverted thinker*, on the other hand, who is also rationally oriented, is characterized by a more theoretical bent and is more concerned with his own subjective organization of the world of ideas. Because he is introverted and subjectively oriented, he is likely to be impractical and rather indifferent to such external things as his appearance and the attitudes of persons around him. This type appears like James's rationalist. The *extroverted feeling type* is oriented toward establishing harmony with the outside world and developing close sympathetic relationships with others, and the *introverted feeling type* is chiefly concerned with his internal harmony, frequently preoccupied with his own dreams and feelings. The *sensation types, both extroverted and introverted*, are principally influenced by pleasure and pain, either externally or interpersonally oriented, as in the case of the extrovert, or internally and subjectively, as in the case of the introvert. The *intuitive types* are affected predominantly by hunches, speculation, and judgments for which no rational or observable basis can be indicated. The intuitive types can also be extroverted or introverted.

Further complicating Jung's eightfold classification is his notion that an individual can be extroverted for one function, say, thinking, but introverted for another, say, sensation. Moreover, an individual can be consciously oriented in the extroverted direction but unconsciously introverted, or vice versa. In other words, a person can believe that he is oriented to interpersonal relations but have a fundamentally introversive personality. Such a discrepancy can plunge an individual into conflict.

Jung seemed to take the view that all persons clearly belonged to one or another of the eight personality subtypes and that the influences determining such membership in a type were largely biological in nature, although these biological tendencies could be somewhat modified by experience. That is, he would expect persons to be distributed predominantly in one of the two poles of the typology, extrovert or introvert. Most modern writers, however, maintain that traits are better viewed as continuously distributed and that most persons probably lie between the two extremes, showing features of both. The term *ambivert* has often been used to refer to persons who could be classified as neither extroverts nor introverts.

Freud's Psychoanalytic Typology

Freud is not usually identified as a personality typologist. Actually, however, in developing his theory of psychosexual development (the elements of which are described in Chapter 6), Freud (1932, 1949) identified three fundamental types of personalities. The type depends on the stage of psychosexual development an individual has reached or upon which a great deal of sexual energy has been fixated. These types are called the "oral-erotic type," the "anal-erotic type," and the "phallic type." If an individual functions primarily at the oral, anal, or phallic levels, respectively, then certain appropriate characteristics can be observed in his behavior.

The *oral* stage of development was considered by Freud to be the infant's first organized form of sexual gratification and involved activity related to the mouth. Oral-erotic persons show an exaggerated degree of erotic pleasures associated with oral activity. During the first part of the oral stage a more passive type of activity is found, characterized behaviorally by sucking. Later, oral activity can shift toward an emphasis on biting. The *oral-passive type* (linked to the sucking period of the oral stage) is identified as a dependent, optimistic, immature person, expecting nourishment from the world and wishing to continue (like an infant) being cared for by his parents or by parent substitutes. His adjustment to the world as an adult is still characterized by the passive, sucking type of orientation, in which he receives his nourishment from some protective figure. The *oral-sadistic type* has reached the level of biting and chewing, and his basic outlook, though like the oral-passive type in seeking sustenance and support from others, is pessimistic about receiving it and suspicious that he will be thwarted in this need. His manner is often sarcastic or bitter, an attitude that is illustrated in the common English metaphor "biting speech," with which this type of person tends to attack others.

The *anal type* is a personality pattern at the stage of development in which a person obtains primary gratification through anal activities. These activities have to do with the expulsion of fecal material through the anus or the retention of these materials in response to the social demands of toilet training. Freud observed that a variety of traits of anal origin seemed to go together and fit into a type, which he called the "anal or obsessional character." These traits included orderliness, parsimony and even miserliness, and obstinacy. The adult of the anal-erotic type is one who is still seeking (often symbolically) the kind of gratification that he

Table 6

EXAMPLES OF FAMOUS PSYCHOLOGICAL TYPOLOGIES

Author	Types		Central psychological characteristics
Hippocrates	Choleric (yellow bile)		Irascibility
	Melancholy (black bile)		Depressed, slow, pessimistic
	Phlegmatic (mucus)		Sluggish, apathetic
	Sanguine (blood)		Cheerful, hopeful, active, quick
James	Empiricist		Practical, realistic, tough-minded
	Rationalist		Abstract and theoretical, tender-minded
Kraepelin	Manic-depressive		Swings of mood, outgoing
	Dementia praecox		Withdrawn, intellectually oriented, introspective
Rosanoff	Antisocial		Criminal tendencies, pathological lying
	Cyclothymic		Mood fluctuations, emotional instability
	Schizoid		Separation of intellect from emotions, withdrawal, chaotic and disturbed sexual adjustment
Spranger	Theoretical		Concerned with abstract principles, concepts
	Economic		Oriented toward material things, money
	Aesthetic		Oriented toward beauty, aesthetic experience
	Social		Concerned with interpersonal relations
	Political		Oriented toward power, laws, government, control
	Religious		Concerned with god, prayer, religious experience
Jung	Extrovert		Generally oriented toward external world
	Rational	Thinking	Concerned with facts, logical classification, practical reality
		Feeling	Desire for harmony with world, warm relations with others
	Irrational	Sensation	Oriented toward social and physical sources of pleasure and pain, demands of others
		Intuition	Responsive to superstition, given to judging others on hunch, investing, gambling

Table 6 (Continued)

Author	Types		Central psychological characteristics
	Introvert		Generally oriented toward self and subjective matters
	Rational	Thinking	Theoretical, introspective about ideas, impractical
		Feeling	Desire for internal harmony, pre-occupied with own dreams and feelings
	Irrational	Sensation	Oriented toward satisfying sensory experience
		Intuition	Given to introspection of a specu-lative nature, ritualistic and respon-sive to own feelings and moods
Freud	Oral erotic		
	Passive (sucking)		Seeking sustenance, dependent, opti-mistic, immature, trusting
	Sadistic (biting)		Seeking sustenance, pessimistic, sus-picious, sarcastic
	Anal erotic		
	Expulsive		Outbursts of aggression, sloppiness, controls others by petulance (defe-cating on the world)
	Retentive		Obstinate, orderly, miserly, parsi-monious
	Phallic		Exhibitionistic, bragging, overambi-tious, narcissistic
	Genital		Altruistic, harmonious, mature

required as a young child from the bowel function, including, for exam-ple, the special attention that came from the parent at toilet time, the praise or punishment that followed cleanliness, and the expressions of hostility toward the parents that sometimes occurred in the form of soiling his clothing. Because he has not fully progressed beyond this childhood level of development, there remains a residue of sexual energy that is still being discharged in adult life in an anal fashion.

The third period of psychosexual development is the phallic period, and it is possible to speak, in psychoanalytic terms, of the *phallic type*. At this stage of psychosexual development a person is struggling with the oedipal problem prior to the transition to a normal, adult sexual adjust-ment. To achieve this transition, the parent must be given up as the object of sexual love and a peer of the opposite sex must become the primary love object. Transition through this early phallic stage leads finally to the highest psychosexual level—the genital level—which characterizes normal or ideal development. The phallic type has been less fully described by psychoanalytic writers than either the oral- or the anal-erotic types, but it is generally characterized as exhibitionistic, full of braggadocio, overambitious, and narcissistic or filled with self-love and adulation. These are typically the characteristics of the early adolescent. He seeks the center of attention and shows little tolerance for frustration. Should he advance beyond the phallic to the genital stage, much of the selfishness will be replaced by altruism and there will be a satisfactory balance of dependency-independence and ambition-restraint.

Freud did not argue that these types represented pure categories in which most persons could be necessarily placed but rather that there are usually present in the same individual features of the oral, anal, and phallic stages of development. The psychoanalytic types tend to reflect extremes in a normally distributed continuum, so an individual cannot be identified as an anal-erotic type unless there is a great exaggeration of the anal characteristics.

Evaluation of the Type Approach

Psychologists have often expressed criticism of the type approach to personality. The main criticism is that, as a classification system, a typology results in a great oversimplification of personality by forcing great varieties of behavior into a few limited categories. Most typologies use a relatively limited number of categories. There are dichotomous typologies, trichotomous typologies, and typologies that, like Jung's eightfold system, utilize a larger number of categories. If the number of categories used is small, much variation between persons is overlooked. If the number of categories is enlarged, the system can become unwieldy and one finds it necessary to refer to hundreds of characteristics in describing and classifying individuals. If one wished to have a classificatory scheme that included every possible variation, then the absurd level could be reached at which a type was postulated for every person in the universe because every person is unique in certain respects even though he shares much in common with others.

Any classification system is likely to be too coarse to do justice to all the variation in personality. The point was made in Chapter 2 that science requires classification, even though it overlooks minor variations in the individual specimen in the interests of having general descriptive principles. It is therefore not proper to criticize the type approach to personality on the basis of its being a simplifying classification system alone. Rather, the question should be: How useful is any particular classification scheme, and how may it be refined and made more effective in description? When we talk about typologies in personality, we are introducing a scientific abstraction, a classification of persons to which any particular individual need not precisely conform. If our problem is the description of a particular individual, then a broad typology will be woefully inadequate. The factor analysts, such as Cattell (1950) and Eysenck (1947), are seriously trying to identify a limited number of basic factors or dimensions that are adequate to describe the basic variations found among different personalities.

Many of the typologies described are particularly useful when we are dealing with an exceptional individual who shows certain extremes in his behavior. For example, if the predominant mode of adjustment of a person involves social withdrawal, preoccupation with his own objective experience, and a disinterest in the social events about him, then we do well to describe him as an introvert because this label says a great deal about him. On the other hand, to the extent that most of us are mixtures of extroversion-introversion, such labels will not work because they require forcing an individual completely into one or another category when he belongs wholly in neither. This particular dimension of personality or typology is clearly insufficient for adequately characterizing large numbers of persons as individuals.

Typologies do serve one very important function that is often overlooked. They are reference points or guides for the examination of dimensions of personality. If we are asked to describe another person, we are all apt to have a wide variety of frames of reference of the kind of characteristics we will look for. Therefore, different persons will give different descriptions, all of which may have a certain validity but which focus on different personality dimensions. However, by reference to a particular kind of classificatory system, we can orient ourselves to any given person in terms of the relevant characteristics to consider. Typologies best serve as anchoring points from which we can examine any individual.

FURTHER CONSIDERATIONS OF TRAIT AND TYPE

It should be recognized also that when we speak of trait and type approaches to personality we are not referring to a specific theory of personality but to ways of looking at it. The notions of trait and type are formal in nature; that is, they do not specify what the traits are that characterize individuals, but merely suggest describing personality by traits or classifying it by types. Thus, two theorists can both employ a trait-and-type frame of reference but have essentially different theories as to what traits exist and how these traits are organized within the individual.

There is one other critical problem with the concepts of trait and type that should be reemphasized here. The description of a human being in terms of certain traits and, in the broader sense, certain types leads us to examine stable attributes *within the person* and deemphasizes the role of *external circumstances* in the determination of behavior. So far as there exist patterns of behavior that are not stable or consistent or that fluctuate with the changing circumstances, a trait or type description is of limited help in predicting behavior. Examination of personal attributes enables us to make probability statements about what individuals may do, because such traits can be looked upon as tendencies or dispositions to act in certain ways. There are other frames of reference, in contrast with the trait-and-type approaches, that emphasize more heavily the external stimulus, or the interactions between personal attributes and the circumstances in which persons behave. The next chapter deals with a more stimulus-oriented frame of reference: association-learning theory.

CHAPTER
4

Association-learning Theory
and Personality

From the association-learning viewpoint the development of personality takes place in accord with the laws of learning. In contrast with the trait-and-type approach, which stresses the stable response characteristics of a person, association-learning theory accords the objective-stimulus situation a very central position. If a person behaves in a consistent or characteristic way, it is because the various situations (stimuli) to which he is exposed are sufficiently similar for the learned response patterns to spread or generalize from one specific stimulus to others. Personality becomes, in essence, the learned habits of response that an individual makes to the stimulus conditions of his internal and external environment.

In connection with the formulation of laws of learning, the great majority of psychologists interested in learning theory have not been particularly interested in the area of personality. They have studied mostly the simplest forms of learning. A few such psychologists, however, have attempted to extend these simple learning phenomena and the theoretical constructs derived from them to the field of personality. These speculative ventures have not always been looked upon with favor by the psychologists specializing in experimental approaches to simple learning. Because a very large percentage of the research from which the generalizations are made focuses on lower animals, to generalize almost exclusively from this type of evidence is always hazardous.

The most ambitious and widely accepted attempt to apply the principles of learning to personality is the book by Dollard and Miller (1950) entitled *Personality and Psychotherapy*. These writers have not formulated an original theory of personality. They have borrowed some of the central descriptive concepts of Freudian theory and translated them into association-learning–theory terms and principles. Many psychologists have considered this an extremely significant contribution, for several reasons. First, it might help to unify two major diverse interests in psychology, one dealing with psychodynamics and psychopathology, the other with normal forms of human and animal learning as viewed by Hull (1943).

Second, it attempted to reformulate certain principles that were difficult to deal with experimentally into terms that lend themselves better to experimentation. Third, the very fact that a translation of this sort can be accomplished suggests that there is much in common in the assumptions of psychoanalysis and of association-learning theory.

Whatever the ultimate status of Dollard and Miller's venture it represents one influential frame of reference about personality theory. Although there are alternative views about the learning process, we shall, in this chapter, examine this single view because it is the only one that has been thus far so systematically applied to personality.

THE FUNDAMENTALS OF LEARNING

Dollard and Miller stated that there are four fundamental factors of prime importance in learning: drive, cue, response, and reinforcement. These concepts are frequently referred to by other roughly equivalent terms. *Drive* means *motivation, cue* refers to *stimulus, response* has to do with an *action* or *thought,* and *reinforcement* (the most controversial of the concepts in terms of its importance in learning) represents *reward.*

In illustrating these fundamental factors in the learning process, Dollard and Miller described an experiment in which a six-year-old girl who is hungry is given the task of finding a piece of candy hidden under one of the books in a bookcase. The little girl proceeds to search for the candy. She looks under some of the books on the top shelf; then she begins to take out the books one by one from the lower shelf. After some unsuccessful attempts in different directions, and after 210 seconds of searching, she finally finds the candy. Responding with an exclamation of delight, she picks it up and eats it. After this, she is again sent out of the room, the candy is hidden under the same book, and she is called back again for another trial. After an 86-second period of search, she again finds the candy. On the third trial she goes almost directly to the right place and finds the candy after only 11 seconds. For several subsequent trials she again takes longer, but she progressively improves until, on the ninth trial, she picks up the correct book immediately and obtains the candy in only 3 seconds. On the tenth trial she again goes directly to the correct book and finds the candy in 2 seconds.

The progressive changes in the child's behavior in this experiment can be plotted in terms of the number of books she examines as a function of her experience at the task during the ten trials. Whereas at the beginning she takes a long time and makes a large number of incorrect responses, at the end of the experiment she is able to go directly to the right book and obtain the candy in two seconds. This progressive change in her behavior is called *learning*. Dollard and Miller illustrated this sequence of

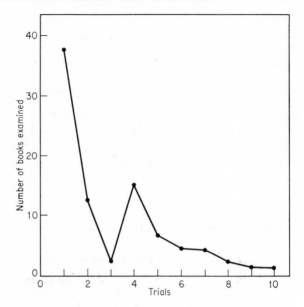

Figure 7. The elimination of errors. On the first trial the child looks under thirty-six wrong books and makes other incorrect responses not indicated on the graph before finding candy under the thirty-seventh book examined. Errors are gradually eliminated until on the ninth and tenth trials the child makes only the one response of going directly to the correct book. (*From Dollard & Miller*, 1950.)

events involving the learning of the correct location of the candy in a simple graph shown in Figure 7.

The learning that took place in this demonstration involved the four factors previously listed as fundamental in learning. The relationship among the four fundamental factors of learning can be summarized in the following way. The drive initiates or impels responses; if the first response is not rewarded or drive-reducing, it tends to drop out and others tend to appear. When some response is followed by reward, the connection between the cue and this response is strengthened; the next time that the same drive and similar cues are present, this response is more likely to occur. The strengthening of the cue or stimulus-response connection is the central point of learning. Learning involves the acquisition of responses to certain cues or stimuli. The responses that are acquired are reinforcing to the drive initiating the response in the first place.

There are a few problems about these fundamental concepts that should be noted. What is the nature of *drive?* Dollard and Miller maintained that any stimulus can become a drive if it is made strong enough, and the stronger the stimulus, the more drive function it possesses. Nevertheless, certain types of stimuli seem to be more important as motivators than others. These have been called *primary* or *innate drives.* They tend to originate from physiological needs essential to the survival and well-being of man. These include hunger, thirst, temperature regulation, pain, fatigue, sex, defecation, and urination, to name the most important ones. The primary drives are contrasted with *secondary* or *learned drives.* These are not innately characteristic of the organism at birth but arise from the social context in which an individual develops. These secondary drives have a social basis and include, for example, approval, achievement, affection, and social contact. They are frequently referred to as "social motives," and they are thought to arise in connection with the gratification of primary drives. For example, we learn to seek approval from others because, in our childhood, approval is one of the conditions under which our primary drives such as hunger and thirst have been gratified. For the infant, disapproval on the part of the parent implies the danger of subsequent pain through the loss of assistance in gratifying primary drives.

Cues, which bring about responses, cannot function in learning unless they are distinctive enough to be differentiated. If the book behind which lay the candy appeared no different to the girl than any other book in the bookcase, it would have been impossible for her to learn regularly to find the candy. In order to learn to find it, the girl had to respond to such cues as color, size, shape, markings on the book, and the position of the book in relation to the rest of the bookcase. Limitations in the perceptual apparatus of organisms serve to limit their ability to learn, because such learning depends upon the ability to make maximum use of different cues in the environment. These serve as sources of information, signifying the means of reducing unsatisfied drive states.

Learning also cannot take place if the correct *response,* which permits the reduction of the drive states, is not or cannot be made. The first thing that must be done to teach a dog to come when called is to get the animal to execute the response of coming and then to reinforce that response with a dog biscuit or a pat on the head. If this response is not made or if it is beyond the capacity of the organism, no learning can take place. The outfielder in baseball may never learn to throw the ball from the center-field wall to home plate because the distance is too far for his physical capacity. However, from a shorter distance, he can readily learn to throw the ball accurately to the catcher. Similarly, a child who has insufficient control of the sphincter muscles associated with defecation cannot be toilet-trained because the response necessary—contracting the sphincter muscles to retain the bowel—cannot be made. It cannot be learned therefore in response to the cues related to the toilet. As a consequence of the biological construction of the organism, some responses tend to be dominant or readily elicited, and others are difficult to produce.

There are some points that must be made with respect to the role of *reinforcement* in learning. For example, reinforcement cannot take place in the absence of a drive because the strength of stimulation cannot be lowered when it is already zero. Moreover, reinforcement that is delayed is less effective than reinforcement that promptly follows the appropriate response. Thus, if the girl removed the correct book but had to wait ten minutes to receive the candy, the reward would be less likely to reinforce the action of removing the appropriate book from the bookshelf. One of the advantages man has so far as learning is concerned is that language and thought increase the possibilities for the organism not only to identify the appropriate cues or drive reinforcements but also to reduce the loss of reinforcement due to delay. If a child is rewarded immediately after committing a desirable act, he will know what he did that led to the reward. If there is a great delay, say, an hour or a day or a week, it is more difficult for the child to identify the reward with the act that he must learn to perform. However, if the parent, in rewarding the child, explains that he is being rewarded for a particular act and asks the child to remember and think about what he did, then the delay is bridged by thinking and, in effect, the reinforcement can be made psychologically contiguous with the rewarded response. The case of punishment is somewhat more complicated (it requires avoidance or escape to be reinforcing), but the basic idea is the same.

FURTHER CHARACTERISTICS OF LEARNING

In addition to the four fundamentals of learning—drive, cue, response, reinforcement—a number of other principles have been developed concerning the process of learning. These principles have to do with how learned responses are eliminated, how they can be generalized from the situation in which they have been learned to a variety of other situations as well, how the process of discrimination between cues or situations occurs, and how we can come to anticipate future reinforcements. Let us briefly examine each of these principles. Following this, we shall discuss how drives or motives themselves can be learned and how previously neutral objects can come to be sources of reinforcement. Finally, we must consider how higher mental processes, such as reasoning and thinking, can be understood in relation to the fundamental processes of learning.

Extinction

Reinforcement strengthens the connection between cues and the rewarded response, tending to make the response associated with the reinforcement more probable on a future occasion. In this way the little girl in our illustration learned the response of picking up the correct book in the bookcase because doing this and performing all the acts prior to it, such as walking up to the bookcase, has led to the reward of finding and eating the candy. When a response is not rewarded, its association with the cue tends to weaken. When a learned response is made without reinforcement, the strength of the tendency to respond decreases. The weakening or elimination of responses previously made or learned is called *extinction*. Stronger habits are more resistant to extinction than weaker ones, and habits acquired as a result of very powerful motivation are more difficult to extinguish than habits of weak motivation. Just as reinforcement is the means by which responses are learned, extinction is the fundamental process by which actions are eliminated.

It should be recognized that extinguished responses are not totally eliminated and that the effects of extinction tend to disappear with the passage of time. The tendency for an extinguished habit to reappear after an interval of time, even in the absence of instances where it has been rewarded, is called *spontaneous* recovery. Extinction does not destroy the old habit but rather inhibits it. However, if extinctions have been repeated often enough, the habit can become so thoroughly inhibited that it has little tendency to reappear.

The importance of extinction in our behavior is very great. If it were not possible for unrewarded responses to be extinguished, it would be difficult to imagine learning taking place, because learning requires the elimination of unwanted acts as well as the strengthening of desired ones. Furthermore, it is unlikely that we could survive biologically because we would be continually making maladaptive responses that did not gratify our primary drives or making responses likely to be followed by physical damage or injury. This does not mean that all the responses that we learn are adaptive, but it does mean that there is a much greater likelihood that adaptive behavior will be acquired due to reinforcement and that maladaptive behavior that is not rewarded or that is punished will be eliminated in the course of our development.

Stimulus Generalization

Responses that have been learned in the presence of one situation or cue tend to transfer to other similar situations. Thus, if we learn to fear flying in one particular airplane, fear is also likely to occur in connection with other airplanes. The transfer of a learned response from one situation to a variety of situations has been called *stimulus generalization*. In general, the less similar the situation, the less the transfer or generalization that takes place; the more similar the situation, the more the generalization.

The importance of generalization arises from the fact that no two situations are ever the same. If, therefore, learned responses were made to a particular pattern of cues that were associated with some reinforcement, learning could not take place because this particular pattern of cues would never occur again in exactly the same way. If, on the other hand, the cues that elicit the responses were totally generalized, learning still could not take place because any cues, regardless of how different, would produce the same response. Thus, generalization involves the spreading of the response from the particular cue from which it was learned to cues that are rather similar to it. The response is more likely to be given when the other cues are very similar and less and less likely to be elicited by cues that are quite different. This grading of degree of generalization as a function of degree of similarity of the cues has been called the *gradient of generalization.*

Figure 8 shows an example of a generalization gradient obtained in an experiment (Bass & Hull, 1934) using electric shock as the reinforcement. When a vibrator was applied near the shoulders of the subject, a shock was administered and a galvanic skin response (a sharp decrease in skin resistance, which reflects a state of arousal of the autonomic nervous system) obtained to the shock. Through conditioning, eventually the galvanic skin response occurred to the vibrator without the shock. The vibrator was then employed a number of times at increasing distances from the original placement, which had been connected with the painful electric shock. The conditioned galvanic skin response was greatest near the original placement of the conditioned stimulus (the vibrator) and became smaller as the distance from this site increased. In other words, generalization occurred from the position of the original stimulus, being greatest when the stimulus was most like the original in its placement on the subject's back.

Consistency in human behavior can occur because our habitual acts, which have been learned in one situation, generalize from situation to situation and can occur in a variety of contexts. An individual who has

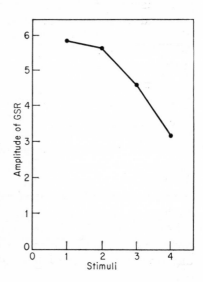

Figure 8. An example of a generalization gradient—generalization of a conditioned galvanic skin response to different stimuli. Stimulus 1 is the conditioned stimulus used during training. All stimuli used for testing differed from the conditioned stimulus only in location. (*From Deese, 1958. Original data from Bass & Hull, 1934.*)

learned an aggressive response to one situation can act aggressively in other situations roughly similar to it. The more generalized this response, the more characteristically aggressively such a person will act; hence we speak of the habit or trait of "aggressiveness."

One interesting point about generalization is that the stronger the drive or motive in the context of which some cue-response pattern has been rewarded and therefore learned, the more likely will generalization take place. That is, if we are extraordinarily hungry and eat at a restaurant, the next time we are very hungry the learned response of going to that restaurant is more likely to generalize to a wide variety of restaurants. We are thus likely to become somewhat indiscriminate in our choice of restaurant. Milder degrees of hunger will make such over-generalization less likely. The stronger the drive, the more stimulus generalization will take place. Similarly, the more similar the cue is to the original, the more likely will a response generalize to it.

Discrimination

The process of discrimination is equally important in learning and is closely related to generalization. Generalization is the tendency for a response to spread from one particular cue to a wide variety of cues. Discrimination is the process by which learned responses are made to a particular and appropriate pattern of cues but not to others. For example, the little girl in our earlier illustration had to learn that one book, and only one particular book, concealed the candy, even though other books in the bookcase were similar to it in size, shape, and coloring. It was necessary for the girl to discriminate a particular cue or pattern of cues that led her to make the correct response. This accentuation of some cues and elimination of others that are irrelevant is the process of *discrimination*. It tends to correct maladaptive generalizations, that is, those that do not produce reward. Whereas generalization decreases the specificity of the cue-response connection and tends to make the response more indiscriminate, the process of discrimination increases the specificity of the cue-response connection and increases the likelihood that the response will be made to the appropriate cue. The more similar are cues, the more difficult it will be to learn discrimination. But without discrimination, learning could not occur.

Anticipation

Responses near the point of reinforcement tend to occur before their appropriate time in the response series; that is, they become *anticipatory*. When the little girl of our illustration was looking for the candy, the response of selecting the correct book, which was the last response and therefore closest to the reinforcement of finding and eating the candy, moved forward in the series and tended to crowd the originally prior responses of selecting the wrong book. The response of reaching for the book or books generalized from the cues that were near to the cues that were further away, and the girl tended to reach for the book before she actually arrived at the bookcase. There was a tendency for the response of reaching for the book to occur before its original point in the reinforced series. Thus, the final act is moved forward and occurs as an anticipation earlier in the sequence of responses than is appropriate.

One of the commonest examples of an anticipatory response is illustrated by attempts to condition a dog by using a puff of air blown on the eyeball to produce an eyewink, which has to be learned to the neutral stimulus of a light. In the course of this conditioning, the dog begins to wink prior to the actual stimulation by the puff of air. In human terms we might say that the dog anticipated the puff of air and thus winked prior to its occurrence. Other examples of anticipatory responses are the child who drops his pants to go to the toilet while he is still in the living room and walks all the way to the toilet with his pants jogging between his feet; or the man who approaches another man with the hand extended for a handshake while he is still all the way across the room.

In learning, particularly in human learning, anticipation is of great importance. Much of our cultural training involves anticipation or anticipatory reactions to future events. These anticipatory responses prepare an individual to react in future situations and to behave so as to facilitate socially accepted reactions. Some such process as anticipation protects us from actions that will have painful or dangerous consequences or from making responses that are socially reprehensible.

Dollard and Miller (1950, pp. 57–58) illustrated the importance of the anticipatory response in the following way:

A child touches a hot radiator. The pain elicits an avoidance response, and the escape from pain reinforces this response. Since the sight and the muscular "feel" of the hand approaching the radiator are similar in certain respects to the sight and muscular "feel" of the hand touching the radiator, the strongly reinforced response of withdrawal will be expected to generalize from the latter situation to the former. After one or more trials, the child will reach out his hand toward the radiator and then withdraw it before touching the radiator. The withdrawal response will become anticipatory; it will occur before that of actually touching the radiator. This is obviously adaptive, since it enables the child to avoid getting burned.

The Learning of Motives and Rewards

It was mentioned earlier that the human being is born with certain primary drives, such as hunger and thirst and reactions to pain and cold, and that habits of response are learned partly because such responses reinforce these primary drive states. One of the primary problems in understanding human behavior is to account for the development of social motives, which seem to arise from our membership in a particular type of society or through certain types of childhood experiences. One of the fundamental premises of association-learning approaches to personality is that these social motives are not innate, as are the primary drives, but are learned or acquired through experiences. This point of view maintains that most of the important drives, such as the desire for money, the ambition to become a scientist or politician, and fears and guilt, are learned during the socialization process through which we progress from infancy to adulthood.

Fundamentally, the way social motives are thought to be learned is fairly straightforward. Certain types of experiences become associated with the reinforcement of some primary drive, and these experiences themselves become sought after because of their connection with this satisfaction. For example, Dollard and Miller (1950, pp. 91–92) wrote:

> In the first year of its life the human infant has the cues from its mother associated with the primary reward of feeding on more than 2,000 occasions. Meanwhile the mother and other people are ministering to many other needs. In general, there is a correlation between the absence of people and the prolongation of suffering from hunger, cold, pain, and other drives; the appearance of a person is associated with a reinforcing reduction in the drive. Therefore the proper conditions are present for the infant to learn to attach a strong reinforcement value to a variety of cues from the nearness of the mother and other adults.

Dollard and Miller argued that such motives as sociability, dependence, need to receive and show affection, and desire for approval from others are learned in this way. They noted, for example, that approval tends to be associated with escape from punishment and with a large number of rewards of primary drives. Disapproval, on the other hand, tends to be associated with nonreward and with punishment. It is, therefore, not hard to see why persons display considerable anxiety at the slightest indication of social disapproval or dislike and why they are rewarded by various signs of approval from others. An individual learns to desire approval because the experience of approval has been earlier associated with the reinforcing of a primary drive. Desire for approval, therefore, becomes an *acquired* or *learned drive* of its own, which, in turn, has the power to stimulate new learning. These social motives, which are learned rather than innate, are of the greatest significance in accounting for human social behavior, even though they have their origin in the gratification of primary drives in childhood and infancy. Depending upon the pattern of experiences of the child, which, in turn, reflects the family and culture in which he has grown, social motives will vary from person to person.

Not only can drives be learned but objects that are innately neutral or have no reinforcing value can come to serve as rewards by means of learning. Food is reinforcing to the hunger drive as a result of the biological construction of man, and although one has to learn that food will reinforce, the reinforcing or reward value of food does not have to be learned. Some objects, however, such as bits of paper with printing on them or round pieces of metal, have no primary or innate reinforcement value but can become rewards or reinforcements. These are therefore called *learned reinforcements*.

Money is the best example of a learned reinforcement. To infants or to persons from other societies coins or paper money are relatively neutral cues with no intrinsic value. In our society, we have learned the value of money, as it were, and these same coins or bits of paper can be used to reinforce the learning of new patterns of behavior and to maintain the performance of old ones. Money therefore functions as a learned reinforcement in the same way that food is an unlearned reinforcement for the hunger drive.

Some very well-known experiments on learned reinforcements have been performed by Wolfe (1936) and Cowles (1937), who taught chimpanzees to work for poker chips, which had acquired learned-reinforcement value. In Wolfe's experiment, hungry chimpanzees were trained to insert poker chips into a vending machine, which presented a grape for each poker chip inserted. After a fair amount of training he found that the chimpanzees could be taught to work for the chips alone by pulling a handle against a weight. The poker chips had developed reward value because they had been previously associated with obtaining grapes (which have primary unlearned reward value) from the vending machine. The poker chips, which had been neutral, now had reinforcement value.

In later experiments, Cowles found that, after the poker chips had become a learned reward, they could be used to reinforce the learning of a variety of new habits. He presented the animals with two boxes. If they opened the one on the left, they obtained a poker chip. If they opened the one on the right, there was nothing. Under these conditions they rapidly learned to open the box on the left in spite of the fact that they were not allowed to exchange the tokens for food until after the end of the day's session. The tokens or poker chips had taken on a reward value that made it possible for the animal to learn new habits by being rewarded by the originally valueless tokens. There is a close analogy between these tokens in the Wolfe and Cowles experiments and money as it is responded to by civilized man.

Higher Mental Processes

From the point of view of association learning, a great deal of human behavior is made up of simple automatic habits. Our responses are made directly to cues in our environment in the presence of internal drives, and we do not take time to think first. In driving a car, for example, we see a person in front of the car and quickly jam on the brakes in a nearly automatic response to a particular cue. The automatic quality of this response is further illustrated by the fact that the passenger in the front seat may also perform the useless response of jamming his foot against the floorboard of the car in response to seeing a person in front of the car.

In a sense, nonautomatic behavior is far more important than automatic learned behavior. The final action can follow a series of internal responses, which might be referred to as a "train of thought." For example, the driver of a car may come to a narrow street on which many children are playing, realize the danger of going rapidly through the street with many cars parked on the side blocking his view of childen or adults trying to cross the street, and decide to slow down to ten miles an hour, at which speed he can come to a rapid stop. Man among all other organisms has the greatest capacity for this thoughtful type of action. These higher mental processes include reasoning, judgment, and concept formation.

One of the characteristics of human beings that contributes heavily to the higher mental processes is their ability to use language (words or symbols, as in mathematics), which can serve as a cue to action. Much human thinking is performed in words and sentences. A person can respond to the words and sentences that he hears from others, reads on a page, or makes internally himself as he thinks. A basic assumption of association learning is that certain laws or principles, which have been discussed with respect to learning at the simpler level, apply also to the higher mental processes and to the use of internal language responses occurring in thought. In the lower or simpler type of learning, acts or responses that produce drive reinforcement are made directly to the pattern of external cues and the internal drive state that is present in the organism. In higher learning, one or a large number of internal *cue-producing responses* (e.g., language) intervene between the external cue and the response. Thoughts are responses that have a cue value in eliciting other responses.

Language has a great value in the higher mental processes because it facilitates generalization and makes us independent of the here-and-now physical attributes of the stimulus. For example, five dimes and a 50-cent piece involve cues that are physically different. Yet these different cues both elicit the same label, or cue-producing response: 50 cents. In other words, through learning they have attained a certain equivalence in our culture. As another example, a child may learn to be afraid of objects that have a sharp edge. By labeling such objects sharp, this fear can be generalized to any relevant new object by simply labeling that object sharp. Verbal labels, therefore, permit us to generalize our actions to a wide variety of cues or situations that have a common attribute, even though as objective stimuli they are quite different. Thus, we can learn to be wary not only of the person who is obviously self-interested and competitive in his relations with us, but also of the person who affects a considerate manner but who has been labeled by others as grasping or self-centered. Though these labels can be misapplied, they serve to orient our behavior, intervening between the stimulus and our response to it.

Attaching different verbal labels to two very similar stimulus objects serves to increase their distinctiveness and our ability to discriminate between them. A $1 bill and a $5 bill are very similar objects from the cue or stimulus point of view, but by the simple expedient of putting a 1 on a $1 bill and a 5 on a $5 bill we can make a very sharp distinction between them. The 1 and the 5 are verbal labels, which facilitate our discrimination *between* the objects. Such labels, which can involve a complex series of internal responses called *thinking*, intervene between the stimulus and the response and tend to make our actions less impulsively responsive to stimuli and more delayed and thoughtful in character. These internal intervening processes increase the power of the human being to adapt to the world and manipulate the circumstances of his life.

LEARNING AND PERSONALITY

Up to this point we have been discussing the fundamental principles of learning. With respect to the development of personality the association-learning theorist simply applies these basic principles to the acquisition of personality characteristics. His assumption is that the important personality attributes are learned through these principles. In the present section, the focus will be primarily on the learning of neurotic patterns of behavior because Dollard and Miller have developed this material most fully. But the same general principles apply to the learning of any personality characteristic.

Conflict

The fundamental factor that must be considered in the development of neurotic symptoms and mechanisms is the learning of unconscious conflicts leading to the acquisition of maladaptive patterns of response. Freud (1924, 1936) was one of the earliest of the modern writers to emphasize the importance of childhood in the development of serious emotional conflicts that were the basis of later neurotic behavior. He maintained that serious conflict in the child usually preceded later neurotic behavior in the adult. Representing the association-learning viewpoint, Dollard and Miller accepted the importance of childhood experiences in the learning of conflicts and neurotic behavior. They pointed out, as have many writers, that the training of children is confused by many irreconcilable demands upon the growing individual. For example, parents try to force the child to be submissive and obedient to the family pressures but to be strong and competitive outside the family situation. Thus, the child must learn to be submissive in some situations and aggressive in other situations, a discrimination that is not an easy one. Relatively little is known about the specific influences of certain patterns of parent-child relationships and of the later effects of conflictual demands that are made upon children, but it is clear that the basic patterns of adult personality tend to be acquired relatively early in life.

A fundamental reason why childhood learning is so important in the development of personality is the physical, mental, and emotional helplessness of children, who are particularly vulnerable to the confusing patterns of childhood training. Children have developed few skills to cope with cultural conflicts. They are smaller and weaker than adults and tend to be helpless to a large degree and dependent upon adults, who can exercise great physical and mental coercion upon them. Children also cannot readily verbalize or use language to label their experiences and are therefore at the mercy of adults, who are capable of more effective understanding and verbal manipulation. The child has strong drives, which impel him to action, and little capacity to control these drives (through the interposition of thought) or to recognize the consequences of them in the near or far future. The parent is apt to impose the tremendous burdens of civilized society upon the child before the child is capable of understanding the instructions he is given or of developing the control he is expected to have over his impulses.

Of special importance in the development of conflicts and the learning of maladaptive ways of coping with such conflicts is the drive of *fear*, the reduction or elimination of which is likely to have a high degree of reinforcement value. The fact that certain responses have reduced or eliminated fear drives is apt to make them strongly entrenched in the behavior repertory of the child, even though they do not permit the gratification of other powerful drives.

Psychologists interested in the dynamics of fear and conflict and the manner in which maladaptive responses are learned have often resorted to experimentation with animals because severe pathological conditions can be easily produced in the laboratory. Miller (1944, 1948, 1951), Maier (1949), and Masserman (1943) are some of the better-known experimenters in the field of "experimental neurosis." By placing rats, cats, and monkeys in fear-producing conflict situations, maladaptive patterns of behavior have been aroused that have at least superficial similarity to human neurotic and psychotic behavior patterns. Masserman (1943) has provided some excellent illustrations of such experimentally produced disorders. These are presented in Figure 9, which pictures one example.

Masserman (1943, p. 60) described the sequence for each picture illustration from *a* to *h* as follows:

a. A normal cat trained to open the food-box to secure food at a light-and-bell signal. The cat readily enters the experimental cage and actively resists removal even between the food-signals. . . .

b. An animal similarly "conditioned" but thereafter made "neurotic" by an air-blast at the moment of food-taking. Despite starvation for 48 hours and the presence of food in the open box, the animal now makes active attempts to escape from the cage at the food-signals as indicated by the flash of light from upper left. . . .

c. Appearance highly suggestive of anxiety in a neurotic animal prevented from escaping the cage. Note piloerection and mydriasis. . . .

d. Continued refusal of food by a neurotic animal which has starved itself for 2 days. . . .

e. Neurotic cat snarling at the signal for food. . . .

f. Compulsive hiding of the head in the food-box at the conditional signal for food (sound of an electric bell). Despite several days of starvation, the animal will remain fixed in this position for from 5 to 30 minutes before leaving the box without touching the food. . . .

g. Phobic reaction accompanied by frantic attempts to escape made by a hungry neurotic cat constricted against the open food-box by the movable barrier. The pilot lights indicate that the visual and auditory food-signals are being given. . . .

h. The neurotic animal persistently presses a switch which actuates the feeding signal (pilot light) but makes no attempt to walk around the barrier to secure the food in the box. . . .

There are a large number of typical training situations imposed upon the developing child that are potential sources of conflict for him. These training situations can readily lead to neurotic manifestations depending upon the way they are handled by both parents and children. Dollard and Miller pointed up four such training situations, and, as it turns out, they are aspects of child rearing that are considered important in personality development by many psychologists. They are the feeding situation, cleanliness training (toilet training), sex training, and the handling of anger. Let us briefly examine the significance of each in the development of conflicts and of various neurotic mechanisms.

The feeding situation: A very young child is totally dependent on the

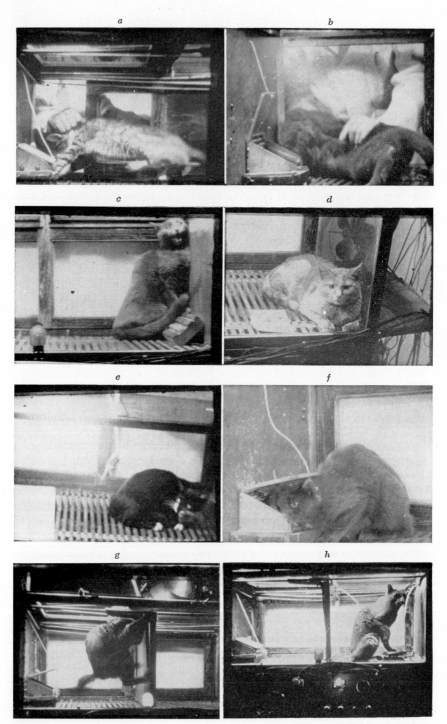

Figure 9. Phenomena of "conditioning" and experimental neurosis. (*Reprinted from Behavior and Neurosis by J. H. Masserman, by permission of the University of Chicago Press, 1943, p. 60.*)

adult for the satisfaction of his hunger drives. He can learn that, when he is hungry, crying can make a great deal of difference in what happens. If his mother comes and feeds him when he cries, a child discovers that something can be done when there is a painful situation; crying is an effective, instrumental act that produces satisfaction of the hunger drive. On the other hand, if a child is left to cry himself out, he can also learn that nothing can be done to change the painful circumstances. Such experiences during the early life of a child could lay the basis for the development of the habit of apathy, on the one hand, or trying to do something when one is in trouble, on the other.

The dependency of the infant upon the parent makes possible the development of secondary needs for sociability and love because a child learns that his hunger is gratified when other persons are around or when other persons, such as the mother, give evidence of feelings of love for the child. Thus, feeding can be linked to social experiences and to love experiences. For Dollard and Miller, this happens because drive reduction is associated with the social and love experiences, although the precise mechanism by means of which secondary needs like love are learned is the subject of controversy among learned theorists. For example, some would minimize the role of reduction of primary drives and emphasize contiguity, that is, the simple fact that loving is contiguous (in place and time in a child's experience) with other satisfying experiences. In any event, a child can also develop pessimistic attitudes toward others as a consequence of its feeding experience or optimistic attitudes when the mother or someone else can be counted on to produce the gratification of the hunger drive. Anxieties can be developed over the prospects of discomfort or pain that follow failure to gratify hunger. Strong degrees of social feeling can arise at this time as well as fears of being alone. Of great importance also is the fact that early conflicts associated with feeding are unlabeled because the child has not developed the use of language. Therefore such conflicts are unconscious and are difficult to discover and identify in later life.

Cleanliness training: One of the earliest demands made upon the growing child has to do with bladder and bowel control, which no child can avoid in growing up. Ordinarily, a young child has no feelings of disgust for feces and urine and, as many a mother will attest, may play with or even eat his excretory materials. Parents encourage in the child disgust for feces and urine and interest in controlling the natural bladder and bowel impulses. Such control is extremely difficult for the child in the absence of adequate understanding of the required behavior and without verbal aids.

Commonly, cleanliness training involves the arousal of strong emotions. A parent himself is apt to manifest strong feeling over the child's successes and failures. Moreover, emotions such as defiance and fear are likely to be directly aroused in the child himself. Aroused fears are likely to produce strong reactions, such as an excessive degree of conformity to the parents' wishes, which can be observed as a passion for cleanliness, neatness, and conformity. On the other hand, attitudes of stubbornness and obstinacy can arise and become habitual as a consequence of strong conflicts associated with cleanliness training. Failures to conform in this period of development can also lead to strong feelings of guilt.

Sex training: One of the greatest sources of conflict in our society is the sexual impulse. Society engenders great anxiety over such impulses and their outward expression. Though it is one of the strongest of the human drives, sex is at the same time one of the most tabooed. It is easy to see how a developing individual will develop anxiety over impulses that are so strongly suppressed and criticized by the society in which he lives.

A wide variety of conflicts can develop concerning sex training, conflicts between sexual impulses and the anxiety-producing suppressions from society. For example, a child's impulse to masturbate often produces emotional reactions in parents and is sharply punished. Masturbatory urges are nearly universal, even in the very young child who discovers that manipulating his genital organs can be pleasurable. The sight of the child masturbating invokes anxiety in the adults of our society, and they often very promptly respond with various sanctions ranging from persistently removing the child's hand from his genital organs to spanking or sharp verbal criticism. Because of the taboo nature of masturbation, labeling or expressing the impulse is likely to produce anxiety and to be punished. Therefore, conflicts over masturbation are generally unconscious.

Another example of conflict arising through sex training is the defining of sex roles for men and women. Homosexual interests are vigorously condemned by most modern societies, and mistakes on the part of the child in sexual identification are carefully corrected by the parents. Boys are expected to have masculine characteristics and girls, feminine characteristics, as defined by the society. The tragedy that can result from failure of the child to show the proper sex identification in his behavior is graphically portrayed in the successful Broadway play and movie, "Tea and Sympathy." The story concerns a boy with effeminate mannerisms who is severely condemned and ostracized in his private-school community.

Factors that increase homosexual impulses include the fears frequently attached to heterosexual approaches. Freud emphasized the Oedipus complex, in which the boy comes into competition with the father because of his heterosexual interest in the mother. One of the results of this family triangle is the fear on the part of the boy of castration or aggressive retaliation by the father. Fears about heterosexual activity, however, can develop in association with approaches to girls on the part of the adolescent boy. There frequently are traumatic experiences, associated with rejection by the opposite sex. Shame can be created by the boy's awkwardness and the social ridicule that may attend clumsy heterosexual approaches.

Again, such conflicts are apt to arouse tremendous anxiety, and they are often poorly labeled at the time they occur. Our culture tends not to give simple or precise names to sexual organs, sexual feelings, or the fears that are attached to them, as is the case with nontaboo experiences. A child may frequently be forbidden to talk to others about his sexual reactions. For these reasons, not talking about such experiences or impulses reduces anxiety and is likely to become habitual. Thus, the sexual conflicts are unconscious and are apt to remain so unless extreme efforts are made to identify and label them.

Handling anger: Anger in response to frustration is characteristic of the human child, and society develops strong attitudes toward it. Generally, society inhibits aggression or at least permits it to take place only under definitely limited circumstances. For example, a characteristic middle-class attitude toward aggression is that verbal anger is more acceptable than physical assault and that aggression is not justified without provocation. Lower-class attitudes, in contrast, are far more favorable to direct assault and less respectful of gentility.

Fear reactions are likely to become attached to feelings of anger because aggressive actions by an individual, particularly by a small, defenseless child, can be conceived as leading to retaliation. Thus, aggressive impulses are likely to evoke fears, and the reduction of the fears can be accomplished by the suppression or concealment of the anger.

Like the other kinds of conflicts discussed, conflicts over aggression are also likely to be poorly labeled. Not only are verbal skills at a low level in the young child, but the child learns that the inhibition of anger (and not thinking and talking about it) tends to reduce the fear associated with it. Like sex conflicts, conflicts over anger are likely to become unconscious and therefore relatively inaccessible. At the same time, aggressive impulses are readily aroused because of the frequency of frustrating experiences and of competition in our society.

The Importance of Conflict

Conflict produces emotional dilemmas in the child to which he must learn to respond. Emotional conflicts are at the basis of the development of neurotic manifestations. Conflicts are particularly apt to occur in certain training situations, which are universal in childhood, the response to which can become an established way of dealing with problems throughout life.

Conflict can arise from pitting one primary drive against another, as hunger versus pain. Strong conflicts can also arise when a primary and a secondary or learned drive are opposed. This is exemplified by the conflict between sexual impulses and the anxiety created by the social taboo about sex. It is further possible to have conflicts when two secondary or learned drives are incompatible, such as anger and the anxiety generated by the cultural attitude toward anger. Of particular importance for the learning of maladaptive reactions is the fact that conflicts developing in early life are likely to be unlabeled and unconscious.

Although all persons experience conflicts, it is possible that the circumstances of life generate severe conflicts in some and less severe conflicts in others. Thus, it is possible that normal and neurotic persons differ to a large degree in the extent of conflict with which they have to struggle. On the other hand, some persons are better able to use higher mental processes than others in resolving the tensions associated with conflict. It is also possible that some persons are more predisposed than others to conflict because they have stronger primary drives or have stronger tendencies to inhibition.

We do not know precisely the conditions necessary for the development of neurotic manifestations in life. Any of the possibilities mentioned could be correct. It is quite clear, however, that neurotic disturbances do arise from conflicts in childhood. For the association-learning theorist, such neurotic manifestations are learned in reaction to conflicts such as we have described. Let us consider more closely how neurotic symptoms and defense mechanisms can be learned as ways of dealing with conflict.

Learning Symptoms

A large variety of symptoms are associated with different forms of neurosis and psychosis. Some of these symptoms are phobias, compulsions, hysterical symptoms (such as anesthesia and paralysis), delusions, and hallucinations. In order to show the application of learning concepts to symptom formation, it is not necessary to deal with each type of symptom. Various pathologies will be described in later chapters. It is desirable, however, to illustrate the learning of symptoms with one or two instances. Let us consider Dollard and Miller's way of handling the learning of phobia and hysterical paralysis, two different types of neurotic symptoms.

Phobia: A phobia is an intense fear of certain kinds of objects or situations, the basis of which usually is not recognized by the phobic person. The phobic person has developed a strong tendency to avoid the feared object or situation because contact with it produces severe disturbance. Some phobias are so common that they have been labeled by the object or situation that is feared: claustrophobia, the fear of being enclosed in a small area; hydrophobia, the fear of water.

In a phobia, a strong fear has been learned originally as a response to a particular cue or pattern of cues and then generalized to other similar cues. For example, Dollard and Miller described the terrifying experience of a pilot who was rescued eventually while floating in the Mediterranean after a series of incidents during which he was exposed repeatedly to death. He had been exposed to intensely fear-provoking stimuli, such as violent explosions close to his plane, the sight of other planes being shot down, and comrades being killed. Other cues, such as the sight and sound of the airplane and thoughts about flying, were attached to the fear experienced by the pilot. The intense fear was learned as a response to all the fear-producing cues, including the sight and sound of the airplane and thoughts about flying. This is the first step in the acquisition of a phobic response.

Recalling the principle of stimulus generalization, we recognize that, when a strong fear has been learned as a response to particular cues, the response will tend to generalize to other similar cues. In the case of this pilot, the fear of this particular airplane and thoughts about flying it generalized to the similar sight and sound of other airplanes and thoughts about flying in them. The pilot became frightened whenever he approached, looked at, or even had a thought about flying in an airplane. Because he had developed a tendency to avoid objects that he feared, he also had a strong tendency to turn away from all airplanes. When he did this, most of the cues that brought on the fear were eliminated and he felt less frightened. The response of avoiding airplanes was reinforced because it reduced the strong drive of fear. Avoidance of airplanes therefore became a strong habit. The pilot also felt anxious when he thought or talked about airplanes and was made less anxious by not thinking or talking about them. The reduction of anxiety succeeded in reinforcing the response of stopping thoughts or speech about airplanes, and he became reluctant to think about or discuss his traumatic experience. Thus, he developed a phobia, including an unwillingness to label the source of his fears.

The only difference between the phobia described for the pilot and the phobias we see clinically is that the development of the former phobia seems to us quite reasonable and understandable, because the causes of the pilot's fear are quite easily grasped and sympathized with. In other phobias the connection between the phobia and the traumatic experience that brought it on is not clear or easy to establish. Because a person has learned to avoid thinking or talking about the subject, he has, in a sense, forgotten the origin of the fear and this forgetting has been reinforced by the reduction in fear that it produces. Thus, a person cannot say why the unreasonable-appearing fear exists. It is therefore difficult to extinguish the fear in the absence of a knowledge of what produced it in the first place. Therapy is usually oriented toward discovering the basis of the fear so that it can be unlearned or extinguished. Any condition, such as a sense of shame or guilt over a response, can increase the likelihood that fear associated with the response and with the cues that elicit the response will become unconscious. This is because the shame or guilt is likely to result in a refusal to talk or think about the situation, thus making the sources of the fear unlabeled and unconscious.

Hysterical paralysis: One of the most interesting types of symptoms is the hysterical symptom in which a part of the body suffers a paralysis that has no organic basis. Such a symptom is learned because it succeeds in reinforcing certain strong drives, most commonly fear. In war, such symptoms are not uncommon; although usually of temporary status, they serve to reduce the soldier's fear of combat and death.

In illustrating the learning of hysterical symptoms, Dollard and Miller cited a case, reported by Grinker and Spiegel (1945), about a soldier who had been directing the fire of an artillery platoon. At the end of the critical phase of battle the soldier was lying on the ground exhausted, when several shells exploded nearby, each time blowing him off the ground. Although he was rather shaken up, he was physically uninjured. Half an hour later his right hand was almost completely paralyzed, and he discovered he could not remove it from his pocket. Instead of reporting sick, he stayed with his company, still suffering partial paralysis, although some of the strength in his arm gradually returned. Later he was sent to the hospital.

After a short series of therapeutic interiews, the paralysis disappeared. When it became obvious, however, that he must return to his company, he developed marked anxiety and tremor in both arms, which had not been present when he went to the hospital. The anxiety seemed directly related to his battle experience. The evidence is strong that the basis of the paralysis and the later anxiety was the escape from combat that the symptoms provided, thus reducing strong fears of the combat situation.

Grinker and Spiegel provide some more general evidence that war neuroses are based on fear of combat by noting that aviators, for example, are likely to develop disturbances in depth perception or night vision (symptoms that are well suited to interfere with flying) and paratroopers are more likely to have paralyzed legs.

In the case of the soldier with the paralyzed arm, the original reward for the symptom must have occurred while the symptom was being learned. The symptom of paralysis reduced the soldier's fear because he knew it would prevent his return to combat. As Dollard and Miller (1950, p. 166) wrote:

As soon as the patient noticed that it was difficult to move his hand, he probably said to himself something like, "They won't let me fight with a paralyzed hand," and this thought produced an immediate reduction in fear. Though the fear reduction probably was mediated by a thought, its reinforcing effect on the symptoms was direct and automatic. In other words, the patient did not say to himself anything like, "Since a paralyzed hand will keep me out of combat, I should try to have a paralyzed hand." In fact, when such a patient becomes convinced of the causal relationship between the escape from fear and the symptom, a strong increase in guilt counteracts any reduction in fear. The reinforcement is removed and there is strong motivation to abandon the symptom.

Dollard and Miller used this illustration as a prototype of all hysterical symptoms, although the war neurosis is easily understood in terms of the traumatic experiences that produce the symptoms in the first place. For association learning, we can view such symptoms as are found in the psychological clinic as learned responses to unusually strong fear-producing cues—learned because these responses tend to reduce the intense fear (that is, are reinforcing). Although the symptom is maladaptive from one point of view—it gets the person into various other difficulties because it prevents him from adequately functioning—it is important to recognize the adaptiveness of the symptom as a means of producing reinforcement. In our soldier illustration, reduction of the fear of combat and removal from the situation that produced the fear is the reinforcement. In the case of nonbattle hysterias, there are other sources of fear, which the symptom reinforces.

Conditions are frequently present for making the origin of the symptom unconscious, because thinking about or talking about the traumatic experiences adds to the fear and not talking or thinking about the experiences reduces the fear. Thus, a patient in the clinic is frequently unable to tell the basis of the symptom or even recognize that the symptom has originated in fears of some sort.

Learning Defense Mechanisms

Not only are certain symptoms characteristic of the different forms of psychopathology, but certain general ways of coping with conflict can become habitual. These are called *defense mechanisms*. Habits of defense have been widely recognized by clinical workers and include such mechanisms as displacement, regression, rationalization, projection, reaction formation, and repression. These mechanisms and their consequences will be more fully described in a later chapter. For Dollard and Miller, they are learned in exactly the same way as symptoms are learned. They are habitual responses, made to certain cues, usually fear-producing, that have been reinforced because they tend to reduce fear or anxiety. The most important of these mechanisms, and the one most frequently alluded to in psychopathology, is *repression*. Let us discuss the mechanism of repression from the point of view of association learning because it is the primary means by which drives and experiences can be made unconscious.

According to Dollard and Miller, drives, cues, and responses that have never been verbally labeled are unconscious. Experiences that have occurred before the child has learned to talk effectively are apt to be in this category. There are many experiences that our language does not adequately label, which are therefore unverbalized and unconscious throughout life.

Repression, from the association-learning point of view, can be understood best by reference to a somewhat similar mechanism, *suppression*, which is a more familiar part of everyday life experience. To illustrate, a group of persons are engaged in conversation at a party. Somehow the subject of conversation turns to persons who have recently had strokes or heart attacks. Members of the group know quite a few cases. The subject is painful, and it raises the general level of anxiety of everyone present. Someone in the group finally says, "How did we ever get on this gruesome subject? Let's talk about something else." The group changes the topic of conversation, and everyone feels more comfortable. The reduction in anxiety tended to reinforce the response of changing the topic of conversation. We tend to suppress or inhibit talking about unpleasant things or saying things that will produce anxiety or guilt.

The process of avoiding painful conversational topics can be a quite conscious and verbalized affair as in the illustration above, in which case it is called *suppression*. However, the same process also tends to occur automatically. Changes in talk or thought content can occur inadvertently without any verbal statement or thought about the desirability of the change. In any case, the reinforcing effect of the reduction in anxiety occurs as a consequence of the change, and thus what has been called "suppression" shades into "repression," in which the elimination of thoughts or speech occurs without awareness.

Repression is similar to suppression, except that it is much more strongly motivated and is automatic and not under the control of verbal cues. In effect, the mechanism occurs unconsciously. Repression is the tendency to avoid certain thoughts. This tendency is unverbalized and reinforced by drive reduction in exactly the same way as are the symptoms already discussed.

Some of the best examples of repression cited by Dollard and Miller are the amnesias of men with combat neurosis, taken from the case material of Grinker and Spiegel (1945). These cases are useful to psychologists because the therapists know the events that have occurred recently and because they can also learn the specific conditions under which the amnesia developed from the man's comrades. This contrasts with the clinical cases of amnesia, where the origin of the symptom is difficult to discover. The patient with amnesia after combat cannot remember certain events and struggles hard to fill in the gaps of his memory. Eventually, however, under treatment, the patient can be made to remember, and the mechanism of repression can be graphically illustrated and closely studied in such cases. Dollard and Miller (1950, pp. 201–202) analyzed learning of the mechanism of repression in the following way:

During combat the soldier is being stimulated by many external cues. He is also producing internal cues by his perceptual responses, his labeling of the salient features of what is going on, and his thoughts about what he is doing. The traumatic conditions in combat attach strong fear to all of these cues. This fear generalizes to other similar cues, and the stronger it is, the wider it generalizes.

Later when the soldier starts to think about what happened, his memories, or, to speak more exactly, his thoughts and the images they provoke, are cues similar to the ones that were present in combat. Hence these thoughts and images evoke extreme fear.

As soon as the soldier stops thinking about his experience in combat, the cues eliciting the fear are removed, and the fear is reduced. This marked reduction in the strength of fear strongly reinforces the responses of stopping thinking. In mild cases this produces a disinclination to think and talk about combat; in severe cases it produces a complete inability to think or talk about the experience.

We would expect the response of stopping thinking to tend to become anticipatory like any other strongly reinforced response. Therefore the patient should tend to stop thinking, or veer off onto a different line of thought, before he reaches the memory of the traumatic incident. He should learn to avoid not only thoughts about the fear-provoking incident but also the associations leading to those thoughts.

Again, as in the case of fear produced in combat, amnesias represent an excellent means of studying the process of repression in general, with the implication that the defense mechanism of repression in ordinary life comes about in the same way and has essentially similar characteristics. The further points should be made that most of the repressions that are important in producing psychopathology in patients seen in clinics arise early in life, probably in childhood, and that the defense mechanism of repression can be learned as a habitual response to a wide range of generalized cues. Thus, some persons can learn to deal with anxiety by means of unconscious mechanisms such as repression, and others can develop other defense mechanisms for dealing with anxiety because these other mechanisms have been reinforced and the conditions for their acquisition have been more suitable. In their analysis of repression, Dollard and Miller simply applied the principles of learning, which we have sketched earlier in the chapter, to the development of mechanisms of defense.

Neurosis

From the association-learning point of view, neurosis, which includes certain defense mechanisms and symptoms, is learned. Neurosis is characterized by what Dollard and Miller called "misery," "stupidity" (that is, failure on the part of the neurotic to understand and solve his problem), and "symptoms," a few of which we have mentioned here. Fear seems to be the strongest of the drives capable of producing neurotic behavior. In the neurotic, fear creates a conflict that prevents the occurrence of goal responses that would normally reduce some other drive, such as sex or aggression. The fear motivates conflicting responses, such as stopping and avoiding. When the neurotic stops and retreats from the goal activity stimulated by normal drives, the reduction in fear reinforces these avoidance responses.

The avoidance responses, however, prevent the other drive-reducing goal responses from occurring, and the unsatisfied drives build up and remain high, producing misery. At the same time, the high drives tend to evoke impulses that elicit the fear. Thus, the neurotic will be stimulated by both the frustrated drives and the fear that these drives produce. The state of conflict itself can produce strong additional stimuli, such as muscular tensions and tremors, which contribute to the misery.

Fear can also motivate the repression of verbal responses that label the elements in the conflict situation. Because certain thoughts arouse fear, stopping these thoughts reduces the fear and repression eliminates from consciousness the verbal responses that are the basis for the higher mental processes. Such repression makes the neurotic behave stupidly. He is less able to differentiate the situations in which he has been punished, and this lack of discrimination retards the extinction of unrealistic fears and helps perpetuate the vicious circle of fear, repression, stupidity, lack of discrimination, and the persistence and even increase of unrealistic fear.

Because the neurotic shows stupidity in the areas affected by repression, he is prevented from finding adequate solutions to his problems and he is driven to maladaptive actions, which further contribute to his state of high drive and misery. The misery tends to interfere with clear thinking and further contributes to his stupidity.

The mechanisms of defense, such as repression, and the learned symptoms that he has acquired result in a partial reduction of the fear that has motivated the neurosis in the first place. However, these symptoms and the defense mechanisms create further dilemmas for which the neurotic must often seek therapeutic help. Moreover, the defense mechanisms and symptoms are likely to be only partially successful in reducing the fear. But their success in at least partially reducing fear makes them difficult to eliminate, especially as the origins of the fear have been repressed and are thus inaccessible to the patient's thought. The purpose of therapy is therefore to help the patient discover the origin of his symptoms and to learn more effective methods of solving his problems. Because of the inaccessibility of much of the material involved in the neurosis, the process is frequently arduous and lengthy.

Overview

Just as the trait-and-type approach is a frame of reference for considering personality rather than a specific theory, so also the association-learning point of view is a general way of looking at personality and not a specific personality theory. For example, it does not propose a new or unique set of constructs with which to describe the substance of personality. In dealing with certain important phenomena of personality, such as the symptoms and defense mechanisms of neurosis, Dollard and Miller took some of the main constructs proposed by Freud (such as repression) and some of the classical symptoms observed in neurotic disturbance (such as phobias and hysterical paralyses) and attempted to apply traditional laws of learning to account for their development. In other words, an already existing set of constructs and observations has been considered in the terms and principles of association learning. This point of view could be applied to any specific theory of personality or psychopathology, just as there are other ways of considering the learning process itself. The fundamental proposition is that any characteristic of personality is learned and that one can profitably examine the specific details of the learning process to answer the question of how any characteristic came into being.

Not all psychologists would agree that learning plays so central a role in the development of personality. Although no psychologists would altogether deny the importance of learning in the development or alteration of personality characteristics, there are those who consider that it has been overemphasized. Psychologists such as Harlow (1953), Maslow (1954), Goldstein (1940), Lecky (1945), Rogers (1951), and Hartmann, Kris, and Loewenstein (1947), to name a few, are critical of the idea that so-called secondary motives (such as curiosity, needs for approval, and problem solving) can only arise out of their connection with the gratification of primary biological drive states, such as hunger or thirst. Developmental theorists such as Freud (1949), Piaget (1952), and Werner (1948), while not denying the role of learning, also maintain that much of man's psychological development comes about as an unfolding of biological processes.

Harlow (1953) experimented with learning and problem solving in monkeys with and without the so-called primary-drive stimulations. He made the observation that, when a hungry monkey is presented with a problem to solve and the solution of the problem is rewarded with food, the monkey ceases to have any interest in the problem again unless the same hunger-drive conditions are present. On the other hand, monkeys with no apparent primary drive aroused learned to solve the problems just as rapidly as the hungry monkeys and, in fact, continued afterward to maintain interest in solving the problems. Presumably they got pleasure out of problem solving for its own sake. He also noted that rewarding a monkey by letting him look out the window at outside passers-by is just as effective reinforcement as feeding him when he is hungry.

Harlow considered it absurd to suggest that higher forms of life, such as man, have only the simple physiological drives at birth that have been credited to him by reinforcement-oriented association-learning psychologists. He suggested that higher drives, such as curiosity or problem solving, may also be innate or primary in man. Thus, from this point of view, the catalogue of primary drives of the human being must be enlarged. Although the form of expression of these drives is learned, their existence as drives is innate.

The growing interest of some learning theorists in problems of personality has been an important development in modern psychology. Personality theorists such as Freud, who often emphasized the biological determination of human development, have also assumed that much of personality organization is acquired through learning. In fact, this side of the question has been increasingly emphasized by the socially oriented psychoanalytic writers, such as Horney (1937), Adler (Ansbacher & Ansbacher, 1956), and Sullivan (1953). But the actual nature of the processes of learning of personality and the mechanisms of adjustment has not been of great interest to these theorists. Attempts to approach the problem of how personality structure comes into being through learning are useful in filling this gap. In this sense, the association-learning approach of Dollard and Miller complements other frames of reference about personality. Its focus is not so much on originating conceptions of the nature of personality itself as on elaborating (in terms of learning theory) the principles of how it got that way.

We have considered, up to now, the trait-and-type approach, which stresses consistent patterns of response independent of the stimulus situation, and the association-learning approach, which emphasizes the establishment of habits of response to an objectively defined stimulus. The stimulus or cue elicits the response, which, through the action of reinforcement, becomes connected to it. But the objective, physically defined stimulus can be apprehended in different ways by different persons. It is possible to argue that some psychological representation of the stimulus rather than the actual external physical object determines behavior. This view in personality theory has been called *phenomenology*, and it represents the essence of a third frame of reference within which personality can be considered. Phenomenologists define the stimulus in subjective terms. We shall examine this point of view in the following chapter.

Personality from a
Phenomenological Point of View

In contrast with the association-learning framework of Dollard and Miller, there is an approach to personality that emphasizes organizing factors within the person, both as the cause of behavior and as important phenomena in their own right. Whereas Dollard and Miller (1950) treated the stimulus to which the organism is exposed in objective, physical terms, the phenomenologists maintain that the important determinant of behavior is not the stimulus object itself but rather the organism's apprehension of it.

Asch (1952, p. 68) made this point in the following way: "To limit investigation to the observation of action alone would be to ignore the paramount fact that the actor is constantly registering in awareness what is happening to him and that this alters his subsequent acts." In other words, the way in which a person perceives events determines how he acts.

In referring to the phenomenal object in contrast with the physical object to which the individual responds, Koffka (1935, p. 78) posed the question: "Why do things look as they do?" As a gestalt psychologist, he wrote: "If things look as they do because they are what they are, then perception would not contain in its very makeup a cognitive problem." In other words, our perceptual representation of objects is not necessarily identical with the objects themselves. If we examine any figure composed of dots, we do not perceive these dots as discrete points in space; rather we react to the pattern of dots belonging together as parts of the contour of a figure. Our senses do not directly mirror the physical object. Koffka went on to say:[1]

When I see a table, this table does not affect my senses at all; they are affected by processes which have their origin in the sun or in an artificial source of light, and which are only modified by the table before they excite the rods

[1] From K. Koffka. *Principles of Gestalt Psychology.* New York: Harcourt, Brace, 1935. P. 79. Copyright, 1935, by Harcourt, Brace and Company, Inc.

and cones in our retinae. Therefore, these processes, the light waves, and not the geographical objects, are the direct cause of our perceptions. . . .

From this point of view, the *representation* of the objects of the world, rather than the physical object itself, serves as the stimulus. The phenomenologists in personality theory have adopted this frame of reference and extended it into the field of personality. They stress the observer-defined stimulus and build their theoretical language around the perceptual process as the essential determinant of human behavior. Whatever this privately apprehended world is called (e.g., "life space" or "phenomenal field"), it is considered the cause of action and must be reconstructed through inference by the phenomenological psychologist in order to understand and predict human behavior. This way of looking at the human being brings together a number of somewhat diverse personality theories, which are summarized in this chapter.

The most influential of the phenomenological theories of personality will be discussed. Not included are many viewpoints that are better dealt with under different categories. The psychoanalytic writers—for example, Freud, Jung, Rank, and Sullivan—although they have things to say that bear upon the phenomenological frame of reference, have special qualities that make it desirable to treat them in other chapters.

MURRAY'S NEEDS AND PRESS FORMULATION

In 1938, Henry A. Murray published a book called *Explorations in Personality*, which contained intensive clinical analyses of normal persons at the Harvard Psychological Clinic. *Explorations in Personality* also included a section called "Proposals for a Theory of Personality." This was an attempt to develop a dynamic conceptual scheme for the description and study of personality. It had a number of phenomenological aspects. In it were included notions that, in various degrees, were borrowed from Freud, Jung, and other dynamic psychologists.

Murray conceived of personality as a hypothetical structure that governs the experience and patterns of action of the individual. The term that Murray utilized to deal with motivational processes was *need*. Need is a construct that stands for a force in the brain region. This force organizes action and perception and other cognitive processes toward the satisfaction of that need. It leads the organism to search for or to avoid relevant environmental circumstances. It is the driving, directing force in human behavior.

Murray gave loving care to the analysis of needs and classified them into a variety of types. For example, there are *primary* or *viscerogenic needs* and *secondary* or *psychogenic needs,* a distinction that is a traditional one in psychology (note Dollard and Miller in the previous chapter). Primary needs include thirst, hunger, elimination, and others, all based upon the organic requirements for physical survival, pleasure, and avoidance of pain. Secondary needs are independent of direct organic processes and include needs for acquisition, achievement, recognition, dominance, autonomy, and aggression, to name a few. Actually, Murray listed and classified thirteen primary needs and twenty-eight secondary ones. This has provided a taxonomy of needs that has been useful for many clinical psychologists in describing an individual personality. Murray's classification and list of needs is shown in Table 7.

Needs can also be *overt* (manifest) or *covert* (latent). The former are permitted immediate and undisguised expression, and others tend to be inhibited by the individual. Overt needs are likely to be expressed in motor behavior, and covert needs can occur in dreams and fantasy. Needs can also be *focal* or *diffuse.* The former require particular kinds of environmental objects; the latter can be directed to a wide variety of objects and expressed in almost any situation.

Murray did more than offer a mere list of needs. He thought that needs are organized within the individual and interrelated in various ways. Some needs or groups of needs can be dominant in an individual or perhaps become dominant with changes in the situation. In other words, there is a hierarchy of needs, with certain need tendencies being stronger or more immediate than others, but this hierarchy can change with changing circumstances. Needs can also be in conflict, with the consequence of considerable personal misery. Needs are likely to become attached to objects, events, or persons. The term, borrowed directly from Freud, for this relation between objects and needs is "cathexis." If an object evokes a positive need (which indicates that the person likes the object), it is said to have a positive cathexis. If it evokes a negative need (indicating that the person dislikes or is threatened by it), the object has a negative cathexis.

Needs can become attached consistently to certain classes of objects, and habits of action can grow out of these connections. Such connections become stable organizations in the brain. Images of these objects in familiar settings and images of preferred modes of behavior become integrated in our minds with the needs and emotions that they usually excite. They sometimes enter consciousness as fantasies or plans of action that can be realized in behavior patterns. These hypothetical organizations connecting objects or patterns of behavior and needs are called "need integrates."

Up to this point the theoretical features that identify a phenomenological approach to personality have not been described. Murray is included

Table 7

Murray's List of Primary (Viscerogenic) and Secondary (Psychogenic) Needs

Primary

A. Lacks (leading to intakes)
- 1. n Inspiration (oxygen)
- 2. n Water
- 3. n Food
- 4. n Sentience

} Positive

B. Distensions (leading to outputs)

Secretion (life sources)
- 5. n Sex
- 6. n Lactation

Excretion (waste)
- 7. n Expiration (carbon dioxide)
- 8. n Urination
- 9. n Defecation

} Negative

C. Harms (leading to retractions)
- 10. n Noxavoidance
- 11. n Heatavoidance
- 12. n Coldavoidance
- 13. n Harmavoidance

Secondary

Actions associated with inanimate objects:

n Acquisition (acquisitive attitude). To gain possessions and property. To grasp, snatch, or steal things. To bargain or gamble. To work for money or goods.

n Conservance (conserving attitude). To collect, repair, clean, and preserve things. To protect against damage.

n Order (orderly attitude). To arrange, organize, put away objects. To be tidy and clean. To be scrupulously precise.

n Retention (retentive attitude). To retain possession of things. To refuse to give or lend. To hoard. To be frugal, economical, and miserly.

n Construction (constructive attitude). To organize and build.

Actions associated with ambition, will to power, and desire for accomplishment and prestige:

n Superiority (ambitious attitude). This has been broken up into two needs: the n Achievement (will to power over things, people, and ideas) and the n Recognition (efforts to gain approval and high social status).

n Achievement (achievant attitude). To overcome obstacles, to exercise power, to strive to do something difficult as well and as quickly as possible. (This is an elementary ego need which alone may prompt any action to be fused with any other need.)

Table 7 (*Continued*)

n Recognition (self-forwarding attitude). To excite praise and commendation. To demand respect. To boast and exhibit one's accomplishments. To seek distinction, social prestige, honors, or high office.

n Exhibition (exhibitionistic attitude). To attract attention to one's person. To excite, amuse, stir, shock, thrill others. Self-dramatization.

Actions associated with defense of status or the avoidance of humiliation:

n Inviolacy (inviolate attitude). This includes desires and attempts to prevent a depreciation of self-respect, to preserve one's "good name," to be immune from criticism, to maintain psychological "distance." It is based on pride and personal sensitiveness. It takes in the n Seclusion (isolation, reticence, self-concealment) which in our study was considered to be opposite of n Exhibition and, for this reason, was not separately considered. The n Inviolacy has been broken up into three needs: n Infavoidance (the fear of and retraction from possible sources of humiliation), n Defendance (the verbal defense of errors and misdemeanors), and n Counteraction (the attempt to redeem failures, to prove one's worth after frustration, to revenge an insult). Counteraction is not truly a separate need. It is n Achievement or n Aggression acting in the service of n Inviolacy.

n Infavoidance (infavoidant attitude). To avoid failure, shame, humiliation, ridicule. To refrain from attempting to do something that is beyond one's powers. To conceal a disfigurement.

n Defendance (defensive attitude). To defend oneself against blame or belittlement. To justify one's actions. To offer extenuations, explanations and excuses. To resist "probing."

n Counteraction (counteractive attitude). Proudly to overcome defeat by restriving and retaliating. To select the hardest tasks. To defend one's honor in action.

Actions associated with human power exerted, resisted, or yielded to:

n Dominance (dominative attitude). To influence or control others. To persuade, prohibit, dictate. To lead and direct. To restrain. To organize the behavior of a group.

n Deference (deferent attitude). To admire and willingly follow a superior allied individual. To cooperate with a leader. To serve gladly.

n Similance (suggestible attitude). To emphasize. To imitate or emulate. To identify oneself with others. To agree and believe.

n Autonomy (autonomous attitude). To resist influence or coercion. To defy an authority or seek freedom in a new place. To strive for independence.

n Contrariance (contrariant attitude). To act differently from others. To be unique. To take the opposite side. To hold unconventional views.

Actions associated with sadism and masochism:

n Aggression (aggressive attitude). To assault or injure another. To murder. To belittle, harm, blame, accuse, or maliciously ridicule a person. To punish severely. Sadism.

Table 7 (*Continued*)

---

n Abasement (abasive attitude). To surrender. To comply and accept punishment. To apologize, confess, atone. Self-depreciation. Masochism.

Actions associated with inhibition:

n Blamavoidance (blamavoidance attitude). To avoid blame, ostracism, or punishment by inhibiting asocial or unconventional impulses. To be well-behaved and obey the law.

Actions associated with affection between people; seeking it, exchanging it, giving it, or withholding it:

n Affiliation (affiliative attitude). To form friendships and associations. To greet, join, and live with others. To cooperate and converse sociably with others. To love. To join groups.

n Rejection (rejective attitude). To snub, ignore, or exclude another. To remain aloof and indifferent. To be discriminating.

n Nurturance (nurturant attitude). To nourish, aid, or protect a helpless individual. To express sympathy. To "mother" a child.

n Succorance (succorant attitude). To seek aid, protection, or sympathy. To cry for help. To plead for mercy. To adhere to an affectionate, nurturant parent. To be dependent.

n Play (playful attitude). To relax, amuse oneself, seek diversion and entertainment. To "have fun," to play games. To laugh, joke, and be merry. To avoid serious tension.

Actions associated with cognitive communications:

n Cognizance (inquiring attitude). To explore (moving and touching). To ask questions. To satisfy curiosity. To look, listen, inspect. To read and seek knowledge.

n Exposition (expositive attitude). To point and demonstrate. To relate facts. To give information, explain, interpret, lecture.

SOURCE: Murray, 1938, pp. 79–83.

---

in this chapter as a phenomenologist because he maintained that the environment *as it is apprehended by the individual* determines behavior. This phenomenological emphasis can best be illustrated by reference to the concept of *press.* The environment or stimulus is phenomenal in nature; that is, it is based on a personal frame of reference. The stimulus is relevant to behavior because of its effect conceived by the individual; that is, the environment or a particular aspect of the environment is apprehended as relevant or irrelevant and as facilitating or obstructing important needs. The conceived harmful or beneficial effect of the stimulus is called "beta press." One may ask: "Does the object physically harm the subject, nourish him, excite him, exalt him, depreciate him, restrain, guide, aid, or inform him?" In essence, the aspect of the stimulus most correlated with behavior is the beta press. The objective situation, called "alpha press," is not the significant determinant of action, although the discrepancies between the objective environment and the perceived environment throw light on the reality-testing capacities of an individual and suggest areas of conflict.

Another feature of Murray's system is the concept "thema," which includes both the need conceived to be operating and the situation relevant to the need (press). A simple thema is a behavioral unit, which includes a combination of a particular need and press. The thema or need-press combination is the unit of personality that Murray considered most adequately handled by the personality psychologist. Thus, in describing actions Murray emphasized the need that impels and guides the action and the beta press under which the need operates.

THE FIELD THEORY OF LEWIN

A most influential and unique phenomenological approach to personality is that of Kurt Lewin (1935, 1936). The central construct of Lewin's system is the "life space." Like Murray, Lewin described the situation to which persons respond in terms of its phenomenal impact rather than in terms of its objective character. The stimulus is a complex field that includes a person's needs, other features of his personality structure, the perceived potentialities to action available to him, and all the recognized consequences of these possibilities. This total psychological environment is the life space. It is the psychological event that must be inferred or reconstructed to comprehend human actions. Along with other phenomenologically oriented theorists, Lewin maintained that the behavior of an individual is a function of the psychological representation of his world rather than the objective world itself. This representation is a complex "field," which includes continuing interaction or interdependence of the internal organization of the person and the environment.

The contents of the life space include the totality of psychological facts that directly determine the behavior of a person at a particular moment. These facts need not be conscious, but they are psychological rather than objective. An individual may be unaware of them in the sense that he cannot verbalize them. One can infer the nature of the life space from a person's behavior in an environmental context.

Lewin distinguished the life space, or psychological environment, of the person from features of the objective or geographical environment to which the individual does not directly respond and which Lewin called the "foreign hull" of the life space. For example, if there are five behavior possibilities in any particular situation and an individual perceives only two of these, then only these two possibilities are part of the life space. The other three unrecognized alternatives belong to the objective environment or the foreign hull (like Murray's alpha press). Although the foreign hull is not part of the life space, it actually can influence indirectly. For example, the tax appropriation for public schools in California is not part of the life spaces of the school children in that state. Their behavior is not directly caused by this tax appropriation. Such an appropriation affects the life spaces only indirectly so far as it has an influence on school conditions and the quality of teachers.

Lewin argued that the life space was changing continually as a result of alterations in the inner-tension states and experience of the individual, as well as in the environment. Thus, if one wished to understand the behavior of an individual at any point in time, it was necessary to describe the life space at that particular moment, because later the entire psychological field would have altered. This emphasis on the forces operating at the particular instant of behavior was referred to by Lewin as *systematic causation* in contrast with *historical causation*, the latter referring to events of the distant past as they determine present circumstances. Lewin did not believe that past events are unimportant in the present structure of the life space. He maintained rather that the understanding of present behavior must be based solely upon the elucidation of the present life space of an individual. The field of forces operating at the instant of action is all that need be known, even though these have been influenced by past history.

Lewin's theoretical system is a dynamic one because the life space is continually changing rather than static. In field theory one cannot think easily of stable traits of a person disposing him to act in particular ways. The dynamics include continuing interplay of environmental and internal psychological structures. In his descriptions of life spaces, Lewin tended to be dependent upon analyses of events after the fact rather than prior to their occurrence. The reason for this is that to know a person's life space requires that he behave in certain ways and that from his behavior an inference be drawn about the momentary organization of the life space. But the behavior has passed already, and it becomes impossible to test the theoretical system in the usual scientific way by using it to predict future behavior. The life space will have changed by then. This has been perhaps the most telling criticism offered of Lewin's field-theoretical system. The system is at its best when one is dealing with descriptions of the momentary interchanges between an individual and his environment; it is less suitable for dealing with personality stability and consistency in predicting future events.

Lewin attempted to represent the life space of a person spatially or graphically, employing a kind of mathematical terminology, which has been called *topology*. His resulting descriptions involved the use of diagrams of direction, distance, and force to represent the characteristics of the life space. The hypothetical construct *force* is used for the motivational aspects of behavior. A force directly produces any reaction and has such qualities as strength, direction, and point of application. Forces can be experienced consciously as urges toward particular goals or as vague restlessness. They are inferred from movements toward or away from objects and situations or by the presence of tensions within an individual. The various objects in the environment of an individual and the different courses of action and goals are described in terms of *valences*. These valences can be positive or negative, depending upon whether the objects are reacted to as desirable or undesirable. They involve the psychological representation of the value of an object in relation to the kinds of needs it is perceived to fulfill for the individual. A further characteristic of the life space is the existence of *barriers* as characteristics of the environmental situation, which block or slow down an individual's approach to a goal.

A person's behavior is seen by Lewin as a resultant of forces operating on him at any moment. The behavior is directed toward goals (called "psychological regions") that have the strongest positive valence and away from regions of negative valence. Conflict can be produced when an action tendency involves both positive and negative valences. Lewin has written extensively about conflict, and some of the forms of conflict that he has described are diagrammatically presented in Figure 10.

Morgan discussed the various types of conflict described by Lewin as follows:[2]

Approach-approach conflict, as the label implies, is a conflict between two positive goals—goals that are equally attractive at the same time. A physiological example of such conflict is that of being hungry and sleepy at the same time. A social example is that of wanting to go to a dance and a swimming party when both are scheduled for the same night. The proverbial donkey is supposed to have starved to death because he stood halfway between two piles of hay and could not decide which to choose. Actually, neither donkeys nor people often "starve themselves to death" merely because they are in conflict between two positive goals. People usually resolve such a conflict by satisfying first one goal, then the other—eating, then going to bed, if one is both hungry and sleepy—or by choosing one of the goals and giving up the other.

A second type of conflict, *avoidance-avoidance conflict,* . . . involves two negative goals, and is fairly common. Little Johnny must do his arithmetic or get a spanking. A student may be forced to spend the next two days studying for an examination or face the possibility of failure. A man may be forced to work at a job he intensely dislikes or take the chance of losing his income. Such conflicts are capsuled in the common saying, "caught between the devil and the deep blue sea." You can probably think of many examples in your own

[2] From Clifford T. Morgan. *Introduction to Psychology.* New York: McGraw-Hill, 1956. Pp. 251–253.

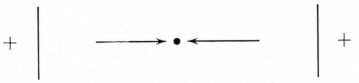

Approach-approach conflict. The individual is attracted by two positive goals that are incompatible with each other.

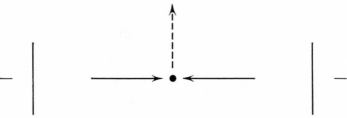

Avoidance-avoidance conflict. The individual is caught between two threats or fears. In addition to the goals shown, there are usually other barriers or negative goals to restrain the individual. Otherwise, in this type of conflict, he is inclined to "leave the field" (dotted line) to escape conflict.

Approach-avoidance conflict. The individual is attracted toward a positive goal, but this goal also has a fear or threat (negative goal) associated with it. Such a conflict is difficult to resolve and tends to evoke more anxiety than the approach-approach or avoidance-avoidance conflict.

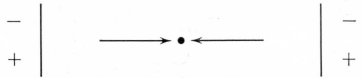

Double approach-avoidance conflict. Many conflicts that appear to be approach-approach or avoidance-avoidance conflicts are really double approach-avoidance conflicts.

Figure 10. Diagrams of types of conflict. (*From Morgan, 1956.*)

experience of things you do not want to do but must either do or face even less desirable alternatives.

Two kinds of behavior are likely to be especially conspicuous in such avoidance-avoidance conflicts. One is vacillation. As we shall see below, *the strength of a goal is greater, the closer one is to the goal*. As a person approaches a negative goal, he finds it increasingly repelling. Consequently, he tends to retreat in the other direction. When he does this, he comes closer to the other negative goal and finds it, in turn, to increase in negative valence. He is like a baseball player caught in a "run down" between first and second base. He runs first one way, then the other. As he runs toward second base, he comes closer to being tagged out, but when he turns and runs back toward first base, he faces the same danger. Such *vacillation is characteristic of avoidance-avoidance conflicts.*

A second important feature of this kind of conflict is *an attempt to leave the conflict situation.* Theoretically, a person might escape avoidance-avoidance conflict by running away altogether from the conflict situation. People do, indeed, try to do this. In practice, however, there are additional negative goals in the periphery of the field, and these ordinarily keep a person from taking this alternative. A child, for example, who does not want either to do arithmetic or to take a spanking may think of slipping away from home. This, however, has even more serious consequences than staying in the situation and "facing the music," so he is wiser not to try it. The adult in avoidance-avoidance conflict, however, may try a quite different way of running away. This is to let his *thoughts and imagination take him away from the uncomfortable situation.* He may spend his time, for example, in day dreaming, instead of facing up to his problem. As a student, you have no doubt found yourself doing this at times when you were supposed to be studying. In extreme cases, a person may conjure up an imaginary world, or re-create in his mind's eye the carefree world of childhood, in which there is no such thing as unpleasant tasks that have to be performed. Carried to such an extreme, this way of leaving the conflict situation is called fantasy or regression, depending on the form it takes. . . .

The third type of conflict, *approach-avoidance conflict,* is the most important of the three because it is the most difficult to resolve. In approach-avoidance conflict, a person is both repelled and attracted by the same goal object. A young bride, for example, may have been brought up in an atmosphere that treated sexual activities as ugly or sinful. As a consequence, sexual matters have for her a negative sign. . . . At the same time, her normal sexual drive, as well as other social values involved in marriage have led her into marriage, thus providing the marital situation with a positive sign. Now, as she enters marriage, she is caught between her sexual motives and the attitudes of her parents, which have become her own values. There is no way out of this situation without altering her motives, which in the diagram means erasing or weakening one of the signs.

The example of the bride in conflict gives us a hint about the way in which approach-avoidance conflicts can develop. Note that the bride's conflict arose because of the social values acquired in her early training. These values serve as obstacles to the satisfaction of motives. Since they are within the person, the process of acquiring them . . . is regarded as one of *internalizing obstacles.* Such obstacles frustrate a person in the same way that the environmental obstacles of childhood do. The fact, however, that they are *internal,* rather than external, makes them much more difficult for the person to deal with. He may find ways of circumventing environmental obstacles, but he can hardly circumvent that which is within himself.

This analysis of frustration . . . permits us to reduce frustrating situations to their simplest elements. In everyday life, however, things are seldom this simple. More typical are conflicts in which there are many different goals, especially negative ones, surrounding a person with pressures he wishes to avoid. There are also some complex combinations of the kinds of situations we have described. One is the *double approach-avoidance conflict*, diagrammed in one of the above figures. In this, two or more goals may have both positive and negative signs. Consider, for example, the student who is in conflict between making good grades and making the college football team. Superficially, this conflict appears to be a simple case of approach-approach conflict—conflict between two positive goals. The student, however, may have considerable social pressure from family and associates to achieve both goals. He may incur the disapproval of his parents if he fails to make good grades, and he may lose the esteem of his comrades if he does not make the football team. Thus failure at either one carries with it a threat. Each goal, therefore, has a negative value as well as a positive one; hence, the student finds himself in a double approach-avoidance conflict.

In diagramming the life space topologically, each behavior possibility available to the person is identified as a "region." To represent forces (motives) Lewin made use of arrows, called *vectors*, which indicate the forces acting upon an individual and the path they tend to induce him to take. The strength of the force is represented by the length of the arrow, direction is indicated by pointing it to the appropriate regions on the diagram of the life space, and the point of application of the force is shown by placing the arrow point against the circle indicating the person as a whole or against the particular region within the person involved. The valence of a region is indicated by plus or minus marks. Strong positive valences may require one, two, or more plus signs, and similarly minus signs indicate negative valences.

The topological field-theory analysis also extends to the structure of personality. Up to now we have tended to view the life space as a field of forces within which the person exists without differentiation or specification as to internal characteristics. Lewin, however, wrote much about the internal organization or structure of the person. In the development of the individual, for example, one of the important concepts in Lewin's theory is that of "differentiation." It involves an increase in the number of parts of the whole. For example, the number of regions or behavior possibilities increases with maturation and experience. The adult has many more differentiated tension systems than the child. Moreover, the psychological environment becomes increasingly differentiated with age. Time becomes differentiated into a present, a future, a near past, and a remote past. Thus, there is considerably more differentiation of parts to the personality structure as development takes place. There also is greater integration or organization of the parts.

This permanent personality structure, just as in the case of the life space, can be diagrammed in topological form. Lewin identified two main classes of regions within the personality: the outer portions, representing the perceptual-motor region, and the central part, representing the inner-personal region, consisting primarily of need systems and cognitive characteristics. The inner-personal region is surrounded by the perceptual-motor area and has no direct contact with the boundary separating the person from the environment. The motor regions operate as a tool in the service of inner-personal needs, which are diagrammed by closed circles within the representation of the person. The interrelations between them are indicated by the thickness of the walls enclosing them in the diagram. Some needs are relatively isolated from others so that they are less likely to influence or be influenced by other need systems within the personality. A need system that can be readily substituted for another to discharge tension has highly permeable boundaries, which can be indicated by thin walls.

The number of regions that can be represented in the life space at any particular moment is determined by the number of separate psychological possibilities that exist at any particular moment in time. If there are only three perceived possibilities at the moment, there are only three regions in the life space. Thus, the diagrams can be enormously complex or relatively simple, depending upon the number of psychological facts to be represented in the life space. One of the criticisms that has been made of Lewin's system, in fact, is that in his topological diagrams he has tended to describe relatively simple psychological events and that a more appropriate analysis of the typical complex psychological event would be totally unwieldy and impossible to use. Lewin, in turn, argued that the behavior of an individual can never be understood if all the relevant pyschological facts are not considered and that an effective analysis of behavior must take some variation of the particular form he suggested.

To understand thoroughly Lewin's description of personality in topological form, it is desirable to examine carefully a characteristic topological diagram. Figure 11 presents a diagram that includes the main constructs essential to Lewin's approach. Beneath the figure is offered a description of the psychological events represented. A careful analysis of this figure will aid the reader to understand what has been described.

Harsh and Schrickel[3] have devised the diagram

. . . to illustrate the man P in the cafeteria who wants to buy strawberry shortcake S for his dessert. S is an object of positive valence, as indicated by the plus sign placed above it. The vector A pointing in the direction of S shows

[3] From Charles M. Harsh & H. G. Schrickel. *Personality Development and Assessment.* (2d ed.) Copyright 1959, The Ronald Press Company. Pp. 359–360.

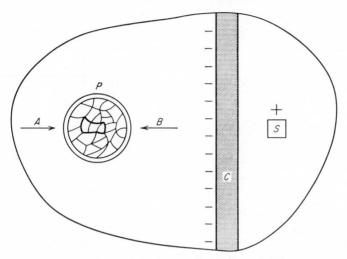

Figure 11. Diagram of field, valences, and vectors in a conflict situation. (*From Charles M. Harsh & H. G. Schrickel. Personality Development and Assessment. (2nd ed.) Copyright 1959, The Ronald Press Company.*)

P's awakened need or tension for *S*, while the barrier *C* (lack of money) is shown as developing negative valence by the minus signs lined along it. The vector *B* indicates the tendency to move away from *C*. The two vectors pointing in opposing directions indicate *conflict* in *P*. The entire figure is enclosed to show that this is the life space of *P* at the moment, just as *P* is enclosed but within the field. As *P*'s locomotion, tensions, etc., and the valences and vectors of the field change, the diagram would be changed to a series of different diagrams, each giving an instantaneous cross section of the dynamics operative within the field at each moment. The sign for the personality *P* is complex and not simply an enclosed homogeneous area. The individual *P* is symbolized as a kind of field or system within the larger field, with its own subareas indicating different tensions or needs, habits, sensory functions, etc. The ego is a dynamic system maintaining its own integrity in ever-shifting equilibrium as it is acted upon by, and acts upon, its environment. In fact, only the integrity of the ego makes possible a life space and a physical space time, or external world. The boundaries of the ego shift, however, so that at one time it may extend no farther than innermost experiences and feelings, such as during periods of silent prayer. At other times it may extend beyond one's skin and include one's clothing, personal belongings, and distant friends. This variability in the boundaries of the ego does not mean that everything and anything can be incorporated into the particular personality.

This is a very brief statement of the field theory of Lewin. A number of excellent treatments of field theory have become available. One of the best has been written by Leeper (1943), and there is another, more recent version by Hall and Lindzey (1957). The reader is encouraged to go to these sources or to the originals for a more elaborate exposition. It is a point of view that has had a major impact on current psychological thought.

ORGANISMIC THEORY: GOLDSTEIN, MASLOW, AND LECKY

The so-called organismic viewpoint is partly an extension of the gestalt movement in psychology initiated by Wertheimer, Koffka, and Köhler. These latter psychologists were concerned especially with the nature of perception. They studied extensively the perceptual field, which they conceived of as an organized whole from which there is differentiated a figure emerging from a larger background. Organismic psychology has extended the gestalt principles (which have been applied mostly to perception) to other psychological functions, including personality.

The reason for including the organismic theorists in this chapter is not so much their "holistic" philosophy as the fact that they are also phenomenologists. Largely as a result of their origins in gestalt psychology, they have made perceptual organization a central theme. The personality is organized around the figure-ground concept, and the behavior of the person is considered to depend upon his apprehension of the world of objects and events rather than upon the physical or objective world. Thus the organismic views of Goldstein (1940), Maslow (1954), and Lecky (1945) are most easily distinguished by their consistent phenomenological orientation.

There are a number of principal features of organismic theory that deserve general discussion before we consider specific formulations characteristic of organismic theorists such as Goldstein, Maslow, and Lecky. For one thing, the unity or coherence of the personality of the normal individual is a cardinal concept of organismic theory. Disorganization, or the isolation or separation of psychological structures, is the essence of pathology.

Second, though the organism must be seen as an organized whole or system, it can be analyzed by differentiating this whole into its various parts. But these parts must never be considered isolated from the whole. The functions of the organized whole cannot be found in the parts, because it is the organization of the parts that determines the qualities of the whole.

Third, instead of postulating, as do many theories, that the organism is motivated by a multitude of needs, organismic theory emphasizes one overriding motivating force. This is self-actualization, which means that man is always striving to express and achieve his inherent potentialities in whatever way he can. There is direction and unity to life because of this single-minded purpose, which orients him.

Fourth, although the external environment plays a role in the behavior and development of the organism, it is less important than the potentialities for growth within the organism, which lead it to select relevant aspects of the environment to which it will respond. If the environment is not too alien, the potentialities of the organism will unfold, producing a healthy, integrated personality.

Fifth, the organismic theorist is inclined to study the organism through the complete examination of one person (an ideographic orientation) rather than through investigation of isolated psychological processes like learning, perception, or emotion in many persons (a nomothetic approach). Thus, there is a special compatibility between organismic theory and clinical psychology, which is also concerned with the functioning of individuals.

In order to see some of the various specific forms of organismic theory, let us very briefly examine the views of several writers who can be classified readily within this framework.

Kurt Goldstein

Goldstein (1940) is an excellent representative of present-day organismic theory. His concepts arose largely from his neuropsychological work with brain-injured patients. Observation of the various disturbances associated with brain injury encouraged him in a holistic conception of the nervous system in contrast with the concept of the localization of function in particular brain tissues or organs. He has extended these more strictly neurophysiological concepts to personality.

Goldstein conceived of the organism as an integrated whole made up of a number of differentiated structures, which normally remain integrated, except under abnormal conditions. The organization of the various structures can be viewed in terms of figure and ground. The figure occupies the focus of activity and awareness. For example, the ideas communicated by the words on this page become the figure against the background of the rest of the page and the total content of the chapter, book, and psychological training that you bring with you from past reading and thinking. Not only perception but all organismic activity can be considered in terms of what is figure and what is background, the figure changing constantly as the nature of the processes in focus also shifts.

An individual's needs and the demands made upon him determine what will emerge from the total background as figure. For example, when the telephone rings, it becomes the figure and the process of reading may fade into the background. The figure-ground organization is constantly changing, although certain consistencies of organization are characteristic of the organism, such as sensory thresholds and intellectual characteristics, and these tend (along with what is produced through experience) to result in a particular kind of organization, more or less stable and characteristic of the person.

Any activity of the organism arises from an unequal distribution of energy between the organism and the environment. A constant amount of energy is conceived to be evenly distributed throughout the organism, which represents a normal or typical tension state. It is constantly being disturbed, and behavior succeeds in redistributing or equalizing the energy state by an "equalization process." Postural changes, eating, sleeping, and socially oriented activity are behavioral examples of the equalization process when the normal tension state (equilibrium) has been disturbed by stimulation of some kind. These disturbances of equilibrium correspond to specific needs or drives.

The concept is a homeostatic one, very familiar in psychology. The central adaptive problem of the organism is to equalize tension, that is, to bring it back to the balance point that is optimal for the organism. During development certain mechanisms appear that tend to maintain the energy balance of the organism and, under favorable circumstances, promote the equalization or "centering" of the individual with respect to energy distribution.

The basic motive in Goldstein's system is *self-actualization*. The various primary drives and secondary motivations are manifestations of this one main purpose of life, to actualize one's self. All persons strive for self-actualization, but the specific goals toward which they strive vary because life experiences differ as well as inherited physical structures.

Self-actualization requires that an individual come to terms with the environment. It must take place in an environment that impinges upon the organism, disturbing its equilibrium and requiring it to act to restore the balance. To actualize itself, the organism must search in the environment for what it needs. Coming to terms with the environment represents a kind of adaptive interaction between the organism and the environment. The environment provides the means by which self-actualization can be achieved, although it can also obstruct self-actualization by excessive demands or by the scarcity of the means to self-actualization.

The normal, healthy organism is one (Goldstein, 1939, p. 305) "in which the tendency toward self-actualization is acting from within, and overcomes the disturbance arising from the clash with the world, not out of anxiety but out of joy of conquest." Successful coming to terms with the environment therefore requires the person either to master it, as is suggested above, or to accept the situation and make the best of it. If the above solutions are not found, an individual either remains in painful tension and becomes disorganized as in temporary catastrophic reactions or gives up and regresses to a lower level of adjustment, as in neurosis or psychosis.

Abraham Maslow

Although not offering a fully elaborated theory of personality, Maslow (1954) wrote a great deal on motivation and personality from a phenomenological and organismic point of view. He severely criticized psychologists for accepting the notion that social motives result from conditioning in relation to primary drives like hunger and thirst. He believed that this leads to a negative conception of man whose virtues are interpreted entirely as efforts to avoid pain or anxiety. He viewed man as taking active steps toward his own high-level development. Maslow is less interested in conflict, misery, and pathology than in psychological health. He attacked psychology for its typical emphasis upon psychopathology.

Man's nature includes a *hierarchy of motives*, which range from the most potent survival needs, such as hunger and thirst, up the scale toward higher needs, including (in this order) safety needs, needs for belongingness and love, esteem needs, needs for self-actualization, cognitive needs such as a thirst for knowledge, and esthetic needs such as a desire for beauty. The higher needs will not be gratified or permitted expression unless more potent primitive needs are satisfied. Thus, if a person is hungry or his safety is seriously threatened, cognitive or esthetic needs will not be expressed. These higher needs will be actualized only when a person is freed from the tyranny of lower-order survival needs.

The *healthy and normal individual* is one who is capable of *actualizing* his fundamental nature, which means fulfilling his potentialities at the highest level of which he is capable. Anything is pathological that frustrates or blocks this. Health is synonymous with the actualization of a person's highest needs so he is capable of love, interested in knowing for its own sake, and in esthetic appreciation. These higher needs in man are less potent than the lower needs, such as hunger and thirst or safety, and are easily overcome by habit or cultural pressure. They never disappear as potentialities, however, and psychotherapy has the aim of freeing the individual so that they can gain expression again.

Maslow believed that psychologists should study healthy persons more extensively and, in particular, the self-actualizing persons. He noted that they are difficult to find, and he has studied some famous, historical persons such as Lincoln, Jefferson, Beethoven, and others who were living at that time, as well as Eleanor Roosevelt and some of Maslow's acquaintances. Maslow sought to determine what distinguishes such self-actualizing persons from ordinary persons. He found them realistic, accepting of themselves and others, spontaneous, problem-centered rather than self-centered, having an air of detachment and desire for privacy, autonomous and independent, novel rather than stereotyped in their appreciation of things and persons, frequently undergoing profound spiritual experiences, identified with and oriented toward mankind, capable of deep and intimate relationships with a few loved persons, democratic in orientation, unlikely to confuse means and ends, having a philosophical sense of humor rather than a hostile one, possessing a high degree of creativeness, and characterized by strong tendencies to resist conformity to the culture.

It is clear that Maslow shares a number of features with other phenomenological theorists and the subgroup of organismic theorists. His theoretical views embrace the total organism. He is skeptical of the secondary-drive concept with its implication of reinforcement through primary drives. Most important to his position in this chapter, he emphasized the private meaning of an experience to an individual and the mediating and organizing structures within the person, which are conceived of as determining behavior.

Prescott Lecky

At a time when the predominant bias of psychology was associationistic in character, Prescott Lecky attempted to formulate a theory of personality that was essentially organismic and phenomenological in character. His ideas were scarcely well developed at the time of his death, and most of his writings were set down in a little book called *Self-consistency* (1945), which represents the only statement of his point of view. It has had, nonetheless, some definite influence in personality theory.

Like Goldstein, Lecky maintained that all psychological phenomena were expressions of a unified personality, which organizes behavior. Man's activities have the purpose of maintaining self-consistency. In other words, his strivings are constantly directed at maintaining a harmonious, organized personality structure, which consists mainly of values consistent with each other. The only source of motivation is, therefore, the *need to maintain* this harmonious organization so far as possible. As a result of efforts along these lines, the personality develops progressively through life into a unified self-consistent organization.

Like Maslow, Lecky attacked the typical psychological conception of motivation that the organism strives to reduce tension as a means of achieving pleasure. Lecky pointed out that the individual actually *seeks to maintain and produce tensions.* Man is a problem solver who obtains pleasure from solving problems and from assimilating new experiences. By way of illustration, he pointed out that a puzzle or problem that is easy to solve is soon discarded and one that is too difficult also is ignored or avoided. Some amount of uncertainty about the outcome, as in a new detective story, is pleasurable for man.

When a problem or conflict is produced by an extremely unfavorable environment, an individual may be under great pressure because he cannot assimilate the experience to the presently existing personality structure without *restructuring* his values. Pain, for Lecky, arises from the organism's failure to assimilate a new experience. Therapy involves permitting the person to reorganize his values to produce a harmonious or integrated totality. If, for example, being accepted by friends is an important part of a system of values and a person has acted in such a way as to evoke severe criticisms from respected and valued friends, such criticism may be difficult for him to assimilate. The individual must in some way handle the experience so that the self picture can be maintained in its present organized form. Reorganizing one's conception of one's self is an extremely difficult and painful thing to do.

The personality arises out of social and physical experiences, and these experiences are molded into a unified structure, an integrated whole. At each step in development reorganization or restructuring of the personality takes place, so the individual is able to move ahead toward other experiences. Pathology arises when an individual has failed to assimilate important aspects of experience to his personality structure, and there remain large areas of experience that cannot be integrated into a self-consistent integrated whole.

Some Comments on Organismic Theory

As has been pointed out by Hall and Lindzey (1957), organismic theory is more of an attitude or frame of reference than it is a systematic theory of personality. In many respects, its general tenets are an accepted part of personality theory. For example, the integrity of the total organism is accepted widely in principle among psychologists of personality.

In their efforts to point out the total or organized nature of any behavioral event, organismic theorists have seemed to go overboard. One can analyze tiny elements in the total behavior act, such as the movement of a single muscle fiber, and one can progressively enlarge the elemental units of behavior to include rather complicated molar events. But where does one draw the line beyond which such holistic emphasis ceases to be useful? The analogy is a little bit like looking at a large-scale map in which an extremely small area is blown up so it can be examined in great detail (a very molecular approach) in contrast with the small-scale map, which includes an entire nation or globe and on which it is impossible to find individual streets, towns, or even roads, but from which one can get a really good grasp of the major land masses and some of their main subdivisions on the earth. There is no right or wrong in using a large-scale or small-scale map. Rather it is a matter of the purpose and the usefulness of these approaches for the problem being analyzed. It seems that we must, at some point, analyze detail, and the size or scope of the detail is a matter of choice, although it seems unlikely that man's actions are best examined at either the most molecular or molar extremes.

The organismic theorists stress the organization of the person, the inseparability of the parts, and the part-whole relationships, but in the process of analysis they frequently lose sight of their very organismic philosophy. For example, Goldstein considered the organism as an entity separated from the rest of the world, with the skin as the boundary line between the organism and the world. To carry the organismic philosophy all the way would require no such arbitrary boundaries. What goes on inside the organism and with its external environment would all be parts of a larger unified system including both.

Perhaps the most serious criticism that has been leveled at the organismic approach is the vagueness of the hypothetical constructs used. How can one deal empirically, for example, with the concept of self-actualization? The concept is so broad (because it includes so many diverse needs, which are organized differently in different persons) that it is difficult to see how it leads to any particular prediction. At their present stage of thinking the organismic theorists have left their concepts shrouded in relative ambiguity. Nonetheless, they have left a deep attitudinal impression on the field of personality theory as it exists today.

SELF THEORY: ROGERS, AND SNYGG AND COMBS

Self theory has much in common with organismic theory and clearly falls in the class of phenomenological approaches to personality. More than most approaches, it is understandable to the lay person because its concepts are couched in the language of our subjective experience (e.g., what we want, how we think and feel).

This section presents two of the main self theories, which differ in certain important respects, although having much in common: that of Carl Rogers (1951) and that of Snygg and Combs (1949). However, the self as an organizing concept does not originate with these writers. One of the most famous discussions of the self was written by William James, in his *Principles of Psychology* (1890).

As Hall and Lindzey (1957) pointed out, the concept of self in present-day psychology seems to have two different meanings. It is used frequently to refer to a person's attitudes toward, his feelings about, and his perceptions and evaluations of *himself as an object*. The second meaning is *self as process* and deals with an active group of processes that do something. When the self is thought of in terms of the regulating or governing processes of the organism, the term most commonly used is "ego," although there is no doubt that many writers have used the terms "self" and "ego" interchangeably or have included both meanings under the term "self."

Self theory is not of recent origin, although it has tended to have its greatest impact in the middle of the twentieth century, particularly in clinical psychology and in the area of social perception. The influence of the self-theory point of view is illustrated by the numbers of well-known writers in psychology who have dealt with or developed views concerning the self. Some examples are the work of Symonds (1951), Sherif and Cantril (1947), Sarbin (1952), Stephenson (1953), Chein (1944), Hilgard (1949), G. H. Mead (1934), and Koffka (1935).

Carl Rogers

The self theory of Rogers (1951) incorporated the viewpoint of organismic theory, features of Freudian theory, and some qualities of Lewin's field theory. It emphasizes the psychological field as the causal agent in behavior. The *phenomenal field* of Rogers is similar in quality to the life space of Lewin. The self is a differentiated portion of the phenomenal field, consisting of conscious perceptions and values of an I or me. The *self concept* includes the central picture of what I am, as a professor, as a student, as a person with a particular history and set of aspirations. The organism reacts as an organized whole to the phenomenal field in order to satisfy its needs. There are a number of specific needs, but there is one basic motive, which we have seen before in the organismic theories, that is, *to actualize, maintain, and enhance the self*. The organism also can symbolize its experiences so they become conscious, it can deny them symbolization so they remain in an unconscious state, or it can selectively ignore its experiences. Thus the phenomenal field can be conscious or unconscious depending upon whether the experiences that are included within it are verbalized or not.

Rogers conceived the self concept as developing out of the organism's interaction with the environment. That is, a person discovers who he is through his experiences with things and persons. Values of other persons can be introjected into the self, or they can be perceived by the self in a distorted fashion. As in the position of Lecky, the self strives for consistency, and the organism behaves in ways consistent with the self concept. Experiences not consistent with the self concept are threats and can produce emotional disturbance. As a result of maturation and learning, the self concept can change. In successful therapy the client's conception of himself undergoes such changes as to lead to a more realistic picture of himself and to free the organism to actualize himself.

Rogers has set forth a series of propositions, which are the fundamental postulates or assumptions of his theory of personality. There are nineteen of them in all, and we shall not elaborate each one here. However, some of the main propositions will provide more of the flavor of Rogers's thought.

Rogers (1951, p. 483) stated that "every individual exists in a continually changing world of experience of which he is the center." This private world of experience can be known in a complete way only to the individual himself. Because not all the phenomenal field is conscious, we have to accept the limitation of what we can learn from a person's verbalizations. The method by which we construct or infer the phenomenal field of a person involves providing a permissive and accepting situation so there will be a favorable atmosphere to obtain candid self reports or introspections from the person.

Rogers (in 1951, p. 484) also maintains that "the organism reacts to the field as it is experienced and perceived. This perceptual field is, for the individual, 'reality.'" In other words, as with all phenomenological theory, an individual responds not to the objective environment but to the environment as he perceives or apprehends it. For that individual, it is reality regardless of how distorted or personalized it may be. In other words, subjective rather than objective reality determines how an individual will behave. For Rogers, these subjective realities basically are tentative hypotheses about reality. The individual can often check the correctness of the hypotheses with other sources of information. This checking of experience against the world as it really is, or "testing reality," provides the person with reasonably dependable knowledge about the world so he can behave appropriately.

Not only does the organism react as an organized whole to the phenomenal field, but, as we have noted before, there is one fundamental motive. As Rogers (1951, p. 487) put it, "the organism has one basic tendency and striving—to actualize, maintain, and enhance the experiencing organism." This single life goal or motivating force involves a basic tendency, inherent in the organism, toward growth, toward actualizing and enhancing one's self. A person is willing to experience pain in this effort toward self-actualization because the innate urge to grow is so strong. The adolescent, for example, seeks independence or autonomy in spite of the fact that it is frightening to leave the protective custody of the parental home, both physically and psychologically. Nonetheless, under favorable circumstances this movement toward autonomy, this actualization or growth process, leads him to develop independence. If a person can discriminate between forward or progressive growth and regressive ways of behaving, he will choose progression rather than regression.

In common with other phenomenologists, learning and development are seen by Rogers in terms of organization and reorganization of the perceptual field. The self concept, as part of the phenomenal field, is the organized picture of the self in relation to the environment. What the person is aware of about himself is figure (clearly conscious). The unconscious (or partly conscious) material is ground. The self concept also includes positive or negative values about the self and its relationship with the world, not only as they exist now, but in the past and future as well. Changes in the self concept come about through reorganizing this picture. In this respect, Rogers sees conflict and the resolution of conflict in a way very similar to Lecky.

To borrow an illustration from Hall and Lindzey (1957), a boy has a self picture of being a good boy, loved by his parents, but he also happens to enjoy teasing his sister, for which he is frequently punished. When he is punished, the punishment involves an experience that conflicts with his self picture and he is called upon to revise his self image and his values in one of several ways. He can say, "I am a bad boy"; he can affirm that his parents do not like him; or he can deny his enjoyment in teasing his sister. If he decides that he doesn't enjoy teasing his sister, he denies his real feelings in an effort to protect his self image as a good boy, loved by his parents. In order to integrate such an experience as punishment for teasing his sister, he must restructure and enlarge his self picture to include negative aspects as well as positive aspects, thus accepting in himself feelings that may be unacceptable or punishable.

The implication here is that there can be two behavior-regulating systems: the self concept and the biological urges of the organism. As we shall see, this has a great deal of the flavor of psychoanalytic thinking, which postulates a kind of warfare between the biological urges of the organism (in particular, the sexual drives) and the ego structure, which inhibits or regulates the expression of these drives to preserve the person or reduce anxiety. When impulses are not accepted but nonetheless guide behavior, there is conflict and the organism does not function harmoniously.

Any experience inconsistent with the self concept will be perceived as threatening, and defenses can be established that deny these threatening experiences to consciousness. The self image becomes, then, less in tune with reality in terms of the actual presence of organismic needs. The person, as a result, is in conflict and becomes maladjusted. Part of the function of therapy is to permit an individual to perceive and accept into his self concept more of his organic experiences that are in conflict with the self concept, so altering the self concept as more readily to permit positive growth.

D. Snygg and A. W. Combs

The self theories of Rogers and Snygg and Combs (1949) are exceedingly similar in fundamental ways. Like Rogers, Snygg and Combs utilized the term *phenomenal field* to represent the psychological environ-

ment. The latter maintain that all behavior, without exception, is determined by, and pertinent to, the phenomenal field of the behaving organism.

As in the case of Lewin, the phenomenal field of Snygg and Combs is
not a constant thing, but it changes with the changing needs of the individual as well as the changing external conditions. But, as is true of
most phenomenologists, Snygg and Combs are not interested in elaborating the laws by which the phenomenal field changes through experience.
Learning is considered as the differentiation of a figure from a figure-
ground matrix. In problem solving, there is increased differentiation of
the field. First, awareness tends to be of gross situations, and the important cues and orientation points emerge into the figure when the behaver
becomes aware of his need for such details. The goal or need of the
behaver and the opportunities for differentiation that are available determine the degree and direction of differentiation. This represents a
description of events that we usually call "learning," in terms of the
concepts of perception. Like other phenomenologists, Snygg and Combs
are influenced heavily by gestalt psychologists, focusing as they do on
the phenomenal (perceptual) field and the structuring and restructuring
of the field with experience.

In Snygg and Combs's development of phenomenology or self theory,
the phenomenal field is divided into two subdivisions, the *phenomenal
self* (which includes all the parts of the phenomenal field that the individual experiences as part or characteristic of himself) and the *self concept*. The self concept is a smaller, more stable subdivision that eliminates what Snygg and Combs considered extraneous factors in the
prediction of behavior. Snygg and Combs (1949, p. 112) wrote:

> Although the tip of my little finger is certainly part of my phenomenal self,
> it is seldom differentiated into figure in the course of my daily life. The same
> is true with respect to many other ideas and concepts which are part of my
> phenomenal self. It is only rarely, for instance, that I have to fix a leaky faucet
> and conceive of myself as an amateur plumber. Nor is my occasional concept
> of myself one likely to be of major importance in understanding my behavior.
> On the other hand, I conceive of myself as a professor six days a week and
> sometimes on Sunday and holidays. This description of myself is very fre-
> quently in figure in my phenomenal field and exerts a very considerable influ-
> ence on my behavior a good deal of the time.

Thus, the self concept is made up of the parts of the phenomenal field
that have been differentiated by the person as definite and stable characteristics of himself. The phenomenal field altogether determines all behavior. However, certain aspects of the field are more important than
others. From the phenomenal field is abstracted the phenomenal self, and
finally the self concept is distinguished as the most important and specific

aspect of the phenomenal field and phenomenal self in determining how a person will behave.

As in the case of Rogers, Snygg and Combs identified one basic human need, which is required to explain and predict behavior; this basic need is the preservation and enhancement of the phenomenal self. Snygg and Combs (1949, p. 61) wrote:

> The soldier in war time is not torn between a desire for self destruction and a desire for self preservation as he faces the coming battle. On the contrary, he is concerned solely with the preservation of or the enhancement of his phenomenal self. Although the situation will vary from individual to individual, it might roughly be described as follows: He may risk death on the one hand to *preserve* his phenomenal self against becoming the kind of person who "lets his buddies down" and on the other hand to *enhance* his phenomenal self by being the kind of person who is "one of the gang," or as "brave as the rest."

Up to this point it is difficult to see much in the way of important distinction between Rogers and Snygg and Combs as self theorists. Both conceptions call for the reconstruction of a person's phenomenal field in order to understand and predict his behavior. However, for Rogers, this reconstruction is based entirely on what a person is able to report about himself, his feelings, attitudes, interests, and goals under the favorable circumstance of psychotherapy. Thus, Rogers utilizes introspection as his primary method.

In sharp contrast to this, Snygg and Combs infer the phenomenal field from introspections of the observer rather than the behaver. The observer asks himself: "Under what circumstances would I have done that?" It is as if the observer says, "If I saw myself as such and such type of person with those types of needs, I would have acted as he does." This kind of reasoning is commonly used in everyday life, but in many ways it is a questionable basis for a scientific theory of personality. To do this accurately calls for a theory of identification, that is, the means by which an observer can put himself in the place of another person and identify himself with the behaver's psychological state. Furthermore, there is the assumption that there is some common frame of reference on the part of different observers and that they are likely to be less biased and more objective in the assessment of another person's phenomenal field than the other person himself. This is a unique kind of method for constructing the phenomenal field of persons and provides one clear distinction between Snygg and Combs's approach to self theory and other formulations.

There is another difference between Snygg and Combs and Rogers. Although Rogers emphasized the phenomenal field and self concept, these constructs are not the only sources of behavior, because he discussed biological or organismic factors that might not be incorporated into the self concept but nonetheless can impel and direct behavior. Thus, Rogers has two systems, the organism and the self, which can be in conflict. Snygg and Combs, on the other hand, considered behavior to be entirely in a one-to-one relationship with the phenomenal field and exclusively caused by this private world.

Some Comments on Self Theory

One of the problems of self theory concerns method. There is abundant evidence that unconscious factors motivate behavior and that what a person says about himself is likely to be distorted by all kinds of defenses. Rogers maintained that a person's internal frame of reference is the best way of understanding behavior, but he depended entirely upon what the person can or will report. In the case of Snygg and Combs, the phenomenology is of a rather unusual sort, dependent upon some kind of consensus in the private worlds of the observers to make inferences about the phenomenal field of the person being observed. Lewin, in contrast, inferred the life space from behavior observation. Many psychologists agree with the use of the concept of self in some form as an organizer of behavior, but they believe that the method of introspection alone poses critical difficulties. Actually, all methods of inference have problems in common, and this criticism cannot be considered unique to phenomenology.

These approaches, with their emphasis upon the individual and his own particular interpretation of events, are most appealing to clinical psychologists and psychotherapists, whose emphasis is on understanding and helping the individual person. The point of view of Rogers, for example, has stimulated a substantial amount of empirical research in psychotherapy. Rogerian students have studied the nature and changes of the self concept during therapy, as well as the relationships between adjustment and the discrepancy between the self concept and how an individual is conceived by others. Rogers's point of view has also strongly influenced the development of the use of recorded interviews, which can be analyzed later, to study the patient's statement about himself and the interplay between the therapist and the patient.

Among the rigorously objective scientists of behavior, self theory is considered vague and not subject to empirical test through the prediction of behavior and the study of the conditions that antecede different kinds of phenomenal fields. Part of this criticism is based on the as yet incomplete development of self theory. It is currently difficult to know to what extent the point of view will develop increased rigor so that specification of the conditions defining the constructs of the phenomenal field can be made.

THE BIOSOCIAL-ECLECTIC POINT OF VIEW OF MURPHY

Many of the theoretical systems presented here overlap in many respects with other similar theoretical points of view, although perhaps differing in certain key respects. Theorists have freely borrowed from the concepts of other theoretical systems. This willingness to utilize systematically the best concepts of varying points of view is called "eclecticism." A successful eclecticism indicates that the sharp distinctions between different theoretical systems, which make them seem incompatible, may not be as great as their proponents imply.

The most successful present-day eclecticism is that of Gardner Murphy, whose book *Personality: A Biosocial Approach to Origins and Structure* (1947) is his fullest statement of a theory that utilizes organismic concepts, field concepts, and concepts of association-learning theory in building a balanced eclectic personality theory. A more recent statement, which is less thoroughgoing and more concerned with his speculations about the future of mankind, is *Human Potentialities* (1958). Because of his eclecticism, it is difficult to classify Murphy in any frame of reference described up to now, although Murphy's predominant emphasis is phenomenological, field-theoretical, and organismic rather than associationistic. Murphy's theory is so elaborate and rich in content that it is difficult to do any substantial justice to it. A few highlights of his thinking will reflect his thoroughgoing eclecticism.

The main components in Murphy's personality theory are physiological dispositions, which develop from genetic and embryological characteristics, canalizations formed early in life, conditioned responses, and cognitive habits, which are produced by both canalization and conditioning.

Physiological dispositions or *organic traits* essentially are tissue tensions transformed into and expressed as symbolic traits through learning. In other words, a person learns to react to a conditioned stimulus or symbol in the same way as he did to the original tissue tension. He learns, for instance, to associate the thought "I am thirsty" with the physical state of thirst, so ultimately the symbolic representation (that is, the thought) can by itself produce search for water and activities related to drinking. Thus, behavior can be guided by physiological dispositions. Here Murphy has borrowed from the experiments of Pavlov and the association-learning theories, which emphasize conditioning as an essential feature of learning.

By *canalization* Murphy means that organic traits or physiological dispositions can be channeled by social pressures and experience into very specific forms of behavior. For example, when we are hungry, any kind of food will be gratifying, but in each society certain types of food, certain ways of preparing the food, and certain ways in which the food is eaten become the specific ways in which the general hunger state can be gratified. The specific mode of gratification, as it is repeated with consequent satisfaction, becomes strengthened as the most desirable way to gratify the need, and many specific forms of behavior become strongly canalized as means of gratifying needs. Particular tastes develop that persist throughout life.

Murphy introduces the term *cognitive habits*, which include such concepts as role, self, and ego. *Role* is a relatively fixed way of behaving, imposed upon an individual by his culture or subculture. Roles become part of the personality structure and orient an individual to act in certain ways. The concept of role permits Murphy's system of personality to reflect the impact of the culture upon the personality.

Murphy also has been influenced by, and has, in turn, influenced, the phenomenologists. He utilized the concept of the *self*, which is defined as a person's perceptions and conceptions of himself; that is, the individual as known to himself. The *ego* has to do with the controlling or regulating processes, including the mechanisms of defense.

Like the developmental psychologists, such as Werner (1948), Murphy sees three stages in the organization of personality: the global stage, in which energy is diffusely spread over the entire personality, which functions as an undifferentiated totality when stimulated; the differentiated stage, in which there begin to be separate structures; and the integrated stage, involving the organization of the discrete parts into a system.

For Murphy, a *motive* is a tension gradient in the tissues, with tension reduction producing satisfaction and tension increase resulting in discomfort. This orientation to motivation is common in psychological theory. As an organismic psychologist, however, Murphy rejected the idea of separate or distinct motives, suggesting that any single motive is part of the total, organized motivational system and anything happening to one is of relevance to the remainder in the system. Moreover, unlike the association-learning approach of Dollard and Miller, Murphy did not separate biological and social needs. For Murphy they are one and the same thing. He rejected the notion that complex adult motives are derivatives of early primary drives. Rather, they are independent and autonomous, arising out of man's construction as well as the present conditions of his life.

A unique feature of Murphy's view of motivation is his emphasis on *sensory and activity needs*. Specific pleasures, like the enjoyment of a musical composition or a sunset and many other esthetic and motor activities, are not learned, but have their origin in characteristics of our sense organs and muscles. Rather than reducing artistic or aesthetic interests to such primary drives as sex or hunger, Murphy maintained that these motivations directly result from tensions in specific regions of the body. For example, musical appreciation arises from organic traits, perhaps the body's capacity to resonate to particular sounds. They are inherent properties of the organism. A particular type of music is appreciated because it is compatible with these organic properties, just as sweet things (even saccharine, which is nonnutritive) taste good without training.

Murphy fundamentally is a field theorist like Lewin. For him, the culture and the person cannot be independently defined. The personality is dependent upon the culture or the environment, and the culture cannot be conceived independently of the personalities of its members. As Murphy wrote (1947, p. 891):

> We can not define the situation operationally except in reference to the specific organism which is involved; we can not define the organism operationally, in such a way as to obtain predictive power for behavior, except in reference to the situation. Each serves to define the other; they are definable operationally while in the organism-situation field.

Murphy's views have produced no real controversies. He has had no militant disciples, as Freud and Rogers have. He has been exceedingly influential in promoting psychologists who have developed their own systems of thought in personality theory. In trying to evaluate Murphy's approach, Hall and Lindzey wrote as follows:[4]

> Biosocial theory has not been a rallying ground, nor has it been a battlefield. Does this mean that biosocial theory is without influence, that it has been passed by, and that it is a dead theory which has been resuscitated for this book? Not at all.
>
> It is our contention that the biosocial approach, as formulated by Murphy, is one of the most vital and influential movements in modern psychology. It does not need ardent proselytizers and it has few critics because it has been built into the sinews of psychology.
>
> Our reasons for reaching this conclusion are these. Biosocial theory is eclectic, functional, holistic, and a field theory. These are all attributes that most psychologists value and that they desire in any theoretical formulation.

In effect, Hall and Lindzey have said that Murphy's views are widely accepted in personality theory as an important synthesis, performed with wisdom and discrimination, and containing emphases most readily accepted among personality theorists. It incorporates the best of divergent

---

[4] From C. S. Hall & G. Lindzey. *Theories of Personality.* New York: Wiley, 1957. Pp. 532–533.

Table 8

PHENOMENOLOGICAL THEORIES AND THEIR MAIN CHARACTERISTICS

Author(s)	Central constructs and motivational forces	Organizing principles	Nature of environment	Bases of inference	Special features
Murray	Viscerogenic and psychogenic needs Need integrates Latent and manifest needs	Thema Need hierarchy Tension-reduction	Alpha press Beta press	Study of individuals through introspection, behavior study, clinical tests	Taxonomy of needs
Lewin	Forces and valences (vectors) Barriers	Tension-reduction Conflict Dynamic ego system Increasing differentiation and organization of structures	Life space Foreign hull Indivisibility of person and environment	Behavior study and reconstruction of life space	Systematic causation Topological representation of forces
Goldstein	Self-actualization	Figure-ground organization Equalization process	As related to maintenance of state of equilibrium	Intensive study of brain-injured	Health equals organization Pathology is disorganization of organismic structure
Maslow	Self-actualization	Need hierarchy from lower to higher Force for growth to highest level	Facilitative or obstructive to development and expression of highest needs	Ideographic study of cases of "ideal adjustment"	Emphasis on the healthy, self-actualizing person

Lecky	Need to maintain self-consistency	Assimilation of new experiences Structuring and restructuring of values into unified system	In terms of assimilability to self picture		Man is a tension producer
Rogers	Need to maintain and enhance the self Biological urges	Figure-ground organization and reorganization Force for growth	As related to the self-concept of the phenomenal field	Introspection of person through therapy situation	Extensive work in psychotherapy Analysis of objective therapy recordings
Snygg and Combs	Need to maintain and enhance the self	Figure-ground organization and reorganization	As related to the self concept	Introspection by observer (putting oneself in place of other)	
Murphy	Organic traits Learned cognitive habits Development of self concept Ego-control system	Progressive differentiation and organization of structures into unified system Tension reduction Canalization and learning	As perceived by person Indivisibility of person and environment	No special form Eclectic	Eclectic synthesis of many other systems

viewpoints, and although no ardent advocate of any specific theoretical system—such as Dollard and Miller's association-learning theory or Rogers's self theory—would adopt Murphy's formulations, the personality psychologists who need not be tied to a specific theoretical system can respond favorably to this complex eclectic integration. It is included here under phenomenology because, although it is identified as eclectic, certain features of Murphy's thinking place him best among the phenomenologically oriented writers.

For most readers, this chapter has presented a bewildering assortment of new concepts attached to many strange names. It is evident that there are major differences between the points of view cited and many similarities and identities. In order to assist the reader to grasp the over-all pattern of theoretical viewpoints, a chart (see Table 8) has been prepared to summarize the main characteristics of each system of thought presented. The chart is only suggestive and tends to be somewhat cryptic because only the key terms have been indicated, but inspection of it may assist in keeping an orderly account of the phenomenological theorists of personality and their fundamental ideas. Only by continuous cross reference to the text or to the primary sources can the chart be maximally useful.

CHAPTER
6

Freud's Psychoanalytic Theory of Personality

It would be inconceivable for anyone to write a textbook on personality without devoting a substantial portion to *psychoanalysis*. The impact of Freud's work upon modern psychological thought, and indeed upon our entire culture, has been enormous. Many of the now commonplace notions about personality (such as unconscious motivation, internal conflict, and defense mechanism), discussed in previous chapters, were either introduced by Freud or influenced by his work. Thus the importance and influence of Freud is such as to require special and extensive treatment.

Another reason for not developing Freudian theory in any of the three previous chapters is that it does not fall clearly in any of the three main frames of reference (trait-and-type, association-learning, and phenomenology). In fact, it contains features of all. For example, there are elements of the trait-and-type frames of reference in psychoanalytic theory. Freud described a number of types, including the oral character and the anal character. Freud also adopted principles that are found today in association-learning theory. For example, the pleasure principle of Freud is analogous to the principle of reinforcement in learning theory. Finally, there are features in psychoanalysis that have something in common with phenomenological theory. Freud's interest in the thought processes and the contents of the mind and his elaboration of the concept of the ego and the ego ideal as guiding or governing forces in human adaptation are relevant.

The scope of Freud's contribution is so huge, its elaboration so rich, and its application so varied that even a single chapter will be a very brief condensation. Other secondary sources summarizing psychoanalysis also exist, to which the reader is referred (Fenichel, 1945; Hall, 1954; Hall & Lindzey, 1957; and Munroe, 1955, to name a few). A fascinating biography of Freud, including what is known of his personal life as well as the development of his theoretical contributions, has been written by Ernest Jones (1953, 1955, 1957), one of his students and close associates.

Freud himself was a prolific writer, and it is possible for the student to go directly to original material (1949, 1953).

As is often the case with an innovator of ideas, Freud was bitterly and widely denounced by the Victorian world when his ideas became known. He lived in the closing period of what has been called the "age of reason." Man was considered a rational animal, who could control and guide his destiny through the use of his intelligence. One of Freud's concepts, which was so difficult to accept, was that man's behavior actually was dominated by hidden or unconscious motives and emotions; in other words, man had little conscious understanding of himself and less control than he believed. Freud also introduced the idea, which was greatly to disturb society, that the basis for adult personality resided in the infant and his experiences, and especially was bound up in the fate of infantile sexual and aggressive urges. Thus, the world was told that the innocent child was a seething cauldron of primitive tabooed urges. Let us consider briefly the development of this revolutionary doctrine.

Freud actually was a neurologist and physician rather than, strictly speaking, a psychologist. Academic psychology, which had just come into being in the 1880s and 90s, was little concerned with human adjustment and psychopathology. Freud, who had made a number of major scientific contributions in the area of neurology, came to specialize in the field of nervous disorders, a relatively little developed field of medicine. In particular, his early work revolved around the study of hysteria, an illness that often seemed neurological in character but which appeared to be associated with no actual structural impairment. In hysteria patients might exhibit such symptoms as anesthesias or paralyses with no evident neurological defect.

Freud's early work with hysteria was much influenced by the French psychiatrist Charcot, who used hypnosis in the study and treatment of the disorder. At the turn of the century, Freud met a Viennese physician, Joseph Breuer, who had developed a cathartic or talking-out method of treating hysteria, in which the patient frequently was relieved of the symptoms by talking about them and their origin. Freud collaborated with Breuer in describing some of the cases they had treated with this talking-out method (1957). The association between Breuer and Freud was short-lived because the latter developed the idea that there was a sexual basis for the illness, and this concept was unacceptable to Breuer. Freud subsequently developed by himself the central ideas of psychoanalytic theory, which he kept revising and enlarging for the rest of his long, productive life.

In contrast with personality theories generated out of the laboratory context, the basis of Freud's theorizing was largely clinical. The concepts derived from his experience first with hypnosis and then later with the free-association method, which involved having the patient lie on a couch in a darkened room talking as freely as possible about anything that came into his mind. From this experience Freud's ideas about psychopathology and the structure of personality emerged. Actually, although Freud studied large numbers of patients, he presented six case studies (aside from those described with Breuer), the rest of his writings dealing with his speculations on personality organization. These six cases were presented to illustrate his concepts and method rather than to serve as empirical support for his thinking.

Psychoanalytic theory, as expounded by Freud, involves the implicit assumption that normal personality can be understood through the study of psychopathology. Most of Freud's insights have been derived from this preoccupation with mental illness on the assumption that illness reflects deviations from normal processes. In addition to gaining information by observing mental patients, Freud attempted a self-analysis over a period of many years and later attempted to verify his ideas about personality against the material obtained from his study of himself. Let us now examine Freud's psychoanalytic theory in its essential outlines.

PERSONALITY STRUCTURE AND DYNAMICS

The main hypothetical *structures of personality* that Freud delineated are three mental systems: the id, ego, and superego, each of which has its own characteristics but all of which are interrelated to produce an organized system. *Personality dynamics* refers to the energy characteristics of the system, which power or energize the structures and become transformed in various ways in the course of the ongoing life processes. As we shall see, concepts such as "instinct," "cathexis," and "pleasure principle" are part of personality dynamics.

It is traditional in discussing Freud's psychoanalytic theory to discuss the mental structure separately from the mental dynamics. However, in the present discussion structure and dynamics will be fused to some degree, because it is easier to see the organized quality of the personality when the structure and the energy principles are dealt with at the same time.

Consciousness and Unconsciousness

In his earlier writings, Freud emphasized the *unconscious* determination of behavior. The primary subdivisions of the personality were the conscious, preconscious (readily accessible to consciousness), and unconscious realms, of which the unconscious was overwhelmingly important as a source of behavior. Gifted with the ability to use a metaphor, Freud likened these subdivisions to an iceberg, which has only a small surface showing above the water and the largest portion, the unconscious, below the surface. Later Freud altered his conception of conscious and unconscious to the status of qualities rather than subdivisions of the personality; that is, a mental act could have the quality of consciousness, preconsciousness, or unconsciousness, and Freud then identified the major subdivisions or structures of the personality as the id, ego, and superego. Activity of the id is normally unconscious; that is, it is never accessible to direct experience. Most of the ego and superego also are unconscious, but portions of them can have the quality of being conscious and preconscious.

The Id

The id is the system of the personality that is most primitive and earliest to develop. It is the source of energy for all mental life. The child inherits its contents from preceding generations, and it is the only mental system present at birth. The contents of the id are (Freud, 1933, p. 105) "instinctual cathexes seeking discharge. . . ." As an unconscious, undifferentiated "cauldron of seething excitement," the id has no direct contact with reality and contains no social values or morality. The operation of the id rests on primitive rules and proceeds without the logic characteristic of the adult mind. Therefore, it is possible for contradictory impulses to exist at the same time within the id. Because the contents of the id are composed of instincts, let us now examine Freud's concept of instinct.

The instincts: An instinct is an inherited source of excitation arising in the tissues (need), which is represented psychologically as a wish. The wish is the motivating force in behavior, although it has a somatic origin in tissue states. Thus Freud differentiated between instinctual impulses or needs (somatic aspect) and instinctual ideas or wishes that arise from them. The total psychic energy of the id consists of the combination of all the instincts.

In the earliest period of life the energy of the id dissipates itself into smooth and striated muscle activity before it has a chance to accumulate. The energy has not become invested in any particular type of object. When the avenue of discharge into the muscle system is blocked, the energy cannot flow directly into the muscles and be dissipated. It builds up and is invested in psychological processes rather than being used up immediately in purely muscular or visceral activities. The energy flows into perceptual, memory, and ideational systems, and these systems (containing percepts, memories, and ideas) become charged with energy. Thus a conception of an object that could permit the discharge of the energy is "cathected," and we have what is called an *object* or *instinctual cathexis*. The energy of the impulse has become invested in an image that motivates behavior by increasing the person's sensitivity to particular kinds of external stimulation.

An instinct can be considered to have four characteristic features: source, aim, object, and impetus. The *source* is a tissue state or need. The *aim* is simply the removal of the excitation or source of tension. The *object* is the activity, thing, person, or condition that produces satisfaction of the need, or wish fulfillment. Finally, the *impetus* of an instinct is the intensity of the need. The greater the strength or intensity of the tissue need, the greater the impetus or force of the instinct.

Freud recognized the existence of many instincts. But he attempted to classify all instincts into two groups, the life instincts and the death instincts, although in the early years of psychoanalysis he had tended to subsume all instincts under a single form of energy, the libido or the sexual instincts. All instincts are distinguished from one another by distinctive somatic sources—for example, hunger versus sex—and distinctive objects—for example, eating versus copulation.

The *life instincts,* such as hunger, thirst, and sex, have the purpose of promoting the survival of the individual and the propagation of the race. For psychological purposes, the sexual instincts are most important. The energy by which they function is called *libido,* which is focused mainly in erogenous zones of the body. Any part of the body can be an erogenous zone—that is, a seat of sexual excitement—but there are particular areas of the body that are unusually sensitive to stimulation and are especially likely to produce pleasurable feelings. The lips and mouth, the anal region, and the primary (penis and vaginal area) and secondary (such as the breasts) sexual organs are particularly important erogenous zones.

The sexual instincts (libido) are the best known and most carefully analyzed group of the life instincts. Because of this great preoccupation of psychoanalytic literature with the sexual instincts, the implication often is drawn that Freud considered sexuality as the only important force in human life and culture. Actually, Freud recognized the existence of many other instincts, which he did not feel obliged to list or explore. Moreover, little was known about the bodily states upon which these instincts depended.

Freud believed that the destructive or *death instincts* are less conspicuous and less understood than the life instincts. Because every person ultimately dies, Freud assumed that the person has an unconscious wish to die and that, as he put it (1955, p. 38), "the goal of all life is death." In other words, there exists in living organisms a compulsion to return to the inorganic state out of which life was formed. In the human being this is referred to as the "death wish." Thus, the aim of the death instincts is the opposite of the life instincts. Where the life instincts aim to preserve life and organization, the death instincts seek to destroy such organization. It is interesting to trace the origin of these ideas about instinctual energy and death urges to the recently established laws of thermodynamics in physics, which greatly influenced Freud's thinking, but we shall have to forego more than a mere mention of this here.

The operation of the death instincts is not readily displayed directly, but they bring about the death of a living thing relatively inconspicuously. However, one important derivative of the death instincts is quite obvious in human behavior and takes the form of *aggression*. Aggressive behavior represents the death instinct that is directed or displaced outwardly against others instead of toward oneself, to whom it is originally directed. Thus, the energy of the death instincts is turned away from the person's self-destruction and projected out on the world, tending for a time to preserve his own life. The blocking of the death wish leads one to fight with others. Freud was greatly impressed by the universality and persistence of wars, and World War I tended to convince him that aggression and the death instincts clearly were as important as the sexual and life instincts.

The problem of the life and death instincts is complicated by the notion that any single act is usually the product of both, including their derivatives. The death instincts are made relatively harmless by fusing with the life instincts. The life instincts neutralize the death instincts and divert them into self-preservative forms, such as mastery, domination, and aggression. Other examples of this fusion occur when love motives utilize mastery to gain possession of an object or when love fuses with hostility in the form of sadism.

The concept of the death instinct has been one of the least acceptable of Freud's concepts. Fenichel (1945), who has written a systematic and respected treatise on Freudian psychoanalysis, while accepting as sound the great majority of psychoanalytic concepts, rejected the death instinct as unnecessary and confusing. Freud believed that it was necessary to postulate the death instinct as a means of accounting for man's destructive behavior. Fenichel, on the other hand, believed that aggressive behavior, even self-destructiveness, can be subsumed under the sexual instincts, arguing that they represent transformations of these instincts in the context of external demands.

The pleasure principle and the primary process: The essential function of the id is to permit and provide for full discharge of the excitations that arise from somatic sources; in other words, discharge of instinctual energy. In doing this, the id follows a principle of tension reduction called the "pleasure principle," utilizing mainly what is called the "primary process."

When there is a failure or delay in the diffusion of instinctual energy through the muscles, an increased accumulation of energy occurs, which is experienced as an uncomfortable state of tension. Such a situation is inevitable because of societal taboos or the lack of a suitable object. The id operates to discharge the tension as immediately as possible and to return the organism to a comfortably low level of energy. The *pleasure principle* is the tendency of the organism to keep increases in tension at a minimum and to obtain immediate pleasure or reduction of pain by discharging the instinctual energy. All behavior, under the pleasure principle, is guided by the striving for immediate tension reduction, tension being painful and tension reduction being pleasurable.

In accomplishing this end of avoiding pain and obtaining pleasure, the id can utilize two processes, reflex action and the primary process. *Reflex actions* are automatic and inherited and include such reactions as defecation. A number of reflex patterns exist for dealing with excitation, but these are adequate for limited kinds of instinctual needs. The predominant method of following the pleasure principle is the *primary process*, in which tension discharge is sought by forming an image or hallucination of an object capable of reducing the tension. If the most primitive operation of the id, that of expending energy immediately in reflexes or other forms of motor activity, cannot take place (many somatic sources of tension, such as hunger and thirst, do not have built-in tension-reducing mechanisms as in urination and defecation), then the primary progress of hallucinating the desired object is put into operation. Thus, the hungry person, through experience, is provided with a mental picture of food, and this hallucinatory experience in which the satisfying object occurs in the form of a memory image is called *wish fulfillment*. Freud considered the dream to be an ideal example of attempted wish fulfillment, as are the hallucinations of psychotic patients. If the organism is capable of perceiving and remembering, then the primary process of hallucinating a desired object can take place as an attempted wish fulfillment. The organism learns and remembers what objects are capable of producing discharge of tension and strives to produce an image that is identical with the original object itself.

The id operates according to the pleasure principle of immediate discharge of tension, utilizing either direct motor or reflex actions and the primary process, which involves a hallucination of the gratifying object as the fulfillment of the wish. The difficulty with this process is that it is not actually, by itself, capable of reducing the tension. As Hall and Lindzey (1957, p. 33) pointed out, "The hungry person cannot eat mental images of food." The mental images can succeed in orienting an individual toward realistic steps to obtaining food. As a consequence of the failure of the primary process to reduce tension, a new or secondary psychological process develops, which is associated with the formation of the ego. The ego is the next subdivision or structure of the personality to be discussed.

The Ego

The ego develops because the infant is not able to gratify instincts through the primary process. In order for gratification to take place a person must have appropriate commerce with the objective world of reality. In the case of needs related to defecation, the infant is able to discharge them reflexly, thus immediately reducing tension. This is not the case for hunger and other needs that are instinctive. For example, the organism must obtain food (the object) and eat it before the tension of hunger can be reduced or eliminated. In other words, it has to learn to distinguish between a memory image of food (primary process) and the actual food, the ingestion of which will reduce the tension. Later on in the infant's existence, even discharge of tension through immediate fecal elimination (reflex action) for example, becomes impossible, because parents and society demand the retention of the stool until it can be eliminated in the appropriate place.

The id operates only through subjective reality and has no transaction with the outside world, whereas the ego can differentiate between a subjective experience and the nature of things in the external world. It does so by means of a process called *reality testing*, by comparing the products of mental activities, such as perception and judgment, with what actually takes place in experience. In other words, the ego engages in a kind of hypothesis testing, checking expectations against what actually takes place. Whereas the id operates according to the pleasure principle and seeks direct and immediate discharge of tension, the ego obeys the reality principle and utilizes the secondary process, which results in the ability to delay gratification.

The reality principle and the secondary process: The ego must do two main things. It must protect the individual against dangers that arise in the external world, and it must at the same time make possible discharge of tension by permitting the gratification of the instincts. In order to preserve the safety of the organism, it must gain control over the instincts, because immediate gratification may endanger life. For example, the direct discharge of aggression through motor activity will be punished by the society, or it can lead to retaliation by the person who is the object of the aggression. The ego thus decides whether, when, and how an instinct can be satisfied. It must prevent the discharge of tension until a safe object is found, appropriate for the satisfaction of the need.

The ego thus operates by the *reality principle*, which temporarily suspends the pleasure principle. In other words, because the operation of the pleasure principle can best be served at certain appropriate times and in particular ways, the reality principle involves the capacity for delay or inhibition of impulse discharge. This substitution of the reality principle for the pleasure principle does not mean that pleasure is no longer the goal of the organism's activity. The reality principle serves the pleasure principle by postponing immediate gratification that is likely to produce pain or danger in order to produce later gratification safely.

All complicated mental activity, such as learning, perception, memory, and reasoning, are functions of the ego, follow the reality principle, and represent the *secondary process,* which is a roundabout way to the ultimate goal of instinct gratification. The development of the ego involves the emergence of thought and the interposition of thought for immediate action. The mature ego mediates between the id and reality, maximizing the opportunity for instinctual gratification through its capacity to bind and control instinctual cathexes, and simultaneously apprehending reality and discovering safe and appropriate avenues of discharge. This process of reasoning out a means of obtaining an appropriate goal object is called the "secondary process." When the organism considers that a satisfactory solution to a problem has been found, the verification of this solution by trying it out is called "reality testing."

According to Freud, the highest achievement of the ego is the mastery of the environment, which is accomplished by the secondary processes of thinking and judgment. The mastery of the environment will permit safe instinctual discharge. Thus, man's creativity and higher mental processes originate in frustration and represent efforts to control the environment so frustration can be minimized. The ineffectual ego is one that cannot find or create the appropriate circumstances for instinctual gratification.

The Superego

The third major subdivision of the personality, and the last to be developed, is the superego. It is the psychological representative of the values and mores of the society in which the child is raised, as represented usually by parents and initially enforced by rewards and punishments. The superego represents morality and the ideals of society, and it is oriented toward perfection rather than pleasure. It is the evaluator of right or wrong in accordance with the moral standards of the society. The superego has two aspects: one, the *conscience,* and the other, the *ego ideal.* Pride occurs when the individual measures up to the ego ideal, and the superego processes continually keep the ego under observation to make sure that it lives up to the ego ideal. Feelings of guilt are produced when behavior does not conform. Thus, the ego ideal represents the standards of ethical conduct, and the conscience represents the processes of judgment, punishing for infractions of the rules.

In order to obtain reward and avoid punishment the child learns to behave according to the rules established by his parents. What the parents disapprove and punish him for doing becomes incorporated into his conscience. Values and behavior patterns of which they approve become incorporated into his ego ideal. The process of incorporation is called *introjection*. Thus, with the formation of the superego, parental control of the child's actions is no longer as necessary because the child has substituted for it self-control.

Because the superego represents parental authority, it behaves toward the ego and the id in the same way that the parents once did toward the child. Its task is to limit instinctual gratification, not in accordance with the reality principle, which is followed by the ego, but in terms of perfectionistic standards identical with those imposed by the value systems or the superegos of the parents themselves. It attempts to block impulses —especially those which are sexual or aggressive in nature—completely and permanently, because the parental rules from which the superego derives involve primarily the suppression of sexual and aggressive impulses.

FREUD'S THEORY OF PSYCHOSEXUAL DEVELOPMENT

Freud was greatly interested in the question: What are the needs and affects that govern behavior and how do they contribute to the development of adult personality? In other words, not only was he interested in the formal structures of personality, but also he was concerned with its content, that is, with the nature of the impulses or motives that guided behavior. In trying to trace the origins of the rational psychological structure of the individual, and the organization of society as well, Freud made one of his major and controversial contributions to psychological thought—the psychosexual theory of development.

The psychosexual theory emphasizes the systematic changes in personality structure in childhood and links these to the development of the adult personality. It stresses the psychosexual aspect of early childhood as the central force in the formation of the personality.

Freud considered the primary and most important force that impelled human behavior to be sexual in nature. The infant is born with a certain amount of sexual energy, called "libido." When this energy is discharged or released, there is satisfaction; but when it is blocked from discharge, there is tension or discomfort.

The theory postulates that the organism goes through a number of stages that have to do with the type of sexual need that is most prominent. During development, three main stages of sexual discharge come into focus successively. These are referred to as the oral stage, the anal stage, and the phallic and genital stages. The terms "oral," "anal," and "genital" refer to the parts of the body whose stimulation makes possible the release or discharge of the libido. Thus, during the first year of life the mouth becomes differentiated as the organ most capable of libidinal discharge, and the child finds pleasure via the mouth, not only as a means of satisfying its hunger, but as an erogenous zone whose manipulation provides pleasure. Thus, the child is observed to put things in his mouth and to suck or bite a great many objects with which he has contact. The focus for the discharge of sexual energy is the mouth, and the period of development in which the satisfactions are derived by oral activities is called the "oral stage."

During the second and third years of life, the focus of libidinal discharge gradually shifts from the mouth to the anal region. During this period, the anal region of the body takes on greater capacity to produce pleasure through sexual discharge, and fecal expulsion and retention serve to stimulate the anal erogenous zone. This period of psychosexual development also tends to coincide with social pressures directed toward toilet training and leads to the association of anal gratification with the social control of the bowel function.

At the third and fourth years of life, the genital organs progressively become the seat of sexual gratification. This is the period in which the universal Oedipus problem arises. The boy adopts his mother as an object of his sexual desires, and the girl chooses the father as love object. The phallic stage of development is the final form of organization of the sexual life of the mature individual. The Oedipus complex produces a family triangle in which the boy is in competition with his father (and the girl in competition with her mother) for the love of the parent of the opposite sex. Fear of retaliation for this competition leads to anxieties over castration, that is, the danger of the destruction by the father of the boy's sexual organ. The story for the girl is more complicated, penis envy occurring as the parallel state to the castration anxiety of the male.

During the preadolescent years that follow, from roughly school age on, the oedipal problem tends to be handled by an abandonment of sexual interest, a period termed the "latency period." For example, the boy becomes interested in masculine things and tends to ignore girls, preferring the company of other boys. The sexual issue is apt not to arise again until adolescence, when the physicochemical changes associated with sexual maturity begin to occur. At this time, the Oedipus complex again arises along with the castration fears that it involves. This anxiety-provoking triangle situation is resolved when the parent finally is given up as a love object and a new love object outside the immediate family is adopted. For the boy, this means relinquishing the mother to the father and finding a girl of his own age to love and marry. In the case of the girl, the father is given up as an object of sexual love, and a boy ultimately is selected as a mate. If this oedipal stage is resolved successfully, true psychosexual maturity is attained.

In addition to postulating universal stages of development, the psychosexual theory stresses underlying structures or processes rather than surface manifestations of personality. The organization of the libido is not observed directly but is inferred from behavioral manifestations. For example, one can directly observe manifestations of the oral stage of development in the infant who sucks his thumb and engages in a wide range of behavior involving the mouth, such as biting, spitting, and stroking the lips with a piece of cloth. Similarly, a child in the anal period of development can be observed to be much preoccupied with bowel activity, often confounding his mother by manipulating fecal matter and decorating the walls of his room with it. In adult life, toilet jokes, concern with constipation, distress over dirt and dirtiness, and sexual interest in buttocks are some of the behavioral reflectors of fixated anal libido. These direct observations can be supplemented by the fantasies of adults under psychoanalysis, which provide sources of information about the underlying psychosexual processes in the personality formation.

Although the unfolding of the psychosexual developmental pattern is biologically determined, deviations from this ideal pattern can occur in a variety of ways. An individual, because of certain traumatic experiences during particular phases of this sequence, can fail to make a full progression from one stage to the next. In this case, some libidinal energy may remain fixated at an earlier level. For example, as an individual progresses from the oral to the anal stage of development, some libido remains focused at the oral stage and, though the individual progresses partly to the anal period, he continues to achieve some libidinal discharge through oral activity. Thus, throughout his life, there will be a residual of libidinal energy fixated at the oral level, which will produce certain types of personality characteristics in adult life. Some degree of fixation at the oral and anal level is common in most persons and, depending upon the degree and pattern of such fixation, leads to normal variation in personality in adulthood.

Freud described the consequences in adult personality of excessive pregenital fixation as the "oral character" and the "anal character," respectively. The anal character, for example, is apt to show such traits as stinginess, obstinacy, meticulousness, and concern about cleanliness. These traits are the expression of libidinal discharge that remains fixated at a period of psychosexual development when anal activity is of primary importance. This anal activity becomes fused with such social behavior as retention or saving of money or other valued objects and leads to the personality trait that we know as miserliness or stinginess. The oral character, on the other hand, arises from fixation at the oral phase of psychosexual development. It includes such behavioral traits as excessive eating, verbal aggressiveness, and other signs that the person is still achieving an excessive amount of libidinal discharge through activities centered on the mouth.

Many personality abnormalities have their origin in pregenital fixations. Not only can a person fail to progress normally to more advanced stages of psychosexual development, but it is also possible to have proceeded to an advanced level and, as a consequence of trauma, regress to a more primitive level of functioning. Freud conceived all abnormal behavior to be a manifestation of either fixation at a primitive level of development (failure to progress normally to a higher level) or regression (going backward) from a higher level to a lower level. Thus, schizophrenia, a severe form of psychotic illness, was considered to be the result of a regression to the most primitive level of development: the oral stage. Similarly, the obsessive-compulsive neurosis involves a regression to the anal level of development.

In the Freudian scheme of things, the reason that the cognitive or intellectual structure develops in such a way as to permit the organism to adapt to external realities is that discharge of sexual energy is not always immediately possible and is often thwarted because of the nature of the external environment. The inevitable fact of delay or frustration of gratification of the libido first leads to the hallucination or image of the desired object by the infant and the gradual emergence of adaptive intelligence and thought as means of achieving gratification within the constraints of the environment. In other words, because the child cannot immediately find discharge or gratification and must therefore often experience pain or anxiety, he searches for ways to obtain such discharge. To solve his problems, he must eventually acquire a knowledge of the environment. Thus, adaptive intelligence and reflective thought, which are identified by Freudian theory as aspects of the ego, arise in consequence of impulses that are essentially sexual in nature, which cannot be immediately discharged. These ego processes mediate between a person's libidinal impulses and the demands of the environment, permitting him to achieve a balance between himself and the external world. (Rapaport, 1951, has written extensively about Freudian theory, emphasizing the origin of the cognitive aspects of personality from the libido.)

PERSONALITY ORGANIZATION

Personality organization refers to the interrelationships between the three main subsystems or structures of the personality: the id, ego, and superego. A few points should be made about this organization and the roles of the three subsystems before leaving the topic.

In discussing such structures as the id, ego, and superego, it is easy to fall into a kind of animistic orientation in which one thinks of these structures as little men or spirits, which operate the personality. Freud himself frequently lapsed into an animistic kind of language in speaking of these structures, as I have in this chapter. For example, we say that the ego does this or the ego feels that. One of the major criticisms that has been leveled at psychoanalytic thought is this tendency to relegate to the structures of the personality the status of a living agent in the image of the man. Actually, the criticism is not quite justified, although the language of psychoanalysis often suggests its substance. The id, ego, and superego should be regarded as names for certain types of psychological processes, which obey certain principles or laws. If the rules of operation and the observable antecedents and consequents of these processes were fully established, there would be no basis for such criticism. One must recognize these terms for what they are: names for hypothetical psychological processes, which have yet to be precisely defined.

A second point must be made. The id, ego, and superego often are described as in conflict with each other. In fact, psychopathology is seen as involving states of conflict between these three personality structures. There are many forms of such conflicts. For example, id impulses can be in conflict with the ego. An individual feels hatred toward someone, say, his employer, but cannot express this hatred because it is recognized as dangerous. Thus the impulse must be blocked and prevented from discharge, or it must be transformed by the ego so that it is no longer dangerous and is discharged in some other form. Thus, the individual can displace his hostility from his employer to his more helpless child, or he can discharge it in socially acceptable ways, such as in competitive sports.

In addition to id-ego conflicts, there are potential conflicts between the ego and superego (that is, between expressions of realistic behavior and perfectionistic or idealistic behavior) and between the id and the superego (that is, between instinctual impulses and the ego ideal). The commonest of these that Freud discussed are those between sexual urges and society's proscriptions about sex.

In his clinical work, Freud was preoccupied with psychopathology and saw mostly patients suffering from various disorders. He therefore wrote about pathology and emphasized conflict between the various subdivisions of the personality. However, he also pointed out that the normal relationship between the id, ego, and superego is one of harmony and organization. In the well-adjusted person, the ego is operating successfully to protect the life of the individual and at the same time to discharge tensions deriving from instincts. The ego is not at war with the id. It is an agency of the id, deriving its energy from the id and obliged not only to protect the safety of the organism but to gratify instinctual impulses. Furthermore, in the well-adjusted person the superego is neither so weak as to permit antisocial psychopathic behavior nor so strong that it severely interferes with adaptation through the ego processes. In other words, the normal and appropriate state of the organism is harmonious and compatible interaction between the three subsystems. These three subsystems are not independent or separate entities unrelated to each other, but they form part of an organized totality.

ANXIETY

Freud was one of the earliest systematic writers to emphasize emotional states as determinants of behavior. We already have discussed the two basic emotional states of love and anger. Also essential in the psychoanalytic theory of Freud is the emotion of fear or anxiety.

As has already been noted, the developing organism must find ways of gratifying its needs through commerce with the external world. The external world is, therefore, a major source of his gratification, but also it is filled with dangers. It can produce pain and increase tension, thus being disturbing as well as comforting. The innate reaction of the organism to threats of pain or destruction with which it cannot cope is to become afraid. Freud theorized that, when the ego is confronted by excessive stimulation, which it cannot bring under control, it becomes flooded with anxiety. The avoidance of anxiety becomes an important motive in the development of the personality and in guiding behavior. Fundamentally speaking, the function of this anxiety is that of a danger signal to the ego to bring into play means to eliminate the danger. The state of anxiety signals the ego that it is in danger and that it must attempt to bring the stimulation under control in order to preserve itself.

Three types of anxiety are usually distinguished: objective anxiety, neurotic anxiety, and moral anxiety. These types of anxiety differ only in respect to their sources, objective anxiety having to do with the relation of the ego to the external world, neurotic anxiety resulting from the relations of the ego to the id, and moral anxiety having to do with the relation of the ego to the superego.

Objective Anxiety

Objective anxiety involves the perception of danger in the external world, something that might paralyze a person, making him helpless to cope with the intense, excessive excitation. A person can avoid the danger by fleeing from it or by attempting to master it, or he can do nothing about it, in which case the anxiety mounts until it overwhelms the ego and the person regresses to a state of infantile helplessness. The helplessness of the infant and the trauma of birth, in which the neonate is suddenly bombarded by intense stimulation with which it cannot cope, represent the origin of objective anxiety, and any condition that threatens a recurrence of this overstimulation and helplessness will produce an anxiety reaction.

Neurotic Anxiety

Whereas objective anxiety has to do with dangers in the external environment, neurotic anxiety involves the fear that the ego will lose control of the instincts and the person will do something that will result in his being harmed. Fear of the id, therefore, is fundamentally fear of what the instincts of the id will cause the person to do and of the consequences of this action. Thus, neurotic anxiety has a real basis, because the child remembers being punished by parents and society for expressing his impulses.

In neurotic anxiety, the anxiety state can be free-floating, involving a general apprehensiveness not linked to any specific situation, although it can attach itself to any suitable environmental circumstance. Neurotic anxiety can also be projected outward as objective anxiety because it is easier to handle an external danger than an internal one. Commonly, the person who experiences anxiety cannot say what is the source of the disturbance.

Moral Anxiety

Moral anxiety has to do with the emotional reaction to the perception of danger from the superego. The ego reacts as in a state of danger when it does something that conflicts with the superego. The person feels guilty or shameful when he does something or thinks of something that is contrary to the moral code by which he has been raised and which he has introjected as conscience. Moral anxiety also has a basis in reality, because the person has been punished in the past for violating the moral code and can be punished again, although the ego perceives the danger as having to do with punishment by the superego (internal punishment as a result of the introjection of society's moral values).

DEFENSE MECHANISMS OF THE EGO

In the development of personality, the individual learns methods of adjusting by discharging impulses and minimizing anxiety. Although Freud considered the development of personality as partly learned, he was never concerned with elaborating the laws of this learning, an interest that has characterized a large segment of modern laboratory psychology. The ego acquires a number of mechanisms by which it can reduce tensions, some of which are normal and relatively successful and some of which were considered by Freud as pathological. Let us first examine the two main normal methods for reducing tension that are available to the ego: identification and displacement. After we have dealt with these, we shall discuss the pathological defense mechanisms.

Identification

The process of identification is important in the formation of the ego and the superego. By this process a person takes over, as his own, characteristics of another person, commonly a parent, and follows his methods of reducing tensions. Freud used the term "identification" because he did not refer to the superficial copying of behavior but wanted to convey the idea of a relatively permanent and unconscious acquisition to the personality, taken over from the person being identified with. The person or persons with whom we identify appear to be successful in gratifying their own needs, and to the child parents appear to be omnipotent.

In the course of development, different objects of identification are accepted by the child. Characteristics of the identified-with object that will be helpful in reducing tension are selected by the child, and through trial and error those aspects are absorbed that are most successful in reducing tension. Actually, the identification can be made with animals, imaginary figures, ideas, and inanimate objects as well as persons. Accumulations of many identifications, made during various times of the person's life, enter into the developing personality structure. Because the mother and father represent, to some degree, the values of the society, the process of identification with the mother and father permits the carry-over of these values from one generation to the next.

Displacement

As we have seen in the discussion of instincts, the energy of an instinctual impulse becomes attached to an object that will permit the discharge or gratification of the instinct. Commonly, however, an original object choice cannot be maintained because of external forces or ego controls (anticathexes). When this happens, a new cathexis or object choice must be formed if the instinct is to be gratified. If this new cathexis also is blocked, its energy can be displaced to another object, and so on until some object is found that produces reduction of the tension. In other words, although the source and the aim of the instinct remain constant, the ego can displace one object with another in order to find gratification.

The substitute objects of the displacement process usually are not as tension-reducing as was the original object, and there remains undischarged tension, which accumulates and serves as a permanent motivating force for behavior. The person always seeks better ways of reducing tension, but in the course of development those objects that represent reasonably successful means of producing gratification become established. It was Freud's view that this process of displacement is essential to the development of civilization, because the original primitive object choices were dangerous and had to be diverted into channels that permitted men to live together in relative harmony and productivity.

One form of displacement has been called *sublimation* and involves the transformation of sexual instincts into cultural achievements. Some of the common forms of sublimation are in artistic expression. The sexual impulses are transformed, and the energy that was originally cathected to erotic activity is diverted into painting, music, or literature.

The capacity to develop substitute-object cathexes is essential for the mature development of personality and is the basis for the development of the complex pattern of interests and attachments that characterizes the normal adult. In lower animals, this flexibility of object choice is lacking. They act in a much more mechanical fashion, driven to perform certain fixed patterns of behavior by unmodifiable instincts. In man, however, his versatility in terms of the object choices that are possible permits the richness and variety that one finds in adult personality.

Let us now examine the defense mechanisms that Freud considered likely to lead to psychopathology. In the context of excessive stimulation, which the ego cannot master, the ego is sometimes forced to take certain measures to relieve the tension, measures that are less adequate than identification and displacement and likely to produce pathological behavior. These mechanisms of defense are pathological because they reduce tension by falsifying and distorting reality and by using up energy that could be employed to better advantage. They operate unconsciously, so the person is not aware of what is happening and can do little about them unless he learns of their existence through psychotherapy. The major neurotic defense mechanisms are repression, projection, reaction formation, fixation, and regression. Anna Freud (1946), who brilliantly discussed and elaborated upon the Freudian defense mechanisms, described other defenses as well, including isolation, undoing, introjection, turning against the self, and reversal. We shall briefly consider the most important defense mechanisms.

Repression

The earliest and most important defense mechanism described by Freud is *repression*, which blocks the discharge of an instinct (by means of an anticathexis) so it cannot become conscious or be directly expressed in behavior. Thus, unlike other defense mechanisms, repression acts directly upon the aim of the instinct, permitting no reduction of tension. In so doing, the ego attempts to eliminate from the id the stimulation that is producing strong anxiety. The repressed impulse is inaccessible to the person in that it is unconscious, and the symptoms resulting from repression are therefore very difficult to treat.

Freud spoke of two kinds or phases of repression. *Primal repression* denies entry into consciousness of the ideational representation of the instinct: the wish. In other words, the threatening impulses in the id remain there unexpressed. However, the id can sometimes transform its content into forms that can be sneaked past the ego. If the ego discovers the true nature of the disguised material, it represses it. *Repression proper*, the second form of repression, involves the repression of these derivatives of the instinct material (disguised forms). In other words, the mechanism of repression can be employed against material that, although neutral in itself, has been associated with the dangerous instincts.

There are certain conditions under which the repressed material does express itself in behavior or become conscious, with the consequence of severe anxiety or the possibility of destruction of the ego. This can happen when the strength of the anticathexis employed by the ego is reduced, as in illness and in sleep; or when the strength of the instinctual cathexis is increased sharply, as in puberty, when sexual impulses are strengthening; or in the climacteric or change of life; or in any circumstances of life that tend to increase the strength of stimulation related to the repressed instinct.

Neurotic symptoms are manifestations of repressed impulses. The symptom expresses and permits some discharge of the repressed impulse as a kind of compromise solution, and although the symptom produces secondary anxiety and a certain disability, this disabling quality and the secondary anxiety are less troublesome than the anxiety that would result if the individual discovered the real origin of the symptom.

Projection

A person can project an impulse that is threatening onto someone else and attribute the impulse to the latter. Thus, the impulse can be attributed to the external world rather than to oneself, objective anxiety or external dangers being easier for the ego to deal with than anxiety arising from within. In this way, projection reduces both neurotic and moral anxiety. Instead of having to face the impulse, "I hate him," an individual maintains that "he hates me." Thus, anxiety is reduced by replacing an intolerable, internal source of danger with a lesser, external one. At the same time, the person who projects can simply express the threatening impulse by making it seem as though he is defending himself against the external danger.

Reaction Formation

In reaction formation, the anxiety-producing impulse is expressed in consciousness by its opposite. The object (a particular person) of the instinct (e.g., hatred) remains the same, but there is a reversal in the conscious impulse; the individual affirms positive feelings (say, love instead of hate). Thus, by falsifying the conscious feeling, the individual reduces the anxiety generated by the real attitude.

Reaction formation often can be differentiated from the genuine expression of an impulse because the expressions of reaction formation usually are extravagant (as in protesting too much) and compulsive. An individual feels obliged, even when it is unnecessary, to manifest the feeling that disguises the true state of affairs.

Fixation and Regression

The understanding of the mechanisms of fixation and regression calls for knowledge of the developmental aspects of Freud's theory, which we have already discussed in Chapter 3, including the three main stages of development: oral, anal, and phallic-genital. These are stages in which sexual urges progressively change in their form of discharge.

As the personality goes through this series of stages until it reaches maturity, each new level may involve deprivation of satisfaction of the new urges or overindulgence, which, if excessive, can halt temporarily or permanently the normal development. The person can become *fixated* at one of the pregenital or immature stages of development because the next step has been associated with severe anxiety. In normal development, small amounts of fixation at pregenital levels of sexuality are likely to take place. Thus we find even in adults a certain amount of sexual discharge at oral and anal levels. A good example is the foreplay prior to sexual climax. In pathological development, so much sexual energy may be fixated at the oral or anal levels that disturbances are produced in normal sexual function and in personality (e.g., oral and anal character types). Fixation can be viewed as a defense, because the individual is protected from the anxieties attendant upon advancing to a higher stage of development by remaining safely at an earlier stage. A child can remain, for example, in the passive or dependent relationships to others characteristic of the oral stage of development, never achieving independent stature and protected continually against the threats of such independence.

Fixation represents a failure to progress from an earlier stage to a later stage, but *regression,* as a defense, involves retreating back to an earlier stage of development as a consequence of traumatic experiences. A child who has been successfully toilet-trained may engage in infantile behavior, such as bed-wetting or soiling, after the birth of a younger sibling or some change in the life experience, such as the disruption of the home. A wife who has recently married and who gets into difficulties with her husband, instead of working them out in a mature fashion, may regress by returning to her parents' home, which offers her more security.

Fixation and regression are related in Freudian theory because the degree of regression was thought to depend upon earlier fixations. The person tends to regress to a stage at which he has been previously fixated to a high degree. Thus, if a child was fixated excessively at the oral level but had moved past this point, leaving a great deal of libidinal energy at the oral stage, under trauma he will regress to the oral level, becoming excessively dependent again when his current anxieties increase to an unbearable degree.

Many pathological conditions were considered by Freud to represent regressive disorders. The severity of the pathology is a matter of the degree of regression. Thus, psychoneurotic disturbances are likely to involve relatively limited regression, to the phallic or anal level of development, and psychotic disorders—which are the most severe forms of pathology—involve much deeper regressions. The regressions in psychosis can result in a person functioning at an extremely primitive or childish level. As we shall see in later chapters, regressed schizophrenic patients may have to be fed and toileted like little children. It is as if the ego has returned or disintegrated to a stage of development when it hardly functioned at all, and instinctual impulses are relatively uncontrolled. The patient must be hospitalized because he becomes a danger to himself and others. Because he cannot master anxiety related to instinctual demands or external dangers at a mature, adult level, the person regresses to a more primitive level of organization of the personality.

THE PSYCHOANALYTIC FRAME OF REFERENCE

In the beginning of this chapter it was indicated that psychoanalysis could not readily be fitted into one of the three chapters on frames of reference in personality because of its varied nature and its independent stature as a theoretical system. Its major concepts are summarized for the

Table 9

Major Concepts of Freudian Psychoanalysis

Personality structures	Instincts	Normal operating principles	Developmental stages	Basis of psycho-pathology
Quality of unconsciousness { Id Ego Superego	Life (sexual most important) Death	Pleasure principle and primary process Reality principle and secondary process Displacement and identification	Oral Anal Phallic Latency period Genital or adult	Conflict between id and ego, ego and superego, id and superego Anxiety Fixation and regression Defense mechanisms: Repression Projection Reaction formation

reader in Table 9. Let us consider, briefly, how Freudian psychoanalysis relates to or compares with the trait-and-type approach, association-learning theory, and phenomenological theory.

In most respects, trait-and-type approaches differ very considerably from the psychoanalytic emphasis, which is on dynamics. A trait or type approach describes static qualities or attributes of persons that determine their actions in a variety of contexts or classifies persons by attributes that they have in common. In contrast, the essence of Freudian psychoanalysis is an organized system of constantly interacting forces within the organism and between the organism and the environment. Thus, behavior in a dynamic theory such as psychoanalysis depends upon a balance of energy distribution, which becomes transformed or discharged through an elaborate system of structures (for example, the ego and superego). External and internal stimuli continually are acting upon this system to produce and influence behavior.

Psychological dynamics is a primary emphasis of Freudian theory. There are elements in the system, however, that parallel a trait-and-type orientation. Just as any system offering a description of a personality emphasizes the stable or consistent qualities that make the person recognizable over a wide range of circumstances, Freud often described persons in terms of personality types. For example, as intimated earlier, Freud spoke of the oral and the anal types, referring to particular stable organizations of personality involving strong fixations at pregenital levels of development. In this sense, he was using a trait-and-type frame of reference in the description of personality.

In recent years, there has been a tendency for clinical psychologists utilizing a Freudian point of view to describe clinical syndromes like hysteria and the obsessive-compulsive neurosis in terms of the predominant defense mechanism characteristic of these disturbances. For example, Schafer (1948) suggested that repression is the defense commonly used by the hysterical neurotic and that mechanisms of isolation and undoing characterize the obsessive-compulsive. Thus, defense mechanisms are viewed not only as processes but also as traits that distinguish an individual over a long period of time. Much of Freudian thinking lends itself readily to a trait-and-type analysis.

The compatibility between Freudian psychoanalysis and association-learning theory is so great that, as we have seen, it was possible for Dollard and Miller readily to translate Freudian theory into association-learning terms. Ironically enough, association-learning theory grew in part out of the stimulus-response formulations of Watson, who was rebelling against the mentalism of introspection psychology and psychoanalysis.

A major point of compatibility between association-learning theory and Freudian psychoanalysis is their mutual emphasis upon a kind of hedonism as a guiding principle in behavior. In Freudian theory this takes the form of the pleasure principle, by which behavior is guided to avoid pain and promote pleasure or discharge through tension release. In association-learning theory, the principle of reinforcement is exceedingly important (although increasingly controversial) in that a response is acquired to a stimulus when there has been drive reduction.

Furthermore, for Freud all social motivation is a derivative of primary biological needs. Similarly, in association-learning theory, secondary drives (the social motives) are acquired because they have been associated with the reduction of tension resulting from unsatisfied biological drive states, like hunger and thirst.

Both Freud and association-learning theory have been strongly influenced by the principle of association; that is, the psychological events are connected by means of their association or contiguity in time and place. Learning theory has emphasized the acquisition of behavior through principles of learning and has attempted to formulate as precise rules as possible for this acquisition. The defense mechanisms postulated by Freud are seen by Dollard and Miller as habits of reaction that reduce anxiety. Both Freud and Dollard and Miller agree that the origin of neurosis lies in the development of fear or anxiety as an acquired drive. It can motivate the organism to engage in behavior that reduces the anxiety, but these anxiety-reducing behaviors often are nonadaptive in some ways and are the symptoms of neurosis.

Where the similarity between psychoanalysis and association-learning theory leaves off, psychoanalysis tends to parallel phenomenological theory. Freud has stressed the internal organization of the person, not only as the mediating step between stimuli and response, but also as a process important to understand in its own right. At the same time, Freud was never completely phenomenological in the sense of Rogers or Snygg and Combs. Because the important determinants of behavior are unconscious, it avails one little, from Freud's viewpoint, to study the personality structure through the subjective experience of the person. The introspections of free association in psychoanalysis are not taken entirely at face value in making inferences about personality dynamics.

In his writings, Freud recognized clearly the importance of motivational factors in determining how reality was likely to be apprehended by the individual. In this sense, he took a position quite compatible with phenomenological theory. The normal, healthy person probably apprehends reality as it is, but in the case of the pathological person—with whom Freud had the most transaction—the ego-defense mechanisms distort reality. Thus, for Freud, the internal structure of the individual determines, to some degree, the apprehension of the stimulus.

In general, Freud utilized a wide variety of forms of thinking in constructing psychoanalytic theory. In some places his point of view contains aspects of a trait-and-type approach; in other places his thinking is similar to that of association learning; in still other instances he parallels the phenomenological frame of reference. It would be impossible to place him squarely in any of the arbitrary categories of theoretical frames of reference that we have set up.

CRITIQUE AND CURRENT STATUS

Freud's conceptual model has the virtue of including a huge variety of phenomena of normal and pathological behavior. The enormous creativity of the model results from its capacity to integrate diverse phenomena under a logical set of propositions. It is the only behavior theory which is so all-encompassing in scope. It has influenced nearly every phase of psychological thought. At the same time, no other psychological theory has been so extensively and bitterly criticized as has psychoanalysis.

When Freud first began to formulate his theory, he met violent attacks from every quarter and at the same time developed a group of followers who, for some time, remained within the orbit of orthodox Freudian thinking. Many of these followers continued to manifest an almost religious reverence toward Freud and his writings, an attitude that Freud encouraged by refusing frequently to be influenced by criticisms and changes that other writers proposed. Although he frequently changed his own views, he did so not on the basis of pressures from others but as a result of his own dissatisfaction with phases of the theory.

Some of the earlier followers of Freud rejected various aspects of Freudian theory and developed psychoanalytic movements of their own. Some of these Neo-Freudians, such as Jung, Adler, Rank, Horney, Fromm, and Sullivan, will be discussed in the next chapter. They frequently are identified as psychoanalysts, although there remains an influential corps of orthodox psychoanalysts who adhere to the fundamental tenets enunciated by Freud and have attempted to elaborate upon, rather than alter, these. Even within the psychoanalytic group proper, there continues to be much theoretically oriented ferment (Gill, 1959). Also now, the persecuted point of view, having become influential, tends often to be intolerant of other theoretical positions.

In every major city of the country there are analytic societies that follow the Freudian tradition, just as in a great many cities there are associations of psychoanalysts who follow the modified point of view. The stamp of Freud's thinking can be found clearly upon all these, both orthodox and Neo-Freudian. Thus, Freud's present-day influence in the profession of psychiatry and in psychoanalysis is very great.

In academic psychology, there has been a slower *rapprochement* with psychoanalysis, although psychoanalytic thinking has certainly permeated the present-day psychological atmosphere. The influence of psychoanalysis is perhaps greatest in the clinical field, where the interest lies in the diagnosis and treatment of psychopathology. It is the rare psychologist who is not familiar in some degree with the basic propositions of psychoanalytic thought.

The most prominent criticisms of psychoanalysis are based less upon the particular content of the theory than they are upon the present vagueness of the theory in specifying the conditions that define the personality processes that Freud speculated upon. There are few rules by which one can arrive at precise expectations about what will happen when certain events take place. For example, we cannot predict through psychoanalytic theory whether repression or some other defense mechanism will be developed by an individual or what exactly will be the traumatic experiences that lead to the development of psychopathology. The past history of an individual is reconstructed from his present status, but rules are not available to construct in the future an accurate picture of his personality from a knowledge of the present circumstances of his life.

One response to this criticism is that it is true also of all current psychological theories and that a theory must first be vague before it can be precise. Many persons regard psychoanalytic theory, in some form or another, as the core from which more precise theorizing will be possible. It is unfair, they say, to criticize the theory for vagueness when a more precise theory of similar scope cannot be put in its place.

There are also a number of criticisms that can be directed at the methodology Freud used to develop and validate his propositions. For one thing, a verbatim record of what the patient and therapist said is rarely available. The material presented at the psychoanalytic session is usually recorded in the form of notes, which the therapist makes at the end of the hour, so it is possible for the therapist to read into the material much that might not have been there or to ignore other items of importance. Because of the absence of objective data, it is not possible to obtain judgments of reliability of the observations of the therapist. This fault is not difficult to correct and, in some instances, is being corrected by the use of verbatim recordings.

The data of psychoanalysis have tended also to depend upon what a patient says about his history, on the assumption that significant incidents would be recalled and ultimately presented by the patient and unimportant ones would be forgotten. Freud studied only patients in trouble, and although much of his work revolves around childhood development, he never studied children directly. The method of analysis is by reconstruction of the patient's history on the basis of what the patient says, a source of information that could well be unreliable. Some of this difficulty is being remedied at the present time by more direct study of children by psychoanalytic researchers.

The inferences that Freud drew from the verbalizations of his patients can be checked continually against observations made in the laboratory and in the clinic. The difficulty with such checking is that the inferences are stated in such vague form that they are difficult to use to derive empirical deductions that would test the propositions in the first place.

In spite of such difficulties, Freud's psychoanalytic theory of personality has had tremendous impact upon both psychological thought and on our culture of today. It has been an extraordinarily fruitful theory in that its propositions have led us to make new observations that we might never have been inclined to make. With all its deficiencies, the psychoanalytic method has been an important addition to the armamentarium of the personality researcher who attempts to understand behavior. Freud has awakened the psychological scientist and the public to a whole realm of ideas and facts that were virtually unknown or unrecognized before 1900. The theory certainly will not survive in its original form indefinitely. No theory does; a theory is an imaginary model, which man creates to understand the world and which is continually changing in the light of new observations and the construction of new or revised models. The importance of Freudian theory lies mainly in the work that it has stimulated, is now stimulating, and will stimulate in the future.

We now are prepared to turn to some of the offshoots of Freudian psychoanalysis, in which new ideas have been introduced that conflict with some of Freud's, and which are currently influential in personality theory.

The next chapter presents the major psychoanalytic theories, which have had their origins in Freudian modes of thought, but which contain major points of divergence.

CHAPTER
7

Modifications of Psychoanalysis

The major concepts of psychoanalysis began to appear in 1895. The unusual and provocative view of personality and psychopathology that emerged created a storm of criticism but also stimulated intellectually a number of brilliant men. These men began to cluster around Freud. They founded the International Psychoanalytic Association in 1910. The group was made up of scientists and physicians through the world and included Ernest Jones, of England; A. A. Brill, of the United States; Sandor Ferenczi, of Hungary; Carl Abraham and Otto Rank, of Germany; Alfred Adler, of Austria; and Carl Jung, of Switzerland. All these men have contributed greatly to the elaboration and spread of psychoanalytic thought. Adler, Jung, and Rank eventually withdrew and developed rival theoretical systems of their own, which have become influential in psychological thought. The theoretical systems of Jung, Adler, and Rank will be described under the heading "Early Revisions of Freudian Psychoanalysis."

A number of later psychoanalytic formulations have developed, which will also be considered in this chapter, although the proponents of these views are not part of the original circle of associates of Freud. These writers include Eric Fromm, Karen Horney, and Harry Stack Sullivan, each of whose views has been influential. The views of these writers will be discussed under the heading of "Later Developments."

In recent years the trend in psychoanalytic thought has been toward a greater emphasis upon the ego, its development, and its functioning. Whereas Freud stressed predominantly the id, that is, sexual energy and its transformations, there is more current interest in the adaptive properties of the ego, which control and direct the discharge of energy. This emphasis will be considered in a special section, followed by an overview of the Neo-Freudian schools of thought.

EARLY REVISIONS OF FREUDIAN PSYCHOANALYSIS

It is a somewhat arbitrary decision to place in the same section the three associates of Freud (Jung, Adler, and Rank) who left the Freudian circle and developed rival viewpoints. Actually, Jung's position is considerably closer to Freudian psychoanalysis than is either Adler's or Rank's. Furthermore, Adler has a great deal more in common with some of the later writers, such as Horney, than he does with Jung or even with Rank.

The historical pattern will be followed by and large, treating Jung and Adler and Rank as examples of early revisions of Freudian theory and Fromm, Horney, and Sullivan as examples of later developments. Although Adler was the first associate to break with Freud, let us discuss Jung's analytic psychology first, because it is more similar to Freud's, and probably more active in current professional movements.

Jung's Analytic Psychology

One of the early associates of Freud who was attracted into the professional circle of the International Psychoanalytic Association was Carl Jung. Jung had a medical degree and had begun a career in psychiatry, working with such eminent men as Bleuler and Janet. He began to correspond regularly with Freud in 1906, and upon the founding of the International Psychoanalytic Association, in 1910, Jung was made its first president, remaining in this position until 1914. About 1912 the personal relationship between Freud and Jung began to cool, and they subsequently terminated their personal and professional correspondence, in 1913. In the next year Jung resigned as president of the Association and shortly after terminated his membership. From that time on, Jung developed his own point of view, which generally has been called "analytic psychology" (1916, 1928, 1933).

It is difficult to assess the causes for the breakup in the relationship between Freud and Jung (as it is in the case of any of the other early associates of Freud). The reasons probably include intellectual as well as personal conflicts. Freud's tremendous and unswerving emphasis on sexuality as a principal motivating force appears to be a major factor. For example, Jung believed that when a person arrives at the late thirties or early forties sexual factors become relatively unimportant in directing his activities. He maintained that, at this time of life, man becomes more oriented toward spiritual matters and turns away from the biologically determined urges. Jung also had a strong purposive point of view (in contrast with Freud's retrospective conceptions of the person as being conditioned by his early history) that the person lives prospectively by aims and aspirations, searching for wholeness and completion.

Jung was a prolific writer, and it is possible here only to sketch the major features of his theoretical system. Let us examine his most basic ideas to communicate the over-all flavor of his system.

The unconscious: The conscious mind was called by Jung the *ego;* it consists of conscious perceptions, memories, feelings, and thoughts. Unconscious processes, however, can be important facilitative or disruptive forces in the organization of the personality, and they play a central role in directing human action and experience.

There are two fundamental divisions of the unconscious structure of the personality: the personal unconscious and the collective unconscious. The *personal unconscious* consists of experiences in the life of an individual that had been conscious but are no longer available to consciousness because of repression or because they had limited psychological impact. The personal unconscious varies greatly from person to person because it is based upon the divergent experiences of life.

The personal unconscious is made up of *complexes*, which are constellations of thoughts, feelings, memories, and perceptions, having a nucleus or core concept that makes certain classes of experience relevant to it and part of it. The core of a complex might be, as an example, the concept of "mother." It is built, in part, from a child's experiences with his mother and, as we shall see shortly, also from what is inherited from the racial past. Ideas, memories, and feelings that relate to the mother are collected and organized together, depending upon the strength of the force emanating from the nucleus. Thus, a person with a strong mother complex is likely to have his thoughts dominated by the concept of "mother," so his conception of his mother, including what she has said and how she has behaved, will guide his actions and feelings and her image frequently will be in his mind. The nucleus of a complex and many of the related aspects commonly are unconscious, though at times they appear in consciousness.

Because these complexes play a strong role in guiding our behavior, it was important for Jung to have a means available for discovering the nature of complexes in individuals. It is in this connection that Jung made use of the word-association test, which had been originated for different purposes many years before by Galton. A given list of words is read to the subject, one at a time, and he responds with the first word that comes to his mind. Jung observed the reaction time for the response and other behavioral and physiological responses, such as changes in breathing and changes in skin color, because of pallor or flushing. Long delays in response to a stimulus word, along with evidences of emotional reactions, suggest that the word has touched or is related to a complex. Such a complex can then be further explored by case study. The word-association test is one of the experimental contributions of Jung that has been taken up extensively by other psychologists. A modification of the original Jung word-association list has been employed clinically by Rapaport, Gill, and Schafer (1946). This list of words, to which subjects are asked to respond with the first association that comes to mind and as rapidly as possible, is presented in Table 10.

Table 10

WORD-ASSOCIATION LIST

1. world	21. suicide	41. taxi
2. love	22. mountain	42. mother
3. father	23. house	43. table
4. hat	24. paper	44. beef
5. breast	25. homosexual	45. nipple
6. curtains	26. radiator	46. race
7. trunk	27. girl friend	47. water
8. drink	28. screen	48. suck
9. party	29. masturbate	49. horse
10. bowel movement	30. frame	50. fire
11. book	31. man	51. vagina
12. lamp	32. orgasm	52. farm
13. rug	33. movies	53. social
14. chair	34. cut	54. son
15. boy friend	35. laugh	55. taxes
16. penis	36. bite	56. tobacco
17. dark	37. woman	57. city
18. depressed	38. dance	58. intercourse
19. spring	39. dog	59. hospital
20. bowl	40. daughter	60. doctor

SOURCE: Rapaport, Gill, and Schafer, 1946, vol. II, p. 13. By permission of publishers. In Shaffer & Lazarus, 1952, p. 256.

A unique feature of Jung's theory is his second subdivision of the unconscious, the *collective unconscious,* which is one of the most potent parts of the personality and, in mental disorder, tends to dominate the ego and the personal unconscious in guiding an individual. The collective unconscious consists of latent memories inherited from the ancestral past of man, which includes the racial history of man as a species as well as his phylogenetic animal ancestry. Man's evolutionary development is inherited in and communicated by the collective unconscious, which is, according to Jung, universal.

All persons basically have the same collective unconscious because of the similarity of their brain structures and the common ancestral experiences in our evolution. The possibility of reviving experiences of the racial past is inherited rather than racial memories themselves. This occurs in such a way that we are predisposed to react to the world in a selective fashion. For example, all persons have had mothers. Therefore, every infant is predisposed to perceive a mother and react to her. There are many such predispositions that come from our common ancestral background, such as our fears of the dark and of snakes and our disposition to develop the idea of a supreme being. The importance in Jung's thought of this discarded and presumably invalid concept of the inheritance of racial experiences has made analytic psychology less palatable to psychologists than it might otherwise have been. Partly as a result of this type of concept, the theory remains fundamentally mystical and difficult to employ in an empirically oriented science.

The collective unconscious is made up of structures called *archetypes,* which are universal ideas containing a considerable amount of emotion. The baby inherits a preformed image or conception of a universal mother (the archetype), which determines how the baby will actually perceive his own mother. This perception is modified or influenced also by a child's actual experiences with his mother, blending compatibly, as a rule, with the racial experience, because mothers have probably maintained similar roles as long as man has existed.

The archetypes of the collective unconscious can come through into consciousness through associative experiences such as myths, dreams, rituals, works of art, and various symptomatic patterns. Jung and his colleagues extensively studied myths and dreams as archetypal representations. Some of the archetypes are so important and have evolved so far that they must be treated almost as separate systems within the personality. These latter systems are the persona, the anima, the animus, and the shadow.

The *persona* is a mask worn by the person (figuratively) in response to social conventions about how we should act and feel. This mask represents the role that society assigns to him and shows that the wearer performs the proper role, regardless of the real, underlying personality.

The *anima* and the *animus* have to do with masculine and feminine components in men and women. Physiologically, the male and female produce both male and female sex hormones; psychologically, both masculine and feminine characteristics are found in both sexes. The feminine side of a man's personality is called the "anima," and the masculine side in women is called the "animus." Man has become partly feminized by living with women throughout the ages, and, conversely, women have become masculinized by living with men. Thus, these archetypes, the anima and the animus, partly govern man's apprehension of women and women's apprehension of men.

The archetype of the *shadow* involves the instincts that man has inherited from lower forms of animals. The shadow is the animal side of man's nature. It contributes to man's sense of his own sinfulness, and it is projected outward as danger, enemies, or evil spirits. Socially tabooed thoughts, feelings, and actions arise from the shadow archetype, but they are apt to be concealed (the persona effects this) from view or repressed so that even the person himself is unaware of them. Thus, the animal nature of man, in the form of the shadow archetype, infuses into the ego and the personal unconscious.

One of the theoretical differences between Freud and Jung is the latter's emphasis on the *self*, an organizing agency or set of system principles within the personality that holds the various subsystems together. It provides unity and stability to the personality This unity and stability is the goal of life, which persons, although constantly striving for it, rarely reach. The search for these goals that is often provided through religion is one of the essential characteristics of Jung's work and gives analytical psychology something of its mysticism and religious quality. The self is, in effect, an archetype that does not strongly manifest itself until the person is in middle life. Then he begins to strive to alter the focus of his personality from the conscious ego to the self, midway between consciousness and unconsciousness. The libido is also deemphasized in favor of spiritual values.

Jung's typology: One aspect of Jung's thought that has been influential is his personality typology, in which two major attitudes are distinguished: *extroversion* and *introversion*. It was described in Chapter 3 to illustrate typologies. The extroverted attitude represents an orientation toward the external world; the introverted attitude involves an orientation toward the inner, subjective world. Both ordinarily are present in the personality, but one is usually dominant and conscious and the other, subordinate and unconscious. The dominant attitude displayed is the basis for classifying an individual by type.

Within these two major attitudes or orientations there are four fundamental psychological functions: *thinking, feeling, sensing,* and *intuiting.* The various functions can be in different relationship to each other, one predominating over the others, and, as noted in Chapter 3, a variety of personality types can be described from the attitudes of extroversion and introversion and the functions of thinking, feeling, sensing, and intuiting.

Jung described the personality in terms of polar tendencies that are likely to be in conflict with one another. For Jung, opposition existed everywhere in the personality. For example, of the four psychological functions, usually one is more highly differentiated than the others and plays a predominant role in consciousness. This is called the "superior function," and the least differentiated of the four functions is called the "inferior function" and is likely to be repressed and unconscious, expressing itself in dreams and fantasies.

Various types of interactions are possible among the various systems of the personality, including the attitudes and functions. One system can compensate for the weakness of another, one can oppose another, or two systems can unite, forming a synthesis. As an example of compensation, if extroversion is dominant, the unconscious can compensate by emphasizing and developing qualities of introversion, which can be expressed when the extroverted attitude is blocked. Opposition tends to exist between all the systems of the personality, between the ego and the shadow or the personal unconscious, and between the persona and the anima or the animus. With the mature development of the self in later life, a synthesis of the polar elements in the personality is accomplished to form a balanced, integrated personality.

Psychic energy: Jung's concept of energy and its origin is formally similar to Freud's. Psychic energy originates from the metabolic processes of the body, and it is this energy with which the activities of the personality are accomplished. Jung used the term "libido" interchangeably with "psychic energy," but his concept of libido is broader than Freud's. Jung's libido includes not only sexuality, but all wishing, feeling, attending, and striving from any biological source as well. Jung's libido might as well be called "life energy," as Munroe (1955) refers to it, or "psychic energy," the term preferred by Hall and Lindzey (1957).

Jung conceived the energy aspects of the personality as a partially closed system. That is, if a particular value in which psychic energy is invested weakens or disappears, the energy invested in that value will not be lost but will reappear in some new value (as in the first law of thermodynamics in physics). No energy is ever lost, except through fatigue, and some additions can take place through rest or eating a meal. Thus, noting some exceptions, Jung treated psychic energy in terms of closed-system principles. A person who loses interest in a hobby will have this added energy available, and it will usually be invested in another activity. If a value is repressed, its energy can be used in the creation of dreams or fantasies. Energy lost from one value can be distributed widely among several other values. Moreover, energy continually flows from one system of the personality to others. The dynamics of personality consists of these redistributions of energy. For example, if the ego develops, it will develop at the expense of some other side of the personality, perhaps the persona, or vice versa.

Jung considered that the distribution of energy in the psyche seeks an equilibrium or balance. Energy will tend to pass from a stronger value into a weaker value in another system until a balance is reached. One of the goals of psychic development is an ideal equilibrium of forces in the personality. A weak system of the personality is likely to obtain energy at the expense of a strong system. This pull from a strong to a weak system creates tension in the personality. For example, if the ego is too much emphasized in relation to the unconscious, tension will be generated because of the attempt on the part of the energy to go from the conscious ego into the unconscious. Similarly, if extroversion is the dominant value, then energy tends to move from extroversion to introversion and the extrovert is pressed to develop the introverted side of his personality. In Jungian psychology, any one-sided development of personality produces conflict and tension, whereas an even development of all the components results in harmony.

Development: Jung maintained that man always moves or attempts to move from a less complete stage to a more complete stage of development. The goal of this development is self-actualization, which is the most complete differentiation and union of all aspects of man's personality. Jung was, therefore, most preoccupied with the future of man and with this purposive conception of man's destiny. Thus, the present is determined not only by the past but also by the future because of this purposive striving, which orients man's actions and development. In contrast with Freud, who appears to some as rather pessimistic and fatalistic about man's development, Jung saw man as continually striving forward toward higher developments.

Just as Jung was less preoccupied with the past than Freud, he was also less detailed about the stages of development than Freud. Jung granted that, in the early years, the libido is oriented toward the activity necessary for survival. Before the age of five, there begin to appear sexual values, which reach their peak during adolescence. The youth and early adult is characterized by the predominance of biological urges, which makes the young person energetic and passionate. In the late thirties or early forties, a change occurs, in which youthful interests lose their value and cultural and spiritual values begin to prevail. When this alteration fails to take place, serious problems occur in later life.

As with Freud, development in Jung's terms can involve progression or regression, forward movement or a backward movement. In progression, opposing forces of the personality are synthesized and harmonious. Frustration interrupts this forward movement, and the libido can regress into the unconscious and become involved in introverted values. Thus, severe introversion is regressive, and the normal progression of the individual is toward the outgoing, environmentally oriented values.

Current status: At the present time there are relatively few practicing psychoanalysts who utilize Jung's concepts and method, although they are an active and vocal group. Jung's influence in traditional psychology has been limited primarily to his work with the word-association test and his theory of types, which has found its way into many general or personality psychology texts. The concept of archetypes is nowhere accepted in modern psychology. Aside from the word-association investigations, Jung's point of view has stimulated little in the way of theoretical elaboration and research in recent years. The emphasis on self-actualization has been taken up by some phenomenological personality theorists, such as Rogers and Maslow. The deemphasis on sexuality is compatible with later Neo-Freudian developments (namely, Horney, Adler, and Sullivan), and Jung's stress on the social and spiritual directions of man past middle life have had considerable appeal. Jung is closer to Freud than most of the other Neo-Freudians in his emphasis on the biological givens in the development of the person, and he is unique in his strong purposivistic emphasis. However, there are some trends evident in Jung's thought that suggest also the beginnings of recognition of the huge impact on man's development of social factors, although this emphasis has been more systematically developed by Sullivan.

Adler's Individual Psychology

Alfred Adler was a Viennese physician, who first specialized in ophthalmology and later became a psychiatrist. He was an early member of Freud's group and later president of the International Psychoanalytic Association for a short while. Adler also was the earliest of Freud's associates to develop ideas that differed from those of Freud. These differences became so marked that he presented them to the Psychoanalytic Association in 1911, and following sharp criticism of his position by Freud and others in the society, he resigned as president and shortly after ended his connections with Freudian psychoanalysis. He formed his own group of associates and developed a system of thought that is commonly called "individual psychology" (1927). He continued active in psychiatry and shortly before his death, in 1937, came to the United States.

Adler was the earliest psychoanalyst to deemphasize the concept of inborn instincts and to give full stress to social factors in the development of personality. This is one of Adler's main contributions, one to which Freud himself never responded warmly. Adler might also be considered one of the forerunners of modern phenomenology, emphasizing as he did a subjective approach to personality and the concept of a creative self, which searches for experiences that will fulfill the individual's highest potentialities. Adler also stressed the uniqueness of personality, a view that Allport (1937) elaborated many years later. One of the major distinctions between Adler and Freud is that, whereas Freud stressed unconscious determinants of personality, Adler considered man as a conscious being, usually aware of the reasons for his actions. Freud pointed up the irrational, emotional, and unconscious sources of action, and Adler conceived of man as capable of consciously planning and guiding his actions toward self-actualization. Thus he also sowed some of the seeds of the later ego-psychology movement. Like Freud and Jung, Adler's experience was in psychiatry. He therefore based his conception of man on his experience with neurotics and later extended his thinking to the normal personality. Let us briefly examine the major ideas that characterized Adler's work.

Fictional finalism: Adler's phenomenological emphasis is illustrated by his use of the concept of "fictional finalism," which was borrowed from a contemporary philosophical writer, Hans Vaihinger (1925, originally published in 1911), and which stated that man's actions are grounded in fictional ideas that do not necessarily conform to reality. Some examples of these "fictions" are belief in life after death or that evil actions are always punished. When such fictions are believed, they seem to help man to cope more successfully with life. They can be used and discarded when no longer valuable.

Adler elaborated the idea that expectations about the future orient man more than events of the past. In other words, the future goals of man affect his present behavior so the fiction of heaven for good persons and hell for sinners exercises an enormous influence on behavior. As in the case of Jung, Adler rejected Freud's retrospective emphasis and added the principle of finalism, in which a future life goal explains man's behavior. Adler believed that the normal person could face reality and ignore these fictions better than the neurotic person.

The style of life: The organized, self-consistent, and unique quality of human personality, as conceived by Adler, is reflected in the concept of "style of life." Adler believed that human aims were the same fundamentally and were embedded in the tendency to strive for superiority. But although every person has this same goal of superiority, there are many ways in which this goal is sought. One person seeks it through social relations, another through education and science, and still others in athletic or economic activities. These different ways of attempting to obtain the goal of life represent a person's unique style of life, the route by which his goal is sought. All aspects of his life and details of his behavior are organized around this style. The style of life is an abstraction that includes every aspect of living within some characteristic plan or means of attaining the life goal.

The style of life is created while the person is very young, perhaps by the age of four or five, and later experiences are assimilated into this style. It is, therefore, difficult to change the style of life later on. Its early development is based upon the kinds of experiences the child has, for example, particular kinds of inferiorities or helplessness which the child experiences in relation to the gratification of his needs. Primarily, however, the style of life grows out of creative efforts of a person to solve the basic problems of early life. In this way, Adler introduced the concept of the *creative self*, which is the consistent organizer of the personality structure. This creative self molds the personality into a unique structure on the basis of hereditary capabilities and life experiences.

Striving for superiority: In Adler's earlier writings he emphasized the struggle for power as a motive, a universal force of behavior based upon the inevitable helplessness of the child to control the circumstances of his life. Later on, Adler gave up the concept of "will to power," replacing it with "striving for superiority." By superiority, Adler did not mean what we normally think of in this connection—leadership or preeminent positions in society—but rather a striving for perfection or self-actualization. Man is pushed by the urge to develop to higher levels. This striving for superiority is innate, but it can manifest itself in many different ways. It transcends the various separate drives that are all part of this striving for perfection.

The concept of superiority suggests some similarities between Adler's thought and that of Jung and later writers, such as Maslow and Rogers, who have used the concept of self-actualization. In this way, Adler rejected the homeostatic or equilibrium principle so characteristic of Freud and the point of view of association learning. The proposition is suggested of a life force, independent of the usual tension-reduction mechanisms, which impels the organism toward higher development and which arises as a given feature of human existence.

The striving for superiority comes into being from innate qualities of the individual but also because of inferiority feelings in the child. In his early writings, Adler had introduced the notion of compensation for bodily inferiorities. He was trying to explain instances of persons who were sick or weak in some biological function but who were able to develop unusual skills in other areas. One of the most often-described examples of compensation is that of Demosthenes, who was believed to have been a stutterer as a child and who eventually became a great orator. Adler drew attention to many such examples of compensation for defects. In his later writings, he tended to regard inferiority feelings as universal, although enhanced by certain experiences, such as physical defects. He regarded subjective feelings of inferiority as the primary basis of human striving. Such feelings of inferiority are normal and helpful in getting man to improve his circumstances, but they can become abnormal or exaggerated by experiences in early life, such as excessive pampering of children or rejection by the parents. Under these circumstances abnormal feelings of inferiority are likely to lead to selfish striving for personal enhancement, which becomes the neurotic person's style of life.

Social interest: In Adler's original thinking, aggression and power were the primary guiding concepts. Later on, Adler enlarged his conception of man to include the notion of unselfish interest, which included such matters as cooperation, interpersonal and social relations, identification with a group, and empathy. Adler meant social interest in the broader sense of the individual helping society toward a goal of perfection. Man in his weakness is capable of banding together to compensate for his individual natural weakness in producing a more perfect way of life.

Social interest is a latent, inborn characteristic of man, although man's embeddedness in the social context further stimulates this inborn social interest. In other words, this innate predisposition would not appear spontaneously without the guidance and experience of a social order. Social interest is the ideal form for the striving for superiority to take. In the neurotic, selfish power goals subordinate healthy social interest. In the normal person, social interest, as a healthy means of attaining superiority, is prepotent over selfish power goals. The neurotic must learn to give up his abnormal style of life, which involves the goal of self-enhancement or power, and must accept a more socially oriented goal, in which empathy and love of fellow man predominate.

Current status: Adler's theory of personality, in contrast with Freud's, gives man greater prospects of mastering his life. Adler emphasized man's natural altruism and creativity, and Freud emphasized man's animal nature. Adler emphasized consciousness, and Freud emphasized the unconscious. For these reasons, Adler's work is far more readily accepted by, and understandable to, the lay person and somewhat more satisfying than Freud's, although for the same reasons it is often regarded by personality psychologists as limited and superficial in contrast with Freud's.

Adler introduced a number of special research methods (as did Jung) suited to his theoretical position concerning personality. His contributions include the study of birth order in personality development, an interest that led, in the 1920s and 30s, to a considerable quantity of research on the personalities of the oldest, middle, and youngest child in the family. Adler pointed out that the familial experiences of these children are different, and this is likely to condition their development in different ways. For example, the oldest child, who initially is given a great deal of attention, is displaced suddenly from the favorite position by the birth of a younger sibling, an experience that can produce hatred and insecurity. The experiences of the second child or middle child are quite different and tend to lead, according to Adler, to ambitiousness and attempts continually to surpass the older child. The middle child is apt to be rebellious and envious but better adjusted than the older or youngest child. The youngest child tends to be spoiled because of the pampering and extra attention he is apt to get when two or more older children have been displaced. However, most of the empirical research on this conception of the significance of birth order has not proved especially fruitful, although child-rearing specialists are now highly sensitized to the concept of "sibling rivalry."

One of Adler's methods, which has not found its way into current psychological research, involved asking a person to report the earliest memory he could recall as a means of getting information about his style of life. Thus, when a person recounts an experience involving a mother, this might suggest a greater interest in mother than in father and further information can throw light on the characteristic kinds of relationships this person has had with mother figures. A Freudian, in contrast, would assume that the readiness of the person to bring out the thought of mother could mean that other, unconscious and more important attitudes exist which are not being expressed.

Adler has had relatively little direct impact on psychoanalytic practice but considerable influence on psychological thought, especially with respect to teachers, doctors, criminologists, and lay persons. He lectured a great deal to the general public and was very active in the schools, juvenile courts, and guidance clinics. An interesting feature of Adler's influence is that it seems to exist in current theoretical formulations of personality without acknowledgement. For example, there is much in common between Adler's and Karen Horney's views, as we shall see later. Adler also was one of the earliest writers to emphasize a phenomenological view of personality, which has been incorporated in many current phenomenological theories. His emphasis on social factors in development is one of the chief modern developments in personality theory and research. His concern with the conscious adaptive properties and resources of the individual and the striving for positive growth has been followed up in ego psychology and in the theories of Rogers, Maslow, and Goldstein. Yet in few instances is the influence of Adler recognized.

One reason for this is that Adler's point of view no longer represents an active system of thought with many current proponents or disciples. Whereas Freud has his disciples and his current formulators, Adler does not. Adler's point of view no longer represents a clear school of thought. The American Society of Individual Psychology, in New York, Chicago, and Los Angeles, remains alive through its journal, *The American Journal of Individual Psychology*, although it is not particularly powerful or influential. A recent and excellent book presenting most of Adler's important writings (Ansbacher & Ansbacher, 1956) may, however, stimulate renewed interest in Adler's contributions.

Rank's Theory of Separation

Otto Rank was also an important member of the emerging psychoanalytic movement. Unlike most of the other participants, his education was primarily in engineering, philosophy, psychology, history, and art rather than in medicine and science. Rank remained for a long time on good terms with Freud, but like Adler and Jung, he eventually became critical of many concepts of psychoanalysis and developed his own views. This is communicated most fully in *The Trauma of Birth* (1952), with perhaps the best over-all statement of his position in *Will Therapy* (1945).

In common with Jung and Adler, Rank emphasized the constructive strivings of the individual. He stressed the efforts of the person to break with his past in order to live independently of it in the present. He also regarded Freud's views as pessimistic because a person's life was seen as a continual repetition of infantile struggles relating to instinctual demands (although often in different forms). In Rank's view, the fact that a neurotic person comes to grief in the struggle to break with the past and exhibit growth or forward movement is no proof that he lacks the tendencies for positive growth.

Birth trauma: In Freud's early thinking, the prototype of all anxiety was the trauma of birth. Birth was considered the first stressful situation, on which later signals of danger or catastrophe were built. The child suddenly is catapulted from the intrauterine environment, where its needs are generally well supplied (this assumption has many times been challenged) and where there is a minimum of struggle on the part of the fetus to adapt biologically, into a world in which he must breathe, go hungry at times, and often be physically very uncomfortable.

Freud's concept of the birth trauma considerably influenced Rank, and the latter elevated it to the status of the primary problem of human life, the universal source of *primal anxiety*. The goal of all human life is the reinstatement of the bliss of the embryonic state, and the greatest source of human fear is *separation*. The primary conflict of all mankind involves, on the one hand, the wish to return to the womb (at least symbolically) and, on the other, the fear of the uterine existence associated with the traumatic experience of birth.

There has been great criticism of the concept of the birth trauma because, in its most literal sense, it assumes a clearer apprehension of the experience of birth than the newborn infant appears capable of. However, if one regards this emphasis on the birth trauma in a figurative sense, then the universal problem of mankind is separation, keynoted by the birth experience, which separates the infant from the security and protection of his association with the mother. Thus, whereas Freud emphasized the sexual and aggressive instincts as the primary sources of conflict in the developing individual, Rank stressed the problem of separation as the primary source of conflict and neurotic adjustment.

The life fear and the death fear: The problem of separation is expressed specifically in the concepts of "life fear" and "death fear." *Life fear* is the fear of separation and individuation. Within the womb the embryo functions in a symbiotic way with the mother's body, and it is protected and secure. This symbiotic union is eliminated at birth, and the old union must be relinquished. As the individual struggles to reinstate a unity between himself and his environment, every advance toward independence is perceived as a threat. The fear of giving up the safety of symbiotic relationships analogous to the prenatal condition and of seeking independent status and existence is called the "life fear."

Death fear, on the other hand, is the fear of the loss of individuality. Any union in the course of the individual's life also becomes a threat because the reinstatement of a symbiotic union (the return to the womb), represents a loss of individuality (death of the individual). The death fear drives the person toward individuation and toward growth and separation from dependency on others, whereas the life fear inhibits this effort and pushes the individual toward establishing dependent relationships similar to that before birth.

These two aspects of basic fear or primal anxiety represent the essential conflict within each individual. Primal anxiety is the very basis of life itself and serves as the fundamental human drive. In Rank's formulation this fear can become a constructive force rather than a crippling one. Separation from the whole implies difference and entails the acceptance of one's self. Union with the environment is a source of support and reassurance. The major ideal of the human race (and also of Rank's psychotherapy) is the constructive, creative integration of these conflicting trends toward union and separation.

The will and the counterwill: Because Rank conceived of life as a struggle between the life fear and the death fear, the outcome of this struggle has to involve a balance of motivational forces in the individual. Thus, Rank discussed the entire process of separation as a conflict of wills. *Will* is the integrative power of the personality, somewhat analogous to the concept of ego. Rank considered the essence of man as an active relationship between himself and the world, conceptualized in terms of will.

As we have pointed out, Rank conceived of the child at birth as completely at one with the mother. The process of separation from the mother begins when the child discovers, through experience, that he and the mother are different individuals. The child must assert himself in a negative way against the parent in order to articulate his own self, and this self-assertion becomes even stronger in later childhood and adolescence. An example of this assertiveness is the negativism so characteristic of a two-year-old. This fighting with the parent has the primary purpose of defining the child to himself. In this differentiation process, there must be a clash of wills, the parent's will and the child's counterwill.

For Rank the will begins negatively as counterwill to the will of the parent, and because the child is fundamentally dependent upon the parent, this counterwill is a source of *guilt*. Guilt is the inherent concomitant of the attempt to become separate. The guilt arising from the counterwill against the parent is called by Rank "ethical guilt" in contrast with "moralistic guilt," which develops when one has committed an act that is disapproved by society.

The problem for the individual suffering guilt because of the conflict of wills is to resolve it by regaining a sense of unity with his world, while retaining his basic independence and the acceptance of his own individuality. In the ideal case, the parent accepts the counterwill of the child as a lovable part of the child's attempts to achieve his own independence but nevertheless remains aware of the child's continual need for support and belonging. Thus, the union between the parent and the child and all other psychological unions of the developing individual are not accomplished at the expense of individuality, nor is the individuality achieved through the loss of a sense of union.

Rank's typology: Rank discussed a number of ways in which the individual can cope with the union-separation problem and the guilt inherent in it. The three principle ways are the solutions of three types of persons: the normal or average man; the neurotic; and the artist or creative man.

The *average man* has failed to assert his will and has instead solved the problem by adjusting or conforming to society and never becoming separated. Such an individual has so identified his will with the will of his parents that he has avoided a great deal of the guilt of separation and the pain of developing his own will to a further degree. There is little effort toward individuation and little conflict about conformity. He spares himself the inner distress of guilt by giving up his own development. This is not a conscious conformity for the sake of expediency, but a natural conformity with no thought of any other type of adjustment. It is the most primitive or easiest solution to the conflict of separation and union. The individual seeks union alone, and in a stable society such a person is well adjusted and a model of social virtue. He has a harmonious relationship to his society, although he is apt to be a victim of social change.

The *neurotic*, in contrast, has developed to the point where he must assert his will, but because of life fear and guilt he is unable to do so successfully. He cannot go forward in positive growth and individuation, and at the same time cannot give up his will or individuality and so is caught in the middle of a conflict. The neurotic fails to win through in his constructive attempt to bring together the conflicting trends. He has achieved so great a sense of separateness that he can no longer accept the union with society. To the neurotic, this union is the realization of the death fear. The counterwill of the neurotic is strong, and he is, in consequence, guilt-ridden and hostile to others. Yet he fundamentally desires the union that will alleviate the guilt. This hostility and counterwill (or resistance, as it is observed in therapy) is conceived by Rank as essentially a constructive force. It must be utilized to permit the neurotic to go beyond the easy solution of the average man to the solution that successfully integrates both forces.

The *artist* has in common with the neurotic the commitment to the pain of separation from the herd. Unlike the neurotic, however, the artist has been able to achieve the highest solution of the problem: integration of his separate will and his need for union. The term "artist" was chosen by Rank to indicate the creativeness of this integrative solution, achieved by the uniquely human qualities that permit the constructive bringing together of the opposite trends within the person.

Current status: Rank, like Adler, has had relatively little impact on traditional psychotherapeutic practice. Of the two men, Rank generally is even less well regarded in academic-theoretical circles, even to the point of sometimes being left out of compendiums of personality theories, although Jung and Adler almost always are included. Much of this disdain undoubtedly is due to the disturbing effect that the concept of birth trauma has had on scientifically oriented theorists, although modern Rankians do not stress the literal aspects of birth trauma but rather the symbolic aspects of it as an instance of the universal problem of separation. When viewed in this way, Rank's theory is immensely interesting and scarcely any more mystical than Jung's.

A major impact of Rank's work has been in the area of social work. A number of schools of social work, for example, some in New York and Philadelphia, have adopted a Rankian position and have utilized his contributions to therapy. Actually, Rank has had considerable indirect influence on the development of Rogerian theory and practice, theoretical parts of which were discussed in Chapter 5.

Perhaps it is Rank's philosophy, more than the actual theoretical details (which are few), that has had the most influence. He emphasized the forces in the individual that guide him toward positive growth. He spoke of the counterwill or resistance as the means by which the individual moved toward individuation. This is the same kind of emphasis that characterizes the work of Rogers and that of Maslow and Lecky. It is in contrast to the homeostatic postulate of Freudian psychoanalysis and association-learning theory, which tends to dominate the field. In these views, the patterns of response are learned because they return the organism to a state of equilibrium. Rankian philosophy—and also to some degree the thought of Jung and Adler—stresses the existence in the individual of forces that lead him to assert himself and to grow positively against materialistic influences, which push him toward an easy and more limited solution.

LATER DEVELOPMENTS

Three writers have had a considerable impact on psychological and psychoanalytic thought in recent years, even though they were not among the circle of Freudians who were involved in the early development of psychoanalysis. These writers have much in common with Adler and Rank in their emphasis on social factors in development, although they still owe a great conceptual debt to Freud. Although the views of Erich Fromm, Karen Horney, and Harry Stack Sullivan are social-psychological in nature and in conflict with some of the Freudian themes, they have close ties with, and spring out of, the theoretical climate stimulated by Freud. For this reason they, like Jung, Adler, and Rank, often are called Neo-Freudians.

Fromm's Conceptions

Of the three writers in this section, Erich Fromm is the only non-medical man, having received his Ph.D. in 1922 from Heidelberg. Fromm was trained in psychoanalysis and in the early 1930s lectured at the Chicago Psychoanalytic Institute. He later took up private practice in New York City as a psychoanalyst, although he has lectured widely and has written several important books, the most well known of which is *Escape from Freedom* (1941), in which his most important conceptual theme is presented. Fromm has not developed a systematic or complete personality theory, but he has elaborated a number of ideas that he considers supplements to, or reemphases in, psychoanalytic thought.

Unlike other psychoanalytic writers, Fromm's emphasis is less on individual character and more on what has been called *social character*, which is the nucleus of character structure shared by most members of a culture. He has focused especially on the nature of society as it relates to the development of social character. One can see how far removed in certain respects are some of the later psychoanalytic writers from the early Freudian emphasis on the biological unfolding of personality.

The main emphasis in Fromm's writings is suggested by the title of his first major book, *Escape from Freedom*. Further ideas can be found in later writings (1947, 1955). As the child develops, according to Fromm, he grows apart from his environment and from his dependence upon and union with other persons and he thus becomes free to express his individuated self. In the unfolding of this need for identity, the individual becomes isolated. For example, as the child is freed from emotional dependence upon his parents, he feels more isolated and helpless. This freedom is itself frightening and produces an intolerable loneliness from which the individual can try to escape by submitting to social authority and by conforming. This condition of isolation is a distinctively human situation, and the basic conflict is between the loneliness and insecurity of freedom and the need to become individuated as a person. The individual can express his freedom and somehow manage to cope with the loneliness, or he can establish secondary bonds through conformity. In these formulations, Fromm has a great deal in common with Rank, who has also emphasized the problem of separation and dependency.

In developing this theme of conflict between feelings of isolation and the desire for freedom and growth, Fromm suggested a parallel between the individual development of the child, as he becomes free from primary ties with parents, and the historical development of societies, in which a similar pattern is manifest. For example, he has traced the structure of human relationships from the feudal Middle Ages to modern times and has given special attention to the Nazi dictatorship as the most powerful force in Germany and Europe at the time he wrote *Escape from Freedom*.

In the Middle Ages man's place was relatively secure in the fixed position of serfdom. With the Renaissance there was an emergence of individualism. Men had to stand on their own and could succeed or fail through their own efforts. Thus, persons lost their place of security and frequently sought secondary bonds to reduce their isolation. Lutheranism and Calvinism, according to Fromm, represented one kind of answer to this problem, in which man accepted his insignificance, gave up his individual self, and submitted to God. However, insecurity always remained in the background, and in Calvinism the values of working took hold as a compulsion rather than as a necessity. Fromm also analyzed Hitler's rise in Germany in terms of his appeal to the German people through the new security that he offered them. The subjugation of the individual to the totalitarian society represents an instance of this basic theme of escape from freedom.

Actually, Fromm conceived that any form of society that man has developed—including feudalism, capitalism, fascism, socialism, or communism—represents man's attempt to resolve the fundamental conflict of being both a part of the social order, and separate from it, with the potentiality for individual growth. Even democracy contains, for Fromm, only the illusion of individuality. Social pressures for conformity tend to destroy the individual's spontaneity and uniqueness. Such pressures toward conformity are characteristic of America, just as they are in totalitarian forms of society.

Fromm was extremely interested in the kind of society that best permits the individuation of man and yet provides sufficient security so that freedom does not become intolerable. He recognized that it is essential that the child's character be shaped to fit the needs of a society in order for that society to function properly. Parents and the educational system attempt to make the child want to act in the ways required for the economic, political, and social systems to be maintained. For example, in a capitalistic society persons must be made to desire to invest or to save and to accept responsibility for economic as well as social obligations.

Fromm believed that there is a basic nature inborn in man, which can be thwarted and warped by a society that makes demands upon him contrary to this nature. In this way, Fromm stigmatized societies as being sick when they fail to satisfy the basic needs of man. There are five basic needs: the need for relatedness or belonging, the need for transcendence (to become a creative person rising above his animal nature), the need for rootedness (to be an integral part of the world), the need for identity (to be a unique individual), and the need for a frame of reference (to have a stable and consistent way of comprehending and perceiving the world). Fromm emphasized in this way, along with the phenomenological theorists of personality, the potentialities in man for certain types of growth. Like Goldstein, Rogers, Lecky, and Maslow, Fromm saw pathology as resulting from the failure of society to permit this growth, and he found no society as yet created that meets the basic needs of man, although he believed it possible to create one. Such a society would be one in which man can have love relationships with other men, being rooted in bonds of brotherliness, but which at the same time permits him to transcend nature by creating and by obtaining a sense of self. In other words, like Rank, Fromm sees the solution of man's basic dilemma as the successful integration of his needs for belonging and love, on the one hand, and his needs for individuation and independence, on the other. Such a proposal is essentially a very general ideal, the empirical conditions of which are not spelled out.

As might be expected, Fromm's impact has been considerable in the areas of social psychology, sociology, philosophy, and religion, and his books have also stimulated the general public. In actual practice, Fromm utilized a modified Freudian psychoanalytic position. He wrote (1947, p. 58), ". . . the fundamental basis of character is not seen in various forms of libidinal organization (Freud) but in specific kinds of a person's relatedness to the world." He emphasized problems of dependency and individuation (like Rank) and helplessness and hostility (like Adler and

Horney). He presented a position that supplements Freudian thought in a philosophical and sociological sense but which lends itself little to detailed elaboration or scientific examination.

Horney's Neo-Freudian Views

Karen Horney also was not one of the early Freudian circle, although she was trained in psychoanalysis in Berlin and for some years practiced analysis under traditional Freudian tutelage. When she came to the United States, she was connected with the Chicago Psychoanalytic Institute and later moved to New York, practicing psychoanalysis and teaching at the New York Psychoanalytic Institute. She became dissatisfied with orthodox Freudian psychoanalysis and, along with others of similar views, founded the Association for the Advancement of Psychoanalysis and the American Institute of Psychoanalysis.

Horney's personality theory falls within the basic framework of Freudian theory rather than being a new or independent approach. Like Fromm, she has attempted to change or deemphasize features of Freudian theory rather than to develop a unique system of thought, as did Adler, Jung, and Rank. Horney's writings, represented in many books but most notably in *The Neurotic Personality of Our Times* (1937), *New Ways in Psychoanalysis* (1939), and *Our Inner Conflicts* (1945), have aimed at eliminating what she considered fallacies in the thinking of Freud. She emphasized social factors in the development of neuroses and rejected the Freudian instinct theory, along with its emphasis on sexuality. She also deemphasized the developmental and historical aspects of Freudian thinking, focusing more upon the current adjustment process of the individual.

Central to Horney's theory is *basic anxiety*, which constitutes "the feeling a child has of being isolated and helpless in a potentially hostile world" (1945, p. 41). This insecurity or helplessness arises from any of the following environmental conditions: domination, indifference, parental inconsistency, lack of respect for the child's needs, lack of real guidance, disparaging attitudes, too much or too little admiration, lack of consistent warmth, conditions that force the child to take sides in parental disagreements, too much or too little responsibility, overprotection, isolation from other children, injustice, discrimination, and a hostile atmosphere. Conditions that interfere with the sense of security of the child and stimulate this sense of isolation and helplessness produce the basic anxiety.

Neurotic patterns were seen by Horney as ways of handling basic anxiety. The neurotic trends arise from the pathological need for security (when the early conditions of life stimulate feelings of isolation and helplessness and the perception of the world as hostile and dangerous). The individual defends himself against basic anxiety by *safety devices*, which are neurotic because they protect him against this inner fear, even though they are not functionally related to realistic dangers that he encounters. Thus, like Adler, Horney emphasized the helplessness of the infant but, in contrast, considered the pathological drives that arise as an exaggerated need for security rather than a drive for superiority. The individual must pile up personal insurances against the danger of being overwhelmed. The neurotic patterns can include an insatiable longing for love, excessive submissiveness, and other pathological ways of seeking security.

Much of Horney's work revolved around the factors in man's experience that produce neurotic conflict. The safety devices, which the individual develops to increase security in a potentially hostile world, further intensify feelings of anxiety and lead to what Horney called a "vicious circle." For example, an individual can attempt to attain safety by moving toward other persons, against them, or away from them; thus he can be compliant, dependent, aggressive, or detached. A compliant person can develop exaggerated fears of his own latent aggressiveness, and the aggressive type can harbor strong dependency needs, which he cannot admit because they involve a weakness that threatens his main strategy of defense. The detached type also harbors latent needs for closeness and relatedness to others. Such strong, unconscious impulses in opposite directions make the neurotic individual impotent. Any of the devices he chooses to reduce anxiety tend to intensify the neurosis because they aggravate the conditions they were designed to ease. For example, a person who is overly demanding of affection alienates others with these demands and, therefore, defeats his own end. This further increases the anxiety, which, in turn, leads to an intensification of the neurotic need for affection. Thus, the neurotic is caught in a vicious circle from which he cannot escape.

The neurotic is likely to solve the dilemma of conflict by repressing one aspect of it. Along with Freud, Horney believed that repression does not eliminate the impulse. Repressed aspects of the personality are likely to function even more strongly in a repressed condition. This solution of conflict (repression), therefore, is ineffective.

Unlike Freud, who emphasized internal biological factors as sources of conflict, Horney stressed factors in the social environment of the individual that produce conflict. She described cultural conflicts that involve incompatible and opposing value systems. For example, in our society we stress such attitudes as loving one's neighbor, but we tend to respect and admire the successfully competitive individual who has succeeded by outwitting or subordinating others. As another instance, we demand maturity and independence in the adolescent and at the same time resist many evidences of maturity that would tend to make the adolescent independent of our authority as parents.

These cultural conflicts become exaggerated problems for the neurotic because of the pathological need for security that he has developed. The normal person (exposed to love, security, respect, tolerance, and warmth) can resolve them, but the neurotic, because of his greater basic anxiety, must utilize irrational solutions. Because of repression, he consciously recognizes only one of the trends, and he creates an idealized image of himself in which the contradictory trend is denied. Whereas Freud and Jung tended to believe that conflict is, to a large extent, an inevitable biological event, Horney believed that it arises out of cultural patterns rooted in a particular society.

It is difficult to assess the current status and influence of Karen Horney's views because, like Fromm, she has not attempted to develop a complete systematic view, remaining essentially within the psychoanalytic tradition. Like Fromm, she has criticized the biological tradition of psychoanalysis, has added concepts here and there, or reemphasized certain aspects of personality where it seems to her desirable. These deletions and additions have found their way into psychoanalytic thought in many groups of less orthodox persuasion. In many communities where there are Freudian groups, there are often analytic institutes that have adopted positions nearer to those of Horney.

The Interpersonal Theory of Harry Stack Sullivan

Among the writers discussed in this chapter, Harry Stack Sullivan is the only American by birth. He was trained in medicine and in 1922 became associated with St. Elizabeth's Hospital, in Washington, D.C., where he was influenced by William Alanson White, an influential person in American psychiatry. Associated for many years with medical schools and neuropsychiatric hospitals in the Washington-Baltimore area, Sullivan has also tended to reflect the views of Adolph Meyer, who developed a psychiatric point of view of his own. Under the influence of White and Meyer, Sullivan became a chief spokesman for the point of view that has been called "the interpersonal theory of psychiatry." He became president of the William Alanson White Foundation and helped found (and became director of) the Washington School of Psychiatry, which is the training institution of the foundation. Sullivan's point of view was promoted for many years by the *Journal of Psychiatry*, of which he later became editor.

Actually, Sullivan wrote relatively little. He gave numerous lectures, which were recorded and which recently have been published in two books: *The Interpersonal Theory of Psychiatry* (1953) and *The Psychiatric Interview* (1954). Other sources also can be found that detail some of Sullivan's concepts: Mullahy's book, *Oedipus—Myth and Com-*

plex (1948), for example, includes some of the writings of Sullivan. Works by other Sullivanians are available under Mullahy's editorship (1949, 1952).

In many other respects, Sullivan does not belong in the same chapter with such writers as Adler, Rank, Horney, and Fromm in that he was not really trained in orthodox psychoanalysis and was, therefore, not strictly speaking modifying or revising psychoanalytic theory with his own formulations. Sullivan elaborated Adolph Meyer's psychobiological theory, bringing it closer to Freudian thinking. His point of view has some similarities to psychoanalysis and has the strong social-psychological flavor of the other Neo-Freudian writers here treated. This special background of Sullivan along with the unique terminology he developed makes his theoretical views distinct in many ways from those of other theorists. His contributions have been regarded widely as brilliant but often rather difficult to follow.

Sullivan's major theme is that personality has to do with relatively enduring patterns of recurrent interpersonal relations. In other words, personality cannot be isolated from social situations, and all behavior is interpersonal. Whereas Rank, Adler, Fromm, and Horney, and even Jung to some extent, recognized that our relations with one another are very important for personality development, for Sullivan interpersonal relations is the main theme of human personality. This is not to say that Sullivan rejected biological givens, such as heredity and maturational processes, in shaping the individual. Rather he believed that social interaction is the distinctly human quality and that interpersonal experiences so alter and fuse with physiological functioning that the individual can no longer be regarded as merely a biological entity. He is a social organism with socialized ways of even breathing and digesting. In other words, the organization of personality concerns interpersonal events rather than intrapersonal ones. Cognitive functioning, such as perceiving, thinking, and remembering, is interpersonal and must be examined not as an attribute of the organism but as an aspect and result of interpersonal relations.

Preoccupation with the interaction between the organism and its personal environment led Sullivan to play down the idea of organized psychological impulses (e.g., instinct, complex) that can be identified as characteristic of the organism itself. He introduced the field-theoretical term *dynamism* to refer to the stable configurations that emerge from the early experience of the organism with his environment. "Dynamism" refers to the stable pattern of energy transformations of the organism, a pattern of behavior similar to a habit and yet always defined in terms of the organism-environment interaction. Habitual hostility toward someone is seen as a dynamism, as is fear of strangers or a sexual relationship. Any habitual reaction to an individual or to a group, either of feelings or actions, is a dynamism.

Dynamisms can revolve around a variety of basic needs of the organism and can be linked to particular zones of the body, such as the mouth, anus, genitals, and hands, such zones involving apparatuses for receiving stimuli and for performing action. Sullivan distinguished a number of fundamental dynamisms, such as the oral dynamism, which involves the fusion of hunger and oral pleasure as a configuration that becomes linked with language. Thus, instead of talking about "orality" (as do the psychoanalysts) as a psychological need or stage of development, Sullivan spoke of the "oral dynamism."

Many dynamisms can be grouped together under the heading of the "pursuit of security," which is largely culturally determined and involves the need for approval and prestige. The infant directly experiences tension through the process of empathy when the significant adults or parents around him are hostile or disturbed. As he identifies the role of his behavior in these uncomfortable attitudes of the adults, he begins to control his behavior in such a way as to reduce the tensions. As a result of this real or imagined threat to the individual's security (the parents' disturbance), anxiety occurs as an experience of tension. Sullivan considered anxiety to be an important educative influence in living, transferred primarily through the process of empathy to the infant by the mothering one who is expressing anxiety in her looks or tone of voice. The infant learns to avoid activities that increase anxiety, and the avoidance of anxiety becomes the motive behind the formation of new dynamisms concerned with the pursuit of security. Sullivan was interested extremely in the vulnerabilities of persons to anxiety in interpersonal relations, far more than in the symptoms resulting from anxiety.

One of the most important dynamisms developing as a result of anxiety is called the *self dynamism*, on which Sullivan laid enormous stress. In contrast to the widespread concept of an inborn self (found in such writers as Rank and later writers such as Maslow and Rogers), for Sullivan the enduring configuration of the self dynamism arises out of the reflected appraisals of the significant adults who influence the infant child. This configuration tends to become established rather permanently very early in life and becomes a main orientation of the personality throughout his later life.

The self dynamism guards the individual against anxiety and includes certain types of protective measures and supervisory controls over behavior. For example, punishment can be avoided by conforming to the parent's wishes. These means of pursuing security form the self dynamism, which approves certain kinds of behavior as the "good me" and disapproves other kinds of behavior as the "bad me." Because the self dynamism protects the individual from anxiety, it is very important to the individual and it is protected from criticism so it resists alteration by any new experiences or forces. As it increases in complexity and independence, it tends to prevent the person from judging events objectively and it conceals contradictions between the self and reality. Therefore, the self dynamism is valuable in reducing anxiety, but it is also a means of distorting reality and interfering with a person's ability to live constructively with others.

The notion of *personification*, which is an image a person has of himself (e.g., "good me" or "bad me") or another (e.g., "good mother" or "bad mother") is one of Sullivan's important concepts. It is an organized collection of feelings and conceptions, which develops out of experiences with anxiety and with the satisfaction of basic needs. Any satisfying interpersonal relationship leads to a favorable personification of the person who is producing the satisfaction, whereas interactions that produce anxiety lead to a negative personification. Thus, the warm, accepting, nursing mother is conceived as the "good mother," and the anxious mother, or the mother who is anxious at some particular time, is personified at that time as the "bad mother." These personifications represent the phenomenological side of Sullivan's theory.

A variety of personifications of the same individual, most importantly a parent, can be formed and can fuse together to form a complex personification. These personifications usually are not realistic descriptions of persons, but once formed, they persist and influence our attitudes toward others. Thus, a child who personified his father as critical and dictatorial may react in later life to persons in authority (such as teachers or employers) as though they were the personification of his father. Sullivan described this carry-over of early attitudes in interpersonal situations to later life situations (including the therapeutic relationship) as *parataxic distortion* (referring to the parataxic mode of thinking), a concept parallel to Freud's notion of transference. The personifications, with their distortions, are important especially when they derive from experiences with significant adults, in childhood these usually being the parents. When a personification is shared by many persons, it is called a "stereotype" and represents consensually validated ideas that are widely accepted.

Sullivan emphasized cognitive (for Freud, ego) processes in personality to a considerable degree. He classified cognitive experience into three modes: prototaxic, parataxic, and syntaxic. These refer to stages in a developmental sequence from primitive or infantile to more advanced adult forms. *Prototaxic experience* involves a discrete series of momentary states of the organism (like James's "stream of consciousness"), sensations, images, and feelings that flow randomly through the mind having no necessary connections among themselves and having no organized or relational meaning for the person. This prototaxic mode of experience is most commonly found during the early months of life and is the precursor for the later cognitive modes.

The *parataxic mode* of thinking involves the conception of causal relationships between events that occur contiguously in time but are not logically connected. According to Sullivan, a great deal of our thinking remains at the parataxic level; that is, we conceive causal connections between experiences that have nothing to do with one another except that they occur together in time. Thus, if I scratch my head and a useful idea for this textbook also pops up at this same time, I might get the idea that scratching my head has made the idea appear and I may persist thereafter in scratching my head whenever I am trying to think up a good idea. In the parataxic distortions referred to above, the person reacts to someone as though he were the same kind of person as a parent simply because of some similarity that results in their being associated together.

The highest form of thought is *syntaxic*. This involves symbolic activity, particularly of a verbal nature, which is shared by the rest of the culture. Words and numbers are excellent examples of symbols, the meanings of which have been agreed upon by a large number of persons. They permit us to introduce logical order into our experiences and communicate this order to others. This abstract ordering is included in the syntaxic mode, which is the last stage of cognitive development.

Sullivan, like Freud, was impressed with the value of viewing personality in stages of development, although the former took a more social-psychological view of the matter. In addition to the three stages of cognitive development, Sullivan identified six general eras of life: infancy, childhood, the juvenile era, preadolescence, early adolescence, and late adolescence. He discussed the characteristic features and dynamisms of each of these stages typical for western societies. Space permits only an allusion to these here and no further description of this material, because it is not as important as other aspects of Sullivan's system.

One of the important features of Sullivan's psychiatry is his optimism about successful therapeutic handling of severely disturbed patients, such as schizophrenics. Freud was pessimistic about the possibilities of treatment of schizophrenics because they could not establish a transference relationship with the therapist. Sullivan was considered rather successful in his therapeutic work with schizophrenic patients and stimulated considerable interest in the treatment of such persons.

Sullivan's views concerning personality are very much in line with increasing interest in interpersonal relations. More and more emphasis is being given to the hospital setting, for example, as a social community, and there is an increasing regard in modern psychology for social factors in psychological development. Social psychiatry is blossoming as never before, and this provides a friendly climate for Sullivan's ideas.

One of Sullivan's handicaps, with respect to his influence on psychological thought, is his somewhat obscure style of writing and the distinctive set of terms that he introduced for nearly every idea, however similar it was to existing concepts. Actually, compared with most of the theorists considered in the present chapter, his most important works have been published very recently. It is, therefore, difficult to tell now to what extent Sullivan's views, and perhaps the views of some of his students and associates, will influence personality theory in the future.

THE RECENT PSYCHOANALYTIC EMPHASIS ON EGO FUNCTIONS AND THEIR DEVELOPMENT

For the most part, Freud's influence has centered on the importance of instinctual impulses and their manifestations in the life of the individual. The instinctual contents that Freud stressed were sexuality and aggression. There is, however, in Freud's writings, a recognition of the importance of the adaptive and defensive functions of the organism and the development of the cognitive structures (the ego) for adaptation. Later, Anna Freud (1946) gave increasing attention to these adaptive and defensive functions of the ego.

Freud maintained that the ego derived most of its energy from the id (instinctual energy). However, it was implied also that the ego had its own available supply of energy as an inherent quality of the organism and that it could emerge and develop without the power source of the id. More recent psychoanalytic writers have further enlarged upon this autonomous growth of the ego structure.

Psychoanalysts have a growing interest in the organism's adaptation to the external world, which emphasizes rational thought, perception, and memory. These processes are considered partly conflict-free rather than entirely dependent upon the instinctual drives of the organism, as Freud tended to maintain. One of the leaders of this latter movement is Heinz Hartmann (1950), who, in collaboration with other analytic writers, such as Kris and Loewenstein (1947), has elaborated theoretically upon these independent adaptive functions of the ego. Another writer who has had considerable influence in this direction is Rapaport (1951).

Hartmann, Kris, and Loewenstein, in particular, suggested that the ego is an emergent part or structure of the human organism, in contrast with the earlier view that the ego originates only because impulses cannot be discharged without commerce with appropriate objects in the environment. They felt that the innate cognitive functions of the ego can mature independently of the delay or thwarting of discharge of the instincts. Thus, the ego does not depend entirely upon the energy of the id but has its origins in inherited predispositions with its own independent course of development. Rational thought can be interwoven with the instinctual drives in the course of living. But it is important also to consider the independent functions and development of the ego. This point of view of Hartmann and his associates does not repudiate Freud's instinct theory or the importance of the defense mechanisms of the ego. Rather the concept is added of the primary autonomy of the ego apparatuses in organizing important aspects of the personality.

It is interesting that this development in ego psychology is occurring within the legitimate, Freudian, orthodox psychoanalytic formulations at the present time, when, as early as 1911, Adler was formulating a point of view, in opposition to Freudian psychoanalysis, which also tended to emphasize many features of an ego psychology. Such a development expressed in opposition to Freud could not then be accepted, a fact possibly related to personal difficulties between Freud and Adler and the nature of the culture of the times. The development of ego psychology today fills a gap long apparent in Freudian psychoanalytic thinking.

OVERVIEW

It is difficult to synthesize the tremendously diverse contents of the Neo-Freudian viewpoints presented in this chapter. The short summaries of each viewpoint tend to reduce greatly the richness of ideas found in the original writings. The reader is strongly urged to go to these original sources if the material presented here intrigues him and to supplement this account with the excellent discussions of Hall and Lindzey (1957) and Munroe (1955). Table 11, which schematizes the basic concepts of each viewpoint, may aid the reader in keeping the similarities and differences in mind.

One of the difficulties in relating one writer to another is that sometimes a close parallel in ideas can be found in one sphere, with great contrast in another. For example, we can note a considerable similarity between Horney's views and Adler's views, both emphasizing at times the helplessness of the child and the struggle for security (through power in Adler's case and through neurotic safety devices in Horney's). But this close parallel may fade when other comparisons are made.

This chapter can be summarized, to some degree, by saying that all the writers presented have been influenced, in some measure, by Freud and have deviated sharply from Freud in the direction of the deemphasis of biological givens in human development and added emphasis on social factors. Such a statement is less appropriate perhaps for Jung, just as the dependence on Freudian formulations is perhaps least applicable to Sullivan.

By and large, most of the writers consider conflict and the anxiety it engenders as the fundamental basis of psychopathology. Psychologically disturbed individuals are forced to develop primitive, ineffective, or pathological means of reducing the anxiety. The theories differ considerably, however, in what impulses or forces are considered to be sources of conflict and anxiety. For Freud the essential struggle involves instinctual impulses (id), primarily sexual and aggressive in nature, and the external forces of reality (ego), as well as the internalized versions of these (superego). For Jung the pathogenic factors are conflicts between the polar tendencies within the organism, for example, attitudes of extroversion and introversion, the archetypes of the collective unconscious in conflict with the ego, or the personal unconscious in conflict with the ego. Many of these overlap with the Freudian instincts. For Adler the primary conflict is a neurotic striving for power versus social interest, such conflict arising because of the exaggerated inferiority feelings in the child who is pampered or rejected. In the case of Rank the essential struggle is between union, as symbolized by the fetus in the uterus, and individuation or separation. For Fromm, in addition to the Freudian instincts, there is the conflict between freedom and security. Horney stressed basic anxiety in relation to the insecurity, isolation, and helplessness of the individual and the neurotic striving for security by means of various strategies. Sullivan also considered the pursuit of security as a potential force in maladjustment and in reality distortion. This leads to the development of the self dynamism that is the principal stumbling block to favorable changes in the personality.

Some writers, such as Adler and Horney, rejected the fundamental psychosexual and libido theories of Freud, and others, such as Fromm, used them, modified them, and added to them where needed. Thus, Fromm is more of a psychoanalyst in the traditional sense than is Adler.

One might say also, in reviewing the various systematic positions, that there are two basic underlying philosophies in conflict. One philosophy emphasizes the biological nature of man and, in particular, the survival side of human behavior. This assumes that what we learn—those characteristics that become established as stable parts of our personality—we learn because they produce survival and reduce tension. This is a *homeostatic* conception of human behavior, in which all action stems from disequilibrium or tension and is aimed at tension reduction or the return of equilibrium. Such a view is taken by Freud and association-learning theorists, such as Dollard and Miller, and to some lesser extent by Fromm, Horney, and Sullivan.

Table 11

MAIN CONCEPTS OF NEO-FREUDIAN THEORIES

	Personality structures	Instincts or basic urges	Normal operating principles	Developmental stages	Basis of psychopathology	Other distinctive features
Jung	Conscious ego Personal unconscious and complexes Collective unconscious and archetypes	Psychic energy, including Freudian type of urges	Equilibrium mechanisms Progress toward self-actualization that involves differentiation and union of all aspects	Not clearly spelled out except for progression toward self-actualization Late in life spiritual values replace biological urges	Regression of psychic energy toward introverted values Conflict between opposing tendencies	Extrovert-introvert typology
Adler	Creative self Primarily conscious orientation	Striving for superiority Social interest	Fictional finalism Style of life Compensation for inferiority	Not emphasized Attempted actualization of superiority (perfection)	Abnormal feelings of inferiority resulting from pampering or rejection, which can lead to selfish striving for power as compensation	Effects of birth order Method of studying earliest memories

Rank	The will The counterwill	Reinstatement of embryonic state of bliss Fear of separation	Life fear Death fear	Not emphasized Increasing self-assertion and attempted resolution of basic conflict between life and death fears	Failure to assert will and avoidance of separation Inability to resolve conflicting wills	Birth trauma as source of primal anxiety Typology based upon method of resolving conflict Average man, neurotic, and artist
Fromm	Not clearly spelled out Freudian structure retained	Five basic needs: relatedness, rootedness, transcendence, identity, stable frame of reference Basic conflict between relatedness and independent identity	Force for growth if permitted by society	Not emphasized	Failure of society to permit man's growth, and thus a whole society may be sick Inability of a person to find conditions that permit gratification of basic needs	Analysis of ideal society
Horney	Freudian structure retained	Need for security Rejection of importance of libido and instincts	Basic anxiety resulting from isolation and helplessness Vicious circle Safety devices (like ego defenses)	Not emphasized	Helplessness resulting from a number of damaging environmental conditions	Analysis of cultural sources of conflict

MAIN CONCEPTS OF NEO-FREUDIAN THEORIES (CONTINUED)

	Personality structures	Instincts or basic urges	Normal operating principles	Developmental stages	Basis of psychopathology	Other distinctive features
Sullivan	Stated in the form of dynamisms rather than explicit structures	Pursuit of security, largely culturally determined. Deemphasis of biological urges	Dynamisms such as self dynamism. Personifications	Cognitive developmental stages, including the prototaxic, parataxic, and syntaxic	Defective parent-child relationship so as to threaten security and lead to anxiety. Avoidance of anxiety by pathological means. Distortion of reality by self-dynamism in order to reduce anxiety	Therapy with schizophrenia. Interpersonal (social) emphasis
Ego psychology	Same as Freud, except postulation of conflict-free ego spheres and their function	Same as Freud, only deemphasis of vicissitudes of instincts and more focus on adaptive functions of ego	Essentially Freudian	Freudian, with greater focus on ego mechanisms	Freudian	Reaffirmation of rational processes in man

The alternative view is that, inherent in man, are *positive forces* for development; that it is basically (instinctually) satisfying to be aware of reality and to solve problems successfully. This is the point of view, for example, of Rank through his promotion of the need for individuation as an inherent quality in man. Similarly, Lecky argues that man is inherently a problem solver, who would find a total absence of tension intolerable. In progressing toward higher levels, man actually is a tension producer rather than reducer. Similar views are also held by such writers as Maslow and Rogers, who have been greatly influenced by the ideas of Rank. This point of view accords to man the unique quality of cognition and symbolic manipulation and deemphasizes the continuity between man and lower animals.

In the light of what has been said, some of the viewpoints presented here can better be classified with the phenomenological frames of reference, and others (e.g., psychoanalysis) have elements that link them to the association-learning viewpoint (e.g., the tension-reduction argument of Sullivan) or even with the trait-and-type formulations. For example, when Rank describes the three main ways of coping with the union-separation problem, he produces a trichotomous typology: the average man, the neurotic, and the artist. Freud, in discussing the oral, anal, and phallic types, also found it convenient to construct a typological model. Yet the placement of these theories in similar categories on the basis of a few common elements is not always true to the fundamental features they possess. If the reader is confused about specific distinctions, as well as points of similarity between the theoretical viewpoints discussed in the preceding chapters, this is not altogether surprising. There are conceptual threads that can be found throughout many or all of the views presented, just as there are unique qualities in the work of each writer. If, however, the reader has developed some feeling for the kinds of distinctions that can be made between some of the major theoretical frames of reference in personality, these presentations will have had real value.

III

PERSONALITY AND ITS DEVELOPMENT

IN CHAPTER 2 we quoted from a physicist named de Klerk, who pointed out that in order to predict the magnetic behavior of a particular piece of metal it was necessary to know the history of the specimen, because what it is like now is a product of its past. The three chapters in this part take up the historical aspect of personality and adjustment in contrast with contemporaneous descriptions.

In Chapter 8 are discussed the concept of development, formal theories of development, heredity as a factor in development, and the concept of instinct. Chapter 9 deals with the significance of biological factors in personality development (for example, the role of the nervous system), especially with respect to their influence on the processes of motivation, emotion, and cognition. In Chapter 10, social factors in personality are taken up, including the impact of culture and social institutions and the mechanisms by which these institutions produce their effects.

8

Principles of Personality Development

In Chapter 2 the nature of personality was discussed, and the question asked was how personality could be described. Pains were taken to clarify the nature of imaginary or hypothetical constructs, which are the theoretical building blocks of personality, and to characterize personality as an inference from behavior. The next step was to examine some of the main frames of reference for viewing personality as well as specific theoretical systems, which make use of particular sets of constructs.

We are now prepared to examine another important dimension, that of personality development. The description of personality has to do primarily with its contemporaneous characteristics, that is, what it is like at maturity. But the fully developed personality is not created instantaneously with the birth of the individual. It develops and has a history. This development implies the question: how did it get the way it is? Although the processes of development have already been mentioned (as we saw in Chapters 3 through 7, they are crucial when theorizing about personality structure and process), the topic of personality development needs to be more systematically treated. This chapter is concerned with the historical aspects of personality, that is, the forces and conditions that have operated in the past to produce the structures and processes of personality that we seek to describe and understand. In the first half we shall take up the developmental frame of reference and its theories, and in the second half heredity and instinct as forces in development will be discussed.

Let us illustrate this distinction and interdependence between the contemporaneous and historical frames of reference by a clinical example. A young man comes to a psychological clinic with the complaint that he is anxious and depressed. In the course of the first interview, it becomes clear that he is not getting along well with his wife. The couple have been married for two years. For many months now they have been quarreling continuously.

Continued contacts with the young man reveal that he presently feels that his wife is inattentive and hostile to himself and his mother. The mother is widowed and lives in another town about twenty miles from the couple. His wife has become increasingly reluctant to visit the mother on weekends, and this has resulted in the young man making the trip by himself much of the time. He also complains that his wife nags and belittles him in the presence of others.

Interviews with the wife confirm the tense and hostile state of affairs. She feels she has made a mistake in her marriage. She has strong feelings of contempt for the young man and is extremely hostile toward her mother-in-law, who, the wife believes, dominates her son. She considers him a mama's baby.

Examination of the personality structures of the persons involved would considerably elaborate the contemporaneous information we have about the relationship. Personality assessment reveals a dependent and immature young man who still is overly attached to a rather domineering, demanding, and overprotecting mother. The young woman also is revealed as domineering herself and inclined to be contemptuous of passivity and inadequacy. She has hostile and competitive attitudes toward powerful and aggressive men but outwardly manifests respect and submission toward them. She is attracted to passive, inadequate men whom she can dominate, but she has little respect for them and can display her hostility toward them without fear of retaliation.

The interpersonal patterns and personalities have been briefly described above from a contemporaneous viewpoint. These descriptions deal with the present situation, but, as we have said, they have a history. It is possible to trace the historical development and the determining conditions of the present situation. The young man, partly because he was brought up by a dominating and overprotecting widow, has developed passive, dependent attitudes toward women (he learned this reaction through experience with his mother) and has been unable to achieve an independent, adult attitude toward marriage. He still remains tied to his mother emotionally. He married because it was the thing to do and unconsciously sought a woman whose personality was similar to that of his mother. The historical determinants of this present state of affairs might be considered to reside, therefore, in the personality structure of the mother (communicated in her behavior toward her son) and in the earlier events, such as the death of the father, that contributed to the particular mother-son relationship, which was influential in the formation of the personality of the young man. This historical perspective could also be supplemented with knowledge of hereditary and physiological factors in the background of the young man were they known.

Similar historical analyses are possible in the case of the young woman and the mother. A far more complete understanding of the present situation can be derived from knowledge not only of the current personalities and interactions of the principal persons, but also of the factors in the past that determined them. The contemporaneous analysis can be used to anticipate the future possibilities, but an understanding of the present state of affairs is facilitated by the study of the past as well as the present. The fullest scientific investigation of personality characteristics requires both contemporaneous and historical data.

Let us now turn our attention to two different aspects of the historical approaches to personality. One emphasizes formal theories of the developmental process, and the other focuses on the empirical conditions (social or genetic and physiological) or determinants of development.

EMPHASIS ON FORMAL DEVELOPMENTAL THEORY VERSUS EMPIRICAL DETERMINANTS OF DEVELOPMENT

The development of the individual involves change. Over the life span of a person, marked changes in the personality structure occur. To take a specific instance, noted in Chapter 2, the degree of inhibition or control of impulses (this is one of the most common hypothetical constructs used in personality theory) progressively increases through infancy and early childhood until a person has considerable command over himself and the direction of his behavior. One can ask about the empirical conditions that influence the acquisition and development of structures of control (ego structures), or one can concentrate on the description and sequences of change of these same structures. One enterprise complements the other.

The *formal developmental theory* approach is concerned mainly with the description of psychological structures and the progressive and lawful changes they undergo in the course of human development. These changes are assumed to occur in a systematic rather than a haphazard way and can be classified in regular stages. Although there are individual differences in the rates and patterns of change in structure, all living organisms appear to pass through certain stages of development. For the formal developmental theorist, these progressions are manipulations of universal biological laws. It is as though the structures follow a universal pattern of creation and development within and between species, the principles of which can be formulated. The developmental principles can be formulated for living organisms in general, or for human beings in particular. They can deal with a process, like inhibition, the emergence and development of perceptual, conceptual, or motor processes, or the development of intelligence or modes of adaptation.

The formal or descriptive developmental approach is not characterized by the search for the causes or conditions of development, but it seeks to describe the processes and principles underlying it. It is postulated, for example, that degree of impulse control increases from infancy to adulthood or that perception is global or diffuse in the young child and progressively becomes differentiated until stimulus forms can be precisely articulated. Such a principle specifies that the perceptual processes normally follow a unidirectional development (from global to differentiated) and that this is a principle of development for all living organisms. In this way, individual specimens can be differentiated by the degree of development along this dimension, and the nature of their perceptual behavior can be related to the level of development that characterizes their perceptual apparatus.

But such formal developmental principles in themselves cannot state what it is that produces such progressive change or deviations from it. To what extent are the dispositions to change or develop in certain ways inherited and carried by the physical constitution of the organism, and to what extent are they the result of experiences that a person can share with other members of the species or have uniquely as his own?

These questions are dealt with by developmental psychologists, who attempt to study the actual empirical conditions that bring about the particular development of psychological structure of the individual or species or alter the form of this development. For example, stern or demanding parents can accelerate the development of inhibitory tendencies, and permissive parents can retard their growth. Similarly, restriction of the range of stimulation of the child can retard or alter the growth of intellectual processes. The use and forms of language in social communication can be facilitated or retarded by the nature of the social contacts available to the growing child. Moreover, genetic or constitutional factors will also play a role in determining the development of psychological structures. Genetic influences will be covered in the second half of the present chapter, but the work on other biological and social factors in development will be surveyed in two separate chapters (Chapters 9 and 10).

Formal theories of development have been less well known and influential in this country. (American developmental psychologists generally have stressed the conditions of development, whereas European workers have leaned toward the more descriptive, formal theoretical emphasis.) Both frames of reference have a great deal to contribute to the understanding of personality and its development. Let us now consider the nature of such developmental points of view.

FORMAL DEVELOPMENTAL THEORY

The formal or descriptive developmental frame of reference can be applied to any biological specimen or tissue and has had much application in such fields as embryology, neurophysiology, and comparative anatomy. It represents a way of systematizing certain observations about organisms and their tissue systems in terms of general principles of growth. One can trace, as Darwin (1859) did, the evolution of biological forms from the most primitive organisms to the most advanced. One observes that, along with changes in the anatomical structure from lower to higher forms of animal, there are concomitant changes in the kinds of functions of which these animals are capable. The varieties of adaptive behavior, for example, increase systematically with the evolution of more advanced types of organisms. Another instance of a developmental sequence is the embryological history of the mammalian fetus, which progresses in certain systematic ways from the one-celled fertilized egg through gradual multiplication and differentiation of cells into the complex organism that appears at birth.

The formal developmental approach rests on the assumption that, wherever there is life, there is growth or development; that is, the formation of structures always occurs in systematic orderly sequence. The behavior of all organisms is examined in terms of similar developmental principles. Ontogenetic development, the development of the individual specimen, is usually considered analogous to phylogenetic development, that is, the progression from primitive forms of life to more complex, advanced forms.

One common, regulative principle of development encompasses the systematic changes in all aspects of living, whether they deal with embryological patterns of tissue formation and growth or the progression of mental activity. The principle states that, wherever development occurs, it proceeds from a condition of relative globality and undifferentiation to a state of greater articulation and organization. Thus, in embryology, the fetus in the early stages of development reacts to stimulation in a diffuse way, the entire fetus responding in a mass reaction. As Hooker (1943) has shown, development in the human fetus proceeds so that stimulation results in a progressively differentiated reaction, later stages of development being characterized by a localized response in the immediate area of stimulation in contrast with the mass, global, diffuse response at earlier stages.

Concomitant with these behavioral changes is the progressive differentiation in the cells as the organism develops. In the beginning of embryological development, there is one cell, which progressively differentiates into specialized tissues so, at birth, the organism has a large number of highly specialized tissue systems including bone and connective tissue, muscle tissue, and nervous tissue. Thus, the analogy that exists between all forms of growth, psychological as well as physiological, is the progressive differentiation of parts from an initial global, undifferentiated state to increasing specialization of function, ultimately reaching a high degree of integration or organization of the parts at later stages. Thus stages of development can refer to the degree of differentiation and integration of the biological specimen we are studying.

Let us consider an example of this principle of development as it is applied to the growing child. The young child is said to have little appreciation of objects external to himself such as furniture, utensils, and persons as distinct from each other and separated from himself. Each person is not seen as a separate entity, different and unique. For example, the mother is just another person, a source of stimulation no different from any other person or object with whom the child has contact. There is only a gradual recognition of persons as distinct. In time, the child comes to articulate the mother and father and other persons as different and separate parts of the external world. Eventually, this differentiation becomes so complex that the child comes to recognize not only the physical characteristics that differentiate the mother from others, but also behavioral or psychological characteristics that are unique to the mother such as the fact that she feeds the child, toilets him, and is temperamentally a particular kind of person.

In this illustration, it should be clear that we are speaking about a theoretical matter (in reference to the progression of perceptual processes from global to differentiated) rather than an empirically observable fact. The characteristic imputed to the perceptual process is an inference, a hypothetical construct such as was discussed in Chapter 2. We cannot ask the preverbal child to tell us how he perceives the world any more than we can ask a dog or monkey about his experience. We can, however, observe the physical stimulus conditions to which the child is exposed, and we can record the varieties of behavior of the child toward the objects to which he is exposed. From these stimuli and response patterns, inferences about the intervening process, such as perception, can be made. Later on when the child becomes able to communicate with verbal language, we can add to these behavioral observations his statements (introspections, as in phenomenological approaches to personality) about his experience with the stimulus objects.

The theoretical principle that the child does not readily articulate objects as separate entities in the early stages of development can be tested. As in the case of any construct, we examine the behavior of the child toward external objects to see whether it is consistent with the theoretical formulation. For example, Piaget (1932) illustrated the fusion of self and object in the child's spatial organization by noting that children perceive the moon as moving with them as they walk.

Wapner and Werner (1957) have observed experimentally such primitive tendencies in children and schizophrenic patients. For example, when normal adults are placed in a completely darkened room, tilted in a chair to the right or left, and asked to judge when a luminescent rod is absolutely vertical, such subjects tend to displace the rod from the plumb line in a direction opposite to body tilt. Young children and schizophrenics, on the other hand, displace the rod in the same direction as the body tilt. In other words, if they are tilted to the right, the latter groups place the rod to the right of vertical on the basis of kinesthetic sensations produced by the body tilt. It is as if they judge objects in space in terms of bodily cues rather than on the basis of visually communicated external relationships. The location of the objects tends to be fused with the child's own body orientation.

Not only are these observations (judgment of the vertical and the child's perception of the moon as following him) consistent with the notion of lack of articulation of objects as separate from the self, but many other observations of a similar sort have been collected by Werner (1948) and Piaget (1952) in their studies of the development of the perceptual process. For example, anyone who has had much contact with young children may have noted the failure of identification of right and left in someone facing them. The child who can raise his right hand on command may be unable to judge correctly the right hand (as opposed to left) in the person facing him. This requires that he imagine himself turned about in space in the same attitude as the other person. But because his apprehension of space is egocentric, or based upon his own body orientation to the world, he may confuse (at an early stage of development) the other person's left and right side. Only later on in development can he perceptually align things in space independently of his own body position.

Development and Time

Formal development always occurs as a function of time. Growth and the progressive changes from diffuse global perceptions to articulated and ultimately integrated perceptions, for example, take place over a period of time. What is especially noteworthy, however, is that time itself is not important; that is, it does not produce change or development. Rather, what happens in time is important. The processes of development take time, but time can pass without certain kinds of developments taking place. It is only incidental that development is examined in the dimension of time. The developmental approach to mental processes is concerned with what kinds of structural changes systematically occur between conception and maturity.

If one is interested not merely in the descriptive aspects of development but also in its determinants, one can look at the time aspect of development in a somewhat different way. Rate can be used to assess the influence of various factors that hamper or facilitate development. For example, one might examine how rapidly perception shifts from the global to the differentiated stage under two conditions: one in which the child is encouraged to adapt independently at an early age (this might facilitate the distinction of external objects in order to adapt), and the other in which he remains overprotected and dependent for a long time. If there are marked effects on the rates at which the two groups moved ahead to later stages of perceptual development, then we would know that the variable studied has an important influence on the development of the perceptual process. In the same way, the social antecedents of ego control could be studied, for instance, in families that are strict and demanding and in those that are permissive. Differences in the rates of development of various processes could provide a good index of the influence of environmental factors.

Achievement and Process in Development

When we considered the nature of personality, it was pointed out that it was possible to describe only a person's consistent actions (a surface approach to personality) in contrast with postulating structures that underlie behavior (substance approach). We can examine development from the same point of view; that is, we can consider obvious changes in behavior patterns as they occur in a developmental sequence, or we can attempt to relate these changes (at the behavioral level) to what we believe is going on at an underlying, structural level.

An excellent example of a systematic surface approach to development is the work of Gesell and his colleagues (1928, 1947). Gesell worked with infants from birth onward, observing the acquisition of certain behavior patterns such as locomotion, prehension (grasping), posture, speech, and motor coordination. Over a period of many years and on the basis of the observations of large numbers of infants and children, this work has led to the establishment of norms of development. These can be used in the diagnosis of organic defects causing mental deficiency or retardation in growth. As a result of this valuable work, we know approximately at what age the average child will crawl, stand, and ultimately walk with an erect posture (see Figure 12). We can chart the development of a large number of skills and the variation in this development. We know the forms a child's speech first takes and the subsequent stages in speech patterns with increasing maturation.

Although the above type of information is of great importance, it is limited in that it establishes neither the material causes of the systematic developmental changes nor the theoretical principles underlying this growth. The underlying structures and processes in the acquisition of speech or their determinants, for example, are not explored in the Gesell type of study as they are in the more formal theories of development. The mere establishment of norms for the development of behavior patterns tends to deal with superficial forms of behavior. It tends to emphasize achievements rather than the processes underlying these achievements.

This distinction between achievement and process is an important one and deserves to be enlarged upon briefly. Achievement refers to the end product of the forces underlying behavior, such as the solution of a problem or the correct identification of the meaning of a word. The main

Figure 12. The motor sequence in human development. (*From Shirley, 1933.*)

209

reason why an analysis of achievements is superficial is that such achievements can come about by means of various processes. Our understanding of the event is unnecessarily limited when we consider only the achievement end product and ignore the manner in which the end product has come about.

For example, let us consider two persons who obtain the same score on a ten-item test of ability. It is altogether possible that these same scores, which reflect the over-all achievement of the subjects on the test, were achieved by totally different processes. For example, the pattern of correct and incorrect answers can differ. One of the subjects may have answered correctly items 2, 4, 6, 8, and 10, whereas the other scored correctly on items 1, 3, 5, 7, and 9. Both have exactly the same score, 5, but they differ in certain ways that can be very important. One is skillful in some areas, and the second excels in others. The use of the simple score of achievement tends to obscure the potentially important patterning of answers, which can reflect different types of intellectual processes.

Another example of the distinction between achievement and process (just as between superficial behavior and underlying sources of the behavior) comes from the observation of children. A child of four was oriented strongly toward time because he would awaken at six o'clock in the morning and had to wait until seven-thirty, when his mother arose to organize the household. He became acutely concerned with knowing at what time on the clock things around him would get into gear. Before long, he had learned to tell time. The process by which this was done, however, was rather primitive and concrete; he had simply learned, over a long period, each combination of hand positions on the clock. He did not know anything about time in minutes or that the numbers were additive and cumulated up to sixty. He simply knew every major combination of hand positions; he had learned by rote that, when the large hand was on the three and the small hand was on the seven, this arrangement was called seven-fifteen. This meant to him only that in a rather short while the spatial position called seven-thirty would occur and mother would get up. Each morning at exactly the right time he arrived at his mother's bedside and announced, "Time to get up, Mommy, it's seven-thirty."

Two and one-half years later, this young child, now well over six years of age, started first grade, where, ultimately, he learned about numbers. In turn, the class went into the matter of telling time. Suddenly, and for several weeks running, the little boy who at four could tell time precisely (at least with respect to the five-minute intervals) could no longer perform this task. Only after several weeks did the skill return. However, now the process by which the performance occurred was quite different. He understood the relations between the numbers, for example, that there were sixty minutes in an hour and that ten past seven is five minutes later than five past seven.

What is especially interesting in this illustration is that both at the age of four and at the age of nearly seven, by superficial achievement-oriented standards, this child could tell time equally well. But what is concealed by noting only that the child could tell time at four (about which the child's parents were extremely proud) is the primitive, concrete nature of the process by which the early achievement occurred. It was only many years later that the concept of numbers became basic to the time-telling task and the concrete, immature process dropped out, to be replaced by one at a more abstract and higher level. In both instances, the answers to the question: What time is it? were the same, but the processes determining the performance were much different. We cannot understand any behavioral event unless we attempt to discover the principles that underlie what is observed. In the same way, we do not understand personality merely by describing behavior in a variety of circumstances. It is desirable to speculate about the underlying structures and processes that make the superficially mystifying patterns of behavior meaningful, as long as these speculations are subject to confirmation or refutation.

Most formal theories of development speculate about underlying structures or processes rather than surface achievements. In Chapter 2, we spoke of motivational patterns and regulative processes as characteristic constructs, which psychologists have used in describing personality structure. Such structures also become the focus of developmental analysis. As we shall see directly, this analysis can involve both forward and backward movement, that is, progression and regression.

Progression and Regression

As we examine systematic changes in structure, we can identify two kinds of change: progressive, developmental changes and regressive changes. Ideal or normal development proceeds in the direction of the gradual formation and elaboration of stable structures, which increase in complexity and organization. However, the formation of structures, or movement from primitive to advanced levels, need not take place in the same way in different persons. Deviations can occur. A person can fail to proceed from one level of development to another. Persons can differ in the rates or extent of development of various attributes, thus producing a different organization of personality.

Of special importance for pathology is the additional notion that an individual who has advanced to a mature level of development can, under certain circumstances (for example, stress), regress to a more primitive level. The developmental process need not be a one-way street. Development can proceed forward and then show regression or backward movement. In such a case there is a dissolution of the structures that have been formed or a reduction in the degree of organization of these structures. Thus, as we shall see more clearly in later chapters, neurosis and psychosis are conceived from the developmental point of view as instances of regression of the personality. Pathology represents the organism moving backward again along the developmental road. Such a developmentally oriented concept of psychopathology was employed by Freud (regression) as we learned in Chapter 6.

By postulating both progressive and regressive changes, the developmental theorist is able to account for pathology. By postulating different rates of development or the attainment of different levels for the various hypothetical personality structures, he is able to account for individuality. Because a particular level of development of a structure implies a specific type of adaptive process, consistency of the personality implies the relative stability of these levels when they have been reached. However, a certain degree of mobility is postulated so the individual is able to function sometimes at a higher level, at other times at a lower level of development. Thus, within normal persons, occasions arise where a person cannot adapt at the highest level to which he has developed, and momentary regressions can take place to permit him to function at a lower level.

Having discussed some characteristics of a developmental or historical approach to personality, emphasizing the general nature of formal theories of development, we now are prepared to take a brief but more systematic look at such theoretical viewpoints.

SOME FORMAL THEORIES OF DEVELOPMENT

Formal developmental theories describe (and ultimately account for) how the individual comes to terms with his environment, that is, the structures with which he adapts and the stages through which these structures emerge and develop. There are certain obvious changes in the adjustment patterns of a person as he matures from infancy to adulthood. These changes typify human development. One can observe, for example, that the child tends to lose some of his impulsiveness as he matures and becomes capable of delaying his actions in response to social and physical pressures and in the interest of future considerations. He develops the capacity to manipulate his environment in a variety of ways. His interests and preoccupations change. He becomes less dependent upon his parents or other significant adults, both emotionally and physically. He becomes capable of reflective thought, in which he can abstractly manipulate objects and events in the world without their actually being present. He develops a concept of who he is and what are his relationships with others, becoming skillful at anticipating how others will react to his attitudes and behavior. He acquires certain stable social-role patterns.

Observations of these systematic changes have led to a number of theoretical approaches to development, which emphasize different aspects of the relationship between the individual and his society. Perhaps the best known of these developmental theorists is Freud, one of whose major contributions to psychological thought was the emphasis placed upon childhood development as a central factor in the formation of the adult personality.

The Freudian theory of psychosexual development already has been described, in Chapter 6, and deals with three main periods: the oral, anal, and genital. These periods represent, for Freud, universal stages of the discharge of sexual energy through which the child progresses. Concomitant with the gradual emergence of these forms of sexual discharge is the progression from the pleasure principle and primary process (as the governing principles of behavior and experience) to the reality principle and secondary processes. The latter are associated with the formation of the ego and superego structures. This psychoanalytic view of development contains all the essential elements of formal theories of development. The basic theoretical constructs are the three psychosexual stages, the primary and secondary process, the id with its instincts, and the ego and superego. These various structures and processes are bound together in the theory by the pleasure and reality principles and by postulating a particular organization of the elements of the personality, which determines their interrelations, that is, how they work together.

Other formal developmental theories are important for the conception of personality but are more limited or less ambitious than the Freudian system in that they are oriented entirely to cognitive processes (thinking, judgment, and perception) and exclude motivational and affective aspects. Two important instances of these are the works of Piaget (1952) and Werner (1948). These points of view will be developed in the remainder of the chapter.

Piaget's Theory of Cognitive Development

Unlike Freud, Piaget was concerned not so much with motivation but rather with the development of the cognitive structures and processes that underlie adaptive behavior. These structures are somewhat analogous to the Freudian ego in that they have to do with knowing and manipulating the self and the world. Piaget assumed that these structures exist in primitive form at conception and progressively develop during the life of the person in certain systematic ways. Whereas for Freud the energy for the development of the ego came from the libido (or sexual drives), Piaget assumed that the cognitive structures themselves contained all the necessary energy for their emergence and development without requiring some separate motivating force.

Piaget's primary principle of adaptation is that behavior is a life process that tends to maintain a state of equilibrium between the person and the environment. This equilibrium is constantly being disturbed by changes in the environment, thus creating a need to reestablish a state of adaptation or balance.

The organism establishes and reestablishes this equilibrium between the external object and itself by means of the processes of assimilation and accommodation. *Assimilation* involves altering or manipulating objects to satisfy the needs of the person, and *accommodation* represents changes in the organism in response to the requirements of objects. Thus, when a toy is placed a certain distance from a child, he accommodates to its spatial location, size, and shape by adjusting the motor movements of his hands or body in such a way that he can reach and grasp it. This is accommodation. On the other hand, the use of the doll for chewing represents the assimilation of this object to the need state of the individual, which calls for oral activity. (See the discussion of accommodation and assimilation in Chapter 1.)

Piaget made continuous observations of children at varying ages. Some of his most extensive observations were made on his own children. He was concerned with how a child conceives the objects in his environment. He wondered how the child acquires the notion that a lollipop is for licking, that pieces of paper can tear, that some objects are combustible and others not, or that some objects, like a pillow, can be compressed and others, like a stone, cannot. He noted that if an object like a watch within the sight of the child is placed behind a cushion of a couch or in the pocket, the child does not, in the early period of his life, have a concept of the watch as a thing independent of its concrete location and its visual appearance. Thus, the child has no idea to look for the watch behind the cushion or in the pocket, for the disappearance of the watch is equivalent to its nonexistence. Piaget observed the stages of development by which objects took on the quality of things independent of the spatial position in which they were localized, so eventually the child could conceive that, even though the watch disappeared from sight, it still existed as the same object in another location.

Piaget also was concerned with the development of the child's concept of causality. He theorized about the emergence of thought and the development of the ability in the child to count and ultimately to manipulate numbers in an abstract way. From observations of children and inferences about their behavior, Piaget developed a theory of intelligence emphasizing the development of structures that permitted an individual to maintain the state of equilibrium between himself and his environment.

For Piaget, the development of intelligence always moved in the direction of increasing the spatial and temporal distances between the person and the objects of his environment. For example, in the early stages of development, the object can be apprehended only in a sensory-motor way, that is, by seeing or touching or in some way manipulating the concrete object through the sensory and motor mechanisms. Eventually, these objects can become psychologically represented (mentally) in the absence of the object itself. Thus, when you read the word "telephone" as an adult, you can psychologically represent the concept "telephone" and manipulate it even though you have no immediate physical contact with it. You can reproduce mentally the entire sequence of operations by which a telephone call is made, including lifting the receiver, dialing the number, and talking into the mouthpiece as you listen through the earphone. An entire conversation can thus be imagined. All this can be done without any immediate contact with the telephone because the capacity has been developed to manipulate objects of the physical and social world in all their ramifications even though they are spatially and temporally quite distant.

The adult organism can manipulate the world symbolically or representationally, but the child must apprehend the world in terms of his sensory-motor apparatus. In early life, a knowledge of the objects of the environment is acquired through sensory-motor manipulation, ultimately leading in later years to the ability to represent these objects, their function, and their characteristics without such sensory-motor contact. In this way, adaptation becomes far more effective because it is no longer dependent upon the concrete, here-and-now contact with objects.

Piaget's constructs, therefore, include types of intellectual operations (for example, sensory-motor and conceptual) cast in the context of developmental stages and studied indirectly by observation of the way in which children at various ages solve various intellectual problems. One of his great gifts was the ingenuity with which he was able to construct tasks for his subjects that permitted the empirical study of the child's processes of adaptation.

Freud and Piaget are two of the most important developmental thinkers in psychology, although there are others, such as Lewin (1935), who have made contributions to developmental psychology. Another important contribution has been made by Werner (1948), who has written extensively about cognitive development. The fundamental premise of Werner is that all life involves growth that can be seen as a progression from a global diffuse state to increasing differentiation and ultimately to the complex integration of the various biological and psychological structures at the higher levels of development.

Werner's Application of Cognitive Development to Psychopathology

Werner has been active particularly in showing the relationships between formal developmental theory and psychopathology. For him, psychopathology represents a *dedifferentiation* of structure (similar to the concept "regression") to more primitive or earlier stages of development. Werner's colleagues and students have shown the parallel between the formal modes of thought found in mentally ill patients and the modes of thought that characterize children at various stages of development.

For example, it has been shown that the perceptual behavior of the most deteriorated schizophrenic patients is analogous in form to the perceptual behavior of children around three or four years of age (Hemmendinger, 1951; Friedman, 1954; Siegel, 1950; Peña, 1953; Freed, 1952; and Phillips & Framo, 1954). Similarly, neurotic patients show perceptual processes like those characteristic of children just prior to adolescence; not so regressed as the more seriously disturbed psychotic patients and yet less mature than those found in the normal adult (Frank, 1951).

In Figure 13 some results of this developmentally oriented research into psychopathology are schematized. A series of ink blots, making up the Rorschach test, were presented to normal adults, children of varying ages, and patients suffering either from paranoid conditions or from hebephrenic or catatonic schizophrenic disorders. The latter two groups represent, theoretically, the most seriously regressed psychotic mental pa-

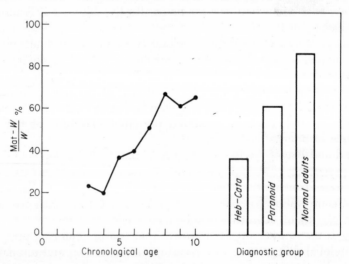

Figure 13. Per cent of developmentally high-level responses in normal adults, children, and diagnostic groups. (*From Werner, 1954.*)

tients. The figure shows the per cent of responses that are considered developmentally the highest level (perceptions of the entire ink blots, made up of part details that are integrated into some organized picture) given by the various groups. As the chronological age of the children goes up, so does the incidence of developmentally high responses. The hebephrenic-catatonic group is most like very young children in the per cent of such responses, with the paranoids next, followed by the normal adults. The developmental progression in perception is clearly evidenced by the changes in quality of responses with age, and the regression is evidenced in the lower (childlike) quality of percepts among the very seriously disturbed psychotic patients.

In other studies, it has been demonstrated that patients who verbally threaten assault or suicide (but never actually attempt it) exhibit characteristics of perception that are higher developmentally than those found in patients who have actually given motor expression to their assaultive or suicidal impulses (Kruger, 1954; Misch, 1954). In other words, one of the characteristics of development is the gradual interposition of reality-oriented fantasy and thought in the place of action; the mature person's behavior is less impulsive and more governed by rational processes. It also has been shown that disturbed children who are hypoactive, that is, who show reduced motor activity (Hurwitz, 1954) are also developmentally higher (in terms of the perceptual process) than hyperactive children (those displaying excessive motor activity). Again, the point can be made that, in the course of normal growth, motor expression of impulses tends to be replaced by ideation and thought.

Although Werner has written most extensively about general principles of development, his application of this frame of reference to psychopathology presupposes that persons can differ with respect to their actual course of development. They can differ in two essential ways. On the one hand, they can achieve different *levels of development,* thus varying in terms of the level of cognitive processes that characterize their adaptations to the world. The neurotic and the psychotic, either because of failure of development or because of dedifferentiation (regression), show perceptual functioning similar in form to that of children. Moreover, Phillips (1954) has shown that persons who have histories of social inadequacies show a lower developmental level in their perceptual functioning than do more successful persons.

In addition to variation in terms of level of development, persons can differ as to the *stability of the levels* of developmental functioning that characterize them. In other words, some persons are more susceptible to dedifferentiation or regression than others. Under stress or unfavorable conditions such persons will more readily resort to lower levels of functioning. For these persons, there is less stability in their developmental level of functioning.

What are the hypothetical constructions of theorists like Werner and Piaget, who are preoccupied with the structures and processes (and their development) that underlie adaptive behavior? For Werner, certain forms of perception and thought are essential parts of the psychological apparatus of the person, and these forms are to be described and their developmental stages mapped. Terms like "diffuse" and "articulate," "rigid-flexible," "labile-stable," "syncretic-discrete," and "concrete-abstract" are used to characterize cognitive processes at various levels of development, just as Piaget uses "sensory-motor," "preconceptual," "intuitive," "concrete," and "formal" to describe the nature of cognitive processes at different developmental stages. These attempts to conceptualize man's formal modes of thought are theories of personality in the same sense as the theories of Freud and the Neo-Freudians. They differ from the psychoanalytic theories with respect to the specific nature of the constructs, and their (i.e., Werner's and Piaget's) emphasis on the cognitive-adaptive properties of man rather than on the motivational and emotional. As in Freudian theory, man is viewed in terms of sequences of development, with each description embedded in a continuously changing pattern of growth, the laws of which are inherent in the biological nature of man and lower organisms.

In the formal developmental mode of thinking, it is clear that the question is not usually asked: What are the conditions that influence the progressive and regressive changes characteristic of development? The assumption is sometimes made that such change is an inherent, biological characteristic of life.

But postulating an analogy, for example, between the modes of adaptation and thought of the psychotic patient and those of the child (with the assumption that a reverse process of dedifferentiation or regression accounts for the similarity) leaves open the question of what produces the schizophrenic regression. Such an analogy is helpful in understanding the processes underlying psychopathology as well as normal development, but it leaves unanswered the question of what conditions are necessary to produce the pathology. In a more general sense, formal developmental theories do not tell us the necessary and sufficient conditions for development. To complete our understanding of how personality structure develops, we will have to consider the biological and social determinants. As a first step in this direction let us now take up hereditary factors in development by examining the blossoming field of behavior genetics.*

---

* Some of the present material has been taken from a more inclusive historical review in an unpublished manuscript by McClearn.

BEHAVIOR GENETICS

The idea of biological inheritance may have existed many thousands of years before Christ, because the dog is known to have been domesticated and probably bred that early in human history. It is certain that the Greeks concerned themselves with breeding animals. Both Plato and Aristotle expressed the conviction that man's behavior reflected, at least in part, a hereditary process. Little development in behavior genetics beyond that found in ancient times took place until the middle of the nineteenth century, although some philosophical and scientific activity, laying the groundwork, began to take place several centuries earlier. For all intents and purposes, the field of modern behavior genetics has its clearest origins in the work of Charles Darwin and Francis Galton.

Modern History

Because children often resemble their parents physically and often even in gesture, manner, temperament, and attitude, mankind was easily convinced that these characteristics are somehow transmitted from parent to child. In the seventeenth century, Spinoza's writings laid an early foundation for the notion of the existence of *innate ideas,* that is, that a child was born with certain types of mental contents. John Locke, in this same period, vigorously opposed this point of view, suggesting that the mind began as a *tabula rasa,* a blank tablet, which gains knowledge through the use of the senses. The inheritance of mental characteristics was again later emphasized vigorously in the work of Darwin and Galton in the nineteenth century.

It is almost a universal temptation among parents to ascribe the desirable characteristics in their children to inheritance from themselves. When it comes to undesirable traits, fathers blame their wives and their wives' families and mothers blame their husbands and their husbands' families. It is widely believed by lay persons even today that attitudes, ways of behaving, and even ideas are inherited directly from parents. Few if any scientists in the modern era deny the fact of inheritance, but the question of what characteristics are inherited and how inheritance takes place continues to be the subject of much speculation and research.

Our task is to clarify the issues of inheritance as they relate to behavior. We are certain that there are strong hereditary components underlying man's behavior, even though these components are complex and interact both with local biological conditions during development and with the nature of man's environmental experience from the earliest time of life. It is not our purpose to inspect the biological mechanism of heredity. This topic is a large and complex one, and if we try to cover it all, we would necessarily have to give it the most superficial and inadequate treatment. The reader is urged to seek a more detailed source of information on the principles of inheritance and evolution (Glass, 1934, 1935; Boyd, 1950). Let us consider some of the highlights in the development of this field from the monumental work of Darwin to the present time.

Two scientific figures can be regarded as having the greatest influence in the nineteenth century on the over-all biological science of genetics and the subfield of behavior genetics. One is Charles Darwin; the other, Francis Galton. Charles Darwin published *The Origin of Species* in 1859, setting forth a theory that the various types of organisms in the world evolved from simpler forms as a consequence of the struggle for life. As a result of this struggle, any variation in biological form, however slight and whatever the cause, will tend to the preservation of that individual if this new quality is in any degree profitable in its adaptive struggle to survive. This was the principle of *natural selection*, and for Darwin it included behavioral characteristics as much as physical characteristics. In a later book, Darwin (1873) compared the mental powers and moral sense of animals and man, attempting to demonstrate that the difference between the mind of man and animals is one of degree, not kind. This issue, which went to the heart of certain traditional religious formulations, led to a sustained and bitter controversy over Darwin's great work. Nonetheless, the theory and the evidence on which it rests have greatly influenced the biological and social sciences in the last century. Darwin wrote (1873, vol. I, pp. 106–107):

So, in regard to mental qualities, their transmission is manifest in our dogs, horses, and other domestic animals. Besides special tastes and habits, general intelligence, courage, bad and good temper, etc., are certainly transmitted. With man, we see similar facts in almost every family; and we now know through the admirable labors of Mr. Galton that genius, which implies a wonderfully complex combination of high faculties, tends to be inherited; and, on the other hand, it is too certain that insanity and deteriorated mental powers likewise run in the same families.

The Mr. Galton referred to in Darwin's statement was Francis Galton, Darwin's half cousin, a man whose influence on many generations of psychologists has been great and whose contributions range from his most important writings, dealing with hereditary genius (1869), to statistical methods, the psychology of intelligence, word associations, and other diverse areas of investigation.

Greatly influenced by Darwin's *The Origin of Species,* Galton subsequently turned to what was to become his central interest, the *inheritance of mental characteristics.* He published a number of major research treatises, presenting evidence for the inheritance of intelligence. He utilized mainly the argument that among the relatives of persons endowed with high mental ability there is to be found a much greater number of extremely able persons than might be expected by chance and that the closer the family relationship, the higher the incidence of such superior persons. Although Galton recognized the objection to this work that relatives of eminent persons would share educational, social, and economic advantages, which are environmental in character, he argued against this interpretation and attempted to provide some evidence, though not conclusive, to refute it. As an indication of his point of view, he wrote (1883, A, p. 1):

I propose to show in this book that a man's natural abilities are derived by inheritance, under exactly the same limitations as are the form and physical features of the whole organic world. Consequently, as it is easy, notwithstanding those limitations, to obtain by careful selection a permanent breed of dogs or horses gifted with peculiar powers of running, or of doing anything else, so it would be quite practicable to produce a highly gifted race of men by judicious marriages during several consecutive generations.

Thus, Galton is the founder of *eugenics*, and further to establish the significance of the hereditary factors in behavior, Galton proposed the co-twin control method of studying the effectiveness of nature (inheritance) and nurture (environment) (1883).

Galton's writings, putting forth a hereditary orientation to problems of intelligence and behavior, appeared at a time when scientists were receptive to such notions, although the specific mechanism of heredity had not yet been explored and the important work of Mendel had not yet been published. However, the climate was clearly ready for a strong genetic orientation, and Galton's work was influential in further pressing the cause of behavior genetics. It is clear, however, that the need was great for a workable theory concerning the hereditary mechanism. Mendel's work filled this gap in knowledge by organizing systematic observations about the inheritance of simple characteristics on pea plants in the garden of a monastery at Brunn, Moravia.

Out of this work of Mendel's came a rapid development of genetics, although the original publication remained mostly overlooked for thirty-four years, until 1900, when it was discovered and its significance recognized. Thus, at the turn of the century, such notions as the gene, dominance and recessiveness, hybrid, and genotype and phenotype had become established. During the next several decades anatomical developments in the study of chromosomes and genes occurred, work on mutation and irradiation producing changes in the genes took place, and increasing sophistication had developed about the complex interplay of genetic structures and the biochemistry of their action.

Since the turn of the century, a great deal of behavior-genetics research has been undertaken with human beings. These studies have employed family biographies, twins of various types, foster children, and correlation of traits among relatives. These approaches can be regarded as methods for dealing with the nature-nurture question, that is, the issue of the relative contribution of heredity and environment in the production of behavior characteristics. Let us consider some of these methods and some of the more significant research activity pertaining to them.

The Methods and Findings of Behavior Genetics

To early workers in this field one of the obvious ways to identify hereditary factors was to show that certain characteristics tend to run in families. There have been many *family biographies,* in which the offspring have been studied for many generations. Galton (1883) had examined a number of different families in order to find evidence for the inheritance of the qualities that make for eminence, but he had not systematically and intensively examined a single family and its progeny.

One of the early single-family studies was made by Dugdale (1877), based upon the "Jukes" family and their descendants, who proceeded originally from two allegedly feeble-minded sisters. In an examination of prison records, Dugdale was impressed by the persistent appearance of one family name, and he began the investigation, covering seven generations and giving the family the pseudonym "Jukes." The investigation yielded a sordid picture of criminality, immorality, feeble-mindedness, and pauperism. Dugdale identified 1,258 surviving and traceable descendents, of which a great number were identified as mentally defective and severely maladjusted. Actually, Dugdale was more impressed with the importance of environmental factors in the determination of the condition of the members of this family, which shows that the family-biography technique can be used to support almost equally well a hereditary or environmental interpretation.

Much later, Goddard (1912) published the results of another study of a degenerate family, which, in Goddard's interpretation, involved a built-in control group. This study of the Kallikak family is another frequently cited example of the family-history approach to behavior genetics. Martin Kallikak was said to have had an illegitimate son by a feeble-minded girl. This formed one branch of the family, which included 480 descendants from this son: 143 supposedly feeble-minded, 292 of uncertain intelligence, 36 illegitimate, 33 prostitutes, 24 alcoholics, 3 epileptics, and 3 criminals, with only 46 definitely known to be normal. Somewhat later, Martin Kallikak married a girl from a good family, from which 496 descendants have been traced. This represents the second, or control, branch of the family, in which only 1 descendant was identified as feeble-minded, 1 as sexually loose, 2 as alcoholic, and 1 as displaying a religious mania. The 491 remaining descendants were considered normal, and a good many of them were successful in business life and in the professions. It must be recognized, in passing, that much of the information concerning both branches of the family was obtained from second- and third-hand accounts of relatives and friends and is based upon impressionistic rather than objective evidence. Yet Goddard maintained that the data were collected in such a way as to err on the conservative side, and he took the evidence to mean that feeble-mindedness was hereditary.

These and other family biographies (sometimes referred to as the "pedigree" method of investigation) have frequently been presented as evidence of the inheritance of behavioral characteristics. The chief difficulty with this type of data is that the hereditary component can never be separated from the environmental one. A child born of feeble-minded or delinquent parents may be inadequate or delinquent not because he has inherited these qualities but because he grows up in a family where the home environment is characterized by these deficiencies. Thus, family histories cannot possibly answer the question of how these characteristics were communicated by the parents. They could be communicated through the genetic structure or via the environment, which the parent created, and probably through both. In the same way, psychoses can be shown to be more prevalent in the offspring of parents who are themselves psychotic than among offspring of healthy parents. But it is not known whether the psychosis came about as a result of genetic factors or because the parents displayed behavioral defects in the rearing of their children.

Recently, there have been somewhat more sophisticated variants of the family-biography approach: for example, *correlations between various relative classes*. The best of these include comparisons of varying degrees of genetic association, for example, identical twins and fraternal twins. They have typically employed intelligence tests, as in the study of Conrad and Jones (1940), who obtained correlations of +.49 between parents and offspring and between siblings on standardized intelligence tests. Similar findings have been reported by Roberts (1941), McNemar (1942), and Thorndike (1944). In 1937, Crook made one of the few studies dealing with personality characteristics and, in discussing his results along with previous work, estimated the correlation between parents and offspring on such traits as neuroticism, introversion, dominance, and self-sufficiency as between +.16 and +.18. For identical twins, the estimated relationship was +.59 and for fraternal twins, +.22. Crook suggested that genetic factors are of relatively less importance in determining variation in personality traits than in intelligence.

One of the most carefully done and highly respected studies along family-biography lines is that performed by Jervis (1938) on the inheritance of a rather rare disorder, which was discovered by Fölling, called "phenylpyruvic oligophrenia" or "Fölling's disease." This is a form of mental deficiency associated with a metabolic defect, resulting in abnormally high secretion in the urine of phenylpyruvic acid. By studying family histories, Jervis demonstrated that the disease followed a Mendelian pattern and was probably caused by a single gene pair inherited in the classical recessive fashion. Thus Jervis successfully employed a family-biography approach supplemented by a careful analysis of frequencies of the disorders in Mendelian hereditary terms. The data left little doubt that the incidence of the disorder (it is extremely rare) is determined largely by a specific genotype.

The obvious defects of the family-biography approach to heredity led to adoption where possible of *studies of twins* and, in particular, the comparison of identical twins with fraternal twins and the co-twin control method. The *co-twin control method* (invented by Galton), in which identical twins are studied who have been reared apart under different environmental circumstances often suffers in practice from the objection that very often the environmental circumstances under which the two twins live are not as disparate as they should be. Ideally speaking, however, the co-twin control method tends to hold genetic factors constant and permits the isolation of the effects of variation in environment. As a corollary approach, in order to study the role of genetics with environmental factors held constant, identical environmental situations must be produced for children having different inheritances. The problem with this method in practice is that identical environments can never be truly created, because inevitably parents or foster parents will develop different patterns of relationships with the different children. Subtle and sometimes even gross differences occur in the psychological environments of the pair of children under study, even though the physical environments are very similar. Unfortunately, the necessary conditions for the co-twin method cannot be created experimentally, because they would work hardships upon the parents and children involved. One must simply wait for social or legal situations that require the separation of children or the rearing of children by foster parents.

Studies along the lines suggested above have been performed, although each of them contains some unavoidable defect, which has prevented its conclusions from being unequivocal. For example, Freeman, Holzinger, and Mitchell (1928) studied a group of 401 foster children, of which 74 had been given intelligence tests before adoption, at an average age of eight years, and retested at an average age of twelve years, two months, after a period of foster placement. Before adoption, the average intelligence quotient was 91.2, and after the approximate four-year interval, it was 93.7. A correction of 5 points gain must be added because of defects of the standardization scale, which resulted in overestimation of the intelligence of the younger children. The study concluded that there was an average gain due to the environmental change of 7.5 IQ points. The study also found that children placed in culturally better foster homes and at younger ages made greater intelligence gains.

A similar study by Burks (1928) obtained findings that agree essentially with those of Freeman, Holzinger, and Mitchell. The evidence suggested that environmental factors play a considerable role in intelligence, although hereditary factors are exceedingly important. In the study by Burks, the Stanford-Binet intelligence test was given to 214 foster children and their foster parents and to a control group of 205 children and their real parents. The control group was closely equated to the foster group on variables such as age and occupational level of the parents. Children were tested from five to fourteen years of age. The correlations of the fathers' and mothers' mental ages with those of the foster children were very much lower than the correlations between the fathers' and mothers' mental ages and those of their biological children. Burks concluded (1928, p. 308), "home environment contributes about 17% of the variance in IQ . . . the total contribution of heredity . . . is probably not far from 75 or 80%."

Few studies have been made in which identical twins have been separated at an early age and reared in different homes. One such study of nineteen sets of identical twins reared apart was reported by Newman and his colleagues (1937). He found that the twins resembled each other just as perfectly as identical twins reared together. There often were great similarities in the incidence and patterns of diseases and in the presence of glandular disorders. Investigation of the results of intelligence tests, however, gave mixed evidence. Twelve of the nineteen twin pairs showed small differences in IQ, three showed moderate differences, and four showed appreciable differences as the result of their separation. In each of the extreme instances, the twin who scored higher had received considerable educational and cultural advantages. In one case a woman with an IQ of 116, who was a college graduate, had a twin with an IQ of 92, who had had no schooling beyond the second grade. Thus, although many physical characteristics showed practically no effect of the separate rearing, intelligence-test scores were more influenced by major variations in the environmental situation.

Since the early 1900s a tremendous literature has grown up around the use of twins and foster children to identify genetic factors in intelligence and personality. This literature has been most ably reviewed by Anastasi and Foley (1949) and need not be repeated here. Characteristics such as emotionality, attitudes, motor skills, eye-movement patterns, epilepsy and electroencephalographic patterns, and autonomic patterns of reactivity have been explored in this research, in addition to intelligence. The results generally suggest (1) that there are hereditary influences, although these interact with environmental ones in determining the behavior traits studied, and (2) that in certain spheres of behavior (e.g., those involving complex qualities of personality) the role of genetic factors is less than in those involving simpler physical traits (e.g., characteristics of the physical constitution).

For those especially interested in abnormal behavior, the work of Kallman (1938) on genetic factors in schizophrenia is worth citing. Kallman applied the method of concordance to the study of the genetics of schizophrenia in an effort to rule out some of the methodological difficulties inherent in other approaches. The method requires comparisons of rates of schizophrenia among identical twins, fraternal twins, siblings, and in the general population. _Concordance_ means the percentage in a large population of pairs of one member of a pair of identical twins, fraternal twins, or siblings who will have the illness when it is known that the other member is sick. Kallman reported that, with identical twins, the index of concordance for schizophrenia is dramatically higher than in the case of fraternal twins, which in turn is higher than among unrelated pairs.

Kallman's approach, although an improvement upon the family-history method, still suffers from the possibility that the environments of identical twins are more similar than those of fraternal twins. It has been argued that parents view identical twins as more alike than siblings in most respects and that the twins themselves have a tendency to imitate each other, wearing identical clothing and considering themselves far more alike than would be the case of fraternal twins or merely siblings. Thus, the role of environmental factors is not entirely controlled by the use of concordance.

If we regard the Kallman data seriously (and in spite of valid criticism of method, they cannot easily be ignored), we can still ask about the nature of the genetic mechanism involved in behavior disorders like schizophrenia. First of all, even if we accept Kallman's probably inflated figures, 14 or more per cent of cases of identical twins do not show concordance (that is, when one twin is ill, the other is not). Why not? Even Kallman does not consider schizophrenia to be directly inherited. Rather, he seems to suggest that certain unknown constitutional characteristics are inherited that predispose a person to develop the illness, given the appropriate environmental circumstances. Thus, Kallman implies an interaction between genetic factors and environmental factors in producing schizophrenia.

This argument is analogous to what has been said about similar concordance data which have been found for tuberculosis. It would be

Table 12

KALLMAN'S DATA ON CONCORDANCE RATES FOR VARIOUS DISORDERS*

Types of psychosis	Half sibs	Full sibs	Fraternal twins	Identical twins
Schizophrenia	7.1	14.2	14.5	86.2
Manic depressive	16.7	23.0	26.3	95.7
Involutional	4.5	6.9	6.9	60.9

* The table entries give the percentages of relatives having the disorder during their lifetime depending upon degree of genetic relationship to the disturbed persons.
SOURCE: Kallman, 1953, p. 124, fig. 36.

absurd to argue that tuberculosis is inherited, for we know without doubt that a person must be exposed to tuberculosis bacteria if he is to become ill. However, a person may inherit some unknown factor that predisposes him to become tubercular if, and only if, he is exposed to the specific bacteria. But no one can identify as yet this unknown factor that Kallman postulates in the case of schizophrenia. For the genetic proposition about schizophrenia to be taken seriously, it is ultimately necessary that this factor be isolated and its mechanism of producing illness understood. In all fairness to Kallman and other geneticists, it can also be pointed out that, just as we do not understand physiologically the genetic component in the illness, if it exists, neither do we have any satisfactory evidence concerning the necessary and sufficient environmental conditions of the disorder.

Although we have emphasized naturalistic research with human beings, there are other ways of studying heredity and behavior, which require experimental animals. It is convenient to study in the laboratory the effects of inheritance over many generations in animals such as the white rat, because the rat breeds so rapidly and in such great numbers. Moreover, rats can be selectively bred for certain physical and behavioral traits, even though there is always the problem of generalizing from such animal studies to man.

In one of the better-known studies, Tryon (1940) selectively bred a group of rats for maze brightness and maze dullness over a period of twenty-one generations. Starting with 142 unselected white rats, he measured their effectiveness in learning a maze and then mated bright rats with other bright ones and, conversely, the dull rats with other dull ones. After as little as eight generations of breeding there was no longer any overlap in the distributions of errors in maze learning between the offspring of the bright and dull rats. In animals like the rat, intellectual processes seem to be susceptible to breeding and therefore greatly influenced by genetic factors.

Many other studies of strain differences among animals have been performed, both in the distant past and in the last two decades, most of these dealing with intellectual capacity. Animal breeders, of course, have known for a long time that physical traits are easily bred. In fact, it is commonly believed that all sorts of behavioral characteristics are associated with breed differences. For example, certain species of dogs are suitable as watchdogs but make poor pets, and vice versa. Thus, in lower animals rather complex behavior patterns can be shown experimentally to have hereditary determinants.

It is commonly acceded that the higher we go in the phylogenetic scale, the more modifiable are genetically determined traits by environmental experience. Because of methodological difficulties in research with human beings, there is a conviction among behavior geneticists that future developments are more likely to be made with animal research, even though the generalization to man will remain hazardous. We have come a long way from the naïve views that characterized the thinking and research on behavior genetics of the nineteenth century, and it is probable that this field, stimulated by rapid increases in knowledge about the hereditary mechanisms themselves and by increasing methodological sophistication, will make important strides toward clarifying the role of genetic factors in behavior and personality.

Heredity and Environment

One of the perennial questions in the area of behavior genetics concerns the relative contributions of heredity and environment. The failure to address and resolve this question adequately has led to much fruitless debate and has retarded our understanding of the factors contributing to human development (see Woodworth, 1941).

One way to state the issue of nature versus nurture is to consider the degree of modifiability of hereditary influences. An old-fashioned view of heredity was that, if the hereditary disposition was transmitted to an offspring, this disposition would produce an invariant result in the structure of the organism. In other words, if the genetic disposition of the individual required a particular stature, say, the height of six feet, he was bound to develop accordingly. Actually, environmental conditions can considerably alter the actualization of hereditary potential. Moreover, experiments have demonstrated that even the genes themselves can be altered by environmental influences. Untold mutations, or changes in the genetic structure, have been produced in organisms such as the fruit fly by means of altering drastically the environmental circumstances of the sex cells. Irradiation (for example, with X rays) can produce all kinds of weird conglomerations: flies with four wings, fewer or extra legs, several heads, and so on. Genes are by no means impervious to environmental influence.

Another type of evidence on this point derives from transplantation experiments on organisms like the salamander (Weiss, 1941, see Figure 14). In the tadpole stage of development, tissues from which limbs were to grow have been grafted to other parts of the body, such as the head. If this is done very early in the development of the tadpole, the transplanted tissues develop in accordance with the characteristics of the surrounding area of tissues that receive the transplant. What would have been a leg will grow into tissues identical with those found on the head. On the other hand, if the transplantation of a limb bud is done later in development, then a perfectly formed limb will appear on the head. Thus, the genetic influence on differentiation of tissues is dependent upon the local tissue environment in which the differentiation occurs.

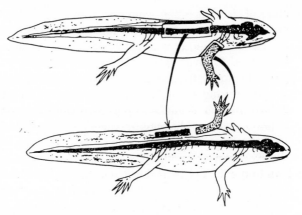

Figure 14. The genetic influences on differentiation of tissues are dependent upon the local tissue environment in which the differentiation occurs. (*From Weiss,* 1941. *In Morgan & Stellar,* 1950, p. 324.)

Similarly, by a somewhat bold analogy, if the human child is separated from his natural culture and transplanted to a radically different culture, the effects upon the development of his personality will probably depend upon the age (and presumably the extent to which the psychological structure had developed) at which the transplantation is made. Thus, if the child is transplanted in infancy, he will grow up almost entirely without reference to his native culture, and if the transplantation is made in young adulthood, important residuals of the early culture will be found, probably throughout his life. This same kind of interaction is always found to a greater or less degree when we examine genetic influences upon behavior.

There is no question that an organism that inherits a tendency to be tall will usually grow to be tall within certain limits. Pathology of the endocrine system early in life, however, can produce stunting of growth or enhancement of growth, even though, genetically speaking, there existed certain predispositions for growth.

Genetic factors play the role of producing dispositions for development rather than directly producing constitutional or behavioral traits. The fulfillment of these dispositions depends upon a wide range of environmental circumstances. Traits are no more produced by inheritance than they are by environmental circumstances. The end product is a function of the interaction of both. At times it is a more useful method in research to emphasize hereditary factors as antecedents of certain characteristics, and at other times an environmental method seems to offer the best chance to study the origins of the process. But this never means that any trait can be considered as either totally inherited or environmentally determined.

One specific version of the problem of behavior genetics can be found in the controversial concept of *instinct.* The assumption behind the concept is that some complex forms of behavior are built into the organism, so to speak, presumably through hereditary mechanisms carried in common by an entire species. The concept appears most useful as applied to lower forms of life (insects, fish, etc.), and it certainly appears to apply to certain primitive forms of human behavior (for example, sucking in infants). Still, anyone who has read even a little of the writings of Freud will recognize that the concept of instinct is also important in psychoanalytic theory. In the recent writings of Maslow (1954) on personality, "instinct," as a term, is also employed and discussed. Let us examine it a bit more closely, recognizing its close relation to the field of behavior genetics.

THE CONCEPT OF INSTINCT

When we look at human and animal behavior and try to formulate organizing principles about it, we must be impressed with certain universal, or near universal, characteristics. For example, sex and mating behavior shows similar if not identical patterns. The same might be said for aggression, a near universal human and animal reaction. Likewise, there is the widespread if not universal tendency for animals to congregate and to care for their young. An elementary solution to the problem of widespread or universal complex behavior in animals and man is to posit the existence of certain universal urges, genetically transmitted through the evolutionary series and presumably through the common biological structures that link all animals regardless of where they are in the phylogenetic series. These universal urges, which have been postulated for thousands of years, have been called "instincts." Thus, when the question is asked: Why does man make war?, the answer often is: Because aggression is instinctive in man. This is to say that it is difficult for him to help himself because he is the victim of his basic instinctual nature.

The crux of this proposal about instincts is that aspects of aggression, or making war, for instance, involve unlearned, inherited responses. The concept of instinct (at least for animals) has had certain religious and philosophical appeal over the past few centuries because it reinforced a conviction that was even more widespread in the eighteenth and nineteenth centuries than it is today. It is that man is somehow marked off from the animal world because his behavior is governed more by rational principles than by animal instincts. In fact, Darwin's concept of evolution was taken as an assault upon this principle because evolution implied that man was merely a further step along a single quantitative continuum, sharing a great deal (even instincts) in common with lower animals. Thus, in terms of this rational concept of man, instincts were generally regarded as bad and leading to irrational conduct, and man was considered capable of controlling the bad, animal instincts in him.

Even Freud viewed the instincts of sex and aggression in a sense as part of man's bad but inescapable animal nature. He pointed out that society came about because these animal instincts, which were often so destructive to human relations, were suppressed or transformed by a kind of tacit social contract into socially acceptable patterns of conduct. Moreover, in Freud's earliest theoretical schemes, man was conceived as developing mental illness because he failed to find adequate means of discharging these socially unacceptable instincts. His dilemma was that of modifying them so that they could be discharged indirectly and without danger and conflict.

The classic story of Dr. Jekyll and Mr. Hyde reflects this implicit philosophy about instinct extremely well. If you will recall, Dr. Jekyll is the all-good portion of man, the kindly, rational soul, and Mr. Hyde is the epitome of evil. If one wonders what is evil about Mr. Hyde, it is that he gives complete license to sexual and aggressive urges. Our modern western society contains elements of this philosophy in its emphasis on asceticism. A common ideal is continence with respect to sensual gratifications, and although aggression is a very widespread feature of human relations in our modern western world, it is publicly denounced and regarded as evil by all major religious systems. The psychologist and psychiatrist are often seen by the lay public as recommending license with respect to instinctual expression.

The idea of an instinctive basis for even human behavior has been popular. As recently as 1923, MacDougall in his social psychology proposed such human instincts as flight, reproduction, self-abasement, parental feeling, and repulsion, among many others. Much human behavior, and certainly behavior of lower forms of life, has been widely and for a long time understood as an inevitable expression of instinctual forces common to all.

One of the chief difficulties with the concept of instinct is that it tends to become a labeling device without any real explanatory power. This need not be so, of course, but to explain behavior by the use of a term that does not designate empirically definable mechanisms is not really explanation at all, although it can be a first step toward locating actual biological processes. Just as we affirm the reasonableness of the existence of a brain center for the control of sleep or some other human activity and then recognize the need to specify the effects of and conditions that activate this center, so is it important to do this with the concept of instinct.

Instinct is usually defined as a complex, unlearned pattern of behavior. There are relatively few patterns of behavior readily observable in man that can be demonstrated as unlearned, and this has resulted in a tendency to consider the concept of instinct as useful only with lower animals. Such a rigid point of view has too readily been accepted in psychology, and the concept of instinct is in disrepute as an organizing principle of behavior, especially in academic circles. Maslow (1954), however, has argued for the value of the instinct concept in human behavior, pointing out that, although it is true that man's behavior is less rigidly determined by totally unlearned instinctual processes, one can regard the organization of his needs as having an instinctual basis. He refers to this basis with the expression "instinctoid needs." It is not as powerful as it is in lower animals, and it is easily overcome by the learning of cultural patterns. But, says Maslow, it never totally disappears as an influence in behavior.

A classic example of an uncontroversial instinct in human beings is the sucking reflex that appears in infants at birth and subsequently disappears. An object, such as a nipple, placed on the mouth of the infant will elicit sucking movements of the lips, which are well adapted to nursing. Little, if any, learning is involved in this act, and it is universal in normal infants, disappearing after a time.

Whereas instinctual behaviors that meet the criterion of the complete absence of learning are unusual in man, in lower organisms there are impressive examples. The homing of pigeons, the migration of birds, bird calls, the mating behavior of insects, the weaving of webs of spiders— these are some of the better-known examples of complex, unlearned patterns of behavior in lower animals that are generally regarded as instinctive. They are considered instinctive not because the physiological mechanisms have been discovered but because the possibility that they have been learned has all but been eliminated.

Little experimental work has been done to specify more clearly the mechanisms involved in instinctive behavior, especially in higher animals. This is not so much the case for lower animals. One of the foremost scientists engaged in such research is Konrad Lorenz. Another whose work in this field is widely known is Tinbergen (1951). Tinbergen's research includes the experimental exploration of the physical mechanisms of instincts in fish, fowl, and insects whose early life has been restricted so the learning of certain patterns of behavior from other members of the species would be minimized or eliminated. In one series of studies, for example, the male stickleback fish was used (see Figure 15). The red color on the male's belly, which develops during the mating season, is the releaser (or stimulus) for built-in instinctual responses in males. When different cardboard models of the male stickleback fish were presented to other male sticklebacks, little else mattered except the red belly of the model. Male sticklebacks attacked very inaccurate models of other sticklebacks that had red bellies, but would not respond to a very well-designed and accurate model of the stickleback without the red belly. In experiments of this sort, Tinbergen has explored the precise meaning of instinct in lower animals, identifying the necessary and sufficient conditions that release the instinctual response.

The dichotomy between instinct and learning places the psychologist in the rather odd position of having a two-class system to maintain: either that a behavior pattern is instinctive or that it is learned (Beach, 1955). Most of what is called "instinctive" in man, however, has some basis in both inherited anatomical structure and learning. In lower forms of animals there is more often determination of behavior through relatively invariant, inherited mechanisms. Thus, the ant, bee, or wasp cannot greatly modify its behavior or readily learn a variety of forms of adjustment in response to new situations. Man's construction permits a far wider range of adaptive patterns of response than is true for lower organisms. We say that man is less governed by instincts than lower organisms.

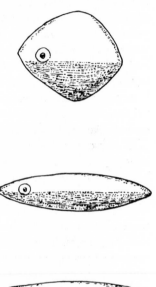

But isn't this exactly the kind of thing we have been saying earlier about the old heredity-and-environment issue? For a long time, the fruitless question was asked: Is such and such behavior determined by inheritance or by environmental experience (through learning)? We recognize today that both heredity and environmental influences contribute toward and interact with the end product that we observe in behavior. We also recognize that the contribution of inheritance is more obvious in certain simple physical traits and less obvious in the complex characteristics for which we usually use the term "personality"; as we have said, the contribution of instinctual forces is more obvious in lower animals ex-

Figure 15. Models used to test attack responses in male sticklebacks. The four models with red bellies release attack responses. A much more accurate model without coloring does not. (*From Tinbergen*, 1951.)

hibiting simpler structures and behavior repertories than in higher animals like man. There is no reason to assume, however, that such a contribution is not there simply because it is less obvious and more subtle.

Perhaps the best-known use of the instinct concept in personality theory is found in Freudian psychoanalysis, as the reader will recall from Chapter 6. Freud postulated the so-called life instincts and death instincts, the latter to account for the destructive qualities in man. Among the life instincts, he was primarily interested in sexual urges, and believing these to be of fundamental importance in the development of psychopathology, he elaborated upon them in great detail. The theory of psychosexual development is a statement of the unfolding of sexual patterns, which Freud regarded as fundamental to the evolution of the adult personality and by means of which it was possible to understand both health and pathology. This emphasis on the unfolding of instinctual patterns was modified or eschewed by later, more socially oriented writers, such as Adler, Rank, Horney, and Fromm.

In any event, having a particular sort of physical structure will probably make certain kinds of behavior easier to acquire than others. Perhaps the physiological construction of man and other animals tends to produce aggression when frustration occurs. The widespread reaction of aggression in response to frustration has been described and discussed by Dollard and his colleagues (1939) in a very well-known series of experiments. The form of this aggression in higher animals like man must be learned, and it varies greatly from society to society and from person to person. For example, it can be displayed through entirely verbal means or by physical assault. Studies by Davis and Havighurst (1952) suggest that middle-class parents teach their children to value verbal aggression or the inhibition of aggression more than physical assault and that lower-class families encourage the opposite value orientation. Wars can be conducted with atomic weapons or cannon or with words or bows and arrows. Competitiveness can be evidenced by the acquisition of property and hoarding or by conspicuous consumption.

The means by which an instinctual impulse is discharged is learned, but this is not necessarily an argument against an instinctive basis for aggression or against the idea that our physiological construction makes it easier for us to respond to frustration with aggression in some form than, say, by turning the other cheek. In this sense, the combativeness of man can be seen to have some instinctual basis. It is possible to learn, although with great difficulty, not to be combative. Clinically it seems that man pays the price for such suppression of his instincts with internal ailments, disturbed behavior, or psychological discomfort. This notion that social maturity brings with it a certain amount of frustration of instincts is very close to Freudian concepts of human development.

Freud was aware that instincts in man manifested themselves differently than in animals, especially because instinctual forces were so modifiable. He argued for the modifiability of instincts by experience and by the development of elaborate controls, such as are characteristic of the ego processes. It has been suggested too that the German word *Trieb*, used by Freud, was unwisely translated into "instinct" (there is no truly exact translation), a term that connotes invariant and unlearned processes, a connotation not intended by Freud. In any event, in psychopathology and personality theory the Freudian use of the word "instinct" has had considerable influence, although it has not yet led to empirical specification, as would ultimately be demanded of any explanatory construct. Those favorable to psychoanalysis might regard it as a useful concept, though still at a primitive stage of scientific development. In the development of personality, instinct remains an important topic.

The problem of behavior genetics and instincts in human development and personality forms a nice bridge to a related topic: biological determinants of personality. The physical constitution of man is very strongly influenced by hereditary factors and, in turn, has a great deal to do with behavior and the underlying structure of personality. We take up these biological determinants in the next chapter.

9

Biological Factors and Personality

Man is a biological creature, made up of tissues; as such, his behavior must obey biological principles. This is the subject matter of the present chapter; more specifically it is about how the physiological characteristics of man influence his personality.

It is not possible to study directly the effects of man's physical structure on personality because, as we have seen, personality itself is a complex construct, which is not directly observable. Therefore, to pursue the problem of physiology and personality, it is first necessary to deal with empirical relationships between physiology and behavior. Only then can we interpret these relationships (by inference) in terms of the theoretical structures and processes that define personality.

A topic as vast as the empirical relationships between physiology and behavior cannot, of course, be thoroughly covered in a single chapter. An anatomical examination of the construction of man alone would be a huge task. The purpose is not to give a lesson in human anatomy and physiology but rather to provide some general understanding of how man's behavior reflects his physical make-up. The reader is referred to chapters on physiology in introductory texts of psychology (such as Morgan, 1956; Krech & Crutchfield, 1958) and to more thorough treatments at a higher level of physiological psychology (for example, Hathaway, 1942; Morgan & Stellar, 1950). In this chapter we shall touch mainly the highlights in this area of research and thought, especially those pertinent to personality.

GENERAL CONSIDERATIONS

It is no surprise that the behavioral repertory of an organism is a function of his anatomy and physiology. To bring home this point at the level of complex, adaptive behavior, we can compare the characteristic behaviors of different types of organisms and relate these to similarities and differences in the nature of their respective brains. For example, man is capable of doing many things that lower organisms cannot; conversely, there are things he cannot do that lower animals can. To illustrate the former point, man has the unique capacity to use language and to communicate with other members of his species in a highly abstract fashion. An examination of man's brain indicates structural features that are not found at all or in the same form or degree in any other organism, including even the anthropoid apes. Figure 16 presents schematic drawings of the cerebral cortex (the outer portion of the brain) of man, chimpanzee, and dog. A comparative approach such as this, which examines different types of organisms as representatives of an evolutionary sequence, is called "phylogenetic."

In spite of differences, there are also great similarities between man and lower animals in the structure and organization of the nervous system. These similarities make possible general behavioral principles that apply to all animals, even the most simple. Thus, we might conceivably learn something about the processes of visual perception in human beings by studying the visual system of the horseshoe crab (as a kind of lowest common denominator), as Ratliff, Miller, and Hartline (1958) have done.

Comparison of man with other animals is relatively easy. It is often a simple matter to relate structure and function by correlating the obvious structural differences and similarities among organisms with the differences and similarities in their behavior patterns. The problem is more complicated when we consider the physiological bases of differences and

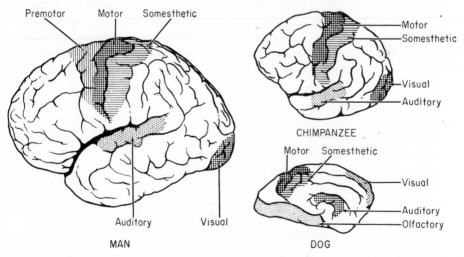

Figure 16. The cerebral cortex of man, the chimpanzee, and the dog. Note the size and positions of the visual, auditory, and somesthetic areas. The diagram also shows the motor areas of all three species and the large olfactory area of the dog. Note, too, how much larger the brain of man is compared with those of the chimpanzee and the dog. (*From Morgan,* 1956.)

similarities in behavior among human beings themselves. Human beings resemble each other in gross physical structure to a high degree. They appear to have similar or identical tissues and organs. Thus, if one person's characteristic behavior differs from that of another, identification of physiological characteristics that might be responsible for the differences is a much more subtle affair.

General Approaches to the Study of Physiological Influences

In order to understand the influence of physiological factors on behavior, the scientist can create temporary physiological states and examine behavioral effects or changes. For example, he can administer drugs that have certain chemical effects on the brain or other parts of the nervous system. Through this chemical action on the brain, behavior can be dramatically influenced.

One example of this type of approach is the research on lysergic acid and mescaline (and other similar drugs), which are capable of producing hallucinatorylike experiences that have a certain superficial similarity to the hallucinations of schizophrenia (Wikler, 1957). Some psychopharmacologists hope that the mechanisms of such disorders as schizophrenia will be better understood if we can learn how these drugs affect the nervous system. It has been suggested, for example, that the partial metabolism in the brain of such naturally produced hormones as adrenalin releases, in turn, substances that have effects similar to lysergic acid and that are capable of producing remarkable pathological effects in human perception, thought, and behavior. Perhaps psychoses result in part from the production of toxins in the brain when something goes wrong with the sequence of metabolic processes in the brain cells. This kind of research is an effort to get closer to the biochemical events that underlie behavior and psychological experience.

In addition to the production of temporary psychological states in an effort to learn about physiological determinants of behavior, we can also examine the stable differences in glandular, neurological, or other organ structures among different persons as possible correlates of variations in behavior. Thus, permanent defects in brain tissues are associated with disorders of intelligence or abnormalities in perception, learning, thinking, and communicating. A little later on we shall illustrate this point with examples of sensory and motor abnormalities and disturbances of communication that have known correlates in structural defects of the brain.

Ways in Which Physiological Factors Affect Behavior

Physiological factors can influence behavior directly and indirectly. *Direct influence* means that some form of behavior is directly produced or caused by some underlying physiological structure or some damage to it. For example, because of particular metabolic effects on the body, glandular secretions (say, an excessive thyroid secretion) can result in hyperactivity. Instances are common of extreme restlessness and hyper-activity (hyperthyroidism), on the one hand, or sluggishness and leth-argy (hypothyroidism), on the other, being produced in this way. Like-wise, damage to the brain through physical injury or the invasion of a microorganism (as in the case of syphilis) produces impairment in adap-tive behavior and intellectual activity. Abnormal changes in mood can also correlate with these structural variations and defects, so a person can be chronically depressed, elated, or uneasy, resulting in major trans-formations in the typical relationships he has with other persons.

It is clear that such disturbances are definitely produced by damage to the brain tissues, but they are not yet explainable entirely in these terms; sometimes we are misled into thinking they are fully understood because we can specify accurately and even control some of the physical condi-tions of the disorder. For example, we know that syphilis, permitted to go unchecked for several decades, will produce brain damage in its third and final stage, which is called "general paresis." We can identify the destruc-tive germ, and before it has affected the brain cells we can cure the dis-ease with penicillin. Even after the brain damage has begun we can ar-rest the deterioration in a similar manner. But the exact manner in which the brain damage produces disturbances of psychological function is not clear and cannot be clear until we fully understand the correlation be-tween the anatomical structure of the brain and the psychological and behavioral functions disturbed by the disorder.

Moreover, as a disease, general paresis is indistinguishable behaviorally from other organic psychoses. The age of the patient, his history, and the discovery of the syphilitic microorganism in the blood determines the differential diagnosis. Similarly, we suspect that a patient is suffering from Korsakoff's psychosis (produced by long-standing alcoholism) when he displays a long history of severe alcoholism in addition to the be-havioral evidence of brain damage (including disorientation and memory disturbance). The personality changes that occur in these disorders seem to be unrelated to the specific nature of the damage to tissues, because one patient can become irascible, delusional, and unpleasant and another with a similar physical disorder (produced by syphilis or long, intem-perate use of alcohol) will become dependent, pleasant, and even euphoric. The best predictor of the personality effects of these brain-damage–based disorders seems to be the premorbid personality of the patient. Thus, although we know for certain that the general behavioral and psychological disturbance is produced by destruction of the tissues of the brain, we cannot yet connect the tissues involved with the specific behavioral aspects of the disorder.

A similar dilemma in the study of the physiological determinants of behavior has been highlighted recently by the experimental use of drugs. Their behavioral effects seem often to depend upon personality factors and the social and environmental conditions to which a person is exposed. For example, we know that alcohol tends to uninhibit persons and lead to a loss of control, first in judgment and social relations and then in physical coordination, but there are individual differences in the extent of this disturbance. Some persons respond with rapid disorganization, and others with similar or even larger amounts of alcohol in the blood show few signs. Also, behavior is apt to deteriorate less when a person is in hostile social circumstances than when he feels safe and at ease with friends. The obvious interactions between the direct effects of drugs (or damage to the anatomical structure of the central nervous system) and the social or environmental conditions to which the person must adapt need to be studied further before they can be fully understood. They greatly complicate research into the physiological factors underlying behavior.

Indirect influence of physiological factors on behavior results from conditions that in themselves produce no specific behavioral effect but produce social consequences that in turn lead a person to respond with altered behavior. For example, the fact that a child is endowed with more physical strength and larger stature than other children can result indirectly in a different pattern of adaptive behavior than in the case of a puny and sick child. Playing with other children, such a youngster discovers that he is stronger than they are and can best them in competition or fighting. He thus develops a different conception of himself than the physiologically less adequate child. Handicaps are also a good example of physical conditions that indirectly affect behavior. The unattractive girl endowed with reasonably high intellectual capacity can compensate for her unpopularity with boys by concentrating on the development of intellectual skills, or she may experience deep feelings of inadequacy or inferiority and react socially by habitually withdrawing.

As a further example of the indirect effects of physiological factors, there is an actual case of a man who had been studying art and began to paint with rather grotesque combinations of colors. On subsequent testing it was discovered that he was color blind. The budding artist reacted to the discovery with great depression, because it meant to him that his life had to be altered and his cherished ambition to paint had to be given up. The physiological influence here is indirect, depending for its impact on occupational (social) consequences of being color blind.

Grace Heider (1959) has been exploring the interactions between the inherent physiological dispositions of infants and the attitude of their mothers toward them. She found, for example, that some infants have difficulty in controlling or reducing stimulation that comes to them from their environments. Such children readily become overstimulated and seem to do best when the mother is able to shield the child from too much in the way of environmental demand. Other children, who readily are able to shut out excess stimulation, are reacted to favorably by the mother, who tends actively to stimulate her child. Heider assumed that the natural physiological tendencies of the infant interact favorably or unfavorably with the habitual patterns of mothering, depending upon how well they are matched. Thus, what is effective mothering for one child is damaging and ineffective for another, depending upon physiological disposition. Such interactions are further examples of the indirect effects that some physiological factors have on behavior (and, inferentially, on the developing personality), because the effects of these factors are dependent upon the (social) reactions they promote in others.

Subsequent discussions of the physiological determinants of behavior are developed around three main classes of psychological process: motivation, emotion, and cognition. Physiological psychologists have focused, in the main, upon the nervous and endocrine gland systems as having the most to do with integrating behavior of all the tissue systems of the organism. In considering motivation, emotion, and cognition, let us assume that the basic details of anatomy and anatomical function are already understood. However, to facilitate understanding of important aspects of the nervous system and endocrine gland system, some simple figures taken from introductory texts and other sources are presented, which diagram parts of the nervous system to refresh the reader's memory about the basic facts of physiology. The purpose here is not to elaborate many obscure facts of correlation between physiological structure and psychological function, but to present a general picture of the current developments in this enthusiastic, vital, and rapidly moving area of psychophysiology, especially as they relate to the field of adjustment and personality.

SOME PSYCHOLOGICAL PROCESSES AND THEIR UNDERLYING PHYSIOLOGY

The Processes of Motivation

As we have seen in Chapter 2, the concept of motivation is central in the field of personality and, indeed, in all of psychology. The core of the idea of motivation is that there are hypothetical forces that energize and direct human behavior toward goals. *Motivation* is the impetus that mobilizes human action toward certain goal objects or states of being.

To approach the question of the physiological mechanisms underlying motivated behavior, we must look to activities of the nervous and endocrine gland systems that might be specific to some particular goal activity, for example, the search for, and consumption of, food or water. Most theories of motivation distinguish between so-called primary or viscerogenic drives, and secondary or social motivations. Most of the progress in isolating the physiological mechanisms underlying motivated activity has been restricted to physiological drives such as hunger, thirst, sleep, and sex. To the personality and social psychologists, social motives, such as the need for affection, esteem, or approval, are of the most fundamental importance. It is, as yet, an article of faith that the physiological mechanisms underlying primary (physiological) drives will turn out to be analogous to, or the same as, those applying to social motivation. As some important progress has been made in exploring the physiological bases of primary drives, let us begin by examining this work, even though its relevance to social motivation and personality is not yet established.

The local-stimulus theory: The concept of motivation that has been influential in psychology for some time is based on an oversimple and outmoded homeostatic model implied by Cannon (1934). In explaining hunger, for example, Cannon and Washburn (1912) suggested a local-stimulus theory, in which hunger sensations were considered to be the result of strong contractions of the stomach walls. The notion was simply that, when there was a deficit in nourishment sufficient to produce stomach contractions, the person felt hungry. How did the organism learn to eat when hungry? It was implied that the discomfort and restlessness associated with the sensations of hunger in the immature organism led to random activity, which by accident led to the act of eating. Thus, the organism learned that, whenever hunger sensations occurred, eating would relieve them.

The Cannon and Washburn experiment (1912) supported the local-stomach-contraction concept of hunger. Washburn swallowed a stomach tube with a balloon at the end of it, which recorded contractions of the stomach wall. Whenever Washburn felt a pang of hunger, this sensation was also recorded and, as it turned out, the subjectively experienced hunger pangs occurred at the same time as peak stomach contractions. However, later evidence (for example, Wangensteen & Carlson, 1931) showed that, even in the absence of a stomach (removed by surgery), sensations of hunger occurred.

The modern, central-motive–state theory: The simple, local-stimulus, homeostatic model for motivation has been replaced by a new theory, contributed to by Lashley, Morgan, and Beach, and recently described by Stellar (1954). A more inclusive and complex view of the physiological mechanisms of motivation was suggested. It included the notion that a number of sensory, chemical, and neural factors are coordinated in a complex physiological mechanism, which regulates motivation and has as its neurological center the hypothalamus of the brain (see Figure 17). The fundamental idea is that of a *central motive state*, which is built up in the organism by combined influence of sensory, humoral, and neural factors. The amount of motivated behavior is determined by the level of this hypothetical central motive state, which is a direct function of the amount of activity in specific excitatory centers of the hypothalamus. The hypothalamus is regarded as the main integrating neural center in motivation. The entire system includes (*a*) inhibitory and excitatory hypothalamic centers, (*b*) sensory stimuli controlling hypothalamic activity by means of the afferent impulses they produce, (*c*) the internal environment of the body (including hormonal secretions and other chemical activities), which influences the hypothalamus through the circulatory system and the cerebrospinal fluid, and (*d*) centers in the cortex and thalamus, which can excite and inhibit the hypothalamic centers associated with the central motive state.

Extensive experimental evidence for the importance of hypothalamic activity in motivated behavior is emerging. From it Stellar (1954) draws three main conclusions.

a. Damage to certain regions of the hypothalamus leads to striking changes in certain kinds of motivated behavior.

For example, in the case of hunger, bilateral lesions in the ventromedial nucleus near the midline produce enormous overeating, leading to

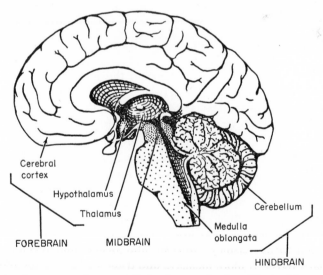

Figure 17. The principal parts of the human brain. (*From Morgan, 1956.*)

doubling of the body weight of rats following operation. Thus it seems that the center affected is an inhibitory one, because removing it eliminates the inhibition of eating behavior. Moreover, lesions of the ventromedial nucleus a few millimeters away completely eliminate hunger behavior. After operation the animals never eat again and die. Therefore, we might call the affected center excitatory in nature because removing it eliminates the excitation or initiation of eating. The same sort of mechanism is found in sleep. With respect to sex, only an excitatory center has been located as yet.

b. Different parts of the hypothalamus are critical in different kinds of motivation.

This means, simply, that destruction of one hypothalamic area can produce behavioral effects dealing with hunger, and another affects thirst, sleep, or sex. Thus, to some degree, there is specialization of function of different structural parts of the hypothalamic brain region.

c. Finally, as we have seen, there are both excitatory and inhibitory centers controlling motivation in the hypothalamus.

In other words, damage to the hypothalamus can sometimes lead to an increase in motivation and at other times to a marked decrease, implying that some hypothalamic tissue is associated with the turning on of motivated behavior and other tissues are essential in terminating the response.

It is no new fact that the internal environment of an animal plays an important part in certain kinds of motivated behavior. It probably does so by changing in some way the excitability of the hypothalamic centers by means of receptor organs, which signal chemical alterations within the body. For example, increases or decreases in blood pressure are known to be signaled to brain centers by receptor organs in the blood vessels so an equilibrium of pressure can be maintained by the activation of excitatory or inhibitory centers within the hypothalamus and via activity of the autonomic nervous system.

With respect to sexual behavior, it is clear that the hypothalamus is not only the main integrating center but also probably the main site of action of sex hormones, another aspect of the internal environment. Experiments on spayed female cats and guinea pigs show that the hypothalamic regions must be intact for sex hormones injected into the organism to arouse sexual behavior. Thus, sexual activity is not simply stimulated by hormonal release; it also relates to the activation of nervous centers in the brain, specifically in the hypothalamus.

Further supporting the modern, more complicated conceptions of the physiology of motivation, there is also evidence that the hypothalamus, though it plays an extremely important role in the control of motivated behavior, is not the only neural center involved. The cortex and thalamus (see Figure 17) are also involved, a fact that should be obvious if one studies even anecdotally sexual behavior in higher organisms such as man. Cognitive activity often turns out to be crucial in determining whether an organism will become aroused sexually; as Ford and Beach (1951) have indicated, it is especially so in the male. There is evidence also that the hypothalamus is under the direct control of a number of different cortical and thalamic centers. The cortex probably exerts both an excitatory and inhibitory influence in motivated behavior, the evidence being clearest in sexual behavior.

A number of physiologically oriented psychologists have recently speculated about human motivation in the light of the sort of developments cited above. Their empirical research has emphasized the autonomic nervous system. Malmo (1959), for example, elaborated on the concept of *activation*, which has many parallels with the central motive state. He alluded to the activity of the reticular formation (a nerve center and pathway below the thalamus) of the brain as a kind of arousing center, which fires impulses to the cortex and alerts or activates the organism to respond to sensory input. Malmo pointed out that an important unsolved problem in psychology is the measurement of drive, which in the past has usually been approached by studying antecedent conditions, such as the number of hours of deprivation of food or water, or certain consequent conditions, such as the rate and energy with which an organism selectively approaches some goal object like food or water. Malmo proposed that a more direct measure of drive might be obtained through some physiological index of activation.

Because level of activation is likely to be reflected in activity of the autonomic nervous system (see Figure 18), which, in turn, innervates various organs of the body (such as the heart, lungs, and sweat glands), autonomic measures might provide an estimate of the general level of activation or drive of the human being. Malmo assumed that, regardless of direction, that is, goal object, motivation or drive can be expressed as a single dimension of activation whose degree can be measured by studying activity of the end organs of the autonomic nervous system. Thus, blood pressure, heart rate, skin resistance, and respiration all might reflect this level of activation.

Another outstanding psychophysiologist, Lacey (1959), also emphasized the autonomic nervous system in the study of motivational as well as emotional processes. He has also been concerned with using the autonomic nervous system to measure level of sympathetic tonus or degree of arousal in man, and he has demonstrated that, when it is high (as measured by heart-rate activity and skin resistance), a person displays a tendency toward impulsivity and lack

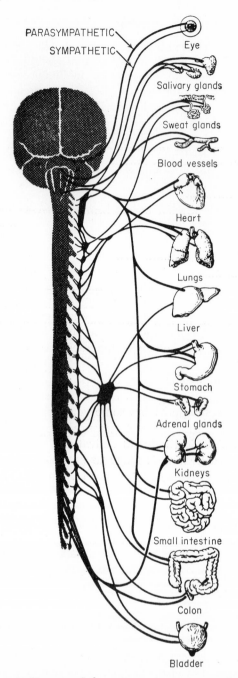

PARASYMPATHETIC
SYMPATHETIC

Eye

Salivary glands

Sweat glands

Blood vessels

Heart

Lungs

Liver

Stomach

Adrenal glands

Kidneys

Small intestine

Colon

Bladder

Figure 18. Schematic diagram of the autonomic nervous system. The autonomic system consists of nerves and ganglia that serve blood vessels, glands, and other internal organs of the body. It has two main divisions: the parasympathetic system and the sympathetic system. (*From Morgan, 1956.*)

of motor restraint (Lacey & Lacey, 1958). There is little doubt that behavior characteristics usually considered as motivationally or emotionally charged are reflected in autonomic nervous system activity.

The evidence that has so far been compiled concerning the importance of excitatory and inhibitory centers of the hypothalamus, thalamus, and cortex in the control of motivation along with chemical factors in the internal environment of the organism and the autonomic nervous system is impressive. But it represents only an early stage in our knowledge of the physiological mechanism underlying motivation and contains certain limitations for a physiological theory of motivation. For one thing, the evidence thus far is restricted to the primary drives, and it is only by extension that we can make it apply to the learned social motives that are so important in the human being. It is an intriguing prospect, nonetheless, to consider the possibility that similar or analogous mechanisms operate. A second limitation is that the work is based mainly on experiments with lower animals such as the rat or the cat, less frequently on primates, and little on man. It is a risky extension to describe the physiological mechanism in human motivation in the same terms, although there is no reason to believe that such an extension, at least to a degree, will not be ultimately warranted.

The Processes of Emotion

The concepts of emotion and motivation are in many respects inseparable. It has generally been assumed that emotional states are distinct from motivation but are intimately related to them. For example, a highly motivated organism is usually observed to be in an emotional state (for example, fear or anger), especially if the motive is likely to be thwarted or gratification delayed. Moreover, from a physiological point of view the same tissue systems seem to be involved in both motivation and emotion. The autonomic nervous system, endocrine system, hypothalamus, and cortex are postulated as basic to emotion, as they are to motivation. In fact, it has been often argued that it is only through the arousal of emotional states that the organism is activated to seek various goal objects. As constructs, motivation and emotion are often confused with each other and used interchangeably.

The role of the central nervous system: As in the case of motivation, the earliest concepts of emotion stressed reactions of the visceral organs of the body as vitally important. Only more recently has the importance of *central nervous system regulation centers* been stressed and systematically studied. We find increasing recognition of the complex network of nervous system agencies in interplay with the internal environment in emotional experience and behavior. As with motivation, the bulk of physiological research on emotional states has employed lower animals. It has been concentrated on fear and anger, two of the most important emotional states.

As long ago as 1892, a German physiologist named Goltz observed that dogs whose cerebral cortex had been surgically removed showed great readiness to display rage by growling, barking, and attacking. Many years later, Cannon (1927) made similar and more extensive observations with cats. He called this reaction of decorticated animals "sham rage," because it was not evoked by the stimuli that normally call forth rage in the intact animal, was not directed toward any specific object, and would cease upon withdrawal of stimulation. Cannon's experiments led him to suggest that the excitatory mechanism of rage was centered in the hypothalamus and that this was normally inhibited by cerebral cortex activity. If the cortex is removed, however, the control over the excitatory hypothalamic center is lost so the slightest stimulation, even gentle handling of the animal, would produce rage.

Although the simple idea of the inhibiting effects of the cortex has been extended in recent years by the notion that the cortex can have excitatory functions as well, there is widespread acceptance of the hypothalamic theory of emotional states. The hypothalamus is also conceived to have both excitatory and inhibitory centers. Other evidence of the importance of the hypothalamus has also been supplied, including the observation that electrical stimulation of the dorsomedial nucleus of the hypothalamus can change a tame cat into a dangerously raging animal, implying some localization of a rage-excitatory center. Conversely, destruction of the ventromedial nucleus (the same center whose removal produced excessive eating) produces a permanently vicious animal, suggesting that the latter hypothalamic area is an inhibitory center for rage. This research makes it quite clear that emotional states involve not only the viscera (bodily organs) but the brain as well, especially the hypothalamus and cerebral cortex.

One of the interesting developments of recent years in the physiology of emotions is the growing specialty of psychopharmacology. This was mentioned earlier in connection with the experimental use of drugs such as mescaline and lysergic acid in attempts to understand the physiological mechanisms of various forms of abnormal behavior. Psychopharmacologists, however, have also been concerned with the effect of drugs on emotional states such as fear and anger. They hope to understand how these drugs affect the various central nervous system centers of emotional behavior. For example, tranquilizing drugs have been known a long time, but they have received great scientific attention in recent years, especially in connection with psychoses in mental hospitals. Two of the most commonly explored tranquilizing drugs are reserpine and chlorpromazine, which seem to calm mental patients who are in excited states and to some degree to relax excessively tense or anxious persons.

Experiments have suggested that these drugs inhibit the action of the hypothalamus so as to lower the body temperature, reduce blood pressure, and, because the hypothalamus includes excitation centers for emotions, prevent agitation and calm pathological excitements.

There is evidence that chlorpromazine (in small doses) blocks impulses from the reticular formation to the cortex. The reticular formation has been found in psychophysiological research to activate or arouse the cortex so it can respond actively to outside stimulation. Thus, in sleep, the organism is relatively unresponsive and normally relaxed or unaroused, and in an alerted or wakeful state stimulation of the cortex by the reticular formation produces a state of attentiveness. These variations can be identified from the pattern of electro-encephalographic (EEG) waves taken from the brain. It has been demonstrated (Himwich, 1955) that these electrical brain waves, which normally are suppressed in amplitude by a painful stimulus, show no such suppression when a subject has taken small doses of chlorpromazine. It is as if the drug renders a person more aloof from his surroundings by inhibiting stimulation of the cortex by the reticular formation, thus placing a block between the environment and its influence on the mind. Such research, although at a relatively early stage, encourages us to believe that science is close to important developments with respect to the physiological mechanisms underlying emotional behavior.

The role of the autonomic nervous system: The most intensive study of the physiological bases of emotional states has been performed on the autonomic nervous system. This is because the bodily effects of autonomic activity are so impressive and obvious and so clearly related to emotion. For example, during the experience of emotion we have an increased or decreased rate of heartbeat, great variations in rate and amplitude of breathing, and many other visceral changes, which are produced directly by stimulation of autonomic nerves. Figure 18 shows the most important visceral organs of the body and the distribution of nerves between these organs and both the parasympathetic and sympathetic branches of the autonomic nervous system. Each branch seems to operate in somewhat different ways and produces different, often opposing, effects.

The activity of tear glands, salivary glands, sweat glands, blood vessels, heart, stomach, adrenal glands, and intestines are controlled by sympathetic and parasympathetic innervation. These organs are known to respond when the organism is activated to deal with any situation or when it experiences a state of emotion. Furthermore, the bodily changes associated with emotion not only affect the adaptive behavior of the organism (as Cannon, 1939, observed, the organism is better prepared for fleeing danger or attacking it) but can also be employed to diagnose states of emotion in human beings and lower animals. Thus, a common method developed by psychologists to determine when a person is under stress or is experiencing an emotional state is the study (by a galvan-ometer) of skin resistance to the passage of electric current. Resistance decreases during arousal probably because of sweat gland activity.

It is not our purpose here to describe the structure and function of the autonomic nervous system. However, there are a few highlights from recent psychophysiological research with emotions that should be men-tioned. One of the most interesting and important of these concerns the differentiation of emotional states by means of their autonomic response pattern. Another concerns autonomic traits; that is, different persons can show different characteristics of autonomic response.

Concerning the *differentiation of emotional states* by means of auto-nomic response patterns, until recently there was little evidence that the nature of the autonomic response pattern was correlated with the quality of the emotional state. The dominant point of view was that the autonomic nervous system showed the same arousal or activation in all emotional states, regardless of quality (for example, fear or anger). The differentia-tion between such states depended upon the observation of behavioral manifestations, such as fleeing from danger or attacking it, or, in the case of human beings, the subjective report of the qualitatively different emotional experiences of fear and anger.

More recently, there has begun to appear evidence that different emo-tional states produce specific, characteristic autonomic response patterns. One such finding has been reported by Ax (1953). At the present time there are other research protagonists of specificity (such as Lacey, Bate-man, & Van Lehn, 1953; Funkenstein, King, & Drolette, 1957). Lacey (1959) speculated, for example, that an activated or aroused organism shows, in general, reduction of skin resistance under stress but that heart rate can increase or decrease, depending upon whether the organism is alerted to take in stimulation from the environment (decrease in heart rate) or desires to protect itself against noxious stimulation by avoiding it (increase in heart rate). Moreover, there is also evidence (Funkenstein, King, & Drolette, 1957) that two different secretions of the adrenal medulla (the central portion of the adrenal gland) are associated with different emotional states—adrenalin with fear, noradrenalin with anger or attack—and that these chemicals have different physiological effects on the organism. The biochemistry of emotions will be dealt with later. In any event, the research supporting the idea that autonomic reaction patterns distinguish between qualitatively different emotional states is the subject of present controversy as well as of great interest, and it may well demonstrate ultimately a much closer parallel between human psychological experience in emotion and physiological patterns of re-sponse.

Concerning traits of autonomic response patterning, some interesting findings have been reported by Lacey and his colleagues (1950, 1952, 1953). Autonomic activity was measured by recording variations in heart rate and changes in the electrical resistance of the skin under resting conditions and under conditions producing states of stress. In some subjects they found patterns of autonomic activity differing from person to person but remaining consistent for each person over varying conditions. One person would react to stress, for example, with an elevated blood pressure and little change in other somatic responses, and another would show little reaction in blood pressure but marked changes in heart rate or skin resistance. Thus, for certain persons, a distinctive or specific pattern of response could be found, which could be regarded as a *constitutional trait*. It is intriguing to consider that psychosomatic-symptom patterns might vary from person to person depending upon the kind of autonomic response pattern characteristically produced in a person as a reaction to chronic stress. Various research teams over the world are currently investigating this possibility. For instance, persons with chronic hypertension (chronic elevated blood pressure) are being examined to discover the characteristics of their autonomic response patterning, which might help to understand and possibly to permit control of this widespread circulatory disturbance.

A similar kind of constitutional trait having to do with the autonomic nervous system can be found in the much older work of Jones (1930) and Macfarlane (1939). Numbers of infants were observed who internalized, that is, who showed their emotional difficulties through autonomic nervous system responses (reflected in visceral changes), and were typically free from overt behavior problems. Others were observed who were inclined to an overt behavioral expression of emotional difficulties and tended to be free of internal organ disturbance. There is, similarly, a widely held hypothesis that adults who react to emotional states with overt expression (for example, when feeling angry, a person lets it out by acting or speaking angrily) are less likely to have psychosomatic disturbances than those who bottle up feelings and inhibit the expression of impulses. A form of this idea is found in Freud's early writings about the value of catharsis as a means of discharging pent-up or repressed emotional states.

The role of the endocrine gland system: Thus far we have dealt only with the nervous system, the central and autonomic systems in particular. No discussion of this topic is complete without reference to the internal environment, especially the *endocrine gland system* (including the pituitary, thyroid, adrenals, and gonads; see Figure 19), which, like the nervous system, plays a major chemical role in emotion. The many chemical secretions of the various endocrine glands are poured directly into the blood stream and are thus circulated to the various tissues and organs of

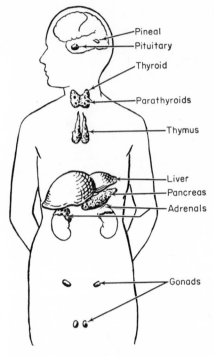

Figure 19. The names and positions in the body of the ductless (endocrine) glands that secrete hormones. (*From Morgan*, 1956.)

the body. The glands even interact with each other (through their secretions), forming a homeostatic system. Thus, each endocrine gland has its own individual function, and each is a member of a total complex of glands whose secretions influence or control the members.

Some of the endocrine glands, for example, the adrenals, can be stimulated by neural impulses; that is, they are dependent upon connections with the autonomic nervous system. Moreover, stimulation by the autonomic nervous system often produces the same effects on the visceral organs of the body as does the chemical stimulation from the secretions of the endocrine glands. For example, during emotional states the autonomic nervous system can stimulate the heart to increase its rate of pumping and its stroke (the volume of blood it handles on each beat); during this same emotional state, adrenalin, one of the hormones secreted by the adrenal medulla, will be poured into the blood stream as a result of this autonomic nervous system activity. The adrenalin also stimulates the heart to beat faster and with a bigger stroke. The initial reaction stimulated by the autonomic nervous system is usually of short duration, but it can be sustained long beyond the period of time produced by nervous stimulation alone, because the adrenalin remains in the blood stream and continues to stimulate the heart action until it is eliminated or metabolized. Thus, long after the immediate crisis that produced the emotion has passed, the body still is reacting as though the danger existed.

The notion has been held for a long time that variation in temperamental and affective qualities in persons (for example, being sluggish and phlegmatic as opposed to excitable and impulsive or being calm and secure as opposed to anxious) are associated with variations in the characteristics of the endocrine gland system.

That such a notion makes some sense is supported, for example, by observations of Williams (1956) on the great variations in glandular structures between individuals. Normal thyroid glands vary in weight from 8 to 50 grams, ovaries from 2 to 10 grams, testes in males from 10 to 45 grams, with a male-sex-hormone output ranging from 0.2 to 7.0 milligrams per day, pituitary gland output from 250 to 1,100 milligrams, and adrenal gland output from 7 to 20 grams. Richter (1959) has observed that the adrenal glands in the domesticated rat are much reduced in size compared with the adrenals found in the same species of rat still living in the wild state and subjected to the normal stresses of living. Disorders of endocrine gland function are associated with major changes or disturbances in temperamental and affective characteristics. But it is now clear that, with respect to motivational and emotional processes, the endocrine gland system, though important, is only part of a complex integrated network of tissue systems, which includes the autonomic nervous system, the reticular formation, the hypothalamus, and the cortex of the brain, and that none of these special organ systems operates in isolation.

Some problems discussed in connection with the autonomic nervous system and emotional states apply to the endocrine system as well. For example, only recently has evidence been provided that the biochemistry of fear and anger is different. A clue to this suggestion comes from the casual observation that in fear a person is likely to grow pale and, as in stage fright, show marked reduction in the fluids usually present in the mouth and other mucous-membrane areas. In contrast, when a person is angry, we expect a red face and considerable mucous-membrane secretion. For a long time only one substance, adrenalin, was known to be secreted by the adrenal medulla and to function clearly in emotional states, but it is now believed that, in addition to adrenalin, a related but different substance called *noradrenalin* is also secreted by the adrenal medulla.

These two chemicals are made extremely difficult to isolate technically, and the distinction can be regarded as still on the frontiers of knowledge about the biochemistry of emotions. But there is reason to believe (Funkenstein, King, & Drolette, 1957) that, when the organism is frightened, adrenalin is the predominant secretion and it produces its own pattern of visceral change. However, when the organism is angry or in a state of readiness for action, noradrenalin secretion is increased, which, while its effects overlap with those of adrenalin, has some unique visceral consequences. In this connection, Funkenstein and his colleagues (1957) have cited the interesting observation that carnivorous animals show a higher proportion of noradrenalin in their systems than do animals that are herbivorous and tend to be timid. Although the current evidence does not completely settle the question, it begins to appear that the endocrine as well as autonomic patterns vary in distinctive ways in different emotional states.

In general it is true that considerable strides have been made over the past few decades in identifying some of the physiological mechanisms that underlie motivational and emotional states in animals and man.

The Processes of Cognition

In many respects, cognitive processes set man off from lower organisms to a greater degree than any other aspect of human function. These include the highest adaptive functions of any organism: learning, problem solving, perception, and thought. In tracing the history of ideas, there is reason to believe that the notion of the brain as important in cognition is an extremely old one, perhaps dating back as far as 3000 B.C. It is universally recognized today that the physiological mechanisms underlying cognitive behavior are found mainly in the mass of tissues composing the brain. The following discussion is to highlight certain current ideas in this field, especially as they pertain to personality and adjustment.

The development of a system of phrenology by Gall and Spurzheim (Boring, 1950) in the early nineteenth century had a dramatic impact on modern concepts of the brain. These German physicians suggested (1) that the brain was the organ of the mind, (2) that different behaviors were controlled by specific parts of the brain, and (3) that the development of the brain was reflected in the shape of the skull. In this way, areas of over- or underdevelopment could be identified and the temperamental characteristics and talents of a person could be identified by an analysis of these brain bumps. The third postulate of phrenology was later rejected, and phrenology in general was discredited, but the work of Gall and Spurzheim successfully emphasized the relationship between the structure of the brain and behavior and set the stage for later attempts to correlate specific psychological functions with particular areas of the brain by elaborate brain mapping. As Morgan (1951, p. 50, see Figure 20) pointed out, "We gradually got away from these maps because there were many human cases of cerebral injury that did not give the symptoms that the maps called for, and also because animal experiments gave the maps no support. So the maps of cognitive areas of the cortex, and the general idea of localization of cognitive function in the cortex, have not been too popular of late."

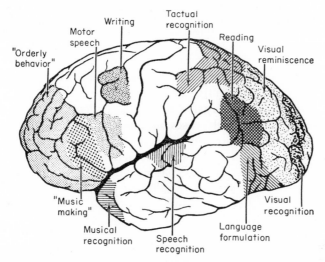

Figure 20. A composite diagram of possible association areas of the cerebral cortex. Localization of memories is undoubtedly not so precise as this diagram would indicate. It gives a general idea, however, of the way in which various areas are more concerned in one memory function than in another. (*From Morgan,* 1956.)

In spite of the disaffection with the extremes to which map makers of the brain went in identifying the particular areas of the cerebral cortex that were involved in the various cognitive functions of learning, problem solving, perception, and thinking, the problem of *cortical localization* remains with us, partly because to some degree there seems to be evidence of general locales for certain types of cognitive activity. Moreover, as we have suggested earlier in this chapter, excitatory and inhibitory areas of the sensory and motor cortex have been pretty clearly identified. Furthermore, as Morgan (1951) suggested, the brain maps have not been given a fair chance because of certain characteristics of the brain and special methodological difficulties.

For one thing, most of the experimental work of this sort has been done with lower animals, on whom it is difficult or impossible to devise methods to get at some of the more complex cognitive functions in which we are interested. More ingenuity and effort has been directed at the physiological techniques than at psychological measurement. The latter requires the construction of tasks for the animal or person to perform that clearly reflect the specific psychological function being studied.

Another problem concerns our lack of knowledge about the areas in the rat, cat, or monkey brain that correspond to the cortex of the human brain. Lateral dominance in the brain also complicates matters. In some kinds of activities, one side of the brain is dominant over the other, that is, plays a greater role in some cognitive activity. Thus, if one side of the brain is injured, either by an accident or by experimental operation, the absence of an effect can be due to the fact that the nondominant side has been injured. Or perhaps both sides of the cerebral cortex are equally prominent in the cognitive function, and thus a lesion on both sides is required to produce the cognitive change.

Finally, as is true of the organization of the endocrine glands, there are considerable individual differences in the sizes and shapes of brains. These individual differences in brain anatomy raise difficult technical questions concerning generalizations from one brain to another when this generalization depends upon the statement that the exactly homologous tissues have been damaged in two different persons. Of course, the anatomical differences between human brains support our article of faith that differences in cognitive behavior and personality can ultimately be traced to differences in physical structure.

In any event, the problem of cortical localization remains alive even though the early extremism of a point-by-point relationship between cognitive behavior and specific cortical tissues has been much modified in favor of the belief that all parts of the cortex are involved in every cognitive activity, at least to some extent. Lashley (1929) introduced the still-influential principle of *equipotentiality*, which asserts that, except for the primary, sensory, and motor areas of the brain, any part of the cortex can do what any other part can do. He also enunciated the corollary principle of *mass action*, maintaining that the adequacy of a brain-injured organism depends primarily upon the total amount of cortex destroyed.

The controversy over localization of brain function reflects the continuing struggle by physiologically oriented psychologists to relate the structural characteristics of the cerebral cortex to cognitive behavior. Although considerable progress has been made in the last fifteen years in our understanding of the anatomy of the brain, there appears to be slow progress at best in relating anatomy to cognitive processes.

Brain lesions and disorders of cognition: One of the main ways in which we study the relationship between the structure of the brain and cognitive activity is through experimental ablation, that is, the systematic removal of particular parts of the brain. After ablation, we can examine losses in the ability of the animal to perform various cognitive tasks. The functions that the animal can no longer perform are then assumed to be sustained by the tissues that have been destroyed. A logically related method is the clinical examination of cognitive functioning in human beings whose brains have been damaged by accident or tumor. Similarly, persons come to the attention of medical authorities because they have unexplained symptoms, and neurological analysis may turn up lesions of the brain. Such brain damage can cause sensory disorders (for example, defects of vision or hearing) and motor disorders (such as paralysis or disturbances of gait, writing, gesture, and speech); among the most interesting and pathetic effects of brain lesions are those that disturb memory, even in the absence of any severe loss in sensation. Such a person can see, hear, and move adequately, but he seems to have lost the meanings of ordinary objects around him.

Neurologists identify three general types of such memory defects: agnosia, aphasia, and apraxia. In *agnosia*, the patient is unable to recognize what used to be familiar to him. The loss can involve certain spheres of meaning rather than others, so one particular patient with agnosia might be unable to recognize parts of his own body and another might show the defect in spatial arrangements, in colors, or in the names of things. The latter disturbance has often been called *anomia* (literally, without names); the individual understands that shoes are used to cover feet and to walk in, but even after being told he cannot call to mind the word "shoes" when they are placed before him.

Aphasia is a disturbance in language. It can be primarily sensory or motor in character. In sensory aphasia the patient cannot formulate words, although he is able to recognize them and to identify their meanings; or, even if he can formulate them, the disturbance can be inability to identify word meanings. In motor aphasia, the patient is unable to speak the words even though he understands what persons are saying and knows the words he wishes to speak.

In *apraxia*, the person cannot perform certain purposeful movements even though the disturbance is not centered about language. The difficulty is in the voluntary control of certain muscles of the body, so he cannot, for example, make intentional movements of the tongue, of the head, or of a part of the body even though spontaneous involuntary movements of that body part are not impaired. In all three types of memory disorder there has been injury to some part of the cerebrum, especially often around the temporal lobe of the cerebral cortex. But, as pointed out earlier, no specific group of tissues has been located for each of these very specific cognitive effects.

There have been large numbers of clinical investigations in man on the effects of brain injury (especially of the frontal lobes of the cerebral cortex) upon complex perceptual and intellectual functions. The interested reader is invited to read reviews by Klebanoff, Singer, and Wilensky (1954) and by Meyer (1957). A great deal of the research has dealt with the proposal by Goldstein (1939, 1941) that cortical injury will produce disturbances in figure-ground discrimination, that is, defects in a person's ability to pick out a specific form (the figure) from a complex of irrelevant details (the ground). Various tests of figure-ground discrimination (such as the famous Gottschalt figures) have been devised to test this function.

Goldstein and his collaborators have published a series of papers over many years attempting to demonstrate this figure-ground defect in patients with lesions in various cerebral areas. Although there is disagreement over the specific importance of frontal-lobe lesions in producing this type of defect, there is rather general agreement that brain damage does tend to disrupt figure-ground perception. Location of the lesion does not seem to be an important determinant, a fact that argues against the position of an extreme localization of function in the cerebral cortex. On the other hand, there is also a wide range of variability in the amount of defect, so changes in figure-ground performance are not an invariant result of cerebral injury.

Another proposal by Goldstein, even more influential and more frequently cited than that dealing with figure-ground disturbance, is that after cerebral damage a person has difficulty in adopting an abstract attitude. This abstract ability was seen by Goldstein as an extension of a basic figure-ground process that when disturbed, manifests (1) an inability to form a set voluntarily and shift it when required, (2) difficulty in grasping the essentials of a whole and analyzing the relationships between the parts, and (3) difficulties in abstracting common properties from stimuli and performing symbolically with these abstractions. Thus a patient with severe cerebral damage is described who was told to look out the window and imagine that it was raining. He could not make this abstraction and responded with the repeated assertion that it wasn't raining. This is an example of concreteness, the inability to get away from the immediate, concrete circumstance. There appears to be general research support for the notion that lesions of the cerebral cortex are often (but not always) associated with impairment in abstract thinking, although here too there is some debate whether the frontal lobes are of greater significance in this regard than other areas of the cortex.

The work of Goldstein on disturbances of figure-ground organization and the loss of ability to form abstractions as a result of damage to the cortex of the brain has resulted in the creation of a number of concept-formation and sorting tests used by clinical psychologists to diagnose the presence of brain damage (Goldstein & Scheerer, 1941). Most of these tests require the subject to sort different kinds of wooden blocks or objects by some abstract principle (for example, color or shape) and then shift to another principle of sorting. One of the best known of these sorting tests is the Object Sorting Test. It consists of thirty-three objects, differing in use, color, form, and material. These must be grouped in various ways by the subject, and the abstract principle of the different

Figure 21. The Goldstein-Scheerer Object Sorting Test. (*Courtesy of The Psychological Corporation.*)

sortings must be verbalized by the subject. An evaluation of performance can not only be used to identify effects of brain damage, but can also be useful in understanding certain aspects of the subject's personality. A version of this test, as published by the Psychological Corporation, is illustrated in Figure 21.

A general review of this type of research on brain lesions and disorders of cognition suggests that neither location nor cause of cortical lesions seems to be important in determining intellectual deficit in man or in chimpanzee. Rather, generalized defects are observed in figure-ground discrimination and in abstract behavior. There is little evidence of a sharp difference between sensory and perceptual deficits, or between perceptual and cognitive disturbances, after brain injury in man. Basic sensory activities are intimately intertwined with more complex functions, which, in turn, depend upon and are essential to the higher cognitive activities, such as remembering, learning, thinking, and communicating. It is difficult to compare studies in man with studies in animals, partly because of the differences in brain structure and partly because the nature of the functions tested and testable in animals and man appears different. The experimental as well as clinical search for correlations between the structure of the brain and cognitive functions continues unabated.

Brain waves and states of attention: Another area of research into brain physiology and adaptive behavior is the more recent field of electroencephalography. A psychiatrist by the name of Hans Berger first demonstrated brain waves in 1929, showing that electrical activity of the brain could be recorded without opening the skull. Since then, many physiological psychologists have considered that the study of brain waves offers tantalizing possibilities for understanding the brain in relation to behavior and cognitive processes, although its contribution in this regard has thus far been quite limited. As it turns out, the current research importance of the electroencephalogram (EEG) lies in the faith that many researchers have that it will some day reveal important secrets. Its primary use is actually clinical, in identifying abnormal brain states (such as tumors), that is, as an aid to diagnosis and surgical treatment.

The brain waves of the human being show a number of patterns or rhythms (having to do with amplitude and frequency of the waves or impulses) that appear to vary under different behavioral conditions. The normal electrical outputs occurring under relaxed conditions are referred to as "alpha waves" and they become more and more irregular and slow as the individual goes through the progression of becoming sleepy, falling asleep, and entering into a deep sleep. Conversely, they become reduced in amplitude and very rapid when a person is excited. As we have seen earlier in this chapter, brain waves also respond to activity from the autonomic nervous system. Thus, they seem to reflect psychological disturbances, arousal, consciousness, and various attention states (see Figure 22).

As Jasper and Shagass (1941) have demonstrated, learning to anticipate a stimulus is accompanied by changes in the pattern of alpha-wave rhythms. Also, if a person attends to a visual stimulus or is given some mental problem to solve, the alpha wave is reduced in amplitude (Davis & Davis, 1936). Thus, mental activity, which includes the cognitive processes of perceiving, learning, remembering, and thinking, seems to be reflected in electrical activities in the brain, and the EEG provides one means of identifying this activity.

Brain chemistry and adaptive behavior: A very recent development in the area of brain physiology and adaptive behavior appears in the work of Rosenzweig, Krech, and Bennett (1959) on brain chemistry. The emphasis of this research is on the adequacy of learning in strains of rats that are genetically different in amount of certain chemical substances thought to be important in nerve transmission. These experimenters, noting the fairly unsuccessful efforts of physiological investigators to find

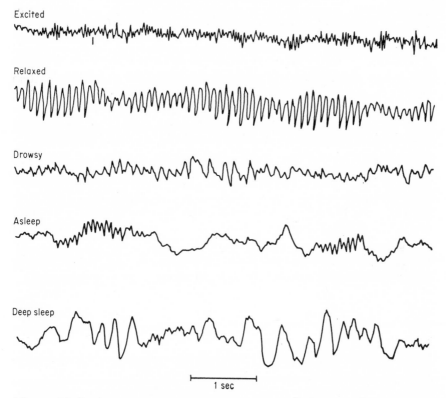

Excited

Relaxed

Drowsy

Asleep

Deep sleep

1 sec

Figure 22. Brain-wave patterns in various states of alertness. (*From Jasper,* 1941.)

structural changes in the brain occurring during learning, maintain that key changes in brain chemistry of a particular sort occur.

It has been known for some time that when an impulse reaches the end of a neuron, it causes a tiny jet of an enzyme, acetylcholine (ACh), to be released into the synaptic space between that neuron and the next. When the ACh has diffused across the tiny synaptic space, it excites the subsequent neuron and therefore results in synaptic transmission. The amount of acetylcholine available in the neuron is probably related to its capacity to transmit impulses. After the ACh has produced excitation across the synapse, it must be eliminated rapidly in order to prepare the synaptic region for the next impulse. Another enzyme, cholinesterase (ChE) breaks up the acetylcholine so it does not accumulate at the synapse. The brain-chemistry research of Rosenzweig, Krech, and Bennett attempts to measure cholinesterase activity as an index of the amount of ACh available in the system for nervous transmission. Some evidence has been presented that it is related to learning and also that there is a genetic determination of the availability of cholinesterase in the rat's nervous system. This type of research is at an early stage of development and is regarded by physiologists and psychologists with mixed reactions; it is mentioned here to illustrate the kinds of effort being made to locate the structural, electrical, and chemical mechanisms in the nervous system that are fundamental to the cognitive processes studied by psychologists.

BRAIN PHYSIOLOGY AND PERSONALITY PROCESSES

It must be clear to the reader that in the study of the physiological bases of motivational, emotional, and cognitive processes, progress has been limited mainly to simple functions in lower organisms. At the present time, the psychologist concerned with personality looks with hope to the physiological psychologist for evidence concerning the physiological determinants of the stable motivational and control processes that make up the personality. But developments in this field tend to promise important discovery rather than provide, as yet, a clear groundwork.

The tempting quality of seeking to understand psychological processes in terms of physiological mechanisms is nicely illustrated by an experiment by Hernández-Péon, Scherrer, and Jouvet (1956), dealing with a physiological mechanism underlying attention and perception and their inhibition. Let us first look at some personality theory, which makes the study to be described of interest to the personality psychologist.

One of the common constructs of personality, already discussed, is ego defense. A great deal of clinical and experimental evidence has been accumulated that the human being is capable of tuning out threatening stimulation either from within, in the form of unacceptable impulses, or from without, in terms of environmental dangers. For example, repression is a mechanism by which a person deceives himself about his true feelings and thoughts and remains unaware of their existence.

If one conceives ego-defense processes physiologically, one must argue that one set of activities in the nervous system must be inhibited by or proceed independently of another. In this way, a person can be selectively oriented to his environment and certain aspects of his past experience can be made available or unavailable to consciousness depending upon their capacity to arouse distress. This is sometimes referred to as "perceptual defense." In a recent discussion of perception, Bruner (1957) proposed neural mechanisms of the perceptual system analogous to defense mechanisms. His discussion included concepts such as "gaiting," which implies that the nervous system can select out of a complex stimulus input some things to send upward to the cortex and other things to ignore or to shut out.

The experiment dealing with processes of this kind performed by Hernández-Péon, Scherrer, and Jouvet (1956) has aroused widespread interest among psychologists who are concerned with physiological mechanisms underlying cognitive processes. In this study, electrical activity in the auditory-nerve pathways was measured under varying conditions of attention. Electrodes were implanted in the cochlear nucleus (an early relay station in the neural pathway concerned with hearing) of a cat by means of a small hole bored in the skull. This permitted the recording of electrical activity at the cochlear nucleus under varying conditions of auditory stimulation.

About a week after the implantation, short clicks were sounded over a loud-speaker near the cat, and these clicks were picked up electrically, showing that neural impulses from the ear were reaching the cochlear nucleus on their way to lower brain centers and eventually to the cortex. Presumably, the cat heard the clicks from the loud-speaker. At this point, two mice in a closed bottle were placed in front of the cat, and immediately, as might be anticipated, the cat became intensely oriented to the mice. The remarkable thing was that the electrically recorded click responses all but disappeared in spite of the fact that the loud-speaker continued to sound the clicks. They returned when the mice were removed.

The evidence meant that neural impulses from the ear were blocked at or before the cochlear nucleus, and though we cannot ask the cat, we might assume it could not hear the clicks because the neural impulses never reached the cortex. When the mice were removed, the cat relaxed and the electrically recorded click response returned in full strength. The same type of finding was obtained by presenting olfactory stimuli such as fish odors, which also suppressed the cochlear nucleus response to the clicking sounds. It is a reasonable assumption that this blocking occurs by means of neural impulses associated with intense concentration, which descend through the reticular formation from the cortex. These serve to inhibit incoming sensory stimuli from ascending through the reticular formation to the cortex. It is also extremely tempting to argue that a mechanism such as this operates in selective attention in human beings and also in the process of ego defense, which protects the individual from recognizing stimuli that are intensely disturbing to him. Thus, the person can shut out the disturbing input by concentrating on something more acceptable or benign. The experiment discussed above seems to be a physiological analog to this kind of defense process, even though it occurs quite peripherally in the nervous system; that is, way out near the ear rather than in the central portion of the brain.

It must be recognized that it is one thing to say that the nervous system is so constructed that such a mechanism *could* operate, as is implied by the experiment, and another thing to say that this *is* the physiological mechanism that underlies ego-defense processes. The evidence produced by Hernández-Péon and his associates indicates that mechanisms of selective attention and ego defense, as postulated by personality psychologists, are neurologically possible. Ultimately, it will be necessary to pinpoint the exact physiological mechanism underlying each cognitive event in which we are interested. Neurophysiologists have known of inhibitory processes in the nervous system for a long time and now recognize both excitatory and inhibitory areas all over the brain. Thus, the idea of ego defense is in itself not remarkable, considering what is known about the structure of the nervous system. In the face of the intriguing research that is reported from systematic efforts to learn more about the physiological bases of adaptive behavior, one cannot fail to be excited at the tantalizing prospects.

This chapter emphasized the physiology of man as a determinant of behavior and, by inference, of the structures and processes of personality. Some highlights of modern research and thought concerning the physiological determinants of motivational, emotional, and cognitive processes have been touched upon. The concern has been with man's internal environment. Let us now turn to an examination of external social environment as a determinant of behavior and personality. The significance of the social context into which man is born is discussed in Chapter 10.

CHAPTER

10

Social Factors and Personality

Most of man's actions are interpersonal. His behavior is oriented
largely to other persons even without their physical presence. His
actions are directed by the expectations of others and by anticipations
of their behavior toward him. Furthermore, membership in each social
grouping within a society requires the playing of a social role. People
are Republicans or Democrats; men or women; rich or poor; educated
or uneducated; they are fathers or mothers or sons or daughters; they
are teachers, doctors, skilled tradesmen, or salesmen. In each case there
are more or less clearly defined definitions of how a person is to believe
and act.

From this point of view, the structure of the society in which man lives
is a very important influence on behavior. To the degree that this behavior reflects the underlying structures and processes of the personality,
the social structure is fundamental to the personality development. That
this is believed by most influential theorists of personality should be
clear by recalling especially the points of view of the Neo-Freudians,
such as Sullivan, Horney, and Adler. There are differences in the degree
to which social factors are emphasized, but no theory of personality
totally neglects social factors as determinants of personality. As was the
case with physiological factors, it is well to remember that the relevant
data consist of correlations between various social variables and stable
patterns of behavior. From these behavior patterns, the hypothetical structures and processes of the personality, such as motives, values, attitudes,
and types of ego control, are inferred. These constructs, in turn, can be
related to the social factors that affect the behavior from which they (the
personality constructs) are derived.

The purpose of this chapter is to examine the influence of social conditions on behavior. We shall be explicitly or implicitly asking what
social factors are important in behavior and also how they produce their
effects.

SOCIETY, CULTURE, AND THE INDIVIDUAL

The essential point in the social analysis of behavior is that man lives in a society of other men. A society is an organized group of persons. There are many forms of society, and they differ in organization and in the number and kinds of persons involved. Within any large society there can be subsocieties of many types.

Culture is an aspect of any society. It consists of the learned and usually organized patterns of behavior characteristic of a particular society. Although the term "culture" often is used by the lay person to mean the nonutilitarian aspects of life that are characteristic of an elite, educated, well-mannered kind of person, to the anthropologist culture involves the artifacts, goods, technical processes, ideas, habits, and values of a society. The values, habits, and ideas of the society, as they are communicated through word or action, are the most important aspects of culture with respect to man's behavior.

A person is influenced profoundly by the culture in which he lives. But although he is a product of the society and its cultural pattern, he remains an individual, with a unique value system and behavior pattern. In other words, he is like other persons in that he shares many of their values and habits; but because his experiences are not identical with those of others, he can have value and action patterns unlike any other individual in precise details.

At this point, it is well to touch upon an interesting question that arises in connection with the use of the expression "membership in a society." Membership can have both a subjective and an objective quality. A person can be classified *objectively* as a member of the lower economic class within a society on the basis of his income. For example, a lower-class person can be defined as one whose income is less than some given amount. Working for someone else rather than being self-employed can be another criterion of lower-class rather than middle-class membership. *Subjectively*, however, such a person can identify himself with middle-class society. Moreover, we can predict his behavior better by knowing his subjective social-class membership than we can from an objective definition. Because he identifies with middle-class society, his patterns of behavior may be more similar to those of a middle-class person than to those of a lower-class person. It will be well to bear in mind this distinction between objective and subjective social memberships as we proceed through this chapter. It is similar to the behavioral-phenomenological distinction we found in personality theory, and we shall have occasion to refer to it again later.

A Little Sociology

Some familiar structural characteristics of society should be considered before proceeding further. In any society the members are classified in certain ways, usually by factors such as age, sex, knowledge, and possessions, and on this basis the members are assigned certain *social roles*, which define appropriate patterns of behavior. Thus, in primitive societies men are usually expected to do the hunting and fighting and women to collect vegetable foods and care for the young children.

All societies tend to be divided into smaller, organized units called "families," which are the means by which much of the culture is transmitted to the individual. Anthropologists and sociologists frequently refer to the *nuclear family*, which is a subgroup within the larger family, consisting of a couple and their children. This nuclear family is contrasted with other groupings within the larger family, which are based upon some type of blood relationship, either real or assumed. Thus, in the western family, for example, there are grandparents, aunts and uncles, and cousins. Certain patterns of behavior are established for the individual within the family. The father commonly plays a different role from the mother, and so on.

Another characteristic of societies is that formal patterned relationships exist into which members of the society can enter voluntarily. Thus, there are unavoidable relationships based upon blood ties, and there are voluntary and avoidable relationships into which we can enter. Societies of teachers, social clubs, fraternities, and local gangs are some examples of the latter. In making the same distinction between voluntary and involuntary group relationships, Linton (1955, p. 32) cited the proverb, "God gives us our relatives, but thank God we can choose our friends."

A final characteristic of societies to be mentioned involves the evaluation of persons and groups in terms of prestige or *status*. Every group whose existence is recognized by society is placed in a hierarchy of inferior or superior status relative to some other group of the same type. Such status characteristics determine the social roles played by the members. Although societies differ in the degree to which the definition of status or prestige is fixed for an individual at birth, all societies have such status patterns. In our own society there is greater fluidity (sometimes referred to as "social mobility") in status patterns than exists in many others. The individual has a greater chance to change his level through his own efforts or by social accident than in other societies, where status patterns are fixed at birth and cannot be altered. When such fixed orderings occur and the individual is relatively powerless to change his

Figure 23. A Negro university student is surrounded by white youths during a sit-in demonstration in a Southern community drug store where segregation is an issue. The incident exemplifies a caste problem characteristic of our society and the tensions created by them. Negroes are seeking service at lunch counters where only white persons now are served. (*Wide World Photos.*)

status, we have what is called *caste*. The Negroes in the United States represent a caste division because there are fixed limits placed by society upon their status and the social activities in which they can participate. A modern example of this caste problem is illustrated in Figure 23.

Any single person can express only part of the total culture of the society in which he lives. No member is familiar with the entire culture, but every member has enough common knowledge to understand and predict the behavior of others to a certain degree. In a sense, persons belonging to different subsocieties within a total society are specialists because they are particularly informed about the value system or technology of a particular social group. For example, neither the psychologist nor the physician is apt to be familiar with more than a small part of the other's field of technological competence, yet there will be mutual influence and a general ability to communicate.

Certain things are shared by all the members of a society. They have a common language, even though there may be great differences in the language styles for different regions or subsocieties. The southerner's speech is easily understood by the rest of us, although the accent and forms of expression may be strange to persons living in other communities. Subsocieties within the total society have special or unique characteristics, which make them different from other social groups, but they also share certain common heritages and social characteristics. They are members of the same society and have a common core of culture.

Society organizes the patterns of behavior of its members by certain rules, which are established by common consent or by law. Persons are expected to play social roles (a social-psychological theoretical construct referring to established interpersonal behavior patterns) of various types, and these roles are organized or instituted by society by virtue of authority. That is, we are permitted or encouraged to play varying kinds of roles depending upon the nature of the social institutions of the society. Employees are subject to certain control by owners and managers, but the roles of employees have changed considerably with the emergence of the labor union and collective bargaining. A soldier is subject to the authority of the commanding officer. He plays a role according to his rank and the type of military unit to which he belongs. Whenever a role configuration (patterns of roles among persons) is so guaranteed or stabilized by some authority or law or social agreement, the configuration is called a *social institution*. The social structure is built up of institutions, which establish the patterns of behavior among the society's members.

Institutions can be classified to enable us to compare the social structures of different societies. They can be classified by size or by method by which the members are recruited. Some sociologists, for example, Gerth and Mills (1953), classify institutions according to their objective function, that is, the ends they serve. They speak of *institutional orders*, which consist of all those institutions within a social structure that have similar consequences or ends and serve similar objective functions. In modern societies of the western world, Gerth and Mills distinguished five major institutional orders, which, although they do not exhaust all the institutional orders that might be cited, include the major social patterns. The institutions dealing with the collective worship of God or gods are called *religious institutions*. Together, all these institutions make up the religious institutional order. Similarly, institutions having to do with power are called *political institutions;* those having to do with violence, *military institutions*. Procreation and marriage involve *kinship order,* and institutions dealing with goods and services are called *economic order.*

Another way to analyze the social structure is by social groupings.

which vary in size and generality. Thus, the social psychologist Queener (1951) distinguishes social class, caste, and sex and attempts to show how membership in these various institutionalized groupings influences the behavior of the individual. We have merely touched upon some of the considerations that must be dealt with in an analysis of social institutions. Our task is not primarily the examination of society but the analysis of the impact of this society upon the developing individual. Having touched upon some sociological questions, we now are prepared to deal with the psychological implications of social structure. We shall begin by examining a number of instances of the impact of society on the individual, as it has been studied by anthropologists and by social psychologists. Later we shall consider how this impact comes about. Our first concern (following Queener) will be with the role of culture, broadly conceived, followed by a consideration of the influence of social class, caste, sex, and smaller groups.

CULTURE AND BEHAVIOR

Variations in culture are systematically studied by anthropologists. These studies often are made by living with the particular society for long enough periods of time to learn the language, observe the customs, and analyze the social institutions. Sometimes when the society is inaccessible to the anthropologist through direct observation, he can interview persons from that society with the aid of an interpreter and construct a conception of the culture of that society.

If we wish to understand the influence of culture on behavior, it is necessary to compare the behavior patterns of individual members of different societies. In this way, the theoretical concept of *social character* (or "basic personality") of a society has been derived, which represents a conglomeration of the value systems and role patterns inferred from the behavior patterns that appear to be characteristic of a particular society. Where differences in social character occur, the implications are that the differences in the cultural pattern are largely responsible. Individual members of any society conform to a greater or less degree to this theoretical abstraction of the social character. The concept is not useful in describing an individual member of the society, but it can be used to describe the dominant personality characteristics arising from it.

Some examples of analyses of social character of particular national groups are Schaffner's (1948) study of the Germans, Kardiner's (1945) examination of an American community, and Benedict's (1946) description of the Japanese personality. Let us examine the excellent summaries provided by Queener (1951, pp. 323–324) of these studies:

Basic Personality in Germany

The child is born into a society with such dominant values as national and family honor, with such dominant techniques (and values too) as order, ranking, self-discipline, the military, and science. Exemplar of these values and master of these techniques is the father, and so his is the highest rank in the family. The motive for being like him is mainly *Ehrfurcht* (honor-fear). He partly earns honor and fear by doing his *duty* by wife and children; he makes more of his duty than his love. The boy with sufficient *Ehrfurcht* will strive to be like him; the girl with sufficient *Ehrfurcht* will strive to be like his version of the woman's role. For the first this means masculine attitudes (particularly respect for higher rank) and skills. For the second this means feminine attitudes (particularly the sanctity of masculine enterprises) and skills. To show insufficient *Ehrfurcht* is to hurt the dutiful father, to earn his stern punishments, and to grow up different from the majority of one's fellows. When one goes to school, he finds himself ranked even down to his seating position in the room; he finds the same demand for order, for respect, for preciseness; discipline is strict. When one goes into the world of business or profession, here too there is thorough ranking with full respect expected and given between ranks. When a boy goes into the army, he finds but an extension of what his family, his school, and his civilian life has been; the army represents no great break with the motives and behaviors to which he has been long accustomed, and its additional rigor of dealing and accepting death is perceived as but the ultimate opportunity to express one's *Ehrfurcht* to the *Fatherland*. There emerges thus a personality frustrated by many a discipline but reserving its aggressions for others than the disciplinarians. The frustration engendered by the father and father-surrogates (teachers, officers, dictators) he has learned to perceive as his due. He will honor them by an almost compulsive expression of orderliness, dutifulness, and nationalist-family ideology. In hard work he will attenuate the tensions that arise when he is not all of these things; in war he may reduce his aggressions against the enemies of his country or find final release in an honorable death.

Schaffner, who had a first-hand knowledge of Germany from living there, also used extensive clinical methods and questionnaires to study more than 2,000 persons in various parts of Germany. There is much variation on the part of individual Germans from the pattern he describes, but Schaffner believed that this description represents a valid abstraction of the German personality or social character.

Queener continues (1951, pp. 324–325):

Basic Personality in an American Community

The most decisive factor is the generally good maternal care, with its effective solicitation of emotional response. Out of the solicitations showered upon him, the child learns to regard himself as important ("positive ego feelings") but at the same time learns that these solicitations are bought at the price of his adhering to certain moral ideals ("strong superego formation"). One of the areas in which the beloved mother, and most of the remaining community, is likely to be threatening, however, is that of the child's psycho-sexual behaviors; he learns here a variety of emotional responses to sexual wants, many of which are conducive to psychic impotency, frigidity, and bizarre compensations for these in later life. Outside of this impediment to efficient personality, he is likely to emerge in adolescence as a fairly well-adjusted person. The well-loved parents have been cuing him to considerable curiosity and aggressiveness all through childhood, and in adolescence they begin gradually to place a greater premium upon practical skills. He stands on the edge of adulthood as an individual with a good opinion of his personal importance, a generous amount of conscience (superego), and probably some one of the skills of a technical culture, but from here on there are characteristic difficulties. For one his status is usually not assured; he must fight for it; he received no rank or calling by birth. As it becomes apparent that very few indeed can achieve the status demanded by their well-developed ego-systems, a variety of aggressions and other compensatory behaviors appear. And then there is the problem of marriage in which years of taboo training are supposed to be set aside by legal or religious rites and in which two people with almost equally well-developed opinions of themselves must live together. Thus in both the areas of work and marriage the individual's self-esteem is challenged. Men with less promising childhoods might take the challenge lying down; these throw themselves into a series of compensatory behaviors and hard labor. Adjustments will be made, of course, but the "tension points" remain to manifest themselves when competitive labor languishes or compensatory mechanisms (for example, sexual or economic aggressiveness) break down. There emerges here, then, a person aware of his importance as an individual, competent in materialistic technology, competitive but often hurt by competition, conscience-concerned but often in conflict with his conscience. For all but a few these motives may be partially reduced in hard work, skill, a battery of rationalizations, and an occasional atypical behavior.

It should be recognized that these concepts were based upon observations of behavior and interviews with community members in a small and relatively backward American community (West & Withers, 1945). A more valid conception of the American personality would have to be based upon a broader sampling of American communities. This qualification represents the chief disadvantage of attempting to abstract social character or basic personality of a society. The picture of the personality that is derived does not apply to any particular person or necessarily to every community within the society. Its appropriateness is based upon the suitability and representativeness of the sample. If the sample is large enough and representative enough to cover the entire society, then the abstraction becomes less applicable to individuals, or even classes of individuals. If the description is limited, as it is in the case of Kardiner's study, to a single community, then the abstraction is less applicable to the society at large but more appropriate to a small segment of this society. Because of these limitations, some social psychologists have been skeptical altogether about the value of the concept of social character.

Queener goes on (1951, pp. 326–327):

Basic Personality in Japan

The growing Japanese becomes aware of a constant concern among his elders; this is the concern for *hierarchy*, for every person behaving according to their station. Within his family he learns that men rate above women, boys above girls, older boys above younger ones. In the larger society he meets the same hierarchy only more so; above all of course, stands the Emperor. One's station, however, is not just a matter of name but more a matter of *behavior;* one does the expected thing in his status, and the worst that can be said of a person is that he does the unexpected. To be sure that the maturing child shall never do the unexpected, he is taught precisely how to behave; nothing is left to chance learning: the mother tilts the infant's head forward in a bow and the father teaches massage by gripping the child's hands and putting them through the precise motions. This is important, for to behave unexpectedly is to be ridiculed and thus to experience *shame; shame* (the contempt of others) and not *guilt* (the contempt of oneself) is the stabbing anxiety within the Japanese. And it is an anxiety reinforced from *every* side; having been ridiculed by the world, one cannot turn even to his family, for they too must reject you. In earlier years dishonoring experiences are avoided as much as possible: in school every child passes and in games everyone is awarded a prize. But by middle school some competition is necessary and in several instances anxiety will mount to suicide. There are more ways than one of doing the unexpected in one's role: first, you may fail to meet an *obligation* (an *on*); second, you may fail to exhibit the perfection expected within your status. Some obligations, to the Emperor or one's parents, can never be repaid, and nothing short of a willingness to make the ultimate sacrifice to them suffices. Other obligations, such as that incurred when a friend (or worse still, a stranger) does you a favor, may eventually be repaid but are a source of anxiety until paid: one word for "thank you" means "this poisonous feeling." Failure to appear perfect in one's position may also incur ridicule, and the professor who has made a statement, the businessman or general who has made a decision, admits to error very seldom—and then only with shame. All is not rigor and shame, to be sure: the child's life involves a minimum of taboos toward sensual delights and has been spent with a father who, though his lord, treats him with warmth. Sex, sleep, food are treated as luxuries to be taken or left as circumstances allow, and the Japanese can do both. The senses are to be hedged only at those points where they might hinder the perfect execution of one's role. *And so what appears here as basic personality in Japan?*

We meet an individual who perceives his own and others' behaviors as the most subtle indicators of position in a hierarchy. To suggest by one's own behavior that the Japanese position is inferior to what he takes it to be is to mount within him his most devastating emotional experiences—shame. For him not to correct this insult is for him to shame the entire hierarchy including himself, his family, his Emperor. Considering the vast array of behavioral nuances by which he may be thus humiliated, he functions at a high level of anxiety and a low threshold of aggression. This latter he can implement with a highly developed executive capacity, although within recent decades he may be turning much aggression inward in the form of a self-destroying pessimism.

Other Studies of Culture and Its Influence on Behavior

Margaret Mead has done extensive studies of various primitive societies and their influences on behavior. One of the most interesting problems she explored is the basis of the turmoil so characteristic of adolescence in our society. In western culture the adolescent period is characterized by a great deal of psychological stress. It has been assumed by many that the behavioral disturbances characteristic of adolescent development are the result of the processes of physical maturation that accompany the adolescent period. The development of secondary sex characteristics, such as menstruation and the growth of the breasts in girls and the formation of a masculine physique in boys, are some of the obvious physical changes characterizing adolescence.

Mead (1928) made an intensive study of the adolescent period in Samoan society. In Samoa, adolescence in girls, dated by the first menses, is heralded by considerable fanfare and celebration. During the period immediately following, the adolescent girl is freer of social responsibility than she has ever been before or will ever be again. Prior to adolescence she was responsible for a great many womanly chores, including the caring for the younger children in the family, and she will after adolescence take on the responsibility of motherhood and rearing a family. But from the time she arrives at adolescence to the time she marries, she is free to court, engage in a considerable amount of sex play, and generally pursue a variety of pleasures with a minimum of social obligation.

The adolescent period for girls in Samoa is not characterized at all by the disturbances found in our own and other societies. Instead, it seems to be a relatively blissful period, after which the girl's lot in life is quite clearly defined and no great source of anxiety. In our own society, the adolescent is regarded as an emergent adult who must become more and more independent and take more and more adult responsibility while remaining essentially a child still heavily dependent upon the family. Thus, our adolescent is pulled in two different directions simultaneously: he is under pressure to grow up and become independent and yet forced to remain a child, still responsive to the dictates of the parents.

Among the Arapesh of New Guinea, another society described by Mead (1935), there is also an easy transition between childhood and adulthood. The adults in this society are affectionate, trusting, and unaggressive and consider the main aims of life to be rearing of children and the growing of food. Boys take over the adult economic and social responsibilities very gradually, after an initiation that involves a great deal of ceremony and very little hardship. The girl is betrothed at the age of 7 or 8 to an older boy and immediately goes to live with his family. Several years later she also participates in initiation ceremonies, but her life goes on essentially as before. Her future parents-in-law are as indulgent to her as her own parents were. She and her betrothed remain members of the same family and community group during the adolescent years and the movement from childhood to married life is very gradual and relatively benign. The behavior of the Arapesh girls reflects the benign quality of growing up by an absence of expressed anxiety and conflict and undisturbed patterns of behavior.

In Tchambuli society, boys of 9 and 10 are pushed away from the protective and supportive groups of adult women and children but are not welcomed by the men, who consider the boys unfit to be trusted with responsible functions. A great deal of strain appears to accompany this status of being neither a man nor a boy and contributes to the subjective turmoil and disturbed behavior characteristics of the preadolescent in Tchambuli society (M. Mead, 1935).

Comparison between the approaches of different societies to adolescence and preadolescence make it clear that the storm and stress associated with western society is not a physiological matter but has to do with the psychological initiation of the child into adult life and the manner in which this initiation takes place. In our own society, where there are conflicting pressures, adolescence often is a difficult period for both parent and child. In other societies, in which the cultural approach to growing up is different, adolescence is often a benign period. Such cross-cultural comparisons throw a great deal of light upon the importance of cultural differences in behavior and, inferentially, in personality development. Fascinating studies of this sort dealing with sexual practices, aggression, social status, cooperation, etc., have been made on many modern as well as primitive societies. Written accounts by anthropologists such as Mead, Benedict, Kardiner, and Linton are rich in their information about cultural variations and the characteristic behavior patterns associated with them.

The Indivisibility of Culture and Personality

We cannot define personality without reference to culture, nor can we properly conceive of culture as independent of the personality structures of those who produce it. There is a reciprocity between the two. When we postulate motivation as part of the theoretical psychological structure of the individual, this motivation is of necessity conceived in relation to goals derived from the society in which he lives. For example, the motivation to achieve develops because the individual grows up in a society in which achievement is given a high value. Attitudes toward achievement are interpersonal and embedded in the culture, and if the culture does not place a high value on achievement, strong motivations to achieve are unlikely to develop. In a society that has no place for achievement, the notion of achievement motivation is meaningless.

Conversely, the values of a society are maintained by its members and a description of these values includes the attributes of the personality structures of the individuals who constitute the society. A person is born into an already existing society with a particular culture. In turn, since he contributes to this culture and to its maintenance, it is totally impossible, except for academic purposes, to separate personality from the culture in which it is embedded.

Concepts of Culture and Personality

It is interesting to see how different theorists have considered the relationships between culture and personality. Freud (1930) took the position that culture was essentially an expression of the biological nature of man. He maintained that there were formal parallels between the development of the individual man, his phylogenetic history, and the development of culture. Thus, man inherits from lower animals certain universal instincts, such as sex and aggression. Just as the development of the individual man (from infancy to maturity) involves the acquisition of certain forms of ego control over these instincts, so the culture represents man's collective attempt to hold these instincts in check so that he can live together safely with other men.

Freud pointed out that in lower orders of animals the male offspring of a sexual union ultimately competed with each other, and with the father, for the available females, which included the mother. Perhaps the reader will recall the excellent nature study, produced by Walt Disney, called "Seal Island," in which the powerful bull seal corners a number of females and develops a harem. He protects his role as the single male in the harem by fighting off competitors. The younger bulls ultimately grow into powerful adversaries and challenge the harem leader, once their father, for control of the harem, which may include the bull's mother. There is a continual struggle between the males, young and old, to procreate with the females.

Freud thought that society was a kind of contract that man made with his brothers to prevent the destructive consequence of inevitable sexual competition as displayed by lower animals. For this reason, societies created taboos against incest (the mating of a son with the mother who bore him or with other blood relatives of close affiliation). The rules of society were formed to control the instincts of man and enable him to live in relative harmony and safety. A limited range of culture could develop as an outgrowth of this control and could serve as means of substitute discharge for the blocked impulses. Education and art, for example, were interpreted by Freud as sublimations of the inhibited sexual drive.

The Oedipus situation, which in the male involves sexual desire for the mother in competition with the father, was considered by Freud to be universal in man, because such patterns were instinctual and inherited by men in the evolutionary progression from lower animals. In the context of social taboos against incest and in order to protect himself against the possibility of dangerous combat with the father, the normal man ultimately gives up the mother as an object of love and finds a mate of his own outside the family circle. He, too, is then protected in this relationship against the destructive competition with his sons by means of this social contract against incest.

The Freudian view of culture and personality has some extremely serious defects. For one thing, it leads to the expectation that most cultures will be basically very similar because men have the same instincts in common, and that certain developmental patterns, such as the Oedipus complex, will be universal in all cultures. It consequently tends to emphasize similarities between cultures and has great difficulty in handling the enormous variation in social institutions among different cultures. It ignores factors other than man's biological heritage, such as economic conditions and climate, which can influence the development of social institutions.

The anthropologist Kardiner (1939) adopted a view of personality that has much in common with that of Freud, but he recognized a larger number of social patterns that permit the successful discharge of human instincts. Kardiner also stressed more than Freud the role of culture in the formation of the individual personality. For Freud, culture as well as man's individual development were products of the human constitution. Kardiner maintained, however, that culture is both the product of man's biology and also a major factor in the individual's personality development. Thus, one society develops certain social institutions that permit the discharge of man's instincts, which influence the personality development of its members in its own unique way; another society finds a fundamentally different way to produce the satisfaction of instincts, which has its own particular consequences for the development of personality.

According to Kardiner, primary variation in culture is brought about by economic or climatological factors. Kardiner analyzed theoretically the personality structure of primitive peoples living in Madagascar, whose culture has been described by Linton, pointing out changes in the behavior patterns in these societies that have resulted from changes in the economic life of the inhabitants. In Tanala society, for example, rice is produced by the more primitive, dry method of cultivation. As a consequence of this, land is used up quickly and has little value. The society tends to be tribal and nomadic. The wealth is shared in a communal way with a minimum of variation in status relationships between persons. Betsileo social structure was once the same as Tanala with the dry method of rice cultivation. However, Betsileo developed the wet-rice method, which means land can be used over and over again. As a consequence, the land became valuable, sources of irrigation became important, and a class system developed in the manner of feudal society.

Of particular importance for our purposes is the fact that major behavioral as well as personality differences now are found between the two societies that originally had been identical. Status problems are particularly important in Betsileo. There is much insecurity among the people and great concern about the preservation of the *status quo* by laws of order and status within the society. Competition is keen and the society far more complex, resulting in a far greater elaboration of social roles than is characteristic of Tanala. The analysis of Tanala-Betsileo culture demonstrates Kardiner's thesis that economic conditions can influence basic social institutions and that these have their differential effects on the behavior patterns (and inferentially, on the personality structure) of the society's members. But the varieties of culture thus achieved are greatly constrained, as Freud assumed, by the physical construction of man.

Other writers have tended to reject entirely the Freudian biological interpretation of culture and even the modifications of the Freudian view presented by Kardiner. They emphasize the role of culture as the primary determinant of personality structure. Such psychoanalytic writers as Fromm, Sullivan, and Horney especially have stressed the nature of interpersonal relations derived from the culture as the predominant causative factor in human behavior. Sociologists like G. H. Mead (1934) and socially oriented personality psychologists like Sarbin (1954) make the social structure of central importance by stressing the concept of social role as a basic construct of the personality. These writers have been less preoccupied with the origins of culture. They emphasized the embeddedness of man in some given culture and the great significance of this for his behavior.

SOCIAL INSTITUTIONS AND BEHAVIOR

In discussing the effects of culture, we have regarded culture in a rather gross sense with little specification of what particular aspects are relevant. A closer look at the role of culture in behavior is afforded by examining the effects of particular social institutions within a single culture, such as our own. Let us examine the impact of social groupings such as class, caste, sex, and small groups upon human behavior.

Social Class

It often is something of a surprise to Americans to be informed that theirs is a class society. Social scientists have made careful studies of social class in American cities and towns, systematically interviewing the residents of these communities as a means of examining the social structure.

A well-known study was performed by Davis, Gardner, and Gardner (1941), who selected a southern community with the disguised name "Old City." At the top of this society they found an *aristocracy* of wealthy persons whose families have a lengthy lineage in the community. Below them in the social hierarchy came the *lower-upper class*, which is financially at least as wealthy as the upper-upper aristocracy, but whose wealth and position are of recent origin through new industries, such as shoes, textiles, silverware, and finance. Below this were found the members of a solid, highly respectable *upper-middle class*, who are financially well off, are extremely active in civic affairs, have high moral principles, and aspire to social contact with upper-class society. The *lower-middle class* consists of clerks and other white-collar workers, small tradesmen, and some skilled workers. Their houses are small, their property limited, and their status essentially inconsequential in relation to the upper classes. The authors also differentiated the *upper-lower class*, composed of poor but honest workers, frequently semiskilled or unskilled laborers. Their income is limited but they are considerably preoccupied with doing the right thing and maintaining respectability in their actions. Finally, the *lower-lower class* has a poor reputation among most of those socially above it. Members typically are evaluated as lazy, shiftless, and impecunious. Their sexual morals are considered by the upper classes to be loose, and they are believed by the rest of the community to have high rates of illegitimacy. The statistical breakdowns of the three main classes, upper, middle, and lower, with their subgroups, yield 1.4 per cent upper-upper, 1.6 per cent lower-upper, 10 per cent upper-middle, 28 per cent lower-middle, 34 per cent upper-lower, and 25 per cent lower-lower class of Old City.

Of considerable interest is the fact that the lower-lower class have only the vaguest picture of the upper classes, tending to merge all those who are reasonably well off financially into one group. In other words, persons of this class do not differentiate the extreme upper subgroups. Similarly, the upper-class citizens tend to assimilate all of the relatively poor groups into one. There is tremendous social distance between class groupings that are not adjacent on the social hierarchy. The findings of Davis, Gardner, and Gardner, as cited above, are presented in tabular form in Table 13.

Membership in a particular social class carries with it certain implications for the behavior of its members toward their children. This produces different social environments for the offspring of the various classes and undoubtedly affects their learned behavior patterns. Davis and Havighurst (1952) studied child-rearing practices and attitudes as a function of class. They found, for example, that middle-class groups tend to emphasize earlier the development of social inhibitions and conformity to social pressures. The middle-class child is apt to be weaned and toilet-trained earlier and with more strictness than the lower-class child. Similarly, the lower-class child is encouraged to be physically aggressive and to respect effectiveness in physical fighting, and the middle-

Table 13

THE SOCIAL PERSPECTIVES OF THE SOCIAL CLASSES

UPPER-UPPER *Class*		LOWER-UPPER *Class*
"Old aristocracy"	UU	"Old aristocracy"
"Aristocracy," but not "old"	LU	"Aristocracy," but not "old"
"Nice, respectable people"	UM	"Nice, respectable people"
"Good people, but 'nobody' "	LM	"Good people, but 'nobody' "
"Po' whites"	UL LL	"Po' whites"

UPPER-MIDDLE *Class*		LOWER-MIDDLE *Class*
"Society" { "Old families"	UU	"Old aristocracy" "Broken-down
"Society" but not "old families"	LU	(older) aristocracy" (younger)
"People who should be upper class"	UM	"People who think they are somebody"
"People who don't have much money"	LM	"We poor folks"
	UL	"People poorer than us"
"No 'count lot"	LL	"No 'count lot"

UPPER-LOWER *Class*		LOWER-LOWER *Class*
"Society" or the "folks with money"	UU LU UM	"Society" or the "folks with money"
"People who are up because they have a little money"	LM	"Way-high-ups," but not "society"
"Poor but honest folk"	UL	"Snobs trying to push up"
"Shiftless people"	LL	"People just as good as anybody"

SOURCE: Davis, Gardner, & Gardner, 1941, p. 65.

class child is taught that physical assault is bad. For example, the middle-class boy is taught never to strike adults and always to be respectful toward them, not to attack girls and to be chivalrous toward them, and that verbal aggression is better than physical aggression. When attacked or when in a competitive situation, he is expected to give a good account of himself but he must never initiate unwarranted aggressions against another child. From these studies we know that there are class differences in child-rearing practices, but the exact effect of these differences on adult behavior is not clear. This is one of the crucial problems of the psychology of personality development. Our information is meager, although suggestive, and much speculation exists about the principles involved.

Social class and the status of the individual in society are intimately related, although in particular situations the relationship does not always hold. For example, an upper-class person usually has high status, but in certain group situations he can be rejected socially and have low status. Among the relatively uneducated army population, for example, the fact that a man has had considerable education can mark him as an egghead and result in isolation from the rest of the group. Such a man may have to play down his education to become accepted as a member.

Status has some interesting effects on the nature of communication between persons. Because, in our society, membership in a particular class or status group is not generally fixed by birth and the individual considers it possible to achieve a higher status, communication tends to be directed to persons of high status. For example, when persons who differ in status, as assigned by an experimenter, are placed in the same social situation, it is possible to observe which persons choose to fraternize with whom. The most frequent choices are those of roughly the same status, but there is a considerable tendency for asymmetry to occur in the upward direction; that is, an individual will communicate with someone of higher status. Thus, at a business party, employees of lower status will more often approach higher-status employees than the other way around.

There have been many studies of objective and subjective class membership and political attitude or voting behavior. Centers (1949) has shown, for example, that liberal attitudes are far more characteristic of lower classes and conservative attitudes more common among the middle class, becoming predominant in the upper class. However, if a person attempts to predict political attitude and voting behavior as a function of class, he might be well advised to define class by subjective criteria, as Centers (1949) did, that is, as the individual sees himself. If an individual is objectively defined as lower class but has identified primarily with middle-class groups, then his voting behavior and political attitudes are apt to conform more with those of the middle class. Because the small shopkeeper often believes that by dint of effort he can become

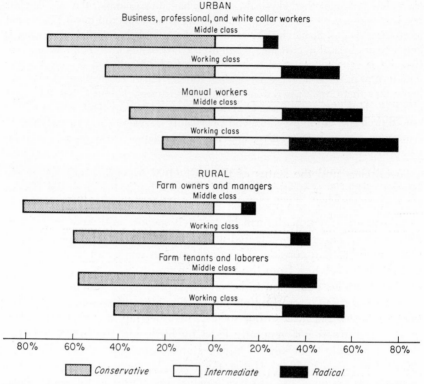

Figure 24. Stratum and class differences in conservatism-radicalism. (*From Centers*, 1949.)

a large industrialist, he is more likely to perceive himself as an upper-class person and behave accordingly.

We have presented some of Centers's findings in Figure 24, which reflect the importance of subjective class affiliation and conservative or radical attitudes as these were displayed in 1949, when the study was first published. Centers (1952) explains these data in Figure 24 as follows:

. . . the attitudes of persons of similar occupational strata, but of different class affiliation, are shown contrasted. It can be seen at once that if people of a given occupational stratum differ in class membership they tend to differ also in attitude. Those identifying with the middle class are more often conservative than those who identify themselves with the working class. The latter tend to be more often radical. *If people's class identifications are the same, their attitudes tend to be similar even though their objective occupational positions are different.*

Caste

Caste is a system by which groups of persons are arbitrarily limited in social privilege, usually because of race. For example, the Negro in our society is restricted educationally, occupationally, and socially because he is Negro. The status of the Mexican in the southwest and the Oriental on the Pacific coast also represents caste subdivisions with concomitant limitation of privilege.

There is no evidence that any differences exist between castes in terms of their intellectual adequacy. A classic study by Klineberg, in 1935, showed that Negro children who were born in the South showed dramatic improvements in their IQs when they moved to New York City, where their educational opportunities were enriched. When they arrived in New York their intelligence scores compared unfavorably with Negro and white children who had been living in the city. During the first five or six years in New York City schools, their intelligence scores increased until the original intellectual discrepancies practically disappeared. Such studies as this suggest that apparent difference between Negroes and whites in intellectual and social adequacy is the result of cultural limitations imposed upon them by the society rather than any biological difference associated with race. Linton (1955) also pointed out that in the modern era there are probably no biological differences in inherent capacity among the variety of races that populate the earth. But the caste restrictions do take their toll in many forms of adaptive behavior and often lead to sharp attitudinal and behavioral differences.

Strong preferences and dislikes exist within our society concerning various ethnic groups that have different racial and national origins. When residents on the Pacific Coast in 1933, the Middle West, in 1935, were asked about the degrees of social intimacy that they were willing to permit with certain ethnic groups, ratings of different ethnic groups were developed. These preferences are illustrated in Table 14. The most-liked group heads the list, and the other groups are ranked in order of preference. Note the striking agreement in such preferences for different parts of the country.

Katz and Braly (1952) have shown that attitudes toward racial and ethnic groups have a strong element of stereotyping. That is, certain characteristics tend to be arbitrarily assigned to ethnic groups as though every member of the group fitted such characteristics. Thus, Negroes are stereotyped as shiftless and superstitious, Germans as intelligent and scientific, Italians as explosive and excitable, and English as austere and formal. The study by Katz and Braly showed that strong preferences or dislikes for racial or ethnic groups were maintained even though an individual had never had any contact whatsoever with the ethnic group. His attitudes toward them were based in part upon verbal stereotypes communicated by the society in which he lives. It generally

Table 14

ETHNIC GROUP PREFERENCES AMONG PACIFIC-COAST AND
MIDDLE WEST POPULATIONS

Pacific Coast	Middle West
Canadians	American
English	English
Scotch	Scotch
Irish	Irish
French	French
Swedes	German
Germans	Swede
Spanish	South American
Italians	Italian
Indians	Spanish
Poles	Jew
Russians	Russian
Armenians	Pole
German-Jews	Greek
Greeks	Armenian
Russian-Jews	Japanese
Mexicans	Mexican
Chinese	Chinese
Japanese	Hindu
Negroes	Turk
Mulattoes	Negro
Hindus	
Turks	

SOURCE: Katz & Braly, 1952, p. 67.

is believed that such attitudes toward minority groups are influential in the behavior patterns of these groups, although systematic empirical studies along these lines do not abound. The effect on the minority group is less often studied than the prejudices within the majority culture itself.

Davis and Havighurst (1952), previously cited as having explored differences in child-rearing practices in different social classes, have also compared such practices in Negro and white families. They interviewed mothers of Negro and white families and observed that Negro society also divides into social classes, which follow white social classes in value systems quite closely. Smaller differences in child-rearing practices were found between Negroes and whites than between social classes within each group. In other words, lower-class Negroes and middle-class Negroes differed from each other in much the same way as lower-class whites and middle-class whites. Middle-class Negro child-rearing practices were essentially the same as those of the middle-class whites. The child-rearing practices followed class rather than caste lines.

Sex

One of the most obvious classifications within a society is based upon sex—the fact of being a man or a woman. There hardly could be any doubt that men behave differently from women and have somewhat different interests. Queener (1951, pp. 205–207) illustrated the differences in male and female roles in social situations by a little playlet about an imaginary dinner party at which three couples are present. The playlet sketches the characteristic type of interplay between males and females:

The women are helped off with their wraps by the men. The women look at the women's gowns. The men look at the women.

DORIS (*The hostess.*):What a lovely gown, Eunice! (*All of the gowns are lovely, and so on.*)

(*The men are over by the liquor cabinet where Alec is mixing.*)

BERT: . . . and then I lost everything I'd won earlier on the State game. . . .

CEDRIC: State still has good material if they'd get rid of that singlewing. . . .

(*And in the women's corner*):

EUNICE: She said she hadn't expected it until December, but when I had *my* first one. . . .

ALEC (*To Bert.*): Well, any salesman for Blank Company can afford to lose occasionally.

BERT: We aren't going under. Did you hear about our killing last month? . . .

DORIS: Let me tell you what Alec, Jr. said in his bath the other day . . .

(*Frances has no children and is listening to the men. She speaks to Bert.*)

FRANCES: I know that's what they say, Bert, but how can you *know?*

BERT (*A little startled.*): Why, I read it in Stavler's column.

FRANCES: Well, Stavler isn't the most unbiased man in the world. Did you read the full report in the *Times?*

(*The men are arguing. The women fall silent and try to appear interested but Eunice begins fingering through a women's magazine and Doris goes out to the kitchen. Frances, however, speaks out occasionally. Bert replies to her.*)

BERT: Well, now, Frances, if you want that sort of thing in this country. . . .

FRANCES: I didn't say anything about wanting it here; I only said you've read only one side!

BERT: Well, if *you* had the prospects of going back into uniform. . . .

FRANCES (*Laughing.*): You mean no one can vote who can't fight?

BERT (*Aroused now.*): Or at least bear some future fighters!

(*Cedric and Frances flush.*)

ALEC (*Embarrassed.*): Oh, come, come now, Bert. . . .

DORIS (*Nervously.*): Politics, politics—it's all beyond me. . . .

EUNICE: Oh me too. Doris, did you see the costume jewelry advertised. . . .

(*The men resume their arguing. Frances is quiet now. Dinner is announced.*)

Certain characteristics of male and female roles are illustrated in this fragment of conversation. You will note, for example, that the men assist the women with their wraps. Visual observation would reveal certain stylistic ways of responding that are strictly male and female, such as characteristic facial expressions and certain manners of physical movement. The women are more preoccupied with each other's clothing, which is the sign of the social and economic status derived chiefly by the husband's occupational success. The women are more concerned with their decorativeness and physical attractiveness. Differentiation between the men and women is obvious also in terms of the topic of conversation representing their respective interest patterns. The men discuss athletics, business, and politics. The women discuss primarily other women, children, and clothes. Then one of the women, Frances, behaves out of role. She seems to lose interest in personalities, clothes, and children. She enters into the conversation about politics and business. She questions a man's knowledge and perhaps his intelligence. If she had lost the argument immediately and quickly confessed her error when Bert spoke up, her conduct would have been more acceptably that of a woman, because a woman's role includes a certain amount of ignorance of important matters. But Frances does not comply and commits the sin of beating a man in his own field. She is attacked severely for this breach of conduct and, interestingly enough, in an extremely vulnerable place when Bert says, "Or at least bear some future fighters!" As she is childless, he has questioned her adequacy as a woman in terms of her ability to bear children.

The sharp differentiation in male and female roles tends to occur in all societies, although it is not always identical in form or constant historically. The roles of men and women in American society have tended to become altered and less clear in recent generations. At one time a woman could not vote or seek a professional or business career. There has been a distinct shift toward an equalitarian position between men and women and a diminution in the conception of the man as the authority, dominator of the home, the social aggressor, and the bread-winner. Many writers have pointed out that this increased ambiguity of sex roles has presented serious adjustment difficulties for modern men and women. A very successful Broadway musical play, "Lady in the Dark," had this problem as its main theme. The successful businesswoman is sarcastically called "boss lady" by one of her male employees, and she is identified as a neurotic on the basis of her rejection of the traditional female role of passivity and softness. After successful psychotherapy, she returns to femininity by giving up her competitive role in business and marrying the male employee.

There undoubtedly are some indirect biological determinants of the sex roles of men and women. The greater strength and size of men fit them better for their traditional role as hunter and warrior. Menstruation and the childbearing function of women further tends to confine them to the more domestic roles. But there also is no doubt that huge variations occur in sex roles from one culture to another, and even within a culture from time to time.

In Manus society, for example, the men are entrusted with the care of the children. Among the Arapesh people of New Guinea, women carry the supplies from the farming area to the village settlement, climbing up and down paths with 60- to 70-pound loads suspended from their foreheads. Men and women both consider this quite proper because (Mead, 1935) "it is appropriate that women should carry heavier loads than men do, because women's heads are so much harder and stronger." Moreover, Arapesh men take as large a part in child rearing as women and even practice a rite in which they express sympathy for the woman in childbirth by duplicating many of her reactions and suffering as she does. Among the Arapesh, women take the initiative in community affairs and in sex as readily as do men. Little distinction is made between masculinity and femininity of personality. In contrast to this, the Tchambuli society of New Guinea considers women as naturally dependable, self-sufficient, and lusty, and men as sensitive, vain, and temperamental. This is a complete reversal from the traditional concepts of male and female in our own society.

The importance of traditional sex patterns in a society for the behavior of subsequent generations should be clear upon a moment's reflection. A person must learn a complicated set of behaviors—a social role—on the very basis of the fact that he is a man or a woman. Very early in life children are indoctrinated in these roles by their parents. For example, in our own society, when a boy shows an interest in masculine things like sports or construction, his parent beams and readily buys him tool kits, toy automobiles, baseball gloves, and so on. Should he play with his sister's dolls, his parent is decidedly unresponsive and even discouraging. "Boys don't play with dolls" may be the response. Boys are told that they will grow into men like their daddy, who does certain things that in our society are considered characteristic of maleness. Girls, in contrast, are informed that ultimately they will become women and mothers and are encouraged to take an interest in their physical attractiveness, household activities, doll play, cooking, cleaning, and child care. Thus certain characteristic patterns of behavior tend to follow from being male or female.

Of considerable importance for the problem of adjustment is the extent to which there are discrepancies between the socially defined sex role and the role an individual actually adopts. Not only will society consider an individual who has not accepted his sex role as maladjusted, but such a person is likely to report internal conflict as well.

The Group

Up to now we have spoken of large-scale and well-established classifications, such as class, caste, and sex. The individual has close contact with only a small number of persons, whereas class, caste, and sex are large impersonal categories. Much of our time is spent in the company of a few other persons, often in small groups. We should not leave discussion of the influence of social institutions upon behavior without discussing a few instances of the direct and intimate influence upon the individual of other persons.

One of the best-known studies of social influence was reported by Asch (1952), whose work was cited in Chapter 1. Asch required subjects to make public judgments about the length of different lines while being a minority of one in a group of eight others. Experiments demonstrated that the subject's judgment often conformed to the group pressure even though the group, whose behavior had been prearranged by the experimenter, made obviously erroneous responses. The fact that everyone else in the group gave one particular answer, even though clearly incorrect, forced many persons to conform. Later interviews revealed that the subject followed the group sometimes to avoid standing out as different from the rest and sometimes without even being aware that he was being influenced. Asch's experiment can be extended to real-life situations where a person is a member of a group that takes a particular political or social attitude and in which he must face the prospect of expressing an unpopular position. Quite commonly in such a context, the individual alters his own view to conform to the others because of the disapproval or perhaps even ostracism that the public maintenance of his own opinion would entail. Stage or screen dramas have depicted often the tremendous direct or subtle pressure that can be exerted in such a situation. Such pressures throughout life tend to shape the individual's behavior. The socialization of the child normally produces a certain degree of conformity, without which a person would be isolated and socially ineffective

A similar type of experiment was performed by Sherif (1935). The task involved presentation of a small light to the subject in a completely darkened enclosure. The room is so totally darkened that no objects can be perceived to serve as reference points for the position of the light. Under such darkroom conditions, the stationary light appears to move. Different persons perceive the light as moving at different rates and in different directions. This phenomenon of a really stationary light appearing to move has been called the *autokinetic effect.* Having measured the apparent direction and extent of movement for several subjects, Sherif then arranged the situation so that two subjects with opposite types of autokinetic effects were placed together in the same experimental situation. The subjects were again to report upon the apparent movement of the light, now knowing the judgment of another person. Under each other's influence, the subjects perceived a greatly modified apparent movement of the light, and its path was the result of the combined subject's judgments. In other words, if one subject had seen the light moving upward and to the right and the other subject had seen it moving upward and to the left, during the situation of interpersonal influence both subjects adjusted the light movement more in conformity to the other's pattern.

Powerful interpersonal influences were present in both Asch's and Sherif's experiments. Often without being aware of it, subjects would modify their own judgment in response to pressures from the group or another person. The studies of Asch and Sherif illustrate the great effects that others have on our behavior. We can see how our behavior can be molded, especially in our most impressionable early years, by such significant persons as parents and teachers. Such social influences are always present throughout our lives. There remains now the question of how this influence manages to produce its effects on behavior. The next section indicates some of the principles by which social factors affect the person.

HOW SOCIAL VARIABLES INFLUENCE BEHAVIOR

The primary culture of a society influences the individual in two main ways. In the first place, the individual is provided opportunities to learn much of his society's culture through formal, systematic teaching. Most societies have self-conscious techniques (schools, books, etc.) to educate new generations. The culture can only survive and progress if there is provision for the transmission of the knowledge and customs gained by preceding generations. In those societies where there is no systematic education, patterns of behavior can be transmitted through imitation, which is the second, or *informal*, type of influence. It is a universal characteristic for children to model their behavior after their parents or elders and in this way acquire behavior patterns appropriate to the culture.

People tend to overestimate the importance of formal education in the transmission of cultural patterns. Actually, although direct teaching is useful, especially in the acquisition of the technology of the society, the most important values and behavior patterns are apt to be acquired by the individual unconsciously and by contact with influential persons. A great deal of this will happen early in life when no formal education exists.

The fact that cultural patterns can be transmitted through both formal and informal procedure results in the opportunity for internal conflicts to be created. These are, of course, known by inference from the person's behavior or his verbal reports about them. There often is a discrepancy between the ideal verbalized values formally subscribed to by the culture and the values manifested in the behavior patterns of the individual members of the society from whom the cultural patterns are absorbed informally.

For example, the parents, school system, or religious organizations can formally teach the child to "love thy neighbor," but such teaching does not have the desired effect on the child's behavior when the dominant behavior pattern of the culture is competitive and aggressive. Karen Horney (1937) has discussed such conflicts within a culture as sources of neuroticism and confusion for the individual. We are taught that wealth is not everything, but our culture tends to respect most highly the wealthy person. We are taught that humility and self-effacement are virtuous, but we adore and respect the self-confident person who stands out in the crowd. The adolescent is told that he is on the threshold of manhood and must become self-supporting, independent, and mature. As he manifests his growing desire to achieve adult status, he is continually reminded that he must be dependent upon and obedient to his parents and that he is still a child in their eyes. The culture of the United States maintains formally the belief in the equality of all men and their rights under the Constitution to equal treatment under the law. However, the child discovers early in life that all men are not treated equally and that some races, ethnic groups, or individuals are, in fact, considered inferior and worthy only of a servile state in society.

The modern educator recognizes that parents expect him to inculcate in their children ideal value systems and behavior patterns, which the parents themselves do not adhere to in their own conduct, and the educator is blamed when he fails in what is nearly an impossible task. The formal transmission of cultural values commonly results in nothing more than verbal exercises, and a person learns the correct words to represent what he should think, while his behavior and real beliefs and attitudes reflect the absorption of informally transmitted characteristics.

Transmission of Social Characteristics through the Parent-Child Relationship

In addition to the formal educational procedures of a society, there is a more important means of transmission of the culture to the growing child. The individual is shaped by what the society's members (acting in accordance with their cultural patterns) directly show to children in their actions. Each society has its own prescribed patterns of infant care and parent-child relationship. In some, children are bound to a cradleboard, swaddled in cloth, and rarely permitted free exercise of their limbs (e.g., Dennis's study of practices among the Hopi and Navaho Indians [1940]). In others, the child is in almost constant physical contact with another person, usually the mother. In still others, relatively little physical contact is permitted with other persons. Children can be fed on demand (that is, whenever they cry), fed by means of a rigid schedule, or on a schedule based strictly on the convenience of the mother. In our society, the tendency toward rigid feeding schedules has given way, within the last generation or so, to demand schedules, following the philosophy that the child should be frustrated as little as possible because such frustration can lead to maladjustments in later life. These are all forms of parental behavior that directly communicate the society's characteristics to the child. Such patterns of child rearing in our own culture recently have been surveyed by Sears, Maccoby, and Levin (1957).

In attempting to comprehend the way in which culture influences the individual, psychologists have emphasized different aspects of the child-parent relationship as important. This matter of understanding how the process of inculcation of the culture, or *acculturation*, works is entirely a theoretical question. For example, Kardiner (1949) argued that the effect upon the personality becomes manifested primarily through the direct child-rearing practices. Kardiner subscribed to the Freudian view of personality development that the individual progresses through the three psychosexual stages of development: oral, anal, and genital. He believed that the child's personality structure develops as a consequence of his opportunities to gratify the primitive needs characteristic of these stages of development. Frustration or indulgence during the oral period will have different consequences for adult personality than will frustration or indulgence during the anal period and likewise during the genital period. For Kardiner, culture is important theoretically in the way it deals with the infant's oral, anal, and genital needs. Thus, weaning and toilet-training practices of the culture are of first importance.

In contrast with Kardiner's view, Fromm (1949) and Sullivan (1949) argued that the specific procedures of child rearing are far less significant than is the atmosphere of the mother-child relationship. Even in the case of the mother who is physically neglectful because she must work in the fields, the relationship between the child and mother can be secure and supportive because she communicates to the child a sense of being wanted or loved during the periods when they are together. (What this means, however, in behavior terms is not at all clear. This is why it is difficult for such writers to tell mothers how to give a child a sense of being loved.) At the present time, systematic research concerning the importance of certain features of child-rearing practices is lacking. We can do little more than point out the difference between views, because it is difficult to find sufficient evidence to support either.

There is general agreement that the culture of a society is absorbed relatively early in the life of the developing individual and that this will occur largely through the relationship between the child and the significant figures of his childhood, usually the parents. The values and behavior patterns of the culture are internalized by the child, and they unconsciously become part of himself. Anthropologists and sociologists have called this process "acculturation." Psychologists have tended to use the term "introjection," "internalization," or "socialization." The child introjects the values and attitudes of his parents so that they become his own and guide his behavior throughout his life even in the physical absence of his parents. This introjection can never be total because the child would then be the image, psychologically, of his parents. Because the child has contacts with more than one significant adult, the processes of introjection are exceedingly complex and permit the development of unique patterns in every person.

The theoretical question still remains as to why the culture is introjected by the child through his relationships with his parents. Perhaps the most widely held view emphasizes the helplessness and dependence of the child during his infancy and early childhood, which make the parent a vital key to the maintenance and enhancement of the child's physical security. The parent provides food, warmth, shelter, and protection against pain and is a primary source of pleasure. It is at the parent's whim that the child is protected from the pains of hunger, the discomfort of thirst, and so on. The child learns, for example, that, if he doesn't eat, he can anticipate great discomfort. If the parent is made angry, anxiety is developed in the child lest this discomfort be permitted to occur. Thus, very early in life he becomes responsive to the approval or disapproval of the parent. Approval means security, and disapproval results in anxiety, associated with the anticipation of the frustration of his fundamental physical needs. In this way, learning the proper behavior will please his parents and reduce the anxiety that disapproval and anticipation of pain tend to provoke.

Davis (1944) compellingly argued the importance of the role of anxiety in the *socialization* of the child, that is, in the acquisition of the cultural patterns conveyed by the parents. The parent manipulates anxiety in the socialization process by rewarding the child when he has been good and has conformed to social demands and punishing the child when he has been bad. The punishment need not involve physical assault; most parents can testify to the extremely powerful effects of mere disapproval or anger directed toward the child. By creating anxiety when the child behaves or thinks in disapproved terms and by relieving anxiety for approved behavior, the parent succeeds in getting the child to acquire the acceptable social patterns. Thus, social needs to be accepted, loved, or esteemed by others become acquired through the intermediate process of anxiety, which is aroused by the anticipation of physical pain or discomfort. Eventually, these social needs become autonomous, that is, cease to be dependent upon the primary physical needs from which they arose (cf. Allport, 1937). Such a view as this is held by such psychological writers as Mowrer (1950) and Miller (1951).

The above view stresses the role of physiological needs in the acquisition of social motives that have to do with relationships between people. Some psychologists have rejected this view of the origin of the higher human motives and values. They maintained that it places tremendous emphasis on physical survival and comfort and little emphasis on the forces of positive growth. These writers, such as Fromm (1949), Sullivan (1949), Harlow (1953), Maslow (1954), Rogers (1951), and Lecky (1945) believed that man as the organism at the highest evolutionary stage is born with tendencies toward positive growth and with basic needs for love and problem solving. They suggested that needs for love, psychological security, and problem solving are not derived from, or dependent upon, physiological gratification (such as hunger or thirst), but exist independently as inborn qualities. However needs for parental approval come about, all writers agree that the values of a society are learned primarily through the parents and that parental approval and disapproval are powerful means whereby this process of introjection of cultural patterns occurs. (The reader is asked to recall the discussion of these matters in Chapters 3–7.)

Types of Parent-Child Relationships

Earlier we emphasized child-rearing practices of different cultures and social groupings as a fundamental way in which cultural values are transmitted to the child. Aside from some of the more specific practices in weaning, toilet training, discipline, and so on, we can examine parental behavior toward children in a variety of interpersonal dimensions. We could describe their behavior as neglectful, arbitrary, democratic, accepting, overprotective, and so on. Research studies at the Fels Research Institute (Baldwin, Kalhorn, & Breese, 1945) have suggested three independent dimensions in which parental behavior toward children can be described. One dimension is that of *acceptance-rejection* and concerns the degree of warmth on the part of the parent toward the child. Another dimension is *possessiveness-detachment*, concerning the extent to which a parent is protective of the youngster. Such behavior can range from overprotective possessiveness to neglect or disregard of the child in relation to dangers or traumatic experiences. A third dimension is *democracy-autocracy*, or the extent to which the child can participate in determining family activities. In the extreme autocracy, the child is handled in a dictatorial way as opposed to a more democratic approach, which involves some degree of participation of the child in family decisions.

Any family can be described within the framework provided by these three patterns of parent behavior, and from the point of view of research, the consequences for behavior can be studied as a function of such variations. Different childhood experiences will occur in families whose patterns along these three dimensions differ. In one family a lack of warmth can be associated with a passive attitude toward the child who is regarded as a nuisance and given only as much attention as absolutely necessary. In another family, the same rejecting attitude can exist, however, not with detachment or indifference, but with hostility and excessive demandingness. The mother may go out of her way to frustrate the child and be unnecessarily strict and unfriendly.

A number of research studies have been performed on the effects of patterns of parent-child relationship on the behavior of the child. Work in this area can be illustrated by summarizing a small number of such studies, dealing with authority relationships, rejection, and maternal over-protection.

Lippitt and White (1952) studied the influence of *democratic and authoritarian leadership* climates in small groups of children upon group functioning and the behavior of group members. In their democratically organized groups, a great deal more independence of action was developed among the group members, so even in the absence of the leader the children were able to proceed constructively. Such groups were more cohesive and had a more positive outlook and a sense of identification with the group. The authoritarian climates, however, resulted in considerably more aggressiveness toward each other and toward the leader, and an attitude of dependence. In the absence of a leader the group could not function adequately at all.

Figure 25 displays some of the main data obtained by Lippitt and White (1952) in their analysis of the effects of democratic versus authoritarian climates on the subjects' behavior and group functioning. They comment as follows: Figure 25

. . . indicates the major differences in the relations which developed between the group members and the adult leaders in the four resultant social atmospheres. In both types of authoritarian atmosphere the members were markedly more dependent upon the leader than in either the democratic or laissez-faire situations, dependence being somewhat greater in the more passive clubs. All other clubs showed a somewhat greater feeling of discontent in their relations with the adult leader than did the members of the democratic clubs, members of the "aggressive autocracy" being outstanding in their expression of rebellious feelings. There is evidence from other sources that the actual "felt discontent" in the "apathetic autocracies" was somewhat higher than indicated by the conversation which was considerably more restricted than was that of the democratic and laissez-faire club members. In both types of authoritarian situations the demands for attention from the adult were greater than in the other atmospheres. It seemed clear that getting the attention of the adult represented one of the few paths to more satisfactory social status in the authoritarian situation where all of the "central functions" of group life were in the hands of the dominator.

The category "friendly, confiding" indicates that the members of the democratic and laissez-faire clubs initiated more "personal" and friendly approaches to their adult leaders, and the data on "out-of-club-field conversation" further indicate the more spontaneous exchanging of confidences about other parts of one's life experience in the democratic club atmosphere.

The data on "group-minded suggestions" to the leader show that the members in the democratic atmosphere felt much freer and more inclined to make suggestions on matters of group policy than in the other three group atmospheres. It is clear from other data that the lower level of suggestions in the laissez-faire situation is not because of any feeling of restricted freedom but because of a lack of a cooperative working relationship between the adult and the other group members.

The much greater responsibility of the members of the laissez-faire clubs to get their own information is shown by the fact that about 37 per cent of their behavior toward their leader consisted of asking for information, as compared to about 15 per cent in the other three club situations.

The final category . . . "work-minded conversation," indicates that a considerably larger proportion of the initiated approaches of the club members to their leaders were related to on-going club activity in the democratic and in the apathetic authoritarian situations than in the other two types of social climate.

Fromm (1947, 1955) theorized about the effects of different authority relationships between parent and child. He suggested that in *democratic* types of authority relationship, the child develops flexibly so he can readily accept authority from others or take over an authority position himself when needed. Authority means simply leadership by the person whose knowledge or skills at any particular moment are most suitable for effective government. In the *authoritarian* parent-child relationships the attitude toward parental authority is one of awe and magic, the parent being vested with superiority and power. Two behavior patterns can emerge from authoritarian parent-child relationships. On the one hand, the child can become characteristically submissive toward persons in authority and be able to function only in a dependent relationship to persons who are symbols of power and authority. In contrast with this, rejection of authority and the need for mastery can develop. The person can never accept authority in someone else but must be in an authoritarian role with someone else as the underling. The authority-rejecting and submissive patterns essentially are immature and neurotic, and the democratic type of authority response is mature and characterized by independence and security.

Research also has been done on the family patterns of delinquent and nondelinquent boys by sociologists such as Sheldon and Eleanor Glueck (1943, 1950). Their data showed that juvenile delinquents come from homes that are far less accepting and much more indifferent and arbitrary than the homes of nondelinquents. Coming from a *rejecting family*, which is essentially lax and inconsistent in supervision, delinquents generally felt unaccepted and unap-

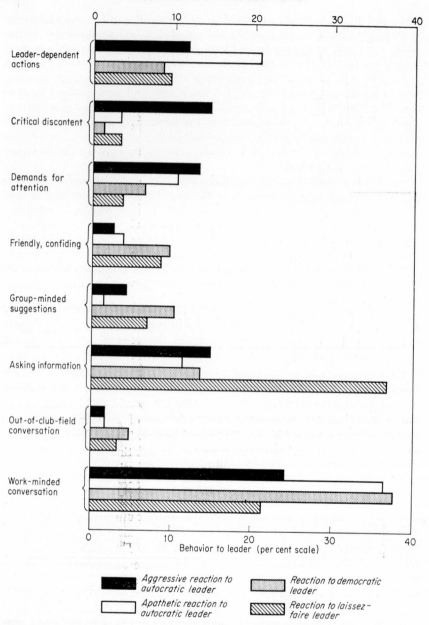

Figure 25. Four patterns of group reaction to the three different types of leadership. (*From Lippitt & White. In Swanson et al., 1952.*)

preciated. They were resentful and suspicious of others and often defiant in their attitudes toward authority. Interestingly enough, however, the delinquents had fewer feelings of anxiety, insecurity, helplessness, and failure. Signs of early anxiety or other fearful attitudes seem to be less frequent in potential delinquents than in other children. Perhaps fear of punishment is the essential basis of proper social behavior. Delinquents are unimpressed with punishment because they have had so much experience with it from their rejecting parents. The delinquents have not introjected as fully the standards of the culture because rejection and punishment have been their only lot in life, and even appropriate behavior on their part has not resulted in the parental approbation needed to encourage socialization.

David Levy (1943) reported research dealing with the behavioral consequences of *maternal overprotection*. Overprotecting mothers were found to have frequent and extended physical contact with their children, caring for them as they would a baby far beyond the age at which such care would be appropriate. In general, they behaved in such a way as to prevent the development of the child's independence.

Two patterns of maternal overprotection were found: one *dominating*, in which the mother produced excessive controls, and the other *indulgent*, in which the mother pampered the child's whims with little attempt to control him. Oversolicitude was characteristic of both patterns. The child was forced to stay within sight or call. The mother was overattentive through even minor illnesses and bathed and dressed the child when he was old enough to assume such responsibility himself.

The *overprotected, indulged children* showed behavior patterns characterized by disobedience, temper tantrums, and excessive demands on others. Such children tried to dominate and tyrannize other children of their own age. They had difficulty making and keeping friends and typically became isolated from everyone except members of their family. Such children did well in school, to a large extent because of the amount of time they spent with their mothers, who stressed the values of adult standards of knowledge. They were anxious and apprehensive about their experiences with peers, and intellectual pursuits seemed more rewarding and safer than social relations. The *overprotected, dominated children* also tended to be anxious and insecure. Such children were obedient, submissive to authority, timid, and backward with their peers.

Both the dominated and indulged children were generally inadequate in social relations; the former were characterized by submissive patterns of behavior, and the latter were characterized by dominating patterns. Because of the continual warnings against danger characterizing the attitude of overprotection (such as "don't cross the street, you might get hurt"; "don't run so much, you might get sick"), these children perceived the world as dangerous and frightening. Other consequences were mistrust of others, as well as a failure to develop independently the skills of interpersonal relations because such relations were handled largely by the mother and the child had not had the opportunity to learn how to function by himself. The dominated children learned to escape or avoid the dangerous world by doing what the mother said.

They could be safe and protected by not exercising initiative. The indulged children learned that protection and safety are obtained by demand. The protector must be coerced by tantrums and manipulation.

These are merely a few examples of patterns of parent-child relationships and their consequences for personality. Varying family patterns are found not only in different societies, but also within our own society as a function of ethnic origins, social class, and individual differences in the personalities of parents themselves. If the parent is neurotic, for example, this disturbance is likely to be manifested in the way in which he deals with his children. Pathological patterns are often perpetuated because the sick parent communicates his pathology in his transactions with his children.

Every person within a culture shares a certain amount of experience with every other person in the same culture. However, there are many aspects of the culture that are not shared by all its members but by members of subsocieties within the larger one. The subdivisions within the society can be drawn finer and finer, until we recognize that there are experiences shared only by members of a particular family. Thus, each family, although showing features of the general culture, can be regarded for certain purposes as an individual society in itself. Moreover, each member within the family has his own unique experiences and biological heritage. Thus, no two persons will be entirely alike.

When we consider the enormous variety of combinations of social and biological factors possible, then we can understand why every person comes out differently. We must realize that an individual is not a simple additive result of the different influences to which he is exposed but a product of the interaction of an enormous number of social and biological factors. To understand an individual, we must know what these factors are and we must trace the course of his life history. It is one thing to attempt to understand how behavior in general is influenced but another to apply this generalized knowledge to a single human being.

Personality structure, as a theoretical proposition, comes about through the interaction of biological and social factors. Many of these biological factors are present at or before birth. What structure the organism has at birth is limited to these biological potentialities. There has been little opportunity for the complex personality structure that characterizes the adult to develop, because the individual's experience with the social world is negligible before birth. One may fancy that the organism at birth has some structure, but it is as yet relatively undifferentiated and unorganized in comparison with what it will be at maturity. Progressively during his life there will be increasing differentiation of psychological structures, resulting from the interaction of biological starting points and the social experience that takes place postnatally. By the time the child is an adult, the processes that have emerged from this interaction will have become relatively ossified, that is, relatively stable or permanent and resistant to change. Although change can always take place, the structure becomes more fixed and immutable with advancing age. Ultimately, senility and death alone can dissipate the well-established personality structure, which has been formed during the entire life history. One can view the development of the personality structure of the organism (as Lewin, 1951, does) from the least structure at conception to the progressively differentiated and integrated organization that develops through life.

Both biological and social conditions are important determinants of human behavior, and inferentially these factors are influential in the development of the personality structure, however it is conceptualized. We can observe directly the correlations between biological and social variables and behavior. This behavior is understood in terms of the hypothetical structure called "personality," which presumably underlies behavior and gives it consistency and meaning. The nature of this conceived structure depends in part upon the theoretical scheme that one has constructed or accepted.

Once it has been formed, this personality structure (a developmental resultant of the effects of biological and social influences) guides and controls behavior. In other words, the personality shows itself to us as dispositions to act and react in certain consistent ways that distinguish one person from another. The momentary behaviors of the person are thus resultants of the interaction of the established dispositions built into the personality and of the situation to which he is exposed. This situation consists of transient physiological states (for example, level of hunger or fatigue) and external stimuli, often interpersonal (for example, an insult or a request to say or do something).

In sum, physiological and social factors not only contribute to the formation of the stable personality structure, which, in turn, impels or disposes the person to behave in certain ways, but they also continually influence momentary behavior by interacting with the already established personality structure. These interactions contribute to the enormous complexity of human behavior and make the task of understanding it a tremendously challenging one.

IV

MORE ON THE ADJUSTMENT PROCESS

WE BEGAN OUR treatment of personality and adjustment in Chapter 1 with a discussion of the nature of the concept of adjustment. A key point was the interdependence of processes of adjustment and personality structure. For this reason we proceeded to examine personality, its nature, theories about it, its development, and the biological and social conditions of life that are influential in its formation. We are now prepared to return to the processes of adjustment in the context of this background.

Adjustment is conceived as continually occurring in response to internal pressures and environmental demands, but special problems are created for the person when these demands become excessive; when an individual is exposed to conditions of stress. It is therefore of great importance to consider the nature of stress and its implications for the adjustment process. This problem of adjustment and stress is the substance of Chapter 11, where adjustment is treated as the processes of coping with stress. Then in Chapter 12 the consequences of inadequate mastery of stress are taken up in the form of failures of adjustment. This chapter is basically a summary of the field of abnormal psychology and deals with the various forms of psychopathology and their causes and dynamics.

In preparing Chapter 12, I have followed, in part, the excellent organization of the field provided by Coleman (1950) in his text *Abnormal Psychology and Modern Life*. Coleman is most useful as a descriptive source, describing the symptoms characteristic of the various disorders without a unified theoretical emphasis or a thorough coverage of the varieties of theoretical points of view about mental illness. Other textbooks, for example, that of White (1956), offer more theoretically oriented treatments of abnormal psychology. To learn fully and specifically how each theoretical system views the causes and dynamics of each disorder will require the reader to seek out primary sources, some of which have been cited. At the end of Chapter 12 a few very brief statements are made, comparing different systems in their general handling of psychopathology.

CHAPTER
11

Adjustment and Stress

The most widespread regulative principle of human behavior is a home-ostatic one, in which the person alters either himself or his external environment when disequilibrium has been produced in order to restore the equilibrium (Cannon, 1939). An alternative or supplementary view involves the postulation of growth tendencies within the individual (e.g., Rogers, 1951). These lead him to seek mastery or control over himself and his environment in order to realize his highest potential and to produce the most harmonious relationship possible between himself and the environment. From either point of view, adjustment refers to the processes of this self or environmental alteration that produce some given state such as equilibrium or self-actualization.

Because the biological and psychological needs of an individual, as well as the external pressures to which he is exposed, are continually changing, adjustment is always taking place. But what if the adjustive capacities are taxed beyond their scope and the demands (internal or external) become excessive? Disturbances in function arise. These disturbances can include such subjective states and behavior patterns as psychological misery, somatic malfunctioning (psychosomatic disorders), abnormal forms of thought, socially reprehensible or deviant forms of behavior, and failure to execute successfully or normally the life tasks within the context of an individual's ability. The processes of adjustment are, therefore, important to us not only because under normal circumstances of living they determine our actions but also because, when they fail under conditions of unusual demand, our welfare is endangered. When this happens, we talk about the existence of a state of *stress*, an extreme instance of disturbed equilibrium.

It is important to study stress states in order to understand their consequences for adjustment and to learn the nature of the (stressor) conditions that bring them about in the first place. We shall discover that the concept of stress is a central one in our conceptions of psychopathology. It is probably also an essential feature of normal human development. For example, Sullivan (1953) considered anxiety as a crucial and even positive force in man's efforts to improve himself and the world. Rank (1945) considered the conflict of wills associated with the life and death fears as a basic part of life itself and as the basis of human creativeness. Davis (1952) also emphasized the importance of anxiety in the normal process of socialization. The crucial problem in normal versus pathological development is the amount of stress and the resources available for mastering it. Let us examine some of the main ways of viewing the nature of stress.

STRESS AS ENVIRONMENTAL CONDITIONS

A wide variety of meanings have been given to the term "stress." One of the most common notions is that stress represents some circumstance or situation *external* to an individual that makes sudden or extraordinary demands upon him. Thus, we might think of unusual conditions, such as anticipated surgery (Janis, 1958) or disasters (floods, storms, fires, explosions, or military bombings) as examples of stress. Also see Wallace (1960).

Figure 26. Parents watch as the school building that housed their children burns and rescue operations take place. The burned bodies of many of them are retrieved. The parents show visibly their stress (in the form of grief and apprehension) over the possible fate of their children caught in the fire. Such disasters are one source of stress in human existence. (*Wide World Photos.*)

One of the most fascinating investigations of such crisis situations was performed by Cantril (1952), who described and analyzed the panic that gripped thousands of persons after the famous Orson Welles radio broadcast, "The Invasion from Mars" (1938). Welles had produced a dramatization of such an imaginary invasion so realistically that large numbers believed it and fled for their lives. Persons all over the country rushed aimlessly through the streets, packed their families into automobiles to flee the danger, cried, or otherwise behaved as though the end of the world were imminent.

Cantril asked what conditions were important in bringing about this extraordinary reaction in so many persons. He observed that panic occurred mostly in persons who tuned in after the program had gotten under way and did not hear the introductory announcement that would indicate that the program was only a dramatization. When such persons attempted to check their hypothesis of a real Martian invasion against other facts, for example, looking out the window or turning to other radio stations, they did not use correctly the information because of their fear. Some noticed the streets were empty and assumed that this was the result of the crisis. Others saw crowded streets and assumed that everyone was fleeing. When they heard regular radio programs on the other stations, they assumed that efforts were being made to reassure the populace. Whatever conflicting information they obtained was integrated into their fear-generating hypothesis of an invasion from Mars.

The essential difficulty with this approach, which defines stress as the threatening situation, is that what is a source of stress for some persons is not necessarily so for others. Although it is true that extreme conditions of actual disaster will severely disturb a high percentage of persons, individual reactions to these situations are extremely varied. Even in floods or military bombings, there are some persons who respond in a cool and collected fashion and others who become disorganized. Moreover, it seems unwise to restrict the term "stress" to those extremely unusual conditions that have a very great impact on nearly everyone. There are many more ordinary conditions of everyday life that can produce great impact.

In the case of the Orson Welles broadcast, only a small percentage of those hearing the broadcast responded to the situation as stressful. In his study of the effects of the program, Cantril also attempted to determine what it was about these persons that made them especially vulnerable. For one thing, degree of education was an important factor. Those whose knowledge was limited had less information against which to check the concept of a Martian invasion. There were, no doubt, important personality factors as well, which made some persons more likely to respond in the fashion they did.

Another study of mass hysteria (Johnson, 1952) concerned persons who believed surging rumors about a killer who struck with a paralyzing gas. It was found that those who reacted with panic had personalities like persons who develop neurotic attacks of hysteria. Most of the reports of attacks came from women. The number affected represented a small part of the total population of the town involved in the supposed crisis.

There have been many experimental attacks on the problem of the effects of stressor conditions. It has been only in recent years, however, that experimenters have begun to explore systematically the factors behind individual differences in reaction. For example, Lazarus and Eriksen (1952) performed an experiment in which a group of subjects were exposed to a situation of failure. The stressed subjects, as a group, seemed not to be affected differently in their performance from a control group, which received no stressor experience. However, a careful analysis showed that the stressed group was much more variable, some subjects showing improvement in performance and others showing impairment. The fact that some subjects were affected in one way and others in the opposite direction cancelled out any obvious group differences. The experimenters then asked what personality factors accounted for the differences in reaction to the stressor condition (Eriksen, Lazarus, & Strange, 1952), but they were unable to find satisfactory evidence in their study. More recent research on the problem has begun to show that differences in motivational characteristics of people determine in part whether stress will occur (Vogel, Raymond,

Figure 27. A funeral ceremony reflecting the common stress connected with the death of a loved one. The man in the center is weeping over his bride-to-be who had collapsed and died while walking to the altar during the wedding ceremony. The problem of death as a source of stress is universal and is dealt with by people in different ways. (*Wide World Photos.*)

Lazarus, 1959). Differences in coping mechanisms are also a basic factor in determining the consequences of stress for behavior and cognition. But there is still relatively little systematic knowledge about the personality and situational factors that influence reactions to crisis or stressor conditions.

There are great differences between individuals in their sensitivity to various situations as stressors, and it is necessary to discover the reasons why one individual is disturbed by a given situation and another is not. We must go beyond the stimulus definition of stress, which treats all persons as essentially alike and assumes that their perceptions of danger or threat are based on exactly the same conditions. We must also consider the ordinary stresses of life, such as getting a job, getting married, the death of a loved one, seeing a disturbing movie, etc. These experiences have different impacts on different persons, and we must come to understand why.

STRESS AS A STATE WITHIN THE INDIVIDUAL

A second major way of viewing stress treats it as a *state of the individual* rather than as an external condition that he faces. For example, the famous physiologist Selye (1956) makes stress synonymous with what he calls the "adaptation syndrome," an organized set of biological reactions to noxious stimulation such as physical injury. If bodily tissues are damaged, certain systematic biochemical changes take place as a result, these changes being part of the organism's efforts to repair the damage. However, these adaptations to the noxious or damaging circumstances in themselves, especially when chronic, can produce further injury to the organism. For example, when a person responds to a chronic fear-provoking situation with an outpouring of adrenalin (a hormonal substance that produces vast changes in metabolism), this outpouring of the adrenal-hormonal substance can be quite damaging to the long-range functioning of the organism. Psychosomatic disturbances such as ulcers, colitis, and high blood pressure are thought to involve this chronic adaptation process to psychological danger (see Chapter 9). Selye's emphasis is on the internal state of the organism and its consequences rather than on the situation that produces it.

This diversity in the meaning of stress can be confusing, because different writers use the term to mean different things. I am inclined to lean toward the latter approach in my definition of stress. However, the problem still remains to identify for any person or class of persons the conditions (internal and external) that can be defined as stressors because they bring about the stress state. One of the consequences of the state is the elicitation of adjustment mechanisms, which are associated with both healthy and pathological behavior.

We are now prepared to divide the area of stress and adjustment into four issues or problems. The first is the conditions or sources of stress. The second is the nature of the stress state itself. The third is the coping mechanisms elicited by the stress. The fourth is the behavioral consequences of stress.

SOURCES OF STRESS

It is especially when the demands upon a person tax him to the limit of his resources or beyond that we speak of "psychological stress." The concept of stress is concerned, therefore, with demands that are in degree more severe than ordinary. These demands must produce thwarting of motives in some way. This thwarting can be in the form of threats to the maintenance of life and the avoidance of pain, or it can restrict a person's opportunity to satisfy motives of great importance to him. Therefore, what is thwarting to one man may not be to another because of different patterns of motivation.

Mahl (1949) made some observations that are very pertinent to this point. He wished to discover the psychological and physiological bases of ulcer formation, and to this end he experimented with the conditions that produce excessive hydrochloric acid secretion (thought to be an important cause of ulcers) in the stomach. Stomach acidity in human subjects was measured just prior to an important college examination and also during nontension control periods. Six of the eight subjects showed a marked increase in acid secretion prior to the examination, but two of the subjects showed no increase; in fact, a slight decrease. Mahl then examined the interview material he had obtained from the subjects during the experiment in order to understand better the reasons for these individual differences. He found that the two students who failed to show an increase in stomach acidity under the stressor condition were rather casual about the examination and did not regard it as threatening. One of them had already been accepted into a medical school of his choice and believed that the examination could not endanger his status. The other was content to obtain the gentleman's grade of C. He too was indifferent to the coming examination. These motivational factors in the two subjects reduced the prospect of their being threatened by the same examination that was a source of stress to the other six.

Another experimental example of the importance of motivation in determining whether a situation will be stressful can be found in a recent experiment by Vogel, Raymond, and Lazarus (1959). They found that subjects who were motivated primarily toward achievement (success academically and vocationally) rather than toward affiliation (establishing warm, friendly interpersonal relations) were not stressed by a threat to the latter motivation but were considerably disturbed by the implication that they were failing on a test of their capacity to succeed academically and vocationally. Conversely, subjects with a strong motivation toward affiliation and weak motivation toward achievement

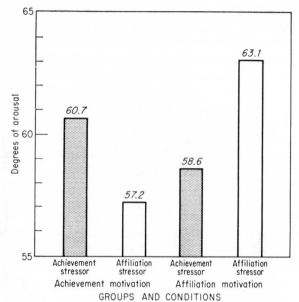

Figure 28. Groups and conditions—degree of arousal and the relevance of the stressor condition to the basic motivational pattern. Shaded bars show degree of arousal when the stressor was relevant to the subjects' motive preference. (*After Vogel et al.*, 1959.)

were disturbed only when their capacity to establish friendly relations with others was impugned and not when they failed in a test of their achievement potential. These results are shown in the form of a bar graph in Figure 28.

Stress must always be regarded in terms of the relation between the pattern of motivations of the person and the life situation to which he is exposed. So far as human beings share similar motive patterns, similar situations produce thwarting. Later on, some of the life situations regarded as typically thwarting, because they impinge upon more or less universal or widely shared motivations, will be discussed.

It is useful to distinguish as sources of stress two kinds of situations; one that produces deprivation of biological needs, or makes extreme physical demands upon the individual, and one that involves threats to the self-esteem of the person. Examples of the former might be exposure to extreme temperatures or to conditions of starvation or semistarvation. Many adventure stories have been built around stress themes of this kind: truck drivers carrying high explosives over treacherous roads; man's struggles with the elements while manning a ship through a hurricane; military battles; in general, man's search for solutions to physical threats to his survival. During World War II, an extensive experimental study of the psychological and physiological effects of semistarvation was made by Franklin and his colleagues (1948). Many consequences of this prolonged physical stress were observed, but these were transitory, disappearing after the body weight of the subjects was restored by a normal diet.

Psychologists generally believe that the second type of stress source, threats to self-esteem, is far more potent in producing maladjustments, including neuroses and psychoses, than the former. Some examples of such sources of stress are the conflict in wartime between a man's wish to escape the dangers of combat and his wish to appear courageous or heroic in the eyes of his fellow soldiers; the conflict between man's hostile impulses toward others and the internalized attitude that such hostility is reprehensible; the conflict between sexual impulses and the attitude that these impulses are wrong or tabooed; or man's wish to be secure and dependent upon some protective persons (often the parents) and his need to be autonomous and independent.

These threats to self-esteem (or "ego motives") are often described as pathogenic conflicts. They result in the *thwarting* of some important motivation of the individual, and this thwarting itself can be viewed as the source or antecedent of stress. The term "thwarting," however, is often applied when a person is deprived in some physical way or when his physical security is in some way threatened. Rosenzweig (1944) applied the term *frustration* to thwartings that have the character of threats to self-esteem in order to distinguish them from simple physical deprivation. I prefer this latter usage because it avoids some of the confusion that arises as a result of these terms (thwarting and frustration) having been frequently used interchangeably.

If we concern ourselves with sources of stress that psychologists generally regard as very common, we can approach the question in two ways. On the one hand, as has been competently done by Mussen and Conger (1956), we could look at periods of development in which characteristically different problems are faced. For example, in childhood there are the problems of weaning, toilet training, social adjustments, and school adjustments. When we study adolescence, we might concentrate on the biological and social changes that take place as the child becomes initiated into an adult role in society. For the period of senescence, new problems emerge from a person's deteriorating physical condition and his reduced usefulness and independence, particularly in our own society.

Although these developmental periods are associated with certain characteristic problems, the exact form and degree of these problems varies from person to person. For instance, some elderly persons are not faced with idleness and are able to function usefully and serenely within society. Similarly, many adolescents are guided through the transition to adulthood in such a way as to minimize or eliminate the stresses common to this period of life. This point is embedded in the anthropological studies of Margaret Mead (1934, 1935), cited in Chapter 10.

In contrast with the analysis of sources of stress by developmental periods, we can approach the field in a second way, by ignoring specific periods of life and considering timeless problems, which psychologists have considered potentially stressful to anyone at any age. The nature of these problems would vary according to the theoretical approach to personality we adopt, although it would not be difficult to obtain some agreement among psychologists about certain focal areas. We can then list as important sources of stress the expression and control of sexual impulses; the containment and appropriate discharge of aggressive impulses; the attainment of social acceptance in the context of competitive behavior; the reaction to the deprivation of love and affection through parental rejection; the conflict between dependency needs and striving for independence; the achievement of social and occupational success in the face of physical and intellectual inferiorities; and the mastery of, or adjustment to, continuing social change (which has become increasingly important in modern times because of the accelerated changes in society and its patterns of living). These sources of stress tend to cut across developmental periods, although they can be accentuated at some periods of life and reduced in others. The relative importance of each varies in the different personality theories discussed.

THE NATURE OF STRESS

The problem now is to consider the effect of these sources of stress upon the individual. Up to now we have theorized that the frustration of ego motives is the general source of stress. There is, moreover, an intimate relationship between frustration and emotion, such that when frustration occurs a person reacts with disturbing emotion (as opposed to positive or pleasant emotion such as delight), probably to the degree of the original motive strength itself. If frustration did not have negative emotional consequences, then we probably would not speak of stress as a special problem. We would consider a person as faced merely with the task of overcoming obstacles to the gratification of motives, and we could apply relatively simple learning principles to understand how he acquires an adaptive solution. When emotions enter into the picture, however, the ordinary course of problem solving is changed in some important respects. There are certain special consequences of the emotional state associated with stress (such as the development of nonadaptive behavior) that make the study of stress of great importance to the understanding of personality and adjustment.

The state of stress is dependent upon the nature of the emotion (i.e., degree and type) aroused and the ways in which persons attempt to cope with it. However, stress is not entirely equivalent to emotion because a person can succeed in reducing or eliminating the disturbing emotional state by mechanisms of defense. In that instance, we may find little or no evidence of emotional arousal, but the person's cognitive behavior in the presence of somatic symptoms may suggest that he is under stress.

In order to clarify this point more fully, let us consider some essential features of emotional states. An emotion is a hypothetical construct in that the emotional process cannot be directly observed but can only be inferred from certain behavioral and subjective consequences.

Generally speaking, there are three classes of observable events that define the state of emotion. One is the *visceral expression,* that is, the many biochemical and tissue reactions stimulated by the activity of the autonomic nervous system. We shall not elaborate these here except to note that emotional states are associated with noticeable visceral changes, such as increased heart rate, respiratory changes, perspiring, and gastric secretions. It was once thought that particular emotional experiences, such as fear or anger, were somatically undifferentiated and that, although persons had different subjective experiences of emotion, the biochemical reactions were the same. The work of Wolff (1950), however, has shown that in anger the mucous membranes of the body become engorged with blood (as in red-faced anger) and bathed with secretions, and in fear reduction of blood flow (paling of the face) and drying out of the tissues is common. Recently Funkenstein and his associates (1957) and Ax (1953) have been able to demonstrate different adrenal gland chemical secretions associated with fear and anger, fear leading to the secretion of adrenalin and anger to noradrenalin (see also Chapter 9).

The second aspect of emotion lies in *motor expression,* the innervation of the smooth and striated muscles of the body sometimes described as "physical tensions." In his studies of stress, Malmo (1953, 1955) and his associates have measured muscle-action potentials, that is, increase in tension in muscle groups of the body as manifested in increased electrical potential. He has observed, for example, that persons who are prone to headaches seem to show their emotional reaction under stress-producing situations in increased tension of muscle groups at the back of the neck.

The third class of activities in which emotions can be expressed has been referred to as *affect,* the subjective experience of emotion, one of the most important of which is anxiety. A person can tell us that he is anxious, uneasy, or apprehensive or that he is delighted, exhilarated, or relaxed.

The field of emotions is one of the most important and baffling in psychology. Relatively little is known about the complex interrelationships between frustration and emotion and between the three classes of emotional manifestation: somatic, motor, and affective. It should be noted that emotions are regarded most often in their negative or uncomfortable sense, with relatively little attention given to positive emotional states, which are also important to behavior. In the field of adjustment and psychopathology, anxiety and fear rather than joy or delight have been given central theoretical positions.

The role of emotion and its manifestations in adaptive behavior has been handled in different ways. Some writers have suggested that mild states of tension are actually sought by man. For example, Lecky (1945) talked about man as a tension-producer rather than as a tension-reducer. Most psychological theories, however, tend to regard tension and affect as unpleasant states, which man attempts to eliminate or reduce by his actions. It is generally agreed that strong affects are unpleasant and can *disorganize* the productive efforts of man. Typically, this disorganization is conceived of as excessive stimulation interfering with cognitive behavior or adaptive functioning; that is, it obstructs the performance of the adaptive tasks at hand.

In contrast, Leeper (1948) argued that emotion actually tends to organize human behavior functionally to avoid danger. Similarly, Freud (1936) and Dollard and Miller (1950) have also stressed the organizing properties of emotion, regarding fear or anxiety as a drive; that is, an unpleasant stimulus, which motivates the organism to discover and apply ways of reducing it. The same point has been developed by social psychologists, such as Davis (1952), who has pointed out that, in the socialization of the child, parents intentionally produce anxiety (a subjective manifestation of stress) by punishing or disapproving socially inappropriate behavior and rewarding or approving acceptable behavior. The child comes to learn the socially approved attitudes and patterns of conduct because failure to do so is associated with disapproval and consequent anxiety (see Chapter 10). In order to be comfortable and free from anxiety, the child learns to adopt the appropriate patterns. As we shall see shortly, when the value systems to which the child is exposed are in conflict, or when they result in the frustration of biologically powerful impulses, various ego defenses can be learned to reduce the anxiety; the behavioral consequences of these defenses, which are maladaptive in certain respects (for example, the distortion of reality), make it appear that emotions disorganize behavior. In reality, anxiety has important organizing properties, but its indirect effects often have the appearance of behavioral confusion.

The evidence of the effects of emotion is consonant with both views of emotion, as a disorganizer, or source of interference, and as an organizer of behavior, depending upon what perspective is employed. In some studies, such as that of Postman and Bruner (1948), perceptual behavior was made poverty-stricken by stressing the subjects (in this case the subjects were required to form hypotheses about the nature of a stimulus presented on a screen too rapidly for complete recognition). In other studies, such as that of Deese, Lazarus, and Keenan (1953), the introduction of a stressor yielded improvements in learning in a particular group of subjects and decrements in another. Two groups of subjects were employed in the latter study, a highly anxious group and one normally low in anxiety. These subjects learned a list of nonsense syllables under control, or nonstressor, conditions, and under a stressor condition, which consisted of a painful electric shock administered whenever the subject made an error. As can be seen from the bar graph in Figure 29, which summarizes some of the data from the experiment, the normally anxious group's performance was actually facilitated by the stressor condition (they gave more correct responses under the electric-shock condition), and the group normally low in anxiety did far worse. Still other patterns were found under different types of stressor conditions. Both the organizing (facilitating) and disorganizing (impairing) effects of emotion can be readily confirmed in experimental research of this sort.

By extension of the above discussion, we can say that stress can affect the process of adjustment in two ways. In the first place, it can interfere with cognition, thus making the ordinary adaptive tasks of life more difficult to perform (the disorganizing effect). Secondly, and perhaps more important, mechanisms of defense designed to reduce the stress are produced (the organizing effect). These defenses in themselves are maladaptive in the sense that they are generally self-deceiving, thus making it difficult or impossible for the person to approach realistically the actual

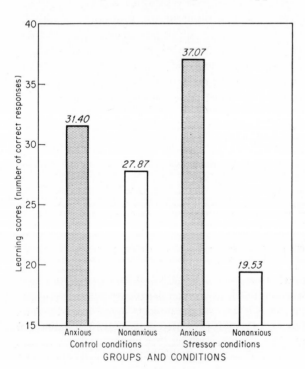

Figure 29. Groups and conditions—effects of stress on learning as a function of level of anxiety. Shaded graphs are those of the subjects who showed a high level of anxiety under normal, nonexperimental conditions as measured by a questionnaire. (*After Deese et al.,* 1953.)

conflict or source of frustration that aroused the state of stress. However, they may be regarded as adaptive in the sense that they serve to reduce anxiety.

It should be understood that the absence of subjective manifestations of emotion (affect such as anxiety) is not in itself a suitable sign of the absence of stress, because defensive operations can reduce or eliminate the emotion at the expense of effective adaptation. For example, if a person deals with stress by repressive defense mechanisms (and is therefore totally unaware of the internal conflicts), he may succeed in reducing anxiety to such a degree that he appears entirely comfortable. The expression *la belle indifférence*, used to describe a characteristic of the disorder known as "conversion hysteria," reflects this absence of anxiety, although the conversion symptom (blindness, deafness, anesthesias, paralysis, etc.) suggests a severe state of stress and the operation of the mechanism of repression. Often we infer a state of stress not from the subjective reports of the person, but on the basis of other evidence such as physiological reactions or the behavioral manifestations of ego-defense mechanisms.

We have considered the sources of, and the nature of, stress, primarily in terms of its relation to emotion. An equally important aspect of the stress state is the attempt to reduce it in some way. We must now consider the ways in which persons cope with stress and the consequences of these coping mechanisms for human behavior and adjustment.

COPING WITH STRESS

Just about all current theories of personality recognize that the individual must find some way to deal with the stress state, which is an inevitable consequence of frustration, regardless of theoretical differences concerning the primary sources of stress. The disturbing emotional state that is part of stress must be tolerated or reduced if a person is not to be overwhelmed by it. Where a conflict of great proportions exists, unsatisfactory solutions can be created. These include the utilization of defense mechanisms of the sort discussed in Chapters 4, 5, 6, and 7 and which need not be enumerated again here. The individual may do everything he can to escape the disturbing situation (as Lewin expressed it, "psychologically leave the field"). For example, if a person has strong fears of meeting other persons, he can avoid situations requiring social interaction. The problem with this solution, however, is that social interaction is often impossible to avoid. Moreover, such avoidance gets the individual into further difficulties in his general life adjustment. If he is a salesman, for instance, his livelihood will depend in part upon his willingness to make business and social contacts.

A number of experimental studies have demonstrated the operation of such defense mechanisms. For example, Levine and Murphy (1943) found that when experimental subjects were given controversial passages to read and remember that were either favorable or unfavorable to their own attitudes, they tended to recall better the favorable material. The upper part of Figure 30 shows the learning and forgetting curves for the people who were pro- and those who were anti-communist in attitude, when the material they had to learn was a pro-Soviet Union selection. In the bottom part of the figure, the same analysis is made employing an anti–Soviet Union selection. You will notice that when the material to be learned was consonant with the subjects' bias, it was more readily learned and less easily forgotten. When it was in conflict, the opposite was true.

Undoubtedly there are other important factors (for example, individual differences in response to conflict and anxiety) that alter the case as shown here, but it is well established that persons defend themselves against the anxiety engendered by threatening material. The Levine and Murphy approach to this mechanism in the area of political conviction is just one example of the general process of resistance to the assimilation of material alien to one's point of view, especially if it is strongly held. It has also long been recognized that persons usually choose to listen to radio commentaries or read newspaper articles that favor their point of view, thus rarely exposing themselves to the other side of the issue. For this reason, it is difficult, in a society in which persons are free to listen to what they choose, to persuade an audience that is hostile. The tensions created by powerful conflicts are often resolved by avoiding them altogether, wherever possible.

The problem of conflict, social tension, and its resolution has been illustrated extremely well by social psychologists such as Lewin (1948), who has written extensively about racial and ethnic prejudice. This work offers so many parallels with stress and the defense mechanisms it elicits that it is worth pointing up here. Imagine, for example, a person with violently anti-Negro feelings. Let us also assume that these prejudicial attitudes are the object of assault or propaganda by certain segments of the society in which this person lives. We now have a case of potential conflict. If someone of low prestige (representing a weak counterforce) attempts to dissuade this person from his strongly emotion-laden views, some conflict is produced, but this conflict is of relatively minor proportions because he can easily disregard the pressures from a low-prestige person with a minimum of tension. There is no reason to take very seriously the opinions of someone who is not highly regarded.

Suppose, however, that someone valued extremely highly by the prejudiced person, such as his minister or perhaps the President of the United States, attempts to persuade him that his views are wrong. The degree of conflict is greatly increased because the two opposing forces are of

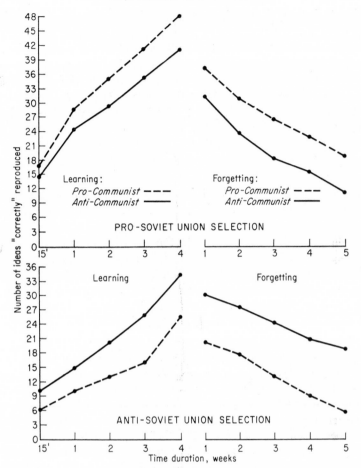

Figure 30. Learning and forgetting curves for "correct" responses for pro-Communist and anti-Communist groups of the pro-Soviet Union and anti-Soviet Union selection. (*Fom Levine & Murphy*, 1943.)

similar strength. The person cannot readily resolve it by altering his own attitudes because they too are strong and well entrenched. In such a situation, the emotional state (Lewin referred to it as "tension") becomes intense. Wherever possible, a person might attempt to avoid such an experience. If it were a sermon in church or a radio program, he might stop listening, turn off the radio, or find reasons for leaving the situation in which the conflict is aroused. Often, however, such a solution is not possible. The person is forced to remain in the situation and must find a solution to the problem in some other way.

In attempting to reduce tension, a person can utilize mechanisms of at least two kinds. He can hear incorrectly the message of the prestige figure; that is, he can *distort* the message and even perceive it as reflecting an opposite viewpoint. Thus, he can say, "The minister (or President) is warning me against rash action with respect to my feelings, but he is also implying that it is perfectly proper to feel this way." Or he can reduce the tension by *dissociating* the message from the prestige figure. For example, he can maintain that the prestige person is merely making an expedient address, the content of which he really doesn't believe, which was dictated by politically oriented writers; and he can justify this behavior by pointing out that, after all, in order for this good man to stay in office, a certain amount of realistically oriented political maneuvering is required. By saying that the prestige figure does not believe what he is saying, the conflict is resolved by an interesting intellectual twist and the basic attitudes of the individual remain untouched.

Under these circumstances, there is also an accommodative solution to the conflict, which equally distorts the realities of the situation. The prejudiced person can deny to others and, most importantly, to himself, that he feels any prejudice. By superficially accommodating his own feelings to the social pressures, he minimizes the discrepancy between himself and others (thus reducing the tension). In such a case he practices self-deception about the feelings he actually has. In the field of psychopathology, this kind of ego defense would be called "denial."

An interesting relevant experiment has been performed by Cooper and Jahoda (1947), using a series of cartoons depicting a character called Mr. Biggott, a highly prejudiced person, in a series of situations that highlighted the absurdity of the bigoted person and placed him in an extremely unfavorable light (see Figure 31). The cartoons were presented to prejudiced and nonprejudiced groups. Instead of altering their attitudes to relieve themselves from seeming ridiculous, the prejudiced subjects went to such lengths to extricate themselves from identification with Mr. Biggott that they simply did not get the point of the cartoons and never saw any connection between themselves and the bigoted person being portrayed. The point or humor of the cartoons was quite readily grasped by the nonprejudiced persons. By unconscious self-deception, it was possible for the prejudiced persons to avoid the disturbing effect that would have followed their awareness of the similarity of Mr. Biggott to themselves.

There is a close parallel between efforts to alter deeply held prejudicial attitudes and the efforts of the psychotherapist to get his patient to alter his conception of himself and recognize his real impulses and ego defenses. Both represent potential assaults on deeply held attitudes or values, assaults capable of producing enormous tension in the individual. A direct attack upon the patient's conception of himself or value system by the therapist might force the patient, in spite of his symptoms, to leave therapy. It is necessary, as we shall see later, to desensitize the

MR. BIGGOTT

"Good heavens! It's not restricted!"

MR. BIGGOTT

Mr. Biggott: "Was it necessary, Reverend, to emphasize the Lord's—er—Jewish background in your sermon?"

MR. BIGGOTT

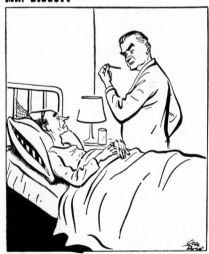

"In case I should need a transfusion, doctor, I want to make certain I don't get anything but blue, sixth-generation American blood!"

Figure 31. Instead of affecting the attitudes of the prejudiced individuals by making them seem ridiculous, the prejudiced subjects went to such lengths to extricate themselves from identification with Mr. Biggott that they simply did not get the point of the cartoons, and never saw any connection between themselves and the bigoted person being portrayed. (*From Morgan, 1956. Courtesy of the American Jewish Committee.*)

patient to certain experiences and attitudes in the context of a permissive rather than a threatening atmosphere. The patient is encouraged, little by little and with relatively tolerable amounts of anxiety, to reach a more realistic conception of himself. The difficulty of this task is reflected, in part, in the great length of time usually necessary to produce such changes. Both these illustrations, the effects of attempts to alter social attitudes and the efforts of the therapist to produce insight in a patient, illustrate the defensive ways in which persons often cope with stress.

Whichever type of solution is used to master stress, it should also be noted that there is an important theoretical difference between the voluntary inhibition of the impulse because it is either dangerous or inappropriate [for example, Asch's (1952) subjects who always realized that they were changing their judgments in accordance with the group pressure] and the unconscious processes by which a person deceives himself about the nature of the forces in conflict. When the latter process of self-deception takes place as a means of coping with stress, there are much more serious consequences for the person's adjustment. Generally speaking, the healthier modes of adjustment involve the resolution of pressures without self-deception, and most theories of psychopathology emphasize the unconscious or unverbalized quality of defensive mechanisms in the development of neurosis and psychosis. Psychologists experimenting with the problem of unawareness are having great difficulties finding suitable empirical indicators of this psychological state (see Eriksen, 1960).

It is also widely believed that defense mechanisms or ways of coping with stress are learned. Variations in defenses are, in large measure, associated with variations in life experience or in cultural patterns. So far as we are members of the same or similar societies, in which we share similar kinds of experiences, we also share many coping mechanisms. In any case, these coping mechanisms are conceived of as efforts to reduce the overstimulation involved in strong emotional states.

The tension-reducing qualities of pathological defenses, even in lower animals, are illustrated by a fascinating study by Masserman (1943) of alcoholic addiction in cats. Masserman argued that alcohol, in anesthetizing higher brain centers, tended to reduce or eliminate the unpleasant emotional state of fear. Cats were exposed to strong fear-producing stimuli (a sudden movement or an electric shock) in the feeding situation, so that a conflict was created between the desire to eat and the fear produced in the eating situation. Masserman then permitted the cats to drink milk containing alcohol in quantities comparable to a cocktail or two for a human being. He was subsequently able to show that when the cats, still in this conflict-produced state of stress, were given the opportunity to choose plain milk (which they ordinarily preferred) or milk containing alcohol, they invariably chose the latter, and continued to do so until the fear-producing conflict was extinguished by later experiences.

The cats' preference for alcohol might be considered analogous to alcoholism in man. It was interpreted as an attempt on the part of the cats to cope with the dreadful conflict produced by the simultaneous desire and fear to eat by reducing the fear side of the conflict with alcohol. It would be similarly argued that persons develop means of coping with stress that succeed to some degree in reducing fear states even though these solutions are maladaptive in other respects. For example, after ingesting considerable alcohol, the hungry cats could not even make the learned responses necessary to obtain the food.

Most readers, as a result of their past contact with psychology texts or courses, will recognize that many types of defense mechanism have been described. It would be undesirable to spell out in detail here these specific defense mechanisms. The great majority of these defense mechanisms were originally conceived and elaborated by Freud, although they have been understood by dramatists for centuries, for example, Shakespeare, and elaborated by other psychoanalytic writers, for example, Anna Freud (1946). We have already discussed repression in the chapters on Freud and association-learning theory. Other important defense mechanisms are projection, rationalization, identification, displacement, and reaction formation. Each of these mechanisms represents a form of self-deception, in which a person fools himself about the nature of his impulses and thus reduces the intense conflict-produced affect (anxiety) that would ensue if the impulse were expressed in a direct fashion.

If a person does not succeed in resolving stress-producing conflicts, or coping with them by means of defense mechanisms, he must remain in a high state of emotion, which can be expressed in the form of severe anxiety, somatic disturbances associated with emotions, or motor tensions. The anxiety disturbs the person's psychological comfort and can itself interfere with his adequate functioning in other spheres. It is also possible that the defensive operations that can be elicited, which were effective under minimum stress circumstances, might cease to be effective or break down under special conditions of increased stress. In this case, a person can suffer a relatively sudden and acute attack of anxiety, which can persist until the defenses are strengthened or until the person is able to escape from the stressor situation.

What happens, however, if a person cannot continue to tolerate, or defend himself against, the stress? In such a case, a more serious defensive process can take place, called regression. A person regresses to a more primitive level of organization of the personality and, in effect, manifests breakdown. He gives up the more mature adaptive functioning characteristic of his highest development. Schizophrenia is commonly thought of as a regressive disorder in which the ill person functions at a relatively childish level, withdrawing from the social field, which is too threatening or disturbing for him to effectively handle. A kind of disorganization is involved, the person giving up many or most of his efforts to deal realistically with the internal and external pressures to which he is exposed. He will be hospitalized and function at a near vegetative level of existence rather than face the unbearable and unmanageable life struggle. Various forms of psychopathology or failures of adjustment are considered in a later chapter. It is sufficient here to recognize that such disorders are generally considered to be stress-produced. A person pays in some way or other for his inability adequately to come to terms with the pressures by which he is beset.

This discussion of defense mechanisms has emphasized the tension or anxiety reduction theoretically associated with them, but we have not elaborated the unfavorable or *pathological consequences (symptoms) of self-deception.* Let us consider some of these briefly. Associated with the mechanisms of defense are distortions of reality, narrowing of experience, and increased vulnerability to each new source of stress. For example, a person misinterprets his own and other persons' behavior and is, therefore, unable to make realistic decisions or act in ways appropriate to the circumstances. The case of the paranoid projection is one of the clearest illustrations. In presumably projecting certain of his own (e.g., hostile) impulses on others, he fails to apprehend correctly the real intentions of others. He often acts as if others were working toward his destruction. As another example, the obsessive-compulsive neurotic, utilizing the defense mechanisms of intellectualization and isolation, is often unable to participate normally in interpersonal relations. Because he cannot permit himself feelings, his relationships remain superficial and distant. To protect himself against stress, he has cut himself off from many rich interpersonal experiences that are possible for the well-adjusted person. The hysterical personality too, who represses threatening impulses, is in continual psychic danger lest these impulses break through to awareness. He must, therefore, continually narrow or constrict his experiences in order to protect himself against this eventuality. He also is not free to develop normally or enrich his experience in any way that might threaten future regressive disorganization.

In addition to these costs of defenses, there are the psychic and somatic symptoms of struggle that beset a person who relies extensively upon defense mechanisms to resolve conflicts. As suggested earlier, somatic manifestations of stress reactions commonly produce wear and tear, so to speak, on the organs of the body. Such symptoms can be painful or debilitating. They are the cause of a very large proportion of consultations in general medical practice. Of further importance is the interference with the pursuit of the person's life goals that can occur as a result of stress and ego defenses. The person's ability to function is impaired and his energy reduced.

Because the defense mechanisms involve distortion of reality and frequently lead to inappropriate behavior in social situations, many secondary problems are also likely to arise. A person may act in such a way that others will avoid his company or employers will depreciate his ability and usefulness. In other words, aside from the internal disturbances connected with stress and the pathological defenses, there is the effect of these defenses on the attitudes of others. As Horney (1937) pointed out, this can lead to a vicious circle. For example, the person who neurotically wants to be loved by others and whose appetite for such a relationship is insatiable (part of the neurotic effort for security and reassurance) may find himself so irritating to others that his desire for love is ultimately thwarted. This further intensifies the neurotic need (see Chapter 7).

Although the defense mechanisms have some value in reducing the strength of the conflict and hence the severity of the emotional disturbance, they are also self-defeating in that they have consequences that make for further difficulties. The stress state has elicited behavior aimed at its reduction or elimination, and yet this behavior in other respects is maladaptive. In many instances a person cannot identify or understand what is happening to him. He is miserable and doesn't know why. He has somatic symptoms and cannot explain them. Other persons react to him in unpleasant ways for reasons he does not understand. He can find no readily available solution to his dilemma.

STRESS AND PERSONALITY THEORY

In Chapters 3 to 7 are outlined a number of somewhat divergent theoretical frames of reference for describing and understanding personality. It would, at this point, be useful to consider how particular personality theories differ in their conception of stress and adjustment. We cannot analyze in detail each of the numerous points of view, but we can illustrate some of the more important similarities and differences in approach to the problem.

There is nothing inherent in the three general frames of reference themselves (trait and type, association learning, and phenomenology) to suggest necessarily different sources of stress in the human being. For example, the trait-and-type frame of reference involves no specified internal or external pressures to which man is exposed. One could adopt a trait-and-type approach and be perfectly free to postulate any source or sources of stress. It is, therefore, necessary for us to disregard the formal theoretical patterns and consider how specific theorists within each frame of reference deal with sources of stress. In many instances these are spelled out in clear and unmistakable terms; in others little is said about the problem. Theoretical systems vary tremendously, as previously noted, in their thoroughness in spelling out the specific internal and external forces to which a person responds.

There do seem to be some concepts about stress that most or all major personality theories have in common. For example, all theoretical viewpoints implicitly or explicitly make anxiety or fear central to the development of defenses and pathological behavior. Similarly, although there are variations in how the coping mechanisms are viewed by different theoretical systems (e.g., safety devices for Horney and ego defenses for Freud), there is probably more similarity than difference between them and most points of view recognize some connection between the way in which a person learns to manage impulses and affects and the quality and caliber of his adjustment.

What seems to differentiate the theoretical points of view most clearly is how they conceive of the various sources of stress or, more particularly, what are the major forces to which a person responds that produce stress. In consequence of this let us consider some sources of stress as conceived in different personality theories. The reader must remember the discussion of these theoretical systems in Chapters 3 to 7.

Association-learning Theory of Dollard and Miller

We might begin by examining briefly Dollard and Miller's (1950) thoughts on this problem. Their basic model for behavior includes the concept of homeostasis or drive reduction and the separation of drives into primary (the biological drives, such as hunger, thirst, and pain) and secondary (e.g., love, achievement, approval, and aggression), which are acquired by reinforcement-learning principles. Fear (a secondary drive) is the primary motivating force in the acquisition of pathological behavior. A person learns to be afraid of certain cues because they have been associated with painful consequences (thwarting of primary drives). The fear, in turn, motivates various means of reducing it; these means of reducing fear are frequently nonadaptive in other respects. When a person resolves conflicts between various primary or secondary drives and fear in favor of reducing the latter (e.g., by repression or other learned mechanisms), maladaptive behavior ensues because the conflict is no longer conscious and available to rational solution. The defense mechanisms for dealing with fear (which are translated to a large extent from the Freudian mechanisms of defense) are seen as learned habits for reducing the fear drive.

But what areas of human experience are particularly important in producing conflict (and therefore stress) and in leading to neurotic defenses? You will recall that Dollard and Miller discussed the feeding situation, cleanliness training, and training with respect to sexual and aggressive drives as especially important, largely because the drives involved are pitted against opposing environmental forces, which tend to frustrate them. For example, society (primarily through the parent) tends to inhibit or punish the expression of sexual impulses. Anxiety is produced when a sexual impulse is aroused, and the child can learn (through parental punishment or disapproval) to reduce the anxiety by repression of the reprehensible impulse. This process is unconscious because the conflict itself may be poorly labeled at the time it first occurs, and the child may also be forbidden to speak about the sexual reactions.

This is not to say that conflicts over feeding, cleanliness, sex, or aggression are the only sources of conflict and stress that lead to pathological defenses or that they are inherent in association-learning theory. Dollard and Miller's purpose was to convert the problem areas investigated by psychoanalysis into concepts of reinforcement learning, such principles of learning being applicable to any conflicts. In other words, they translated Freudian conceptions of the sources of stress and the mechanisms for coping with stress into association-learning terms, adding nothing about the nature of these sources. They conceptualized these forces somewhat differently than the Freudian psychoanalysts and emphasized the learned quality of conflict and adjustment mechanisms, but they appear to be in fundamental agreement about the internal and environmental forces that are sources of stress because they produce conflict.

Phenomenological Theories

In general the so-called phenomenological theories give us little in the way of detailed analysis of the sources of stress from which pathological behavior arises. Their analysis tends to be of a formal nature without specifying in concrete terms the organism's needs that conflict with environmental forces.

Lewin (1935), like most theorists, also represented stress in terms of emotional states (labeled "tension") produced by conflicts, but he did so in a particularistic way. He said that the nature of these forces must be examined individually for each person. He wrote a great deal about conflict not in terms of the typical content of conflicts but in terms of a formal analysis of types of conflict, for example, with respect to the direction of the forces of approach and avoidance.

Similarly, the organismic theorists, such as Goldstein (1939), referred to the process of homeostasis (which Goldstein labeled the "equalization process") and emphasized, in addition, a general need for self-actualization without specifying what it is in the organism that must be actualized. Goldstein wrote of the failure of the environment often to provide the conditions necessary for self-actualization. A person then cannot come to terms with the environment. There exists a discrepancy between personal goals and the realities of the life situation; the organism can be described as disorganized or in a pathological state. But this formal analysis leaves out the particular dynamics, which include an analysis of the specific impulses that cannot be suitably realized in the face of the environmental obstacles. Thus we cannot learn from Goldstein what are the general sources of stress for man. We must discover these specifically for each individual as a function of his physical construction and particular experience.

Many phenomenologists (such as Lecky, 1945; Rogers, 1951; and Snygg and Combs, 1949) emphasized the need to maintain and enhance the self concept of the individual, and they viewed each experience as either harmoniously integrated with the self picture or in conflict with it. Thus if an impulse or experience is in conflict with his self concept, a person is under stress, especially if he is unable altogether successfully to assimilate the impulse or experience into the self picture. But here again the self concept is viewed in a rather particularistic sense; that is, it is unique because of each person's particular life experience, and it is difficult to speak of universal sources of stress. If they exist, they are not spelled out by the phenomenologists, who emphasize the unique nature of every person.

The maintenance and enhancement of the self concept (and the need for self-actualization) are rather vague abstractions from which it is difficult to specify the specific components. Therefore, it is never possible to identify the conditions or sources of stress, except by intensive analysis of the individual and the reconstruction of his phenomenal field. The model offers a formal guide but not a clear map as to when a person will be under stress. We must accept the task of identifying for each particular person the nature of his self concept so we can predict the impact of environmental situations upon it.

Freudian Psychoanalysis

The Freudian (1949) conceptions of sources of stress involve primarily the two basic instincts of sex and aggression, which in their direct expression inevitably run counter to environmental pressures or to the internalized prohibitions of the environment (the superego structure). The forms of these basic instincts vary developmentally so, with respect to sexuality, for example, the nature of the stress-producing conflict depends upon the psychosexual stage at which a person is traumatized: oral, anal, or phallic. Thus sexual conflicts can arise in the oral period (the feeding situation), in the anal period (the toilet-training situation), and in the phallic period (the Oedipus situation and the attendant fear of castration).

In Freudian terms, conflict produces anxiety, and the development of particular ego-defense mechanisms is thought to depend upon the psychosexual period during which conflict arises. Thus, the mechanisms of intellectualization and isolation arise when the sexual impulses are anal in form, and the repressive mechanism arises at the phallic level, when the main sexual impulses are oedipal in nature. The reason for the conflict can be a straightforward struggle between a person's biological urges and the environmental proscriptions of these urges. These environmental pressures become internalized so some of the most serious conflicts occur between the id and the superego and often come to represent entirely internal struggles. Freud regarded the physical demands of life as less important psychodynamically than conflict over sex and aggression (the important sources of stress).

Neo-Freudian Theories

Jung (1933), like Freud, conceptualized the personality in terms of continuing intrapsychic conflict but, like the phenomenological theorists, also postulated a self, which attempted to harmonize the conflicting subsystems of the personality. This harmony could be achieved in Jung's theory only in later life by the reduction in importance of the libido (including most of the vital life urges) and by the development of a religious, esthetic orientation that turned a person outward toward the society. For Jung, the sources of stress in early life were all the conflicting trends within the organism; archetypes from the ancestral past; his present experience, including the personal unconscious; and the struggle between introversive and extroversive dispositions. He placed less emphasis on the sexual drive than Freud did, and more on the wide variety of biological needs that characterize the human being.

For Adler (see Ansbacher & Ansbacher, 1956), the primary stress of life arises from the inferiority and helplessness of the individual, particularly in childhood, and his struggle to compensate for his helplessness and master his environment. The neurotic solution to this helplessness is the striving for personal power. Healthy adjustment can only take place when a person gives up his neurotic power strivings and actualizes his needs for superiority in an idealistic sense; a person must develop his capacity for social interest, which is continually stimulated by his lifelong social experiences.

The sources of stress for Rank (1945) are outlined in the concept of separation. Conflict exists between the life fear and the death fear. This is expressed in a struggle of wills, on the one hand pulling the individual toward a return to the dependency and security of the womb and on the other hand directing the individual toward increasing autonomy. The successful solution to this struggle (in the case of the artist) lies in the harmonious integration of the individual's effort toward automony and his need for belonging (return to the womb). All other conflicts are manifestations of this one basic problem.

Fromm (1941) accepted, for the most part, the Freudian system of thought but increased the emphasis on cultural forces producing a sense of isolation, loneliness, and insecurity, which are accentuated by man's freedom and autonomy in modern society. This conflict tends to force a person to seek dependent relationships with others to allay his sense of isolation and loneliness (escape from freedom). The special source of stress for Fromm, aside from those that are strictly Freudian, is a person's struggle for self-expression and individuality and the anxiety produced by the isolation that such independence produces. In this respect, there is considerable similarity between Fromm and Rank.

Horney (1937, 1939) postulated, in a way somewhat similar to the thinking of Adler, that basic anxiety (stress) is produced by a sense of isolation and helplessness in the individual. This isolation or helplessness leads to the development of various neurotic safety devices, which are ways of reducing the anxiety. The devices do not succeed because of the vicious circle they produce. Horney also emphasized, more than other writers, the cultural conflicts that accentuate stress by making the task of minimizing the sense of isolation or helplessness more difficult.

Sullivan (1953) also believed that anxiety was derived from threats to the security of the individual, which in man, who is interpersonal by nature, is achieved by social approval and prestige. The individual acquires various self dynamisms, which represent learned ways of reducing the anxiety resulting from his personal insecurity. Thus, for Sullivan, the primary source of stress is insecurity, as it is helplessness for Adler, isolation and helplessness for Horney, isolation and loneliness for Fromm, and separation for Rank. Like the concept of self-actualization, the problem of security or safety, emphasized by these latter theorists, is difficult to pin down. The basic force in human life is the individual's need for security or safety, usually defined as support and approval from others. It is not biological urges in conflict with environmental pressures, as Freud, Dollard, and Miller believe. The individual is conceived as struggling to overcome anxiety resulting from perceived lack of security or safety. Any condition that threatens a person's sense of security is a source of stress. For Horney, it would be one that accentuates helplessness or isolation; for Sullivan, disapproval or failure; and for Fromm, social rejection. The distinctions between these are not always easy to draw, especially because their exact meaning depends upon the individual.

In spite of divergences among the theories, there is one basic formal model of stress that seems to apply to all of them. Conflict (whatever its origins) leads to anxiety or fear, which, in turn, is dealt with either by successfully coping with the conflict or by tolerating the anxiety. In the case of neurosis, the response to anxiety is the utilization of pathological modes of reaction, commonly referred to as "defense mechanisms." In psychosis, even these mechanisms fail and the individual regresses to more primitive forms of adjustment. In the next chapter the problem of adjustive failure is elaborated. Various forms of psychopathology, most of which have their origin in stress and in efforts to master it, are surveyed.

CHAPTER

12

Failures of Adjustment

During the course of their lives, some persons are exposed to greater amounts of stress than others, making their task of adjustment more difficult. In addition, the resources they have developed for coping with stress may be too limited to permit them successfully to master these excessive demands. Failure of adjustment is the consequence.

It is interesting to speculate whether these failures are most clearly traceable to exaggerated degrees of stress or to inadequate mechanisms developed to cope with stress. In the latter case it would be argued that the psychologically disturbed persons among us have been exposed to essentially the same degree of stress as those who have developed healthy personalities but have simply been less fortunate, either in their heredity or in their life experiences, which are unfavorable for the acquisition of effective techniques of stress mastery.

It is probable that both interpretations are partially correct. The disturbed person has probably had more difficult life experiences with which to deal and, perhaps because of this, has not had the opportunities to acquire adequate techniques of mastery. But if we examine the life histories of schizophrenic patients, it is often difficult to find evidence of excessive degrees of stress in their past to account for the pathology we observe. Similarly, if we examine the life histories of relatively healthy persons, we often observe extremely pathogenic circumstances in their histories, which, theoretically, should have led to adjustive difficulties. Still, it seems plausible that behavior disorders can arise either from excessive degrees of stress or from the failure to develop satisfactory means of coping with normal life stress, although the reasons for such failure are not clear. We can combine both explanations and suggest that failure to develop adequate coping mechanisms can have its origin in too much stress, or even too little stress, at certain critical stages of life. Psychology has yet to explore this problem thoroughly and to obtain the information necessary for a suitable answer.

Failure of adjustment is the subject matter of abnormal psychology. It converges upon the area of personality and adjustment, but its focus is on pathology rather than the dynamics of the healthy personality. In a topic as large as this only the highlights can be sketched in a single chapter. Such topics as the nature of adjustive failure, the classification and description of adjustive failures, the extent of the problem, and adjustive failure and personality theory will be dealt with.

THE NATURE OF ADJUSTIVE FAILURE

In Chapter 1 we differentiated between adjustment as process and adjustment as an achievement. It was noted that the term "failure of adjustment" implies some standard of values for considering the adequacy of adjustment. We also discussed some criteria of the adequacy of adjustment. These included degree of psychological comfort, the presence or absence of physical symptoms, the social acceptability of behavior, and the effectiveness of the person's functioning in skilled or intellectual tasks. It is common to regard inadequacy by any of these traditional criteria as a sign of maladjustment. The healthy or adjusted person is often conceived of as adequate by these criteria, although the definition of mental health exclusively by the absence of signs of maladjustment is far less than satisfying.

It is generally believed that most symptoms of psychopathology arise from the inability to resolve stress-producing conflicts. They reflect the development either of inadequate solutions to this conflict or of defensive mechanisms, which themselves have unfavorable consequences. In other words, *psychopathology* is a manifestation or symptom of the dynamic processes by which a person attempts unsuccessfully to deal with stress. When mastery is generally successful, the personality is healthy. When mastery is partially or wholly inadequate, different degrees of pathology are manifest, the kind of pathology being associated with the particular coping method the person employs. The origins of defective coping methods lie both in the life experiences of the person and in his physical constitution.

It is appropriate now to turn to the classification and description of the various forms of psychopathology.

CLASSIFICATION AND DESCRIPTION
OF ADJUSTIVE FAILURES

The traditional classification of psychopathology is based not on a clear theoretical understanding of the disorders themselves but rather on the observed pattern of symptoms that distinguishes the various types of disturbances. The fundamental scheme for classification, which we use in modified form today, was developed originally by Kraepelin (1937). Although it has undergone modification in subsequent years and although it has many recognized inadequacies, it is still the basic system for describing and classifying abnormal behavior. It will help to consider briefly some of the categories most commonly found in this type of classificatory scheme.

A classic distinction is between so-called *functional* and *organic disturbances*. This distinction is particularly relevant when dealing with the psychoses, the most severe forms of psychological disturbances. The implication is that the organic psychoses are based directly upon disturbances of the physiological apparatuses or structures of the body and that the functional psychoses have no such organic basis. An excellent example of the former is general paresis, which is produced by damage to the central nervous system by a syphilitic infection in a very late stage. The organic structural basis of the disorder, damage to the brain, is undeniably associated with the psychotic symptoms, although these symptoms can vary greatly from person to person.

No one quarrels with the evidence that organic psychoses such as general paresis have direct structural origins. The difficulty with the functional-organic distinction is the implication that the former (such as schizophrenia) involve no demonstrable physiological or biochemical disturbances simply because such disturbances are not now known. There is no reason to assume that, because specific physiological or biochemical conditions of the disturbance are not now known, they do not exist. (At one time the physiological origin of general paresis was also not recognized.) Nor, for that matter, are the socially oriented adaptive problems found in the organic conditions explained by mere reference to structural defects in the organism. Adaptation is an organism-environment interaction at both levels, social and physiological.

It has been suggested that, rather than speaking of functional and organic disturbances, we should consider certain disorders (usually those that are now labeled "organic") as irreversible in the sense that damage to the brain tissues cannot be repaired and other disorders as reversible because the physiological malfunctioning or degenerative process can be stopped or reversed so normal function can again be restored. Because of the interactional property (organism and environment) of adjustment, however, this is only a partially satisfactory solution.

In spite of the general distress about the distinction between functional and organic psychoses, the classification tends to persist. Even though some textbooks do not use the distinction formally, the so-called organic psychoses tend to be discussed separately from the so-called functional psychoses. There is undoubtedly a rational basis for this distinction as long as its imprecise and tentative meaning is not misunderstood.

Another common distinction in the classification of the behavior disorders is between *psychosis* and *neurosis*. Although there are both quantitative and qualitative distinctions to be made between the psychotic disturbances and the psychoneuroses, these disturbances are commonly regarded as shading off into each other, the neuroses representing a more integrated and higher level of functioning and the psychoses representing a more severe and regressive degree of disturbance, in which a person functions at a far more primitive level of personality organization.

Nowadays it is common to find further distinctions with respect to the classification of disorders. We recognize that some psychopathologies are transient reactions to unusual or acute stressors and that their duration matches the duration of the stressor. Thus combat neuroses commonly disappear when the person is removed from the combat situation; if the disturbance fails to disappear after such a removal, it is assumed that combat has simply precipitated a chronic or potential disturbance of long standing. As another example, the mourning reactions of persons who have lost loved ones are akin to neurotic or psychotic depressions, but we regard these disturbances as normal in a sense, or at least reactive to realistic stressor conditions and generally temporary. Many of the transient reactions are difficult to distinguish from long-term psychoses or neuroses (except in duration) and probably have many similarities in regard to process.

It is also common to distinguish a condition known as *character disorder* from neuroses, psychoses, and reactive disturbances. Rather than inadequately facing severe stresses, a person with a character disorder has not acquired mature patterns of social behavior. Included here also are antisocial or criminal patterns and certain sexual deviations. Alcoholism and drug addiction are frequently separated from the character disorder because they are often considered as reactions to stress. Quite unique in some respects from any of the above categories are *defects of intelligence,* which may or may not be associated with emotional disturbances at all but which produce inadequate adaptation.

This is the basic classification scheme we shall use here. It includes six major categories: (1) the transient reactions to acute stress, (2) psychoneurotic disorders, (3) psychotic disorders, (4) character disorders, (5) alcoholism and drug addiction, and (6) defects of intelligence. Although this classification scheme follows in the tradition of Kraepelin's categories and the more recent classification system developed by the American Psychiatric Association, it represents in particular a modification developed by the U.S. Army. It is a relatively simple and reasonable scheme, and it permits us to describe the major forms of behavior disorder in an organized fashion. It is also the scheme adopted by a major textbook in abnormal psychology, written by Coleman (1950), which is a well-organized secondary source. Coleman's organization of psychopathology forms the basis of the present chapter outline. We must remember, however, that the individual categories include disturbances that, although similar in symptomatology, can have considerably different causes. Moreover, it is often difficult to utilize these labels reliably because there is a great deal of overlap between the conditions described. That is, patients commonly manifest symptoms that are included in several categories. Such a descriptive labeling system per se does not imply an understanding of the psychodynamics of each disorder, but it offers a useful starting place for the consideration of adjustive failure.

TRANSIENT REACTIONS TO ACUTE STRESS

The transient reactions to acute stress are of less significance than long-term neuroses, psychoses, and character disorders because they disable the person for a relatively small proportion of his total life. But they are also especially interesting. Because we often know the conditions that bring them about (e.g., wars and other disasters), these transient stress reactions are more amenable to controlled study than are long-term disturbances. They provide a kind of miniature model of psychopathologies, giving us important insights into many abnormal processes.

The common external cause of the transient stress reactions is some serious crisis (stressor) with which a person cannot effectively cope. A most common crisis is military combat; there are also numerous crisis situations not uniquely associated with wartime, for example, tornadoes, hurricanes, earthquakes, and fires. In some ways, however, these latter stressor conditions often lack something that is found especially in war; the severe demands on the person in combat can continue for months or even years, but most of the other crises mentioned are more often relatively short-lived, although their consequences can persist. Severe economic depressions, such as that of the 1930s, would represent for many persons, like the combat situation, a fairly long drawn-out source of stress.

It must be recognized that the external crisis itself does not altogether explain the disturbances that persons can display under these conditions, because the largest majority of persons exposed to such situations do not develop marked pathological patterns of behavior. As suggested in the preceding chapter, it is necessary to understand the predisposing characteristics of a person that make him respond to such a situation with a behavior disorder.

Personality disorders associated with combat were clearly recognized during World War I, when such traumatic reactions were frequently called "shell shock." The term "shell shock" reflected the prevailing notion that these disorders were primarily organic in character and produced by small hemorrhages of the blood vessels of the brain. It was later recognized that this explanation did not hold, and in World War

II new terms such as "battle fatigue," "war neurosis," and "combat exhaustion" were introduced.

There is no simple descriptive statement that will entirely cover these pathological reactions to battle-induced stress. The symptoms vary with the individual and with the circumstances. For example, among ground troops exposed to severe battle conditions, men commonly developed such symptoms as loss of weight, pallor, terrifying battle dreams, tremor, and various degrees of disorientation, which sometimes even reached the level of stupor (Henderson and Moore, 1944). On the other hand, Levy (1945) described typical anxiety symptoms associated with long experiences of combat flying, which included depression, phobic reactions to the combat missions, and excessive tendency to startle with little cause. It has also been pointed out that the symptoms associated with an acute and short-lived traumatic situation were often different from those produced by chronic, long-term stressors.

An illustration of an extreme instance of combat exhaustion of a transient variety, cited by Coleman (1950), is presented by Grinker and Spiegel (1945, pp. 18–19) who intensively studied such reactions:

A 20-year-old platoon Sergeant in the infantry had no anxiety in civilian life, and none in the six major engagements prior to the Battle of Mateur, where he developed acute anxiety in a very confused military situation. His platoon had orders to take a hill and had been told that they would meet with no opposition. The reverse proved to be the case and most of the men were wiped out by enemy machine gun fire. The patient and a friend wandered about trying to get back to their own lines, when they were caught in the fire of their own artillery. They finally made their way to a foxhole, where they found a dead German and a dead American soldier, the latter having been a member of their company. The patient's friend threw the bodies out, and got into the foxhole. Shells were falling all about them and there was no room in the foxhole for the patient. He then developed intense anxiety and did not know what to do; finally he lay prone on the ground and flung the dead bodies of the two soldiers over him for protection. He lay there for a long time, trembling and terror-stricken, until finally an artillery shell exploded very close by and blew the two bodies off the patient, ripping off his shirt at the same time. The two dead soldiers had actually saved his life. His mind at that point went blank. He wandered about, and was picked up by some men from his company, who brought him back to the bivouac area, from where he was returned to the rear. When he entered one of the forward hospitals he had acute anxiety, persistent tremor, great restlessness, loss of appetite, and insomnia with battle dreams. After a few days of rest these symptoms improved considerably. The acute anxiety and tremor disappeared, and he was sent back to our hospital. On admission he complained of restlessness, lack of appetite and a shaky feeling in his body. He had only very fine tremors of the hands. There were terrible dreams, in which he relived his battle experience, and also nightmares, in which he saw himself being attacked by gorillas. After pentothal therapy all anxiety disappeared, as did the battle dreams, and he was shortly sent back to non combatant duty.

In this case the symptoms are not severe. On the other hand, some battle disturbances are nearly indistinguishable from psychoses, at least during the period of acute behavior disorganization. A description of such an instance has also been provided by Grinker and Spiegel (1945, pp. 5–7) and presented in Coleman's text (1950):

A 32-year-old infantryman had taken part in the severe fighting in Northern Tunisia. Nothing was known of his past history beyond the fact that his company had been subjected to heavy mortar fire and dive bombing while attempting to take a height strongly defended by the enemy. When brought into the hospital he was unable to speak, and presented the typical picture of severe terror. He had coarse, persistent tremors of the hands and lips and started violently when any part of his body was touched. At times he seemed about to speak but nothing came of it but inaudible whispers. He made no effort to get out of bed or to help himself in any way but lay in a flexed posture with his body curled up like an intra-uterine fetus. . . . At the end of two weeks the clinical picture had undergone considerable change. The patient was now out of bed, but walked with a peculiar simian gait. His knees were bent and his shoulders stooped, his arms hung lifelessly at his side to below the knees, and his head and neck jutted forward at a peculiar angle. His facial expression was one of anxious, puzzled apprehension. He squinted and frowned at his attendants as if trying to make out who they were and what he had to fear from them. If an attendant made a sudden or unexpected motion, the patient would start back with fear. With much stammering, he asked simple questions about who he was, where he was, and what had happened to him. He asked these questions over and over again, never receiving satisfaction. From time to time a fatuous smile would cross his face, he would laugh, and, leaping upon his cot, he would jump up and down on the springs and shout "Dive bombers! Dive bombers!" as if it were a huge joke. Apparently an accomplished accordion player in the past, he had his instrument with him and enjoyed playing it. He repeatedly played the song "Maybe," singing the words to his accompaniment without a trace of his usual stammer. When he sang, his whole face lit up in a kind of ecstasy, tears ran out of his eyes, and the apprehension disappeared, only to return as soon as he put away his instrument. There was considerable stereotypy, and various bizarre mannerisms reappeared in a regular routine. . . . After treatment, this patient made a good recovery.

In these illustrations we see differing degrees of breakdown of the individual's capacity to master the stress produced by the battle conditions. Almost all varieties of symptom patterns, neurotic and psychotic, have been observed. One can see too that, in these transient reactions to acute stress, we know a little more about the precipitating circumstances, which the person has difficulty mastering, compared with the chronic neurotic and psychotic patterns, where the precipitating conditions must be inferred from the total life situation of the patient. A very useful discussion of the stress-producing factors of various aspects of military life and combat can be found in an article by Haggard (1949).

No doubt persons vary in what they are sensitive to as sources of stress and in the resources they have available for coping with it. These considerations probably determine which men will break down under crisis conditions and which will not. Moreover, almost always in the transient reactions, when the stress-producing circumstances have been eliminated, the person returns to a more mature level of functioning.

THE PSYCHONEUROSES

The transient reactions to acute stress involve a person's struggles to deal with stress produced by a relatively temporary crisis, but the psychoneuroses represent continuing struggles to cope with chronic states of stress. A most fascinating problem concerns the extent to which different neurotic syndromes (symptom patterns) are associated with particular sources of stress or with different coping mechanisms. Some theories have emphasized the nature of the stress-producing conflicts as the essential determiner of the different neurotic reactions, and others have emphasized the ways in which persons attempt to master stress. For example, Freud conceived of the hysterical neuroses as based upon a heterosexual conflict related to the Oedipus complex. In contrast, the obsessive-compulsive neuroses were thought to originate from struggle with aggressive impulses associated with the anal stage of development. Freud also believed that the type of coping mechanism (ego defense) was closely linked to the nature of the conflict or source of stress. For example, repression goes with oedipal (heterosexual) impulses, whereas isolation and undoing are the defenses against anal-aggressive urges. One of the relatively unsolved theoretical problems in psychopathology is whether particular modes of coping are always associated with particular problems or whether any stress-producing conflict can be connected with any type of defensive mechanism.

A good descriptive classification of neuroses includes nine subclasses of neurotic patterns: anxiety reaction, asthenic reaction, hypochondriacal reaction, conversion reaction, dissociative reaction, phobic reaction, obsessive-compulsive reaction, neurotic depressive reaction, and psychosomatic disorders. Several subclasses of these patterns can be combined into larger classes, depending upon the theoretical viewpoint. For example, anxiety reaction, asthenia, and hypochondriasis are instances of a general *anxiety state,* and dissociative reactions and conversion reactions are often considered manifestations of the general category of *hysteria.* We shall separately treat each subclass of neuroses, as listed above, although they will be discussed under the major categories in which they are often included.

Anxiety States

Anxiety reaction: This is one of the most common of the psychoneurotic syndromes and to some extent, tends to be a kind of wastebasket category, used when the primary symptoms involve general manifest anxiety and when other more specific symptom patterns do not predominate. The main complaint of the person is usually chronic anxiety, with occasional attacks of acute anxiety or panic. He describes himself as continually uneasy, and there may be secondary complaints, usually of insomnia, inability to concentrate, and various autonomic nervous system signs of chronic disturbance (see Chapter 9).

An interesting feature of the anxiety is that, although it can be occasionally directed to specific objects or situations, the patient commonly cannot identify an objective source for the apprehension. This kind of anxiety is usually called "free-floating" because it is not fixed to a single situation and seems free to attach to a wide variety of circumstances.

The measurement of anxiety has been a problem of increasing theoretical interest among psychologists because it is a central concept in psychopathology and also of practical interest (for diagnosis). Various approaches have been employed, each suffering from some inadequacies because the manifestations of anxiety appear to be variable and depend upon individual ego-defensive characteristics. One method, which has as many defects as any but which has attracted widespread attention, is a questionnaire developed by Janet Taylor (1953). A group of clinical psychologists were asked to sift through a larger personality questionnaire to pick out all the items that seemed to refer to manifest anxiety. It is not appropriate to discuss in detail here the problems connected with the measurement of anxiety. The Taylor scale is reproduced in Table 15; it includes a variety of symptoms common to neurotics that have seemed to professional workers to reflect, by and large, the experience of, and bodily reactions to, anxiety.

In the panic state or acute anxiety reaction, a person senses an impending catastrophe without being able to specify its nature; his distress can be so severe as to require sedation or considerable reassurance before the attack subsides. These panic states are usually brief, lasting anywhere from a matter of minutes to days, but they usually subside. Occasionally such panic reactions are precursors of a more severe disturbance, such as a psychosis.

The usual conception of the *mechanism* of the more acute and severe states of panic is that strong, conflictful impulses have been stimulated that previously had been weak enough for the individual to subdue. His reaction is one of panic lest these dangerous impulses break through to consciousness or into overt behavior. Frequently when previously existing neurotic defenses are unable to master the stimulation, these defenses tend momentarily to dissolve, placing the person in a state of panic. Thus, in the decompensation of the neurotic as a psychotic breakdown begins, the neurotic defenses drop out. There is a short period of panic, and the person then either regresses to a more primitive level of functioning characteristic of the psychoses or mobilizes stronger defenses to prevent breakdown. During this decompensation or disorganization process the person remains in an acute state of anxiety or panic until he can restore the original defenses, get out of the situation that he cannot handle, or regress to a psychotic level of personality organization.

The most common general view of the *dynamics of the chronic anxiety reaction* is that the person is in a state of stress because of some internal conflict and has not developed a reasonably successful anxiety-reducing defense mechanism. In a sense, one might say that such a state, though far more uncomfortable than one in which defensive operations have been interposed, is a more mature reaction, inasmuch as the person is still struggling to master the anxiety without the extensive use of neurotic defense mechanisms. In an earlier reference to the studies of Masserman (1949), in which cats were made neurotic, it was noted that the cats discovered that drinking milk containing alcohol reduced the anxiety, the alcoholism being a defense against the painful anxiety state. The person with an anxiety reaction is miserable because no anxiety-reducing device has been adopted and the conflict-produced sources of the anxiety have not been eliminated.

Asthenic reaction: This pattern of symptoms used to be called *neurasthenia* because it was thought to be caused by the depletion of the nerve cells of the body (nervous exhaustion). Rest and relaxation were the prescribed cure. The predominant symptoms of the asthenic reaction are physical and mental fatigue. A person has difficulty concentrating, is easily distracted, and does not have sufficient energy to carry on the ordinary tasks of life. Often this patient sleeps a great deal but remains chronically tired. He can feel extremely fatigued in the face of many of the boring and conflictual tasks he has to perform, but he often shows ample energy for anything interesting and pleasant, like play. Along with this chronic fatigue there are frequently somatic complaints, including headaches, indigestion, pain, and dizziness. But fatigue and anxiety are the predominant complaints in the asthenic reaction, and the person is unable to function effectively as a result. Most commonly he blames his failure to function on the fatigue and generally assumes that the fatigue has some organic basis that excuses his inadequacy.

This latter rationalization gives us a clue to the *dynamics of the as-*

Table 15

TAYLOR'S SCALE OF MANIFEST ANXIETY

1. I do not tire quickly. (False)
2. I am troubled by attacks of nausea. (True)
3. I believe I am no more nervous than most others. (False)
4. I have very few headaches. (False)
5. I work under a great deal of tension. (True)
6. I cannot keep my mind on one thing. (True)
7. I worry over money and business. (True)
8. I frequently notice my hand shakes when I try to do something. (True)
9. I blush no more often than others. (False)
10. I have diarrhea once a month or more. (True)
11. I worry quite a bit over possible misfortunes. (True)
12. I practically never blush. (False)
13. I am often afraid that I am going to blush. (True)
14. I have nightmares every few nights. (True)
15. My hands and feet are usually warm enough. (False)
16. I sweat very easily even on cool days. (True)
17. Sometimes when embarrassed, I break out in a sweat which annoys me greatly. (True)
18. I hardly ever notice my heart pounding and I am seldom short of breath. (False)
19. I feel hungry almost all the time. (True)
20. I am very seldom troubled by constipation. (False)
21. I have a great deal of stomach trouble. (True)
22. I have had periods in which I lost sleep over worry. (True)
23. My sleep is fitful and disturbed. (True)
24. I dream frequently about things that are best kept to myself. (True)
25. I am easily embarrassed. (True)
26. I am more sensitive than most other people. (True)
27. I frequently find myself worrying about something. (True)
28. I wish I could be as happy as others seem to be. (True)
29. I am usually calm and not easily upset. (False)
30. I cry easily. (True)
31. I feel anxiety about something or someone almost all the time. (True)
32. I am happy most of the time. (False)
33. It makes me nervous to have to wait. (True)
34. I have periods of such great restlessness that I cannot sit long in a chair. (True)
35. Sometimes I become so excited that I find it hard to get to sleep. (True)
36. I have sometimes felt that difficulties were piling up so high that I could not overcome them. (True)
37. I must admit that I have at times been worried beyond reason over something that really did not matter. (True)
38. I have very few fears compared to my friends. (False)

Table 15 (*Continued*)

39. I have been afraid of things or people that I know could not hurt me. (True)
40. I certainly feel useless at times. (True)
41. I find it hard to keep my mind on a task or job. (True)
42. I am unusually self-conscious. (True)
43. I am inclined to take things hard. (True)
44. I am a high-strung person. (True)
45. Life is a strain for me much of the time. (True)
46. At times I think I am no good at all. (True)
47. I am certainly lacking in self-confidence. (True)
48. I sometimes feel that I am about to go to pieces. (True)
49. I shrink from facing a crisis or difficulty. (True)
50. I am entirely self-confident. (False)

SOURCE: Taylor, 1953, p. 286.

thenic person. He is able to escape from threatening situations and tasks by his somatic complaints, and he can excuse his life failures on these grounds. Thus asthenia can be understood not only in terms of the debilitating effects of chronic internal conflicts on a person's energy and motivation but also in terms of the considerable psychological gain because the fatigue enables him to excuse his own inadequacies and escape from painful circumstances. The asthenic reaction has a great deal in common with the anxiety reaction and appears to have similar dynamics. When fatigue, rather than anxiety, aspects of the neurotic disturbance predominate, we speak of an asthenic reaction, although anxiety is almost always present to some degree.

Hypochondriacal reaction: This condition represents another variation within the general category of anxiety state, but in this case the anxiety has been focused on the person's state of bodily health. Anxiety is a predominant symptom, but it is anxiety about peculiar organic symptoms or sensations. A person is often fearful that he may die or be seriously ill.

From a *psychodynamic point of view* the hypochondriacal reaction includes defenses similar to the asthenic reaction. These protect the person from a recognition of his inadequacies, offering him excuses for his failures and permitting him to escape painful situations. The real source of anxiety tends to be displaced toward a preoccupation with his body and its functioning. Like the asthenic, he can use his symptoms to manipulate others by obtaining sympathy or support.

Phobic reaction: As most persons recognize today, a phobic reaction is an intense and chronic fear of something. The fear seems irrational in terms of the actual reality. A phobia often interferes with the everyday activities. A patient with a phobia about balloons can be perfectly comfortable in most situations, but is never able to go to a party because of the probability that balloons will be used as decorations, the sight of which elicits terror.

Phobias can involve fears of a wide variety of objects and situations, and various names have been given to such phobic reactions, some of which are very well known. For example, claustrophobia involves the fear of enclosed places; acrophobia, the fear of high places; zoophobia, the fear of animals or some particular animal. The patient recognizes the irrationality of the fear but can deal with it in no other way than to avoid or remove himself from situations that elicit it.

Psychodynamically speaking, phobias are thought to be acquired from an early life experience of strong fear in the presence of some object or circumstance associated with shame or embarrassment or with some impulse or act that would be punished. If a person is so frightened and shamed about talking about the experience, the actual event can be repressed and any stimulus situation that resembles it can take on the character of a phobic object or situation.

From the psychoanalytic point of view, phobias represent displacements of the original anxiety to some object or idea that symbolizes a feared impulse so the patient remains completely unaware of the real source of his anxiety. The phobia permits the person to focus on a relatively innocuous object or circumstance, thus avoiding the recognition of the true nature of the impulses associated with the repression. In addition to a strong fear experience early in life, there must be some reason why the person refuses to verbalize further or label the experience so a phobic person usually cannot say why such a strong irrational fear exists.

Hysteria

Conversion reaction: One of the most dramatic neurotic manifestations is the conversion reaction, usually classified as a form of hysteria. It is dramatic because the patient commonly suffers from severe physical symptoms that have no organic basis. For example, there can be anesthesia (the loss of sensitivity of some part of the body), with the patient being unable to feel pain or any sensation in that part. Hysterical blindness, deafness, convulsions, or the inability to talk or to swallow are other examples of conversion symptoms. These symptoms are entirely real; the patient actually is unable to see, hear, or feel, and there is no structural (organic) basis for the disturbance. Very commonly the conversion symptom takes a form inconsistent with the actual physical patterning of the nervous system. For example, in the classic glove anesthesia the entire hand up to the wrist loses all sensitivity, as though covered completely by a glove. Such an anesthesia is a neurological impossibility, but the person nonetheless feels nothing when cut or stuck by a pin or touched by an examiner. At times the conversion symptom disappears for a period or changes its locus so the anesthesia or paralysis occurs in one part of the body today and tomorrow shifts to another.

The conversion reactions were first discovered by neurologists because, so commonly, the pattern of symptoms suggested a neurological disturbance. The disorder played a large part in the development of Freud's psychoanalytic theory. It is interesting to note that the word "hysteria" comes from the Greek word that means "uterus." Hippocrates and other ancient Greeks thought that this disturbance occurred only in women and was caused by the wandering of the uterus (which had been deprived of children) to various parts of the body. Hysterical conditions were thus linked, in Greek thought, to sexual difficulties. Freud elaborated this *dynamic* concept, believing that conversion reactions originated in sexual conflict related to an unresolved oedipal conflict, and that the energy of repressed sexual impulses was converted into the physical symptom. The symptom was thought to reflect or symbolize the particular nature of the sexual conflict.

True conversion hysterias appear to be less common today than they were years ago, possibly because we have become, through education, more sophisticated about neurology and about the psychogenic aspects of somatic symptoms. If it is true that the conversion reaction has a heterosexual basis, it may also be that changes in our concepts of sex and in our family structure since the late 1800s and early 1900s have reduced somewhat the potentiality of sexual conflicts as a source of stress. However, it is widely held that the conversion symptom arises from the defensive process of repression. So successful may the repression be at eliminating conflict-produced anxiety that it is common to find in conversion patients what has been called *la belle indifférence* (beautiful indifference), in which the patient shows relatively little overt concern or anxiety to indicate that he is indeed under stress. The conversion patient may report that all is well psychologically; that he is simply suffering from some mysterious symptom that he wishes cured. The symptom frequently gives him such secondary gains as sympathy and escape from unpleasant situations, but it also reflects stresses that he cannot face directly, which are expressed as a physical symptom.

Dissociative reactions: This remarkable group of disturbances is often considered a form of hysteria and includes amnesias, fugues, multiple personalities, and somnambulisms. The common quality is a dissociation of disturbing memories or thoughts from the rest of the personality. In a sense the disturbing thoughts or impulses are simply not recognized or are forgotten or separated out as alien because they cannot be successfully integrated with the rest of the personality.

In *amnesia,* a person cannot recall certain past experiences of his life. Some amnesias are based upon brain damage, but the "functional" amnesia involves no such injury. The forgotten material remains unconscious, although it can often be restored after a time or with treatment. Because the patient cannot cope with this threatening material, it is thought to be eliminated from consciousness by repressive mechanisms.

In the case of the *fugue state,* there is also a general amnesia for a person's entire past, including who he is or where he lived. This amnesia, however, is associated with a flight (fugue), in which the patient wanders away from home and then, days, weeks, or sometimes years later, finds himself in a strange place, not knowing how he got there and not remembering anything about the period of the fugue. In some cases, a person has lived away from his original home for ten or more years, starting a new occupation, building a family, only to reawaken later, missing his place of origin.

Multiple personalities are relatively rare, but the problem has recently been brought to the attention of many people because of the successful book by Thigpen and Kleckley (1957), *The Three Faces of Eve,* which has been made into a movie. Like the classic descriptions of multiple personalities by Morton Prince some years ago (1920), this book describes a case of a woman who alternates between several personalities, with one frequently unaware of the existence of the others. It is as if several sections of the personality that have not been successfully integrated become separated or dissociated from each other, the person frequently shifting abruptly from one to the other. There appear to be several complete systems of personality, with each system having distinct emotional and thought processes, dramatically different from each other. Commonly, one personality is free and impulsive, and another is very inhibited and responsible.

Another type of dissociative reaction is *somnambulism.* Here, systems of ideas that are normally kept out of consciousness are so strong during sleep as to determine the patient's behavior. The sufferer usually rises and carries out some act, which can be rather complex. In many respects somnambulism is similar to multiple personality in that there is a dissociation of some subsystem within the personality, which gains expression during sleep and for which there is usually no memory during the waking state.

The *dynamics of the dissociative reactions* are considered fundamentally comparable with those of the conversion reaction, both being manifestations of the repressive mechanisms of hysteria. A system of impulses or ideas that is dangerous or unacceptable to the person is repressed or segmented off from the rest of the personality and gains expression in some special way. In the case of the conversion reaction, it is through a physical symptom, such as a paralysis, and in the case of dissociative reactions, it is through amnesias, fugues, multiple personalities, or somnambulistic actions. The repressive defense inhibits discharge of these ideas or impulses, which can then be expressed by dissociation from the rest of the personality. Why the repressed material is expressed in the particular symptom pattern of one or another of these dissociative reactions is not clearly understood.

Obsessive-compulsive Reactions

The obsessive-compulsive patient recognizes the irrationality of his behavior, but he seems to be forced against his desire to think about something (obsession) or to engage in unwanted actions (compulsions). This tendency to have obsessional thoughts or engage in compulsive acts is quite common among many persons without its reflecting a severe neurosis. For example, a tune keeps repeating itself in our minds, or we may, for a time, keep thinking about an examination or an anxiety-producing trial through which we must go in the near future or which we have experienced in the recent past. Or we may feel impelled to do some ritualistic act like regularly straightening up our desk or drumming our fingers on the table in some symmetrical or rhythmical pattern. In the neurotic version of these obsessive or compulsive behaviors, the thoughts or acts involved are more difficult to get rid of or control. They seem to serve no useful purpose and are regarded as silly and unwanted by the individual, yet impossible to prevent. The person is obliged to perform some usually senseless act or think some irrational and repetitious thought. If he does not do it, he is overcome with intense anxiety.

A common example of compulsion of a more or less normal variety is frequently found in children who engage in various rituals, like stepping over the cracks on sidewalks, doing things by twos so a room must be entered twice, or walking around a ladder instead of under it. In the neurotic compulsion, the acts are more persistent, appear absurd to the patient, and can very seriously disrupt his everyday behavior. A classic instance is the hand-washing compulsion, in which patients have been known to wash themselves needlessly many dozens of times a day. The compulsive act seems to reduce anxiety to some degree, but there is an insatiable need to persist in the ritual continually. Shakespeare, in *Macbeth*, has captured the essence of an obsessive-compulsive reaction with great vividness and insight; after the murder of the king, Lady Macbeth is obsessed with the idea that she still has blood on her hands and cannot wash it off.

In terms of *dynamics,* the obsessive-compulsive reaction, like the phobia, involves the displacement of certain unacceptable or threatening impulses into another form. In the case of obsessions, the thinking of certain thoughts keeps other more terrible thoughts from being expressed. Such thoughts can involve the expression, frequently in disguised fashion, of dangerous hostile or sexual impulses, with the emotional aspects of these thoughts eliminated or disguised by means of reaction formation. Masserman, for example, cited an instance of a patient who defended himself against repressed aggressive impulses toward his family by developing fears concerning their safety.[1]

A successful executive who for various reasons hated the responsibility of marriage and fatherhood, was obsessed many times a day with the idea that his two children were "somehow in danger," although he knew them to be safe in a well run private day school to which he himself brought them every morning. As a result, he felt impelled to interrupt his office routine twice daily by personal calls to the school principal who, incidentally, after several months, began to question the sincerity of the patient's fatherly solicitude. Similarly, the patient could not return home at night without misgivings unless he brought some small present to his wife and children, although, significantly, it was almost always something they did not want.

Compulsions, in a sense, represent attempts to deal with danger by ordering everything in such a way that the person will be safe. Compulsions can also represent attempts to undo unacceptable impulses, for example, washing one's hands because they are somehow unclean, perhaps because of guilt over masturbation or, as in the case of Lady Macbeth, murder. For the neurotic person, having the wish or impulse is as threatening and reprehensible as having actually performed the tabooed act. The compulsions represent defensive reactions against impulses and the continual undoing of the situation in order to make things right. Sometimes the actions are direct representations of the guilty impulse or act, or they can be disguised or symbolic representations of it. The compulsion tends to establish controls, which protect the patient from the impulses he fears. We frequently speak, for example, of someone who works compulsively. He may follow an exhaustive schedule of daily activities, which make sexual interests or activity impossible and thus protect him from any impulses in that direction. As another instance, unreasonably strong fears of syphilis can prevent a person from ever engaging in sexual activities, the fear rationalizing the exercise of controls, which protect him from doing that of which he is most afraid.

Neurotic Depression

Some depressive reactions are extremely severe, as in the psychotic depression. They can occur without any basis in the external circumstance of the person's life. The manic-depressive psychotic, for example, for little

---

[1] From J. H. Masserman. *Behavior and Neurosis.* Chicago: University of Chicago Press, 1949. P. 43. Copyright, 1949, by the University of Chicago.

or no apparent reason, shows fluctuations between an extremely excited euphoric condition and a deep depression, in which there exist feelings of worthlessness and guilt. Other depressions (the neurotic or reactive type) can be of a milder variety and clearly *reactive* to specific circumstances of the person's life. Like psychotic cases, the symptoms include dejection, discouragement, and sadness. There are commonly feelings of worthlessness and guilt and some hopelessness about the situation. But in the neurotic or reactive depression there is usually a precipitating cause, and when this cause has been removed, the depressive reaction eventually disappears.

Although a precipitating circumstance can often be discerned, neurotic depressives are regarded as especially predisposed to such feelings. They are hypersensitive to circumstances that tend to elicit in them feelings of dejection. Because of unconscious feelings of hostility, such persons are especially prone to react with guilt when there has been a death of someone close. The depression is overdetermined and excessive; that is, it is not a normal response to a personal loss, but it is more extreme and generally complicated by the person's guilt feelings about the loss.

Psychosomatic Disorders

This term refers to conditions in which psychologically produced states of stress have led to organic symptoms that are either defenses against anxiety or consequences of chronic stress. The symptoms include ulcers, colitis, high blood pressure, asthma, migraine, skin disturbances, and other less common conditions that can be aggravated or produced by chronic states of stress.

There are fundamentally two, not mutually exclusive, ways of interpreting the psychosomatic disorders; the first emphasizes the notion that particular types of conflict or emotional states (e.g., fear or anger) are associated with particular somatic mechanisms. Thus, for example, peptic ulcers have been considered to result from conflicts over dependency. The patient is characterized as ambitious, driving, struggling for independence, but unconsciously seeking a dependent relation with someone who will serve as a maternal figure.

One difficulty with this hypothesis is the lack of clarity about how the particular psychological disturbance is centered in particular organs of the body. Moreover, much of the empirical personality research in psychosomatics has not been very successful in relating specific psychological conflicts to specific psychosomatic disorders. There are occasional findings that are extremely provocative, but they do not fully answer the question of cause and effect. Malmo and his colleagues (1951, 1953, 1955) have produced evidence suggesting that, under stress, headache-prone patients are susceptible to a greater degree of muscle tension in the back of the neck. It has also been suggested by other research that the migraine personality is one who has defective techniques of managing and discharging strong hostile feelings. These feelings and the efforts to control them appear in the form of increased muscle tension and headaches. The data here, however, are not definitive.

A second, more widely held notion concerning psychosomatic disturbances is that the constitutional characteristics make a person prone to express psychological tension from any source in particularly vulnerable organ systems. From this point of view, a patient has an ulcer not because he has a specific conflict (say, concerning dependency), but because he is in a chronic state of stress. This, in turn, produces biochemical changes within the stomach of a predisposed person that can produce ulcerative damage to the stomach wall. Mahl (1949), for example, has shown that, under chronic stress, increased amounts of hydrochloric acid are secreted in the stomach. Other changes probably occur in the ulcer-prone individual that reduce the effectiveness of the stomach lining in resisting the corrosive effects of the stomach acid.

Psychosomatic symptoms are conceived as evidences of wear and tear on the organism and represent signs of stress in an organism constitutionally predisposed to respond to stress in certain ways. From this point of view, the psychosomatic reactions are similar to the anxiety reactions, but they represent instances where tissue damage to various organ systems of the body has been produced.

THE PSYCHOSES

Because the so-called organic psychoses are clearly associated with damage to the tissues of the brain, we shall not dwell at length upon them, although it is important to indicate their general characteristics and the psychological problems they raise. We shall deal with these first.

Organic Psychoses

Organic psychoses as a rule have a large variety of causes and range from relatively common sources of brain damage to some that are exceedingly rare. Regardless of the specific cause, the various disorders have one common quality: damage to or interference with the functioning of the brain. To some degree the nature of the symptom pattern is related to the degree of brain damage and to the area of the brain affected. But even a knowledge of the exact lesion (injury) will not permit, in most instances, precise prediction of the cognitive or personality changes resulting from it. In the case of general paresis, for example, the personality symptoms seem to depend upon the premorbid personality structure of the patient; that is, the characteristic personality before brain damage occurred. Some patients, as the deterioration develops, will be depressed, paranoid, apprehensive, and generally unpleasant; others will manifest excitement, abandon, and expansiveness.

Organic psychoses usually have in common impairment of the intellectual functions; unspecified emotional changes; the lowering of impulse control; deterioration of conduct; general carelessness in personal appearance; loss of interest; sensory-motor disturbances, which frequently include aphasia (disturbances in comprehension), paralysis, incoordination, and other neurological manifestations; and general disorientation (confusion as to who the person is and where he is).

The classification of the organic psychoses is atypical in principle from most other mental-disease classifications, because it is not based upon symptom patterns but rather upon the agent that presumably caused the disease. For example, there are psychoses associated with *infectious diseases,* such as general paresis (syphilitic infection), encephalitis, and meningitis. Each of these disorders can produce a psychosis because of damage to the brain or parts of the brain.

There are psychotic disorders produced by *brain tumors* located at a large variety of possible sites and with a consequent wide variation in the specific symptom pattern. There are psychoses associated with *head injuries;* again the nature of the disturbance can vary greatly both with the nature and extent of the injury and the previous personality characteristics of the injured person.

Another category includes disorders associated with *toxic and metabolic disturbances.* The toxic states that sometimes accompany infectious diseases such as diphtheria, pneumonia, typhoid fever, uremia, and pernicious anemia can produce damage to brain tissues. The ingestion of drugs or inhalation of gases can produce psychotic effects, of which some are temporary and others involve permanent damage to the brain or even death. *Fevers* that accompany pneumonia, typhoid fever, malaria, smallpox, etc., can also produce psychotic disturbances.

The delirium following *extreme exhaustion* has psychotic qualities, which are usually transient, although a longer-standing disorder can be precipitated. *Nutritional deficiencies* and *endocrine disturbances* are also occasional causes of psychotic manifestations.

Another instance of a disorder usually classified as organic is the *epilepsies,* of which there has been increasingly greater control by the use of various drugs, which reduce or eliminate the seizure patterns. The causes of these may be brain injuries, although the common ideopathic epilepsy is not presently understood as to cause and seems to have some hereditary basis.

One of the largest categories of organic psychoses is associated with *aging.* With the advancing average age of the population, the frequency of senile psychosis is increasing, and the number of patients in mental hospitals with senile psychosis resulting from the deterioration of the brain tissues characteristic of old age is extremely large. Damage to the brain in the elderly patient can occur through the blocking of the blood supply to brain tissues, through hemorrhage, or through the poorly understood deteriorative biochemical condition of the brain cells.

Finally, there are organic conditions the cause of which remains unknown or unclear. *Huntington's chorea* is a relatively rare disease of the nervous system involving progressive deterioration and ending in death. The most common explanation of Huntington's chorea is a hereditary one, although the disturbance does not appear in adults until between the ages of thirty to fifty years. The disorder runs in families and appears to follow Mendelian ratios, which strongly suggests a hereditary basis for the disease.

Although the organic psychoses are irreversible (there being no way of regenerating brain tissues), they represent interesting challenges to the physiological psychologist in terms of the possibility of relating brain functioning to adaptive behavior. There are, of course, many other problems of more psychological import. For example, one of the most serious problems of our present generation is the progressive increase in the aged population. Aside from the deterioration of function with age, there are the adjustment problems associated with the loss of vigor and sense of usefulness in the elderly person. When brain damage occurs in children at birth or when still young (such as cerebral palsy), there is the serious problem of the consequence of these injuries for the child's psychological development. There is clearly an interplay between the physically produced symptoms of the organic patient and the socially oriented adjustive patterns or personality characteristics of such persons. Yet because of their clear structural basis, the organic psychoses represent a special group of disorders, different in origin from the functional group, with somewhat distinct theoretical and empirical implications.

The Functional Psychoses

There are three main classes of functional psychoses: the schizophrenias, the paranoid disorders, and the affective disorders. As with the neuroses, there is a great deal of overlap between the classes, many cases showing combinations of symptoms that cut across categories. Although there are many considerations pertinent to the psychoses in general, some brief descriptions of the specific psychotic patterns are offered first.

Schizophrenia: No more puzzling or serious group of mental disturbances exists than the schizophrenic disorders. They represent about 50 per cent of all hospitalized neuropsychiatric patients and about 25 per cent of the hospital beds utilized for any reason in the United States. The condition has been known since ancient times, although knowledge about it has increased rapidly in the late nineteenth and early twentieth centuries.

One of the earlier modern terms for schizophrenia was dementia praecox. It was popularized by the German psychiatrist Kraepelin, who borrowed it from a Belgian psychiatrist, Morell, who had first used the term in 1860. The term, meaning mental deterioration (dementia) beginning early in life (praecox), was employed on the assumption that the disorder was essentially limited to youths. Some years later, in 1911, Bleuler (1950) introduced the modern term, "schizophrenia," partly because it became clear that the disturbance was not limited to young persons and partly because he believed that the disturbance was characterized by the splitting or separation of emotional processes from thought processes. "Schizophrenia" has been retained, although the conception of the disorder introduced by Bleuler has been much modified and the concept "splitting of the personality" is no longer in common usage except among lay persons.

The term "schizophrenia" now applies to a rather wide variety of disorders that have in common disturbances of thought processes; the severe distortion of reality; frequently bizarre behavior patterns and ideas, which can include delusions and hallucinations; and the loss of integrated and controlled behavior. It is the most serious of the functional disturbances, the most devastating to the total personality, and the most baffling, and it has the poorest outlook for treatment of all the functional disorders. It commonly results in long periods of hospitalization and, in many cases, continual deterioration in hospitals over a long period of years.

Theorists have often distinguished between two main types of schizophrenia, *process* and *reactive*. Process schizophrenia refers to an insidious disturbance of long standing with clear origins early in life and a gradual onset of the symptoms. It is often possible to discover signs of the disorder many years before hospitalization is required. In such cases one can observe in the school life of the person general inadequacy of functioning and the failure to establish normal interpersonal relations. Such a person may never have shown evidence of a normal level of functioning at any stage in his development. Many researchers regard this type of schizophrenia as organic in origin and cause.

In reactive schizophrenia there is an acute major disturbance of sudden onset in a person who has, in the past, functioned on a reasonably adequate or even high level. Thus, reactive schizophrenia is more analogous to the transient reactions to acute stress, mentioned earlier. The outlook for this kind of disturbance is generally better, the disorder commonly being short-lived and disappearing when the crisis to which it is a reaction has been alleviated.

There is a widespread suspicion that, although there are formal similarities between the symptom patterns of the reactive and process types of schizophrenia, classifying them together as the same disturbance misleads us into thinking that they are the same. It is quite possible, and it remains one of the current research problems of the clinic, that the cause or causes of process and reactive schizophrenia are distinct and different, even though there are many parallels in behavior pattern.

The most usual classification of schizophrenic disorders is based on symptom complexes (descriptive) and includes four types: simple, catatonic, hebephrenic, and paranoid. Some writers in this field assume that there is somehow a continuity between these types, regarding the simple and paranoid schizophrenias as early or high-level stages in the progressive schizophrenic deterioration and the catatonic and hebephrenic types as later or end stages in the deterioration processes. In actual experience, however, a patient can become catatonic without proceeding through any evident earlier stages.

In *simple schizophrenia* there is a gradual narrowing and loss of interest, emotional flatness, and social withdrawal. There may be periods of moodiness or irritability, and there is over-all increasing indifference and, along with it, deterioration of personal appearance. The simple schizophrenic displays an unreadiness to assume normal obligations and often appears content to lead an irresponsible and dependent existence. Many such patients can get along outside of the hospital because of the good will of others or the embarrassment of their families, who often conceal and support them. They may also manage to get along for some years as vagrants, although such persons occasionally run afoul of the law because of sexual assaults and other antisocial activity. The simple schizophrenic seems to belong to a large general class of inadequate personalities, commonly showing a long history of inadequacy and irresponsibility. He commonly lacks the more colorful symptoms of other schizophrenics (delusional systems, hallucinatory experiences, and bizarre qualities of thinking).

The *catatonic schizophrenic* usually shows one of two dramatic patterns: stupor or excitement. In stupor there is a loss of animation and a tendency to remain motionless in certain stereotyped positions or postures, which are sometimes maintained for hours or days. There is minimal contact with anyone and frequently mutism (the refusal to speak), which can continue in some cases for months or even years.

There are many varieties of patterns of stuporous categories; for example, the patient may automatically obey commands, imitate the actions of others, or repeat phrases in a stereotyped way. "Waxy flexibility" can be observed; when the patient's arm is raised to an awkward position, it can be maintained this way for long periods or until the position is changed. Often there is a stubborn resistance to any effort to change his position or posture. He may refuse to eat, pay no attention to bowel and bladder controls, and have to be washed, dressed, and cared for as an infant. While apparently out of contact with other persons, such a patient can notice a great deal of what is going on, demonstrating this after recovery from the stuporous condition.

In the catatonic excitement, the patient seems to be under great pressure of activity. He may talk excitedly and incoherently, pace back and forth rapidly, masturbate publicly, mutilate himself, attack others, and, in general, exhibit a frenzy of activity that requires restraint. This excitement can last hours, days, or weeks and can even alternate between periods of stupor.

The *hebephrenic schizophrenic* shows the most severe disintegration of personality. Progressive emotional indifference and ultimately infantilism in his reactions are characteristic. The patient is silly and incoherent in thought, speech, and action. There is little connection between expressions of emotion, such as laughter and crying, and the circumstances under which they occur. As with the catatonic, hallucinations and delusions are common. The deterioration of behavior is so severe that the patient must be cared for as if he were an infant (feeding, cleanliness, toileting, dress, etc.)

Cases of *paranoid schizophrenia* shade off in various degrees into the disturbance called *paranoia*. The extent to which paranoid or schizophrenic qualities predominate varies. The most common symptoms are delusional systems, usually involving the idea of persecution, in which the patient is suspicious of being watched, followed, poisoned, or influenced in some way. Delusions of grandeur can also be found, in which the patient believes he is some famous figure such as Napoleon or Jesus Christ.

If the schizophrenic pattern predominates, these delusions are bizarre, illogical, and changeable, now taking one form, now another. There will often be hallucinatory experiences, loss of contact with reality, deterioration of the personality in general, and disorders of thought. As the paranoid elements predominate, the delusional system is more logical and encapsulated in the sense that other forms of thinking and reality testing are not disturbed and thought disorder is less prominent. The more unpredictable and changeable is the delusional system, the more clearly is there a schizophrenic process involved. In such cases the behavior and appearance of the patient are more likely to deteriorate.

Paranoia: In paranoid disorders, the main common quality is the delusional system, usually persecutory or grandiose. The word "paranoid" itself refers to a quality of thinking, an intellectualized system of defenses, characterized predominantly by delusions, which can shade off in less disturbed paranoid personalities into a general sense of grandiosity or suspiciousness. Such patterns of behavior are not uncommon among persons functioning within relatively normal limits. They can be hypersensitive and readily assume that other persons are talking about, or plotting against, them, but the delusional system never takes complete hold of the personality and can be kept under sufficient control to prevent serious trouble. It is a frequent characteristic of paranoids that they have sufficient judgment and self-control both to avoid hospitalization and to maintain limited social functioning. The suspicious or exploited inventors, the persecuted businessmen, extreme reformers and prophets, and crank letter writers are often cases of paranoid conditions, which do not necessarily lead to hospitalization unless their behavior creates a serious public disturbance or danger.

In the true and rare paranoia, the intellectual defense system has been elaborated to such a degree that a highly systematized delusional system is created. This often makes the person a serious homicidal risk, and he must be hospitalized. Aside from his delusional system, the paranoiac's general functioning is apt to be normal. The person is logical and coherent, and the delusional system may not appear in casual contact, asserting itself only when he begins to feel secure in a relationship.

The delusional system itself tends to be logical, but it is built on some false premise. If one could accept the premise as sound, then frequently everything else the paranoid says follows in a reasonable way. The paranoid may call upon considerable intellectual and educational resources in constructing the delusional system, sometimes making superficial use of physical or electronic concepts (believing, for example, that his mind is being influenced by some new invention which sends out invisible waves on the same wave length as his own nervous system). He is completely convinced of his delusional system and cannot be dissuaded from it. The delusional system itself is an extremely well-entrenched ego-defense mechanism, but he frequently has sufficient contact with reality to recognize that others do not accept it. When hospitalized or imprisoned, he may inhibit expression of it because he has recognized that attempting to convince others gets him nowhere and in fact leads to punishment.

Affective psychoses: In contrast with the schizophrenias, in which the predominant symptom is bizarre ideas and thought disturbances, and the paranoias, which also show up in disorders of thinking, the affective psychoses involve primarily disturbances of mood or emotion. Such disturbances of mood are not necessarily qualitatively different from the normal mood fluctuations that take place in most of us—periods of euphoria or gaiety and periods of depression—but they are so severe as to make a person dangerous to himself or to others, a public nuisance, and perhaps even a public charge.

There are two major forms of the affective psychoses: manic states and depressive states. A patient may have a single manic attack or a large number of attacks over a period of years and never exhibit the depressive reaction. Another may show the same pattern with respect to depression; still another may oscillate between manic states, periods of relative tranquillity, and depressive attacks. The outlook for such disturbances is generally good. In most cases they are transient, although they can recur.

In the *manic reactions* there is elation, often grandiosity, extreme overactivity, and distractibility. In milder disorders of a similar sort (hypomania), the disturbance can involve moderate elation, flightiness and overactivity, tremendous energy, and oversociability. If the condition is more severe, the elation can get out of hand, creating public disturbances, and the patient's mood can change to irritability or great anger. He may exhibit wild flights of ideas and incoherence of speech and may make business decisions that seriously endanger the economic welfare of himself and his family. The manic ideas can reach the point of transient delusions and perhaps even hallucinations, but the predominant characteristic is an affective disturbance rather than a thought disorder.

Depressive reactions manifest loss of enthusiasm and slowing down of mental and physical activity. There is commonly dejection and discouragement and feelings of unworthiness, sinfulness, and hopelessness. Although there is mental and motor retardation, there is usually no disorientation or disturbance of thinking. The patient is in excellent contact, his memory is unimpaired, and if allowed sufficient time, he is able to answer intellectual questions in a fashion consistent with reality. The psychotic depression differs from the neurotic version primarily in degree.

In severe depressions, mental and motor retardation can be extreme, the patient becoming inactive, isolated from others, unapt to speak unless spoken to, and extremely slow in reaction. Feelings of guilt, hopelessness, and worthlessness are very pronounced, and he may even hold himself responsible for social disasters of all kinds. The depression then shades off into delusional and even hallucinatory experiences. In this state of mind the patient is a great suicidal risk and must be cared for, usually in the extremely restrictive, protective setting of the hospital.

Psychotic depressions are difficult to distinguish from a disorder called *involutional melancholia*. Involutional melancholia is differentiated from other depressive reactions by its occurrence during the involutional or climacteric period of life, associated with the loss of sexual potency and the biochemical alterations of the change of life. In women this involutional period occurs generally from forty to fifty-five years of age, and in men from fifty to sixty-five. The term "involutional melancholia" assumes that the disturbance is connected with biochemical changes, although it might equally well be argued that it is the psychological import of these changes—the loss of vigor and the prospects of old age—that are the primary sources of stress producing a psychotic disturbance.

The depressions of the involutional patient can be of the *stuporous variety,* in which the predominant pattern is mental and motor retardation and depressive feelings, or of the *agitated type,* in which there is commonly crying, wringing of the hands, and inability to sleep or relax. The outlook for the involutional patient, as in the case of the depressive in general, is good, the condition usually being transient and clearing up after a period of weeks or months. Again, as in the case of the ordinary depressives, the greatest dangers are from suicidal attempts.

Some general considerations: The functional psychoses in general can be compared with the neuroses in a number of ways. For one thing, the deterioration of the personality in the psychosis is far more severe; the patient is often so seriously incapacitated that hospitalization is common. Thus, in terms of the general involvement of the personality and the severity of the disorder, the psychosis is far more serious. With respect to symptoms, the neuroses and functional psychoses overlap in somatic manifestations and the presence of anxiety and ego defenses. However, hallucinations and delusions, thought disorders, destructive behavior, and the extreme absence of impulse control are common in the psychoses but are not found in the neuroses. The neurotic does not understand the nature of his disturbance, but he is often aware that something is wrong. The psychotic usually lacks insight into the nature of his behavior. He will frequently protest, however disturbed his behavior may be, that he does not belong in the hospital and that he is perfectly well. From a social and legal point of view, the psychotic is often—though not always—a danger to himself and the community because he lacks insight and control over his destructive impulses; the neurotic is rarely dangerous. It is largely because of this difference that the psychotic is often treated in the hospital setting, where external controls can be introduced over his behavior.

One of the most fascinating questions about the neuroses and psychoses has to do with their theoretical relation. There are many obvious differences in symptom pattern, and the psychoses are often considered as qualitatively different from the various neurotic patterns. However, in some instances, such as depression, the difference is one of degree rather than kind as we move from a neurotic depression to a psychotic depression. The question we might ask is: "Are the neuroses an entirely different class of disorders with different causes, or are they simply milder forms of basically similar reactions to stress?"

The most frequent answer to this question is that, although the neuroses seem qualitatively different, they represent more integrated attempts to retain personality organization and to reduce anxiety produced by conflict. If neurotic defense mechanisms succeed in permitting a person to master, even at a neurotic level, the enormous stimulation (stress) to which he is exposed, he can continue to function as a reasonably integrated person, in fairly good contact with reality.

However, when this adaptive effort is inadequate or ineffective, a regression to a more primitive level occurs and a psychosis is manifest. The deeper the regression, the more formally similar it is to a child's way (primitive) of functioning. If the ego strength or adaptive resources of the person are not sufficient for psychological survival at the healthy or neurotic level, the more mature controls characteristic of the adults are dissolved in favor of more primitive psychotic levels of functioning. In other words, the neuroses are a kind of first line of defense to control the anxiety-producing impulses or stimulation, the failure of which results in the regression of the personality to a psychotic level.

If we can conceive of the development of mature healthy personalities from childhood to adulthood as the progressive imposition of more effective and reality-oriented controls over behavior to permit the safe gratification of impulses, then we can consider the psychoses as representing a regression to earlier, less mature, levels. The regression can be slight, as in the case of the neurotic disorders; more severe, as in the case of paranoid disorders; or extremely severe, as in the manic-depressive and schizophrenic disturbances.

Some support for this kind of conception comes from the observation of formal similarity of cognitive processes at various chronological age levels to the thought processes characteristic of the various disorders. For example, one study of the development of the perceptual and conceptual process as a function of chronological age provided norms against which various psychopathologies could be compared. It was found that the normal adult showed the highest perceptual level of functioning, the neurotic next, followed by the paranoid and the catatonic and hebephrenic schizophrenics, who functioned at a level similar to that of the three- and four-year-old child (see Figure 13, presented in an earlier discussion). The guiding principle that emerges is that of levels of organization or development, with the more severe deterioration or regression of the personality to early forms of functioning observed in the psychoses. Thus there is conceived to be continuity between the neuroses and psychoses, even though there appear to be qualitative differences in the modes of coping and their adequacy.

THE CHARACTER DISORDERS

In speaking of neuroses reference was made to unresolvable internal conflicts dealt with by various ego-defensive processes aimed at the reduction of stress (or anxiety). In psychosis, it was suggested, there was a breakdown of such defenses and a regression to primitive modes of functioning. The character disorders, in contrast, involve failure to acquire effective habits of living and mature ways of mastering the stresses of life. There is commonly a lifelong pattern of overt pathological behavior associated with an absence of anxiety or signs of internal struggle. There is often a failure of socialization such that the person behaves in antisocial ways. The troubles do not seem clearly to arise from internalized conflicts and the consequences of defense mechanisms against anxiety, but rather from a faulty or inadequate ego development. Unlike the neurotic, who is overtly inhibited in the expression of his impulses, the person with a character disorder acts out in the sense that his behavior represents more or less direct, impulsive, and often socially unacceptable expressions of these impulses.

Many types of behavior patterns have been included under the heading of character disorders. For example, such mild conditions as stuttering, nail-biting, and enuresis (bed-wetting) can be cited. Examples of emotional instability, passive dependency, passive aggression, and aggressive reaction can also be included here.

In *emotional instability*, a person reacts to minor stresses with excitability and ineffectiveness. His emotional reactions are poorly controlled, resulting in fluctuating emotional attitudes in his relations with others; he flies off the handle readily.

Passive dependency is characterized by an attitude of helplessness, indecisiveness, and a tendency to cling to others for emotional support and help in any small crisis.

The *passive-aggressive personality* has many of the qualities of the passive-dependent type but is consumed with hostility toward others, expressed not directly but in passive ways, such as pouting, passive obstructionism, stubbornness, inefficiency, and procrastination. Instead of reacting directly with "I dislike you" or "I am angry," such a person overtly maintains a passive, benign relationship with others, but he shows hostility in indirect ways. He seems to ask for help but continually rejects it by throwing into question the suitability or appropriateness of it.

In an *aggressive reaction*, a person is apt to express overt hostility in relatively childish ways—through irritability, temper tantrums, and destructive behavior. Immaturity is displayed in the infantile fashion in which his resentment toward those in authority is continually expressed.

All these above types of character disorder have in common childish and inadequate ways of solving personal problems, which lead a person into nonadjustive behavior patterns that are unsuccessful in maintaining healthy interpersonal relations. The person's adjustive problem is not one of great anxiety or severe internal conflict that is resolved defensively but rather the failure to develop mature methods for dealing with life and the world. The absence of such mature methods makes a person fundamentally incompetent and inadequate, even though his intellectual capacity should result in higher levels of functioning than are manifested.

One of the more widely recognized forms of character disorder is the antisocial personality, or, as he has sometimes been called, the *psychopath*. This category includes persons who get into conflict with the law and often wind up repeatedly in the courts and jails. The failure of adjustment is symptomatically expressed in criminal behavior. Such persons are frequently above average in intelligence. They seem to know the rules of society and the ways of influencing others, but they are deficient in moral and ethical values. Thus, like the other character disorders, there is a relative absence of internal conflict and anxiety and inadequate ego development, particularly in the area of conscience (superego).

The psychopath fails to identify with the most basic values of society and often appears unable to forego immediate pleasures in the interests of worthwhile long-range goals. He shows the immature reactions already described as well as impulsiveness, or lack of impulse control. When he is caught and punished for his crimes, the antisocial person regrets not his crime but his capture. It has often been suggested that there are deeper meanings behind the psychopathic pattern because many psychopaths foolishly leave a clear trail toward their capture. One such depth interpretation is that the criminal activity represents a compulsive and repetitious pattern aimed ultimately at self-destruction.

It should be pointed out that actual criminals represent a mixed assortment of personalities, so some might better be classified as neurotic or psychotic persons, dealing unsuccessfully with severe internal conflicts, and others—a relatively small percentage—represent true psychopathic personalities in the sense that there is a real absence of social identification and conscience. Because the cause of the latter type of disturbance is unknown, the term *constitutional psychopath* has often been used to reflect a deficiency either in constitution or in the early processes of identification that make for normal socialization of the personality.

Another form of character disorder, the *sexual deviate*, is marked by sexual disturbances. Of course, the definition of normal sexual functioning varies from culture to culture and even within the culture between social classes. Often included in this category of sexual deviation are persons with a diversified pattern of socially disapproved behaviors, including homosexuality, rape, sadism, voyeurism (the Peeping Tom), and exhibitionism. Sexual deviations are often separated into three general groups: (1) deficient sexual activity or desire, such as impotence; (2) normal sexual patterns that occur under antisocial conditions, such as promiscuity; and (3) those involving unusual or abnormal sexual objects, such as homosexuality or bestiality.

Our attitudes toward these various deviations have been considerably influenced by recent explorations of the typical American sexual practices by Kinsey and his associates (1948). Many socially disapproved forms of sexual behavior are far more common than most persons had supposed, and the question of sexual deviation is a good example of the problem of the cultural determination of pathology. If homosexuality is a normal and accepted practice in some societies or groups, regarding it as a pathological manifestation in our own represents a culturally bound definition of adjustive failure. It is considered pathological mainly because of the proscriptions against such behavior in our society, and perhaps because it is not the predominant sexual pattern. The difficulty of assessing the adequacy or healthiness of a behavior pattern is well illustrated in this case, although the problem goes far beyond the issue of sexual deviation.

It might be worth offering one concrete illustration of patterns of sexual behavior that are often regarded as deviant but which have been shown by Kinsey and his associates to be common, especially among young American males. Kinsey and colleagues (1948, pp. 168–170) wrote concerning homosexual activity:

About half of the older males (48%), and nearer two-thirds (60%) of the boys who were pre-adolescent at the time they contributed their histories, recall homosexual activity in their pre-adolescent years. . . .

The order of appearance of the several homosexual techniques is: exhibition of genitalia, manual manipulation of genitalia, anal or oral contacts with genitalia, and urethral insertions. Exhibition is much the most common form of homosexual play (in 98.8 percent of all the histories which have any activity). . . . There are teenage boys who continue this exhibitionistic activity throughout their high school years, some of them even entering into compacts with their closest friends to refrain from self masturbation except when in the presence of each other. In confining such social performances to self masturbation, these boys avoid conflicts over the homosexual. By this time, however, the psychic reactions may be homosexual enough, although it may be difficult to persuade these individuals to admit it.

Exhibitionism leads naturally into the next step in homosexual play, namely the mutual manipulation of genitalia. Such manipulation occurs in the play of two-thirds (67.4%) of all the pre-adolescent males who have any homosexual activity. . . .

Figure 32 presents some data on the incidence of homosexual as well as other sexual activity of preadolescent boys as reported and schematized by Kinsey and his associates (1948). They are interesting in the light of our usual attitudes toward homosexual behavior.

Alcoholism and *drug addiction* are also treated as forms of character disorders, although they include features of a unique sort. The consequences of extreme use of *alcohol* over a short time are acute disturb-

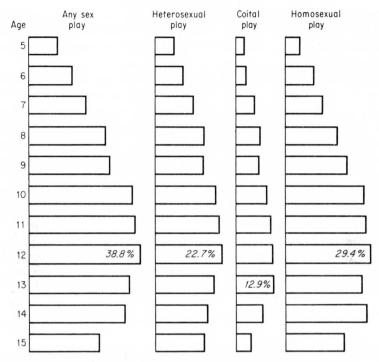

Figure 32. Per cent of males involved in sex play at each preadolescent age. (*From Kinsey et al.*, 1948.)

ances such as temporary psychotic symptoms (delirium tremens), including disorientation, hallucinations, fears, and tremors. The attack is relatively short-lived, lasting about three to six days, after which there appear to be no residual symptoms.

If the person has drunk excessively for many years, perhaps fifteen or twenty, there may develop an organic condition known as *Korsakoff's psychosis,* in which there is damage to the tissues of the brain leading to progressive mental deterioration. The acute alcoholic state itself is dangerous because the resulting disorientation can lead to injuries and can have disastrous consequences for the person's social and occupational functioning. Loss of job and general deterioration of behavior can ensue. The craving for alcohol can get an individual into difficulty with the law and can lead to a depletion of physical and financial resources.

The causes of alcoholism are not at all clear, although the condition is generally believed to reflect underlying personality maladjustments and to be a means of escaping temporarily from impossible-to-solve problems (stress). Why some persons become addicted to alcohol and others do not is a presently unsolved problem. The psychogenic view emphasizes inadequate character development and the importance of alcohol as a means of reducing anxiety. Others hold that in some persons there are organic (biochemical) factors that make alcohol a greater metabolic necessity than for others and make it difficult or nearly impossible to give up.

Popular treatments of the subject in plays and movies have made the lay person quite familiar with the problem of alcoholism. Cases occasionally have been demonstrated of well-known personalities who suffered from alcoholism for long periods of their life but who have successfully overcome it, sometimes through the help of such religious-therapeutic agencies as Alcoholics Anonymous. Most professional therapeutic approaches to alcoholism have not been conspicuously successful. In fact, the general category of character disorder is considered rather difficult to treat successfully.

Related to alcoholism but representing a somewhat different problem is *drug addiction*. Alcohol can be taken in mild or moderate doses by many persons throughout their lives without the development of addiction or later brain damage, but the use of any narcotic drugs derived from opium, such as morphine and heroin, or cocain will invariably lead to addiction within a relatively short time. The problem of drug addiction is a serious one (Menninger, 1948, estimated there were about 40,000 drug addicts in the United States) because it invariably leads to a severe deterioration of behavior. It is difficult to treat because, like alcohol, the drug produces an escape from severe problems, and the cessation of its use produces severe withdrawal symptoms, which are so terrifying that an addict, unless hospitalized, will commit any criminal act to prevent them.

The first symptoms of withdrawal of the drug are yawning, sneezing, sweating, loss of appetite, and an increasing desire for the drug. There follow increasing restlessness, depression, feelings of impending doom, and irritability. There may be chills alternating with excessive sweating, vomiting, diarrhea, abdominal cramps, pains, and tremors. In severe cases there may even be cardiovascular collapse, which can result in the death of the patient. The administration of the drug at any point during the withdrawal syndrome shortly ends the distress, but then the patient must continue to have more and more of the drug to prevent the recurrence of the withdrawal syndrome. The withdrawal syndrome itself usually lasts about a week or more, with its peak around three to five days. The tolerance that the patient has built up for the drug during the addicted period disappears after the withdrawal symptoms have ceased, and if the patient returns to his addiction, he must begin with smaller dosages all over again.

As in the case of alcohol, there is a deterioration of moral behavior, a reduction in health, ostracism by society, and frequent criminal behavior in an effort to obtain the expensive doses of the drugs. If the drug addict could maintain a well-balanced diet and an adequate supply of drugs (this is, of course, difficult because the law makes narcotics illegal), he might remain in this addicted state for many years without deterioration, but such a benign situation is extremely rare. This type of approach is actually being followed in Great Britain by physicians, who are legally able to administer such drugs routinely. The treatment of drug addiction is also difficult because, even after the immediate addiction has been eliminated by withdrawal of the drug, the same characterological problems push the person to return to the habit. If a person after treatment is still unable to face his problems, he will again seek some such escape and the cycle will begin all over again.

MENTAL DEFICIENCY

The lack of intellectual adequacy characteristic of the mentally deficient person reduces his capacity to master the problems of living. However, it is a vastly different basis of adjustive failure than is the case in neuroses and psychoses, because the problem is strictly based upon inadequate inherent capacity rather than defects resulting from conflict-produced stress. We can only touch briefly upon some of the important considerations in mental deficiency. The reader is urged to consult a fuller treatment, such as that of Sarason (1949), which is one of the best recent surveys of the area. There are various grades of defect ranging from what is often called the "dull-normal" category to morons, imbeciles, and idiots, the latter cases representing the most severe grade of mental deficiency.

The diagnosis or measurement of mental deficiency is by no means an easy task. The typical approach involves the use of standard intelligence tests, but the difficulty here is that many persons who have IQs below 70 (the usual cutoff score for serious mental defect) are able to function independently and learn the necessary skills to be reasonably self-sufficient and some persons with IQs well above 70 must be institutionalized because they cannot care for themselves independently in the community. There is a general relationship between intelligence-test level and the ability to adjust without institutionalization, but there are many exceptions in which social adjustment or adequacy does not accord precisely with test intelligence. As a consequence many researchers in this area have recommended broader criteria for diagnosing mental deficiency, of which intelligence-test score is only one and social competence or maturity is another (Doll, 1941). As Director of Research of the famous training school at Vineland, N.J., Doll (1946) created a social-maturity scale to be used in the assessment of the social as well as intellectual functioning of the mentally defective person to determine to what extent he might have sufficient competence to function outside an institution. The scale contains items that emphasize social functioning such as writing letters, perform-

Table 16

The Items from the Vineland Social Maturity Scale Arranged by Age Level

---

Age level 0–1

1. "Crows"; laughs
2. Balances head
3. Grasps objects within reach
4. Reaches for familiar persons
5. Rolls over
6. Reaches for nearby objects
7. Occupies self unattended
8. Sits unsupported
9. Pulls self upright
10. "Talks"; imitates sounds
11. Drinks from cup or glass assisted
12. Moves about on floor
13. Grasps with thumb and finger
14. Demands personal attention
15. Stands alone
16. Does not drool
17. Follows simple instructions

Age level 1–2

18. Walks about room unattended
19. Marks with pencil or crayon
20. Masticates food
21. Pulls off socks
22. Transfers objects
23. Overcomes simple obstacles
24. Fetches or carries familiar objects
25. Drinks from cup or glass unassisted
26. Gives up baby carriage
27. Plays with other children
28. Eats with spoon
29. Goes about house or yard
30. Discriminates edible substances
31. Uses names of familiar objects
32. Walks upstairs unassisted
33. Unwraps candy
34. Talks in short sentences

Age level 2–3

35. Asks to go to toilet
36. Initiates own play activities
37. Removes coat or dress
38. Eats with fork
39. Gets drink unassisted
40. Dries own hands
41. Avoids simple hazards
42. Puts on coat or dress unassisted
43. Cuts with scissors
44. Relates experiences

Age level 3–4

45. Walks downstairs one step per tread
46. Plays cooperatively at kindergarten level
47. Buttons coat or dress
48. Helps at little household tasks
49. "Performs" for others
50. Washes hands unaided

Age level 4–5

51. Cares for self at toilet
52. Washes face unassisted
53. Goes about neighborhood unattended
54. Dresses self except for tying
55. Uses pencil or crayon for drawing
56. Plays competitive exercise games

Table 16 (*Continued*)

Age level 5–6

57. Uses skates, sled, wagon
58. Prints simple words
59. Plays simple table games
60. Is trusted with money
61. Goes to school unattended

Age level 6–7

62. Uses table knife for spreading
63. Uses pencil for writing
64. Bathes self assisted
65. Goes to bed unassisted

Age level 7–8

66. Tells time to quarter hour
67. Uses table knife for cutting
68. Disavows literal Santa Claus
69. Participates in preadolescent play
70. Combs or brushes hair

Age level 8–9

71. Uses tools or utensils
72. Does routine household tasks
73. Reads on own initiative
74. Bathes self unaided

Age level 9–10

75. Cares for self at table
76. Makes minor purchases
77. Goes about home town freely

Age level 10–11

78. Writes occasional short letters
79. Makes telephone calls
80. Does small remunerative work
81. Answers ads; purchases by mail

Age level 11–12

82. Does simple creative work
83. Is left to care for self or others
84. Enjoys books, newspapers, magazines

Age level 12–15

85. Plays difficult games
86. Exercises complete care of dress
87. Buys own clothing accessories
88. Engages in adolescent activities
89. Performs responsible routine chores

Age level 15–18

90. Communicates by letter
91. Follows current events
92. Goes to nearby places alone
93. Goes out unsupervised in daytime
94. Has own spending money
95. Buys all own clothing

Age level 18–20

96. Goes to distant points alone
97. Looks after own health
98. Has a job or continues schooling
99. Goes out nights unrestricted
100. Controls own major expenditures
101. Assumes personal responsibility

Table 16 (*Continued*)

Age level 20–25

102. Uses money providently
103. Assumes responsibility beyond own needs

104. Contributes to social welfare
105. Provides for future

Age level 25+

106. Performs skilled work
107. Engages in beneficial recreation
108. Systematizes own work
109. Inspires confidence
110. Promotes civic progress
111. Supervises occupational pursuits
112. Purchases for others

113. Directs or manages affairs of others
114. Performs expert or professional work
115. Shares community responsibility
116. Creates own opportunities
117. Advances general welfare

ing household tasks, managing spending money, and performing skilled work. Such an approach adds greatly to the information that can be derived from standard intelligence tests, because the social-maturity items appear more closely related to kinds of activities a person has to perform if he is to live independently in a social community. The Vineland Social Maturity Scale is presented in Table 16.

In classifying the varieties of mental deficiency, one group has been identified in which the defect is mild, appears to run in the family, and seems to have no complication, such as brain injury, disease, or other organic condition, that might be causal. The suggestion in these cases is that a hereditary factor might be responsible for the mental inadequacy, although this is by no means unequivocally demonstrated. Many terms have been given to this variety of defectives. Sarason (1949) has used the term "garden variety."

Other types of mental deficiency are associated with the presence of organic disease, metabolic disorders, congenital injuries, and special hereditary defects. In apposition, therefore, to garden-variety mental deficiency is this second large category, in which one of the above factors is considered basic to the defect. It is generally assumed that factors such as metabolic disturbances or neurological damage to the brain are the causal agents of the mental defect in this second category, but the precise mechanism through which the retardation of intellectual development is produced is not really clear. Much more work must be done on brain functioning and adaptive behavior before these conditions are fully understood.

It is important to make a distinction between mental deficiency that involves the failure of the intelligence to develop to normal levels and what might be called *intellectual deficit*, damage or impairment to a person that has previously developed adequately. In the early days of neurology and psychiatry no clear distinction was made between these failures of adequate development (sometimes called "amentia") and disorders that produced intellectual impairment after a person had manifested normal development to mature levels ("dementia"). Frequently the psychotic person displays intellectual defects that are associated with the psychotic process, although it is often clear that he had once attained high or at least normal levels of mental growth prior to the illness.

In mental deficiency the inadequacy is usually present at, or shortly after, birth and becomes manifest to the clinical observer or the parents within the first few years of life. Thereafter, there is retardation of development. The defective person is always far behind the normal child and never catches up. This failure of intellectual development goes along with inability to solve the normal problems of living, to learn the skills necessary to master life situations, and to be self-supporting rather than a public or private charge.

In most cases the treatment of this particular adjustive failure is to accept the handicap and attempt to rehabilitate the person by providing a minimally demanding environment and by teaching some of the basic skills necessary for independent survival. This training is normally accomplished in special training institutions for the feeble-minded. In contrast, in neurosis and psychosis it is typically the case that the person has the necessary intellectual resources so treatment can capitalize on those potential resources not effectively utilized because of the psychopathology. It should be noted that sometimes neurotic or psychotic disturbances are interwoven with a genuine condition of retardation. In this event, the identification of the basis of the adjustive failure presents special difficulties. In fact, the interrelationship between intelligence and psychodynamics in general is one of the most fascinating problems with which psychologists interested in adjustment have been concerned.

Table 17 is a very general summary chart that indicates the main classes of adjustive failure, the main symptoms of each, and the possible dynamics or causes of each. It should be clear that relatively little is currently known about the causes of each clinical disorder, although concepts about these causes have come from both biological and social frames of reference. In the column on dynamics and causes are only very general ideas about the nature of the defense mechanism usually postulated and the condition that produced the disorder, for example, brain damage in the case of the organic psychoses. These should be regarded as what they are, merely vague hypotheses. This is not the place to inquire deeply into all the

Table 17

MAJOR FORMS OF MENTAL DISORDERS, THEIR SYMPTOMS, AND POSSIBLE DYNAMICS OR CAUSES

Disorder	Main symptoms	Possible dynamics or causes
Transient reactions to acute stress	Variable, including severe anxiety, psychotic disorganization, and neurotic behavior patterns	Precipitating factors are acute stressor conditions such as war conditions (bombings); civilian disasters (explosions and floods); any temporary personal crisis or personal loss (death of loved one); predisposing factors not clear
The psychoneuroses: Anxiety states	Chronic or acute severe anxiety	Either unresolved internal conflict for which no adequate defense has been developed, or the temporary dissolution of a previously adequate defense
Hysteria	Neurological-appearing physical conversion symptom (e.g., paralysis) and dissociations	Repression of strong, unacceptable impulses expressed as symptoms
Obsessive-compulsive reactions	Obsessions and compulsions	Threatening thoughts or impulses displaced or transformed into less disturbing ideas or actions
Depressions	Dejection and discouragement, with or without agitation	Acute personal loss; could also be classed as transient reaction to stress
The psychoses: Organic	Loss of memory and impulse control; disorientation	Brain damage produced by various causes
Schizophrenia	Disorder of thought; withdrawal; bizarre behavior; variable delusions and hallucinations	Various theories, but in the main, no clear, well-supported causal hypothesis; this is the

		most severe disorder, often considered to be the end stage of overwhelming and continuous stress
Paranoia	Systematic delusions of grandeur or persecution	Defense of projection against unacceptable impulses, such as homosexuality
Affective	Manic excitement of mood or depression (stuporous or agitated)	Another consequence of inadequate coping with stress the origins of which are not clear; often thought also to have genetic or constitutional basis; simply exaggerations of neurotic depressions
The character disorders	Variable, including impulsivity, emotional instability, passivity, antisocial behavior, and addiction	Failure to acquire adequate habits of living and relating to others; not characterized primarily by internal conflict and stress
Mental deficiency	Inadequate ability to solve problems and learn to function without social-welfare support	Lack of intellectual development resulting from genetic factors or congenital injury or disease

369

possible etiological theories, and it is hoped that the interested student will go more fully into the question by seeking primary or more advanced sources in abnormal psychology. In any event, most researchers in this field would agree that we have hardly begun to understand the various conditions of pathology and that the vagueness found in Table 17 in the third column accurately reflects our current ignorance.

THE EXTENT OF THE PROBLEM OF ADJUSTIVE FAILURE

No discussion of adjustive failure, however brief, would be complete without some statement about the amount of adjustive failures in the population, at least within our own culture. It is clear to most educated persons today that adjustive failure in its many forms is shockingly widespread. In recent years a great deal of publicity has been given to the problem. The increasing recognition of the extent of the problem has stimulated the development of institutional resources and the training of specialized personnel, primarily psychiatrists, psychologists, and social workers, to study and deal with the problem. The demand for services, however, far outstrips the supply of trained clinical personnel, and at the moment the outlook is poor that the supply will catch up with the demand in the foreseeable future.

There is no really accurate way of estimating the number of mentally ill persons because failures of adjustment vary from extremely mild to severe, and lumping these together produces a statistic that is extremely hard to interpret. Moreover, our figures are mainly based upon records derived from hospital admissions; it is nearly impossible to judge without extensive systematic study how many patients are being seen privately. There are now government-supported agencies attempting to explore this problem. However, a high percentage of those who need clinical assistance never seek it or get it, and any objective figures could be gross underestimates. Another difficulty in making estimates is the transiency of some adjustive failures; that is, some disorders occur for a relatively short period of time.

One way to discuss the problem is to consider the various major categories of disorder and give some brief estimates of their incidence in the population. Nearly any up-to-date textbook in abnormal psychology provides figures along these lines, and although the estimates vary, the pattern seems to be similar.

With respect to transient reactions to acute stress, the largest instance of which are combat exhaustion and military maladjustment, there seem to have been approximately 750,000 such admissions to Army hospitals. It is also reported that about 37 per cent of all Army medical discharges were for neuropsychiatric reasons. Over 50 per cent of all patients in Veterans Administration hospitals are psychiatric cases (Menninger, 1948). Relatively little systematic statistical work has been done with civilian crises, although individual studies have been made, for example, of the panic following the Cocoanut Grove fire in Boston in 1942. Adler (1943) reported that over half the survivors of this fire required treatment for severe psychological shock, although in the overwhelming majority of cases the disturbance was relatively mild and transient.

The incidence of psychoneurotic disorders is extremely difficult to determine, although a conservative estimate is that more than eight million persons in the United States can be classified as psychoneurotics. It has been suggested by many privately practicing physicians that anywhere from one-third to two-thirds of those who go to doctors with physical complaints are suffering from some form of psychoneurotic disturbance. Although psychiatry got its first impetus for growth from the more severe disturbances, the enormous development that has taken place in the past several decades can be traced to the recognition of the importance of the milder psychological disturbances, which partially incapacitate persons and make them unhappy.

There are useful statistics available with respect to the organic psychoses. About 4 per cent of all first admissions to mental hospitals are based upon general paresis, which represents approximately 5 per cent of all untreated syphilitic persons. But the incidence of paresis is dropping sharply and has dropped a great deal over previous decades because of the use of penicillin in the treatment of syphilis. Diseases such as encephalitis are extremely rare, accounting for approximately 0.1 per cent of first admissions to mental hospitals. Although it is a little more common, the same can be said of cerebral spinal meningitis. Head injuries are extremely common in ordinary life, resulting from falls, automobile accidents, or intentional blows on the head, many of these injuries actually involving penetration of the cranium. But few patients with brain injuries enter mental hospitals, the percentage being approximately 0.4 per cent of first admissions. The metabolic and toxic causes of mental-hospital admission are likewise not a sizable source. Huntington's chorea is also rare. Epilepsy as a disorder is relatively common, probably affecting up to one million persons in the United States in some form or other. However, epilepsy ordinarily does not lead to psychotic disturbances for which hospitalization is necessary; only 1.2 per cent of first admissions involve epileptic disturbances.

By far the most common cause of admission to mental hospitals for organic disturbances is aging. There has been a progressive increase in the percentage of aged persons in the United States. Senile dementia is a psychosis based upon the degenerative changes of the brain in old age. The senile psychoses constitute about 10 per cent of hospital first admissions and an even larger percentage of the chronic hospital population, because there is no improvement in the disorder over time (brain tissue does not regenerate) as in the case of other acute functional disorders. The senile patient usually lives out the rest of his life in an institutional setting. Psychoses associated with cerebral arteriosclerosis (the hardening of the arterial walls of the brain), which occurs earlier in life than the senile disturbances, make up approximately 12 per cent of first admissions to mental hospitals. More public attention has been paid to cerebral strokes and coronary heart diseases based upon arterial changes and degeneration than to the psychotic consequences of these changes.

The functional psychoses involve a very high percentage of hospital admissions, with schizophrenia leading the list with about 20 to 25 per cent of the total admissions. The manic-depressive and involutional psychoses produce close to 14 per cent, and the paranoid disorders yield the lowest figure for the functional group, with 1.5 per cent.

The statistics for the character disorders are also hard to estimate because they are confused with criminology data, and many persons never reach the mental hospital. In general, perhaps 6 per cent of first admissions to mental hospitals are based upon a combination of the psychopathic personality (criminal patterns), behavior disorders, such as sexual assault, and alcoholism. This figure excludes the large prison population among which is a large percentage of psychologically disturbed persons.

From Malzberg (1959), in the American Handbook of Psychiatry, comes a comparison of first-admission rates of all forms of mental illness in the New York State hospital system (the largest in the world) for each year from 1910 to 1950. These figures are interesting because they show a continual rise over the years in the rate of mental disorder in general per 100,000 population. Malzberg attempted to analyze this rise by estimating and eliminating the increasing contribution of first admissions due to old age. He found that, although the percentage of aged persons being admitted has indeed gone up sharply, the increase in over-all admissions cannot be entirely accounted for in this way. There appears to be a genuine trend toward increased incidence of other forms of mental illness, as found in the state hospitals. It is not possible, however, to say whether this increase represents a higher actual incidence of mental illness or results merely from the fact that greater attention is now being paid to this field, leading increasingly often to the hospitalization of any person who appears mentally disturbed. Table 18 presents Malzberg's data on first admissions for all reasons during the several decades studied. The figures do not include the milder, nonhospitalized disorders, such as neuroses and character problems. They consist mainly of psychoses, organic and functional. Objective data on the milder forms of disturbance are very difficult to obtain in the absence of systematic records.

Table 18

FIRST ADMISSIONS TO NEW YORK CIVIL STATE HOSPITALS, 1910–1950, PER 100,000 POPULATION

Fiscal Year	Males	Females	Total
1910	63.7	57.0	60.4
1912	65.5	59.4	62.5
1914	68.1	61.2	64.6
1916	70.0	63.7	66.9
1918	70.4	64.9	67.7
1920	67.8	62.5	65.2
1922	69.3	61.0	65.1
1924	68.2	61.3	64.7
1926	71.8	61.5	66.4
1928	77.1	63.1	70.1
1930	78.9	64.9	71.9
1932	90.8	74.2	82.4
1934	99.0	82.9	91.0
1936	102.9	88.3	95.6
1938	107.8	92.3	100.0
1940	108.2	95.5	101.8
1942	110.9	97.2	103.8
1944	102.8	102.7	102.7
1946	100.7	103.4	102.1
1948	104.4	101.4	102.9
1950	109.9	102.4	106.0

SOURCE: Malzberg, 1959, pp. 161–174.

While any sophisticated discussion of the statistics of mental disorder or adjustive failure involves complicated issues, the enormity of the problem can be grasped from even the meager information presented. No exaggeration of the actual data is necessary to bring this point home to the lay as well as professional public.

ADJUSTIVE FAILURE AND PERSONALITY THEORY

One of the great dilemmas in the psychology of personality is why the development of a person should somehow go wrong and adjustive failure occur. There seem to be two general points of view on this question. On the one hand, it can be argued that the stress-producing experiences of life interfere or disrupt the learning of appropriate adjustment mechanisms. In the previous chapter we have pointed out the long-standing concept that emotional states interfere with or disorganize the cognitive processes, which are essential in the adjustive process. From this point of view, failures in adjustment represent essentially nonadaptive behavior through the disruptive action of stress.

The other alternative is to regard failures of adjustment as occurring because the wrong coping mechanisms (adaptive efforts) have been acquired in the struggle to reduce stress. From this point of view, the organism is not able properly and rationally to solve his problems because defenses against anxiety make inaccessible the underlying conflicts or problems. In other words, the neurotic and psychotic adjustment patterns are not total failures, because they do serve to reduce stress. However, they produce secondary consequences for behavior that reduce a person's effectiveness from a biological and social point of view. The latter notion seems to be the predominant one in most theories of pathology. A person cannot progress to healthy and high-level solutions to life's problems because he has learned to cope with stress in inadequate ways. He therefore lacks insight into his problems and the capacity for rational judgment about his life situation.

The two points of view can be integrated by suggesting that common to all functional maladjustments is the failure to develop adequate rational modes of control. This failure is the result of tremendous and unfortunately timed overstimulation (stress) that produces immature defense mechanisms. Thus we might conceive adequacy of adjustment on a continuum from the healthy personality to the less mature neurotic or character disorder to the severe psychotic. The more stress to which a person has been exposed before mature modes of coping have been developed, the more likely there is to be interference in the learning of healthy modes. The problem is the acquisition of effective techniques of mastery, but these techniques can never develop satisfactorily unless the stresses during development can be successfully mastered at each stage. Stresses are a natural part of the life experience of a developing individual, and such stresses force the organism to develop means of mastery. Too great stress at the wrong time will interfere with the development of these techniques of mastery, just as too little stress will also retard the acquisition of such techniques.

Adjustive failures (at least in the neuroses and psychoses) therefore are usually a consequence of the acquisition of pathological modes of coping with stress; the various types of neurosis are synonymous with various types of immature methods of coping. The predominant method by which a person handles stress varies with the nature of the pathology. But these acquired methods, though unsatisfactory to some degree, always resist change because the adjustive mechanism does reduce stress to some degree. The person develops what appear to be nonadaptive coping mechanisms, but these are, in reality, coping methods that have a certain value in reducing the pain of a stress state.

Most of the important theories of personality have arisen from the clinical context in which psychopathology is observed. Few have started with a conceptualization of the healthy personality. Some, such as Rank, offer very general guiding principles for understanding neurosis, and others, such as Freud, offer elaborately worked-out schemes for considering the origins of each symptom pattern. All these cannot be reviewed here, and some of this material has already been covered in the discussion of the personality theories themselves. However, let us illustrate some of the differences in a few cases.

The previous chapter compared briefly some theoretical systems with respect to sources of stress in the development of the individual. This remains a primary theoretical basis of distinction concerning psychopathology. For Freud, the development of effective ego-control mechanisms (e.g., sublimation) over sexual and aggressive impulses is the primary problem in human psychological development, and the vicissitudes of this struggle determine the personality structure as well as the neurotic and psychotic symptom patterns.

The Freudian system is the most thoroughly worked-out one available to us. It specifies the psychodynamics and developmental stages through which every form of personality organization passes. The ego defenses (and hence the pathological manifestations) depend upon the stage of psychosexual development in which personal crises take place. For example, in the anal period of development the mechanisms of intellectualization and isolation characteristic of the obsessive-compulsive neurotic pattern are formed and become the characteristic means by which a person deals with threatening anal impulses. Repression characterizes the stage of ego development that is simultaneous with the struggle to master oedipal conflicts. Thus, in Freudian theory, the various neurotic manifestations are understood in terms of particular ego-defense characteristics aroused by particular kinds of conflict related to the stages of psychosexual development. One of the best treatments of this relationship between instinctual conflict, ego development, and neurotic manifestations is found in Fenichel (1945), who has systematically represented the Freudian scheme for understanding the neurosis.

As pointed out earlier, the association-learning frame of reference of Dollard and Miller is mainly a restatement of the Freudian system in association-learning terms, pointing to similar types of conflict and elaborating the mechanisms of learning by which the various defense mechanisms are acquired. The system rejects some of the original Freudian assumptions, such as the universal and instinctual nature of sexual and aggressive drives, and the Freudian levels of psychosexual development. Freud's implicit assumption that defense mechanisms are learned has been elaborated in learning-theory terms. As in the case of Freud, Dollard and Miller made fear or anxiety the cornerstone of the development of pathological modes of coping. It is fear that leads a person to develop the mechanisms of repression, reaction formation, etc. Thus a person acquires inadequate ways of mastering stress because fear drives him to develop pathological mechanisms for its reduction, and these mechanisms deceive the person about the unlabeled (unconscious) or unverbalized sources of fear.

The point of view most in contrast with the Freudian and association-learning approaches has been called the "self-actualizing school," elaborated in one form by Otto Rank and developed in various other forms by later writers such as Goldstein, Rogers, Lecky, and Maslow. Rank emphasized the conflict between the life fear and the death fear and the individual's need for union or dependency and his need for individuation or growth. From this point of view, all neurotic manifestations represent consequences of this struggle in which the two forces could not be successfully reconciled. Every form of human conflict and every neurotic symptom represented an instance or version of this fundamental struggle.

But Rank is vague about the relationships between this general guiding principle and the specific varieties of symptoms of psychopathology. His typology is a gross one, including the average man, who has suppressed the forces for self-expression in favor of the safety of loss of identity and membership in the group; the neurotic, who has suppressed neither force, although these may alternate in their ascendancy, and who is continually struggling unsuccessfully with the basic conflict; and the artist, who has realized his individuality but yet somehow reconciled it successfully with his dependency needs. The nature of the neurotic pattern reflects in part the ineffective striving on the part of the individual to actualize in various ways both of these forces.

The aspect in which Rank differs from Freud, which was elaborated by later self-actualizing writers, is the assumption or proposition that there exists in the individual a force for growth or self-actualization. The self-actualizing writers use this assumption as a cornerstone of their theoretical systems, which, like Rank's system, do not spell out the specific dynamics of each neurotic pattern but offer very general guiding principles of development. The essential proposition is that adjustive failure represents failure to reach the highest levels of which a person is capable because the circumstances of life have inhibited the normal growth process. Neurosis is seen as inhibited development, and treatment is oriented toward improving the opportunities for a person to grow or move forward toward self-actualization.

Similar comparisons can be made between many of the different theoretical systems, and it will be discovered that great similarities also exist. There is fundamental agreement that conflict produces anxiety (or fear or states of stress), which interferes with the normal process of learning and development. A person often adopts more primitive or pathological ways of adjusting than he should in the attempt to master the stresses.

For Freud, no special force for growth is postulated, and development, particularly of the ego processes, occurs primarily because instincts need to be gratified; they are obstructed in this gratification by social forces external to the individual. The person must find ways, sometimes pathological, to permit sufficient instinctual discharge, and the reality-oriented adaptive resources of an individual develop out of this struggle to find safe and successful forms of discharge. For the self-actualizing school, the human organism is so constructed that normal development involves growth and the actualization of man's highest cognitive potentialities (for Maslow these include esthetic and problem-solving capacities). Positive growth does not occur out of the struggle for survival or in the effort to discharge biological urges but because it is inherent as a force within the organism. Positive growth, rather than being stimulated by the struggle for survival and adequate biological discharge, can be inhibited by it so development is stunted. These two points of view highlight an essential philosophical distinction, which is probably one of the basic points of divergence among personality theories and theories of psychopathology.

The important general point to be gained from this discussion is that failures of adjustment are somewhat differently understood by different theoretical systems of personality theory. As the student becomes more familiar with the intricacies of the various theoretical systems, he will become better able to conceptualize the dynamics of particular psychological disorders.

It must be recognized that we have emphasized theories presented at the psychological-social level of analysis; it is also possible to consider all psychopathology at the physiological level of analysis, that is, in terms of biochemistry, genetics, and neurological models of behavior. One level will never, of course, supplant the other because behavioral laws must ultimately be related to physiological laws. Personality theories represent attempts to describe and conceptualize behavior and behavior disorder psychologically. This is, after all, the primary concern of the psychologist of personality.

PART
V

ASSESSMENT, TREATMENT, AND OTHER PRACTICAL APPLICATIONS OF THE FIELD

NOW WE COME TO what might be called the "pay-off" section, in which is discussed how the knowledge accumulated about adjustment and personality might be employed to solve some of the pressing psychological problems of mankind. We begin with the field of personality assessment and clinical diagnosis in Chapter 13. Once we have learned about modes of adjustment and their consequences and successfully identified the most important aspects of personality and their observable qualities, it is a logical next step to attempt to measure these and employ them in practical application. As a matter of fact, the task of measurement and the task of acquiring knowledge are mutually interdependent, because if we could not find even gross indicators or measures of personality and the adjustment processes, we could not, in turn, have a science of personality.

Another major area of theory and application is psychotherapy, which is dealt with in Chapter 14. Here is discussed the nature of the psychotherapeutic process as a means of reducing or eliminating the psychic and economic cost of psychopathology. Finally, Chapter 15 is concerned with application of psychological knowledge in general and additional forms of application than those implied in the chapters on assessment and psychotherapy.

Our objective in this last section is not so much to catalog and detail the areas of application as to outline and assess the problems underlying them. Furthermore, this is not a manual to teach the reader how to diagnose and treat but rather a treatise on the fundamental concepts underlying the methods of assessment and treatment.

To some readers the inclusion of these areas of psychological concern, although obviously related to adjustment and personality, may seem specialized and technical. However, nowadays the lay person (including the beginning student as well as those who have had no formal psychological training) is aware of diagnosis and therapy as he has never been before. The mass media frequently touch upon these subjects, and it is in the interest of a high level of education to inform properly the student of psychology about these very fundamental areas of inquiry and application. As with other topics treated in summary fashion, there are additional sources (such as those referred to in the chapters themselves) that give more elaborate treatments of specific subject matter.

CHAPTER

13

Personality Assessment and Clinical Diagnosis

Personality assessment is the determination of personality characteristics for theoretical or practical reasons. Theoretically, personality assessment requires the translation of the hypothetical processes of personality into behavioral referents that can be directly measured. In this
way it is possible to test our theories of personality through the techniques of assessment.

Aside from this theoretical significance, the task of assessment has
practical value. For example, if we need to select men who will be
most effective in wartime combat situations, we not only must know the
personality characteristics that determine combat efficiency, but also must
be able to measure these characteristics. The same applies to any kind of
personnel selection where the problem is to fit individuals to work conditions. Personality assessment is an important enterprise both to theoretical and practical psychology.

The title of this chapter refers also to clinical diagnosis. Actually this
is the task of assessing personality in the very special context of the clinic
or hospital. Professional clinical workers must determine the severity of
a patient's mental disorder, the resources he has available to profit from
treatment, and the nature of the forces that lie behind the manifest disturbance. Clinical diagnosis has these particular aims in mind, but it is
really only a special case of the general problem of personality assessment.

In this review of personality assessment, the purpose is not to describe
thoroughly the special measuring techniques that have been developed
nor is it to prepare the reader to be an assessor or diagnostician; it is to
provide an over-all grasp of the problems of assessment and the methodological and theoretical issues that underlie them. These will be illustrated
with examples of the assessment techniques available to psychologists.

THE PROBLEM OF ASSESSMENT

We can approach the problem of assessment by distinguishing two main approaches. One is *empirical* and the other *theoretical*. The procedures of these two approaches often coincide, but there is also considerable difference in their aims.

Empirical Prediction

Many psychologists consider the basic aim of assessment to be the prediction of behavior. One of the essential features of personality assessment is that it offers the possibility of predicting a person's future behavior on the basis of what we know about him now or in the past. From this point of view, the construction of assessment procedures will be based upon correlation between behaviors. That is, if we observe that in a particular situation a person acts in a particular way, we can often say that in another future situation he will act in some predictable, if not similar, fashion. We can then check the predictive ability of our assessment procedures by whether, in truth, the predicted behavior does occur.

For example, suppose we wish to predict the future academic standing of any sample of students. The empirical question here is: What are the behavioral antecedents of academic success? In other words, what kinds of information do we need to have about a person to make a predictive statement about his future grades? A classic solution to this empirical problem has been the development of intelligence tests.

In the late nineteenth century, there was no real agreement about what sorts of tasks reflected the level of intelligence. Many psychologists in those days (such as J. McK. Cattell & Farrand, 1896) believed that one should seek out the simplest neurologically oriented functions as the basic building blocks of mental capacity, and accordingly they extensively studied sensorimotor tasks such as reaction time. But in order to evaluate this approach to the measurement of intelligence, some behavioral criterion of intellectual capacity was needed. A student of Cattell, Clark Wissler, attempted to find the correlation between Cattell's simple mental tests and the course grades obtained by college students (1901). There turned out to be little more than a chance relationship. This aborted the effort to study intelligence through simple sensorimotor tasks.

During the same period, European psychologists like Binet and Simon (1905) had been experimenting with more complicated tasks like imagery, comprehension, and perceptual judgment. These experiments showed not only that performance improved with age, but that it was substantially correlated with teachers' estimates of brightness in children and with school grades. Thus, a practical set of measures was developed in the form of the Binet tests of intelligence, which became the basis of the famous Stanford-Binet Intelligence Scale. This scale and other, similar ones could predict school grades and related types of performance.

This statement of the relationship between the Binet test score and school grades is the essence of empirical prediction in personality assessment. One set of test behaviors is observed or measured, and some other behavior, in this case, school grades, is predicted. Actually there need be no theoretical interpretation of this relationship; the validity of the assessment is based entirely upon its predictive efficiency. The empirical relationship does not depend upon theory, although our conceptual schemes, for example, the way Cattell or Binet tended to define and operationalize intelligence, may lead us to look for certain types of behavioral predictors rather than others. Moreover, once found, the relationship requires explanation or understanding. As soon as we label performance on the Binet tests or on school examinations as a manifestation of intellectual capacity, we are venturing into the theoretical realm by attempting to identify the nature of the processes that underlie task performance.

Such relationships between observable variables constitute the facts of psychology (and any science), and although they are often useful in the prediction and control of behavior, they lack the meaning a theoretical conception can give to them. Many psychologists might be called "empiricists," because for them the only really significant aspect of psychology is its body of empirical relationships. Attempting to understand the process underlying the prediction through theoretical speculation is considered by some to be a futile exercise in imagination (Skinner, 1950).

Constructs of Personality

In Chapter 2 we differentiated surface (behavioral) definitions of personality from substance (those emphasizing underlying hypothetical structures) definitions. Thus, in contrast with the emphasis in assessment on empirical prediction, greater emphasis can be placed upon identifying these underlying or substance characteristics through assessment techniques. Included here might be such hypothetical constructs as motives, attitudes, and defense mechanisms, all of which represent inferred characteristics. They are not directly measurable and are the conceptual elements of personality theory.

It has been argued that we can actually predict behavior better when we have a sound theoretical system from which to deduce relationships between behavioral patterns. But the main reason for approaching the problem from a substance point of view is not based entirely upon the practical value of predicting human behavior. The hypothetical constructs of personality theories represent our understanding or interpretation of empirical relationships, and this attempt at understanding represents an equally important part of psychological science.

If one accepts this point of view, then the decision about what to assess in personality assessment is not determined entirely by the practical consideration of prediction, but rather by its relevance to the conceptual system that one adopts. Thus a Freudian description of a person is likely to involve different descriptive terms and units of measurement than one developed by Rogers, Jung, or Rank. Rank would assess the personality in terms of the life and death fear, and Freud's emphasis would naturally be placed upon the level of psychosexual development attained and its implications for intrapsychic conflict.

Different conceptual systems are likely to use different tools of measurement. For example, a depth psychologist, concerned with unconscious processes that influence behavior, would use the depth interview or the projective technique to make inferences about underlying processes. On the other hand, a phenomenologically oriented theorist, such as Rogers, would be interested primarily in introspections. These can be derived during therapy; the patient discloses his self concept by talking about himself and his related attitudes. A more empirically oriented scientist will choose objective techniques that require less inferential judgment, such as the questionnaire or direct behavioral observation of objectively definable behavior (which can be readily counted and quantified).

Diagnosis as a Special Case of Assessment

The term *diagnosis* merely refers to the assessment process when focused upon symptoms and dynamics of adjustive failure. The problems of diagnosis are fundamentally no different from those of assessment in general. Diagnosis should not only be a description of symptoms but also a conceptual representation of personality organization and a statement about the dynamic conflicts and their sources underlying the disorder. One difficulty with the term "diagnosis" has been that, over many years, it has tended to mean labeling in the strictly descriptive sense (usually employing Kraepelin's categories).

When diagnosis means an exploration of the structures and forces that led to a patient's present difficulties and differentiate him from other patients, it becomes a highly elaborate personality assessment of the construct type. It can be oriented primarily toward understanding the disorder in conceptual terms, or it can be aimed toward utility in predicting the outcome of the disorder. In the latter case the term "prognosis" is usually used. We say, for example, that schizophrenia has a poorer prognosis than a manic-depressive disorder because, in general, persons suffering from manic-depressive attacks usually recover and schizophrenia more commonly leads to a chronic and deteriorating condition.

This discussion is not intended to divorce prediction from theoretical understanding entirely. Any theoretical statement about personality organization can only be made on the basis of objective behavior and can only be evaluated as to its usefulness by deducing (or predicting) empirical relationships. The point is, however, that behavioral consequences themselves are not the only or even primary objective of personality assessment. We are often interested in conceptualizing personality by using some theoretical model to make inferences from a person's behavior pattern. But any inferred hypothetical process, such as a need or defense mechanism, must be evaluated in some way; this special kind of validity has sometimes been referred to as "construct validity" in contrast with "predictive validity." The test of a statement about a process inferred from our assessment device can only be made by deducing from it how a person will act under certain circumstances.

In the same way, if we assume that an intelligence-test score gives us an index of mental energy (as Spearman, 1937, was inclined to conceptualize the fundamental principle underlying intelligence), then we must be able to deduce from this concept of mental energy how a person will act. One of these deductions may be that he will perform better in a learning situation.

Thus, if we are interested merely in empirical prediction, we are not deeply concerned about what it is we are measuring with our intelligence test (theory), because, after all, it does permit us to predict scholastic achievement. On the other hand, if we are interested in the theoretical concept of intelligence, the fact that an assessment of this characteristic predicts scholastic achievement is important primarily because it supports our theory or throws additional light on the nature of the concept of intelligence. In a sense, we are dealing with the difference between strict interest in practical application of knowledge and understanding human beings. This difference in orientation is the subject of bitter conflict between psychologists (and indeed, representatives of every science) who strongly espouse either value.

Assessment and Trait Orientation

All personality-assessment procedures tend to emphasize a trait orientation to personality. Tests are given to subjects on the assumption that their scores, or the inferences made from the scores, represent stable characteristics or dispositions that will apply in a wide variety of contexts. The role of the stimulus situation as a determinant of behavior is apt to be ignored or deemphasized in contrast with the role of enduring traits as the primary determinant of behavior. However sophisticated such techniques become, they must always represent a probabilistic approach to the prediction of behavior because they depend upon the consistencies of human personality. Thus, without field-oriented research, relating personality traits to situations, one can only make a probabilistic statement that, given such and such an attribute, a person will perform or behave in such and such a way regardless of external conditions. Scientific prediction of behavior must ultimately be based upon both personality traits and the social and physical conditions under which behavior occurs.

SOURCES OF INFORMATION

The psychologist who is concerned with personality assessment is a seeker of information about the behavior of the individual and his private experiences. Regardless of the theoretical approach he follows, behavior and the situations in which behavior occurs represent the only basis for predictions of future behavior or for inferences made about the personality. But there is so much taking place in the course of even a very brief sampling of behavior that some theoretical guide is extremely important in telling the psychologist where to look; that is, which behaviors to emphasize and which to ignore.

Let us press this point further. In the course of a single hour's interview there are large numbers of gestures, complicated and varied facial expressions, elaborate patterns of muscular movement, and various physiological concomitants, which can sometimes be measured through psychophysiological equipment or directly observed (e.g., sudden pallor, flushing, tremor). To describe all this would be extremely difficult and would produce an unwieldy set of materials. If one further considers a person's entire life history, some choice must be made of which features of an enormously varied and rich set of experiences and actions to note and which to ignore. This selecting and organizing task is facilitated by some conceptual system for describing and understanding personality. The first step, however, is access to the necessary information.

There are three main sources of information for the study of personality. These are the case history, the interview, and the psychological test. These sources of information have similarities, but there are particular assumptions and technical problems specific to each one. Let us consider them separately.

The Case History

A case history is essentially a story about a person's life. The main facts about his development and the events and reactions leading up to his present status are obtained from a wide variety of sources. These facts must then be organized and analyzed along with other kinds of data as antecedents to the present personality.

The fundamental assumption is that a person's present personality is part of a continuous process of development. The past history provides clues to the life experiences that have molded it and yields evidence of the consistent ways in which a person has adjusted and continues to adjust. The past history provides data that is predictive of present and future patterns; even more important, it must be seen as functionally related to the present. In other words, the present personality is determined both by the circumstances of the moment and by past history.

If we have a theory of personality development, we can analyze the past events in a person's life in terms of it. Certain experiences will assume a certain influence in development. We can look for certain types of family relationships or of child-rearing practices to result in certain types of adult behavior patterns or adjustive processes. These expectations can be then empirically checked. We may find, for example, that rigid toilet-training practices in early life (or severe discipline) are associated with meticulous, orderly, rigid, and compulsive behavior patterns in later life. Our theories are constantly being suggested by empirical observation and, in turn, tested by subsequent observation and experimentation.

One of the great technical problems concerning the case history is the reliability of the information obtained about a person's past. The data frequently depend upon a person's memory or the memory of persons who knew him, and this information is extremely fallible. Studies, like that of Doering and Raymond (1935) on the reliability of information given by mothers of sixty patients of the Boston Psychopathic Hospital, show that, even in factual items like date of birth and high-school grade, errors of information were made by 11 per cent of the mothers. In more threatening and ambiguous items involving hereditary factors (for example, incidents of mental disease in the family), 26 per cent of the mothers gave incorrect information. Thus the information derived for the case history is frequently biased and in error, and one source must be continually checked against another. The use of objective records, such as baby books, school records, police-court records, and military information, offers some checks on the reliability of the information.

In a behavioristic view of the impact of the life situation, it is of vital importance to discover the objective facts about the event. Only then can the role of the objective stimulus be assessed in the determination of the future behavior patterns. On the other hand, in a phenomenological orientation, the actual facts are not as important as the person's conception of them. In other words, it may not be so crucial to know whether a person had an accepting or rejecting mother as whether he conceived of his mother as rejecting or accepting. Of course, the comparison of the objective and subjective information can be extremely informative about personality characteristics, often revealing a person's tendencies to distort reality in certain ways.

Far more difficult even than the identification of facts is the problem of interpreting the data obtained. Developmental psychologists must develop adequate conceptions of developmental processes and the conditions that determine them if the case-history method is to be a useful one in personality assessment. For example, one must be able to answer the extremely complicated question: What significance for a person's life pattern can we attribute to parental divorce when the person was, say, nine years old? If we say it is an important and damaging influence, then how do we deal with the observation that many apparently well-adjusted persons have a history of parental divorce? Divorce in one family is severely traumatic to one or several of the children, and in another it is dealt with effectively and can even give rise to the development of certain personality strengths.

The problem of the significance of past events is extremely complicated and presents a great challenge to the research psychologist. Each single event in a life history must be considered in relation to other events as well as to resources within the person. It is much easier to explain mental disorder after we have noted that a mentally disturbed patient has had certain pathogenic experiences than it is to predict in advance the impact of such events.

The technique of the case history and the problems associated with it require, for a thorough exposition, a more detailed discussion than is feasible here. There are many sources to which the reader can go to explore the problem. Some of these sources have been listed by Shaffer and Lazarus (1952), who reprinted some standard outlines for the case history, one of which is found in Louttit. Such an outline can be greatly expanded or varied. Louttit's version of a case-history outline (1947, p. 68) is as follows:

A. Personal history
    1. Present
        a. Description of behavior
        b. Physical condition
        c. Performance ability and achievement
        d. Living conditions
    2. Past
        a. Birth and infancy
        b. Health
        c. Education
        d. Other experiences and activities

B. Family history
    1. Parents, siblings, and others living in the home
    2. Grandparents and collateral relatives not living in the home

Another version of a case-history outline is presented by Richards (1946, pp. 22–25):

Identifying data
Genetic history
Personal history
    Environmental factors
    Infant habits
    Physical illness
    School history
    Work history
    History of delinquency
    Psychosexual development
    Social history
    Behavioral history
    Use of drugs

A much fuller history is in a form for an autobiography illustrated by Shaffer and Lazarus (1952, pp. 74–76). It shows the kinds of data regarded by psychologists as important antecedents of the present personal status:

FORM FOR AUTOBIOGRAPHY

DIRECTIONS. Please glance over this outline to get a general idea of what is required, and then write your autobiography without consulting it. When you have finished writing, read over the outline carefully and add, as a supplement, whatever information you omitted in your original account.

FAMILY HISTORY

(a) Parents: (1) Race, education, economic and social status, occupations, interests, opinions and general temperament, state of health. (2) General home atmosphere (harmony or discord). What was the attitude of each of your parents toward you (affectionate, oversolicitous, domineering, possessive, nagging, anxious, indifferent, etc.)? Attachment to family (close or distant), favorite parent; fantasies about parents; disappointments and resentments. Which parent do you most resemble? Discipline in home, punishment, reactions to punishment.
Moral and religious instruction.
Special enjoyments at home.
(b) Sisters and brothers:
Order of birth; characteristics of each.
Attachments and resentments; conflicts.
Do you feel superior or inferior to sisters and brothers?

(*c*) Larger family circle. Grandparents and relatives.

(*d*) Physical surroundings of youth. City or country; nature of home.

PERSONAL HISTORY

Date and place of birth.

Nature of birth (natural or Caesarean; short or long labor).

Time of weaning.

First experience you can remember.

Recollections of each parent during your early years. Did you feel secure and at peace in your relationship to them?

(*a*) Early development. Was it precocious or retarded? When did walking and talking begin?

Illnesses.

Habits: Thumbsucking, nail-biting, bed-wetting, stammering, convulsions; tantrums, fears, nightmares, sleepwalking, revulsions, finickiness about food.

Play: Toys and animals; other children.

Fantasies of self; favorite stories and heroes.

General attitude: Was your general attitude adaptive (cooperative and obedient); aggressive (competitive and assertive); timid (sensitive and fearful); guileful (teasing and wily); refractory (negative and resistant)?

(*b*) School and college history:

Age at entrance; age at graduation.

Scholastic record; best and worst subjects.

Friendships (many or few, casual or deep); quarrels; moodiness and solitariness.

Association with group (shy, submissive, genial, confident, forward, boisterous, aggressive).

Ambition and ideals.

Hero-worship: Were there any particular people (historical or contemporary) whom you attempted to imitate? What qualities did you particularly admire?

Interests and amusements.

SEX HISTORY

(*a*) Early knowledge. Curiosity about the body, especially about sex differences.

What theories did you hold about childbirth?

When did you discover about the sex relations of your parents? Were you shocked?

Sexual instruction.

(*b*) Early practices: masturbation, relations with the same or the opposite sex. Did you play sex games with sister or brother? Did you want to see others naked or display your own body?

(*c*) Puberty experiences of a sexual nature. Have you ever been in love? How often? Did you quarrel? What type of person was selected?

(*d*) Erotic fantasies; reveries of ideal mate. What kind of activity was imagined as specially pleasurable?

(*e*) What emotions accompanied or followed sex experiences (anxiety, shame, remorse, revulsion, satisfaction)

(*f*) What is your attitude toward marriage?

MAJOR EXPERIENCES

Positive (events accompanied by great elation; success and joy).

Negative (events accompanied by great depression and discomfort; frights, humiliations, failures, transgressions).

Aims and aspirations: What are your chief aims for the immediate future? If you could (within reason) remodel the world to your heart's desire, how would you have it and what role would you like to play in such a world?

Estimate of self and world: State briefly what you believe to be: (1) Your general estimate of and attitude toward the social world; (2) The world's estimate of and attitude toward you; (3) Your general estimate of yourself.

This autobiography indicates the kinds of past experiences that have generally been considered relevant in personality development. Different theoretical systems emphasize or deemphasize various features of this history. Undoubtedly, events not categorized in this autobiography can also be relevant, although the outline permits the inclusion of almost anything a person conceives to be of significance or to have had an important impact upon him.

The autobiography is phenomenologically oriented because it depends upon how a person conceives his past history and his life orientations. Undoubtedly changes in theoretical bias will alter the nature of an autobiographical technique. For example, the inclusion of a large section on sexual history reflects the Freudian influence on clinical thought and technique. A cognitive developmental point of view might lead to a greater emphasis on evidences of social adequacy and maturity (developmental level), as exemplified in the social maturity scale of Phillips and Cowitz (1953), which is a somewhat different case-history approach (see Table 19). A Rankian approach would place greater stress on the dependence-independence struggle.

It is possible that, for some persons, dependency conflicts are the most important consideration in the adjustive struggle; for others, sexual factors should be emphasized; for still others, the management of hostility is the most important single factor underlying the psychological development. In studying a person, it is important to consider which of the many sources of conflict have played primary roles in the development of the present personality and how this can be integrated within a com-

Table 19

Occupation-Education

	Rating
1. *Educational level*	
Some postgraduate work	6
College graduate	5
Completed technical school or one or more years of college	4
High-school graduate	3
Some high school	2
Six to eight grades of school	1
Five or fewer grades of school	0
2. *Job level*	
Managerial, professional	3
Skilled (D.O.T.* 4 and 5)	2
Semiskilled (D.O.T. 6 and 7)	1
Unskilled (D.O.T. 8 and 9)	0
3. *Job responsibility*	
Inventive-creative; e.g., artist; research worker, but not technician	3
Wide range of freedom, must adapt to changing conditions; e.g., office manager; insurance salesman	2
Sets up own job but supervisor available for unusual conditions and emergencies, e.g., production worker; radio repairman	1
Routine work, minimum of individual freedom; e.g., postal clerk; assembly-line worker	0
4. *Level of supervision*	
Head of company which employs ten or more workers; head of department which includes skilled workers	4
Head of company which employs less than ten workers; head of department which includes semiskilled workers	3
In charge of a group of unskilled workers	2
Has helper when needed	1
Never has command	0
5. *Gain in job level (1942–1952)*	
Upper third of distribution	2
Middle third of distribution	1
Lower third of distribution	0
6. *Salary increase (1942–1952)*	
Upper third of distribution	2
Middle third of distribution	1
Lower third of distribution	0
7. *Striving for advancement*	
Desire and intense activity; e.g., letters written about jobs; interviews applied for; contacts for better position actively sought	3

Table 19 (*Continued*)

Desire and tentative activity; e.g., is interested in another job if offered; keeps eyes open; does not seek a job; does not write, although may look through ads; has vague long-range goals   2

Desire but no activity; e.g., says he would like a change but does nothing   1

No desire and no activity   0

8. *Time spent in off-the-job work*

Additional job   3

Often does part-time work but no regular additional job   2

Sporadic part-time work   1

No part-time work   0

Father-subject comparisons (scales 9 through 12)

Scores on these scales are obtained by subtracting father's rating from subject's rating on the following scales: (1) Education level, (2) Job level, (3) Job responsibility, (4) Level of supervision.

Brother-subject comparisons (scales 13 and 14)

Scores on these scales are obtained by subtracting the median score of the subject's brothers from that of the subject on the following scales: (1) Educational level, (2) Job level.

Sex and marriage

---

15. *Psychosexual level*

The following criteria are used:

a. Age of marriage within three years of the median of the total group

b. Age of first sexual intercourse within three years of the median of the total group

c. Length of courtship between 6 months and 3½ years

All criteria met   2

Two criteria met   1

Less than two criteria met   0

16. *Marital status*

Married   1

Divorced, separated, or single   0

17. *Independence from parents after marriage*

The following criteria are used:

a. No financial assistance from parental figures

b. Has not lived with parental figures

c. Sees parental figures less than once a week (includes working with father)

Number of criteria met: All, two, one, none are rated respectively 3, 2, 1, 0.

Table 19 (*Continued*)

Parental figures are defined as subject's parents, wife's parents, or, if own parents are dead, older siblings. A brief stay with parents while subject is moving is not considered a violation of criterion *b*.

18. *Planning for children*

The following criteria are used:

    a. All children planned for, past and future

    b. One child born within five years of marriage

    c. Plans for, or has, two or more children

All criteria met	5
Criterion *a* and either *b* or *c*	4
Criterion *a* and neither *b* nor *c*	3
Criterion *a* but one birth not planned, and either *b* or *c*	2
No planning in the past but planning for the future regardless of whether *b* and *c* are met	1
No planning, regardless of whether *b* and *c* are met	0

19. *Disciplining of children*

Parents share disciplining; e.g., "Whoever is around does it"	2
Assumes responsibility for most disciplining; e.g., "We both do, but mostly me"	1
Rarely assumes the responsibility for disciplining	0

20. *Family finances*

The following criteria are used:

    a. Mutual consideration of expenditures

    b. Subject pays some bills other than characteristically male expenditures, such as car, workshop

Both criteria met	2
Either criterion met	1
Neither criterion met	0

Social relations

21. *Type of organization*

If subject belongs to more than one organization, the organization with the higher rating determines his score

Belongs to organizations where membership results in service to community; e.g., PTA, Community Chest, Red Cross	1
Belongs to organizations where membership is primarily beneficial to self; e.g., Elks, Knights of Columbus, sports clubs	0

22. *Number of organizations*

Belongs to four or more	2
Belongs to two or three	1
Belongs to one or none	0

Table 19 (*Continued*)

23. *Organizational attendance*
    Regular   2
    Infrequent   1
    Never   0
24. *Organizational leadership*
    Within the past year has held:
    Executive position   2
    Minor position; e.g., committee member   1
    No position   0
25. *Habitual recreational activity*
    The following criteria for habitual recreational activity are used:
    a. Self-educative; e.g., course work, home study
    b. Constructive; e.g., repairing equipment, building, painting
    c. Requires training or skill; e.g., choral singing, playing musical
        instrument
    Meets any of the above   2
    Meets none of the above, but engages in participant recreation;
      e.g., fishing, golf, chess, cards   1
    Meets none of the above, and activities restricted to spectator
      recreation; e.g., viewing television, casual reading   0
26. *Social participation and leadership*
    The following criteria are used:
    a. States he has at least one close friend
    b. Participates in social gatherings at least once a month
    c. Indicates he is more than just a passive follower in social groups
    Number of criteria met: All, two, one, none are rated respectively
      3, 2, 1, 0.

---

* *Dictionary of Occupational Titles*, Vols. I and II, Washington, D.C.: Superintendent of Documents, 1949. SOURCE: Phillips & Cowitz, 1953.

prehensive theory. The scientific study of human personality development and one of its most important tools, the case history, are both still in the early stages.

The Interview

The interview is one of the most important techniques of personality assessment. It offers tremendous versatility, because the interviewer is free to roam over a wide variety of topics. At the same time he can be responsive to direct evidences of stress and ego defenses on the part of the interviewee, and he can tailor his procedures to these signs. For the same reason, however, the problem of the reliability of the information and the interpretation of it is most difficult, for rarely will two interview procedures be the same. Its very flexibility is its greatest source of confusion.

There are many types of interviews and many uses to which an interview can be put. Interviews can be therapeutic in purpose, a means of giving information, or a technique for obtaining information. In personality assessment, the interview is a source of information.

As in the case history, the information from the interview can be approached as potentially objective in nature; it can be assumed that the person tells us the facts of his behavior and the truth about his attitudes and beliefs. Such an assumption of objectivity is always hazardous, because these facts are likely to be distorted by personal defenses. Also we can regard the interview as an opportunity for a person to give us his personal view of himself, the world, and his past experience through introspections about them. Thus, to some extent, the interview provides us with a picture of how the individual conceives of these things (and what he is willing to tell about this) rather than an objective representation. A person must first be willing to expose his feelings and conceptions, and he must also have reasonable insight in order to describe his phenomenal self accurately.

Various devices of interviewing can be utilized to maximize the likelihood that a person will present an undistorted picture. One of the best treatments of the interview process from this point of view has been provided by Carl Rogers (1942), who stressed nondirectiveness and an atmosphere of acceptance to facilitate a person's examination of his phenomenal field. Rogers has effectively codified the wisdom of therapeutic interviewers of many different theoretical schools into important principles of interviewing. These insights are so basic that they can be illustrated in the ordinary interplay that might take place between friends.

Bill is having family troubles and is expressing some of these to a friend, picturing his dilemma and describing the impossibility of the situation. He describes an impasse with his father over his relationship with a girl, and his father's unreasonable insistence that he give her up. He expresses his bitter feelings toward his father and the difficulty he is having in dealing with the conflict.

Imagine the situation if the listening friend, John, begins to criticize Bill's disobedience and hostile attitudes toward the father. Bill is likely under such circumstances to become defensive or even hostile and to terminate the discussion because of John's criticism.

In contrast, suppose that John questions Bill's acceptance of the paternal control and criticizes him for not simply ignoring it, continuing the relationship with the girl, and possibly even leaving the family home to establish adult independence. Again the discussion is likely to bog down in an argument over what is the right or possible thing to do, and little progress will occur beyond the initial statements.

On the other hand, if John responds with sympathy and acceptance of his friend's dilemma, reflecting without criticism, as Rogers suggested, only the feelings and content of what has been said, deeper explorations of Bill's feelings are more apt to occur, because he has less need to be defensive and appears to have the interest and support of his friend. It may then be possible for him ultimately to discover the nature of his dilemma; that he cannot accept the passive and dependent role in his relationship with his father any more than he is freely able to move out on his own and lose the paternal support and approval.

By accepting what a person says in an interested and sympathetic manner and by reflecting his feelings, Rogers believed that the way is gradually paved for the uncovering and understanding of his real feelings and attitudes.

In order to reduce the unreliability of the interview as an assessment tool, standardized interviews have been developed in which each interviewee is approached in the same fashion or with the same questions. This procedure makes the stimulus to which each interviewee must respond more uniform. Under these conditions, personal differences under assessment can less often be attributed to differences in interviewer technique and to the type of material being covered.

The evidence shows clearly that the standardized interview yields higher agreement between interviewers. The difficulty, however, is that such an interview does not allow for a free interchange between persons on the detailed problems of the subject's unique feelings (which often reveals underlying patterns in conflict with initially expressed verbalizations).

The differential consequences of the two approaches to interviewing is beautifully illustrated in a recorded interview by Redlich and Gill (1954). A woman patient in an initial interview at an outpatient clinic bitterly complains about the failure of her marriage, which she considers the result of her husband's inadequacies. During the interview the therapist probes her feelings extensively and skillfully presses her to consider what her own role in the marital failure has been. About halfway through the interview the discussion shifts from her husband as the agent of the marital discord to her own personal problems. Ultimately, through the persistence of the therapist, the patient reveals a fact that had been concealed for three-quarters of an hour of the interview and one that she has the greatest difficulty talking about. After long, suspenseful pauses and digressions, she finally indicates that she was pregnant by another man while she was going with her present husband. After a miscarriage of that baby, she and her husband were married, and she has continually felt that he held her illicit affair and pregnancy over her head. The episode further indicated a loveless relationship from the start.

In her struggle to bring up this fact, which was so difficult for her to discuss, she points out that she had an earlier psychiatric interview that was quite different from the present one. She describes it as the usual kind of question-and-answer affair, and she confesses that she had a tendency at that time to cover up. In the earlier interview the opportunity had not been provided for her to elaborate her deeper feelings fully and in her own way. The personal interaction provided by the later interview, with its flexible techniques and opportunity to follow the patient and probe each important feeling, revealed a totally different picture, not only of the attitudes of the person, but also of the actual facts of her relationship with her husband.

The importance of the interview to the personality psychologist cannot be overstressed. It probably plays the most significant role of any clinical procedure in eliciting personal information. Used to its fullest advantage, it is an interpersonal experience that has qualities quite different from any other sources of information available. It is potentially the most flexible technique available, although this very flexibility tends to decrease the reliability of the observations and judgments made from it.

The importance of the interview is highlighted by the fact that it is often the chief means of evaluating other assessment techniques or diagnostic tools. It is used in psychotherapy, where the interview procedures are extended over a long period of time, intensively sampling the behavior patterns and feelings of the person under study. In therapy, the interviewer is concerned less with getting information and more with producing changes in the personality of the patient.

Used as a flexible interpersonal interaction rather than a standardized test, the interview fits well into a depth-oriented personality theory. It assumes that a skillful interviewer can infer a person's stable personality organization. It is usually less concerned with the direct data of what the patient says and more oriented toward the underlying hypothetical processes or substance characteristics of the personality that such statements reflect. It emphasizes the judgment of the clinician in interpreting the behavior of the person within the context of personality theory. The psychologist must focus his observation on certain features of what a person says, ignoring or deemphasizing others. He must integrate the various statements and behaviors of the interviewee into a pattern that provides some understanding of the underlying structure and dynamics of the individual.

This does not mean that this analysis, which is essentially a theoretical construction about an individual case in relation to some general theoretical system, is not subject to empirical consequences. The ultimate basis of the inferences derived by the interviewer must be in empirical relationships consonant with theoretical derivations.

Although it is true that, like the case history and autobiography, the interview can be, and often is, a source of factual information about past history, it may not be the most important kind of information sought in the interview situation.[1] We are often less interested in what actually happened at some particular time than in the attitudes of the patient to these events in his life. The accuracy or inaccuracy of the patient's report is important only so far as it gives us some insight into the interpretation of the experience, for it is the interpretation that determines behavior rather than the event itself. By noting, in the face-to-face situation, what a patient avoids in his discussion, what he believes, and what his emotional reaction to the material is, a great deal of information can be derived concerning his motivations and his ego-defense mechanisms.

A simple illustration might be in order here. A student complained that he could not seem to get any pleasure out of his studies. In the course of the interview he explained that he was particularly pained about this because in high school studying was a great source of satisfaction to him. Now it was all he could do to force himself to sit down and read his textbooks. Later in the hour he further elaborated, by way of illustrating what he could really do academically, that for a while in high school he had been doing very poorly. He became ashamed of himself, suddenly made a very intensive effort at studying, and by dint of extraordinary effort pulled his average up to the highest in his class. "Of course," he added, "I nearly got a nervous breakdown doing it."

Seeing in this statement and in other material that came out in the interview the possible recognition of the true state of affairs (that this student really did not enjoy studying but was being pushed very hard to be intellectually successful by his mother and by his strong feelings of inadequacy), the interviewer responded, "Then you really never did enjoy studying, inasmuch as it was such a great effort for you in high school." The student's response to this interpretation was most vehement. "Oh," he said, "but I loved to study. It's just that *now* I can't seem to get any pleasure out of it."

It becomes clear from this interview that the student did not realistically perceive his motivation to study in high school or college. It was too important to him to believe that he was intellectual, just like his self-taught mother, whose intellectual virtues he extolled for about fifteen minutes. He could not yet afford to recognize that he had been able to work in high school only with the exertion of tremendous effort, almost to the point of the development of a nervous breakdown. The diagnostic aspect of the interview produced mainly some information about the student's motivations, sources of anxiety, and defense mechanisms. It hardly produced a realistic picture of his high-school experience with studying, if we were to take his descriptions completely at

[1] Most of the material on pp. 399–400 has been adapted from G. W. Shaffer & R. S. Lazarus. *Fundamental Concepts in Clinical Psychology.* New York: McGraw-Hill, 1952. Pp. 83–84.

face value. This is where the diagnostic interview shines—in giving us a picture (by inference from verbal inconsistencies, etc.) of an individual's personality dynamics rather than factual data about his previous experience.

With respect to valid judgments of an individual case, not only is every case embedded in the general rules of human behavior, but also there is an opportunity to verify these judgments in succeeding sessions with the same person. In long-term psychotherapy, for example, the interviewer can continually check and revise his early inferences against what develops in subsequent sessions. Thus, the therapist has one tremendous advantage over the typical personality assessor, because the latter may see a person for periods as short as a total of thirty minutes up to perhaps a forty-eight–hour period and the former can work with a patient for thousands of hours over a period of years.

The Psychological Test

In a sense psychological tests are standardized interviews. They allow us to measure the ability, achievement, or personality characteristics of an individual with reference to other comparable persons. The content and procedure of an interview vary with the person being assessed as well as with the interviewer, but tests are given under essentially similar conditions. The items given to each subject are identical or equivalent. The data, showing how many persons of particular kinds do on the items (these are called *norms*), enable us to compare an individual with others without dependence upon memory and frequently with a minimum of subjective judgment. The essential difference between the test and the interview is in this standardization, which increases the objectivity of the measurement and minimizes situational factors in the behavior observed. We can illustrate these qualities of tests as follows: if we wanted to know how much information a man has, we might ask him a number of questions, such as: Who is President of the United States? or What is the equator?[2] The answers we would get from our series of questions would tell us very little by themselves. What we usually want to know is how much this man knows compared with other men. We may wish to compare him with men of a certain age range, or with men with a given amount of education, or with men who have sustained injuries to their brains. In any case, knowing how much absolute information he has is of no value unless we can relate it to some standard. Therefore, it is also necessary to find out the amount of information other men with the specified characteristics have.

[2] Most of the material on pp. 400–401 has been adapted from G. W. Shaffer & R. S. Lazarus. *Fundamental Concepts in Clinical Psychology.* New York: McGraw-Hill, 1952. Pp. 85–86.

To Jones we might put the question: What are diamonds made of? We might ask Smith: What is the capital of Afghanistan? We next observe that Jones does better than Smith, and we might conclude that he has more information. If we are assessors of wide experience, we can call upon our memory of conversations with other persons and note that Jones appears to have more information than Smith but less than about one-quarter of the others. By now the acute reader has begun to see some of the basic reasons why we use standardized tests. In the first place the question we asked Jones was a great deal easier than the one we put to Smith. In this case the discrepancy is obvious, but in other instances we might not be able to make an accurate guess without empirically determining the difficulty of the questions. If we try the same items on everyone, we might do better. However, then we run into the problem of finding questions that do not favor one man over another because of his occupation or specialized education. We relied on our memory to tell us where Jones stood with respect to other men. But our memory is fallible, and our experience is limited. Consequently we need standards that we can always refer to in making statements about our subject's standing in a group. These standards are called "norms."

Just as our memory is limited, our judgment is subject to bias. Because our estimate of Jones's level of information was a subjective one, if we did not like Jones's manner we might unwittingly think less of him and rate him lower than we ought to. The element of subjectivity is therefore a source of error in clinical evaluation. One way to eliminate this bias is to use objective tests that reduce or eliminate subjective judgment in scoring. However, because these kinds of tests are often not the most fruitful for gaining information about personality, it is possible to use tests in which the subjective element is present but can be measured. For example, we can measure how much agreement there is between several assessors' interpretations of subjective-test performance. We might call this way of assessing a test's objectivity "observer reliability."

There are many important characteristics of tests. Two of the most important have to do with what the test measures; these characteristics are *reliability* and *validity*.

Test reliability: A single administration of a test represents one sample of a person's behavior. If we repeated these measurements on other occasions, we would arrive at a different score each time for the same attribute. This variation is the result of accidental factors and inaccuracies in the measuring instrument. The problem, of course, is to obtain as close an estimation of the subject's true score as possible; if the test is unreliable, the subject may be at the top end of the distribution of subjects today and tomorrow he may fall near the bottom. Whether we said he scored high or low in some characteristic would then depend upon which day we tested him. Consequently, high reliability in a test is an essential characteristic.

The reliability of the test can be estimated in a variety of ways. It is often represented by a correlation between two administrations of the same test, by the use of equivalent forms of the test, or by correlating equivalent halves of the test. In order to make accurate estimates of a person's true score, the reliability of the test must be high; otherwise interpretations of an individual score on a single administration are hazardous and can actually give the wrong information. When we construct psychological tests assessing personality characteristics, we attempt to reduce this error or variation around the true score, making the reliability as high as possible. An unreliable test can never give us a valid measure of a personality attribute because we can never know how far the actual measurement deviates from what it would be if the test were a reliable measure. Low reliability might mean that the characteristic being measured was extremely subject to the influence of transient conditions. In personality assessment, we are interested in traits that operate consistently over a wide range of circumstances.

Test validity: It is affirming the obvious to say that, to be useful, a test must measure what it is supposed to. If a test is reliable, we know it measures something consistently even if we cannot say what it is. A test is valid if we have evidence that it measures some specified variable. A test has predictive validity if we can show that the score on the test predicts some aptitude in which we are interested. For example, in a test for aptitude for college work, we must be able to show that, when administered to college freshmen, it really permits us to predict with reasonable accuracy how students will do in their later academic work.

However, if the test is intended to measure some hypothetical structure within the individual, such as a particular motivation or mechanism of defense, we speak of the test validity as *construct validity.* That is, the test is not necessarily devised to permit empirical prediction of behavior but rather to assess the usefulness of some hypothetical process of the personality. This is a somewhat different sense of the term "validity," because the validity of the construct can never be absolutely proved in this way but only evaluated as to usefulness in terms of its consonance with empirical observation. To determine the construct validity of the test, we must be able to deduce from the presence of the hypothetical process how an individual should behave. Thus, if we assume we are measuring motivation to succeed or to achieve, as opposed to motivation to be accepted and liked by others, then we can deduce how a person should act in certain situations as a consequence of this motivation. A person with a high achievement motivation (as inferred from some test behavior) should exhibit more active and intense striving toward success, perhaps in college by giving evidence of a great deal more effort in study-ing. On the other hand, if we are inferring strong affiliation motivation, such a person should be consistently oriented in his behavior toward others, knowing them well, being liked by them, and, in turn, liking others. If this type of prediction fails, then our inference is inadequate.

It must be remembered that the other sources of information that we have discussed, the interview and the case history, have characteristics that make them similar in some ways to tests. From both we are trying to assess personality characteristics from which predictive statements about future behavior can be made. The problems of measurement men-tioned with respect to the interview apply equally well to them, just as the same problems are relevant to the measurement of blood pressure, metabolic rate, the weight of some chemical compound, or the thickness of hair. Such measures must first be reliable. They must also be valid in the sense that their interpretation can be supported by other deduced observable behavior characteristics.

Types of Tests

There are many ways of classifying personality assessment tests. For example, they can be classified by the kind of process they are supposed to measure, such as general intelligence, special aptitudes, interests, at-titudes, degree of pathology, motive patterns, and defense mechanisms. Another classification is on the basis of types of items, for example, those emphasizing the manipulation of words (called *verbal tests*), or those dealing with designs and geometric forms (*nonverbal* or *performance tests*). Mode of administration is another basis of classification, as in in-dividual tests versus group tests. Or they can be classified into speed tests and into those in which speed is not a factor (power tests).

One fundamental basis of classification is the opportunity provided for variable responses by the subject. Some tests are designed to elicit pri-marily a yes or no answer or a choice from several clearly designated alternatives, such as multiple-choice items. In these cases the stimulus is relatively unambiguous, and the response required of the subject leaves little room for individual differences in personality to be expressed. These are called *psychometric* or *objective tests*. In contrast with psychometric tests are those designed so that the variability of response between per-sons is great. The stimuli are usually ambiguous and permit each subject to interpret or structure it in his own way, thus evoking personality char-acteristics that are somewhat unique to him. These are called *projective tests*. They attempt to obtain more information about the person's unique way of looking at the world, and because of this, the assessor or diag-nostician must use his own judgment a great deal in interpreting the responses. The projective tests tend to sacrifice such virtues of the psychometric tests as objectivity, simplicity, and economy in favor of behavior that potentially reflects the subject's unique orientation to the world and his psychodynamics.

In discussing personality assessment by means of tests, let us classify them into three types, which tend to cut across some of the distinctions just made. The use of direct observation of behavior in *naturalistic and standardized situations* is discussed first, then the *self-report techniques* (primarily questionnaires) are dealt with, and finally the *projective techniques* are considered.

Direct behavior study: The behavior-study approach to personality assessment involves making inferences about personality, or predictive statements about behavior, on the basis of direct observations of how a person behaves in sample situations. We can distinguish two types of situations in which it is possible to make observations of human behavior. One involves observation of an individual in a *natural setting;* that is, in a situation in which he behaves in his real-life circumstances without any necessary awareness that he is being observed. The second may be referred to as the *standardized test setting,* in which the observer produces a somewhat more artificial setting, simulating real life, and standardizes it so that all the subjects are exposed to essentially the same external stimulus conditions.

The advantage of the naturalistic observation lies in its uncontrived qualities and the fact that the scientist's observation does not greatly alter the behavior of the person being studied. We all know that being watched, for example, by a superior evaluating our work, provides a very different atmosphere than is the case when working without such external constraining influences. The observer in the naturalistic observation tries not to interfere with the event he is attempting to observe.

On the other hand, the advantage of the standardized test situation is that, like any test, it always approaches a constant for every subject, and we can more legitimately compare the reactions of different persons because the circumstances to which they are exposed are the same. Moreover, we need not wait until the event takes place naturally, but we can construct beforehand the situation in which we desire to examine a person's reactions. Thus, we can make behavior observations in the laboratory under far better control than might be the case in the field. However, it is often dangerous to assume that we can make the interpretive jump from the laboratory situation to the naturalistic situation, and it is often difficult to know to what extent our assessments are determined by the contrived quality of our experimental observation.

An excellent example of the comparison between the naturalistic and the laboratory approach to problems in personality is reflected in some of the research dealing with psychological stress. Various public health research agencies have sent teams of professional psychologists and psychiatrists to areas of the country where disaster had struck in order to understand better the impact of the stressor conditions on those involved (Wallace, 1956). Just after the destructive tornado of June, 1953, in Worcester, Mass., the reactions of the victims, some of whom were either severely injured or had lost family and home, were observed (see Figure 33). Similar studies were made in Texas City following the terrible explosion there in 1947, of the Cocoanut Grove fire in Boston, and of other similar disasters. These are all examples of a naturalistic approach. Janis (1958) has made observations of persons facing the stress of surgery, especially of one woman who was undergoing psychoanalysis at a time when major surgery was required. In most respects, these studies of Janis's were also naturalistic because the observations were made at a time when the natural stressor conditions were prevailing, and the observer did his best to avoid biasing by his presence the information received.

This is in sharp contrast with laboratory experiments in which subjects have been systematically exposed to experimentally induced stresses in

Figure 33. Effects of the Worcester tornado of 1953. The picture shows rescue workers locating a dazed and injured woman in the debris of her home following the tornado. The stress produced by the disaster frequently yielded confusion and bizarre patterns of behavior which lasted for many hours. (*Wide World Photos.*)

an effort to understand similar processes. But the advantages of both approaches, as well as their disadvantages, are well remarked here. The naturalistic observers (such as the public health teams) had to wait until the disaster conditions happened in order to study the problem. They could not usually be on the spot until after the first shock had taken place and had to depend upon the reports of untrained observers. They could not produce conditions whose effect could be predicted on the basis of earlier information about the participants. However, they did deal with a completely true-to-life situation of great intensity and poignancy, whereas the laboratory worker can only produce relatively mild disturbances (for practical as well as ethical reasons) under the artifical setting demanded of an experiment. It must be said, in any case, that the laboratory scientist could maintain a much higher degree of control over the circumstances so generalizations could be made without the confounding influence of many diverse and difficult-to-measure conditions not directly related to the stressor conditions. It should be clear that there is a place for both kinds of assessment procedures. One is not likely to replace the other because each contributes a different perspective on the problem.

Difficult as it is to produce satisfactory standardized test or laboratory situations in which there is adequate realism, it is equally difficult to find adequate ways to observe and measure the nature of the subject's reactions. If the task of any observer were to count up the number of hits a subject makes on a target-pursuit test or to determine how many questions on a pencil-and-paper test he has answered yes to, little difficulty in measurement would be encountered.[3] Yet even this kind of observation is subject to some error. Special difficulties can be created by the problem of the interpretation of the results. However, when the task of the observer is to select from a complex behavior situation those features that are relevant or significant and then to interpret them in accord with some theoretical system, the problems encountered by the scientific observer are really multiplied.

One of the chief problems of observation and measurement is observer reliability. Observers not only make many errors of observation of what has actually happened, but they tend to focus on different aspects of the event and frequently interpret the subject's reactions in different ways. The use of motion pictures and tape recordings greatly facilitates the task of the observer in that he has a permanent record and can check up on his remembered impressions. When such permanent recordings are available, the problem changes from one of observing to one of judging. It is necessary to obtain a reasonably high degree of agreement between

[3] The material in this paragraph has been adapted from G. W. Shaffer & R. S. Lazarus. *Fundamental Concepts in Clinical Psychology.* New York: McGraw-Hill, 1952. P. 210.

several judges who are rating the behavior of persons under observation or making inferences about underlying processes. If the judges cannot agree about what is going on and what it means, then any conclusions must be of doubtful value.

In the behavior-study technique, the observer becomes the instrument of measurement and evaluation, and an important methodological problem arises—to discover something about the characteristics of observers, the kinds of things on which agreement is possible, and the training required to obtain reasonable agreement. The evidence is clear (Wolf & Murray, 1937) that higher agreement will be obtained when judgments are made about outward characteristics like aggressiveness than about characteristics of a person's private experience. Social psychologists are now becoming extremely interested in the very important problem of how we form personal impressions (e.g., Tagiuri & Petrullo, 1958).

Another problem in the behavior-study approach is an adequate sample of an individual's reactions. It is important to know whether a person's reactions on a particular day or in a particular situation are representative, and it is clear that some forms of behavior are more stable than others. We are often placed in the position of having to generalize about a person's behavior or inferred personality structure from a limited sample of observations, and we rarely are in the position of being able to follow a person about in order to assess the consistency of these characteristics in a variety of situations. The more limited the sample of observations, the more limited must be our generalizations. For this reason, the psychotherapist is in an excellent position to make inferences about the personality of his patient, because he sees the patient often over a long period of time and is thus obtaining a considerably larger sample of his reactions.

The behavior-study technique requires, as does any other assessment procedure, adequate normative data or a reference standard by which to compare an individual's reactions to a situation either with himself in other situations or with other persons in the same situations. These norms can be informal in that an experienced personality-assessment psychologist can keep them in his head, so to speak, having developed them out of lengthy experience with persons in certain types of situations. On the other hand, the science of assessment requires elaborate and explicit normative information for systematic research, and this requirement is no less applicable to the behavior-study technique than it is to any other type of psychological test or assessment procedure.

Psychologists interested in personality assessment have developed many techniques designed to solve some of these problems. These techniques are discussed more fully in textbooks of clinical psychology or personality assessment (e.g., Shaffer & Lazarus 1952; Ferguson, 1952). The problem of quantifying and objectifying observations of the activities of persons in naturalistic and test situations can be handled in a variety of ways. Two techniques have been devised that are particularly applicable to children, especially in their nursery schools, but they might readily be employed in some adult situations as well. These techniques are called *time* and *episode sampling.*

In the case of *time sampling,* a person or a group is observed carefully and inconspicuously a specified number of times for a brief period each time. A decision is first made as to what categories of child behavior will be concentrated upon, for example, social participation, leadership, or sympathy. During each of the sampling periods the child's activities are classified; at the end of the series of observations, the number of time periods occupied by a particular type of behavior is evaluated. By such methods it is possible to study human or animal activities, as they are related to particular types of experimental situations, or to consider the stages of development in which these activities emerge. The difficulties in the technique involve the precise and adequate description of the complex behavior pattern observed, and, of course, the technique leads the observer to ignore everything else that is going on except those behavior patterns previously determined as important.

In the similar technique of *episode sampling,* some discrete form of behavior—an episode—such as an argument, a temper tantrum, or asking a question, is studied over a longer period of time than in the case of time sampling. Daily observations might be made for an hour or so over a period of days or weeks. The score is the number of times the episode occurs. The technique is useful only when the episode represents a conspicuous form of behavior that is not readily missed by the observer and occurs frequently enough to justify the lengthy time-sampling procedures. Both the techniques of time sampling and episode sampling are costly in time. With children it is not difficult to make such observations without constraining the children by virtue of the very observation itself, whereas with adults there might be an unfavorable response if it were known they were being observed. Recent use of one-way screens, which permit the subjects to be observed without knowing it, reduce or eliminate the influence of the observer on the behavior. The technique is also ideally suited to the study of groups in social situations or in therapy, where it is not uncommon to have an observer watching the interactions that take place between the persons concerned.

In the clinical diagnostic situation, a variant of time and episode sampling is the use of the *sign approach.* The clinician utilizes a variety of signs or indices in evaluating the status of any particular individual. These signs are like behavior episodes, so to speak, and provide clues to the psychodynamics of the person being considered. The validity of the use of signs depends upon prior observations that the behavior being observed is indicative of the personality characteristics or forms of psychopathology. Thus, observing examples of thought disorder in which there is distortion of the logical processes of thinking can give the clinician a clue that he is dealing with a schizophrenic process, because a hallmark of a schizophrenic disorder is disturbance of the thought process.

Rating scales are also formalized devices for evaluating persons. Such scales permit us to translate our impressions about behavior or personality into roughly quantitative terms. Generally, rating scales contain a list of traits, which judges are asked to consider in relation to a particular person. A person is placed on a scale, for example, of aggressiveness, indicating the degree to which this trait is displayed in certain observational situations (see Figure 34).

The problem of reliability of measurement is dealt with by using several judges and permitting the experimenter or assessor to determine the degree of agreement between the judges. When the judges disagree sharply, there is low reliability and, therefore, a high degree of subjectivity in the ratings. Where the judges manifest a high degree of agreement, we consider the ratings to have a reasonable degree of objectivity. Such objectivity, or agreement between judges, will depend on the simplicity of the characteristic being judged and the clarity with which the behavioral manifestations of the trait are described.

The rating-scale technique can be standardized, and a great deal of

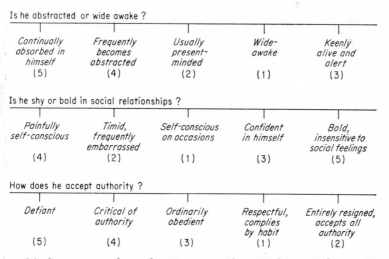

Figure 34. Some items from the Haggerty-Olson-Wickman Behavior Rating Schedules. (*From M. E. Haggerty et al. Haggerty-Olson-Wickman Behavior Rating Schedules. Yonkers, N.Y.: World, 1930. By permission of the American Council on Education.*)

information can be developed about the characteristics being rated because they are the same for a wide variety of samples of persons and situations. There are many such standardized rating scales available. Standardization adds to our information, not only about the reliability of such rating methods, but concerning their validity as well, and it provides norms against which any person can be compared with respect to the characteristics being rated.

There are many classic studies of personality assessment involving the use of standardized test situations and in which a variety of measuring procedures have been employed. One of the best known is a study performed by Hartshorne, May, Maller, and Shuttleworth, published over several years between 1928 and 1930. Techniques were devised for studying honesty and self-control in children in a variety of contexts.

Another extremely interesting study, which highlights the great difficulties that psychologists must meet in this area of behavior study, was conducted by the Office of Strategic Services during World War II (OSS Assessment Staff, 1948). This was an elaborate attempt to work with adults for the specific purpose of identifying in soldiers the qualities that would make a good undercover agent in enemy territory. The OSS assessment staff attempted to study characteristics that might be relevant in espionage, such as leadership, initiative, reaction to authority, and cooperation. Many ingenious situation tests were created and the men involved were evaluated over a period of three days. Continuous observation during these three days was made by the OSS staff, at the end of which time each man was given a total rating.

One of the most interesting and amusing of the situation tests involved putting up a wooden structure. The subject had as assistants OSS psychologists who masqueraded as ordinary GIs and heckled his work while they observed his reactions to this bitterly frustrating situation. The OSS report described a typical dialogue held between a candidate and his two assistants, Kippy (a negative and lazy fellow) and Buster (an eager beaver who is also a constant source of annoyance). The humor of the situation and to some degree its poignancy has caused it to be cited widely in introductory and personality-assessment texts and makes it worth reporting here (OSS Assessment Staff, 1948, p. 105):

CANDIDATE: Well, let's get going.
BUSTER: What is it you want done, exactly? What do I do first?
CANDIDATE: Well, first put some corners together—let's see, make eight of these corners and be sure you pin them like this one.
BUSTER: You mean we both make eight corners or just one of us?
CANDIDATE: You each make four of these, and hurry.
KIPPY: Whacha in, the Navy? You look like one of them curly-headed Navy boys all the girls are after.
CANDIDATE: Er, no, I'm not in anything.
KIPPY: Just a draft dodger, eh?

CANDIDATE: Let's have less talk and more work. You build a square over here and you build one over there.

KIPPY: Who are you talking to—him or me? Why don't you give us a number or something—call one of us number one and the other number two?

CANDIDATE: I'm sorry. What's your name?

BUSTER: Mine's Buster and his is Kippy. What's yours?

CANDIDATE: You can call me Slim.

BUSTER: Not with that shining head of yours. What do they call you, Baldy or Curly? Did you ever think of wearing a toupee?

SLIM: Come on, get to work.

KIPPY: He's sensitive about being bald.

SLIM: Just let's get this thing finished. We haven't much more time. Hey, there, you, be careful. You knocked that pole out deliberately.

KIPPY: Who, me? Now listen to me, you ——, if this —— thing had been built right from the beginning, the poles wouldn't come out. For ——, they send a boy out to do a man's job.

There is little doubt that the highly motivated candidate for acceptance into the OSS team was deeply frustrated and threatened by this situation, in which he knew he was being assessed in terms of leadership potentialities. His reaction might be one of disorganization or anger, and his strenuous efforts to enlist the cooperation of the two observers were important sources of information about how such a person might function in a disastrous situation.

The technical problem here, of course, is validly and reliably assessing the subject's reactions on the assumption that they might help predict future level of functioning in the actual conditions of field operation. Here all the problems of measurement mentioned earlier are brought into sharp focus—problems of what should be observed, what inferences about a person's adaptive resources can be made (construct validity), what agreement is possible between the two judges of the subject's reactions (reliability), and how successfully the assessors can predict future behavior in the field (predictive ability).

The method of direct behavior observation is obviously expensive, because large numbers of personnel are required and relatively small amounts of information are obtained in a given period of time. Psychologists have not yet been outstandingly successful in utilizing this method, but it is clear that its potentialities are very great. We must recognize that we are dealing here with the whole man, a most complicated organism, in a complex social context, and it is a highly ambitious undertaking to attempt this type of assessment. In spite of the ingenuity of such test situations, there is always the problem of whether it represents real-life conditions, with which one is always concerned. There is also the problem of behavioral consistency; that is, what is the range of conditions over which the observed reaction patterns will be found. Yet, more meaningful kinds of behavior can be studied by means of direct observations in naturalistic or test situations than through any other systematic approaches to assessment. The challenge of the behavior-study approach to personality assessment is a great one partly because of the multiplicity of variables to be considered, but the fruits of effective and systematic research into it are potentially very large.

Self-report techniques: Psychologists have developed self-report tests of personality in an effort to be as objective as possible and to avoid some of the obvious pitfalls in the behavior-study approaches. Simply stated, the self-report techniques involve attempting to measure aspects of human personality on the basis of what a person can say, or is willing to say, about himself. They usually consist of a series of printed objective questions presented to the subject or to a group of subjects. Such inventories of questions can be used to study interests, attitudes, and various other facets of personality. They are objective because the subject must respond usually with a "yes," "no," or "I don't know" answer to each question. Thus, little judgment is required of the assessor, who can simply count, for any particular category of the questionnaire, the pattern of answers. These answers yield a single score or a multiple series of scores that can be compared with norms derived from various populations on which the test has been standardized.

The Woodworth Personal Data Sheet, which appeared in 1918, is the modern grandfather of the personality questionnaire. It was actually devised in an effort to select emotionally unstable recruits during the first World War as an antidote to the costly and, at that time, impractical psychiatric screening interview. The questionnaire involves 200 neurotic symptoms, the score being the number of items answered in a pathological direction. The idea seemed so useful that the technique became very popular, and dozens of instruments patterned after the original Woodworth test subsequently appeared. Freeman (1950) pointed out that there are probably around five hundred or so personality questionnaires, the largest number of these duplicating each other. They vary greatly in the amount of systematic research performed on them. Some items from the Woodworth Personal Data Sheet and the more modern Minnesota Multiphasic Personality Inventory are presented in Table 20.

The self-report technique has three major virtues to account for its popularity. These are economy, simplicity, and objectivity. It is economical because it can be administered in groups and, therefore, many persons can be tested at the same time. Because of the simplicity of the answering system it is possible to score such tests by IBM machine or, at the very least, by hand templates, which permit very rapid evaluation of a subject's performance. Performance can often be expressed in a

Table 20

SOME SAMPLE ITEMS FROM THE OLD WOODWORTH PERSONAL DATA SHEET, AND FROM THE MORE MODERN MINNESOTA MULTIPHASIC PERSONALITY INVENTORY

Personal Data Sheet

Have you failed to get a square deal in life?
Is your speech free from stutter or stammer?
Does the sight of blood make you sick or dizzy?
Do people seem to overlook you, that is, fail to notice that you are about?
Do you sometimes wish that you had never been born?
Are you happy most of the time?
Do you find that people understand you and sympathize with you?
Would you rather be with those of your own age than with older people?
Do you nearly always feel that you have strength or energy enough for your work?
Do you feel that you are a little different from other people?
Do people find fault with you much?
Have your thoughts and dreams been free from bad sex stories which you have heard?
Do you feel tired and irritable after a day or evening of visiting and pleasure?
Do you suffer from headaches or dizziness?
Do you ever imagine stories to yourself so that you forget where you are?

SOURCE: Woodworth, 1918.

Minnesota Multiphasic Personality Inventory (mark items true or false)

I work under a great deal of tension.
I have diarrhea once a month or more.
I seldom worry about my health.
Most any time I would rather sit and daydream than to do anything else.
These days I find it hard not to give up hope of amounting to something.
I am certainly lacking in self-confidence.
The sight of blood neither frightens me nor makes me sick.
I frequently find myself worrying about something.
I work under a great deal of tension.
At parties I am more likely to sit by myself or with just one other person than to join in with the crowd.
I very seldom have spells of the blues.
People often disappoint me.

SOURCE: Hathaway & McKinley, 1943.

single or, at the most, a limited number of objectively determined scores. Because of the simplicity of the multiple-choice responses called for, the technique is highly objective. There is no problem of observer reliability to deal with. Except for errors of carelessness in transcribing the scores or counting up the number of answers in each category, there is no basis for disagreement between persons evaluating the test performance. In fact, completely untrained persons can administer and score these tests and often make the standardized interpretations called for by using the normative data. However, the use of such tests by untrained persons is exceedingly dangerous because such persons do not understand fully the limitations of the techniques; the advice or information provided can lead the unwary lay person to act against his best interests.

Along with the advantages of economy, simplicity, and objectivity, there are also some serious disadvantages in the self-report techniques. For one thing, the results of such tests provide no understanding of the basis of the patterns of answers obtained. At best they simply provide a statement about the presence of certain behavioral trends, but the same trends in the patterns of scores can originate for very different reasons in different subjects.

It must also be recognized that a fundamental assumption in the self-report technique is that the introspections of a person, as they are communicated in a test situation, are a sound basis for inferences about his personality. We are dependent, in the self-report approach, on what a person is willing and able to tell us about himself in his answers to various questions. At the same time most of these questionnaires are constructed with striking transparency of meaning, so it is easy for the subject to recognize what the examiner is getting at. It is often clear to the subject which answers are good and which are bad, and he can produce at will nearly any kind of personality picture depending upon how he is motivated. If he wants to create a favorable picture because he is a job applicant, he can usually affect the score accordingly. If he wants to be rejected from military service because of psychopathology, he can make himself look sick and only further assessment may reveal this.

But even assuming that the subject wishes to present an honest picture of himself, this depends upon his knowledge of his own attitudes and his own behavior in various situations. The overaggressive subject may actually conceive of himself as quite compliant by a self-deceptive mechanism. Moreover, because he must answer usually with a "yes," "no," or "I don't know," there is little opportunity for qualification or elaboration of the answers, so a great deal of information is either lost or distorted. Thus, if asked whether he is outgoing and sociable, the subject must say yes or no without being able to specify the conditions under which he is outgoing and the conditions under which he tends to be withdrawn. Finally, there is a considerably high literacy requirement in most of these tests, and if the subject fails to understand the wording of a question, he can misinterpret it and give a false answer.

At one time psychologists were extremely impressed with the advantages of the self-report technique and went overboard for this approach. Psychologists with a behavioristic bent were particularly delighted with the method because its objectivity was high, and they were able to ascertain the predictive validity of the tests without the danger (as they conceived it) of referring to hypothetical and untested personality processes. Additional sophistication and experience showed that the self-report technique of personality assessment did not live up to this early expectation, and for some years, especially in clinical diagnosis, the questionnaire was disavowed and in some instances even considered useless. There appears to be a return to a more realistic point of view on the part of assessment psychologists. They recognize the clear advantages of the self-report technique and, at the same time, the appropriate place of such techniques in the over-all task of assessment. The self-report technique is no longer viewed as a panacea or disregarded entirely. It has an important place in the battery of tools available to clinical and personality-assessment psychologists.

Great improvements have been made over the early self-report techniques that have increased the complexity of the information derived and clarified better the nature of the personality characteristics being measured (e.g., the Minnesota Multiphasic Personality Inventory, Hathaway & McKinley, 1943, and Welsh & Dahlstrom, 1956; and the Edwards Personal Preference Schedule, Edwards, 1954). The problem of the transparency of the questions has been approached, and ways have been devised to reduce or detect the amount of deception that occurs in the answers. There is more sophistication about the conditions that affect scores on the questionnaires, and the scope of questionnaires has been enlarged to include patterns of traits. The best of the modern self-report questionnaires are making a serious bid for primacy of usage in many clinics and personality-assessment centers.

Projective techniques: When personality psychologists became interested in the model of human behavior that emphasized unconscious dynamisms (an outgrowth of the Freudian impact on psychological thought), a very special type of assessment technique began to develop. It was necessary to find a means whereby inferences could be made about the organization of needs and coping mechanisms within an individual. The depth psychologists assumed that such important processes were often not accessible to an individual, so he would not and could not report them to the examiner. The projective technique was a logical outgrowth of this interest in the underlying determinants of behavior. Such inferences could be made from the direct study of behavior in naturalistic and test situations and to some extent from the self-report techniques, but more suitable procedures were still needed.

The rationale for the projective test rests upon the depth psychologist's assumption that, where the reality constraints are limited, as they are in ambiguous stimuli, unconscious dynamics will be reflected in the interpretations and fantasies of the subject. This process by which a person contributes his unique personality in an interpretation of ambiguous stimulus material has been called *projection*. In a sense, a person projects his past experiences and personal dynamics into the stimulus material, so inferences about the underlying dynamics of his personality can be made from the individual differences in this apperceptive process. This is a slightly different use of the term "projection" from "projection" as a defense mechanism, although the two processes are related.

Although projection occurs any time a person must interpret any ambiguous situation or stimulus, special projective tests have been created in which the ambiguous stimuli have been standardized in order that the interpretations of many persons of different personality organization could be used as norms. Let us look a bit more carefully at the theoretical rationale for the projective test.

In attempting to explore approaches to the underlying personality dynamics of neurotic patients, Freud developed the technique of "free association." He assumed that, under the appropriate circumstances, the unconscious motivations and defense mechanisms at the root of the patient's illness must eventually appear in his verbal associations. These associations were, in fact, thought to be controlled or determined by unconscious processes and the nature of these unconscious processes could be inferred. Dreams and slips of the tongue (Freud, 1922, 1938), for example, are manifestations of these unconscious processes. The concepts underlying the use of free association, dreams or fantasies, and slips of the tongue became the theoretical antecedents of projective testing.

If we are asked to view some common and unambiguous object, such as a chair, a pencil, or a book, the perception of these objects is constrained or determined largely by our common experience with them. However, in the case of ambiguous stimuli, such as blots of ink, cloud formations, or objects presented under weakened illumination or clouded conditions, the interpretation varies with a person's past history. These differences reflect characteristics of the perceiver (such as needs, defenses, and the habitual ways of orientation to the world) rather than exclusively reflecting characteristics of the stimulus object.

Moreover, many interpersonal situations have this ambiguous quality. For example, consider the interpretation of motives in a complex interpersonal relationship and the varieties of interpretations obtained for most human social situations. Because the stimulus information is unclear or ambiguous, we project our own personal needs and characteristic ways of apprehending the world upon this material. The paranoid patient, for example, readily assumes a hostile or destructive attitude in others on the basis of little or no information. If we ourselves have self-aggrandizing motives or hostile attitudes, we are likely to interpret other persons' motives and attitudes in a similar fashion. If we conceive of our own mothers as domineering and destructive, we are likely to react to any middle-aged or elderly woman in these terms, projecting our own conception of mothers to any relevant stimulus we may observe, sometimes even when the behavior of such a person justifies a quite different interpretation.

For example, a girl has just bought a new dress, which she feels is somewhat too daring because of the low neckline.[4] Now that she has put it on to go to the party, she regrets buying it and begins to develop a strong sense of embarrassment about it. That evening she is certain that the other girls are looking scornfully at her immodesty, whether this is actually true or not. In fact, no one else might have even considered the dress to be in bad taste. A strong personal need has made her interpret the other girls' behavior in a way that, in this particular situation, may be quite far from the facts.

Just as we might infer something about the personality dynamics of the embarrassed young lady on the basis of her interpretation of the social situation, so we can obtain similar information by the use of projective tests in which a variety of ambiguous stimulus situations are presented to a person for interpretation.

The concept of projection has received considerable impetus by recent laboratory research dealing with the personality determinants of the perception of ambiguous stimuli. Most of the early work of psychologists on perception was concerned with the role of the physical stimulus in determining the perceptual experience or behavior of the subject. Personality and clinical psychologists later began to emphasize the importance of perception as a manifestation of the personality dynamics of the individual.

Early work by Sanford (1936, 1937) produced evidence that hunger increased the likelihood that ambiguous figures would be perceived as relevant to food and eating. Later work has continued to demonstrate that need states could be reflected in various kinds of apperceptive fantasy and perceptual behavior, although the precise mechanisms by which this takes place have not been fully clarified. Lazarus, Eriksen, and Fonda (1951) showed that the psychodynamics associated with hysterical and obsessive-compulsive neuroses

[4] The material in this paragraph has been adapted from G. W. Shaffer & R. S. Lazarus. *Fundamental Concepts in Clinical Psychology.* New York: McGraw-Hill, 1952. P. 249.

led to altered perceptual recognition thresholds for threatening sentences presented auditorally on a wire recorder. When aggressive, sexual, and neutral sentences were played against a background of noise that permitted only about 50 per cent of the material to be correctly identified, it was found that the particular defense mechanisms of these two types of patients determined to some extent the nature of the perception of the threatening material (aggression and sex). Obsessive patients, who are thought to deal with threatening material by the mechanisms of intellectualization and isolation, showed significantly higher accuracy of recognition of the emotionally toned sentences compared with neutral ones; on the other hand, hysterical patients, presumably dealing with threat by repression (avoiding threatening concepts), showed poorer recognition of the sexual and aggressive sentences than the neutral material. Experimental work of this kind, which has supported the theoretical basis of projective techniques, has been reviewed by such writers as Allport (1955), Eriksen (1954), and Jenkin (1957).

Many types of projective techniques have been developed, and it is not difficult to produce stimuli that are sufficiently ambiguous so responses to them will reflect unique personality characteristics of the subject. The wide range of projective techniques produced has been very adequately reviewed by Bell (1948). We cannot here describe all the varieties of projective techniques, although we can illustrate two of the most frequently used types, the Rorschach Ink Blot Test and the Thematic Apperception Test.

The *Rorschach test* consists of a series of ink blots, which were developed by a Swiss psychiatrist named Rorschach (1932) and which have since been used extensively with large varieties of populations. The task of the subject is to observe, one at a time, a series of ten ink blots and interpret what each ink blot might be. The examiner attempts to identify, through a special inquiry, the location of the particular percept (for example, what part of the blot is seen as a man running, an animal, or a bug) and what aspects of the ink blots determined the subject's particular association. Thus the subject's percept might be based on the color or shape of the blot; it might include action; it might involve picking out precise small details within the blot; or it might represent a response to the entire blot as a whole. The individual differences in the way subjects go about performing the task are the basis of inferences about personality structure.

In the *Thematic Apperception Test* (Morgan & Murray, 1935), a series of drawings or pictures, usually of persons in various situations, is presented. The subject has to tell a dramatic story about each picture, indicating what he imagines the persons are doing, thinking, and feeling, what has led up to the particular situation depicted, and what the outcome of the story is likely to be. There are some common themes that are typically given to each of the stimulus cards, but there is a great diversity

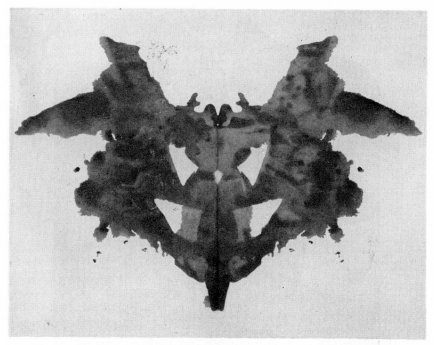

Figure 35. An example of a Rorschach ink blot. (*Rorschach,* 1942.)

in the kinds of stories told and in how the problems and attitudes of the significant characters of the story are characterized. Interpretations are made by the psychologist on the assumption that the subject is, in part, identifying himself with the characters in the story, reflecting his own wishes, fears, and conflicts, and projecting them into the thematic material.

The Rorschach test and the Thematic Apperception Test emphasize different aspects of projective behavior. In the Rorschach test, analysis is made largely on formal grounds. That is, it is not so much what is seen as how and where it is seen that determines the interpretation of the subject's personality structure. The emphasis is on the styles or processes of perception, which are believed to be associated with aspects of personality structures (for example, ego-defense systems and different developmental stages).

The Thematic Apperception Test solicits primarily the content of a subject's fantasy, asking him to construct an imaginary story and to populate the story with particular kinds of characters. Although these stories can also be analyzed from a structural or formal point of view (such as their logic, sequence of ideas, sentence structure, and the conformity of the story to the stimulus picture itself), the primary reason for

Figure 36. An example of a Thematic Apperception Test stimulus card. (*Reprinted by permission of the publishers from Henry A. Murray. Thematic Apperception Test. Cambridge, Mass.: Harvard University Press, Copyright 1943, by The President and Fellows of Harvard College.*)

presenting the test is to get at the contents of a subject's wishes, fantasies, and ways of thinking about the significant persons in his life. The test is given on the assumption that a person often cannot or will not report these things on direct examination, that is, by introspection, or at least will not do so except under time-consuming free-association therapy. However, when given the task of constructing a story ostensibly about others rather than about himself, the more inaccessible aspects of his personality can be inadvertently communicated just as the professional writer of fiction frequently reveals his own personality in his novel or play (for example, Eugene O'Neill's autobiographical play "Long Day's Journey into Night"). Thus, the projective test cuts through the surface level of behavior, theoretically permitting a more direct access to unconscious processes and making it easier to build inferences about an individual's personality organization. While the effort is to get at need states or wishes, there is increasing awareness that such information in the story-telling approach is contaminated not only by the stimulus characteristics but by the intervention of ego or cognitive characteristics of the personality as well. A treatment of this problem can be found in a new publication on apperceptive fantasy by Kagan & Lesser, which is now in preparation.

There are many problems associated with the projective approach to personality assessment, which the clinical psychologist and personality-assessment psychologist must ultimately solve if they are to be used effectively and improved. Many of these problems are common to all assessment methods. For example, the question of reliability is an important one, because we hope to sample, in a single sitting, generalized personality characteristics. Moreover, responses from the subject must be interpreted in some way, and psychologists must be able to agree on these interpretations if we are seriously to consider them as sound inferences. The validity of these inferences is of great significance, both in predicting behavior and in attaining a sound conception of a hypothetical personality organization. A great deal of effort has been expended by psychologists in studying the problems of the projective techniques. There is relatively little disagreement that the projective test is an important source of information about personality structure, but there is great disagreement whether the particular kinds of inferences traditionally drawn from a particular type of record are valid. These problems, which are typical for the entire field of assessment, can only be solved by continuing systematic and intelligent research.

Regardless of the approach, behavior study, self-report, or projective, there are two overriding sources of information about personality: direct observation of behavior and introspections. To greater or less degree, any type of test can be approached from a behavioral or introspective point of view. In the self-report technique we can ask a person to give information about his attitudes or behavior. In a behavior-study approach we watch what a person does in various contexts (although we can also listen to what he says). In the projective techniques we again obtain observations of perceptually and fantasy oriented behavior and sometimes make use of what the subject reports about his feelings.

The differences between the methods lie mainly in what we try to do with them. The varied testing techniques can be treated in various ways depending upon the theoretical and methodological orientation of the assessment psychologist. In the same way, the interview and case history can either be treated as instances of behavior from which predictive statements can be made directly or be used to make inferences about hypothetical underlying processes.

The theoretical frames of reference sketched in earlier chapters apply very readily to the assessment situation. How one will use the available tools and the behavioral and introspective information they produce, and, in fact, what tools will be created or preferred, will tend to depend upon the frame of reference. Moreover, our interpretation of the material will further depend on the specific theoretical system with which we are concerned. For example, it can be centered on the orthodox Freudian model or on the ideas of Rank, Sullivan, or Jung. The objective evidence will commonly be similar or the same, but the nature of the inferences drawn is always determined by the theoretical model of the assessment psychologist.

THE IMPORTANCE OF ASSESSMENT

The assessment of personality is of enormous importance to psychologists for many reasons. Chief among these is the fact that, although all persons have much in common, every human being differs in constitution and experience. These differences, which include intellectual and personality characteristics, are important determinants of reaction in a wide variety of situations. The same situation produces different effects or is responded to in different ways by different persons. In order to understand the contribution of these individual differences in intelligence and personality to behavior, it is important to be able to make valid assessments of a person as an individual in comparison with others.

In addition to the study of the role of personality in human behavior, there is the problem of the origin of this personality, that is, how it came about. In order to study how persons develop in various ways, it is necessary to have tools with which to assess their past and present personality status. The question of what factors influence human development in general and the development of personality in particular cannot be answered satisfactorily without adequate tools of assessment or measurement.

There are, of course, very practical as well as theoretical reasons why it is important to develop personality-assessment methods to a high degree. Since World War I, when Woodworth developed his personal data sheet as a means of screening out men who were psychologically unfit for military service, the problem of personnel selection for industry, the military services, the appropriate school grade, etc., has grown in importance at an accelerated rate. Centuries ago Plato had conceived the idea of finding the right man for the right job on the basis of a knowledge of individual differences.

The assessment of skills and aptitudes has already been highly developed and represents a case similar to personality assessment. No one questions any longer the desirability of selecting men with the desired skills or aptitudes for military or industrial organizations. Industrial leaders not only need to select men with the necessary knowledge or aptitude for acquiring certain trade skills, but they face the harder job of selecting executive personnel for top-level positions. It is certain that the cartoonist, Al Capp, would agree that effective methods of selecting candidates would add to the caliber of some of the United States legislators and that versions of Senator Phogbound, satirized in Capp's comic strip, would be less frequent if the necessary intellectual and moral resources were at least one criterion for high political office.

One place where assessment procedures (under the name of "psychodiagnosis") have been of great importance is in the area of clinical psychology. In the clinic there is the problem of evaluating incoming patients in terms of potential disposition and therapy. For example, it is important to know the severity of the pathology and whether the patient should be hospitalized or treated as an outpatient; seen intensively many times a week or given relatively superficial support. Sometimes the problem of diagnosis becomes a life-and-death matter in cases of homicidal or suicidal patients. One must decide whether the patient can be left without the control and security of the hospital. Mistakes can be extremely costly. The play and movie "The Shrike" was a bitter account of this problem. It concerned refusal to grant a man freedom to return to his family and work, largely because of the judgment that he was a suicidal risk, having recently attempted to take his life. The general problem here is parallel to the use in medicine of the electrocardiogram and blood tests in addition to the patient's report of symptoms in order to improve the diagnosis and make a better guess about outcomes and necessary treatments.

Related very closely to the question of disposition in the clinical setting is the value of diagnostic or assessment information for decisions about therapy. It is often very helpful to know something about the psychodynamics of the patient and his psychological resources when planning the strategy and goals of therapy. It is beginning to be clear that certain types of therapeutic approaches are poor choices for some patients, and if the therapy is to be tailored to the psychodynamics of the patient, these must be known accurately.

In the field of rehabilitation counseling, similar problems arise. For example, when the patient leaves the hospital, what type of employment and interpersonal situations can he cope with adequately and what situations should be avoided lest they overwhelm him and produce a recurrence of the acute disturbance? Again a knowledge of the strengths and weaknesses of the personality permits wiser decisions.

There is hardly much disagreement about these worthy theoretical and practical objectives for personality assessment or psychodiagnosis. The real problem is the success of assessment programs. Empirical research has shown that assessment techniques now in use have value, but only in a limited statistical sense. That is, we can improve our guesses about future behavior or the course of an illness to a certain degree, meaning that a higher percentage than chance will follow the clinical prediction. This is not much consolation to the clinical or industrial practitioner who must deal with single persons or with real industrial problems and is committed to doing the best he can to help. It is sobering to think that, even if he is correct 70 per cent of the time, in 30 out of 100 cases he will make the wrong judgment.

Thus, the assessment psychologist's statements are probabilistic ones, and the tools he uses can improve his educated guesses to a significant degree, but in any individual case there is never any certainty that the appropriate inferences or prognostications have been made. Far more research is needed in techniques of assessment; as it is, the probability levels at which we presently work are not impressive. A factor limiting this research is that the psychological practitioner can ill afford, for his peace of mind, to worry or ruminate about each judgment he makes. If he looks squarely at the facts, he can become dismayed, especially if he holds the untenable view that he is approaching every clinical case correctly. So strong is this need to assume correctness that seldom is systematic study of the validity of clinical judgments encouraged. The function of research seems too rarely to intermingle with the aspirations for expertise of the practitioner. The result is that extremely important opportunities for systematic research in personality assessment are being continually passed over for lack of interest, lack of time, or lack of conviction.

It must be clearly affirmed again and again that personality assessment must follow scientific principles. It is dependent upon sound concepts and unambiguous empirical data. The development of a science of assessment is at a very early stage. The concepts involved need sharpening and elaboration, and the tools need continual improvement. The instruments available today should be considered really beginnings in the science of human assessment; in many instances they are ingenious, but they must not be regarded as sacred. Nor must we get the notion that we have reached the end of the line so far as the development of old and new tools of personality assessment is concerned. These tools should, furthermore, be embedded in some theoretical conception of human psychological organization. It is probable that the basic sources of information will remain variants of the case history, the interview, and the psychological test.

The ultimate question is: Are we making statements that logically cohere within some accepted theoretical framework and do these statements lead to legitimate scientific prediction of how a person will react under certain specifiable conditions? The improvement of the science of personality assessment, independent of parochial arguments, will have momentous implications for theoretical psychology in general and for applied psychology, which depends so heavily upon such assessment in selection, in training, in diagnosis, and in treatment.

CHAPTER
14

Psychotherapy

Once aware of the problem of adjustive failure, a natural next question is how to deal with it. Emotionally disturbed persons were recognized in antiquity, and men have realized since the beginnings of recorded history that there are great variations in individual ability to make satisfactory living adjustments. In modern times these adjustive failures have become the object of not only intensive study but systematic efforts at treatment. This chapter concerns these systematic attempts to promote more effective adjustments.

The earliest therapeutic programs were usually directed at the most severe kind of psychological disturbance: the psychoses. In more recent years we have realized that a high percentage of persons who are able to function successfully outside the mental hospital show symptoms of psychological disorder—of a milder and less pervasive degree but nonetheless partially incapacitating for the everyday tasks of life. Such persons either are unhappy or less effective than they might be or exhibit somatic symptoms that have no observable organic or structural basis, which are painful and damaging to health over long periods of time. With the recognition that therapy could help such persons, a great impetus was given to the professions that could offer therapeutic services.

The main reason for the rapid development of therapy was the possibility of alleviating suffering, but there are other important reasons for an interest in the processes of therapy. Attempts to produce personality change can also yield increased understanding of the structure of personality and the causes of psychopathology. Thus the therapeutic process offers a special kind of laboratory in which the personality of an individual can be laid bare for study. Indeed, many of our present concepts of personality and its development have arisen from the therapeutic situation. For example, the theories of Freud and the Neo-Freudians are largely an outgrowth of attempts to understand and treat psychological disorders.

SOME TERMS AND DISTINCTIONS

Before we proceed further it is important to be clear on the meaning of some of the most common terms in the area of therapy and some of the professional considerations concerning the practice of therapy.

Therapy is the general term for treatment of pathology of any kind. *Psycho-* comes from the Greek word *psychē,* which has come to mean the mind or mental processes. Thus, *psychotherapy* is a general term applied to any efforts to treat mental or psychological disturbances by directly influencing the personality structure of the person.

We must recognize at the outset that there are forms of treatment characterized by manipulation of the environment of the person (rather than directly altering the personality). In recent years there has been a tendency to narrow the definition of psychotherapy to exclude this indirect treatment, or environmental manipulation, and refer to the latter as *sociotherapy* or *milieu therapy.* On the basis of this distinction, psychotherapy is the method of talking with a patient, often for a long period of time, in an effort to get him to understand his troubles and to reorganize his patterns of reactions from pathological ones to some pattern considered more healthy. Although there is confusion over what the term *psychotherapy* delimits, current usage emphasizes this direct *face-to-face* relationship involving conversation between a psychologically trained person and the patient.

The lay person often cannot differentiate between the terms "psychotherapy" and "psychoanalysis." The latter is both a systematic theory of personality and a specialized technique of psychotherapy. In other words, *psychoanalysis* is one orientation to personality and psychotherapy. It contains its own special concepts and techniques, although these have been taken over into the general field of psychotherapy to a high degree. A psychoanalyst is a psychotherapist who utilizes the psychoanalytic approach to treatment and has met certain professionally defined (by psychoanalytic societies) criteria.

As we have seen in earlier chapters, there is no single form of psychoanalysis itself, for many analytically oriented psychotherapists have deviated from the original Freudian scheme and have modified analytic theory and technique. In general, traditional psychoanalysis represents an intensive approach to psychotherapy, because the patient in psychoanalysis must be seen four to five times a week, for hour periods, over several years. In psychotherapy in general the treatment can be as infrequent as a single session per week for several weeks. The essential point is that "psychotherapy" is a more general term for direct manipulation of the personality, which involves a wide variety of therapeutic approaches including also any of the various forms of psychoanalysis.

There is also confusion concerning which professional persons practice psychotherapy. On this point there is some professional disagreement between *psychiatry* and *psychology*. At the present writing, the official policy of the American Psychiatric Association is that only a medically trained practitioner is qualified to practice psychotherapy. This position is contested by psychologists and other professional groups, including social workers and ministers, and there has been evolving, for some years, an increasing social and legal recognition that psychotherapy is not the field of any particular specialized group.

In actual practice, many professions contribute to the field of psychotherapy, and the laws throughout the country concerning who may practice psychotherapy are quite variable and even nonexistent in many states. It is clear, however, that the important professions in psychotherapy include psychiatrists, psychologists, and social workers, all of whom can function in clinical settings, such as hospitals or outpatient clinics, and many of whom have a certain amount of private practice as well. It will be some years before the relationships between these three professions are clearly worked out, but the great demand for psychotherapy, which cannot be met by existing personnel resources, is spreading the practice of psychotherapy more and more among the different professional groups.

There are also other groups who practice psychotherapy or counseling in the course of their everyday activities, although their point of view may be different from that of the professions officially concerned with adjustive failure. The clearest example of such a group are the ministers and rabbis who for centuries have been ministering to the spiritual and psychological concerns of their congregations. Such persons often play extremely important roles in the lives of persons who come to them with personal problems and, as such, are in a continuing position to practice some form of psychotherapy whether they are psychologically trained or not. For example, the Christian Science practitioner may spend a great deal of therapeutic time with clients suffering from all manner of psychological disturbances. This fact has stimulated the development of *pastoral psychology* or pastoral counseling, which has permitted religious leaders to become psychologically more sophisticated and better able to utilize available knowledge about psychotherapy and psychopathology in their day-to-day contacts with members of their religious groups. Such persons are practicing some form of psychotherapy, whether it is based on religious philosophy or on any other doctrinaire psychological principles, and whether it is sound or unsound.

This spread of psychotherapeutic practice, which results from the great demand for such services and the relative lack of supply of professionally trained persons, is further evidenced in the use of various ancillary services such as nurses and ward attendants in mental hospitals. Most nurses and attendants see a great deal more of the patients in such hospitals than does the psychiatrist, psychologist, or social worker. Nurses and attendants, therefore, become extremely important persons in the general treatment process. In recognition of this, more and more effort is being made to give at least a minimum of psychological training to such personnel, because their day-to-day contacts with the patient can be either positively psychotherapeutic to the patient or potentially harmful. The professionals have tended, more and more, to play a supervisory role rather than a directly psychotherapeutic one.

OBJECTIVES OF PSYCHOTHERAPY

Discussion of the objectives of psychotherapy is complicated by the fact that different theoretical systems define these objectives in terms of their own unique formulations. Thus the process of psychotherapy and the steps leading to its ultimate goals are somewhat differently conceived. The relationships between personality theory and psychotherapeutic practice are discussed later on in the chapter; let us restrict ourselves now to general considerations about objectives.

Generally speaking, it is possible to distinguish between *supportive* and *insight psychotherapy* (see Shaffer & Lazarus, 1952). In the former, the patient is given psychological supports by the therapist to help tide him over a temporary crisis or to provide some slight help when more ambitious objectives seem unnecessary, impossible, or dangerous. In other words, supportive psychotherapy makes no attempt to produce a major reconstruction of the personality of the patient through intensive and long-term probing into the basis of the patient's trouble; rather, it utilizes the therapeutic relationship in a simple supportive fashion. Such an approach to psychotherapy is used for two kinds of patients: (1) persons whose general mental health is good and whose present difficulties seem largely situational and (2) persons who are so disturbed that the effort to probe the basis of the disturbance would be too traumatic, with such an effort possibly precipitating the patient into a more serious breakdown. In supportive psychotherapy, the therapist's friendly interest and acceptance, and his regular availability and reassurance, add a measure of strength to the patient in his efforts to overcome a psychological crisis or to keep his head above water in the continuing struggle for psychological survival.

The aims of insight therapy, on the other hand, are far more ambitious, because they represent the joint effort by a patient and therapist to lay open the patient's psychological organization. An attempt is made to ex-

pose the anxiety-provoking impulses and conflicts, to undercut the pathological defenses of the patient, to expose these to his critical examination,
and to produce a restructuring of the personality so more healthy modes of
handling impulses and coping with threats can be ultimately acquired.

One must recognize that insight therapy also can vary from the formida-
ble aim of exposing a person's earliest and deepest-lying experiences and
feelings (as in orthodox psychoanalysis) to a more limited attempt to
understand more superficial difficulties and their ramifications for a person's immediate adjustive problems. It may be sufficient to deal psychotherapeutically with features of the personality that are less deep or infantile in order to produce significant relief from pathological symptoms.

The frequency of contacts between therapist and patient often reflects
these differences in the depth of objective. The severity and nature of the
problem, the resources of the patient, and the point of view of the
therapist all tend to determine how ultimate, intermediate, or immediate
the objectives of insight therapy will be. There are continuing debates
about the efficacy of more limited psychotherapeutic programs and to
what extent therapeutic efforts aimed at the ultimate objective of major
reconstruction of personality succeed along these lines.

THE THERAPEUTIC PROCESS

This section concerns the basic theoretical question about psychotherapy: How does it work? One must recognize immediately that the
question is apt to be answered in various ways depending upon the
theoretical formulations of personality that one employs. It is not possible
for us here completely to develop this problem. At times, especially in
systematic discussion of personality theory and therapeutic practice,
some differences in emphasis with respect to the therapeutic process will
be pointed up. The concepts with which we shall deal have originated in
psychoanalytic thought, although they have also become infused into general thought about psychotherapy (Alexander & French, 1946). We must
remember that psychoanalysis has played a most central role in the development of modern concepts of psychotherapy, and even those workers
who are not primarily psychoanalytic in systematic orientation utilize concepts like resistance, catharsis, transference, insight, and working through.
We shall, therefore, concentrate on these concepts; the interested reader
can avail himself of a variety of divergent sources.

Before we proceed further it should be noted that we are begging the
extremely important question of whether or not psychotherapy works. For
the purpose of this exposition let us assume that important changes do
take place in patients in the psychotherapeutic process, although the empirical evidence on this point is scarce and difficult to assess. There is

relatively little in the way of systematic evaluation of the results of psychotherapy and still less in the realm of comparison of the different forms of psychotherapy practiced today. It will not be fruitful here to ruminate about the effectiveness of psychotherapy, but it is well for the reader to understand that it is a question of great significance. The problem is complicated by the difficulties of assessing personality and personality change.

Catharsis

People have long recognized that the verbal expression of their feelings can have a very helpful effect in relieving tensions. The wise lay person senses that, when such feelings have been bottled up, giving vent to them is therapeutic. This release of feelings is one of the oldest and most important processes recognized in psychotherapy. Because Freud considered this expression of previously unexpressed feeling as a kind of release or purging, he introduced the term *catharsis*. In the early stages of his theorizing, catharsis was considered the primary agent of therapy, the idea being that failure to express deep-lying feelings was responsible for the neurotic symptoms. It is now well recognized that far more is required for successful therapy than this process, but catharsis remains an important feature of psychotherapy.

A first and essential step in any psychotherapeutic approach is the requirement that the patient talk about his problems. Usually the patient will begin with a story, so to speak, that he is prepared to tell. This story is often colored by rationalizations of his behavior and other self-deceptions and frequently consists of factual statements that may not be associated with the expression of feeling. It is usually feelings, however, that the therapist wishes the patient to express. Catharsis can be considered essential to the therapeutic process as a whole for two reasons: (1) because the therapy cannot proceed if the patient does not lay before himself and the therapist the feelings and impulses that lie behind his trouble and (2) because this very discharge of feelings can be the means of relief for some of the discomfort and anxiety associated with them.

Resistance

Resistance is the process by which patients protect themselves from the painful discoveries or insights into the real nature of their problems (see, for example, Reich, 1949, Hendrick, 1939, or Freud, 1935.) Basically resistance is the operation of the varied mechanisms of defense that are fundamental to the neurosis itself. It is one of the most remarkable concepts in the area of psychotherapy. It implies that, although the patient comes to the therapist voluntarily for help, he actually resists such help by refusing to say anything he thinks and dig into impulses and attitudes that are at the core of his problem.

But the concept is not nearly so remarkable if we truly understand what is meant by mechanisms of defense. These mechanisms are aimed at the reduction or elimination of overwhelming anxiety that would follow from the recognition or expression of impulses that are dangerous or unacceptable. The therapist is asking the patient to give up the very props and self-deceptions that have permitted him to retain his integrity and to perform the painful task of reorganizing his perceptions of himself. The present organization of his personality, however pathological, has been achieved over a period of many years and with considerable struggle, and it is not easily altered or given up. The patient has come to the therapist for relief from his symptoms, and the therapist tells him, in effect, that such relief can only come about by the even more painful process of faithfully examining himself and exposing things he has not been able to face.

The process of resistance is manifested by refusal on the part of the patient to associate freely without censorship of his thoughts, by digressions from painful subjects, by complete blockage of speech when the patient can think of nothing to say, and by a variety of maneuvers, usually unconscious, that relieve him of the obligation to examine every facet of himself. If the resistance is stronger than the discomfort of the pathological adjustment, it can even result in the patient leaving the psychotherapeutic situation altogether.

One of the tasks of therapy is to overcome the patient's resistance, but it cannot be overcome by direct attack. The psychotherapist must be careful not to press the patient so hard that it is impossible for him to remain in therapy. He must utilize to the fullest the patient's motivation to get well. There is the assumption on the part of many therapeutic theorists, such as Rogers (1951), that there is sufficient force for growth in a person that, if given certain optimal conditions, he will ultimately progress in a positive direction in spite of the counterforces of resistance and ego defense.

A force that can help to keep the patient in the therapeutic situation is the positive effect of catharsis. Another is the uncritical acceptance of the patient's feelings by the therapist and the permissive atmosphere that the therapist provides as well as the interest he expresses in the patient's troubles. These conditions of therapy have been heavily stressed by Rogers and other writers and represent what most therapists, regardless of therapeutic school, do if they are experienced and competent.

Transference

One of the key therapeutic processes that helps to overcome the patient's resistance is the *transference relationship*. During the course of long-term psychotherapy it is not surprising that the therapist becomes an extremely important person in the life of the patient. For one thing, there is the sense of promise provided by the therapist that important changes will take place, which will relieve the patient of his neurotic suffering. Moreover, if, as in psychoanalytic therapy, a patient sees the therapist five days a week for an hour at a time in an atmosphere of intimacy, in which the patient's most private feelings are expressed, his relationship with the therapist is likely to reach major proportions compared with the ordinary run-of-the-mill relationships that normally do occur between persons.

The concept of transference arose from certain observations that Freud and other psychoanalysts began to make concerning this intense emotional relationship between the patient and the analyst. The emotional interest of the patient for the analyst develops gradually, but in its full-blown state has many of the qualities commonly associated with the relationship of parent and child. The patient may develop erotic fantasies about the therapist or resent his interest in other patients, whom the patient regards as rivals for the analyst's approval and affection. He becomes preoccupied with pleasing the analyst and in many instances behaves as though he were wholly dependent upon him for guidance, protection, and support, just as he was upon one or both of his parents. Although the intensity of this relationship can be relatively mild, in some instances it is very strong.

Freud called this relationship, which appeared so often in psychoanalytic therapy, *transference* because it seemed to be a reenactment of the child-parent relationship (Freud, 1924). The patient transfers to the analyst emotions that he has experienced with the most significant adult figures in his life, especially parents. The analyst, in a sense, represents to the patient the persons who have been important in his life, especially during childhood. The relationships reenacted can have positive aspects, in which the predominant emotion is one of affection and dependency, or negative, in which a hostile attitude dominates.

For the analytically oriented therapist, the transference relationship is important in two main ways. In the first place, the nature of this relationship and the behavior of the patient in regard to it can give him important clues concerning the childhood patterns of identification and the way in which the patient continues to establish relationships with others. Thus, the analyst learns from this so-called reenactment of childhood some of the fundamental features of the patient's personality and strives to acquaint the patient with these as well. Transference is therefore a learning experience.

Secondly, the analyst uses this strong affective relationship to encourage the patient to overcome resistances that conceal the underlying neurotic problem. Because the patient's dominant wish at this time may be to please the therapist and because he also obtains a form of protection and support from the therapist, it is not so difficult for him to bring up material that, in the absence of this relationship, would be too overwhelming or anxiety-producing for him to tolerate. Thus the transference is not only useful diagnostically but is also a motivational tool in the therapeutic process.

Therapeutic schools of thought emphasize or deemphasize or treat in different ways the transference relationship. In psychoanalytic therapy the transference is considered to be the core of the psychoanalysis. In Rogerian therapy transference is deemphasized. In most therapies, however, the relationship between the therapist and the patient, however it is conceived, plays an important role.

Because Freud believed that the seeds of the neurosis are planted in the very earliest years of childhood, he considered it essential that the emotional relationships of childhood be reenacted in order to be understood and revised in an adult undergoing therapy. For Freud, only certain kinds of persons were capable of this kind of transference relationship, and for this reason he believed that psychoanalysis was only suitable for those neurotic disturbances where this *transference neurosis* was possible. For example, patients with hysterical disturbances were considered ideally suited for therapy, but those with character disorders, such as the psychopath (or antisocial personality), and psychoses, such as schizophrenia, could not be treated by the psychoanalytic method.

The most important factor considered to determine the possibilities of transference is the personality organization of the patient. With the therapist seated behind and out of the view of the patient lying on a couch and minimally intruding himself as a real person with particular objective qualities, the process of transference takes place most readily. The patient is free to engage in infantile fantasies about the therapist regardless of the sex of the therapist or his objective characteristics as a stimulus. It is probable that many conditions impede or enhance the possibilities of the transference relationship, and the therapeutic approaches that minimize the transference relationship as a tool of therapy have many means to reduce a patient's inclination to establish such an intense relationship.

The fact of the transference relationship in terms of therapeutic observation is incontestable, but there is considerable room for controversy over our understanding of the nature and basis of this relationship. The psychoanalyst conceives this relationship as a repetition of earlier infantile relationships, but it is also possible to interpret it from other points of view. For example, Sullivan interpreted transference in a way far more compatible with learning theory, as a generalization to the therapist of ways of reacting to the significant figures of childhood or to any person who in any way resembles these early significant figures. In other words, a patient has learned to respond as a child to certain types of adults in certain ways and now, as an adult, knows no other way of interacting. Sullivan spoke of this relationship as *parataxic distortion.* Learning theorists utilize the concept of *stimulus generalization,* suggesting that the therapist places the patient in a situation similar in certain ways to important earlier relationships with other persons and similar responses are now made to the therapist. Generalization from parental stimuli to the similar stimuli provided by the therapist takes place.

However transference is conceptualized, it is widely regarded as an important feature of the therapeutic situation, particularly when that situation is intensive and of long duration. The patient can learn from this relationship and must come to regard it as an artificial one, brought about by the conditions of therapy. The therapy cannot be brought to a satisfactory conclusion until the transference relationship has been dissolved. That is, the patient must see the relationship for what it is, an instance of the way in which he relates to many other persons and once related to his parents, and he must ultimately give up the relationship in order to function without it when therapy is terminated. In this way he may be better able to establish mature adult relationships with the important persons (wife, children, employers, parents) in his current life situation.

Insight and Working Through

Not long ago it was believed that the mere bringing up of unconscious memories and feelings ("catharsis") was the primary therapeutic agent. Later, the transference relationship itself was emphasized as the important feature of therapy and therapeutic success. Eventually, the importance of understanding insight on the part of the patient about his life pattern became the objective of therapy on the assumption that this insight or understanding is essentially all that is necessary for therapeutic success. It was assumed that, if the patient fully grasped the significance of this behavior, he would be freed of the neurotic difficulty.

In more recent years there has developed the conviction that *insight* or self-understanding is only an intermediate, although significant, step toward the resolution of neurotic conflict. If neurosis involves defensive operations against anxiety, then it is clear that these defense mechanisms must be given up in order for the patient to comprehend clearly, and to come to grips with, the problem. Because they are unconscious, they must be brought to awareness before he can begin to deal with them in a more rational fashion.

At least one further step must be accomplished when reasonably good insight has been achieved. This is the step of *working through* or, as some writers identify it, reeducation. A person must learn new and more adequate ways of dealing with the neurotic conflicts before he can function successfully. He must apply the insights he has learned about the sources of his difficulties in a wide variety of situations that are part of his everyday life.

The purpose of therapy is not ordinarily to assist a patient to solve a very specific problem but to aid the patient in developing resources with which to solve any emotion-producing problem. His capacity to make satisfactory adjustments to new as well as to old interpersonal problems must be enhanced. This means that whatever insights are gained in the psychotherapeutic situation must not only be applicable to a single problem but also be available to the patient in his dealing with a wide range of stress-producing circumstances throughout his life. The ultimate goal of psychotherapy is to increase a person's capacity to do this without necessarily having recourse again and again to the psychotherapist. This is a reeducational process, which seems to be possible only when the patient, in the later stages of therapy, has examined and understood his reactions under a wide variety of circumstances and applied what he has learned about more successful mastery of stress. These new modes substitute for the pathological defenses that characterized his adjustment prior to successful psychotherapy. This is not to say that a person who is successfully adjusting is without problems or conflicts; rather these conflicts are accessible to him and are satisfactorily resolved without the interposition of symptom-producing mechanisms of self-deception.

It is now appropriate to look at the therapeutic situation itself to see what conditions permit these processes to occur.

THE THERAPIST'S STRATEGY

The previous section dealt with some essential concepts concerning the therapeutic process, that is, theoretical statements about what actually takes place during therapy. These concepts do not tell us directly what the therapist does, but they tell us what he thinks is happening. Certain attitudes and forms of behavior on the therapist's part are generally regarded as means for permitting this therapeutic process to take place.

One of the oldest therapeutic techniques is *suggestion*, which enters into almost all situations in which one person attempts to influence another. Because of the prestige or authority of the therapist, it is possible for him to play upon the suggestibility of the patient to help him eliminate some of his symptoms and pathological modes of conduct. It should be pointed out that any therapeutic interpretation, even in modern therapy, can have aspects of suggestion, whether the therapist desires it or not, because the patient may accept what the therapist says as valid because of his presumed expertise. As a general medical practitioner suggests to a patient that the prescribed medicine will have a desired effect, a psychotherapist can suggest the probable success of a certain line of action or reassure the patient that many of his apprehensions are not warranted. This can play some part in alleviating the patient's anxieties. But therapists today are no longer so impressed with the value of suggestion as a very significant feature of the psychotherapeutic approach, even though it can play some relatively minor role.

One form of suggestion, called *autosuggestion,* was popularized some years ago by the Frenchman Coué. This involved having the patient repeat, over and over again, various phrases such as "day by day in every way I am getting better and better." Coué believed that the continued application of encouragement by this means, even in the absence of a therapist, would ultimately win the patient over. If one vividly imagined a state of health, pathological reactions would be excluded. Although this method gained considerable attention in its time, it is not currently used as a therapeutic technique, but it called attention early to the limitations of intellect and will power as opposed to emotion and imagination in the adjustment process.

Another approach related to suggestion is *spiritual healing,* which has a long history in practically every religious group. It depends upon the profound belief in the power of spiritual forces to correct adjustive failures or abnormalities, and there is no question that such phenomena as convulsive seizures, fainting spells, paralysis, and hysterical sensory losses have been removed or alleviated in many cases, at least temporarily, through religious experience. This type of approach has rarely been applied by professional workers in psychotherapy. One early attempt to treat alcoholism by religious conversion is reported by Forel (1907). Alcoholics Anonymous has had considerable success in treating chronic alcoholics. Their method includes a mixture of personal support from other persons and spiritualism. Christian Science has also functioned in this way, with the Christian Science practitioner acting as a quasi therapist as well as spiritual guide. The difficulty with suggestion is that it is superficial and symptom-oriented. The relief, if any, is usually temporary, with the symptoms returning in similar or varied form. It rarely gets to the core of the patient's problem, and it does not permit the patient to develop any insight. There is some agreement, however, that, where the symptoms are not grounded in major personality disturbances, various forms of suggestion can be effective. Some cases of mass panic, where considerable numbers of persons have been severely frightened by suggestions of impending doom or danger, support the notion that immature persons of low intelligence and education and a hysterical personality structure are most responsive to suggestions.

Another relatively old approach to psychotherapy is *persuasion* (Dubois, 1907; Dejerine & Gaukler, 1913). The therapist exhorts the patient to approach rationally or morally the false ideas and bad mental habits upon which his symptoms depend. The emphasis is on the appeal to the rational capabilities of man, and to a limited degree such persuasion could conceivably have some value in relatively minor disturbances. Its value, however, is considered so limited that it is rarely employed as a therapeutic technique or adjunct at the present time.

One of the most interesting and baffling early approaches to psychotherapy, which is gaining renewed attention, is the technique of *hypnosis*, which has had a fascinating history since the time of Mesmer, who called the process "animal magnetism." We cannot develop the history of hypnosis here, although it is a most interesting story. Freud, influenced by the great French psychiatrist Charcot, first used hypnosis in an attempt to treat cases of hysteria with seeming neurological symptoms, and he discovered that it is possible in many cases to uncover unconscious processes through the technique, and even to remove symptoms, at least temporarily, through posthypnotic suggestions.

Freud abandoned hypnosis for many reasons, one of the most important of which was that, although the therapist discovered a great deal about the patient under hypnosis, the patient himself was not participating cognitively and, upon awakening, he recalled little or nothing of what had taken place. If insight is essential for successful psychotherapy, hypnosis by itself seems not to provide much opportunity for it. There are other contraindications to hypnosis that limit its use to certain types of patients. It was after these experiences with hypnosis that Freud developed the techniques of free association.

Some modern psychotherapists utilize hypnosis as an adjunct to the therapeutic process, because it can be used to speed it, particularly where the problem is not especially deep-seated or the objectives of therapy not too ambitious. An interesting treatment of the use of hypnosis as a therapeutic adjunct is presented by Wolberg (1945), who has used the term "hypnoanalysis" for his combination of psychoanalytic procedures and hypnosis. In recent years there has been a reawakening of interest in hypnosis and the possibilities of its use. It has been successfully used in childbirth without anesthesia and in surgery, and today some dentists use hypnotic techniques to relieve the pain of dental work. The process of hypnosis has also been recently reinterpreted by Sarbin (1950) as an instance of role playing by the hypnotized person.

Let us now consider some key features of modern therapeutic strategy, which are followed more or less by the large majority of experienced psychotherapists.

The Principle of Minimum Activity

One of the primary problems in psychotherapy is to get the patient to talk about his problems and himself. In the course of the presentation of his story it is natural for the patient to wish the therapist to guide or direct him in some way as to what he thinks is important or what he wishes to hear. Moreover, the patient will undoubtedly say things the therapist does not consider fruitful or important or about which the therapist may wish clarification. The therapist will also, implicitly or explicitly, subscribe to some conceptual framework about personality and psychopathology, thus having his own ideas about the causes of the disorder that a patient manifests. The principle of minimum activity simply asserts that the therapist should avoid leading the patient in such a way that what emerges is the product of the therapist's bias and interests rather than those of the patient. Yet the patient must be prodded to talk and to follow certain pathways that the therapist considers important. The therapist must direct the patient, but he should do so by careful and subtle means.

For example, it is not desirable to say to the patient, "Now let me hear about such and so." Rather the message should be conveyed by selective nods of the head, attentive but noncommittal remarks, or leaning forward in the chair when the patient is talking about something that is of interest and relevance. When the therapist wishes clarification, he should ask in a very general way, such as "Tell me some more about that" or "I don't quite understand." The objective is to guide the patient into therapeutically profitable areas of exploration without therapy developing into a question-and-answer interview in which the patient comes to expect complete guidance from the therapist concerning what to say. It is the patient's mind, and not the therapist's, that is being explored.

The principle of minimum activity has been made explicit by such psychiatric writers as Jacob Finesinger (1948). A more extreme injunction against too much direction in the psychotherapeutic situation is offered by Rogers (1942), who has developed a series of therapeutic principles called "nondirective therapy." In nondirective therapy, the therapist never goes beyond what the patient himself has stated, never offers interpretation, and never prods the patient in any particular direction by any verbal statement. The patient is permitted to determine what is discussed and when it is discussed, although feelings rather than intellectual statements are subtly encouraged. Most therapists do not follow a strictly nondirective approach to therapy, and their strategy can better be characterized as consisting of minimum direction, in which the therapist does lead the patient to some degree and even at appropriate times asks questions and offers interpretations.

Following the Patient

Just about all psychotherapists agree that good rapport is established with a patient when he sees that the therapist understands him and knows what he is saying. Simply listening silently is not sufficient as a sign that a patient's story is understood, and the therapist finds he must give signs that he is following or going along with what the patient is saying. The Rogerian technique for following the patient is often called "reflection" because the therapist rephrases the feeling content of what the patient has said in similar or slightly different fashion. For example, if the patient has said, "It bothers me when other people get ahead and I don't," the therapist can reflect this statement by responding, "You are troubled when others are successful and you are not." This paraphrase reflects to some degree understanding and attention to what the patient has said. The therapist could equally well have said, "You resent other people's success," but this might have been slightly more interpretive; or he might have simply nodded his head or said, "I see"; or if he wanted further elaboration or clarification of this statement, he might have simply responded, "Oh?"

Fundamentally, the question of following the patient is a matter of communication and giving signals to the patient that communication is taking place. Gill, Newman, and Redlich (1954) presented a very interesting recording of an interview between an experienced psychotherapist and a young schizophrenic woman. The therapist is having great difficulty throughout the interview in following the patient because he cannot quite grasp the innuendos and complicated, confused ideas of the schizophrenic girl. He tries very hard, but it is clear to the listener that he is not quite getting it. Interpretations of what the patient is saying involve not only listening but understanding what lies behind what is being said. Generally speaking, evidence that the therapist is following the patient is responded to warmly by the patient, and absence of such evidence will frequently make him resentful or make him feel as though he is getting nowhere. We all know that this is also true of our day-to-day relations with other persons.

Emphasis on Feelings

In presenting his thoughts and experiences, a patient will say a great many kinds of things, including factual descriptions of what he thinks happened at a particular time and feelings he has about these experiences. Psychopathology, at least theoretically, is built around emotional states (like fear or anger), and it is therefore widely recognized that the patient's feelings are the most important things to be dealt with in the psychotherapeutic process. Thus the therapist will focus on or emphasize these feelings and seek to elicit them from a patient when he does not normally present them.

Even in Rogerian nondirective therapy, when the patient makes a complicated statement, the therapist chooses what features of the statement to reflect; this choice consists usually of statements about feelings rather than description or fact. Similarly, when Finesinger referred to minimal direction of the patient by showing interest or disinterest and by responding to some things said by the patient and not to others, he made it a point to encourage the patient to talk about his feelings rather than intellectual material. Thus, the therapist will reserve his nods of the head, or leaning forward with interest, for the feeling-oriented statements, and he will ask for elaboration more readily when the patient is discussing how he feels about something than when is is simply telling an intellectual story. Soon, in relation to the greater or less interest expressed by the therapist in feelings and facts, the patient will learn what kinds of things it is that the therapist desires him to talk about without the exact content being influenced too greatly.

Acceptance and Support

Perhaps the most important strategem of the therapist is his acceptance of anything the patient says without criticism or evaluation and the kind, understanding support he offers. Rogers (1942) has most clearly described this feature of therapeutic strategy, and almost all therapists will concur in its value in producing a truly therapeutic atmosphere.

Previous to his contact with the psychotherapist, the patient will have complained to, or sought help from, friends, associates, or family. He has found ready evaluation of his behavior by these persons, who are only too willing to offer advice, to criticize his behavior, or to support the patient by agreement with his course of action. The woman who, for example, feels continually abused by her husband, whom she accuses of being alcoholic and indifferent to her, will find some persons anxious to attack the husband and all men, wondering how she has put up with this for so long. She will find others who imply that, if the husband is alcoholic and inattentive, she must be doing something wrong herself. As she describes her woes to still others, they will often, in turn, tell her how difficult things have been for them, implying that hers is not a real problem next to their own.

The therapist's attitude, however, is something new for the patient. The therapist listens, he seems attentive, he seems to follow what the patient is saying, he accepts the patient's attitudes without evaluation, even the most reprehensible ones, which the patient is ashamed to tell others and even to express to himself. The emphasis is on the exploration of the person's feelings and attitudes without censorship. The patient is thus encouraged to perceive the therapist as an accepting paternal figure who is there to offer support and who will not desert him regardless of what he says or does.

This acceptance and support offered by the therapist encourage a kind of parental conception of the therapist by the patient and the development of strong positive attitudes previously described as transference. The therapist can use this dependent relation (infantile, as conceived by the psychoanalyst) to encourage the patient to dig into areas that he could not communicate to others or even to himself. Because the attitude of criticism and evaluation is missing and the therapist offers support in the trying period when some of the unacceptable impulses and feelings of the patient have been expressed, the patient can go deeper into his unconscious fantasies than he could in any context where he feels less safe.

SUITABILITY FOR PSYCHOTHERAPY

It would be ideal if no limitations existed on the suitability for psychotherapy of persons suffering from any type of adjustive failure. However, psychotherapy, as we have described it here, is only possible with relatively limited types of patients. The criteria of suitability include, for example, an emotional disorder severe enough that a person is motivated to seek help but not so severe that he lacks contact with reality, as in the case of the deeply regressed psychotic. Furthermore, psychotherapy is largely a verbal process in which the patient must communicate at a high level of abstraction with the therapist, and he must be intellectually competent to understand the subtleties of personality dynamics and be able to label his experiences accurately. It would not be legitimate to say that the intellectually dull person could not profit to some degree from psychotherapy, particularly the cathartic aspects, but there is little doubt that intellectual capacity sets limits within which a person can profit from the psychotherapeutic experience. The bright person has more chance to comprehend his problem successfully, although intelligence alone will not necessarily produce effective therapeutic progress.

Earlier in this chapter mention was made of supportive therapy for a person who lacks sufficient ego strength to tolerate, without breakdown, the exploration of his psychological conflicts. For this kind of person a more modest objective is necessary, which further attests to limitations on the kind of patient suitable for insight psychotherapy. The psychotic person, who is out of contact with reality and thinks bizarrely and illogically, will also have great difficulty developing and maintaining a suitable psychotherapeutic relationship. In such instances primarily support is offered until the patient has sufficient contact to be able to profit from the more intensive and exploratory psychotherapy.

Similar difficulties are often encountered with the character disorders. The psychopath, for example, rarely considers himself responsible for his difficulties or in need of help, just as the paranoid patient does not seek psychotherapeutic assistance because the nature of his defense mechanisms leads him to project his troubles onto others. He does not consider himself emotionally disturbed or out of contact with reality. In the case of patients with character disorders who have a history of adjustive inadequacy through most of their lives, the psychotherapeutic approach seems to have limited value, as with cases of intellectual inadequacy. It is not merely a matter of a person discovering through psychotherapy the unconscious conflicts and self-deceptive mechanisms that have defeated his adjustive efforts, but it is a matter of a whole lifetime of failing to develop mature and adequate ways of solving problems and getting along in society. Although the problem is not always insurmountable, the character disorder involves severe obstacles to a successful psychotherapeutic effort.

There are also more subtle factors that sometimes limit the possibilities for successful psychotherapy. Hollingshead and Redlich (1958) have pointed to social-class factors in determining the type of disorder, who seeks therapy, and who is selected by psychotherapists in the hospital setting for therapeutic attention. Lower-class members of society do not often acquire an introspective orientation, which is required for psychotherapy, and such persons find it difficult to approach their problems in the fashion characteristic of modern psychotherapeutic practice. It is largely the educated middle class that finds the psychotherapeutic situation meaningful.

Similarly in the understaffed hospital (and this means most hospitals throughout the country), the psychotherapist cannot work intensively with every patient. He must therefore select those patients who seem to have the qualities that offer the best possibilities of a positive outcome. Those patients are selected who can verbalize their problems and who seem to have sufficient ego strength to undertake the psychotherapeutic process; the regressed or chronic patient is more likely to be ignored. The same is undoubtedly true in private practice because a person must be able to afford psychotherapy, be motivated to undertake it, and be educated enough to recognize its possibilities.

Another factor determining suitability for psychotherapy is age. An elderly person is likely to be far less ready or capable to change the personality structure that has been developing and ossifying for so many years. Therefore, above the fifties, a patient is generally less suited to a psychotherapeutic approach to emotional disturbances. On the other hand, a person must be old enough to profit from the therapeutic relationship. A small child is seldom able to verbalize and conceptualize his experiences and feelings sufficiently well, and other therapeutic approaches must be considered for him. It is common, when children are brought for treatment, for the therapist to treat the parents as well as the child. This is because the difficulties, presumably, are centered in the relationship between the child and the parents, and there is often a better chance of directly helping the parents, which, in turn, can have an indirect salutary effect on the child himself. In the case of an early adolescent, it is not often possible for the young patient to have sufficient control over his life situation to profit from whatever insights he might gain from psychotherapy. He must continue to live at home, dependent upon his parents. In this situation the youngster can be placed in a foster home (indirect or milieu therapy), while attempts are made simultaneously to help him in a direct way through a psychotherapeutic relationship.

It must be clear from the foregoing that psychotherapy as an approach to failures of adjustment tends to be limited to a particular age group of sufficient intelligence, with a limited degree of pathology, and to those who can accept the implicit value system of the therapeutic process, which is based so heavily upon a verbal and introspective approach. This still leaves a tremendous field for psychotherapeutic practice, but it means that other or modified approaches must be sought for a large percentage of persons suffering from disorders of adjustment. It is quite possible that many failures of psychotherapy have to do with the unsuitability of the patient for the particular kind of therapeutic approach employed. A primary reason for diagnostic work-ups prior to deciding what therapeutic approach to follow is the need to suit the patient to the therapeutic technique. A great deal more must still be learned along these lines.

SPECIAL PSYCHOTHERAPIES

Clinicians interested in psychotherapy have been very inventive in developing special types of psychotherapy to suit particular patient populations or to fit special needs in the clinical setting. Among these special psychotherapies, three have been especially important. These are play therapy, role playing and psychodrama, and group psychotherapy.

Play Therapy

Because of the difficulties in establishing the usual kind of verbal psychotherapeutic relationship with children, techniques of play therapy have been developed. These techniques have in common placing a child in some play situation to provide opportunity for the relief of tensions, the production of diagnostic information about the sources of stress in his family situation, and sometimes even the development of limited insight on the part of the child concerning his problems. Such activities as puppet shows, finger painting, drawing, modeling with clay, and play with toys and dolls have been used in this fashion.

Frequently the child will not or cannot verbalize problems directly to the therapist, but he can reveal a great deal about these problems if allowed to play freely with toys. The child can indirectly express his fears and conflicts, his ambivalent attitudes to parents and siblings, his feelings of unwantedness and insecurity, and the repressed aggression that he cannot express or verbalize in a direct fashion.

A child, who could not or would not talk about his car sickness might deal with the problem quickly in the play room. In one particular case, for example, a child placed a mama doll and a boy doll in a toy street car and said that the little boy felt sick. He further stated that the boy was sick because he feared a truck would hit the car and hurt the mama. In another situation he played with a small boy doll, who would not go to sleep alone in a dark room for fear that the father doll, who did not live with the mother doll, would come and steal him. In the skillful handling of such play situations it is possible for the therapist to develop dynamic understandings that might otherwise be impossible. In addition, as the child is enabled to reveal his strivings, his tensions, and his reactions to family influences, he may himself gain some important insights.[1]

Various writers have emphasized different features of the play therapeutic situation. Some, such as Levy (1939), have stressed the role of catharsis in play. For example, hostility to siblings or parents can be discharged in play with dolls that represent members of the family. Others, such as Thom (1937), have emphasized reeducation of the child and habit training, which requires a high degree of authority and control over the child's behavior.

Axline (1947), in contrast, utilized Rogerian nondirective principles, pointing out the importance of an atmosphere of permissiveness and acceptance in which the child is the most important person in command of the situation, without being nagged or told what to do, free to test out his own ideas and to express himself fully without the constraint of adult authority. It is assumed that the child will bring his feelings to the surface in his play and will learn to face them, control them, or abandon them. In time, he becomes emotionally relaxed in play and will develop self-acceptance and self-sufficiency in the presence of an accepting, permissive, and understanding adult. If the therapist follows what a child expresses in his play, he can help him gain understanding or insight by reflecting back to him his attitudes, and this can make the child realize that these attitudes are accepted by someone else. At the same time the necessity of placing limitations on a child in the play situation is fully recognized. Although these limitations are few, they are considered important. For example, there is a time limit to the therapeutic situation, and at the end

---

[1] The material in this paragraph has been adapted from G. W. Shaffer & R. S. Lazarus. *Fundamental Concepts of Clinical Psychology.* New York: McGraw-Hill, 1952. Pp. 391–392.

of the prescribed time the play session is over. Moreover, a child is not permitted to attack the therapist or other children, nor is he permitted to be destructive of equipment. Beyond these limitations, however, the therapist is permissive and accepting and offers little restraint to the play activities.

Role Playing and Psychodrama

There is widespread recognition that a person's adjustive difficulties develop primarily in the context of interpersonal relations and involve, at the very least, difficulties between an individual and the other persons with whom he has contact. There has, therefore, been increasing emphasis on the aspects of therapy that concentrate on the nature of the social roles the patient plays.

Excellent examples of the importance of social roles in adjustment are the cases of patients who have been in mental hospitals and must now return home to live with their families again and to locate employment. For such patients there are special difficulties that are simply the result of their having been hospitalized and of the attitudes of fear and hostility that the public commonly expresses toward the former mental patient. Such a patient faces the difficulties of being questioned by a prospective employer concerning the period of time in his occupational history during which he was hospitalized. An employer may react with distrust and rejection of the patient when it is learned that he has suffered a mental breakdown. Similarly suspiciousness, fear, and hypersensitivity toward any symptomatic displays on the part of the patient, which are likely to occur among the patient's family and friends, are also very trying experiences for him in the period of his rehabilitation.

These problems can be prepared for in the hospital setting by having the patients enact scenes in which these events are likely to take place (Herriott & Hogan, 1941). One patient can play the role of the employer or a member of the family, and another patient can play himself in the situation he is about to face as he leaves the hospital. In this way, by role-playing techniques, he can become accustomed to the embarrassments produced by such situations and learn to respond to them wisely and without excessive emotion. When he leaves the hospital, he will be better prepared for these experiences and know how to act when they occur. In general, through the role-playing procedure, he can gain additional understanding of the feelings and behaviors of others.

The role-playing technique has been adapted in recent years to problems of human relations in industry and has been widely utilized in this context (Coffey, 1950).

A rather specific and elaborate version of this role-playing technique, in which some problem is acted out in anticipation or in restrospect, has been developed by Moreno (1947) and called *psychodrama*. In psychodrama a patient is asked to come upon a stage and portray his feelings and problems. He can begin by acting out situations that are a part of his daily life, and he is encouraged to act freely and spontaneously in the situation. He can enact his fantasies on the stage, and later real persons can take the place of those imagined by the patient. A staff of therapeutic actors portray the roles required by the patient's private world, and the therapist directs the drama and analyzes the situation as it develops.

Group Psychotherapy

A form of psychotherapy that is becoming increasingly important is group therapy (Slavson, 1943; Corsini, 1957). It involves a therapist and, instead of a single patient, a group of patients, approximately five to fifteen in number. One of the primary reasons for the increasing use of group-therapeutic techniques is the shortage of trained psychotherapists in relation to the number of patients who require therapy. Group therapy offers the therapist the opportunity to see a fairly considerable number of patients in a therapeutic situation at the same time. In mental hospitals, a single ward can be divided into several groups and seen by a therapist for an hour or so every week, thus spreading professional services much more widely among patients. Individual therapy is so time-consuming and inefficient that there is an increasing tendency to utilize group-therapeutic situations more and more as a treatment method.

There are many reasons other than efficiency of time for the rapid development of group-therapeutic techniques. In the group-therapeutic situation a patient is expected to interact with other persons with similar or diverse problems, and this interaction itself has certain values that individual psychotherapy lacks. For example, the simple exposure of a person to the problems and experiences of others can lead to the recognition that others are similarly unhappy or disturbed and can increase the confidence of a person who feels inadequate in the face of his problems. The group situation also offers opportunities for a person to improve his relationship with others by learning how to relate better to them and their feelings.

The therapist in the group situation commonly remains in the background, permitting and encouraging a free flow of interpersonal relationships between the members of the group. As a patient discusses his problems or symptoms, others offer their points of view or present some of their own experiences. Discussions ensue that include interpretation of the meaning of the symptoms and often criticism of each other's attitudes. The therapist can enter the discussion to clarify or summarize some of the important issues, or he can draw out those who are not actively participating. He also has the opportunity to observe the interaction of the members, learning a great deal about their characteristic social roles or styles of life and perhaps even utilizing this information later in individual contacts with the patients.

The group situation is a fluid affair, which raises an enormous number of scientific problems concerning the therapeutic process. These problems include, for example, selecting the members of the group; that is, what kinds of persons can be put together in a group situation and how many. There are also problems of methods for the psychotherapist in a group situation to use in successfully classifying and interpreting the interactions of the persons in the group. The therapist may observe that one patient plays the role of the doctor's helper, siding with the therapist in his interactions with the other patients, acting as a kind of surrogate therapist or lieutenant and attempting to interpret the therapist to the other patients. Powdermaker and Frank (1953), who have written extensively about the group-therapy situation, also describe the "help-rejecting complainer" patient, who acts as though he is continually seeking advice or assistance in his dilemma but continually rejects any suggestions or interpretations made in response to his pleas. These roles seem to be rather consistent in that an individual tends to play them repeatedly over a long period of time, and they give considerable insight into the patient's relationships with others outside the therapeutic situation.

Group therapy is a relatively new special approach to the therapeutic problem, and although it has gained great interest among professional workers, there is still a great deal to be learned about the processes of group interaction that are inherent in it. The method, however, offers tremendous opportunities for research and promises to have great value in a wide variety of contexts, both in the hospital and outside.

PHYSICAL AND CHEMICAL THERAPIES

In a sense, the physical and chemical approaches to therapy do not strictly belong on the same dimension as psychotherapy, which has been narrowly defined as involving direct interpersonal contact between patient and therapist, usually by verbal interaction. However, they are closer to psychotherapy than to sociotherapy or milieu therapy because, unlike the latter, they do not involve attempts to alter the environment of the patient but are oriented toward producing alteration of the personality structure through physical or chemical rather than psychological means. It is important that some mention be made of them because, in one form or other, they are widely used, and they are most appealing to the clinician who views psychopathology as a biochemical or physiological anomaly.

Physical and chemical therapies have had a long and checkered history. Until recently, one of the most important of these approaches was the so-called shock treatment, which was used primarily with the most severely disturbed patients in mental hospitals, and especially with those where the duration and extent of the illness seemed to make unlikely the recovery of the patient. In 1928, Meduna (1935) produced convulsions in schizophrenic patients by intramuscular injections of camphor in oil; shortly after he turned to a substance called *metrazol*, which produced epilepticlike seizures immediately and reliably. These seizures, however, involved continual danger of fractures and other serious damage. Metrazol was abandoned, partly because of the danger of injury and the great anxiety that its use seemed to promote in patients. It was replaced by *electroshock-induced* convulsions by Cerletti and Bini (1938). Electroshock has been used very widely up until recent years with relatively few complications or discomforts to the patient, especially with manic-depressive psychosis. Such treatment, however, has been found relatively inadequate with the schizophrenias, and the use of *insulin* to produce convulsions or comas was stimulated by the work of Dussik and Sakel (1936). Insulin produces a coma and convulsions by severe reduction in the blood sugar content of the blood, and it was, until recently, very commonly used in schizophrenic disorders.

There has long been considerable controversy over the effectiveness of the various shock therapies with their history of conflicting claims and research findings. Moreover, there is little agreement on the theoretical basis by which shock therapies produce improvement in psychotic disturbances. Shaffer and Lazarus (1952) have reviewed a considerable amount of this research and some of the theoretical interpretations of the effects of the shock treatment.

Along with shock therapies, surgical procedures have also been utilized in attempts to produce improvement in psychotic patients, especially the most seriously regressed. A particular form of *psychosurgery*, often referred to as the "prefrontal lobotomy," was first introduced by Moniz (1936) and enthusiastically received in the United States by Freeman and Watts (1937). It involved destruction of certain tissues of the brain, especially the nervous pathways that connected the frontal lobes of the brain with the thalamus. As in the case of shock therapies, there has been little agreement on the value of psychosurgery and substantial concern that great damage was also incurred, or at least risked, by this drastic procedure.

Other procedures, such as the use of *deep narcosis* produced by sodium amytal and other narcotic drugs, were less common but not infrequently found. Physiotherapy, such as relaxation and massage, baths to quiet excited patients, and diathermy, is also long-standing physical therapeutic procedure employed in the mental hospitals.

In recent years, a dramatic change has taken place in the physical and chemical approaches to mental disorder, which has almost resulted in the abandonment of all the above techniques for treatment. This change has resulted from the development of so-called tranquilizing drugs, including such patented versions as Reserpine, Chlorpromazine, Thorazine, and drugs such as Miltown or Equinol, which are used in huge quantities by very mildly disturbed persons.

The use of tranquilizing drugs is so recent that it is as yet difficult to assess their real worth and effectiveness as a treatment of mental disease. Moreover, relatively little is yet known about their precise chemical effects on the nervous system. The tranquilizing drugs cannot genuinely be conceived as the basis of cure of psychopathology, but in many instances they seem to have produced the quieting of usually disturbed hospital wards and placed previously inaccessible patients in sufficiently good contact to be amenable to other forms of psychological treatment. There has been a wave of enthusiasm among clinical personnel for these drugs, so it is difficult to tell whether the ameliorative effects result from this enthusiasm and its suggestive effect upon patients or whether the chemical reaction is the primary basis by which they work. Research studies remain, at the present time, somewhat inconclusive on these questions, some yielding apparently exciting results and others, discouraging results. Nowhere is there more need for cool and precise experimentation and theory than in this area.

The use of tranquilizing drugs is part of a renewed interest in the biochemistry of the brain in the hopes that the biochemical correlates of mental disorder and of human adaptation in general can be better understood. One must always remember, however, that psychopathology is, in part, defined by a context of social interaction, which cannot be reduced entirely to biochemical or physiological terms. The psychologist, sociologist, or psychiatrist, who views psychopathology as ineffective social interaction, tends to be skeptical that a strictly physiological approach can adequately deal with the pervasive problem of adjustive failure. On the other hand, there are substantial numbers of scientific and professional persons who are convinced that the reduction of behavior disorders to the physiological level of analysis, at least in part, is both possible and fruitful, and these persons tend to view psychopathology as disturbances of cellular structure and function in the nervous tissues.

THERAPEUTIC COUNSELING

Until now emphasis has been on attempts to treat adjustive failures by direct therapeutic procedures based upon the interview or physical interaction, with the aim of producing personality reorganization. Such procedures deemphasize the environmental situation in which the patient is embedded and focus upon the process of personality change as it takes place through direct conversations (or physical treatments) between patient and therapist. It is possible to place greater emphasis on the circumstances of a patient's life, attempting to change these so the internal pressures motivating the individual can be better actualized or the external demands that overwhelm him can be reduced.

This manipulation of the environment has been practiced for a long time and is one of the earliest forms of therapy, broadly conceived. This is what happens to some degree when a person is hospitalized. He is physically removed from the direct and continuing influences of his family, his community, and his job. In a sense it is like the old-fashioned medical prescription of a rest cure—getting away from things—so a person can change his perspective or replenish his resources for coping with difficult adjustmental problems when he returns to his old haunts. A child having difficulties in a pathological family context and placed in a foster home is an example of such environmental manipulation. Likewise, when it is recommended that someone change jobs or occupations to one more suitable to his abilities or personality characteristics, the therapeutic agent involves an environmental change.

In the case of the physically handicapped person, the environment can be controlled or limited in some way to fit better an individual's adjustive limitations, or he can be trained again to cope with environmental demands on a new basis. For example, a blind person can be taught to read braille, and his household and interpersonal contacts can be rearranged to permit him to function better. A mentally deficient child can be placed in a special school, which recognizes and deals with his handicap, just as the unusually bright child can be placed in special classes or provided with enriched programs to permit better actualization of his intellectual potential. These environmental manipulations are often referred to as *milieu therapy,* or *sociotherapy.*

The difference in emphasis between direct efforts at manipulating the psychodynamics of an individual and approaches that are more oriented to environmental control is represented by another type of professional psychologist in the clinical field: the therapeutic counselor. Just as there are training programs for the clinical psychologist, there are separate training programs for the *counseling psychologist,* although, as we shall see, the overlap between them is so great that the distinction is often difficult to apply in actual professional practice. Milieu therapy and psychotherapy go hand in hand and are often thoroughly intertwined.

Counseling psychology seems to have had its origin as a distinct field in the process of educational and vocational guidance (Brayfield, 1950; Porter, 1950; Hadley, 1958). Guidance experts recognized that persons differed considerably in their intellectual capacities to handle certain types of educational and vocational demands. On the basis of appropriate information about these capacities, a counselor could frequently advise a person on the levels and types of education and occupation suited to his level or pattern of abilities.

It was also soon recognized that intellectual capacity alone was an insufficient basis for educational and vocational decisions. A person's interests and motivations were important, and there were personality attributes that were consonant with some types of work and not with others. More and more it became evident that the task of suiting the individual to educational and occupational demands required a thorough knowledge of psychological processes and personality dynamics. The value of professional guidance or counseling became recognized in such areas as marital relations and work with handicapped persons.

The major distinction between counseling psychology and clinical psychology is that the latter began to develop primarily in terms of interest in the personality dynamics of the individual and the psychotherapeutic process, whereas the former originated in a concern with environmental demands upon the individual. Moreover, the clinical psychologist, with his accent on psychotherapy, tended to see more seriously disturbed persons, and the counselor tended to work more extensively with mildly disturbed or relatively healthy persons who needed guidance.

It was inevitable, however, that the clinical psychologist should move in the direction of increasing recognition of the importance of environmental factors and toward a greater concern for the relatively healthy or only mildly disturbed person. In the diagnostic work of the clinical psychologist the fact had to be faced that the patient was living in a particular environment. If he were hospitalized, he had to have some organized program of activity that was therapeutically important, over and above the usual direct psychotherapeutic contact. Such patients ultimately would be discharged to return to their families and to either an old or a new occupation. A patient could not be regarded simply in terms of internal (trait) concepts of personality structure, but he had to be seen as an adjusting individual in an environmental context.

Similarly the counseling psychologists had to recognize more and more that any environmental control or manipulation had to be considered not only in relation to such factors as level of intelligence and pattern of interest but in terms of the entire personality. This personality determined what was threatening or supporting in the life circumstances of an individual and what resources were available to him, allowing him to cope appropriately with these demands.

The result of these insights on the part of mature clinical psychologists and counseling psychologists has led to a progressive disappearance of the distinction both in the training situation and in the clinical settings themselves. There is still a profession of counseling psychologist as opposed to clinical psychologist and the American Psychological Association still offers diplomates (or special boards) in clinical psychology and counseling psychology, but it is becoming increasingly difficult to find a sensible distinction between the two fields. Thus therapeutic counseling is likely to include in practice what has been discussed as psychotherapy but with a primary concern with the environmental context in which an individual makes his adjustments.

PSYCHOTHERAPY AND PSYCHOLOGICAL THEORY

Until now psychotherapy has been considered as a means of solving one of the great human problems: personal and social maladjustment. It is also important for another reason. Psychotherapy is a kind of laboratory for exploring personal psychological organization. We can therefore ask the question: What does the process of psychotherapy contribute to psychological theory, including our conceptions of personality? and conversely: What do our theoretical conceptions about persons contribute to psychotherapeutic practice?

It would seem that psychotherapy has contributed more to psychological theory than our theories have contributed to psychotherapeutic practice. Most of the great systems of personality theory have originated in the clinical context, with a creative theorist struggling to understand psychopathology and its treatment. For example, Freud was a physician and neurologist who attempted to deal with and understand hysterical phenomena. His personality theory was built out of the observations he made of patients with various types of personality disturbances. Most of the systematic points of view concerning personality discussed earlier, which are the most influential and important systems of thought, have originated in this way. The emotional disturbances of clinical patients require explanation and also invite comparison with normal functioning. The attempt to understand psychopathology and to conceptualize personality change through psychotherapy inevitably leads to the construction of some theoretical model of human behavior and development.

If we turn to the question of the impact of our theories of behavior on psychotherapeutic practice, it becomes abundantly clear that this has been slight. There is a large gap between our theoretical conceptions and psychotherapeutic practice, and it is only with the greatest of difficulty that we can show, on occasion, that a particular therapeutic practice is closely integrated with theory. Good psychotherapists, to be effective, utilize similar approaches in actual practice, regardless of whether they are Freudian, Sullivanian, Adlerian, Jungian, or Rogerian. What these clinicians say about the process of therapy can differ considerably, but their actual behavior is often quite comparable and not consistently related to their diverse theoretical orientation.

There are some systematic differences that can be highlighted. For example, the traditional Freudian psychoanalyst is likely to insist on a minimum of three to five hours per week of psychotherapy and to regard the therapy as inadequate and incomplete unless it is carried on over a considerable period of time, a minimum of two years and usually far longer. The patient almost always lies on a couch with the therapist behind him, and there is a minimum of direct interaction between the therapist and patient, especially early in therapy. On the other hand, those psychologists with a more social orientation, such as Adler, Horney, and Sullivan, are less concerned with the patient reliving his childhood experiences, especially those within the first four years of life, and emphasize more the meaning of the present relationship between the therapist and the patient in the context of his current life situation. Thus, the therapy can take place over a far shorter period. Furthermore, the therapist and patient are more likely to sit facing each other and interact as two real persons.

Most therapists, regardless of conceptual framework, agree that interpretation must be minimized and presented carefully (at least with neurotics) so the patient presents his own picture of his problem and is not frightened away. On the other hand, where interpretation is used, it cannot help but be somewhat slanted by the theoretical position of the therapist. And, of course, there are some very special features of some theoretical systems, which, when they are applied in psychotherapy, lead to very particular kinds of therapeutic action. For example, Rank's conception of the neurosis (built around the problem of separation) leads him to the technique of "end setting," which means that the therapist establishes a date for the termination of the therapy (for the separation of the patient and therapist), which the patient is expected to abide by. The Rogerian conception (of forces for growth within a person that will operate when the external constraints of a repressive society are removed or reduced) leads him to eschew interpretation entirely and to emphasize the accepting and permissive quality of the therapist's behavior and the reflection of the patient's statements about himself.

Although there are some differences in therapeutic practice that arise from varying theoretical conceptions of man, these differences are not nearly so great as one would imagine from the different points of view themselves. There is less articulation and integration of the theoretical system with the therapeutic practice, and one must always differentiate between what the therapist says about the therapeutic process and what he actually does in a series of therapeutic interviews.

Up until recently it was uncommon practice to record interviews, and it was therefore also difficult to analyze objectively the therapeutic process in terms of what actually took place. More and more interest is now being displayed by clinicians in studying the actual process of therapy and the nature of the interpersonal interaction that takes place. To some extent, by an objective approach to the problem, we can temporarily ignore what the therapist thinks is happening and focus upon what the patient and therapist are actually saying. With considerably more research effort in this direction it should be possible to develop closer ties between actual therapeutic practice and theories of personality. The opportunities for elaborating and sharpening our conceptual systems for understanding behavior are greatly enhanced when we can study *in vivo* the interaction of the patient and therapist as they work together on the problem of maladjustment.

PSYCHOTHERAPY: A DOUBTFUL PANACEA

In the profession of clinical psychology, speaking broadly to include all workers concerned with the amelioration of suffering produced by adjustive failure, there is a tendency to seek desperately and to apply any methods that genuinely seem to have promise in this effort toward increased human welfare. To the person who remains sensitive to human suffering, this task of helping persons solve their problems sometimes seems overwhelming. For one thing, there are so many in need of professional assistance and so few professionally trained persons available or even in prospect.

Psychotherapy, as a direct verbal method of approach to personality change, really got its impetus in the early 1900s from the Freudian psychoanalytic movement and was further stimulated by the theoretical variations on psychoanalysis that later developed. It is not our intention here to trace the history of psychotherapy, but since World War I, and especially following World War II, there has been a tremendous increase in interest in psychiatric and clinical psychology training and psychotherapy has become established as a potent force in the mental-health fields. There remains some unresolved conflict concerning psychotherapeutic practice between the two professions of clinical psychology and psychiatry, but the trend has been toward greater participation on the part of all relevant professions, including social work and counseling psychology, in the area of psychotherapy.

There have been times when those professional workers first discovering psychotherapy made grandiose statements concerning its value in the solution of mental-health problems. Professional persons sometimes referred to whole societies as sick and recommended psychotherapy for every human being who could possibly obtain it. Although intensive work with psychotherapy was earlier directed at the severe emotional disorders, it soon became recognized that many persons could profit from it who were only mildly disturbed. Then the horizons for psychotherapy opened wide to include nearly everyone. Psychotherapy was often considered a kind of panacea, which could solve not only the minor and serious emotional disturbances that afflict persons in our society but even the problems of international tensions and war.

Among some professional and lay persons this grandiose conception of psychotherapy continues, but there is developing a gradually increasing realization that the values of psychotherapy in the solution of emotionally based problems are not as great as once anticipated. There is increasing recognition that psychotherapy, at least as described in this chapter, is suitable for only certain kinds of persons, and is, in addition, a terribly costly enterprise. As pointed out earlier, large segments of the population cannot enter into a psychotherapeutic relationship for one reason or another, although it is always possible to assume that changes or improvements in our techniques will increase the scope of the population that can be treated psychotherapeutically.

It is interesting to recall that Freud himself became extremely skeptical near the end of his life that psychotherapy could be performed with any but a very limited number of persons who met certain psychodynamic criteria. Of course, Freud had in mind psychoanalytic psychotherapy, which is perhaps the most restrictive of the psychotherapeutic approaches in its applicability. Moreover, all psychotherapists experience a considerable percentage of failures in the psychotherapeutic process. Patients under their care do not improve or improve in only very limited ways and to slight degree. Many patients who begin psychotherapy terminate it early in the process before any help can be realized. Large numbers will not come for help, although it is safe to say they need it. It is also quite conceivable that a patient who can make substantial progress with one psychotherapist or one type of therapeutic orientation may not progress successfully with another. We are flirting here, of course, with the entire question of the assessment of the results of psychotherapy, a problem that has scarcely been touched in clinical research.

We cannot answer the question of how successful psychotherapy is, in general, because the needed information is fundamentally lacking and the issues of the values of psychotherapy are tinged with emotional and economic considerations. There are those writers, such as Eysenck (1952), who maintain that there is little or no evidence that psychotherapy does any good at all. Most psychotherapists and many patients will attest anecdotally to significant improvements under psychotherapy, but it is quite true that these claims are not yet buttressed by competent research and competent research is difficult in this area because of a wide range of methodological problems and social pressures.

Clinical manuals and textbooks in abnormal psychology and personality usually present psychotherapy in its most positive light, but there is beginning to be greater realism in the clinical professions about what psychotherapy can and cannot do. More than ever clinical persons are searching for other forms of approach to the problem of mental health, and this search, in itself, is a reflection of the recognition that psychotherapy alone does not totally solve our problems. But there is a considerable cultural lag, so that students of psychiatry, clinical psychology, and social work are often unaware of this trend and frequently still regard psychotherapeutic practice as the most desirable and ultimate goal of their training. They underplay, for example, many other more mundane approaches, such as rehabilitation counseling, the use of drugs, and the preventive approach to mental health through social change and more adequate child-rearing practices. Professional workers are taking increasing interest in community-health projects and in the developmental and education processes central to the production of health or disorder. The exaggerated and uncritical enthusiasm for psychotherapy has begun to wane, and in its place there is arising a more sensible orientation, which recognizes the limitations inherent in the current psychotherapeutic approaches.

Above all, real progress can never be made by preoccupation exclusively with how, without a continuing concern for why. In other words, the first and most important problem is to understand failures of adjustment and why certain kinds of experiences have a corrective or harmful influence on further development. Psychotherapy seems to be an experience that for many persons is corrective, and we should be most preoccupied with understanding when and why it has a positive effect. The problems to be understood are important ones, and the psychotherapeutic relationship offers a vital and exciting arena for the scientific study of man as much as for the actualization of our humanitarian motives to help those in trouble.

CHAPTER 15

Other Applications

There are two main reasons why the professional psychologist undertakes the study of personality and adjustment. The inquisitive scientist in him hungers for understanding about the human being. This understanding is reflected in theories of personality, which are designed to organize and make comprehensible the multitude of facts about human beings that he and others before him have recorded.

The ultimate test of this understanding lies in the ability to predict behavior under specified conditions. The theories must be stated in such a way as to be subject to confirmation or disconfirmation through predictions. Personality research involves efforts to enlarge the scope of known facts and to test predictions derived from the concepts of personality theory.

The second main reason for the psychologist's concern with personality and adjustment is a completely practical one. Should he achieve sufficient information and understanding as to be able to predict with reasonable success, he is then in a position to influence the psychological world that he studies. In other words, the ability to predict behavior successfully implies the ability to control it. In the field of psychopathology, for example, adjustive failure and great human suffering might be either prevented or relieved. In the field of international relations tensions might conceivably be reduced and war abolished. There are great areas of human endeavor where the application of understanding of the processes of personality and adjustment could prove tremendously important. The purpose of this chapter is not to detail these but to consider the implications of such application and offer some current examples.

IMPLICATIONS OF CONTROL OVER HUMAN BEHAVIOR

Before we proceed further, it would be well to linger for a moment on the implications of these possible applications. Whenever human beings have the power to influence their destinies and the destinies of others, we must ask whether, in any specific instance, this is a good thing or a bad thing. In other words, it is necessary to decide what kind of world we want before we seriously try to influence it. Psychologists who are committed to the reduction of human suffering resulting from mental illness are regarded as pursuing a humanistic and laudable goal. But the greater the possibility of influencing their patients, the more crucial becomes the question: What kind of person should be produced?

Actually, psychotherapists have tended to avoid this value-oriented question; yet it is continually before them, at least implicitly. They are able to justify this avoidance because they generally deal with clearly disturbed persons who are either unhappy or deviant with respect to their society. But the decision to hospitalize a patient, for example, is usually made not merely because the patient is disturbed but because this disturbance involves either a danger to himself and others or a great nuisance or threat to social proprieties. Although advising is not by any means a main activity of the psychotherapist, the advice that is given is predicated on some conception of the pathological personality and of what the healthy person ought to be. In the same way, the objectives of psychotherapy must be grounded in similar conceptions and cannot help but influence the attitudes and behavior of the patient. This is not a criticism of psychotherapy but merely the recognition of an ethical problem that is inevitable any time we try to influence a person, even if we are guided by the most benign motives. As we shall see, this problem is inherent in any of the psychological applications and is often not recognized clearly by psychological practitioners.

Think for just a moment about what would be implied if psychologists were truly able to predict and control human behavior to a high degree, say, to the same degree as the physical scientists and engineers can predict and control the physical world.

In Aldous Huxley's *Brave New World* (1932) and in George Orwell's *1984* (1949), the frightening prospects of a psychologically controlled society are held before us by the gifted imaginations of two writers. If this kind of prospect has not produced more alarm, it is because few persons have taken seriously the scope and predictive power of psychological theories. Few persons yet believe that enough is known to effect such control. This is probably a proper estimate for the moment, but the fantastic development of the physical sciences and the recent strides in the biological sciences suggest that psychology will someday be much more potent in the prediction and control of human behavior. Think of the enormous responsibility this will entail. Should this happen, there can be no refuge from the value-oriented questions that psychological scientists have, in the main, avoided.

PERSONAL APPLICATIONS

But let us bring the discussion of application more clearly into the context of this book. Most readers will not be professional psychologists but persons interested in the more immediate applications of knowledge in the field of personality and adjustment. Especially, they will look at the subject matter rather personally and evaluate it, at least in part, from their individual points of view.

For some, there will be great disappointment. These are the ones who have been oversold on what constitutes present knowledge in this area and who have perhaps expected or hoped for a profound personal effect from reading in this area. Because most of us suffer more or less from some psychological distress and would like to increase our comfort and interpersonal effectiveness, we are drawn irresistibly to the subject matter of personality and adjustment.

The disappointment is that what has been read cannot be used in any direct way. If an intellectual knowledge of the principles of human behavior and personality could markedly alter adjustment and interpersonal relations, then all the professional workers who are steeped in this material and who have gone far beyond the introductory level of this book would be paragons of mental health. Surely the reader knows better than this. Psychologists, psychiatrists, social workers, educators, and so on, are, as groups, no healthier mentally and emotionally than workers in other fields. Many live happy, effective lives, and many suffer psychotic breakdowns or chronic neurotic disturbances.

There is a large discrepancy between knowing the principles of psychology and applying them in any particular case, especially to one's self. But why should this be? One answer is that the very mechanisms of ego defense, to be effective, must permit us to deceive ourselves. Thus, although we can recognize paranoid projections, hysterical denials, or obsessive-compulsive intellectualizations in others, we are likely to be unaware of them in ourselves.

The many books that promise peace of mind or a happier life in one way or another merely by virtue of reading them tend to mislead, however we might wish otherwise. The advice they offer can have the ring of truth or can include fine statements of some practical, ethical, or religious position with which we can concur. They give us a momentarily positive experience but scarcely any profound or long-lasting effects. It simply violates the recognized principles of personality dynamics to propose that intellectual knowledge about personality and adjustment will have a deep impact on our own personality dynamics and way of life. Let us consider some concrete examples.

Because so many of us seek guides for behavior, books and newspaper columns offering advice on mental hygiene proliferate. They bombard us with wise sayings and bits of advice similar to the half-truths found in all great literature and in the wisdom of ancient philosophers. For example, one spokesman for Roman civilization, Horace, advised, *"carpe diem,"* which means pluck the flower of the day, or seize the present moment and enjoy it. Surely this sounds like a good principle, except for somebody who is so impulse-ridden that he cannot put off momentary pleasures in order to plan for greater gains in the future (e.g., the character disorders). Besides, do we imagine that the extremely inhibited, compulsive person who cannot let go heedlessly under any circumstances will take this piece of advice to heart? Extreme conservatism is so deeply embedded in his character structure that such advice would be rejected even if he wanted to follow it.

Let us look at another, more modern, example. Figure 37 presents a famous cartoon column called "Let's Explore Your Mind" (Duvall & Duvall, 1959), which indeed, in this particular instance, makes a most sensible plea to be yourself. We can read the statement and assent, "Yes, that's true—it is so right—don't put on an act; be yourself without pretense or sham." The advice is clearly based upon the fact that many persons are so tied in knots with inhibitions and poses that they cannot permit themselves to express their impulses, even when, in fact, such expression might have desirable effects on their interpersonal relations, reduce tensions in themselves, or ease psychosomatic symptoms. In that sense, it appears perfectly sensible.

The trouble is, however, that the person who most needs to heed this advice cannot. The inability to express freely impulses and feelings often

Figure 37. A famous cartoon newspaper column called "Let's Explore Your Mind," which offers advice and inspiration concerning problems of adjustment. (*Reprinted, permission National Newspaper Syndicate.*)

is rooted in inaccessible conflicts. The existence of certain impulses produces severe anxiety, and a person can have acquired all sorts of defenses to avoid their expression. Control over such dangerous impulses
may have become terribly important and relaxation of these controls all
but impossible. Such a person can even recognize that he is excessively
inhibited and can see the point in the plea to "be yourself." Others can
be totally unaware that they play-act in most interpersonal situations.

The cartoon column further states, "Most important of all, get in the
habit of becoming really interested in others." This, as the public long
ago recognized as good advice in the best-selling book by Dale Carnegie,
How to Win Friends and Influence People (1937), is a fine thought. But
a person who lacks genuine interest in others cannot so easily revamp
his narcissistic personality in order to become interested. He can often
affect such interest, although this imitation of the real thing is often
spotted as such, and the constant maintenance of a false role can hardly
be very satisfying, nor can it promote a comfortable way of life. A person who does this with ease in order to manipulate others can succeed
in such manipulations but also suffers from a disorder of character that
in itself is likely to promote other troubles.

This does not mean that advice or the kind of knowledge contained in
this book is never of any value. In a basically healthy personality, discoveries can be sometimes made or given by counselors that are helpful.
This is especially true when the problem is based upon a lack of knowledge of some method or skill for accomplishing ends. A mother who has
been having difficulty disciplining her child can sometimes get help from
information about other techniques she either did not think of or did
not know about. A student who is having trouble studying effectively
or taking notes can gain from applying information provided by books
or pamphlets on how to study. But this is only the case when the problem is superficial and not based upon serious internal conflicts. In the
latter instance, a mother, for example, might not be able to accept the
good advice, or the student the technical information, because deep
problems interfere. Most of the important problems of adjustment are
of the latter kind and are refractory to all wise sayings based upon either
common sense or psychological sophistication.

In the application of principles of personality and adjustment by a
person who has intellectually absorbed them and tries to apply them to
himself, the prospects for success are not very great. But there is also
the matter of the professional who attempts to apply knowledge to specific cases. Here, our control of human behavior is still at so early a stage
that application remains somewhat limited. As was pointed out earlier,
our predictions are probabilistic. That is, because we cannot usually
have command or knowledge of all the relevant conditions with which

to make predictions, we must make the best-educated guesses about what is to happen as a result of our interventions in the lives of others. We will be often wrong, but sometimes right. The greater our knowledge, the less will be the amount of error in our efforts.

For some readers the absence of final and absolute statements throughout this book will have been disappointing, and for others the problems posed will have stimulated the excitement of a great challenge. Such readers will recognize that the answers depend upon continued research. This introduction to the field will represent for them not really a conclusion at all but a beginning or preface.

SOME OTHER FIELDS OF APPLICATION

In the remainder of this chapter, let us consider a number of different areas of human endeavor in which there are present and potential applications of our knowledge of personality and adjustment. We might begin with one of the most obvious—the broad field of mental health.

Mental Health

Broadly speaking, this field includes the business of understanding, preventing, and curing adjustive failure from the minor neuroses and behavior problems to the most severe disorders, such as schizophrenia. In a sense, it might be better to say that the mental-health field is concerned with promoting healthy personalities, but, as noted in Chapter 12, there has been a greater tendency to define mental health as the absence of symptoms of pathology than to attempt to develop a useful conception of positive mental health.

The bulk of the professional resources concerned with mental health is concentrated in *clinics and hospitals*, although there are many in other public-health institutions, schools, prisons, and private practice. The greatest active pressure comes from agencies responsible for the obviously disturbed person needing diagnostic and therapeutic services. There are, however, an increasing number of outpatient clinics (which see patients who live outside the clinic and come under their own power for therapeutic assistance) and inpatient hospitals over the country. In the chapters on personality assessment and on psychotherapy, applications in these settings were discussed.

Another mental-health area in which applications are important is the *school system*. Here application consists in spotting a disturbed child and in providing treatment for him. There is also the ever-present question of the kind of educational atmosphere desired to promote mental health. This latter sentence conceals a multitude of decisions that must be made about children in the educational system, independent of a concern with the educational process itself. For example, what should be done with the exceptional child (bright or dull)? Should he be advanced, held back, or put in special classes? How permissive or disciplined should the classroom situation be? Appropriate decisions about these questions require a knowledge of the relations between childhood experiences and adult personality. Finally, there is the task of educating teachers to the mental-health role they play with the children in their charge. Most education curricula for teachers now include systematic courses in the psychology of personality and adjustment.

Still within the area of mental health there are the ever-present sociological and psychological problems of *delinquency* and *criminality*. The reader will recall current debates about whether juvenile delinquency, for example, is increasing, and if so, what social factors are contributing to it? The field of personality and adjustment provides some answers, and professional workers use psychological principles in making decisions about how the criminal should be treated and what opportunities are provided for rehabilitation.

The ever-increasing percentage of our population in the aged category presents other problems in applying principles of personality and adjustment. Some of these problems, of course, are strictly physiological, although even these can have psychological import, as when we ask about the capabilities and limitations of older persons to hold jobs, drive cars, and carry responsibilities.

But many, and perhaps the most serious, problems of aging are entirely psychological, especially those relating to the adjustment of elderly persons in a society that provides decreasing opportunities for the older person to be active and useful. Mandatory retirement ages of a fixed and arbitrary sort work great hardship on the person who is still active and effective. The aged person requires financial security and interesting things to do. There is the problem of facing death, now closer than ever before. Moreover, individual differences in physical and mental capacities as well as needs of elderly persons vary greatly, which means that the proper approach to each case depends upon a knowledge of personalities. Public efforts to solve some of the problems of aging are becoming increasingly frequent and effective. Senior Centers catering to elderly people have been springing up all over the country. The increase in this sort of attempt to find a partial solution to the social and psychological problems of aging is reflected in the fact that *Life* magazine ran a full story about centers of this kind on July 20, 1959. Figure 38 shows a group of elderly men and women active in one such organization.

There are also problems of application in marriage and divorce. For good reason, getting married is regarded as one of the crucial decisions that men and women make in their lifetimes. It is a decision that can

Figure 38. The man seated at the left celebrated his one-hundredth birthday by playing three tunes for square dancing on his fiddle. He also shook hands with about twelve hundred friends who greeted him at a community center for senior citizens. Other elderly members of the center also participated. Organizations such as this, designed to give meaning and activity to the remaining years of elderly persons, are becoming increasingly common. (*Wide World Photos.*)

result potentially in a lifetime of family mutual gratification and harmony. It can be one that, in the less unfortunate instance, involves pain only for the two participants; in the more unfortunate case, it can have painful and psychologically damaging ramifications that extend to several children. The problems include the choice of mate, disturbances of communication, and failures to provide the mutual gratification of very important needs of the marriage partners. Principles of personality and adjustment are required for sound decisions by the courts, by attorneys, by ministers, by marriage counselors, and by psychotherapists. For better or worse, such services are continually given, based usually on what is known generally about marital discord and on the extensive specialized experience of professional workers.

In addition to these extremely large-scale and pervasive problems in our society, there are a number of special mental-health fields for which principles of personality and adjustment are relevant and in which they are continually being applied. The field of *adoption* is one. Adoption agencies, through their social-service workers, are concerned with placing infants and children for adoption with families that are appropriate for the task of child rearing. They are thus continually making judgments about factors important in child rearing, one of which is the mental health and personality of the potential parents. They also attempt to anticipate the potentialities of the child being adopted. A complex tangle of legal and social issues is part of the problem. These issues often bear upon the theoretical and empirical questions of personality and adjustment.

The *handicapped child or adult* represents another instance of a mental-health problem requiring the discovery and application of psychological principles of adjustment and personality. Psychologists in this field are being employed more and more by organizations that are concerned, for example, with the cerebral-palsied child, the blind, and the deaf. The problems involved go beyond the clinic or the hospital. They include finding ways of making the adjustment of the handicapped person in his life setting less painful and more effective and of working with relatives, friends, and associates to help them behave more wisely toward such a person and his problems. Professional workers have recognized, for example, the great psychological dangers of the hardship and guilt often experienced by the parents to the development of the handicapped child and his siblings. By studying their attitudes, these workers have also appreciated the importance to the handicapped person of seeing himself as adequate and not essentially different from others. Often well-meaning sympathy or efforts to assist are displayed by relatives or friends in a clumsy way that makes the task of adjustment even more difficult.

In all these instances where application of principles of personality and adjustment are made to some mental-health problem, decisions are continually being made that imply a rich understanding of personality as well as the specialized adjustment problem itself. It is not desirable here to attempt to assess the adequacy of this application in each or any specialized area. This, indeed, might be difficult to do because little or no definitive information is available in most instances concerning the outcomes of psychological practice. It is mainly important to make the point that the value of what is being done is tied to the adequacy of our knowledge and that in every one of these areas there is always the danger of misapplication, however well intentioned. Professional persons who provide services cannot disregard the misery they find on the grounds that they have inadequate information and understanding to be confident of the effects of their efforts. Yet, as in psychotherapy, discussed in Chapter 14, these other areas of application involve considerable groping, guesswork, and uncertainty about outcomes and will continue so until our research knowledge develops far beyond its present level.

Personnel Selection

There are fields other than mental health where the subject matter of personality and adjustment is highly relevant and leads to applications of various sorts. One of these is *personnel selection*. This field overlaps greatly with industrial psychology, because one of the largest buyers of personnel-selection services is industry.

The problem in personnel selection is selecting (where there is a choice) the right persons for certain jobs. This requires a knowledge of the job requirements and the personal attributes relevant to them. In addition, such personality characteristics must be successfully assessed or measured.

In Chapter 13 was mentioned the effort of the Army in World War I to screen out of military service men who were likely to develop serious adjustive disturbances during their enlistment. The Woodworth Personal Data Sheet was the first large-scale attempt to do this. This type of personality assessment was also utilized far more extensively during World War II and is still used at the present time by the military services. The techniques involved have been applied to the selection of men for pilot training, for radio operators, for undercover agents, and for many other tasks. They have found their way into industry and are employed by psychological consulting firms and sometimes by a department of the industrial organization itself. A wide variety of assessment procedures is used, including those which stress abilities and aptitudes and those which emphasize personality characteristics considered relevant to the successful performance of some given duties. Efforts at personnel selection in industry range from semiskilled and skilled jobs to the hiring or advancement of executive personnel.

As always, the problem is to discover through research which personality characteristics are desirable, and which are not, for the position being filled. This latter problem is well illustrated by recent efforts to select men to be the first travelers into space. It was necessary to select from a larger number of volunteers the men who have the physical and psychological characteristics necessary to function effectively under these unusual conditions. In cases like this, it is usually necessary to guess what characteristics are important, because relatively little can be known about the kinds of physical and psychological problems these first space travelers would meet in undertaking their flight. In some instances, experiments were performed with animals in early models of the space ships. Also, in the laboratory, men were exposed to conditions of intense heat, weightlessness, and great acceleration because these conditions were known or assumed to be expected in a space flight. But much personnel selection takes place when only rough guesses can be made about the important attributes. Ideally, it should be possible to experiment in advance with persons of many different qualities in the actual situation to be predicted in order to obtain clear evidence concerning the kind of person who functions well or badly under the specified set of circumstances.

Interpersonal and Intergroup Relations

This is another area in which the field of personality has actual and potential application. It concerns the nature and determinants of the interpersonal relations that take place when persons interact or attempt to solve problems together. In labor-management relations, for example, knowledge in this field could make a great deal of difference in the negotiations for wage contracts and in the handling of strikes. Consultants to industry employ a knowledge of the psychology of personality and group processes in decisions about incentive plans and in the analysis of the communications, morale, and organizational structure.

The same could apply in politics, especially in the field of international relations, where persons of different language backgrounds, personalities, and cultures must work out their problems peacefully or risk continued international tensions and war. It is reasonable to think that advanced application here could have some value, especially in cases where disagreement arises from misunderstanding rather than a real conflict of interests.

Advertising and Merchandising

In recent years, increasing attention has been given to another area of application of principles of personality and adjustment. This is the field of advertising and merchandising. Vance Packard's best-selling book called *The Hidden Persuaders* (1957) includes a discussion of motivation research and manipulation in advertising and merchandising. Here the emphasis has been on using concepts from the field of personality to determine how to make a product appealing to different types of potential customers and how to communicate this appeal. This kind of approach is not new, although it has become more widespread and effective and of more public concern lately. Such efforts include the arousal of, and appeal to, feelings of insecurity to get persons to use large quantities of mouth washes in order to prevent bad breath or underarm deodorants to avoid social failure due to the odor of perspiration. Or they involve associating a product with some irrelevant but prestigeful or glamorous public figure. In the ad shown in Figure 39, some interesting efforts are made to enhance the marketability of the product by associating it with certain widespread human motives. The lowly sock is called "The Governor," lending it a certain distinction which is further supported by the arresting thought, "Men who wear The Governor are millionaires by forty." If the reader does not believe that wearing The Governor sock will lead him to his first million by forty, the advertiser has at least succeeded in making the connection between Esquire Socks and wealth. Moreover, according to the pictorial material, elegant women belong with the men who wear such a garment. All in all, the ad conjures up images of lovely women, wealth, elegance, distinction, prestige, and so on—take your pick as you look at it. These advertising machinations depend sometimes upon actual research data which suggest the kinds of appeals which will tap people's motivational mainsprings, for example, the desire to be rich, esteemed, or successful with the opposite sex. Whether or not any adequate evidence exists that such appeals really work, the business man and advertiser are certainly sold on the value of these kinds of approaches to the presentation of their products. A large industry (advertising) is based upon this conviction.

Applications of principles of personality can have a more lofty and humanistic orientation than simply selling a manufacturer's product. The U.S. Public Health Service is continually struggling to improve the health conditions of the population in a number of different ways. With the

"MEN
WHO WEAR
THE GOVERNOR'
ARE MILLIONAIRES
BY FORTY!*
"

*This statement is not the result of a survey. It is merely our own biased opinion—based on a simple fact. The Governor is America's best selling one-size all-nylon rib sock! $1 pair. (Sanitized® for hygienic freshness.) 'The smartest thing on two feet'.

ESQUIRE SOCKS®

Another fine product of Kayser-Roth

Figure 39. An example of the use of principles of motivational psychology designed to transform the lowly sock into an object of elegance and sex appeal. (*Kayser-Roth Corporation.*)

development of the Salk vaccine against polio, for example, the problem was to get reluctant persons to use the vaccine, sometimes during a polio epidemic. Here a knowledge of personality and motivational processes is crucial to overcoming enormous resistances found among large numbers of persons. The fears and attitudes that sustain these resistances must be understood, and effective pressures applied to change them. The community struggles that have taken place over the issue of fluoridation of the water supply provide another clear instance of the importance of understanding the processes of personality, both in comprehending and in dealing with attitudes opposed to developments that can improve the public health.

Social Engineering

Perhaps the most grandiose example of potential application of the subject matter of personality and adjustment is an effort which might be called "social engineering," the business of designing a better society. Some theorists in the field of personality and social processes, like Erich Fromm (1955), have been greatly concerned in their writings with the problem of what kind of society is most likely to promote happy and productive lives for its members. Fromm has argued that none of the many forms of society man has developed over centuries of human history has been fully successful in both permitting man to be free and individuated and simultaneously giving him a sense of belonging or union.

Whether or not one agrees with Fromm's thesis or his prescriptions for a better world, it is clear that the high incidence of adjustive failure and the extensive misery and suffering that one can find in all societies arise, in part, from the ways in which the human being and human society are constructed. It would seem odd that persons could deny that important improvements in society could be made, although it is quite clear that wide disagreement would be found as to how to change it. Those who wrote the Declaration of Independence and who helped establish the American form of democracy were attempting to evolve a more successful society. Societies are continually evolving and changing; our values and institutions today are by no means the same as they were twenty, fifty, or a hundred years ago, and they will also be different some years from now. In social engineering we are thinking of the lines along which we would wish society to evolve to meet certain criteria of a satisfying and productive (these two are not necessarily synonymous) way of life for the largest possible number of its members. Any major effort along these lines would have to depend upon a very complete knowledge of the human personality and its determinants, as well as on agreement concerning the important values to be achieved.

Psychologists generally are suspicious of the application of psychological principles to social engineering. This is because the scientist's main task is to describe and understand events as they are, and the effort to produce a better world involves, to a high degree, differing value systems that are difficult to evaluate objectively. One can be objective about describing the nature of the social or personal world of man, but one cannot be objective when it comes to specifying what is good and what is bad.

Yet increasing numbers of social scientists have recognized that they are, in fact, actively involved in the very process of social evolution, just as physical scientists and engineers have recognized that the enormous control exercised over the physical world by recent developments in their fields catapults them continually, and in spite of their reluctance, into social and political problems. The recent debates about continuing or discontinuing atomic explosions (involving concern over the seriousness of the radiation hazard) reflect this changing role of the physical scientist. The same problem exists for the social and biological scientist (psychology has a foot in each field). When he finally comes to understand the conditions that bring about psychopathology, the psychologist will in fact be presenting an argument against these very conditions. The problem up to now has been not so much the unwillingness on the part of psychologists to advise against social engineering as the uncertainty of their knowledge about such matters. We still cannot say that we understand the conditions (e.g., the early childhood experiences) associated with the development of schizophrenia or any other type of psychopathology. However, it is surely only a matter of time before we do, at least well enough to take effective prophylactic steps.

Lest the reader think that these statements are fanciful and that the psychologist of personality and the social scientist in general does not play or has not played a role in social engineering, we need only point to the issue of racial segregation and the Supreme Court decision that ended it. The issue of separate but equal facilities for Negroes and whites rested before the Supreme Court not only on legal grounds, but partly on the question of whether psychological harm was being done to Negroes (and possibly even to whites) by virtue of the enforced segregation. Expert psychological testimony was taken in this case. Here, in our generation, is an instance of a psychological issue (involving the impact on personality development of segregation) that was important in determining a political and sociological decision. It is probable that this kind of application will occur more and more frequently, influencing the nature of the social world in which we live.

It was previously suggested that, in surveying the sampling of knowledge about personality and adjustment reflected in this book, some will be disappointed because our knowledge is as yet so tentative; yet others will be challenged and excited by the growing prospect of increasing our understanding, with its implications for prediction and control. This field is a very young one in comparison with the physical sciences, and like other biological and social sciences, it is rapidly expanding and developing. The student of personality and adjustment in the present-day college classroom is a member of a generation that stands on the threshold of exciting and important new insights. As research efforts increase in the exploration of personality and the processes of adjustment, our knowledge will become more sure and complete and the application of this knowledge will have greater impact on the world in which we live.

Bibliography

Adler, A. *Individual Psychology*. New York: Harcourt, Brace, 1924.

―――. *The Practice and Theory of Individual Psychology*. New York: Ha court, Brace, 1927.

Adler, Alexandra. Neuropsychiatric Complications in Victims of Boston's Cocoa nut Grove Disaster. *J. Amer. med. Ass.*, 1943, **123**, 1098–1101.

Alexander, F., & R. M. French. *Psychoanalytic Therapy*. New York: Ronald, 1946.

Allport, F. *Theories of Perception and the Concept of Structure*. New York: Wiley, 1955.

Allport, G. W. *A Study of Values: Manual of Directions*. (rev. ed.) Boston: Houghton Mifflin, 1931.

―――. *Personality*. New York: Holt, 1937.

――― & H. S. Odbert. Trait-names: A Psycho-lexical Study. *Psychol. Monogr.*, 1936, **47**, No. 211.

――― & P. E. Vernon. *Studies in Expressive Movement*. New York: Macmillan, 1933.

―――, P. E. Vernon, & G. Lindzey. *A Study of Values: A Scale for Measuring the Dominant Interests in Personality*. (rev. ed.) Boston: Houghton Mifflin, 1951.

Anastasi, Anne, & J. P. Foley. *Differential Psychology*. (rev. ed.) New York: Macmillan, 1949.

Ansbacher, H. L., & Rowena R. Ansbacher (Eds.) *The Individual Psychology of Alfred Adler*. New York: Basic Books, 1956.

Asch, S. E. Effects of Group Pressure upon the Modification and Distortion of Judgments. In G. E. Swanson, J. M. Newcomb, & E. L. Hartley (Eds.), *Readings in Social Psychology*. New York: Holt, 1952. Pp. 2–11.

―――. *Social Psychology*. Englewood Cliffs, N.J.: Prentice-Hall, 1952.

Atkinson, J. W. The Achievement Motive and Recall of Interrupted and Completed Tasks. *J. exp. Psychol.*, 1953, **46**, 381–390.

Ax, A. F. The Physiological Differentiation between Fear and Anger in Humans. *Psychosom. Med.*, 1953, **15**, 433–442.

Axline, Virginia M. *Play Therapy*. Boston: Houghton Mifflin, 1947.

Baldwin, A. L., Joan Kalhorn, & Fay H. Breese. Patterns of Parent Behavior. *Psychol. Monogr.*, 1945, **58**, No. 3.

Bass, M. J., & C. L. Hull. Irradiation of a Tactile Conditioned Reflex in Man. *J. comp. physiol. Psychol.*, 1934, **17**, 45–65.

Beach, F. A. The Descent of Instinct. *Psychol. Rev.*, 1955, **62**, 401–410.

Bell, J. E. *Projective Techniques.* New York: Longmans, 1948.

Benedict, Ruth. *The Chrysanthemum and the Sword.* Boston: Houghton Mifflin, 1946.

Binet, A., & T. Simon. L'Application des méthodes nouvelles au diagnostic du niveau intellectuel chez des enfants normaux et anormaux d'hospice et d'école primaire. *Année psychol.,* 1905, **11,** 245–366.

Bleuler, E. *Dementia Praecox.* New York: International Universities Press, 1950.

Block, Jeanne, & J. Block. An Interpersonal Experiment on Reactions to Authority. *Human Relat.,* 1952, **5,** 91–98.

Boring, E. *A History of Experimental Psychology.* New York: Appleton-Century-Crofts, 1950.

Boyd, W. C. *Genetics and the Races of Man.* Boston: Little, Brown, 1950.

Brayfield, A. H. (Ed.) *Readings in Modern Methods of Counseling.* New York: Appleton-Century-Crofts, 1950.

Breuer, J., & S. Freud. *Studies in Hysteria.* Edited by J. Strachey. New York: Basic Books, 1957. (First German edition, 1895.)

Brozek, J., H. Guetzkow, & Marcella V. Baldwin. A Quantitative Study of Perception and Association in Experimental Semi-starvation. *J. Pers.,* 1951, **19,** 245–264.

Bruner, J. S. Neural Mechanisms in Perception. *Psychol. Rev.,* 1957, **64,** 340–358.

Burks, Barbara S. The Relative Influence of Nature and Nurture upon Mental Development. *Yearb. nat. Soc. Stud. Educ.,* 1928, **27,** Part I. Pp. 219–316.

Cannon, W. B. The James-Lange Theory of Emotions: A Critical Examination and an Alternative Theory. *Amer. J. Psychol.,* 1927, **39,** 106–124.

———. Hunger and Thirst. In C. Murchison (Ed.), *A Handbook of General Experimental Psychology.* Worcester, Mass.: Clark University Press, 1934. Pp. 247–263.

———. *The Wisdom of the Body.* (rev. ed.) New York: Norton, 1939.

——— & A. C. Washburn. An Explanation of Hunger. *Amer. J. Physiol.,* 1912, **29,** 441–454.

Cantril, H. The Invasion from Mars. In G. E. Swanson, T. M. Newcomb, and E. L. Hartley (Eds.), *Readings in Social Psychology.* New York: Holt, 1952. Pp. 198–207.

Carlson, V. R., & R. S. Lazarus. A Repetition of Meyer Williams' Study of Intellectual Control under Stress and Associated Rorschach Factors. *J. consult. Psychol.,* 1953, **17,** 247–253.

Carnegie, D. *How to Win Friends and Influence People.* New York: Simon and Schuster, 1937.

Cattell, J. McK., & L. Farrand. Physical and Mental Measurements of the Students of Columbia University. *Psychol. Rev.,* 1896, **3,** 618–648.

Cattell, R. B. *Description and Measurement of Personality.* Yonkers, N.Y.: World, 1946.

———. *Personality: A Systematic, Theoretical, and Factual Study.* New York: McGraw-Hill, 1950.

Centers, R. *The Psychology of Social Classes*. Princeton, N.J.: Princeton University Press, 1949.

Cerletti, V., & L. Bini. L'Elettroshock. *Arch. gen. Neurol., Psichiat. Psichanal.*, 1938, **19**, 266–268.

Chein, I. The Awareness of Self and the Structure of the Ego. *Psychol. Rev.*, 1944, **51**, 304–314.

Coffey, H. Roleplaying in Exploring Relationships. *Publ. Hlth. Nursing*, 1950, **42**, 267–272.

Cohen, L. H., E. R. Hilgard, & G. R. Wendt. Sensitivity to Light in a Case of Hysterical Blindness Studied by Reinforcement, Inhibition and Conditioning Methods. *Yale J. Biol. Med.*, 1933, **6**, 61–67.

Coleman, J. C. *Abnormal Psychology and Modern Life*. Chicago: Scott, Foresman, 1950.

Conrad, H. S., & H. E. Jones. A Second Study of Familial Resemblance in Intelligence: Environmental and Genetic Implications of Parent-Child and Sibling Correlations in the Total Sample. *Yearb. nat. Soc. Stud. Educ.*, 1940, **39**, Part II. Pp. 97–141.

Cooper, E., & Marie Jahoda. The Evasion of Propaganda: How Prejudiced People Respond to Anti-prejudice Propaganda. *J. Psychol.*, 1947, **23**, 15–25.

Corsini, R. J. *Methods of Group Psychotherapy*. New York: McGraw-Hill, 1957.

Cowles, J. E. Food-tokens as Incentives for Learning in Chimpanzees. *Comp. psychol. Monogr.*, 1937, **14**, No. 5.

Crook, M. N. Intra-family Relationships in Personality Test Performances. *Psychol. Rec.*, 1937, **1**, 479–502.

Darwin, C. *The Origin of Species*. London: J. Murray, 1859.

———. *Expression of the Emotions in Man and Animals*. New York: Appleton-Century-Crofts, 1873.

Davis, A. *Deep South: A Social Anthropological Study of Caste and Class*. Chicago: University of Chicago Press, 1941.

———. Socialization and Adolescent Personality. In *Adolescence: Forty-third yearb. nat. Soc. Stud. Educ.*, 1944, **43**, Part I. Pp. 198–216.

——— & R. F. Havighurst. Social Classes and Color Differences in Child Rearing. In G. E. Swanson, T. M. Newcomb, & E. L. Hartley (Eds.), *Readings in Social Psychology*. New York: Holt, 1952. Pp. 539–550.

Davis, H., & P. A. Davis. Action Potentials of the Brain. *Arch. Neurol. Psychiat.*, 1936, **36**, 1214–1224.

Deese, J. E. *The Psychology of Learning*. New York: McGraw-Hill, 1958.

———, R. S. Lazarus, & J. Keenan. Anxiety, Anxiety Reduction, and Stress in Learning. *J. exp. Psychol.*, 1953, **46**, 55–60.

Dejerine, J., & E. Gaukler. *Psychoneurosis and Psychotherapy*. Philadelphia: Lippincott, 1913.

de Klerk, D. Magnetic Properties below One Degree K. *Physics Today*, 1953, **6** (2), 4.

Dennis, W. The Effect of Cradling Practices upon the Onset of Walking in Hopi Children. *J. genet. Psychol.*, 1940, **56**, 77–86.

Doering, C. R., & A. F. Raymond. Additional Note on Reliability. In *Schizo-*

phrenia: Statistical Studies from the Boston Psychopathic Hospital (1925–34). Reprint No. 6, 1935.

Doll, E. A. The Essentials of an Inclusive Concept of Mental Deficiency. *Amer. J. ment. Defic.,* 1941, **46,** 214–219.

————. *Vineland Social Maturity Scale.* Philadelphia: Educational Test Bureau, 1946.

Dollard, J., L. W. Doob, N. E. Miller, O. H. Mowrer, & R. R. Sears. *Frustration and Aggression.* New Haven: Yale University Press, 1939.

Dollard, J., & N. E. Miller. *Personality and Psychotherapy.* New York: McGraw-Hill, 1950.

Dubois, P. *The Psychic Treatment of Mental Disorders.* New York: Funk, 1907.

Dugdale, R. W. *The Jukes.* New York: Putnam, 1877.

Dussik, K. T., & M. Sakel. Ergebnisse der Hypoglykämie: Schockbehandlung der Schizophrenia. *Z. ges. Neurol. Psychiat.,* 1936, **155,** 351–415.

Duvall, G. M., & Evelyn M. Duvall. Let's Explore Your Mind. *Oakland Tribune,* Sunday, Jan. 4, 1959. John F. Dille Co., 1959.

Edwards, A. L. *Manual: Edwards Personal Preference Schedule.* New York: Psychological Corp., 1954.

Eriksen, C. W. The Case for Perceptual Defense. *Psychol. Rev.,* 1954, **61,** 175–182.

————. Discrimination and Learning without Awareness: A Methodological Survey and Evaluation. *Psychol. Rev.,* 1960, **67,** 279–300.

————, R. S. Lazarus, & J. R. Strange. Psychological Stress and Its Personality Correlates: Part II. The Rorschach Test and Other Personality Measures. *J. Pers.,* 1952, **20,** 277–286.

Erikson, E. H. *Childhood and Society.* New York: Norton, 1950.

Eysenck, H. J. *Dimensions of Personality.* London: Routledge & Kegan Paul, 1947.

————. The Effects of Psychotherapy: An Evaluation. *J. consult. Psychol.,* 1952, **16,** 319–324.

Fenichel, O. *The Psychoanalytic Theory of Neurosis.* New York: Norton, 1945.

Ferguson, L. W. *Personality Measurement.* New York: McGraw-Hill, 1952.

Finesinger, J. E. Psychiatric Interviewing. *Amer. J. Psychiat.,* 1948, **103,** No. 3.

Foote, N. N., & L. Cottrell. *Identity and Interpersonal Competence.* Chicago: University of Chicago Press, 1955.

Ford, C., & F. Beach. *Patterns of Sexual Behavior.* New York: Harper, 1951.

Forel, A. *Collected Papers.* Baltimore: Phipps Psychiatric Clinic, 1907.

Frank, I. *Perceptual Structurization in Certain Psychoneurotic Disorders: A Genetic Evaluation by Means of the Rorschach Test.* Doctoral dissertation, University of Texas, Austin, Texas, 1951.

Franklin, J. C., B. C. Schiele, J. Brozek, & A. Keys. Observations of Human Behavior in Experimental Semistarvation and Rehabilitation. *J. clin. Psychol.,* 1948, **4,** 28–45.

Freed, E. *Perceptual Differentiation in Schizophrenia; A Tachistoscopic Study of Structural Rorschach Elements.* Doctoral dissertation, Syracuse University, Syracuse, N. Y., 1952.

Freeman, F. S. *Theory and Practice of Psychological Testing*. New York: Holt, 1950.

Freeman, G. N., K. J. Holzinger, & Blythe C. Mitchell. The Influence of Environment on the Intelligence, School Achievements, and Conduct of Foster Children. *Yearb. nat. Soc. Stud. Educ.*, 1928, **27**, Part I. Pp. 103–217.

Freeman, W., & J. W. Watts. Prefrontal Lobotomy in Treatment of Mental Disorders. *Sth. med. J.*, 1937, **30**, 23–31.

Freud, Anna. *The Ego and the Mechanisms of Defense*. New York: International Universities Press, 1946.

Freud, S. *The Interpretation of Dreams*. New York: Macmillan, 1922.

————. *Collected Papers*. Vol. II. London: Hogarth, 1924.

————. *Civilization and Its Discontents*. London: Hogarth, 1930.

————. Libidinal Types. *Psychoanalyt. Quart.*, 1932, **1**, 3–6.

————. *New Introductory Lectures on Psychoanalysis*. New York: Norton, 1933.

————. *Autobiography*. Translated by J. Strachey. New York. Norton, 1935.

————. *Inhibitions, Symptoms and Anxiety*. London: Hogarth, 1936.

————. *The Problem of Anxiety*. New York: Norton, 1936.

————. The Psychopathology of Everyday Life. In A. A. Brill (Ed.), *The Basic Writings of Sigmund Freud*. New York: Modern Library, 1938.

————. *An Outline of Psychoanalysis*. New York: Norton, 1949.

————. *Beyond the Pleasure Principle*. In J. Strachey (Ed.), *The Standard Edition of the Complete Psychological Works*. Vol. XVIII. London: Hogarth, 1955. (First German edition, 1920.)

————. *The Standard Edition of the Complete Psychological Works*. Edited by J. Strachey. London: Hogarth, 1953–1959.

Friedman, H. Perceptual Regression in Schizophrenia: An Hypothesis Suggested by the Use of the Rorschach Test. *J. genet. Psychol.* 1954, **81**, 63–98.

Fromm, E. *Escape from Freedom*. New York: Rinehart, 1941.

————. *Man for Himself*. New York: Rinehart, 1947.

————. Psychoanalytic Characterology and Its Application to Understanding of Culture. In S. S. Sargent, & Marian W. Smith (Eds.), *Culture and Personality*. New York: Basic Books, 1949. Pp. 1–12.

————. *The Sane Society*. New York: Rinehart, 1955.

Funkenstein, D. H., S. H. King, & Margaret Drolette. *Mastery of Stress*. Cambridge, Mass.: Harvard University Press, 1957.

Galton, F. *Hereditary Genius*. London: Macmillan, 1869.

————. Inquiries into Human Faculty and Its Development. London: Macmillan, 1883.

Gerth, H., & C. W. Mills. *Character and Social Structure*. New York: Harcourt, Brace, 1953.

Gesell, A. *Infancy and Human Growth*. New York: Macmillan, 1928.

———— & C. S. Amatruda. *Developmental Diagnosis: Normal and Abnormal Child Development*. New York: Hoeber-Harper, 1947.

Gill, M. The Present State of Psychoanalytic Theory. *J. abnorm. soc. Psychol.*, 1959, **58**, 1–8.

Gill, M., R. Newman, & F. C. Redlich. *The Initial Interview in Psychiatric Practice.* New York: International Universities Press, 1954.

Glass, B. *Embryology and Genetics.* New York: Columbia University Press, 1934.

———. *The Scientific Basis of Evolution.* New York: Norton, 1935.

Glueck, Eleanor, & S. Glueck. *Criminal Careers in Retrospect.* New York: Commonwealth Fund, 1943.

——— & ———. *Unraveling Juvenile Delinquency.* New York: Commonwealth Fund, 1950.

Goddard, H. H. *The Kallikak Family.* New York: Macmillan, 1912.

Goldstein, K. *The Organism.* New York: American Book Co., 1939.

———. *Human Nature in the Light of Psychopathology.* Cambridge, Mass.: Harvard University Press, 1940.

——— & M. Scheerer. Abstract and Concrete Behavior: An Experimental Study with Special Tests. *Psychol. Monogr.,* 1941, **53** (239), 151.

Goltz, F. Der Hund ohne Grosshirn. *Arch. ges. Physiol.,* 1892, **51**, 570–614. Cited by D. Krech & R. S. Crutchfield, *Elements of Psychology.* New York: Knopf, 1958.

Grinker, R. R. *War Neuroses.* New York: McGraw-Hill–Blakiston, 1945.

——— & J. P. Spiegel. *Men Under Stress.* New York: McGraw-Hill–Blakiston, 1945.

Hadley, J. M. *Clinical and Counseling Psychology.* New York: Knopf, 1958.

Haggard, E. *Psychological Causes and Results of Stress: Human Factors in Undersea Warfare.* Washington, D. C.: National Research Council, 1949. Pp. 441–461.

Hall, C. S. *A Primer of Freudian Psychology.* New York: World, 1954.

——— & G. Lindzey. *Theories of Personality.* New York: Wiley, 1957.

Harlow, H. F. Mice, Monkeys, Men and Motives. *Psychol. Rev.,* 1953, **60**, 23–32.

Hartmann, H. Comments on the Psychoanalytic Theory of the Ego. In Anna Freud et al. (Eds.), *The Psychoanalytic Study of the Child.* Vol. 5. New York: International Universities Press, 1950. Pp. 74–96.

———, E. Kris, & R. M. Loewenstein. Comments on the Formation of Psychic Structure. In Anna Freud et al. (Eds.) *The Psychoanalytic Study of the Child.* Vol. 2. New York: International Universities Press, 1947, pp. 11–38.

Hartshorne, H., & M. A. May. *Studies in the Nature of Character.* Vol. 1. *Studies in Deceit.* New York: Macmillan, 1928.

———, ———, & J. B. Maller. *Studies in the Nature of Character.* Vol. 2. *Studies in Service and Self-control.* New York: Macmillan, 1929.

———, ———, & F. K. Shuttleworth. *Studies in the Nature of Character.* Vol. 3. *Studies in the Organization of Character.* New York: Macmillan, 1930.

Hathaway, S. R. *Physiological Psychology.* New York: Appleton-Century-Crofts, 1942.

——— & J. C. McKinley. *The Minnesota Multiphasic Personality Inventory.* (rev. ed.) Minneapolis: University of Minnesota Press, 1943.

Heider, Grace M. *A Pilot Study of Vulnerability to Stress in Infants and Young*

Children: The Coping Project. Topeka, Kans.: Menninger Foundation, June, 1959.

Hemmendinger, L. *A Genetic Study of Structural Aspects of Perception as Reflected in Rorschach Responses.* Doctoral dissertation, Clark University, Worcester, Mass., 1951.

Henderson, J. L., & M. Moore. The Psychoneuroses of War. *New England J. Med.,* 1944, **230**, 273–278.

Hendrick, I. *Facts and Theories of Psychoanalysis.* New York: Knopf, 1939.

Hernández-Péon, R., H. Scherrer, & M. Jouvet. Modification of Electrical Activity in Cochlear Nucleus during "Attention" in Unanesthetized Cats. *Science,* 1956, **123**, 331–332.

Herriott, F., & M. Hogan. The Theatre of Psychodrama at St. Elizabeth's Hospital. *Sociometry,* May, 1941.

Hilgard, E. R. Human Motives and the Concept of the Self. *Amer. Psychologist,* 1949, **4**, 374–382.

———— & G. R. Wendt. The Problem of Reflex Sensitivity to Light Studied in a Case of Hemianopsia. *Yale J. Biol. Med.,* 1933, **5**, 373–385.

Himwich, H. E. The New Psychiatric Drugs. *Scient. Amer.,* 1955, **193**, 80–86.

Hollingshead, A. B., & F. C. Redlich. *Social Class and Mental Illness.* New York: Wiley, 1958.

Hooker, D. The Reflex Activities in the Human Fetus. In R. G. Barker, et al. (Eds.), *Child Behavior and Development.* New York: McGraw-Hill, 1943.

Horney, Karen. *Neurotic Personality of Our Times.* New York: Norton, 1937.

————. *New Ways in Psychoanalysis.* New York: Norton, 1939.

————. *Our Inner Conflicts.* New York: Norton, 1945.

Hull, C. L. *Principles of Behavior.* New York: Appleton-Century-Crofts, 1943.

Hurwitz, I. *A Developmental Study of the Relationship between Motor Activity and Perceptual Processes as Measured by the Rorschach Test.* Doctoral dissertation, Clark University, Worcester, Mass., 1954.

Huxley, A. *Brave New World.* London: Chatto & Windus, 1932.

Jahoda, Marie. *Current Concepts of Positive Mental Health.* New York: Basic Books, 1958.

James, W. *Principles of Psychology.* New York: Holt, 1890.

————. *Pragmatism.* New York: Longmans, Green, 1907.

Janis, I. L. *Psychological Stress.* New York: Wiley, 1958.

Jasper, H., & C. Shagass. Conditioning the Occipital Alpha Rhythm in Man. *J. exp. Psychol.,* 1941, **28**, 273–388.

Jasper, H. H. Electroencephalography. In W. Penfield & J. Erikson (Eds.), *Epilepsy and Cerebral Localization.* Springfield, Ill.: Charles C Thomas, 1941.

Jenkin, N. Affective Processes in Perception. *Psychol. Bull.,* 1957, **54**, 100–127.

Jervis, G. A. The Genetics of Phenylpyruvic Oligophrenia. *Proc. Ass. ment. Def.,* 1938–1939, **44**, 13–24.

Johnson, D. M. The "Phantom Anesthetist" of Mattoon: A Field Study of Mass Hysteria. *J. abn. soc. Psychol.,* 1945, **40**, 175–186.

Jones, E. *The Life and Work of Sigmund Freud,* New York: Basic Books, 1955. 3 vols.

Jones, H. E. The Galvanic Skin Reflex. *Child Develpm.*, 1930, **1**, 106–110.

Jung, C. G. *Analytical Psychology*. New York: Moffat, Yard, 1916.

———. *Psychological Types*. New York: Harcourt, Brace, 1922.

———. *Contributions to Analytical Psychology*. New York: Harcourt, Brace, 1928.

———. *Modern Man in Search of a Soul*. New York: Harcourt, Brace, 1933.

Kagan, J., & G. Lesser (Eds.). *Contemporary Issues in Apperceptive Fantasy*. Unpublished manuscript.

Kallman, F. S. *The Genetics of Schizophrenia*. New York: Augustin, 1938.

———. *Heredity in Health and Mental Disorder*. New York: Norton, 1953.

Kardiner, A. *The Individual and His Society*. New York: Columbia University Press, 1939.

———. *The Psychological Frontiers of Society*. New York: Columbia University Press, 1945.

———. Psychodynamics and the Social Sciences. In S. S. Sargent & Marian W. Smith (Eds.), *Culture and Personality*. New York: Basic Books, 1949. Pp. 59–74.

Katz, D., & K. W. Braly. Verbal Stereotypes and Racial Prejudice. In G. E. Swanson, T. M. Newcomb, & E. L. Hartley (Eds.), *Readings in Social Psychology*, New York: Holt, 1952. Pp. 67–73.

Kinsey, A. C., W. B. Pomeroy, & C. E. Martin. *Sexual Behavior in the Human Male*. Philadelphia: Saunders, 1948.

Klebanoff, S. G., J. L. Singer, & H. Wilensky. Psychological Consequences of Brain Lesions and Ablations. *Psychol. Bull.* 1954, **51**, 1–41.

Klineberg, O. *Race Differences*. New York: Harper, 1935.

Koffka, K. *Principles of Gestalt Psychology*. New York: Harcourt, Brace, 1935.

Kraepelin, E. *Clinical Psychiatry*. Translated by A. R. Diefendorf (Ed.). New York: Macmillan, 1907.

Krech, D., & R. S. Crutchfield. *Elements of Psychology*. New York: Knopf, 1958.

Kruger, Alice. *Direct and Substitute Modes of Tension-reduction in Terms of Development Level: An Experimental Analysis of the Rorschach Test*. Doctoral dissertation, Clark University, Worcester, Mass., 1954.

Lacey, J. I. Individual Differences in Somatic Response Patterns. *J. comp. physiol. Psychol.*, 1950, **43**, 338–350.

———. Autonomic Response Specificity and Rorschach Color Responses. *Psychosom. Med.*, 1952, **14**, 256–260.

———. Psychophysiological Approaches to the Evaluation of Psychotherapeutic Process and Outcome. In *Research in Psychotherapy*. Washington, D.C.: American Psychological Association, 1959.

———, Dorothy E. Bateman, and Ruth Van Lehn. Autonomic Response Specificity. *Psychosom. Med.*, 1953, **15**, 8–12.

——— & Beatrice C. Lacey. The Relationship of Resting Autonomic Activity to Motor Impulsivity. *Proc. Ass. Res. nerv. ment. Dis.*, 1958, **36**, 144–209.

Lashley, K. S. *Brain Mechanisms and Intelligence*. Chicago: University of Chicago Press, 1929.

Lazarus, R. S., & C. W. Eriksen. Effects of Failure Stress upon Skilled Performance. *J. exp. Psychol.*, 1952, **43**, 100–105.

———, ———, & C. P. Fonda. Personality Dynamics and Auditory Perceptual Recognition. *J. Pers.*, 1951, **19**, 471–482.

——— & N. Longo. The Consistency of Psychological Defenses against Threat. *J. abnorm. soc. Psychol.*, 1953, **48**, 495–499.

——— & J. C. Speisman. A Research Case History Dealing with Psychological Stress. *J. psychol. Stud.*, 1960, **11**, 167–194.

Lecky, P. *Self-consistency.* New York: Island Press, 1945.

Leeper, R. W. Lewin's Topological and Vector Psychology: A Digest and Critique. *Univ. Ore. Publ. stud. Psychol.*, 1943, No. 1.

———. A Motivational Theory of Emotion to Replace "Emotion as Disorganized Response." *Psychol. Rev.*, 1948, **55**, 5–21.

Lerner, E. *Constraint Areas and the Moral Judgment of Children.* Menasha, Wis.: George Banta Publishing Co., 1937.

Levine, J. M., & G. Murphy. The Learning and Forgetting of Controversial Material. *J. abn. soc. Psychol.*, 1943, **38**, 507–517.

Levy, D. M. Release Therapy. *Amer. J. Orthopsychiat.*, 1939, **9**, 713–736.

———. *Maternal Overprotection.* New York: Columbia University Press, 1943.

Levy, N. *Personality Disturbances in Combat Fliers.* New York: The Josiah Macy, Jr., Foundation, October, 1945.

Lewin, K. *A Dynamic Theory of Personality.* Translated by K. E. Zener & D. K. Adams. New York: McGraw-Hill, 1935.

———. *Principles of Topological Psychology.* Translated by F. Heider & Grace Heider. New York: McGraw-Hill, 1936.

———. *Resolving Social Conflicts: Selected Papers on Group Dynamics.* Edited by Gertrude W. Lewin. New York: Harper, 1948.

———. *Field Theory in Social Science: Selected Theoretical Papers.* Edited by D. Cartwright. New York: Harper, 1951.

Lindner, R. *Prescription for Rebellion.* New York: Rinehart, 1952.

Linton, R. *The Tree of Culture.* New York: Knopf, 1955.

Lippitt, R., & R. K. White. An Experimental Study of Leadership and Group Life. In G. E. Swanson, T. M. Newcomb, & E. L. Hartley (Eds.), *Readings in Social Psychology.* New York: Holt, 1952. Pp. 340–355.

Louttit, C. M. *Clinical Psychology.* (rev. ed.) New York: Harper, 1947.

McClearn, G. E. *The Inheritance of Behavior.* Unpublished manuscript.

McClelland, D. C. *Personality.* New York: Sloane, 1951.

———, J. S. Atkinson, R. A. Clark, & E. R. Lowell. *The Achievement Motive.* New York: Appleton-Century-Crofts, 1953. P. 266.

McDougall, W. *An Introduction to Social Psychology.* Boston: Luce, 1923.

Macfarlane, J. W. The Guidance Study. *Sociometry*, 1939, **2**, 1–23.

McNemar, Q. *The Revision of the Stanford-Binet Scale: An Analysis of the Standardization Data.* Boston: Houghton Mifflin, 1942.

Mahl, G. F. Anxiety, HCl secretion and Peptic Ulcer Etiology. *Psychosom. Med.*, 1949, **11**, 33–44.

Maier, N. R. F. *Frustration.* New York: McGraw-Hill, 1949.

Malmo, R. B. Activation: A Neuropsychological Dimension. *Psychol. Rev.*, 1959, **66**, 367–386.

————, D. J. Belanger, & A. A. Smith. Motor Control in Psychiatric Patients Under Experimental Stress. *J. abnorm. soc. Psychol.*, 1951, **46**, 539–547.

———— & C. Shagass. Studies of Blood Pressure in Psychiatric Patients Under Stress. *Psychosom. Med.*, 1952, **14**, 82–93.

———— & A. A. Smith. Forehead Tension and Motor Irregularities in Psychoneurotic Patients Under Stress. *J. Pers.*, 1955, **23**, 391–406.

————, H. Wallerstein, & C. Shagass. Headache Proneness and Mechanisms of Motor Conflict in Psychiatric Patients. *J. Pers.*, 1953, **22**, 163–187.

Malzberg, B. Important Statistical Data about Mental Illness. In S. Arieti (Ed.). *American Handbook of Psychiatry*. Vol. 1. New York: Basic Books, 1959. Pp. 161–174.

Maslow, A. H. *Motivation and Personality*. New York: Harper, 1954.

Masserman, J. H. *Behavior and Neurosis*. Chicago: University of Chicago Press, 1943.

Mead, G. H. *Mind, Self, and Society*. Chicago: University of Chicago Press, 1934.

Mead, Margaret. *Coming of Age in Samoa*. New York: Morrow, 1928.

————. *Sex and Temperament in Three Primitive Societies*. New York: Morrow, 1935.

Meduna, L. V. Treatment of Schizophrenia with Induced Convulsions. *Z. ges. Neurol. Psychiat.*, 1935, **152**, 235–262.

Menninger, W. C. *Facts and Statistics of Significance for Psychiatry*. The Hogg Foundation, University of Texas, 1948.

Meyer, V. Critique of Psychological Approaches to Brain Damage. *J. ment. Sci.*, 1957, **103**, 80–109.

Miller, N. E. Experimental Studies of Conflict. In J. McV. Hunt (Ed.), *Personality and Behavior Disorders*. Vol. 1. New York: Ronald, 1944.

————. Learnable Drives and Rewards. In S. S. Stevens (Ed.), *Handbook of Experimental Psychology*. New York: Wiley, 1951.

————. Studies of Fear as an Acquirable Drive: 1. Fear as Motivation and Fear-reduction as Reinforcement in Learning of New Responses. *J. exp. Psychol.*, 1948, **38**, 89–101.

Misch, R. C. *The Relationship of Motoric Inhibition to Developmental Level and Ideational Functioning: An Analysis by Means of the Rorschach Test*. Doctoral dissertation, Clark University, Worcester, Mass., 1954.

Moniz, E. *Tentatives opératoires des le traitment de certaines psychoses*. Paris: Masson, 1936.

Moreno, J. L. *The Theatre of Spontaneity: An Introduction to Psychodrama*. New York: Beacon House, 1947.

Morgan, C. D., & H. A. Murray. A Method for Investigating Fantasies: The Thematic Apperception Test. *Arch. Neurol. Psychiat.*, 1935, **34**, 289–306.

Morgan, C. T. Some Structural Factors in Perception. In R. R. Blake & G. V. Ramsey (Eds.), *Perception: An Approach to Personality*. New York: Ronald, 1951. Pp. 25–55.

————. *Introductory Psychology*. New York: McGraw-Hill, 1956.

————— & E. Stellar. *Physiological Psychology*. (2d ed.) New York: McGraw-Hill, 1950.

Mowrer, O. H. *Learning Theory and Personality Dynamics*. New York: Ronald, 1950.

Mullahy, P. *Oedipus—Myth and Complex*. New York: Hermitage, 1948.

—————. *A Study of Interpersonal Relations*. New York: Hermitage, 1949.

————— (Ed.). *The Contributions of Harry Stack Sullivan*. New York: Hermitage, 1952.

Munroe, Ruth L. *Schools of Psychoanalytic Thought*. New York: Dryden, 1955.

Murphy, G. *Human Potentialities*. New York: Basic Books, 1958.

Murray, H. A. *Explorations in Personality*. New York: Oxford University Press, 1938.

Mussen, P. H., & J. J. Conger. *Child Development and Personality*. New York: Harper, 1956.

Newman, H. H., F. N. Freeman, & K. J. Holzinger. *Twins: The Study of Heredity and Environment*. Chicago: University of Chicago Press, 1937.

OSS Assessment Staff. *Assessment of Men*. New York: Rinehart, 1948.

Orwell, G. *1984*. New York: Harcourt, Brace, 1949.

Packard, V. *The Hidden Persuaders*. New York: McKay, 1957.

Peña, C. A Genetic Evaluation of Perceptual Structurization in Cerebral Pathology: An Investigation by Means of the Rorschach Test. *J. proj. Tech.*, 1953, **17**, 186–199.

Phillips, L. Case History Data and Prognosis in Schizophrenia. *J. nerv. ment. Dis.* 1953, **117**, 515–525.

—————. *Developmental Theory and Social Adaption*. Talk presented as part of a symposium, "Developmental Approach to Problems of General and Clinical Psychology," at a meeting of the Massachusetts Psychol. Ass., Mar. 31, 1954.

————— & B. Cowitz. Social Attainment and Reactions to Stress. *J. Pers.*, 1953, **22**, 270–283.

————— & J. L. Framo. Developmental Theory Applied to Normal and Psychopathological Perception. *J. Pers.*, 1954, **22**, 464–474.

Piaget, J. *The Language and Thought of the Child*. London: Routledge & Kegan Paul, 1932.

—————. *The Origins of Intelligence in Children*. New York: International Universities Press, 1952.

Porter, E. H. *Therapeutic Counseling*. Boston: Houghton Mifflin, 1950.

Postman, L., & J. S. Bruner. Perception Under Stress. *Psychol. Rev.* 1948, **55**, 314–323.

Powdermaker, Florence, & J. D. Frank. *Group Psychotherapy*. Cambridge, Mass.: Harvard University Press, 1953.

Prince, M. Miss Beauchamp—The Theory of the Psychogenesis of Multiple Personality. *J. abnorm. soc. Psychol.*, 1920, **15**, 82–85, 87–91, 96–98, 102–104, 135.

Queener, E. L. *Introduction to Social Psychology*. New York: Dryden, 1951.

Rank, O. *Will Therapy*. Translated by Julia Taft. New York: Knopf, 1945.

—————. *The Trauma of Birth*. New York: Brunner, 1952.

Rapaport, D. The Autonomy of the Ego. *Bull. Menninger Clin.*, 1951, **15**, 113–123.

———. The Conceptual Model of Psychoanalysis. *J. Pers.*, 1951, **20**, 56–81.

———, M. Gill, & R. Schafer. *Diagnostic Psychological Testing*. Vol. 2. Chicago: Year Book Publishers, 1946.

Ratliff, F., W. H. Miller, & H. K. Hartline. Neural Interaction in the Eye and the Integration of Receptor Activity. *Annals N.Y. Acad. Sci.*, 1958, **74**, 210–222.

Reich, W. *Character Analysis*. Translated by J. P. Wolfe. (3d ed.) New York: Orgone Institute Press, 1949.

Richards, T. W. *Modern Clinical Psychology*. New York: McGraw-Hill, 1946.

Richter, C. P. Rats, Man and the Welfare State. *Amer. Psychologist*, 1959, **14**, 18–28.

Riesman, D. *The Lonely Crowd: A Study of the Changing American Character*. New Haven: Yale University Press, 1950.

Roberts, J. A. F. Resemblances in Intelligence between Sibs Selected from a Complete Sample of an Urban Population. *Proc. int. genet. Congr.*, 1941, **7**, 252.

Rogers, C. R. *Counseling and Psychotherapy*. Boston: Houghton Mifflin, 1942.

———. *Client-centered Therapy*. Boston: Houghton Mifflin, 1951.

Rorschach, H. *Psychodiagnostics*. Translated by P. Lemkau & B. Kronenberg. New York: Grune & Stratton, 1942. (First German edition, 1932.)

Rosanoff, A. J. *Manual of Psychiatry and Mental Hygiene*. New York: Wiley, 1938.

Rosenzweig, M. R., D. Krech, & E. L. Bennett. *Heredity, Environment, Brain Chemistry and Learning*. Pittsburgh Symposium on Current Trends in Psychology, March, 1959.

Rozenzweig, S. An Outline of Frustration Theory. In J. McV. Hunt (Ed.), *Personality and the Behavior Disorders*. New York: Ronald, 1944.

Sanford, R. N. The Effect of Abstinence from Food upon Imaginal Processes. *J. Psychol.* 1936, **2**, 129–136.

———. The Effect of Abstinence from Food upon Imaginal Processes: A Further Experiment, *J. Psychol.* 1937, **3**, 145–159.

———. Surface and Depth in the Individual Personality. *Psychol. Rev.*, 1956, **63**, 349–359.

Sarason, S. B. *Psychological Problems in Mental Deficiency*. New York: Harper, 1949.

Sarbin, T. Contributions to Roletaking Theory. I. Hypnotic Behavior. *Psychol. Rev.*, 1950, **57**, 255–270.

———. A Preface to a Psychological Analysis of the Self. *Psychol. Rev.*, 1952, **59**, 11–22.

———. Role Theory. In G. Lindzey (Ed.), *Handbook of Social Psychology*. Reading, Mass.: Addison-Wesley, 1954. Pp. 223–258.

Sawrey, W. L., J. J. Conger, & E. S. Turrel. An Experimental Investigation of the Role of Psychological Factors in the Production of Gastric Ulcers in Rats. *J. comp. physiol. Psychol.*, 1956, **49**, 457–461.

Schafer, R. *The Clinical Application of Psychological Tests*. New York: International Universities Press, 1948.

Schaffner, B. *Fatherland*. New York: Columbia University Press, 1948.

Sears, R. R., Eleanor Maccoby, & H. Levin. *Patterns of Child Rearing*. White Plains, N.Y.: Row, Peterson, 1957.

Selye, H. *The Stress of Life*. New York: McGraw-Hill, 1956.

Shaffer, G. W., & R. S. Lazarus. *Fundamental Concepts in Clinical Psychology*. New York: McGraw-Hill, 1952.

Sherif, M. A Study of Some Social Factors in Perception. *Arch. Psychol.*, 1935, No. 187.

———— & H. Cantril, *The Psychology of Ego-involvements*. New York: Wiley, 1947.

Shirley, M. M. The First Two Years, A Study of 25 Babies: Vol. II. Intellectual Development. *Inst. Child Welf. Monogr.*, 1933, No. 8.

Siegel, E. L. *Genetic Parallels of Perceptual Structuration in Paranoid Schizophrenia: An Analysis by means of the Rorschach Techniques*. Doctoral dissertation, Clark University, Worcester, Mass., 1950.

Skinner, B. F. Are Theories of Learning Necessary? *Psychol. Rev.*, 1950, **57**, 193–216.

Slavson, S. R. *An Introduction to Group Therapy*. New York: Commonwealth Fund, 1943.

Snygg, D., & A. W. Combs. *Individual Behavior*. New York: Harper, 1949.

Spearman, C. *The Abilities of Man*. New York: Macmillan, 1927.

Spock, B. *Baby and Child Care*. New York: Pocket Books, 1951.

Spranger, E. *Types of Man: The Psychology and Ethics of Personality*. Translated by P. J. W. Pigors. Halle: Niemeyer, 1928.

Stellar, E. The Physiology of Motivation. *Psychol. Rev.*, 1954, **61**, 5–12.

Stephenson, W. *The Study of Behavior*. Chicago: University of Chicago Press, 1953.

Sullivan, H. S. Multidisciplined Coordination of Interpersonal Data. In S. S. Sargent & Marian W. Smith (Eds.) *Culture and Personality*. New York: Basic Books, 1949. Pp. 175–194.

————. *The Interpersonal Theory of Psychiatry*. New York: Norton, 1953.

————. *The Psychiatric Interview*. New York: Norton, 1954.

Symonds, P. M. *The Ego and the Self*. New York: Appleton-Century-Crofts, 1951.

Tagiuri, R., & L. Petrullo (Eds.) *Person Perception and Interpersonal Behavior*. Stanford, Calif.: Stanford University Press, 1958.

Taylor, Janet A. Personality Scale of Manifest Anxiety. *J. abnorm. soc. Psychol.*, 1953, **48**, 285–290.

Thigpen, C. H., & H. M. Kleckley. *The Three Faces of Eve*. New York: Harper, 1949.

Thorndike, E. L. The Causation of Fraternal Resemblance. *J. genet. Psychol.* 1944, **64**, 249–264.

Thom, D. A. *Habit Training for Children*. New York: National Committee for Mental Hygiene, 1937.

Tinbergen, N. *The Study of Instincts*. London: Oxford University Press, 1951.

Tryon, R. C. Genetic Differences in Maze-learning Ability in Rats. *Yearb. nat. Soc. Stud. Educ.*, 1940, **39**, Part I, 111–119.

Vaihinger, H. *The Philosophy of "As If."* New York: Harcourt, Brace, 1925.

Vogel, W., Susan Raymond, & R. S. Lazarus. Intrinsic Motivation and Psychological Stress. *J. abnorm. soc. Psychol.*, 1959, **58**, 225–233.

Wallace, A. F. C. *Human Behavior in Extreme Situations*. Washington, D.C.: National Academy of Sciences–National Research Council, 1956. Publication 390.

———. *Tornado in Worcester*. Washington, D.C.: National Academy of Sciences–National Research Council, Disaster Study No. 3, 1956. Publication 392.

Wangenstein, O. H., & H. A. Carlson. Hunger Sensations in a Patient after Total Gastrectomy. *Proc. Soc. exp. Biol. Med.*, 1931, **28**, 545–547.

Wapner, S., & H. Werner. *Developmental Changes in Perception: An Experimental Investigation from the Viewpoint of Sensori-tonic Field Theory*. Worcester, Mass.: Clark University Press, 1957.

Weiss, P. Autonomous versus Reflexogenous Activity of the Central Nervous System. *Proc. Amer. phil. Soc.*, 1941, **84**, 53–64.

Welles, O. *The War of the Worlds*. A long-playing record. Audio Rarities, produced by Bill Forest, LPA No. 2355, a Kinor release.

Welsh, G. S., & W. G. Dahlstrom. *Basic Readings on the M.M.P.I. in Psychology and Medicine*. Minneapolis: University of Minnesota Press, 1956.

Werner, H. *Comparative Psychology of Mental Development*. New York: Harper, 1940.

———. *Comparative Psychology of Mental Development*. (rev. ed.) Chicago: Follet, 1948.

———. *Developmental Approaches to General and Clinical Psychology*. Paper read as part of a symposium, "Developmental Approach to Problems of General and Clinical Psychology," at a meeting of the Massachusetts Psychol. Ass., Mar. 3, 1954.

West, J., & C. Withers. *Plainville, U.S.A.* New York: Columbia University Press, 1945.

White, R. W. *The Abnormal Personality*. (2d ed.) New York: Ronald, 1956.

———. Motivation Reconsidered: The Concept of Competence. *Psychol. Rev.*, 1959, **66**, 297–333.

Wikler, A. *The Relation of Psychiatry to Pharmacology*. Baltimore: Williams & Wilkins, 1957.

Williams, R. J. *Biochemical Individuality*. New York: Wiley, 1956.

Wissler, C. The Correlation of Mental and Physical Tests. *Psychol. Rev., Monogr. Suppl.*, 1901, **3**, No. 6.

Wolberg, L. R. *Hypnoanalysis*. New York: Grune & Stratton, 1945.

Wolf, R., & H. A. Murray. An Experiment in Judging Personalities. *J. Psychol.*, 1937, **3**, 345–368.

Wolfe, J. B. Effectiveness of Token-rewards for Chimpanzees. *Comp. psychol. Monogr.*, 1936, **12**, No. 5.

Wolff, H. (Ed.) Life Stress and Bodily Disease. *Proc. Ass. Res. nerv. ment. Dis.* Baltimore: Williams & Wilkins, 1950.

Woodworth, R. S. *Personal Data Sheet.* Chicago: Stoelting, 1918.

————. Heredity and Environment. New York: *Soc. Sci. Res. Council Bull.,* 1941, No. 47.

Name Index

489

Subject Index